COMMERCIAL LAWS & BUSINESS REGULATIONS OF THE PEOPLE'S REPUBLIC OF CHINA

COMMERCIAL LAWS & BUSINESS REGULATIONS OF THE PEOPLE'S REPUBLIC OF CHINA

VICTOR F. S. SIT (Editor)

TAI DAO PUBLISHING LTD

Publisher: Tai Dao Publishing Limited

Address: 113, Wanchai Road, Tak Lee Commercial Bldg.,
13/F., Block D, Hong Kong
Telex: 71942 MCTDP HX
Cable: 4718 HONG KONG
Telephone: 5-8910493

Printed in Hong Kong
ISBN 962 7084 01 8

INTRODUCTION

Legal Clarification for the Potential Investor

The worldwide interchange of technology and investment for productive purposes has always been a feature of international liaison and cooperation, enhancing the development of international trade, goodwill and understanding. With the rapid development of new technology since World War II which has amounted to a virtual explosion of new ideas, concepts, discoveries and their myriad applications, the pace of economic and social advance across the world has been phenomenal. The result of this technological revolution has been to encourage the reduction of national and regional barriers to trade and to improve communication between nations. This in turn has made all countries increasingly dependent on each other for their continued economic and social development. Cultural, social and ideological differences between people and countries have had to be bridged in order to allow greater cooperation for mutual benefit. There has never been a time in history when communication and interchange of information have been at a higher or more productive level. So it must continue if the world economy and world trade are to be allowed to expand and provide us all with an improved standard of living and opportunity.

Hong Kong and the People's Republic of China have had a long and productive partnership despite being at opposite ends of the ideological rainbow. We have managed to support the development of each other because it has made good economic sense in doing so. China has directly assisted Hong Kong's development in a variety of ways, too numerous to mention in this introduction. Hong Kong, in turn, has reciprocated with wide ranging support for certain aspects of China's development.

In recent years, the P.R.C. has modified its policy towards foreign investment and participation. A great many foreign companies have responded with thousands of new productive ventures in China. This development has been rapid particularly in the creation of business and industrial joint ventures. The new policies and their results have brought in their train a need for foreign companies to be aware of the implications, limitations and, conversely, the opportunities provided within the Chinese legal system. This has seen substantial changes and additions in recent years to keep pace with the development of new outward looking economic, trade and investment policies by the P.R.C. Not unnaturally, the new legislation needs to be explained in languages other than Chinese, and explained as comprehensively as possible, if it is to encourage further foreign participation in Chinese economic progress.

This publication seeks to do just that and I believe that it will help to provide a more comprehensive understanding of this rather complex (at least to the layman and even the businessman) but essential subject. I commend the book to those interested in taking part in Chinese economic development and wish the editor every success.

J.D. McGregor
Director
The Hong Kong General Chamber of Commerce

PREFACE

Before 1978, China was reluctant in developing normal international business exchanges. Her import-export trade was insignificant. It amounted to less than 10% of her national income and was related mainly to trade with the communist bloc. In that period when a pronounced anti-capitalist and self-sufficient feeling prevailed in the country, direct investment by foreigners was impossible. However, this attitude began to thaw after the fall of the Gang of Four in 1976. China's trade volume as a percentage of national income rose steadily to about 15% in 1980. This trend has resulted in some relaxation towards foreign financing, and the introduction of vigorous foreign trade promotion programmes. In fact, the turning point – 1978, was also the year when historical changes occurred in many important policy considerations in China. One of these was the recognition that if the PRC is to become a powerful socialist country with modern agriculture, industry, national defense and science and technology by the end of the century, her foreign trade would have to be developed to full advantage.

The new 'open door' policy was advanced a step further in 1979 by the promulgation of the "Law of the PRC on Joint Ventures Using Chinese and Foreign Investment" and the creation of the Special Economic Zones in Guangdong and Fujin. These developments cleared away some of the many doubts in foreign businessmen's minds regarding direct investment in China. The "Income Tax Law on Joint-ventures" and the "Individual Income Tax Law" complimented the investment law and were similarly welcomed by the non communist business world. Indeed, we are advised that these are but early examples of a series of legal reforms that will provide an adequate and stable legal framework and administrative guidelines for doing business with China.

Of course, it was the state policy on foreign trade rather than the absence of foreign investment laws or the like that had inhibited the growth of Chinese foreign trade and direct foreign investment in China before 1978. Since the PRC was established in 1949, over 250 laws and regulations regarding business activities within the country were promulgated. Some of these have since become obsolete, some are in the process of being amended to meet changed circumstances, but many are still being enforced. The reorientation of the national goal and changes in foreign trade policy have made the adoption of new commercial laws and regulations imperative, especially those that are directly related to foreign participation. These new additions supplement the existing legal framework and help to provide a more concrete picture than before of the business environment of China. However, the Western business world seldom paid attention to laws and regulations brought into effect in earlier years. Only those laws that have a direct bearing on foreign investment attract interests from foreign companies and investors. Such is the natural outcome of two factors: (1) information of previous laws and regulations is not readily available for quick and easy reference, and (2) the general belief that the methods by which domestic businesses are run and regulated are of little relevance to the foreign investor. Given that all foreign business participation in foreign trade or direct investment in China requires some form of local partnership, laws and regulations that regulate the behaviour of local Chinese businesses are likely to have an influence on the success or failure of joint-venture and other forms of foreign participation. The coexistence of the foreign element and the local socialist business system will persist for as long as China continues to be a socialist country. It is therefore the intention of this volume to bring together both sets of business laws of China: (1) those that apply specifically to foreign businesses and (2) those that apply to all businesses in China. In the volume are also included laws and regulations that may not be directly related but are essential to business operations within China, such as laws affecting immigration, science awards regulations and so on.

There is as yet no complete collection of Chinese business laws and regulations covering 1949 to the present. The most comprehensive set of PRC laws covers only 1949-1965 and is restricted to laws and regulations approved or adopted by the five National People's Congresses and the State Council. It is a twin-serial of 18 issues published in Chinese between 1956 and 1966, entitled *Collection of Laws and Decrees of the Central Peoples' Government* (中央人民政府法令滙編) *and Collection of Laws and Regulations of the People's Republic of China* (中華人民共和國法規滙編). The content of the serial is arranged chronologically. A reprint up to No. 9 of the serial covering laws and regulations adopted up to 1959 is now available. More recent laws and regulations are contained in two other publications, one of which can be subscribed from outside since 1979 and the other since 1983. The *Announcements of the State Council* (國務院公佈) appears irregularly being issued in 20-30 issues a year. Most of the contents are laws and regulations adopted or approved by the State Council. A similar publication, the *Announcements of the Standing Committee of the National Peoples' Congress* (人大常委會公佈) will be available to outside subscribers in 1983. However, all these existing collections contain only laws and regulations promulgated by the State Council or the National Peoples' Congress and have excluded those adopted or announced by the lower rank state organs. Some of these latter documents appeared in local newspapers and/or magazines. In the compilation of the present volume search has been made in all these secondary sources and additional information has been obtained through assistance of friends in China. Despite our efforts, there are inevitable gaps. It is our hope that the publication will be improved in its next issue.

In the present collection, the laws and regulations are basically arranged by economic and/or activity sector for easy reference. Within a sector, the order of subgroups are alphabetical while within a subgroup, it is again chronological. The documents are somtimes called 'laws', 'regulations', 'measures' and other times labelled as 'announcements', 'rules' and 'circulars'. The differences between the terms are related to the different authority which promulgated them as well as being due to the varying levels of refinement of the document within the law from which they originated (See Diagram). In China, the power to make law principally rests with two authorities: the Standing Committee of the National Peoples' Congress (NPC) and the Standing Committee of the Communist Party of China (CCP). The NPC, as listed in the Chinese Constitution (article 22), possesses 10 functions and powers, of which one is 'to make laws' and the other 'to supervise the enforcement of the Constitution and the law'. In a review of the commercial laws and regulations announced in 1978-80 (see table) all the five laws announced were found to have been adopted by the NPC. In two of the laws which related to income tax the Ministry of Finance is named as the agent to devise detailed regulations for implementation subject to the approval of the State Council. In one the agent named is the Ministry of Forestry, and in another, the State Council; while there is no such mention in the foreign investment law. In fact, the State Council is the authority for approving regulations derived from existing laws though it may not always be the agent for their formulation and implementation. This has been spelled out in Article 32 of the Constitution. i.e. of the nine functions and powers of the State Council, the first two are:

(1) to formulate administrative measures, issue decisions and orders and verify their execution, in accordance with the Constitution, laws and decrees;
(2) to submit proposals on laws and other matters to the NPC or its standing committee.

Schematic Chart of Law Making Agents in the PRC

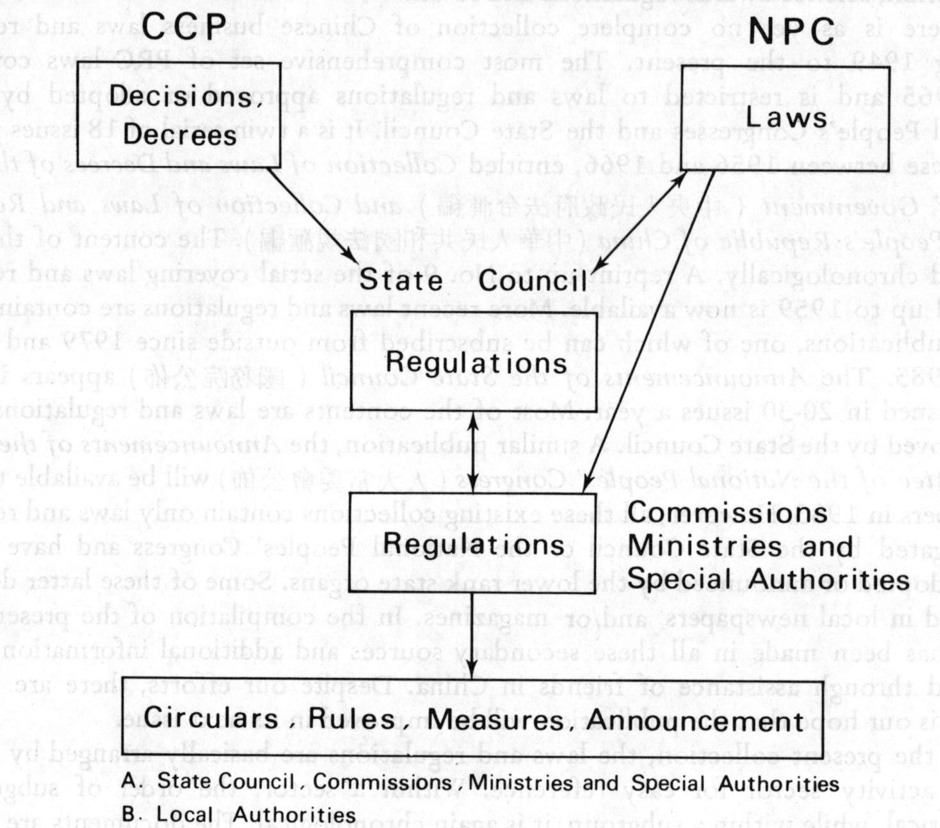

Classification of Commercial Laws and Regulations Promulgated in 1978-80 and Contained in the Almanac of the China's Economy 1981

Document Label	Promulgating/Approving Authority			
	NPC	CPC	State Council	Others
Law	5	–	–	–
Regulations	1	–	21	13
Rules	–	–	–	1
Decisions	–	2	–	–
Announcement	–	–	1	–
Circulars	–	–	1	–
Measures	–	–	1	–
Total*	6	2	24	14

* The total pieces of document number 42. Four of which were promulgated by 'others' but approved by the State Council. Hence, there is a double counting element given rise to the present listed total of 46.

From the previous table, it is obvious that the State Council is the main organ responsible for establishing business regulations in China.

The second authority in law making is the Central Committee of the Communist Party of China. Decisions or decrees of that organ sometimes have the power of law. These often appear as broad principles or policy guidelines that the State Council would follow for fabricating regulations for their implementation.

Administrative units under the State Council, such as the various commissions, ministries and special authorities may be delegated power to make regulations and administrative measures to implement existing laws and for regulating the businesses or facets for which they are responsible. In many of the business regulations promulgated by the State Council, there is a common clause that delegates power to local authorities for adopting measures which fit circumstances for local implementation.

China is a vast country. The enormous possibilities for business in China are being more and more appreciated by foreign businessmen. For successful business penetration into this vast market, however, one of the indespensible factors is an understanding of the legal framework for business operations within China. In meeting such a demand the present volume has been compiled with two considerations in mind: timeliness and comprehensiveness. This is, understandably, a difficult task. We are conscious of the comparative lack of comprehensiveness and other faults, such as translation mistakes, that may appear in the volume. We sincerely wish to receive criticisms from readers so that we shall be able to produce an improved and up-dated version in future.

We do believe, however, that this publication will be of help to those companies and individuals contemplating doing business with or investing in the Peoples' Republic of China, and, indeed, possibly also to companies already involved in China.

Victor Fung Shuen Sit
Editor

March 5, 1983

EDITOR'S NOTES

1. This collection includes all relevant laws and regulations promulgated by the PRC up to May 1983 and which are still being enforced.

2 Due to constraint of size of the volume, we have included mainly laws and regulations that have clear relevance to foreign business and joint-ventures, and those that are directly concern China's current economic policies.

3. The English translation of this collection is unofficial. Readers are advised to refer back to the Chinese original as promulgated by the PRC government whenever there are points in doubt.

4. The laws and regulations are categorized into sections base on major economic and administrative sectors. The sections are arranged in conventional order for easy reference. The subsections are in alphabetical order, for example, under the section on 'Industries' the subsections are in the order : "Combination of Enterprise", 'Competition', 'Enterprise Autonomy', 'Responsibility System' etc. Laws and regulations with a subsection are arranged chronologically.

5 Whenever possible, the date and the name of the promulgation authority have been noted.

6. Some of the laws and regulations have been slightly amended since their promulgation. We have made relevant notes and revisions whenever such cases arise.

ACKNOWLEDGEMENTS

We thank the following people who have supported our work with their encouragement and expert advice on the editing and translation of this book.

Mr. Wong Mincan, officer of the Ministry of Justice of the People's Republic of China.

Mr. J. D. McGregor, Director of the Hong Kong General Chamber of Commerce.

Mr. William W. S. Lo, Solicitor of the Supreme Court of Hong Kong.

Mr. Fredric M. Kaplan, President and Publisher, Eurasia Press, Inc.

EDITORIAL STAFF FOR ENGLISH EDITION

Chief Editor: Dr. Victor Fung Shuen Sit

Editors: William Wai Shing Lo
Fredric M. Kaplan
Albert Hok Man Wong
Louis Wing Hong Wong

Managing Editor: Albert Hok Man Wong

Editorial Staff: Windis Fu
Tracy Wu
Clara Wong

Cover Design: Leung So

CONTENTS

SECTION III: FINANCE AND BANKING

SECTION IV: INSURANCE

SECTION VII: TAXATION

SECTION XVII: MEASUREMENTS

SECTION XVIII: STANDARDIZATION AND QUALITY CONTROLS

SECTION XIX: AWARDS AND PROTECTION OF INVENTION

SECTION XX: LABOUR WELFARE AND ORGANIZATION

SECTION XXIII: STATISTIC

SECTION XXIV: ENVIRONMENTAL PROTECTION

RESOLUTION OF THE STANDING COMMITTEE OF THE NATIONAL PEOPLE'S CONGRESS CONCERNING THE EFFECT OF LAWS AND DECREES FORMULATED SINCE THE FOUNDING OF THE PEOPLE'S REPUBLIC OF CHINA

(Adopted by the 12th Meeting of the Standing Committee of the Fifth National People's Congress on November 29, 1979)

For the purpose of strengthening and perfecting the socialist legal system and ensuring the smooth advance of the socialist modernization construction, in the spirit of the resolution of the First Session of the First National People's Congress in 1954 that the current laws and decrees of the People's Republic of China shall remain in force, we now resolve: the laws and decrees formulated or approved by the previous Central People's Government since the founding of the People's Republic of China on October 1, 1949 and the laws and decrees formulated or approved by the National People's Congress and the Standing Committee of the National People's Congress since the formulation of the Constitution of the People's Republic of China at the First Session of the First National People's Congress on September 20, 1954 shall remain in force with the exception of those which go against the constitution and laws formulated by the Fifth National People's Congress and against the decrees formulated or approved by the Standing Committee of the Fifth National People's Congress.

1

INDUSTRY

Combination of Enterprise/ Competition/ Enterprise Autonomy/ Responsibility System/ Transport

PROVISIONAL REGULATIONS CONCERNING THE PROMOTION OF ECONOMIC COMBINATION

Adopted by Executive Meeting of the State Council (July 1, 1980)

Following the preliminary reform of the system of economic management, certain forms of economic combination have emerged in many places. Such combination helps to make full use of the advantages of each economic unit, while making up for its deficiencies, achieving greater economic results and speeding up production and construction. It helps to channel the material and financial resources of local governments and enterprises into serving the urgent needs of the nation's construction. It helps to build up the horizontal connections between different areas and departments according to economic laws and to break down regional blockades and unreasonable division of production and distribution by the various departments. It facilitates the reorganization of industry according to the principle of specialized co-operation, avoiding such practices as small factories squeezing out big ones, duplication in the building of plants and blindness in production. To take the path of combination and to organize various forms of economic combination is a requirement of the readjustment of our economy and of the further reform of our economic system. It represents an inevitable trend of development in our national economy. With a view to promoting economic combination, the following provisional regulations have been worked out:

1 In organizing economic combination, one must proceed from the urgent needs of the development of production, adhere to the principle of voluntary participation and not use administrative orders to force various enterprises to combine. Generally, the combination of enterprises should start at the lower level, although in some cases it may also begin at the top. It should proceed gradually, from the easier to the more difficult and should expand step by step. The combination should not be accomplished in haste.

The combination of enterprises should not be restricted by trades, territories and ownership or by their relationship of subordination. However, the ownership, relationship of subordination and financial relations of the combined enterprises must not be changed arbitrarily. These enterprises must not change their original arrangement for handing over their income, or their credit and debt relationships with banks. If changes must be made, they should obtain the prior agreement of the relevant financial department and bank.

Combination must be effected according to the principle of equality and mutual benefit, and consideration must be given to the economic interests of all parties concerned. On the basis of their respective contributions, including funds, raw materials, technology, labour power, sites, equipment and installations, the parties to the combination will determine the proportion in which the proceeds of their operation (profit and products) will be divided among themselves and an agreement or contract will be signed accordingly.

The form of combination should conform to actual conditions. Many different forms are allowed and no one particular type should be enforced.

2 Provided that targets set by the state are met, the combinations of various types may dispose of their products in excess of the planned targets, as well as products manufactured with materials arranged by themselves, in the following ways: They may ask the commercial and supply departments to purchase certain kinds of their products. For others, they may market them directly according to state policy, with each supplying what the others need.

3 Combinations of producers and processors of raw materials should be promoted. First of all, the tasks set by the state for the transfer of raw materials must be fulfilled. For some raw materials it has supplied to the processer in excess of planned targets, the producer may be compensated through consultation by receiving a suitable share of the profit or processed goods from the processor. As for others, they may be processed on the spot under the joint management of the processor and the producer of the raw materials.

If one of the combined enterprises requires raw materials produced by another, it may obtain them directly from the latter without going through the intermediate links of commercial, supply and marketing and materials distribution departments. As for certain kinds of materials that are distributed by the state, these can still be sent to the processor by the producer directly, or through the commercial, supply and marketing and materials distribution departments. This is to be done according to the original relation of subordination of each party and according to principles of economy and rationality.

4 All combined enterprises must guarantee their payment of taxes and profits to the state so as to fulfil their obligations. They are not allowed to make inroads in state revenue.

The parties to the combination should continue to carry out their original regulations concerning wages and welfare benefits for the workers and staff, and may not change these regulations as they please.

5 The leadership of the combined enterprises should practice democratic and scientific management in a spirit of cooperation and of taking joint responsibility. The enterprises should have a combination committee as the organ of authority consisting of the representatives of all parties concerned. None of these parties has the right to change the decisions made by the committee, and arbitrary interference by the administrative departments is not allowed.

The parties to a combination shall not interrupt their cooperative relationships with other departments without mutual agreement through consultation. While fulfilling their contracts of cooperation, they may establish business relations with other enterprises outside the combination. Enterprises which have joined a combination for specialized cooperation should not "eat the rice cooked in one big pot" and each should be responsible for its own income and expenditure.

6 After an agreement on combination has been reached, each party to the combination should report to its own department in charge and to the concerned department of administration of industry and commerce for the record. The combination agreement and contract signed by the parties to the combination shall be protected by the law of the state, and its funds, equipment and materials shall not be appropriated or transferred by any person or organization. If any party to the combination fails to fulfil the agreement or contract or in the event of a dispute in the process of executing it, the department in charge will mediate between the parties. Should the mediation fail to produce any result, the dispute shall be settled by arbitration by the court.

7 With regard to an economic combination involving several provinces, municipalities or regions, or of different trades, the constituent parties may work out temporary arrangements on problems of administrative leadership, material supply and the distribution of products.

8 The governments at all levels should give competent leadership to economic combination. They should support and encourage all forms of economic combination which facilitate the development of production, accelerate supplies and marketing and promote economic prosperity. The governments should respect the power of the enterprises to make their own decisions, and should not cause any unjustified administrative interference in the affairs of the enterprises. To speed up their socialist construction, the governments at all levels should be good at guiding the enterprises to adapt their enthusiasm for economic combination to the sound development of production in society.

Along with the development of various types of economic combination, a series of new problems may crop up which require the departments concerned to make corresponding improvements in policies, regulations and measures so as to promote the consolidation and expansion of economic combination. The planning departments should strengthen overall balance. The departments in charge of the administration of industry and commerce should improve their work to make the various forms of combination beneficial to the readjustment and development of the national economy. The banks should use such means as credit and interest rates to support the different combinations, giving priority to those that operate more successfully. The banks should organize account-settling work and try out various kinds of trust agreements according to the characteristics of the various forms of economic combination. The financial and tax authorities should improve the taxation system and solve the problem of double taxation on components which are produced by one of the enterprises within the economic combination, and which are used in the assembly of a complete piece of equipment produced by another, etc. Promoting economic combination is an important policy of our country. All localities and departments should enthusiastically protect and support it and continuously sum up experiences so as to enable this policy to develop healthily.

We hope that all localities and departments will carry out the present provisional regulations in light of their specific conditions.

PROVISIONAL REGULATIONS CONCERNING THE DEVELOPMENT AND PROTECTION OF SOCIALIST COMPETITION

(Adopted by Executive Meeting of the State Council on October 17, 1980)

Since the Third Plenary Session of the 11th Central Committee of the Chinese Communist Party, competition has developed steadily with the implementation of the policy of "readjustment, restructuring, consolidation and improvement" of our economy, especially with the expansion of the rights of enterprises to make their own decisions and the utilization of the regulating role of the market. Having displayed its vitality in our economic life, competition is giving an impetus to economic development and technological progress. There are essential differences between socialist competition and capitalist competition. The former, being developed on the basis of the public ownership of the means of production and under the guidance of the state plan, serves the socialist economy. It plays an important role in bringing into play the initiative and creativity of production and business units and of the workers, in making full use of their strong points and avoiding their weaknesses, in promoting the combination of enterprises and further activating our economy so as to constantly meet the people's demands and speed up the four modernizations. We should gradually reform the existing system of economic management, energetically develop competition and protect its smooth progress. For this purpose, the following provisional regulations have been worked out:

1 In the course of developing competition, all production and business units should ensure the fulfilment of their production and sales plans as set by the state and make great efforts to improve management, strengthen business accounting, increase the varieties of their products, raise their quality, reduce the consumption of energy, raw and processed materials, cut down costs and expenses, raise labour efficiency and improve their services. They should try to compete with each other, steadily raising the level of production and technology and the level of business management so as to achieve good economic results.

2 To develop competition, an enterprise must be granted greater power to make its own decisions and its status as a relatively independent commodity producer should be respected. No local authority or department is allowed to interfere with the rights which an enterprise is entitled to enjoy under government policies, laws and regulations, rights with regard to production, supply and marketing, personnel, finance and materials. Agreements and contracts concluded between enterprises will be honoured by both parties and protected by the laws of the state. If a party breaks a contract, it shall be held responsible economically and legally. An enterprise may work out its own production plan or undertake tasks in co-operation with other enterprises according to market demand, provided that such plans ensure the supply of goods as required by the state. In addition to materials to be allocated by the state, an enterprise may purchase the materials it needs from other areas and units, insofar as this is permitted by government policies and laws. The areas and departments concerned must not hinder them. As for materials that are allocated by the state according to plan, steps should be taken gradually to give enterprises some freedom in choosing where to buy them. An enterprise has the right to resist all attempts to violate its power to make its own decisions and may lodge complaints with higher authorities.

3 While the socialist public ownership plays the dominant role in the economy, competition shall be allowed and encouraged among the various economic sectors and among the enterprises, enabling each to bring its own advantages into play. In economic activities, no monopoly of commodities shall be allowed, except those which the state has specified to be handled exclusively by certain departments and units. Tenders may be invited and submitted for the construction of production and business projects which can be undertaken by contractors. Those collective and individual economic units which are beneficial to the national economy and the people's livelihood should be given help after they have registered and started business. With overall arrangements in place, they should be given lenient treatment with regard to the supply of goods, payments for goods, taxation, labour power, marketing of products, etc. Their legitimate rights and interests should be protected by the laws of the state. No department or person shall appropriate their assets, impose irrational burdens on them or encroach on their interests.

4 Channels of commodity circulation shall be increased to open ground for competition. In principle, an enterprise may market products that are its own in excess of the planned target, those turned out with raw and processed materials arranged by itself, and goods it has trial-produced. Goods in short supply and those to be purchased, marketed and allocated exclusively by the state must be first of all purchased by the state. The enterprise may be permitted to market a portion of certain products itself. The prices of the products thus sold should be fixed according to the relevant stipulations. Distribution channels shall be increased while the number of intermediate links is reduced. The enterprises shall be permitted to use various distribution channels and to reduce the number of intermediate links, to adopt diverse forms of operation to link up production with demand and to speed up the circulation of commodities. With a view to promoting the marketing of their goods, enterprises of a certain area may set up marketing offices in other areas, hold trade fairs there, or commission others to act as their agents. Urban enterprises may do the same in rural districts, and vice versa.

5 To develop competition, irrational prices must be readjusted gradually. The prices of certain commodities selected by the state are allowed to fluctuate within a prescribed range. In accordance with state policies and the changes in the condition of supply and demand on the market, the enterprises have the power to lower the prices of the capital goods they have turned out, provided that this will not affect their delivery of profit to the state. If an enterprise wants to raise the prices of its goods, it must obtain the approval of the relevant authorities as stipulated by the division of power in price management. The price of all major commodities which are closely related to the people's livelihood must be kept basically stable.

6 To promote competition, regional blockades must be broken and the partition of the market by different departments must be stopped. No area or department is allowed to enforce a blockade or to forbid the sale of outside products in its own area or department. It must ensure the export of the raw and processed materials it produces according to the state plan, and any blockade is impermissible. To facilitate competition, the departments in charge of industry, communications, finance and trade must revise that part of existing regulations and rules which hinders competition. It is illegal to adopt administrative means to protect the backward and to restrict the advanced, obstructing the normal circulation of commodities; such practices must be abolished.

7 In order to encourage technological innovation and inventions, and to protect the economic benefits due to the departments and personnel concerned, compensation should be made for the transfer of the possession of important technological achievements. For this purpose, the State Council departments concerned shall draw up relevant policies and regulations. Before such documents are formulated, the problem should be solved through consultation between the enterprises. In the course of competition, we should promote technical exchange in the spirit of socialist co-operation.

8 To engage in competition, enterprises should strictly observe government policies and laws and practise lawful means. Attention should be paid to building up reputation and observing business morality. It is impermissible to practise fraud, to offer and accept bribes, to engage in speculation and seek exorbitant profits at the expense of the interest of the state and the people. Those who violate law and discipline should be dealt with by law according to the severity of the circumstances.

9 Government at all levels and the departments in charge of different enterprises should deepen their understanding, keep abreast of the current situation and give better leadership to competition as the circumstances demand. They should work in a down-to-earth way to render services, coordinate, plan as a whole and supervise, grasp the new situation and resolve new contradictions and problems in good time. In order to ensure that competition develops soundly, they should learn to master the law of economics and work out the necessary economic laws and regulations by making use of such economic links as prices, taxes, credit and rates of interest. Those enterprises which consume less energy and materials in turning out good-quality products at low costs should enjoy priority in obtaining raw and processed materials and energy resources. With regard to backward enterprises, some should be consolidated and helped to improve their management and administration so as to catch up with the others. In the course of readjusting the national economy, others shall be reorganized, change their line of production or merge with other enterprises. They shall be encouraged to take the path of combination. The economically developed areas should pay attention to helping the underdeveloped areas. Economic management departments at various levels must give better guidance to plan-

ing and market management, do a good job in making market investigations and forecasts, make comprehensive analyses of the trends of development of products and the market situation so as to guide the enterprises to improve their production and management, and avoid blindness in production and construction that may arise in the course of competition.

10 It is hoped that all economic enterprises will earnestly try out the above provisional regulations in the light of their specific conditions. Every area and department may work out implementing rules on the basis of these regulations, to protect the development of competition.

TENTATIVE MEASURES CONCERNING THE SHARING OF PROFITS IN STATE-OWNED INDUSTRIAL ENTERPRISES

Issued by the State Economic Commission and the Ministry of Finance
(Approved by the State Council on January 22, 1980)

In July 1979 the State Council issued the "Regulations on the Sharing of Profits in State-Owned Enterprises," and the Ministry of Finance, the State Economic Commission and the People's Bank also published the "Opinions Concerning Some Concrete Problems in the Experimental Work Of Putting into Effect the State Council Document on Restructuring the Enterprise Management System." These two documents have helped to bring into play the initiative of enterprises and to encourage enterprises to show interest in production and increase their profits.

In order to improve the experimental work, ensure the collection of state revenues and give consideration to the interests of the state, the enterprises and individual workers, the measures concerning the sharing of profits in state-owned industrial enterprises were revised after problems and opinions collected from various parts of the country in the course of the experiment were discussed at the National Planning Meeting. The revised measures are as follows:

Article 1 State-owned industrial enterprises which have maintained normal production order and management after consolidation, retained independent economic accounting and have profits may, with approval, try out the profit-sharing system in accordance with the Measures.

Article 2 The original method of drawing shares from the total profit is changed to the method of drawing shares from the basic profit and the increase in profit. If the profit of an enterprise in the current year is bigger than that in the preceding year, the enterprise may draw a share from the basic profit, which is equivalent to its profit in the preceding year, according to the assessed proportions, and then draw another share from the increase in profit, that is, the part above the profit in the preceding year, according to the proportions defined by the state.

If the profit of an enterprise in the current year is smaller than that in the preceding year, the enterprise may draw a basic share from its actual profit in the current year according to the assessed proportions. In calculating the shares to be drawn from the basic profit or from the increase in profit, the amount of increased profit attributable to technical measures adopted with depreciation funds and funds pooled by the enterprise itself should be included.

An enterprise may use the shares drawn from the basic profit and the increase in profit for its production development fund, workers' welfare fund and workers' bonus fund.

Article 3 When an enterprise obtains approval to start the experiment, the proportions of shares it draws from the basic profit shall be determined by the percentage of the following expenses in the preceding year to the total amount of profit in the same year:

(1) Enterprises assigned to develop new products may, on the whole, calculate the cost of new product development at 1% of the total profit. Those enterprises which have been assigned to develop more new products may calculate the cost of new product development at 2% of the total profit. Machine-building plants may calculate the cost at 3% of the total profit. Enterprises which are not assigned to develop new products, e.g., coal mines, oilfields, power plants, power stations, lumber centres, railways and other communications, and other mining enterprises, shall not calculate this cost.

(2) An enterprise's expenses for scientific research and for workers' technical training are calculated on the basis of the government's actual allocations to the enterprise (not including the three special appropriations given by the government for scientific and technical work and expenses for adopting technical measures). The expenses not included in the production cost of an enterprise or its business turnover shall be calculated according to the formula stated above.

(3) The workers' welfare fund to be drawn from the cost of production shall be calculated at 11% of total wages.

(4) Workers' bonuses, paid from the cost of production as a whole, shall be calculated at 10% of the total basic wages of an enterprise. The percentage may be raised proportionately for a limited number of advanced enterprises, but it shall not constitute more than 12% of total basic wages.

(5) The percentage of enterprise funds to be drawn from the profit by a basic level enterprise shall be stated separately by the authorities and shall constitute no more than 5% of total wages, depending on varying conditions in enterprises.

The sums in items (1) and (2) constitute the production development fund. The amount in item (3) and 80% of the amount in item (5) constitute the workers' welfare fund. The amount in item (4) and 20% of the amount in item (5) constitute the workers' bonus fund, Proportional shares of profits to be drawn by enterprises shall be assessed separately for the three funds.

The total profit for calculating the proportional share from the basic part is the amount of profit after the loan for technical measures to be returned is deducted. After the system of drawing the workers' welfare fund and bonus fund from the cost of production is replaced by the system of drawing them from profit, the total profit for calculating the proportion share from the basic part should be increased correspondingly.

After the profit-sharing system is introduced, the government shall no longer make appropriations for the expenses which should be paid from the share of profit, and enterprises shall no longer include expenses as part of the production cost nor draw enterprise funds.

Article 4 The proportions of shares which enterprises will draw from the increased part of profit are separately stated for different industries as follows:

(1) 10% for petroleum, power, and petrochemical enterprises and enterprises with complete plants imported from abroad which earn considerably more profits;

(2) 20% for metallurgical, machine-building, electronic, chemical, light industry, textile, building materials, timber, railway and other communications and other enterprises;

(3) 30% for coal mining, post and telecommunicatons, civil aviation and farm machinery enterprises.

Article 5 The proportions of shares from the basic part of profit shall be assessed level by level from top to bottom. The total proportions of shares of profits retained by the provinces, municipalities, autonomous regions and the ministries in charge of production shall be assessed by the State Economic Commission and the Ministry of Finance. The provinces, municipalities, autonomous regions and the ministries in charge of production may separately assess the proportions of shares of profits retained by the enterprises (or corporations) under them within the limits of the total proportions of shares assessed by the state.

Article 6 The assessed proportions of shares from the basic part of profit shall, in principle, remain unchanged for three years. Adjustments may be made under the following circumstances:

(1) The readjustment of the prices of products, the prices of major raw materials and the restructuring of the taxation system lead to big increases or decreases in the profits of enterprises;

(2) The readjustment of the enterprises in the industrial reorganization leads to big increases or decreases in the profits of enterprises;

(3) The operation of workshops, branch factories and attached factories that are newly-built or expanded with government investment leads to big increases in the profits of enterprises;

(4) The profits of enterprises decrease after they pay taxes on fixed assets and interest on fixed loans.

Article 7 An industrial enterprise can draw a full share of profit as stated only when it reaches the four planned targets for output, quality, profit and fulfilment of its contracts to supply goods. If an enterprise fails to reach one of the four planned quotas, a deduction of 10% shall be made from its share of profit (including both the share from the basic part of profit and the share from the increased part of profit).

Quotas for assessment in the railway and other land and water transport, post and telecommunications and civil aviation enterprises shall be defined separately by the ministries in charge of these enterprises and the Ministry of Finance through consultation.

Article 8 An enterprise shall draw a full share from the basic part of profit as stated if it fulfills its monthly target; it shall draw 80% of its share in advance for the month if it fails to fulfil its monthly target. An enterprise may draw 50% of its share in advance from the increased part of profit as stated if it fulfills 50% or more of its annual quota in the first six months, but it is not permitted to draw any shares from the increased part of profit in advance if it fails to fulfil 50% of the annual quota. The share of profit an enterprise is entitled to shall be included in its final accounts at the end of a year. A surplus shall be refunded and a deficiency made up when the final accounts are settled after an examination by the department above in charge and by the financial department at the same level.

When an enterprise draws a share of profit, the profit shall be calculated after the enterprise repays its loan for technical measures.

Article 9 An enterprise shall draw its share from the basic part of profit according to the assessed percentages separately for the production development fund, the workers' welfare fund and the workers' bonus fund, and shall also manage and use them separately for these purposes. The amount drawn by an enterprise from the increased part of profit to be used for development of production shall not be less than 60% and the amount used for workers' welfare facilities and bonuses shall not be more than 40%. The production development fund may be used together with the capital fund for replacing or revamping old equipment, but not for workers' welfare or bonuses. The bonuses issued to workers shall be paid from the workers' bonus fund, except the savings bonus stated separately by the government. An enterprise should draw the workers' bonus fund before using it and the bonus fund shall not exceed the quota. Total bonuses issued to the workers of an enterprise which draws a greater bonus fund than others, calculated on the basis of the enterprise as a unit, shall not exceed an amount equivalent to the basic wages of the workers in the enterprise for two months. The surplus of the bonus fund shall be carried over to the following year.

Article 10 An enterprise's plan for the use of the funds drawn from profit must be submitted to the workers' congress of the enterprise for discussion. The funds must be placed under full democratic management and mass supervision.

Article 11 The quantity of materials and equipment needed by an enterprise for adopting production measures or for improving welfare facilities with the retained share of profit should be reported to the planning commissions and departments in charge of surplus at all levels and should be included in the plans for settlement.

Article 12 In practising the profit-sharing system, enterprises must conscientiously carry out the party's policies and principles and state plans, and must adhere to financial guidelines; they must not resort to fraud and deception. If an enterprise violates the guidelines, the departments above in charge of the work should make a deduction from the share of profit accruing to the enterprise or suspend the enterprise's right to draw the share of profit in a given period, depending on the severity of the case, and the leaders of the enterprise and other people involved shall be dealt with sternly.

Subject to approval, these measures shall be adopted on an experimental basis in state-owned industrial enterprises beginning in 1980. Enterprises which have already started the experiment according to local measures must all change to adopt these measures as of 1980.

PROVISIONAL REGULATIONS OF THE STATE CAPITAL CONSTRUCTION COMMISSION, THE STATE PLANNING COMMISSION, THE MINISTRY OF FINANCE, THE STATE BUREAU OF LABOUR AND THE STATE ADMINISTRATION OF SUPPLIES ON PROBLEMS RELATED TO THE BROADENING OF THE MANAGEMENT DECISION-MAKING POWER OF CONSTRUCTION ENTERPRISES

(May 4, 1980)

It is essential to broaden appropriately the decision-making power of construction enterprises in matters of management in order to operate them as basic units of material production with independent management and accounting, to further arouse the enthusiasm of the construction enterprises and their workers and staff, to improve management, to increase economic returns, and to fulfil capital construction tasks with greater, faster, better and more economic results. Following are the relevant regulations:

1 Broaden the power of decision of the enterprises in the management of production. The drafting of production plans for construction enterprises should, under the guidance of the unified state plan, be changed over step by step to the practice of taking contracts as the basis. While assigning construction tasks to the enterprises, the department in charge should guarantee the material conditions they require in order to fulfil the tasks. So long as they guarantee the fulfilment of the tasks assigned by the state, the enterprises should have the right to contract on their own certain construction jobs or to develop the provision of multiple services to construction work in the light of their own conditions and social needs. No unit or individual should interfere with the normal business of production and management within the enterprises.

2 Reform the methods of material supply. Building materials, forms, tools and materials for erecting large provisional facilities needed in capital construction projects should be supplied within the overall consideration of manpower, funds and materials supplies. Before major reforms are made in the entire system of material supply, the following three methods can be adopted in the contracting of jobs and material supplies for construction enterprises:

A. Materials needed by construction enterprises under the ministries of metallurgical, coal, power, railways, communications, petroleum, second machine-building and chemical industries are allocated to the ministries concerned according to existing regulations and then distributed by the ministries directly to the construction units in line with the needs of the projects to be built.

B. With regard to projects whose budgets are covered by the central government, the materials needed are to be determined by central government in accordance with the progress of the projects, and the practice of delivering materials to the construction sites is to be adopted step by step.

C. The supply of materials for construction projects undertaken by enterprises under the State Bureau of Building Industry is to be handled in the following ways:

For local projects belonging to provinces, municipalities or autonomous regions, the practice of allocating materials to the departments in charge of construction or directly to the construction units is to be adopted by the related departments in the provinces, municipalities or autonomous regions concerned; for projects directly belonging to various departments under the State Council, the departments in charge may earmark quotas for material consumption or supply materials to the construction units directly; the construction units may use the materials in a flexible way in line with the order of priority of the projects.

3 Restore the practice of retaining legal profits. All state-run construction enterprises that practice independent accounting are entitled, beginning from 1980, to draw a legal profit equivalent, for the time being, to 2.5% of the budgeted cost of the project. The legal profit does not have to be turned over to the higher authorities but is kept entirely by the enterprises themselves in the first three years. After the first three years, the profit will be handled according to the ratio of distribution specified in Item 4. Following the adoption of the practice of retaining the legal profit, construction units will no longer charge the departments owning the projects for funds to operate schools for workers' children.

4 Introduce the practice of reserving part

of the building cost saved in construction. The amount of building cost saved by the construction enterprises together with other income that remains after non-business expenditures and stipulated enterprise funds are duly deducted, will be divided in half, one of which is to be turned over to the financial authorities and the other to be kept by the enterprise. When the profits to be turned over by an enterprise to the higher authorities on a 50/50 basis exceed the amount handed over in the previous year, the enterprise is then required to hand over only 20% of the excess portion while retaining the rest. In order to foster development in areas populated by national minorities and in remote provinces, construction enterprises belonging to the provinces and autonomous regions of Yunnan, Guizhou, Tibet, Xinjiang, Qinghai, Ningxia and Inner Mongolia, together with enterprises for constructing hydroelectric projects under the Ministry of Power Industry, are allowed to hand in to the financial authorities only 30% of the year's profits while keeping the rest. They do not have to follow the practice of reserving part of the excess portion of above-quota profits.

Those units which have been authorized by provincial, municipal or autonomous regional governments to practice the system of sole responsibility for profit or loss may continue to act according to existing rules.

The legal profit and the share of saved building costs reserved by construction enterprises should be used mainly for expanding production and for the workers' collective welfare facilities.

5 Replace the practice of receiving government investments by charging fees for construction tasks as payment for technical equipment needed by local state-run construction enterprises. Beginning from 1981, the government will no longer make investments to cover the expenses of technical equipment for local state-run construction enterprises. They can charge fees equivalent to 3% of the budgeted cost of the projects contracted and, if this is insufficient, borrow money from the Construction Bank to cover the balance. This practice may be introduced this year (1980) in those provinces, municipalities and autonomous regions which generally have not yet allocated funds for the purchase of technical equipment for construction enterprises. Fund earmarked for technical equipment must be used for this purpose only. The surplus left over from one year can be used during the following year. Departments in charge of construction enterprises in various areas should control an appropriate amount of such funds in their hands, make an overall arrangement and use them flexibly according to the level of equipment and the tasks of different enterprises under them.

Regulations governing the equipment funds of those construction units directly under the departments of the State Council will be studied and formulated separately.

6 Introduce a quota system for expenditures on large temporary facilities and building materials. Specific quotas will be determined by the State Planning Commission, the State Capital Construction Commission, the Ministry of Finance and the State Bureau of Supplies in line with the circumstances of different construction enterprises and will be assigned to them separately. Surpluses can be used by the construction enterprises for building houses to improve the workers' living conditions.

7 Broaden the scope of authority of the enterprises in the management of labour and wages. In view of the fact that construction tasks change frequently, that workers are constantly on the move and are scattered and that construction projects often involve work high above ground and field operations, the enterprises may recruit temporary workers directly through local labour departments to meet the needs of the projects. When recruiting permanent workers in line with the state employment plan, the enterprises have the right to choose the best through examination according to the needs of production. In view of the characteristics of construction enterprises, the labour departments should allot to them as few women workers as possible. The enterprises may, on the principle of "to each according to his work" and in the light of specific tasks, adopt the system of time-wages plus bonuses or piece-rate wages. Bonuses may be given to those who complete their projects ahead of schedule while meeting the requirements for engineering quality, material consumption and safety in operation; bonuses are to be paid by project-owning units out of their own revenues. Bonuses may also be given to those who economize on the three major categories of building materials — 8 to 15% of the cost saved for timber; 3 to 8% of the cost saved for cement; and 1 to 3% of the cost saved for rolled steel. These bonuses are to be paid out of the money saved. The specific regulations for these matters will be drafted by the State Capital Construction Commission after consultation with the Ministry of Finance and the State Bureau of Labour.

8 Reduce the added burdens on construction enterprises. No unit or individual is permitted to apportion expenses to construction enterprises

or to transfer their personnel, equipment or funds to other uses beyond the explicit stipulations of the state. Or, the enterprises have the right to reject them. When personnel are transferred with authorization, their wages and expenses are to be borne by the units that employ them.

9 Uphold the principle of combining right and responsibility and fulfil obligations strictly. All enterprises must, under the leadership of the department in charge and under the supervision of the workers' congresses, correctly exercise their rights and strictly fulfil the following obligations:

A. Uphold the four basic principles (Communist Party leadership, the dictatorship of the proletariat, the socialist road, and Marxism-Leninism-Mao Zedong Thought); conscientiously implement state principles, policies, laws and decrees; and safeguard state property from encroachment.

B. Try in every way to fulfil the state construction plans, conscientiously honour contracts and strictly observe financial regulations.

C. Keep to the work processes of capital construction, continuously improve management, raise the quality of projects, shorten construction time, lower building costs, accelerate the turnover of funds and increase work efficiency.

D. Strive to train qualified personnel, adopt advanced technology and scientific managerial methods, and work hard to raise technical and managerial levels.

E. Make rational use of basic depreciation funds, funds for major overhauls, legal profits and shares of saved building costs, tap potential and revamp enterprises systematically so as to expand production.

F. Ensure safety in operation, improve environmental protection, and improve the workers' physical fitness.

G. Correctly handle relationships among the state, the enterprises and the individual workers with regard to their material interests, and improve the workers' livelihood and welfare amenities step by step on the basis of expanded production.

H. Strengthen political and ideological work, continuously raise the workers' ideological awareness and communist ethics, educate them to observe state laws and decrees and labour discipline in an exemplary way.

The broadening of the decision-making power of construction enterprises in matters of management, which involves a wide range of complex problems, must be done actively and appropriately. All departments concerned should closely coordinate their efforts while consciously summing up experience so as to achieve success.

INTERIM CONCRETE PROCEDURES TO IMPLEMENT AND FULFILL STATE COUNCIL DOCUMENTS CONCERNING POWER EXPANSION AND TO CONSOLIDATE AND IMPROVE POWER EXPANSION

Jointly printed and distributed by the State Economic Commission, the System Reform Office of the State Council, the State Planning Commission, the Ministry of Finance, the Ministry of Commerce, the Ministry of Foreign Trade, the State Bureau of Supplies, the State Bureau of Lobour, the State Bureau of Prices and the People's Bank of China (May 20, 1981)

The Central Working Conference in December of 1980 fully affirmed reforms of the economic system since the Third Plenary Session of the 11th Central Committee of the CPC and explicitly pointed out that the direction of reform was right and that the results were remarkable. Meanwhile, it pointed out that current economic work should be centered on regulation and that reform should be subordinate and be advantageous to the regulation. Those reform measures that had proved effective in every respect should be maintained continuously and should not be allowed to be turned back. The results of reform should be consolidated and developed and a small number of new experiments in reform should be taken step by step under the leadership. The leading comrades of the State Council have recently pointed out that we shall not lose sight of the beneficial effects of the reform on regulation and that many regulating measures can work only if they are coordinated with the reform; some reform measures are closely related with and cannot be separated from the regulations and the reform measures which are advantageous to the regulations and which help invigorate the economy shall vigorously be carried out.

More than two years' practice of experiments in expanding the powers of enterprises to act on their own has proved that Documents No.23 and No.226 (1980) of the State Council embody the Party's policy, accord with the actual conditions of the industrial and communications enterprises in our country and do play a positive role in ensuring the fulfillment of state plans and in invigorating the economy and increasing economic benefit. However, the present power-expanded enterprises (including the corporations and head plants with experiments made in power expansion) have mainly put the profit reserves into practice, but have not yet fulfilled the other contents of reform. In order to further fulfill the due expansion of enterprises' powers to act on their own so as to enable various reform measures to go on simultaneously and completely, help consolidate and improve power expansion experiments, give full play to the potentialities of more than 6,000 power-expanded enterprises and further invigorate the microscopic economy while at the same time strengthening the planning directions for the macroscopic economy, the State Economic Commission, the System Reform Office of the State Council, the State Planning Commission, the Ministry of Finance, the Ministry of Commerce, the Ministry of Foreign Trade, the State Bureau of Supplies, the State Bureau of Labour, the State Bureau of Prices and the People's Bank have jointly worked out the Interim Concrete Procedures to further implement and fulfill the documents Nos. 23 and 226 (1980) and No. 48 (1981) of the State Council in accordance with the spirit of the related instructions of the Central Committee and the State Council and with experiences in the practice of reform of every area and every department. Now they are distributed among all areas and departments for implementation among power-expanded enterprises.

I Planning

(1) The plan of an enterprise shall be worked out in accordance with the requirements transmitted by the state, the demands of the market, the productive capacity of the enterprise itself and variables in the supply of fuel and raw materials. After it is submitted from below to above, considered jointly by the higher and lower levels, synthesized and balanced and dovetailed with the plans of other enterprises, it shall be transmitted as an enterprise plan by the department in charge in a uniform manner in accordance with its subordinate relationships. The enterprise shall ensure the fulfillment of the production plan

and the allocation and transfer plan transmitted by the state. The department which transmits the production plan shall make appropriate arrangements for the production conditions required by the enterprise for the fulfillment of the state plans. An enterprise shall try in every possible way to increase the production of light industrial or textile products which are salable in the market, energy output and processed materials; an enterprise shall not produce any products in excess of the limits fixed in the plan and the supply of energy resources and raw materials shall be controlled in accordance with limited output. A production plan transmitted by the department in charge shall be positive and reliable and should have some margin left for the enterprise to readjust the variety, produce new products on a trial basis and make a good job of the combination of production and demand. When the planned targets are found not to be in conformity with actual conditions in the course of implementing the plan, the enterprise shall submit a report to the department transmitting the plan and put forward suggestions to amend them; with regard to an instructive plan, the enterprise shall be entitled to make proper regulations and supplements and submit them to the department in charge for record. The division of orderly and instructive targets shall be put into trial effect in some departments and on some products as of 1982.

(2) The planning department at each level shall implement the principles of choosing and arranging for what is better and of choosing and purchasing what is better when drawing up a plan. Priority shall be given to an enterprise with small consumption, low cost and good quality in the arrangement for and the purchase of the same product.

(3) A power-expanded enterprise shall ensure the fulfillment of the state planned tasks (including production, supply and marketing tasks). With the prerequisite to ensure the fulfillment of the state planned tasks, the enterprise shall endeavour to increase the production of the short supplied products, light industrial or textile products and export products needed by the state and by the market in accordance with the conditions of fuel, power and raw materials; make good jobs of processing with supplied materials, assembling business and technical services; and adopt a variety of forms such as cooperative operation or joint operation to bring productive capacity into play.

(4) In order to make clear the economic responsibility, the producing, supplying, marketing and transporting parties shall sign and strictly fulfill contracts for the products included in state plans and purchased by the state. An enterprise shall organize the production in accordance with quality, quantity, category and date of delivery as stipulated in the plan and in the sales contract and deliver the product monthly or quarterly; material, commercial or trade and transportation departments shall do their best in the supply of raw materials, the purchase of products and in their transportation as stipulated in plans and contracts.

Parties in violation of a contract shall bear the economic responsibility. Amendments to contracts shall be discussed and agreed upon by both parties. If any dispute occurs in the execution of a plan or a contract, both parties shall consult with each other and settle it by proceeding from the whole situation. If no agreement can be reached through consultation, it shall be handled in accordance with the provisions in "The Joint Notice of a Number of Problems in the Administration of Economic Contracts" of the State Economic Commission, the General Administration for Industry and Commerce and the People's Bank of China on August 8, 1979.

(5) The planning department at each level shall regularly circulate to enterprises the developments and tendencies in the national economy. Each industrial or communications ministry shall undertake tasks to provide enterprises with economic information and market forecasts and assign special organizations and personnel to take effective forms and measures to provide enterprises regularly with the information on the productive capacity, output, main economic and technical targets, price, sales, stock and changes in social demand for each major product within the same trade. Enterprises shall also keep abreast of social needs on their own initiative and do a good job in jointly coordinating between production and demand.

II Profit Reserves

(6) Provisions for the reservation of profits stipulated in Document No. 23 (1980) of the State Council shall continue to be implemented. Each province, municipality or autonomous region shall make an earnest summary of the procedures which were formulated by itself and put into effect in the past and make proper readjustments for some enterprises which reserve too many profits on the basis of doing ideological work well.

(7) A small number of power-expanded enterprises with insufficient tasks and great loss of profits shall first be regulated, reorganized or

merged and the structures of their products shall be regulated so as to get into the swing of the production. If normal staff's welfare and minimum rewards cannot be ensured through normal endeavour, proper measures shall be taken to look after them. They should not withdraw from the experiments nor return to the practice of "messing together" (distribution not according to contribution).

(8) If major changes occur in the profits of an enterprise owing to such factors as state regulation of the prices of raw materials or products, the base profit reserves of the enterprise shall be readjusted in accordance with the provisions in Document No. 23 (1980) of the State Council.

(9) For the purpose of settling the unequal share of rewards or hardships among various enterprises due to objective conditions, the bureau (or corporation) in charge shall make proper adjustments according to the appropriate management level, the relative merit of objective conditions, the possibility of an increase in production or revenue and the degree of the contribution to the state of each power-expanded enterprise in that trade. But these adjustments shall be made from the sums kept in reserve by the bureau (or corporation) in charge or from the financial resources obtained by gathering parts of the profit reserves of the enterprises under it, although such expenditures shall not be increased. Internal settlement prices shall be put into practice wherever feasible.

(10) The expansion of enterprises' powers to act on their own shall be combined with industrial reorganizations and mergers. Each area or department shall choose some qualified corporations in the nature of enterprises and make power expansion experiments with the corporation after approval. The unit with the experiments made by the corporation shall properly handle the relations of power centralization and power division between the corporation and the factories under it and rationally distribute the economic interests within the corporation. The corporation shall safeguard the due powers of the factories under it to act on their own, aiming at the invigoration of grass-roots enterprises; the factories shall respect the unified leadership of the corporation, submit to the overall arrangements of the corporation and vigorously support the achievement of the specialized reorganization. Accounting by levels shall strictly be put into practice within the corporation and equalitarianism shall not be practised. The corporation shall amass part of production development funds for the purpose of making technological transformations in a planned and focused way. A grass-roots enterprise shall also preserve a certain amount of production development funds. Staff welfare funds and rewards funds shall, in principle, be reserved by enterprises, but the corporation shall also gather a certain part of them to be used for the purpose of adjustments.

(11) In order to urge an enterprise to strengthen its business management and enhance its sense of economic responsibility, the power-expanded enterprise shall put the repaid expenditure of fixed funds and current funds into practice and the procedures for this shall be implemented in accordance with the relevant provisions of the Ministry of Finance. The economic effects of the expenditure of these funds shall be regularly checked and examined.

(12) An enterprise that belongs to a system or trade that has not undergone power expansion shall continue to put the system of enterprise funds into effect. For the enterprises with a little profit or running at a loss, different procedures shall be adopted respectively such as undertaking to accomplish a limited amount of profits and sharing the excessive part of the limit or incurring losses within allowed limits, obtaining no subsidies in case of excessive losses and reserving the funds saved from the reduction of losses so as to help arouse their enthusiasm and invigorate production.

In a large or medium city, the procedures for profit reserves shall be put into trial implementation by the trade step by step and in a planned way.

A small enterprise shall gradually implement the procedure of paying taxes instead of turning over profits and assuming sole responsibility for its own profits or losses.

(13) With regard to an enterprise of collective ownership in the second light industrial system (mainly referring to the handicraft industry), the state responsibility for its profits or losses shall gradually be changed into independent accounting and its sole responsibility for its own profits or losses; in general, the proportion of the profits kept in reserve by the enterprise after paying taxes shall not be less than 50 to 70 percent. With the approval of the people's government of the province, municipality or autonomous region, such procedures shall be implemented with the taxable income of the enterprise in the year 1980 used as a base which shall be fixed for several years without changes and with the annual increments in income tax or turned-over cooperative operating funds reduced by a certain proportion.

III Expenditure of Profit Reserves

(14) An enterprise has the power to dispose of profit reserves on its own. The enterprise shall rationally use the reserves in accordance with the state plans, policies, decrees and the guiding principle of regulation. With the prerequisite to ensure the renewal and overhaul of equipment, the enterprise shall use the production development funds in combination with the depreciation funds, overhaul funds or medium- or short-term equipment loans. It shall be put under the direction and supervision of the department in charge so as to prevent repeated construction. The production development funds of the enterprise shall mainly be used to save energy, reduce consumption, improve the quality of products, produce new products on trial basis, control "three wastes" (waste water, waste gas and individual residue) and take safe production measures as well as undertake technological transformations and equipment renewals related to these transformations; and to make up the deficiency of current funds in order to serve the needs of the development of production and make greater economic benefit of the limited funds. The projects completed by enterprises with the production development funds or other funds as required in the local or departmental plans shall be reported to the localities or the departments in charge for record; major projects shall be submitted to the higher authorities concerned for examination and approval as stipulated in Document No. 162 (1980) of the State Council, i.e. "Interim Procedures Annotated and Passed On by the State Council for the Strengthening of the Potentialities-tapping, Innovation and Transformation of Existing Industrial and Communications Enterprises."

(15) The profits obtained from the products of the comprehensive utilization launched for the purpose of eliminating pollution and controlling the "three wastes" shall not be turned over within five years as stipulated by the state and shall be left with the enterprise to continue to use them as expenditures in this respect.

(16) If a tapping, innovating, transforming, closing or transferring project arranged for by an enterprise with the depreciation funds and profit reserves over the years needs surplus deposits of the previous years to draw upon the bureau (or department) of finance, the economic commission, the planning commission and other departments concerned of each province, municipality or autonomous region shall form a combined examination group and strive to clearing them up. Priority shall be given to the light industrial, texile or energy-saving projects or those serving them for the release of the deposits.

(17) In order to better implement Document No. 10 (1980) of the State Council, a power-expanded enterprise shall make a serious summary and rectification of the granting of rewards. Those which are rational and advantageous to the mobilization of the staff's enthusiasm and the promotion of production shall be maintained; it shall resolutely be corrected and checked to arbitrarily apportion costs under all sorts of pretexts, recklessly give rewards, allowances, subsidies and material objects or resort to dishonest means. The welfare funds and rewarding funds of an enterprise shall be drawn and properly and rationally used strictly in accordance with the reservation proportion checked and determined by the state for the enterprise. Rewards shall be given in accordance with the controlled sums checked and determined by the bureau (or corporation) in charge with some margin left so as to make up for a deficiency with a surplus. A little more of reward funds shall be spared for building staff dormitories, canteens, bathrooms, nurseries, kindergartens, reading rooms, cultural or recreation places and other collective welfare facilities. The principle of the distribution according to work shall resolutely be implemented and equalitarianism shall be opposed. The procedures for the distribution of rewards shall be formulated and perfected and the system of job responsibility, that of assessment and that of rewards and punishments shall be combined so as to persist in the practice of reckoning the rewards by recording the points or practise excessive piece rate rewards for small collectives such as production groups or units composed of operators in co-ordinated processes of production machines and benches for the purpose of distributing different sums of rewards according to the relative merits of economic effects and enabling the rewards to play a realistic role in encouraging and rewarding the advanced. Piece rate wages shall be practised as far as possible without giving any rewards with the approval of the labour department in an enterprise which is normal in production, full of tasks, perfect in management, advanced in quotas and suitable for reckoning by the piece.

(18) The financial supervision over enterprises shall be strengthened. Jointly with the financial department, each department in charge shall make at least two examinations per year of enterprises' execution of financial and economic discipline and

resolutely object to illegal and discipline-violating activities.

IV The Sales of Products

(19) Commercial, material and industrial departments and the enterprises under them shall support and be closely coordinated with each other and jointly make good jobs of the dovetailing of production, supply and marketing. The reform of the forms of purchase and sale and the channels of circulation in the commodity circulation field shall be maintained and perfected. A variety of forms shall vigorously be put into trial practice such as industrial and commercial joint operations, direct partnerships between factories and stores, fixed production by selecting samples or patterns and coordinated processes of the purchase, supply, wholesale and retail sale of products not under plan so as to enlarge distribution channels, reduce intermediate links, speed up the circulation of commodities and make the market prosper.

(20) An industrial enterprise shall sell part of its products by itself in accordance with the self-selling scopes of different products stipulated by the state after ensuring the fulfillment of the state plans and purchase contracts. Self-selling scopes include those products kept in reserve as stipulated, those produced in excess of the plans (except for those otherwise stipulated by the state), those made from or of major raw materials organized and obtained by the enterprise itself, new ones produced on trial and those which are not purchased by the material or commercial department or which are overstocked. The material and commercial departments shall vigorously organize the purchases, duly provide industrial departments and enterprises with the information on the changes of the demand in the market and support enterprises in selling parts of their products by themselves as stipulated. The responsibility shall be investigated if any enterprise sells its products by itself before fulfilling the state plans or going outside stipulated scopes.

(21) Four forms of purchase and sale shall be practised for industrial products dealt with by commercial departments: (1) the commodities monopolistically purchased and sold (or distributed) by the state shall be purchased and dealt in by commercial departments in a unified way (excluding clothing exempted as materials in direct-supply experiments approved by the state) and the new products among them shall be market-tested by the enterprises themselves in the period of market-testing. (2) Commodities purchased according to plan shall be delivered by enterprises and purchased by commercial departments in accordance with the purchasing plans stipulated by the state, and overproduced ones shall be sold by enterprises themselves or purchased by commercial departments through negotiations. In the case of commodities purchased as planned which are seriously short of supply, such as sugar, cigarettes, matches, soap, pencils, etc., the overproduced parts shall first be purchased by commercial departments as in the present situation where the market is insufficiently supplied and in cases where the enterprises shall sell those products which are not purchased by the commercial departments by themselves. (3) With regard to the commodities ordered, both industrial and commercial parties shall dovetail production with marketing in accordance with the demand of the market. The production plans shall be transmitted down by the industrial department and the purchasing contracts shall be discussed and signed by both industrial and commercial parties. (4) The commodities chosen shall be sold by enterprises themselves and chosen and purchased by commercial departments. The disputes arising between the industrial and commercial parties in matters of specific implementation shall be settled by the people's government of the province, municipality or autonomous region (the classification list of specific commodities in four forms of purchase and sale is attached hereinafter).

(22) Enterprises shall not sell on their own initiative crude oil, finished oils, timber, tin and thermal industrial products falling under the products as means of production which are distributed by the state in a unified way. The procedures for full-quantity division of products and increase division of products shall be implemented for coal, copper, aluminum, lead, zinc, nickle, magnesium, tungsten concentrates, molybdenum concentrates, cement, plate glass, sulphuric acid, caustic soda, soda ash, rubber and short categories of steel products and the specific procedures shall otherwise be considered, formulated and transmitted down by the State Planning Commission, the State Economic Commission and the State Bureau of Supplies. The products obtained through division shall only be sold by enterprises themselves in our country and if they are required for export, applications shall be made to the State Bureau of Supplies and the Ministry of Foreign Trade for approval.

(23) An enterprise shall register the establishment of self-selling salesrooms with the administrations for industry and commerce and adopt a

variety of forms for self-selling such as partnership between factories and stores and entrusting stores with commissioned sales, distributions, display sales, market-testing, etc. For self-sold products, taxes shall be paid according to regulations, tickets shall be collected and prices shall not be raised without authorization, nor should enterprises permit shoddy work or use inferior materials, pass inferior products off as good ones or use other unjust means to seek illegal gains. The profits obtained from the products self-sold by enterprises shall be put under independent accounting and brought into the totals of the enterprises' profits so as to draw profit reserves in a unified way. Profits to be turned over shall not be intercepted and retained.

(24) The goods and materials which are intersupplied shall be directly settled between both parties of supply and demand and material supply and marketing departments shall not collect any charges for such dealings; the material supply and marketing departments shall only collect management fees if the goods and materials do not go through material warehouses; they shall not collect any storage fees.

V New Products

(25) A power-expanded enterprise shall vigorously increase the variety of styles and designs of its products, test produce and popularize new products and do a good job in updating and generation-renewal of its products so as to suit the needs of both domestic and foreign markets.

(26) New products shall be as follows: notably improved and enhanced in one or several of such aspects as structure, performance, quality, technical features, etc. as compared with the old ones, or with original creation; possessing advancement and practicality, capable of increasing economic benefit and worth being popularized; products which are successfully test produced for the first time within a province, a municipality or an autonomous region and have been appraised and confirmed by the departments concerned in charge. Those which are only improved or enhanced in such aspects as designs, colours, appearances, surface decorations, packages, etc. without any changes in structure, performance, etc. shall not be listed as new products.

(27) Appraisals and confirmations for new products shall be organized by such deparments as the central or local scientific and technological commission, economic commission, ministry, department or bureau in charge on the principle of administration by levels and in accordance with their degrees of importance and their levels of technology. Such grass-roots units as an enterprise, an institute (or a laboratory) shall not launch new products on their own accord.

(28) With regard to the test-producing expenses of new products, if major test-producing projects are planned and arranged for by the state or by the department in charge, funds shall be allocated by the departments which assign the tasks; if any test-producing project is arranged for by an enterprise itself, the expenses required shall be expended from the profit reserves. With regard to the materials and equipment required for the test-production of new products, the department in charge and the material department shall give energetic support to the enterprise and give priority to the arrangement for their settlement.

(29) New products shall go through appraisals and confirmations before being put into production and market-testing. The period of market-testing shall be determined by the department in charge jointly with the departments concerned according to specific products, the period generally being one year and not more than two years at most.

(30) The market-testing prices of new products shall be prescribed by enterprises in accordance with the costs of production and in the light of the prices of the products of the same kinds and reported to the price administration department for record. Among them, those that are major new products shall be submitted to the price department of the province, municipality or autonomous region for examination and approval. If they are put into large scale production at the expiration of market-testing, the enterprise shall submit a report to the department concerned for the prescription of official prices.

(31) Financial and tax departments shall adopt the policy of energetic support in an enterprise's test-production of new products. If the cost of a new product is high, if its profit is low or if it incurs loss during the market-test, the tax on it shall be reduced or remitted with the examination and approval of the financial or tax department of the province, municipality or autonomous region.

VI The Expansion of Exports and the Allocation of Foreign Currencies Obtained

(32) If a power-expanded enterprise has

favourable factors, it shall vigorously expand the production of export products so as to create more foreign currencies for the state. Both industrial and foreign trade parties shall conscientiously carry out the principle of "Four Combinations and Two Openings" (i.e., handling official business in combination, arranging for production in combination, negotiating with foreign businessmen in combination and dispatching groups to go abroad for inspections in combination; the prices of foreign trade export commodities shall be opened to industrial departments and the costs of industrial production shall be opened to foreign trade departments), engage themselves in close cooperation with each other and work in unison in the fields of external relations. Foreign trade departments shall vigorously support power-expanded enterprises to take part in foreign trade activities and provide the enterprises with overseas technical and economic information and with news of developments in foreign markets so as to enable the enterprises to duly improve their products in accordance with the needs and changes in the international market and strengthen the suitability and competitive capacity of export products.

(33) Power-expanded enterprises shall be entitled to apply for the right to export of their own products, participate in countersignatures on contracts when transactions are concluded with foreign firms and entrust the foreign trade corporations concerned with the handling of export business. Qualified power-expanded enterprises shall directly deal in export business with the approval of the State Import and Export Commission and the Ministry of Foreign Trade and after going through registration. They shall carry out independent accounting in financial affairs by assuming sole responsibility for their own profits or losses and undertake appropriate export planned tasks and foreign currency collecting tasks. The relevant practice shall be handled as stipulated by the State Import and Export Commission and the Ministry of Foreign Trade. Qualified enterprises shall combine themselves with foreign trade departments so as to "integrate industry with foreign trade." If any export products are not purchased by the local foreign trade department, an enterprise shall negotiate the export or supply of them in other ports with the consent of the department in charge in the people's government of the province, municipality or autonomous region in accordance with the state unified foreign trade prices and provisions. Foreign trade departments shall reduce intermediate links, simplify the formalities of approval and improve their efficiency.

(34) The domestic pricings of export products shall be rational. According to the provisions in "The Report of the State Bureau of Prices Asking for Instructions, Annotated and Passed On by the State Council, Concerning Several Problems in the Supply and Pricing of Export Industrial Products" as Document No.206 (1979) of the State Council, the basic principle shall still be to price them on the basis of the industrial products for home sales, the same price for the same quality and a better price for better quality, but full consideration shall be given to some characteristics of the export industrial products. In the case of some products with great industrial profits and high ex-factory prices and which have good prospects for export, if the foreign trade department still suffers from large losses under conditions of rational operation, the departments concerned shall consult with each other and the ex-factory prices of the parts supplied for export shall be reduced; in the case of some other products with little industrial profits but with high ex-factory prices and big export losses due to rather high tax rates, the foreign trade department or the industrial department shall make applications for the reduction or remission of the taxes on the exported portions in accordance with the relevant provisions of the State Council to the Ministry of Finance or the people's government of the province, municipality or autonomous region for the approval of its practice. Some industrial products are salable in the overseas market and have high rates of exchange for foreign currencies if they are exported, but as their domestic ex-factory prices are on the low side, the producing enterprises can only recover the cost, make little profit or even incur losses under conditions of normal production and rational operation. With regard to these products, if it is not suitable to raise their prices for the time being, or if the costs of the producing enterprises in the production of the parts supplied for export increase due to such special requirements as small batches, great variety, etc. although their prices for home sales are basically reasonable, the industrial department shall consult with the foreign trade department and provide the parts supplied for export with extra-price subsidies or properly increase their ex-factory prices with approval – on the principle that a producing enterprise shall have proper profits.

(35) Power-expanded enterprises with export tasks shall be entitled to obtain their shares of foreign currencies as stipulated by the state. The procedures for the division of the foreign currencies obtained from export shall be implemented in accordance with the "Notice Issued by the State Council Concerning the Provisions for a Number

of Problems in the Energetic Development of Foreign Trade to Increase the Income of Foreign Currencies" as Document No. 202 (1979) of the State Council. In the case of the projects financed with foreign-currency loans, if domestic materials and equipment can be used to replace those to be imported, the enterprises which supply the materials and equipment shall be entitled to obtain the deserved foreign currencies with approval under the prerequisites to ensure the fulfillment of the state plans relating to foreign currencies income.

(36) Enterprises shall be entitled to use their own shares of foreign currencies and entrust the foreign trade corporations concerned with the handling of import business in accordance with the state policies, regulations and decrees relating to foreign currency administration and import and export administration. But the approval of the use of foreign currencies shall be obtained from the departments concerned as stipulated so as to avoid blind importing practices. The formalities of approval shall be simplified as far as possible so as to make things convenient for grass-roots enterprises. The enterprises' shares of foreign currencies shall mainly be used to develop the production of export products, to introduce some necessary advanced techniques, materials, parts, accessories, testing and measuring instruments, technical patents, books, periodicals and data and also for necessary overseas inspections.

VII Prices

(37) Power-expanded enterprises shall strictly execute the state policies of prices so as to maintain the basic stability of prices. The prices stipulated by the state shall be implemented for the means of the production of industrial products and Class 1 and Class 2 daily industrial products allocated and transferred as planned by the state and Class 3 industrial products priced in a unified way by the state or local price department, including overproduced and self-sold products, and no negotiated prices shall be allowed. The principle of fixing prices according to quantity shall be carried out – high prices for good quality and low prices for inferior quality. In the case of products sold at floating prices, enterprises shall strictly implement price policies in accordance with the categories and floating ranges of prices stipulated by the price administration department. Prices set beyond the stipulated ranges shall be submitted to the original stipulating department for approval.

(38) With regard to some abundant products which have excessive profits or for which the supply exceeds the demand and to overstocked materials, their prices shall be lowered with the approval of the price department but the extent of the reduction shall not be too great.

(39) If some products make some profits for the commercial department but cause losses to the industrial department or vice versa due to unreasonable ex-factory prices, the departments concerned of the State Council and the people's governments of the province, municipality or autonomous region shall regulate and settle them in the present case that it is not suitable to change the market prices. If both industrial and commercial parties suffer from losses but the products are required to be produced, industrial and commercial enterprises shall endeavour to improve their business management, reduce costs and transform losses into profits. If there are still any losses through endeavours, the financial department shall give proper subsidies according to policies so as to arouse the enthusiasm of the industrial and commercial enterprises for production and operation.

(40) The prices stipulated by the state shall be implemented for the products self-sold by enterprises. If no prices are stipulated by the state, the prices shall be prescribed in the light of those of the products of the same kinds and checked and determined by the price department in accordance with the limits of authority of the administration of prices.

VIII Taxation and the Experiments of Paying Taxes Instead of Turning Over Profits

(41) With regard to enterprises which have been permitted by financial departments to undertake experiments in "paying taxes instead of turning over profits, independent accounting and assuming sole responsibility for their own profits or losses," each area or each department shall necessarily strengthen its leadership and resolve to obtain results and experience. With the exception of existing experimental units, the scope, in general, shall not be expanded this year. In case a few new experiments are suggested, they shall be reported to the Ministry of Finance for approval.

(42) An enterprise's trial implementation of paying taxes instead of turning over profits shall be handled as stipulated in Document No. Cai-Shui-Gai 1 (1981) of the Ministry of Finance. With regard to those enterprises which adopt experi-

ments of paying taxes instead of turning over profits as stipulated by the locality, the tax or due rates paid to the state and the forms of payment shall be unchanged for the time being so as to facilitate the summary of experience. If a few enterprises retain too many profits after paying taxes, thereby affecting financial revenues, necessary adjustments shall be made on the basis of getting them to comprehend the implications of this practise.

(43) After an enterprise has paid taxes and dues instead of turning over profits, the limits on cost expenditures, the guidelines for expenses and extra-business revenues and expenditures shall still be handled in accordance with current financial and accounting regulations. The enterprise's staff welfare funds, rewards funds, new product testing expenses and scientific research outlays which are originally included in the cost shall be expended out of profits retained after paying taxes, and no longer calculated into costs or used to reduce the amount of taxable income. Fixed fund spending fees and current fund spending fees which have been brought into base profits retained by the enterprise shall be paid out of profits retained after paying taxes.

(44) In order to promote industrial reorganization and combinations, repeated tax payment shall be cancelled and incremental taxes or other procedures shall be put into trial implementation for corporations or head factories as in the case of those enterprises which have been approved by the State Council and the province, municipality or autonomous region to conduct experiments and which practise independent accounting, and in respect of internal cooperation for the purpose of forming complete sets among the factories under them (including the products of cooperation of technological cooperative centres). The specific procedures shall be transmitted to lower levels by the Ministry of Finance in a separate document. The procedures for trial implementation which have been approved by the people's government of the province, municipality or autonomous region shall continue in force so as to obtain experience.

(45) For the purpose of supporting specialized cooperation, corporations and those enterprises under them which spread the cooperation of products to enterprises other than the corporations or enterprises which process and supply the products to the original spreading units at cooperative prices shall enjoy two years' exemption from taxes.

IX Bank Loans

(46) Banks shall make use of such economic means as credit, settlement, etc. to support and supervise power-expanded enterprises so as to develop production, use funds rationally, improve business management and increase economic benefit. They shall grant loans and regulate the interest rates on the principle of "dealing with different enterprises in different ways and fostering those which are better" so as to suit the activities of the enterprises to the requirements for economic regulation. They shall properly organize medium- and short-term equipment loans and current fund loans and energetically support light industrial, textile and building material enterprises and those serving the light and textile industries so as to do a good job of tapping potentialities and promoting innovations and transformation. They shall make great efforts to increase the production of consumer goods and export products required by urban and rural markets.

(47) Contracts shall be entered into for the loans to enterprises with time limits determined so as to obtain repayment on schedule. Additional interest shall be paid for the loans taken up by overstocked materials and financial expenditures. Additional interest shall be paid out of profit reserves. If a bank finds the loans are not used in conformity to the provisions of the contract, it shall recover them ahead of schedule or stop them.

(48) Newly increased profits earned after a project built by an enterprise with a medium- or short-term equipment loan is put into production are a component part of the results of the work of the staff of the enterprise, and welfare and rewards funds shall be drawn from them in proportion to base reserves as previously checked and determined. Principal and interest on the loan shall be paid out of the newly increased profits after the related project is put into production and shall not take up profits which were to be originally turned over. If the newly increased profits are inadequate for the on-schedule repayment of a light industrial or textile special loan, it shall be handled in accordance with the provisions in the "Report of the State Economic Commission, the People's Bank of China and Other Units, Annotated and Passed On by the State Council, Concerning the Request for the Approval of the Procedures for the Trial Implementation of Medium- and Short-term Special Loans to Light Industry and Textile Industry" as Document No. 9 (1980) of the State Council.

(49) In order to clear channels and invigorate the economy, with the consent of the bank an enterprise shall dispose of the mechanical and electrical products overstocked for a long time by means of sale on credit or by installments if the enterprise is in real need, but it has no sources of funds for the time being and it is able to pay off the loan within one or two years on the principle of avoiding lengthening the front of capital construction. An enterprise shall be allowed to collect earnest money in advance or collect the money by stages according to the progress of production for large mechanical or electrical equipment or special-purpose equipment with a long production cycle.

(50) Experimental enterprises which practise "Paying taxes instead of turning over profits, independent accounting and assuming sole responsibility for their own profits or losses" shall vigorously participate in property insurance.

X. Establishment of an Enterprise, Personnel and Labour

(51) A power-expanded enterprise shall be entitled to decide on the establishment of the enterprise and the provision for various personnel within the limits of the fixed-personnel establishment according to the needs of production and on the principle of simplification and efficiency. It shall be allowed not to coincide completely in organization with the higher department in charge under the prerequisites of ensuring the fulfillment of tasks.

(52) A power-expanded enterprise shall be entitled to appoint or dismiss the cadres at or below the medium level and report the appointments or dismissals to the higher department in charge and the local personnel department for record. Under the prerequisites of the allowances of the authorized size of the enterprise, the avoidance of increasing the total of wages or the existence of the quotas of natural decreases in personnel, the enterprise shall advertise for and employ through appraisals or examinations those scientific and technical personnel and management personnel who are really needed by it. A worker who is elected or appointed to be a cadre at the medium level shall enjoy the same political treatment as a state cadre not engaged in production during his or her tenure of office and job allowances shall be put into trial implementation according to the conditions of the enterprise for such workers. Such workers shall return to their original working posts after removal from office.

(53) A power-expanded enterprise shall employ staff by choosing the best personnel through overall examinations in morality, intellect and physique within the regional limits determined through negotiations with the labour department according to the enterprise's requirements for the employment of staff in accordance with the labour plan transmitted down by the state. An enterprise shall enter into training contracts with apprentices and living expenses shall be given during their apprenticeship. They shall only become the workers of the enterprise after passing examinations at the expiration of their apprenticeship. Those who fail shall have their apprenticeship extended or even be removed from the enterprise. Military personnel demobilized or transferred to civilian work who are assigned to enterprises as required shall go through centralized specialized training before specific arrangements are made for their work assignments. The labour department and other departments concerned at each level shall open all avenues for obtaining employment and make appropriate arrangements for those who wait for employment. Personnel who are not required by virtue of their special skills shall not be forced to join a given enterprise.

(54) A power-expanded enterprise shall strive to achieve a fixed number of staff and fixed quantity of production, organize production strictly in accordance with the fixed number of staff and the fixed quantity of production and enhance its labour productivity. Staff shall be trained in turn by stages and in groups by leaving production temporarily, studying political knowledge, learning to read and write, learning techniques and studying management, so as to enhance their political quality and educational and technical levels.

(55) A power-expanded enterprise shall be entitled to record merits for, give rewards to and make promotions of members of staff with excellent achievements and outstanding contributions. It shall also be entitled to impose different punishments on staff who violate laws or discipline and refuse to mend their ways despite repeated admonition according to the degrees of the seriousness of their offences, or even suspend or directly discharge them. The original wages of those punished by suspension shall be reduced as the enterprise thinks fit and no rewards shall be given to them. Those who really repent and mend their ways after a period of labour shall have their ranks redefined and be given wages and rewards.

XI. Easing the Extra Burdens of Enterprises

(56) Except for those stipulated in explicit

terms by the state and the province, municipality or autonomous region, an enterprise shall be entitled to refuse any unit or individual apportionment of various expenses to it, indiscriminate transfer and extortion of various products, materials or equipment.

(57) Without the approval of the higher department in charge, it shall not be permitted to transfer personnel, equipment, materials or funds from an enterprise. The equipment, materials and funds approved to be transferred shall be transferred at cost and the wages and other expenses for the personnel on loan shall be paid by the unit having the loan.

XII. Democratic Management

(58) The expansion of the enterprises' powers to act on their own is in essence the enlargement of the powers of the mass staff to manage the enterprises. A power-expanded enterprise shall make a good job of democratic management, establish and perfect the system of the staff's congress under the leadership of the Party committee and bring it into actuality. The four basic principles shall be upheld, ideological and political work shall be strengthened relations of interests among the state, the enterprise and the staff shall be well handled and the mass staff's sense of responsibility as masters shall be enhanced so as to ensure the fulfillment of various tasks of the enterprise.

(59) The system of the factory director's responsibility under the leadership of the Party committee shall be maintained continuously. The factory director shall assume the overall responsibility for the production, operation and administration of the enterprise. The factory director shall regularly report the work to the staff's congress and put himself or herself under examination and supervision. Such major problems shall be discussed and examined by the staff's congress as the formulation and revision of the long-term plans, annual plans, financial final accounts, the plans for production technological transformations and important regulations of the enterprise. The problems of immediate concern to the staff such as the distribution and use of welfare and rewarding funds shall be discussed and decided upon by the staff's congress.

(60) The staff's congress shall be entitled to supervise each department or the cadres at each level to carry out Party and state guiding principles and policies and support their work; to make suggestions as to the praise or reward and the punishment or dismissal of the leading cadres of the enterprise to the higher leading authorities for examination and determination.

The above Interim Concrete Procedures shall continuously be supplemented and perfected in practice with the development of power expansion, and each area or each department is requested to make serious investigations and duly sum up experience in the implementation. We hope that new situations or new problems occurring in the power expansion and the opinions as to these Procedures shall duly be reported to the State Economic Commission and the System Reform Office of the State Council.

PROVISIONAL REGULATIONS CONCERNING QUESTIONS OF ADOPTING THE ECONOMIC RESPONSIBILITY SYSTEM IN INDUSTRIAL PRODUCTION

Approved and issued by the State Council

(November 11, 1981)

In the past two years, the economic responsibility system in the industrial and transport departments has been gradually adopted, and its orientation is correct and results are remarkable. However, many problems remain unsolved due to the short period of its adoption, insufficient experience and imperfect methods. According to the spirit of relevant Party Central Committee and State Council instructions and practical experience gained in the various localities, the following detailed regulations for the solution of some problems deserving our attention in the further adoption and improvement of the system are set forth.

(1) A comprehensive understanding of the economic responsibility system in industrial production should be fostered. The system is a production and management system aimed at raising the economic results and closely combining an enterprise's responsibility, power and interests under the guidance of state planning. It requires that enterprises' management departments, enterprises, workshops, work groups as well as workers and staff should all be clear on their respective economic responsibilities for the state, and that each enterprise should set up and improve its responsibility system in production, technology and management and for each work post, and provide the state with high-quality, marketable products and more accumulation. It also requires that the relationships of interests between the state, the enterprises and workers and staff be correctly handled, that the economic responsibilities and economic results of the enterprises and workers and staff be combined with their own economic interests, that the principle of "from each according to his ability, to each according to his work" be earnestly implemented and that there should be more pay for more work and both awards and penalties given appropriately. Moreover, the responsibility system requires that enlarged power be further granted to enterprises in their management and necessary conditions for production and management be guaranteed to them, so that all enterprises can be gradually transformed into relatively independent economic entities.

(2) Units that have adopted the economic responsibility system should ensure the overall fulfilment of state plans and cater their production to the needs of society. They should not go singlemindedly after production that yields big profits to the neglect of products yielding low profits, which, if unchecked, will bring production out of line with demand. They should make sustained efforts to improve the product quality, lower the production costs and raise the economic results. They should assess their work in a comprehensive way ranging from profits delivered to the state to output, product quality, variety and costs. When the management departments work out the targets for such assessments, they may change them in the light of the specialities and emphases of the different enterprises and set forth specific targets for each enterprise. Enterprises that have met all the targets may, according to prescribed stipulations, keep part of the profits or part of the surplus incomes. For each target an enterprise has failed to fulfil, a certain percentage of the part of the profits or surplus income that ought to be retained by it will be deducted according to regulations in the State Council Document No. 23 (1980).

(3) Relevant policies should be adopted to encourage and support enterprises producing small commodities or products that are in short supply on the market but yield low profits. When deciding the portion of the profits kept by these enterprises, their basic contracted quotas for profits or losses and the portion of the surplus incomes they are entitled to, the management and financial departments should give them special consideration. Planning, pricing and tax departments and banks should, after careful studies, work out policies encouraging the production of small commodities and play their roles as economic levers.

(4) Departments concerned may refuse to purchase the unauthorized excessive and unsalable products by enterprises that go singlemindedly after profits to the neglect of state plan, goods-supplying contracts and output-limiting regu-

lations; the bank may refuse to grant them loans and may charge additional interests on the above-quota loans they have borrowed. Enterprises are not allowed to shift their unsalable products by unjustifiable means; if they do so, the profits resulting from this should be deducted and they are not allowed to keep any part of the profits or the surplus incomes thus earned.

(5) All enterprises must first ensure the fulfilment of their financial quotas to the state so as to facilitate a yearly increase in state revenue. The portion of annually increased profits handed over to the state by enterprises which have instituted the economic responsibility system should be bigger than that retained by themselves.

For units which are allowed to keep part of their profit and assume the responsibility for certain amounts of profits or losses, the portion of the profits retained by them, the basic contracted quotas of profits or losses and the portion of surplus incomes retained by them should be reasonably fixed and brought in line with the production plans and financial tasks allotted to the relevant localities and departments by the state.

For enterprises which keep part of their basic profits and retain a portion of their surplus incomes, the basic profits should be the average profits of the previous three years instead of the profits made in the previous year.

Generally speaking, the contracted basic profit quotas for profit-making enterprises whose production is in normal conditions should be higher than those of the previous year, and different progressive rates of increase should be fixed in accordance with the enterprises' potential ability of expanding production and increasing incomes; the contracted basic quotas for losses for enterprises losing money should be lower than those of the previous year, and should be reduced progressively on a yearly basis. If the prescribed contracted basic quota for an enterprise is on the low side, it should be properly adjusted by the management department and the financial department at the same level.

No less than 60% of the surplus incomes and reduced losses of enterprises which assume responsibility for fixed amounts of profits or losses should be delivered to the state; the portion retained by the enterprises should generally not exceed 40%. For enterprises making low profits from the production of articles for daily use, their portion may be properly increased. Enterprises which fail to fulfil the quotas they have contracted for should make up the differences from their special funds.

(6) Enterprises granted bigger decision-making powers and keeping part of their profits and experimental enterprises that substitute tax payments for profit deliveries and bear the responsibility for their own losses or gains should, in principle, carry on the original experimental methods. Enterprises whose period for the experimental method of retaining a portion of the profits have expired may, upon decision of the financial departments and the management departments, continue their original method or experiment with other methods so as to gain experiences. For enterprises whose production and profit decrease by big margins due to economic readjustment, if their retained portion of profits cannot ensure the normal welfare of their workers and staff, the management departments should consult with the financial departments and give them special consideration. As to enterprises whose profits have dropped by big margins as a result of the readjustment in the product mix although their production has not been affected, the normal welfare of their workers and staff should be guaranteed and appropriate amounts of bonuses fixed.

(7) An enterprise may adopt either the method of keeping a portion of its profits or the method of assuming the responsibility for fixed amounts of profits or losses; it may not use the two methods simultaneously. Enterprises retaining a portion of their profits cannot keep part of the incomes in excess of the contracted amounts; enterprises that assume the responsibility for fixed amounts of profits or losses cannot retain part of their profits or deduct money for their enterprise funds. Those which have retained money according to both methods should stop doing so and return the additional sums they have kept.

Where appropriate conditions exist, the practice of retaining a portion of the total profits earned by the whole trade shall be vigorously promoted. As to which method an enterprise should adopt, that of retaining a portion of the profits or that of assuming the responsibility for fixed amounts of profits or losses, this shall be decided by the financial departments together with the management departments in the light of the enterprises' actual conditions. Once a method is adopted, this should be kept unchanged for three or four years. For enterprises whose production is in abnormal conditions or whose keeps changing erratically, the contracted amounts of profits or losses may be decided every year.

(8) Enterprises should repay the loans granted to them for adopting technical measures

with profits gained after the related projects are put into operation instead of with original profits. They are not allowed to delay the repayment when new profits have been made, nor should they increase their profits in this way so as to keep a larger amount of the profits.

(9) The level of bonuses of an enterprise should be increased or lowered alongside the fluctuations of its production and profits, product quality and production costs. Bonuses should be reduced or no bonuses whatsoever should be issued for enterprises whose production and profits went down, quality of products declined and production costs went up.

(10) The issuance of bonuses should be controlled in accordance with the State Council Document No. 10 (1981) and its supplementary regulations. The various localities and departments should decide bonus quotas in the light of management and contributions of the various trades and enterprises. The bonus quotas should vary from enterprise to enterprise; they should not be the same regardless of the efficiency of their management. The enterprises should, within the quotas fixed by their leading bureaus, follow the principle of "to each according to his work." Those who do more get more bonuses, those who do less get less and those who do not work at all get nothing. There should also be both rewards and penalties, and egalitarianism should be overcome. Once the quotas for bonuses are fixed according to the above-mentioned State Council stipulation, they should not be exceeded. Surplus from bonuses already issued may be used to improve public welfare facilities or labour protection facilities or to set up reserve funds for making good possible deficiencies in the future. Enterprises that have not had their bonus quotas examined and fixed should get it done as soon as possible. Bonus quotas that have been fixed but do not accord with the State Council stipulation should be corrected. Provinces, municipalities and autonomous regions and industrial and transport ministries that fix their bonus quotas higher than the stipulated level due to their special situations should report to the State Council for approval.

(11) Funds used for bonuses should be withdrawn strictly according to stipulations and they should not be withdrawn repeatedly. Enterprises that have issued bonuses monthly in accordance with fixed quotas should not issue year-end bonuses with funds obtained from part of the surplus incomes and other funds.

(12) The institution of piece rate wage system should be controlled. On the basis of summing up experiences and doing a good job in fundamental work, its popularization should be examined and approved strictly according to requirement and proceed in a planned and systematic way.

The requirements for enterprises that can adopt the piece rate wage system are: There are a strong leading body and plenty of production tasks; the relationships between production, supply and marketing are relatively normal; the products can be counted by piece; there are average advanced quotas, rational prices for piece goods and a relatively healthy system of scientific management. Enterprises applying for the adoption of this system should go through strict procedures of examination and approval; no enterprises should adopt this system without the approval of its leading department.

Enterprises that have instituted the piece rate wage system should sum up their experiences, consolidate it and make necessary readjustments according to the above-mentioned requirements. The adopted piece rate wage system should be discontinued in the enterprises that do not qualify for these requirements and those whose quality of products has gone down and costs have shot up, whose absolute amount of wages in the cost per unit product has been increased, whose production is not linked with the ultimate products, resulting in uneven production and incomplete sets of products, or whose overall production quotas have not been fulfilled. They should undergo conscientious consolidation. When the consolidation is successful they may adopt this system after being examined and approved by the leading departments.

In view of the fact that quotas for labor in the majority of enterprises are not accurate or fall short of the average advanced level, the extra pay for work done in excess of the quotas in the piece rate wage system should, generally speaking, be limited to 30% of the enterprise's average standard wages. In enterprises that give extra pay for the amount of work done in excess of the quotas, those who fail to fulfil the quotas should have their basic wages properly deducted. On condition that average advanced quotas have been fixed, a good job has been done in maintaining the equipment and attention has been paid to safety in production, there can be no limitation whatsoever to extra pay for underground coal-miners and longshoremen of sea ports under a piece rate wage system.

The piece rate should be decided in accordance with standard wages and it should not include factors other than the standard wages. Piece rate that has included such factors should be corrected.

Workers receiving piece rate wages are not entitled to comprehensive production bonuses. No extra wages should be paid for extra work hours except for approved extra work hours during legal holidays.

(13) Apart from the amount issued to individuals according to state stipulations (such as subsidies for those in financial difficulties), enterprises' welfare funds are mainly used for the collective welfare of the workers and staff.

Apart from revision by state regulations, no change should be made with regard to the proper labor insurance benefits and welfare of the workers and staff and their personal benefits stipulated in the labor insurance and other regulations. If some stipulations need to be improved in view of actual conditions, experiments may first be made upon approval by the provincial leading departments.

From now on, the items of welfare expenditures and their standards should be formulated by the leading departments in a unified way and approved by the people's governments of the provinces, municipalities and autonomous regions. Items and standards under the category of unified state stipulations can be changed only upon State Council approval. No one is allowed to add new items or issue "products for welfare purposes," pay for extra work hours, allowance and subsidies under any pretext. Financial departments, banks, labor departments and trade unions should co-operate with the leading departments of the enterprises in examining and supervising the use of enterprise welfare funds. Enterprises that have widened the scope of welfare expenses, raised their standards, excessively issued welfare funds or even divided them up among the workers and staff should be resolutely stopped and corrected. Those who have done this with serious consequences should be held responsible.

(14) Units that have adopted the economic responsibility system should strictly carry out the economic policies of the state and abide by its financial and economic discipline. Financial departments and banks should work in close co-operation with the leading departments of the enterprises to strengthen financial supervision of enterprises and examine how the financial and economic discipline is being observed in these enterprises at regular intervals, at least twice a year. Enterprise's lawful rights and interests should be protected; those abiding by discipline and laws should be commended; those having violated financial and economic discipline, engaged in cheating, concealed, withheld or exaggerated their profits, scamped work with insufficient materials, lowered the quality of products, evaded tax, arbitrarily raised prices or divided products among themselves without authorization should be required to pay back whatever economic gains they have obtained by illegal means. The portions of profits or surplus incomes that ought to be retained by these enterprises should be reduced or stopped. Depending on the seriousness of their cases, the enterprise leaders and persons involved shall be held economically or legally responsible for their actions.

(15) In instituting the economic responsibility system, it is imperative to strengthen the Party leadership, give first place to ideological work and strive to eliminate feebleness and slackness in the ideological and political work. It is necessary to strengthen the ideological and political work in a down-to-earth way,educate the workers and staff to foster the concept of seeing things from an overall standpoint, correctly handle the relationship between the state, the enterprise and the individual and the relationship between the immediate and long-term interests, heighten their sense of responsibility as masters of the country and make as much contribution as possible to the state. It is necessary to have faith in the masses and rely on them, strengthen democratic management and give full play to the role of the congresses of workers and staff. It is necessary to conscientiously implement the principle of combining moral encouragement with material rewards, direct the enthusiasm of the workers and staff to consolidating the enterprises, improving management and raising the levels of production, technology and management, and continuously improve the economic responsibility system — all for the purpose of raising the economic results in a sustained way and speeding up the four modernizations.

PROVISIONS FOR THE PURSUIT OF THE SYSTEM OF ECONOMIC RESPONSIBILITY IN CONSTRUCTION ENTERPRISES

Promulgated by the State Capital Construction Commission, the Ministry of Finance, the State Bureau of Labour and the Chinese People's Construction Bank

(December 15, 1981)

Since the Third Plenary Session of the 11th Central Committee of the Party, the construction enterprises throughout the country have done a lot of work and made certain achievements in the implementation of the Party's line, guiding principles and policies, in the elimination of the "Left" ideological influences and in the conduct of their consolidation. Some enterprises have even put various forms of the system of economic responsibility into trial practice, preliminarily overcome equalitarianism, changing the phenomena of messing together and mobilizing the enthusiasm of the enterprises and their staffs. In a word, the orientation is right and the results are satisfactory. However, such problems as poor quality, high cost and prolonged building time in projects still exist in a considerable number of construction enterprises. This state of affairs shall be promptly changed and the system of economic responsibility shall be further perfected in the light of the construction enterprises' own features and in the spirit of the "Notice Annotated and Passed On by the State Council Concerning the Interim Provisions for a Number of Problems in the Implementation of the System of Economic Responsibility in Industrial Production" as Document No. Guo-Fa 166 (1981) of the State Council. For this reason, the following provisions are made:

1 Understanding shall be deepened. The exercise of the system of economic responsibility is aimed at increasing economic benefit and making a good job of the business management of an enterprise under the direction of state plans so as to enable the enterprise and each member of the staff to be clear about the economic responsibility borne by itself or himself or herself for the state. The system of economic responsibility is both economic and political. A proper balance shall be maintained in the relationship of interests between the state, the enterprise and the staff, and the relations between immediate and long-term interests and between partial and general interests shall be put right. The economic responsibility of the enterprise and staff shall be combined with economic results and benefit and the principle of each doing the work according to his ability and each getting the benefit according to his work shall conscientiously be implemented so that those who do more will get more and there will be rewards and punishments accordingly. It requires the further expansion of the enterprise's powers in business management to act on its own to ensure the conditions required for the production or business of the enterprise so as to enable the enterprise to gradually become a relatively independent economic entity.

The pursuit of the system of economic responsibility shall proceed from actual conditions with the persistence in being practical and realistic and being suited to local conditions. It shall advance steadily as if crossing a river by feeling about for stones underneath. Experience shall conscientiously be summed up and macroscopic direction and supervision shall be strengthened so to be constantly perfected and to develop healthily.

The construction units which have not practised independent accounting shall gradually be changed into economic units which conduct the independent accounting of profits and losses and the system of economic responsibility shall be practised so as to change the situations of "barter system" or "massing together."

2 To undertake the tasks of building projects, the construction enterprises shall practise the system of contracting. Before the start of work, both parties shall sign an economic contract to define clearly the rights, responsibilities and interests of each party. The project unit shall guarantee "five sure makings" (i.e., making sure of funds, materials, designs, building site and the external water and power supply and roads), while the construction enterprise shall practise "five undertakings" (i.e., undertaking the time limit according to time limit rates, undertaking the project quality according to the assessing standards for quality, undertaking the building cost according to the budget of the working drawing with the addition of coefficient, undertaking the materials according to the budget of the working drawing and undertaking the entire completion), which shall be fixed at one go as far as possible and guaranteed or undertaken to the end. The project unit or the construction unit

shall be punished if the former affects the "five undertakings" because it has not accomplished the "five sure makings" or if the latter does not fulfill the "five undertakings" as stipulated in the contract. The penalty for each party shall be the same.

If several independent accounting construction enterprises are doing construction on the same site, the system of the division of labour with individual responsibility by general contracting and subcontracting shall be put into effect, with the construction enterprise which undertakes the major and key works of the project as the general contractor and the other units as subcontractors. The general contractor shall hold itself responsible to the project unit and the subcontractors shall hold themselves responsible to the general contractor. The economic contracts of "five sure makings" and "five undertakings" shall also be signed between the general contractor and the subcontractors so that each of them can fulfill its own contract responsibility.

The system of making tenders shall be put into trial practice for the projects with favourable conditions. General contracting shall be put into effect by the block for an urban housing construction project and the building cost shall be undertaken within the limits per square meter.

3 A state-operated construction enterprise shall undertake to turn over the profits made to the state on time. In addition to the reduction of cost reserves in accordance with the "Interim Provisions for the Problems Concerning the Expansion of the Powers of State Construction Enterprises to Act on Their Own in Business Management" as Document No. Jian-Fa-Shi 185 (80) jointly promulgated by the State Capital Construction Commission, the State Planning Commission, the Ministry of Finance, the State Bureau of Labour and the State Bureau of Supplies, the following shall also be adopted:

(1) To fix the base for the undertaking of profits, which shall still be turned over accordingly even in case of losses (that is to say, to turn it over with the enterprise's own funds), and the profits in excess of the base shall belong to the enterprise itself;

(2) To fix the base for the undertaking of profits and those in excess shall be shared;

(3) To determine a fixed proportion of the profits to be turned over in the net profits of the enterprise and undertake its turnover;

(4) To practise the undertaking of profits by the same trade;

(5) To undertake losses within limits, no supplements to be obtained if the losses exceed the limits and those less than the limits to be shared or retained for use.

With regard to the question of which way shall be taken by each construction enterprise, each area or each department shall study and determine it with the construction bank (or the financial department) at the same level according to actual conditions in accordance with the subordinate relations. A base for the undertaking shall be advanced and rational. In brief, it shall proceed from actual conditions with consideration given to the interests of the state, the enterprise and the staff so as to give full play to the initiative of the enterprise and the staff in the increase of production or revenue and improve economic results constantly. In the distribution of interests among the three, more earnings for the state shall be taken for the prerequisite and no selfish departmentalism shall be practised. An enterprise shall only practise one of the ways of profit reserves or the undertaking of profits or losses and shall not use two ways concurrently. It shall not draw reserve funds repeatedly and this shall be put right if it has been done.

4 A construction enterprise shall properly handle its internal relations of distribution. The system of economic responsibility shall be well combined with the principle of the distribution according to work so as to link the income of the staff up directly with the results of labour, resolutely overcoming equalitarianism. The measures which are now put into trial practice in various places are all effective and shall be vigorously put into trial implementation, for example, the measure of "fixing, undertaking and rewarding" by levels, that of organizing a mixed team and making the undertaking of budgets by the building number, that of the piece rate system for high standard overall excess and that of high work excess rewards in the nature of piece rates and so forth. No matter which measure will be taken, the distribution according to work shall certainly be implemented so as to embody the spirit that those who do more will get more; the quality of the project shall certainly be guaranteed and its cost shall certainly be reduced; mental encouragement and material reward shall certainly be well combined. The levels of rewards in an enterprise shall be raised or lowered with the increase or decrease of production and profits, the superior or inferior quality of products and the reduction or increase of cost. The increase of the rewards in an enterprise shall be lower than that of its production and profits. No maximum limit shall be fixed for the excess wages obtained by the workers in an enterprise which contracts in accordance with the state uniform labour rates

and on the ground of the six standards for an all-fine project. If the rated undertaking is practised in accordance with the supplementary rates for the enterprise or temporary estimated labour, the excessive wages shall not exceed 30 per cent of the average standard pay of the enterprise. Those who cannot fulfill the rates shall have proper parts of their basic wages deducted. There shall be both rewards and punishments. The implementation of piece rate wages shall be controlled and the enterprises which implement them shall be those which have sufficient tasks of production, rather normal supply of materials, various perfects systems of business management and profits and which are capable of reducing the contents of wages in the costs of projects. In the control of excessive wages, cautious consideration shall be given to neighbours and an individual shall not be overpaid. If the excess is too much, the member of staff shall be persuaded to turn it over to collective welfare funds or reserve funds or to spend it in the following year.

5 The powers of state construction enterprises to act on their own in business management shall continue to be expanded.

(1) They shall have the powers to utilise the profit reserves (or those after the fulfillment of the undertaking to turn over, the same hereinafter mentioned) on their own. The profit reserves, enterprise funds and staff welfare funds drawn by an enterprise and the legal profits obtained through reckoning shall be used to establish four kinds of funds, i.e. production development funds, staff welfare funds, staff rewarding funds and reserve funds (used for the expenses of return visits and repairs undertaken by the construction enterprise and the fines concerning the contracts). With regard to the proportions of various funds, the manager of an enterprise shall make a plan in accordance with the specific conditions of the enterprise, submit it to the staff's congress for examination and decision after obtaining the consent of the construction bank (or the financial department) and then submit it to the higher department in charge for record.

(2) With the prerequisites to put itself under the direction and supervision of the department in charge and to ensure the purposes of various special funds, an enterprise shall be entitled to pool overhaul funds, reform and transformation funds and production development funds together for use in an overall way.

(3) An enterprise shall be entitled to choose and employ the good contract workers and casual labourers as required by the project.

Besides, in the supply of materials, each area or each department shall directly distribute them to construction enterprises as far as possible so as to enable the construction enterprises to undertake the fulfillment of their work according to the materials supplied; in addition, in some areas where "the allotment of materials by the state" and the distribution of the quotas of Class 2 materials to project units have been put into effect, it shall be energetically implemented that the construction units apply for orders and the organization of supply in accordance with the economic contracts signed with project units and the quotas of materials accepted (project units will no longer apply for orders nor control materials) so as to reduce transfer links as far as possible, decrease turnover expenses and create favourable conditions for construction enterprises to practise the system of economic responsibility.

It is a new thing that construction enterprises practise the system of economic responsibility and will certainly undergo a course of development, substantiation and perfection. Each area or each department shall surely strengthen the leadership, duly sum up experience, use the experience of selected units to promote the work of the entire area or department and push the work forward so as to smoothly and healthily pursue the system of economic responsibility in construction enterprises.

PROVISIONAL REGULATIONS ON STRENGTHENING THE WORK OF TAPPING POTENTIAL, RENOVATION AND TRANSFORMATION IN EXISTING INDUSTRIAL AND TRANSPORT ENTERPRISES

(June 21, 1980)

China has established the beginnings of an independent and fairly comprehensive industrial complex through 30 years of socialist construction. Relying on existing enterprises, tapping their potential, renovating and transforming them and giving full play to their role – this is the starting point of our modernization programme and the "base area" from which we set out on a new "Long March." During the period of the readjustment of the national economy, in particular, the growth of our industry and transport, the increase of commodities for the domestic market and for export, and the expansion of accumulated funds will mainly rely on the tapping of the potential of existing enterprises. Adhering to the principle of "production before capital construction and tapping potential before building new enterprises" and doing a good job of tapping the potential, renovating and transforming existing industrial and transport enterprises is, therefore, a cardinal issue which has a direct bearing on the overall situation. It is of special importance for winning success in the first campaign of the new "Long March" and for accelerating the advance of the modernization programme.

1 The potential-tapping renovation and transformation of existing enterprises must be linked up with the restructuring of our country's system of economic management, with the broadening of the decision-making power of the enterprises in matters of management. Along with the restructuring of the system of economic management, the enterprises should be given greater decision-making power in management, including the right to improve their production techniques continuously and to accelerate the expansion of production through the tapping of potential, renovation and transformation in line with the state plans, market demands and their own economic interests.

2 The tapping of potential, renovation and transformation of existing enterprises means carrying out technical renovation and transformation of present factory buildings and equipment by adopting new technologies and processes while maintaining simple reproduction so as to tap the production potential of the enterprises to the fullest possible extent and increase their economic returns comprehensively.

3 In tapping potential and in carrying out renovation and transformation during the period of economic readjustment, emphasis should be placed on: A. Saving energy by giving first priority to such measures as reducing oil consumption, substituting coal for oil in use as boiler fuel, using exhaust heat for power generating and other purposes, developing central heating and conserving power; B. Giving priority to the development of light, textile and handicraft industries; C. Strengthening weak links in communications and transport, chiefly the bottleneck sections of several old railway lines and several harbours; D. Improving the quality of products, increasing varieties and designs, raising the production of raw and other materials in short supply and expanding the production capacity of export commodities.

4 Formulation and examination of programmes for tapping of potential, renovation and transformation:

Programmes should be drawn up before projects for these purposes are carried out. All areas and departments should conscientiously map out their own programmes for tapping of potential, renovation and transformation in line with the aim of the readjustment of the national economy and the principles and tasks of the long-range programme, in the interest of coordination between different specialities and the requirements for the reorganization of industry and in conformity with the orientation and emphasis of the national drive for tapping potential, renovation and transformation. All areas and departments should provide guidelines for their subordinate enterprises in drafting their programmes for these purposes, be responsible for examining these programmes and organize efforts to carry them out.

All enterprises which need to carry out such projects should draw up their own economical, rational and practical programmes in accordance with the requirements specified in the programmes of their areas and industries, and with reference to their own orientation in production and specific circumstances and in the light of the problems that exist in their production and management, technological processes, factory buildings and equipment. These enterprises should try to make their products readily marketable while avoiding increases in their average consumption of fuel, power and raw materials. They should not try to expand themselves into integrated enterprises. No project should be included in such a programme unless the related geological resources have been clearly established, the technological processes and techniques are up to standard, the supplies of fuel, power and raw materials and transport facilities are guaranteed and the problems of environmental pollution have been solved. No projects of tapping potential, renovation and transformation involving large amounts of work are allowed to start unless they have been included in the programmes of an area or department so that blindness in action can be avoided.

Unified programmes should be drawn up by the relevant local authorities or departments in charge for certain comprehensive regional projects and those involving several industries. Local authorities and relevant departments of the State Council should cooperate closely and support each other in this regard. Before assigning projects to various areas, the departments concerned should first obtain approval from the planning and economic commissions of the relevant provinces, municipalities or autonomous regions; on the other hand, various localities should submit for examination to the departments in charge those projects they intend to apply for inclusion in the national programme.

All areas and departments should map out programmes and annual plans for tapping potential, renovation and transformation with the following contents: A. Names and contents of the projects; B. The funds needed and their sources; C. The equipment and materials needed and their sources; D. The sources of fuel, power and raw materials needed and ways to achieve a balance in their supply; E. The economic returns expected; F. The time limits set for the projects.

Systematic steps should be taken to carry out the projects included in the programmes and plans according to their order of priority, on the principle of easy ones before difficult ones and with a view to minimizing the cost, shortening the time, increasing returns and achieving satisfactory results. Efforts should be made to acquire the funds, equipment, materials and labour power needed for those projects already included in the annual plans. Those enterprises which cannot solve the problem of labour power may request the capital construction commissions at various levels to make an overall arrangement.

As to the procedures of examining and approving programmes and plans for tapping potential, renovation and transformation, those projects which fall in line with the requirements of regional and departmental programmes and whose expenses can be covered by the sponsoring enterprises out of their reserve funds need only be reported to the local authorities or departments in charge for the record; those projects which need to go through the procedures of requisitioning land, call for a unified balance in the supply of fuel, power and raw materials or have to apply for bank loans or government subsidies, should first go through examination by the departments in charge (and by the bank as well in instances where loans are required) and then be submitted for approval to the economic and planning commissions and financial departments at various levels. Major projects should be handled with reference to the procedures for capital construction. Small loans and odd construction items are to be handled according to existing rules.

In drafting their programmes and plans for tapping potential, renovation and transformation, the enterprises should fully practise democracy, follow the mass line, adopt the "three-in-one combination" of leading cadres, technical personnel and workers. The programmes and plans should be submitted to the workers' congresses for discussion and approval, and their execution should be reported to the congresses regularly.

5 Ways of acquiring and using funds for tapping potential, renovation and transformation: Pending an all-round reform of the system of economic management, funds needed for these purposes may be obtained from the following sources:

A. That part of the basic depreciation funds reserved for these purposes. The State Council document Guo Fa (1978) No. 12 and the document Cai Qi (1979) No. 675 jointly issued by the Ministry of Finance and the State Economic Commission, stipulate that a certain portion of basic depreciation funds should continue to be set aside in the state budget mainly for the purpose of ensuring the conservation of energy and other such important projects. Basic depreciation funds in the hands of various departments and local authorities should be spent entirely on the renewal of existing equipment and major projects of tapping potential, renovation and transformation. Similar funds reserved by the enterprises and those deducted according to the quantity of production should also be spent entirely on renewing and transforming fixed assets (including development and extension in mining) and must not be diverted to other purposes.

In order to accelerate the renewal and technical transformation of machinery and equipment, those enterprises which have been authorized by the State Economic Commission and the Ministry of Finance to experiment with the broadening of their decision-making power in management may raise their rate of basic depreciation for machinery and equipment by 0.05% in 1980 on the basis of increased profits.

B. The share of profits kept by the enterprises that may be used for the purposes of tapping potential, renovation and transformation.

C. Loans that may be provided by the banks (including small loans for introducing technological measures and loans for special purposes).

D. Small sums in subsidies granted by the state or local authorities.

E. Funds pooled in partnership. Comprehensive regional projects like central heating may be started with funds pooled by the enterprises being benefited. Specialized items, such as the multiple utilization of timber, can be started as joint ventures between central and local authorities, between different provinces, between different cities and counties within the same province, or between enterprises under ownership by the whole people and those under collective ownership by breaking the bounds of different localities, trades and systems of ownership. The products, profits and other revenues of such joint ventures may be shared among the partners on the principle of mutual benefit and according to reasonable proportions agreed upon through consultation. Enterprises may apply for reduction or exemption of tax on those products they have increased through the treatment of industrial wastes and may reserve part of the profits thus increased in accordance with relevant state regulations.

Those enterprises which carry out technical transformation in connection with major overhauls may combine the use of funds for major overhauls with funds for the renewal and transformation of equipment. Funds for the purposes of tapping potential, renovation and transformation not in use for the time being should be deposited in banks under separate accounts; departments in charge of the enterprises may cooperate with the banks in using such deposits as loans to those enterprises which are short of funds for these purposes. Enterprises that raise loans should make sure to repay them. A low rate of interest is to be adopted on both deposits and loans in this regard. No department has the right to transfer or to divert to other uses funds of enterprises for the said purposes.

6 Enterprises should first of all make full use of over-stocked goods in their warehouses in providing the equipment and materials needed for the said purposes. In case such goods fall short of needs, central or local departments in charge of the enterprises should draw up unified plans for supply on the principle that whichever level provides them with funds shall provide materials as well, and shall apply for help separately to departments of supplies at various levels in accordance with the present system of material distribution. Departments of supplies at various levels should, in line with plans for tapping potential, renovation and transformation approved by the central or local authorities, treat materials needed for these purposes in the same way as production, maintenance and capital construction, open separate accounts, include them in the plans for the distribution of materials at different levels, give them priority and see to it that the relevant plans are carried out. When various areas, departments and enterprises under them start up projects for the said purposes using funds raised by themselves, they should in principle solve the problems regarding equipment and materials on their own; those which cannot solve these problems may apply for help. Projects for which the materials needed cannot be obtained should not be included in the annual plans. Economic commissions at various levels should participate in examining and approving plans for distributing materials and should assist departments of supplies with the work of coordination in the course of executing the plans.

7 Enterprises should make full use of existing labour power, improve their labour organization and raise labour productivity in tapping their potential, renovating and transforming themselves. If it becomes essential to increase the numbers of some workers, the quotas should be examined and determined by labour departments at various levels through consultation with the planning and economic commission at the same level and should be included in the plans for the distribution of labour power at different levels.

8 Projects for the said purposes should be linked up with the popularization of advanced techniques developed in China and the introduction of advanced techniques from abroad. Importance should be attached to the systematic application of existing advanced techniques in China to the technical transformation of old enterprises. Imported advanced technologies and equipment should be used first of all in the transformation of old enterprises.

9 Funds for the said purposes are to be

managed by the Construction Bank. Special loans issued by the People's Bank for introducing technical measures should continue to be managed by the People's Bank. Funds raised by enterprises on their own should be used on the principle of depositing before using.

Foreign exchange needed by enterprises for importing technical patents and equipment should be included in the state plan for balance in foreign exchange, and the enterprises concerned should raise loans in foreign exchange in accordance with the "Regulations Governing Short-Term Loans in Foreign Exchange" approved and transmitted by the State Council.

10 Strengthening of leadership: Economic commissions at various levels are responsible for supervising the entire work of tapping potential, renovation and transformation. They should supervise the drafting of programmes and plans, organize efforts to carry them out and strive for good economic results. All industrial and communication departments under the State Council should also take practical steps to do this work well. Financial departments and banks at various levels should strengthen management and supervision of the use of funds for these purposes. Departments in charge of enterprises should report to the economic commissions and financial, banking and statistical departments at the same level on the results of the use of funds. Provincial, municipal and autonomous regional economic commissions and financial bureaus should pool information on the way local enterprises use their funds for the said purposes and report it to the State Economic Commission and the Ministry of Finance. Statistical departments and departments in charge of enterprises at all levels should strengthen their statistical force and establish or improve their system of statistics and reports on the implementation of plans for tapping potential, renovation and transformation.

INTERIM REGULATIONS ON COORDINATED TRANSPORT

(Promulgated by the State Economic Commission on November 6, 1981)

Transport has such features as crossings between regions, continuity, multiple works and many links. The whole-journey transport of goods and passengers usually requires the dovetailing with each other of several means of transport for its completion. To develop coordinated transport can tap the potentialities of transport, increase its benefit, improve its service and simplify its formalities so as to satisfy as best as possible the demands of industry and agriculture and the life of the people for transportation. For this reason, its development shall be energetically encouraged and vigorously supported.

The present coordinated transport of our country not only includes that between various modes of transport (or between the same means of transport) such as railway-waterway, railway-highway, marine-land-air, sea-river or other coordinated transport, but also includes the transport cooperation between producing, supplying, transporting and marketing parties and within the transportation industry, for example, the cooperation between railways (or highways) and ports, highways (or railways) and factories, railways (or highways) and mines and between railways (or highways) and forests, the collecting and distributing transport at ports or stations, load allotment to empty return vehicles or vessels and the organization of the common use of special-purpose railways and special-purpose wharves, etc. These Interim Regulations are formulated for the purpose of offering some rules and regulations to be followed in coordinated transport.

Chapter I Principal Tasks of Coordinated Transport

1 The marine-land coordinated transport of large-quantity goods and materials shall be energetically developed. In addition to continuing to expand coordinated transport business in accordance with the "Rules for the Coordinated Transport of Railway and Waterway Goods," favourable conditions shall be vigorously created to organize "continuous" transport lines composed of scheduled vehicles and vessels, scheduled routes and points, to constantly improve the transport efficiency of vehicles and vessels, pick up load-transferring speeds and shorten the times of idling of vehicles and vessels.

2 The coordinated transport of odd loads and planned car loads shall be energetically developed and such a coordinated transport method shall be popularized step by step as "consigning at one go for shipment, checking them separately, counting freight and carriage by sections, handling transfers as agents, delivering and taking delivery to and from the doorstep and being responsible for the whole journey."

3. Good service shall be made of clearing ports and stations. At the ports and stations which are very busy with load-transfers, the planned balance and the coordinated dovetailing shall be strengthened according to the circulating directions and volumes of goods and materials and the relay transport with transport capacity shall be well organized so as to ensure the smooth running of ports and stations.

4 Coordinated transport networks and points shall be established in economically developed areas with the county seats as centres and the main and feeder coordinated transport services shall be developed for the purpose of connecting main transport lines with people's communes, production brigades and teams so as to promote the development of industry and agriculture and stimulate the interchange of urban and rural goods and materials.

5 The linking between vehicles and vessels, direct load-transfers and load allotment to empty return means of transport shall be energetically organized so as to save transport capacity and energy.

6 The common use of special-purpose railways and special-purpose wharf facilities shall be energetically organized so as to tap the potentialities of transport facilities.

7 The transport cooperation between all transport departments and enterprises shall be strengthened and the system of handling official business in combination shall be established and perfected so as to improve handling efficiency and ensure the fulfillment of transport plans and production tasks.

8 Containerized (containers, cases, cartons,

baskets, bags and pallets) and coordinated transport shall be energetically developed and the "door-to-door" transport shall be realized step by step so as to save packaging and reduce damage and shortage of goods. In the places where "door-to-door" transport cannot be accomplished for the time being, proper container dismantling and loading places shall be set up so as to speed up the containerization of the transport of package and combination goods.

9 The commission booking of the passenger tickets for various modes of transport shall be energetically developed so that it can be achieved step by step to get the passenger tickets for several modes of transport at a time and it shall be developed to handle transfer passenger tickets and arrange accommodation for passengers and to carry out tourist coordinated transport so as to give facilities to passengers as far as possible.

10 Favourable conditions shall be created to expand international coordinated transport.

Chapter II The Coordinated Transport of Goods

11 The coordinated transport of goods shall be handled according to plans. With regard to the car load (batch) coordinated transport goods consigned for shipment or to be transferred, the coordinated transport service shall put forward a plan to the carrying unit concerned, handle consignment and payment of transportation expenses and accept goods in accordance with the dispatching plan of the carrying unit.

12 In the coordinated transport of odd goods, their circulating directions and volumes shall be well known. In principle, the goods shall be shipped or transferred as soon as they are received. In order to make a good job of the dovetailing between two modes of transport and moderate the warehousing pressure of the transfer ports and stations, the coordinated transport service shall organize the balanced dispatch in a planned way to the best of its ability according to the dispatching directions of the main transport lines concerned. The main lines shall duly accept the goods and duly dispatch them.

13 When the owner of goods entrusts the coordinated transport service with the coordinated transport of the goods, he shall fill in a waybill as stipulated and affix the official seal of the shipping unit (or the private seal of the individual) on it. The packages of the goods shall conform to the provisions promulgated by the state or a ministry concerning the packing standards for transportation. The coordinated transport service shall check and accept the goods against the waybill, weigh them and collect the charges; if the waybill is found not to accord with the goods or if the packages are found to be inappropriate, it shall be amended or they shall be renovated and reinforced before the service accepts them for shipment.

14 The coordinated transport service at the location of a transfer port or station shall recheck the transferred goods against the waybill, accept them, duly get in touch with the relay carrying unit and go through the formalities of consignment. The carrying department shall make out the ticket, collect the charges and organize the transfer.

15 If the consignee entrusts a coordinated transport service with the receipt of goods on his behalf, such a service at the destination shall promptly organize the relay transport upon receipt of the notice of the arrival of goods from the port or station and notify the consignee to take delivery of them. In the areas where conditions exist, the direct delivery of goods to the doorstep shall be developed.

16 A strict transfer system shall be put into effect for coordinated transport goods. The transfer procedures shall strictly be handled between the port, shipping, highway, railway, civil aviation, short-distance transport by lighter and other links of the whole course and the transfer "on credit" shall be stopped.

17 If damage or shortage of coordinated transport goods or the inconsistency of the goods with the waybill is found at any of such links as acceptance for shipment, transportation, load transfer, etc. of the whole course from the acceptance for shipment by the coordinated transport service up to their delivery at the destination, both handing-over and taking-over parties shall duly work out freight transport or commercial records, dispatch them with the goods and send their copies to the dispatching unit of the goods.

18 If any damage or destruction or loss of coordinated transport goods is found at the time of delivery, the coordinated transport service at the destination port or station shall work out

freight transport or commercial records jointly with the consignee and give them to the consignee for use as the basis to claim compensation; the copies shall also be sent to the responsible units concerned for inquiries. The units inquired of shall cooperate closely and shall not find any excuse to shirk the responsibility. When the responsibility is not clear, the unit which finally signs receipt of the goods shall undertake to compensate and shall be responsible for the compensation within the time limit stipulated by the department concerned.

19 The consignee shall claim compensation from the coordinated transport service at the destination within the time limit to claim compensation and attach the freight transport or commercial records and the certificates of prices to the claim. If the responsibility lies on the coordinated transport service, the compensation for the goods shall be calculated by adding the transportation and sundry expenses on the whole journey and packing charges (without adding packing charges if they are already included in the prices for allocation and transfer) to the state prices for allocation and transfer at the place of the dispatch.

20 In case coordinated transport goods cannot be delivered, the carrying unit or the coordinated transport service shall not dispose of them without authorization and shall try in every possible way to trace the owner so as to return the goods to their rightful owner as far as possible. The procedures for their disposal shall be handled in accordance with the "Provisions for the Disposal of Undeliverable Goods at Ports and Stations" promulgated by the State Economic Commission.

Chapter III The Coordinated Transport of Passengers

21 The port, station or coordinated booking office in each area shall vigorously develop the forward or commission booking of passenger tickets for various modes of transport so that passengers can get all the tickets at a time for more than two of such modes of transport as railway, highway, waterway and civil aviation and change to vehicles or vessels (or aircraft) by sections and shall handle such services as the consignment of luggage, meeting or seeing-off, etc.

22 In the cities with larger transfer numbers of passengers, the coordinated transport services shall take the coordinated transport of passengers for their key work, set up passenger coordinated transport service centres and develop such services as the commission booking of transfer passenger tickets, the introduction of provisional accommodation, etc.. Favourable conditions shall also be energetically created on trains or ships to develop such services on them as selling transfer passenger tickets for changing to other means of transport, introducing accommodation, etc.

23 With the day-by-day improvement of the cultural life of the people and the development of tourism, the tourist coordinated transport services including transportation, board and lodging shall be energetically developed in the places where favourable conditions exist.

Chapter IV Coordinated Transport Service Companies

24 A coordinated transport service company (department or centre) is a specialized independent accounting service enterprise, serving the society mainly by means of offering personal services. It shall not only serve passengers or owners of goods, but also serve transportation enterprises. Therefore, these companies generally do not deal directly in the business of vehicle or vessel transportation, but they shall expand their warehousing and load-transferring capacity as required. Their services mainly include: commission booking of passenger tickets, commission consignment of luggage or goods, transfers or load transfers, paçking and rearranging, warehousing and custody, taking delivery and delivering, handling financial settlements as agents and containerization services, etc.

25 In order to constantly expand coordinated transport, the formation of a coordinated transport service network all over the country shall be sped up and coordinated transport services shall be energetically guided so as to develop in the direction of specialized operation. The opening of a coordinated transport service company (department or centre) shall be examined, approved and registered with the administration concerned for industry and commerce.

26 The establishment of a coordinated transport service company (department or centre) shall be suited to local conditions and current circumstances. In areas where the conditions for its establishment are not ripe, a coordinated transport service centre (or team) concurrently

managed by each transportation enterprise or by the coordinated transport headquarters shall first form an independent accounting enterprise step by step. Partnership in joint business operation shall also be put into practice on the principles of voluntary participation and mutual benefit. In the areas where the conditions are ripe, especially at key ports and stations, railway, waterway and other transport main lines shall be organized to participate in the partnership joint operation of coordinated transport services with local transportation enterprises concerned.

Chapter V Transport Cooperation

27 In order to prevent obstruction of ports and stations and speed up the clearing of goods and materials, the port, railway, highway, shipping, urban transport and material departments shall cooperate closely with each other to make good jobs of forecasts, accurate reports, transfers and load-transfers and organize the direct transfers of goods between vehicles and vessels in a conditional way so as to shorten the times of idling of vehicles, vessels and goods.

28 The transport cooperation of each transportation department with the enterprises concerned shall be strengthened, various regulations for the administrative bodies of transport cooperation shall be established and perfected and the information on the state of affairs shall be duly exchanged. Good jobs shall be made of loading, unloading, transport and other links so as to fulfill the transport plans jointly.

29 Between the cities with close economic connections and frequent traffic of vehicles and vessels, economic means shall be adopted with the supplement of necessary administrative interventions (such as certification) to energetically organize the load allotment to empty return vehicles and vessels and pick up transportation so as to increase the real load rates of vehicles and vessels and save energy.

30 The common use of special-purpose lines and special-purpose wharves shall be energetically developed. The stations, ports and enterprises concerned shall create conditions for each other and adopt such procedures as signing agreements (or contracts), paying rational charges, etc. to achieve the coordination of handling machinery, power and labour so as to tap the potentialities of existing equipment and moderate the pressure of warehouses and freight yards at stations and ports.

Chapter VI Financial Settlements

31 The transportation and sundry expenses occurring in the coordinated transport of goods shall be calculated in accordance with the current rates of transportation and sundry expenses and the standards of the assigned transfer charges at each transfer port or station.

32 The settlement of charges shall be handled according to the different conditions in the receipt and payment of funds and in accordance with the methods stipulated in the settlement regulations of the People's Bank and in the agreements (or contracts) signed by the coordinated transport services with the units participating in coordinated transport. The people's bank in each area shall strengthen the supervision of the coordinated transport services in their handling of the settlement of coordinated transport charges and accurately and duly make the settlements. If an agreement (or a contract) is violated by delaying in paying transportation and sundry charges, the responsible party shall pay the fine for late payment.

33 Coordinated transport services shall strengthen financial administration and economic accounting and strictly execute financial and accounting regulations and financial and economic discipline. The settlement funds of each carrying or consigning unit shall be separately entered in different accounts and strictly checked and calculated so as to prevent mistakes or confusion of funds.

To organize coordinated transport, the regulations and procedures for the business management of transportation departments shall be followed so as to guarantee the economic benefit for each transport enterprise stipulated by the state.

Chapter VII Organising Leadership

34 The State Economic Commission shall form a national coordinated transport leading body together with such units as the Ministry of Railway, the Ministry of Communications, the General Administration of Civil Aviation of China, etc. and its main tasks are as follows: To consider and formulate the guiding principles and policies for national coordinated transport; to work out the procedures and regulations for national coordinated transport; to plan the construction of the national coordinated transport service network; to organize the interchange of experience

in national coordinated transport and examine and direct coordinated transport, etc.

35 Each province, municipality or autonomous region shall establish or retain the original transport headquarters as required, which shall be responsible for organizing, examining and urging all departments concerned to develop coordinated transport, carry out transport policies, fulfill transport plans, execute agreements (or contracts) and make good jobs of the planned balance and coordinated dovetailing between all departments concerned.

A prefecture (or a city) or a county shall set up coordinated transport headquarters and carry out the work in the light of the organizational principle of the coordinated transport headquarters at the provincial level. The prefectures (or cities) or counties with less coordinated transport shall not set up coordinated transport commanding organs.

The coordinated transport (or transportation) headquarters or coordinated transport office at each level shall not take on what shall be done by the transportation department separately, but shall mainly play a good role of the "synthesizing department" between several transportation departments and between production, supply, transport and marketing.

36 Coordinated transport administrative organizations shall be set up at stations, ports and the cooperative points between highways (railways or ports) and factories (mines or forests) which are busy with coordinated transport and each transportation department and units concerned shall dispatch professional personnels to join them. These grass-roots transportation cooperation offices (centres or teams) are the component part of the on-the-spot production commands and shall therefore be perfected and strengthened.

37 At present, the personnel who are not within the fixed establishments and who have been transferred from various units to join the provincial, prefectural (or city) or county coordinated transport offices shall be kept relatively stable and the original units shall still be responsible for their political treatment, wages, rewards, welfare benefits, etc.. The leaders of the coordinated transport offices shall regularly let the original units know the situations of the transferred personnel as matters really stand so as to be used as the main basis for examinations and appraisals.

Chapter VIII The Others

38 In order to make a good job of coordinated transport, each unit shall not only make good jobs of unity and cooperation, but also strictly enforce financial and economic disciplines. The coordinated transport headquarters at each level shall organize and urge the transportation units and the material units to sign various agreements (or contracts) between them to make clear the limits of duties and economic responsibility of each other. Economic sanctions shall be taken against those who violate the agreements (or contracts) as stipulated.

39 The coordinated transport services shall prescribe the charging standards for collecting coordinated transport service charges, commission transfer expenses, assigned transfer charges, etc. in the spirit of "small profits but more transport" or "charging more for more service" and "charging less for less service" and put them into effect after the approval and transmission of the department concerned in the province, municipality or autonomous region. It shall be strictly prohibited to concoct various pretexts and collect charges at will.

40 Coordinated transport enterprises shall strengthen the political and ideological work and make technical and professional examinations of the staff. The members of the staff with excellent achievements at work shall be rewarded. Rewarding funds shall be drawn from the profits of the enterprises. The amount of a reward shall be determined by referring to that of the neighbouring enterprises.

These Regulations shall be put into effect as from January 1, 1982. Each province, municipality or autonomous region shall work out the rules for the implementation in the light of the local actual conditions and by referring to the provisions of the departments concerned. If the documents printed and distributed in the past concerning coordinated transport go against these Regulations, these Regulations shall prevail.

INTERIM PROVISIONS FOR THE IMPROVEMENT AND STRENGTHENING OF THE ADMINISTRATION OF HIGHWAY TRANSPORTATION

(Promulgated by the State Economy Commission and the Ministry of Communications on June 11, 1982)

Highway transportation is an important component of the communications and transportation of our country. Within the regulation of the national economy, it shall be regulated energetically, rectified in earnest and developed in a well planned manner so as to provide the socialist modernization construction with safe, good-quality, high-yield and low-consumption transport capacity.

Each province, municipality or autonomous region shall attach great importance to highway transportation, conscientiously strengthen their leadership over it, gradually reform the administrative system of motor transportation, regulate the division of labour in transportation, bring into full play the initiative of all quarters and keep highway transportation in good order and invigorate it on the principles of contributing to production, saving energy, being rational in economy and organizing in a unified way so that highway transportation can serve industrial and agricultural production and the people's life better.

I Regulate the Division of Labour in Highway Transportation

In order to improve and strengthen the administration of highway transportation, highway transportation motor vehicles shall be divided into two kinds: i.e., for business transportation and for non-business transportation, and different signs shall be designated for them for the sake of distinction.

Non-business transportation vehicles mean the self-owned vehicles of a unit which serves the production and the living of the staff in the unit itself and does not have various types of carriage settlements with other units or individuals; all others are business transportation vehicles.

Business transportation vehicles shall undertake transportation jobs within the regions or along the routes delimited by the province, municipality or autonomous region. The business transportation vehicles of communications departments shall serve all trades and professions, especially ensuring the transportation of key point, large-quantity, port and station goods and materials for collection and distribution. The business transportation vehicles of non-communications departments shall mainly serve the needs of the department owning them for transportation and shall be allowed to undertake social material transportation jobs if surplus transport capacity is available.

The vehicles self-owned with approval by Party and government organs, bodies, schools, armed forces, enterprises and institutions shall undertake the transportation of internal production and living goods and materials for the units owning them. They shall take part in business transportation with the unified organization of communications departments as required.

Agricultural motor vehicles and tractors shall mainly serve the agricultural production and the ranges for their engagement in non-business transportation shall be implemented in accordance with the provisions in the "Notice of the Ranges for the Engagement of Agricultural Tractors in Non-business Transportation" as Document No. Guo-Ban-Fa 38(1982) of the State Council.

II Strengthen the Administration of Highway Transportation

The department in charge of communications at each level shall conscientiously strengthen the administration of highway transportation. Any unit or individual engaged in highway transportation or transport and handling business shall:

1 Only commence business after the application has been examined and approved with signing and annotating comments by the department in charge of communications at or above the county level according to the demand of transportation, and checked and approved by the administration for industry and commerce and after the business licence has been issued and the account has been opened with a bank;

2 Abide by the State policies, decrees and relevant provisions for communications administration and be put under the supervision of the department in charge of communications;

3 Use the uniform driving waybills and

vouchers of carriage clearing (separate provisions shall be made for international transportation) and execute the uniform carriage-counting standards, otherwise the financial department shall not make any reimbursements; the formalities should be simple and easy when handling driving waybills and vouchers of carriage clearing;

4 Submit transportation plans and statistical data to the local department in charge of communications;

5 Pay management expenses as stipulated by the province, municipality or autonomous region.

The department in charge of communications at each level shall cooperate closely with industrial, commercial, financial, tax, price and banking departments and conscientiously make good jobs of supervision and inspection. Jointly with the administration for industry and commerce, the department in charge of communications shall deal separately according to different conditions with those in violation of the provisions for transportation administration by making criticisms, taking economic sanctions, revoking or suspending licences, ceasing business, etc.

In the spirit of the "Instructions to Strengthen the Market Administration and Crack Down on Speculation, Profiteering and Smuggling" of the State Council, private citizens shall not be allowed to buy motor vehicles or tractors for the purpose of engaging in business transportation.

III Strengthen the Administration of Taxes, Profits and Carriage Rates

In order to urge highway transportation enterprises to improve business management and fulfil their economic responsibilities, all enterprises and individuals dealing in transportation or transport and handling business shall strictly implement the carriage rates stipulated by the state and pay taxes or turn over profits to the state as stipulated.

For the sake of overcoming the trend that each unit blindly increase its number of self-owned motor vehicles, the economic procedures for the use at cost shall be put into effect in addition to the strict control in the allocation of motor vehicles in future. The Ministry of Communications and the Ministry of Commerce shall select a prefecture (or a city) in a province (or an autonomous region) as soon as possible so as to experiment with collecting motor vehicle using fees and work out the relevant procedures. The motor vehicle using fees shall be turned over to the state at each level.

The communications and price departments at each level shall strengthen the administration of the current motor vehicle carriage rates and gradually rectify the irrational ones. The Ministry of Communications shall formulate the procedures for the administration of the national motor vehicle carriage rates and uniform carriage-counting standards jointly with the Ministry of Finance and the State Bureau of Prices. The communications department (or bureau), the department (or bureau) of Finance and the bureau of prices of each province, municipality or autonomous region shall formulate appropriate detailed rules for the implementation and carriage rates in the light of the actual conditions of their own areas, put them into effect after the approval of the people's government of the province, municipality or autonomous region and report them to the Ministry of Communications, the Ministry of Finance and the State Bureau of Prices for record.

IV Organize the Combined Operations of Motor Transportation Enterprises

The practice of combined operations in the motor transportation industry is advantageous in overcoming the blind development, repetitious construction and waste of energy and transport capacity brought about by scattered operations. On the principles of voluntary participation and mutual benefit, the motor transportation enterprises with different subordinate relations and of different ownership shall gradually be organized into combinations so as to practise combined operations.

In the organization of motor transport combinations, each area or each unit shall adopt different forms according to different conditions by proceeding from the actual conditions. The joint operations shall be practised by means of "unified operations, administration by levels, buying shares through evaluation of the capital and drawing bonuses according to shares;" combined operations shall also be practised by means of "combined operations, income decomposition, separate accounting and respective responsibility for profits or losses;" the enterprises shall also be directly organized for the purpose of the unified management of the sources of goods and the unified arrangement of transport capacity so as to practise combined transportation. The forms shall be in a great variety.

V Practise Planned Transportation and Start Combined Transport Services

The guiding principle of planned transportation with principal and market regulation as its supplement shall be executed in highway transportation, the idle use of vehicles shall be strictly controlled and various methods shall be adopted to seriously and properly organize rational transportation. In the case of state key points or large-quantity goods and materials or those in lots extending across prefectures or counties or those collected and distributed at ports or stations, the department in charge of communications in the people's government at each level or the unit assigned shall be responsible for balancing the sources of goods and transport capacity well and arranging for rational allocation of loads. Preferential carriage rates shall be implemented for the goods transport which offers a two-way source of goods. The transportation enterprises which provide others with return sources of goods shall be given certain commissions.

Combined transport service corporations shall be opened vigorously. They shall not only handle transport business for the owners of goods, but also organize the allocation of loans for vehicles belonging to transportation enterprises. A good job shall vigorously be done in combining transport services.

VI Do a Good Job of Reserving Vehicles and Saving Oil

The people's government of each province, municipality, or autonomous region shall conscientiously make good jobs of reserving vehicles and saving oils in accordance with the "Notice of Saving Petroleum" No. Zhong-Fa 20 (1981) of the Central Committee of the Chinese Communist Party, the State Council and the Military Commission of the Central Committee of the CPC, the 1981 Energy-saving Order No. 3 of the State Council and the provisions in other relevant documents. The number of trucks provided for its own area shall conscientiously be checked and determined in accordance with the situations of social transport capacity and transport volume and the surplus vehicles shall be reserved in good order. The surplus trucks of the enterprises or institutions directly under each ministry or commission of the Central Government shall be reserved in good order by the people's government of the province, municipality or autonomous region where they are located. During reservation, licences shall be returned, the supply of oil shall be stopped and the trucks shall be kept in good custody. Old cars used for many years, in poor technical condition and with high oil consumption shall be rejected after appraisal and their fixed assets shall be written off. They shall not be transferred for further use. In future, the new increase in number of trucks in each unit shall be approved by the department assigned by the people's government of each province, municipality or autonomous region, otherwise they shall not be brought in. In the areas where the transport capacity exceeds the transport volume, if new trucks are bought, appropriate old ones shall be put in reserve or their use shall be stopped in order to prevent the waste of energy and transport capacity.

VII Improve Business Management and Raise the Quality of Service

In order to contribute to the promotion of specialized cooperation, improve transportation efficiency and save transport capacity and energy, the business transportation vehicles of communications and non-communications departments shall be organized to carry out independent accounting. The enterprises shall be rectified in an all-round and planned way and the system of economic responsibility shall be put into practice so as to increase economic benefit. The departments in charge in the State Council and each province, municipality and autonomous region shall give business transportation enterprises preferential treatment and make the supply to what is better in such aspects as the allocation of vehicles, the extension of loans, the supply of oil, etc.

The transportation enterprises of the communications departments are the backbone of highway transportation in our country. They shall be fostered and supported energetically and developed in a focused manner. The department in charge of communications at each level shall gradually practise the separation of enterprises from the administration in its subordinate transportation enterprises, expand the enterprises' powers to act on their own and bring the initiative of the enterprises into full play. Each transportation enterprise shall update its vehicles in a planned manner and increase big-tonnage diesel vehicles, small trucks and various special-purpose vehicles so as to suit the needs for the transportation of various goods and materials in the society. Meanwhile, the departments and enterprises concerned shall conscientiously overcome the "official-businessmen's style of work," improve the attitudes in attending to customers, enhance the transportation quality, establish a good reputation and serve the socialist modernization construction and people's life better.

Each province, municipality or autonomous region shall formulate the detailed rules for implementation in the spirit of these Provisions and in the light of the local actual conditions.

2 AGRICULTURE

THE NOTICE OF THE STATE COUNCIL THAT AGRICULTURAL TAXES SHALL BE LEVIED ON ALL RECENTLY-EXPANDED FAMILY PLOTS AND FORAGE FIELDS

(July 13, 1981)

According to the report of the Ministry of Finance, after the Notice of the Central Committee of the Communist Party of China and the State Council of March 30 this year to transmit the "Report on the Vigorous Development of the Rural Diversified Economy" of the State Commission of Agriculture reached to lower governmental levels, telephone calls, telegrams and letters have come from many parts of our country, asking whether agricultural taxes shall be exempted for the family plots and forage fields properly expanded in accordance with the above notice in the places without fixing of farm output quotas for each household and requesting the State Council to clarify. After consideration, in order to maintain the balance in the policy of agricultural tax liabilities between the places without fixing of farm output quotas for each household and those with such fixing, and in consideration of the actual situation that the state now has difficulty in finance, the State Council has resolved that agricultural taxes shall continue to be levied on the parts of land originally bearing them after they are taken up due to the proper expansion of family plots and forge fields in each area and shall not be reduced or exempted. The specific procedures for the collection shall be determined by the people's government of each province, municipality or autonomous region according to local conditions. At present, the actual tax liabilities of agricultural taxes are rather light comparatively, so commune members should pay a little more agricultural taxes because of their increase of family income on account of their acquisition of more family plots and forage fields. We hope each area shall conscientiously strengthen propaganda and education and collection services on receipt of this Notice so as to endeavour to fulfil the state tasks of the collection of agricultural taxes.

INTERIM (DRAFT) PROCEDURES FOR THE ADMINISTRATION OF PRICES FOR NEGOTIATED PURCHASES AND SALES OF AGRICULTURAL AND SIDELINE PRODUCTS

(July 30 1981)

To develop the negotiated purchases and sales of agricultural and sideline products under the direction of the state plans is an important policy for promoting the agricultural production and invigorating the market. The following provisions are made in order to strengthen the administration of the prices for negotiated purchases and sales, level down country fair prices and maintain the basic stability of market prices:

I The Scope of the Commodities to Be Purchased and Sold through Negotiations

The scope of the commodities to be purchased and sold through negotiations shall be restricted to the agricultural and sideline products in Class 3 and those in Class 1 or Class 2 which shall be permitted to go on the market after the fulfilment of the purchasing quotas. No negotiated prices shall be allowed for the important industrial raw materials, animal by-products, large quantities of vegetables for large or medium cities or for industrial or mining areas and Chinese medicinal materials (including 34 kinds of precious medicinal materials) among the agricultural and sideline products in Class 1 and Class 2; no negotiated prices shall be allowed as well for the essential products of foreign trade commodities bases provided with the materials sold in reward or purchased for barter. A small number of important agricultural and sideline products in Class 3 shall be assigned with purchasing quotas for part of them in their major producing areas. Those beyond the limits of the purchasing quotas shall still fall under the range with negotiated prices.

In order to strictly control the scope of the commodities with negotiated prices, the division of the agricultural and sideline products in Class 1 and Class 2 shall by and large consistent throughout the country (the current list of the agricultural and sideline products in Class 1 and Class 2 attached). Some adjustments in all areas should be made between the categories of Class 2 and Class 3 in the light of particular conditions on the approval of the people's government of the province, municipality or autonomous region. Suggestions shall be obtained from the departments concerned of the State Council in accordance within the limits of authority for the division of administration of commodities for the agricultural and sideline products in Class 2 which shall be purchased or sold through negotiations after the fulfilment of the purchasing quotas or be brought down into Class 3. With the exception of those approved by the State Council, no proportions of the planned purchasing quotas of the agricultural and sideline products in Class 2 shall be transferred for the purchase with negotiated prices which leads to the combined purchases both at par and at negotiated prices.

II The Pricing Principles of the Commodities to Be Purchased and Sold Through Negotiations

The prices of the commodities to be purchased and sold through negotiations shall be fixed in consideration of the interests of the state, producers and consumers so that they can not only invigorate the market but maintain the basic stability of market prices.

(1) **The Prices of Negotiated Purchases:** They shall be discussed and determined together with the producers on the basis of the situations of supply and demand in the market, for the purpose of protecting and putting resources to rational use and in consideration of the parities of related products. In the case of the commodities of which the supply and demand are in balance on the whole or of which the supply falls short of the demand, their prices of negotiated purchases shall be a little less than the country fair prices in that locality and at that time. Meanwhile, the management department shall make up another's deficiency from one's surplus so as to keep down the country fair prices through purchases and sales. In the specific control, the prices of negotiated purchases shall be properly higher for the perennial mountain and forest native and special products and major aquatic products which are in large demand in both domestic and overseas markets or which do not vie with grain and cotton for land or which are produced with complicated techniques; the prices of negotiated purchases shall be lower for the agricultural and sideline products of which the supply and demand are basically in balance or of which the demand in both domestic and overseas markets is going less or which vie with grain or cotton for land; the prices of negotiated purchases shall be kept down as low as possible for the unsalable or

overstocked commodities which still have certain use values but do not suit the needs of the market so as to promote the better suitability of the production to the demand. The prices of negotiated purchases of cereals and oils shall be determined on the principles of complying with the lines of business and with the market and making them a little lower than market prices, by referring to their country fair prices and according to different areas, different annual harvests, seasons, categories or qualities.

The extent of the prices of negotiated purchases of agricultural and sideline products to be higher than market quotations shall be controlled separately according to different conditions. Those of some categories of grain and oil shall be lower than or equivalent to the over-purchasing prices and some others shall be a little higher than them but they shall not be too high so as to prevent the market prices from being stimulated to rise. In general, the extent of the negotiated purchased prices of other agricultural and sideline products shall not exceed 30 per cent; that of a very few categories with rather low unit prices or with the prices differing greatly from quoted market ones shall be higher than 30 per cent; the prices of negotiated purchases of the categories of which the supply exceeds the demand shall be a little lower than the quoted purchasing prices. For the purpose of protecting the farmers' interests, the negotiated purchased prices of some important agricultural products shall not be lower than the minimum protective prices. The prices of negotiated purchases shall duly be readjusted according to the situations of supply and demand and to the changes of seasons. The negotiated purchased prices of agricultural and sideline products in contiguous areas shall be discussed and made consistent as far as possible.

(2) **The Prices of Negotiated Sales:** They shall be fixed generally in accordance with the principle of small profits and quick turnover, that is, by adding necessary expenses and small profits (the profit rates calculated as a whole to at 2% to 3%) on the basis of the prices of negotiated purchases in accordance with the rational circulating directions of commodities and, in general, they shall be lower than the country fair prices in that locality and at that time. In respect of the negotiated sale prices of cereals and oils, there shall be rational regional or seasonal price differences. Both profits and losses shall concurrently be allowed for different categories or different seasons so long as there are some profits left when they are calculated as a whole in the year. The disparities between the prices of purchases and sales, or the disparities between wholesale and retail prices or the rates of expenses in the prices of allocated or transferred goods shall generally be lower than those of the commodities at par of the same categories. The amount of the profits from the commodities with negotiated prices shall not exceed that from the commodities at par of the same categories. The negotiated sale prices of meals, cooked food, pastries, snacks, non-staple food, etc. made of the commodities with negotiated prices as raw or supplementary materials shall be controlled as low as possible and, in general, their ex-factory or selling prices shall be determined by calculating the producing and processing costs in accordance with the prices of the products at par of the same categories with the addition of the differences between the parities and the negotiated prices of the raw materials with negotiated prices and of the taxes. The negotiated prices of fresh or live commodities shall flexibly be controlled according to their qualities and the changes of supply and demand in the market and some difference in prices shall be allowed between different enterprises in the same market and in the same category so as to be helpful to competition.

In order to strengthen the administration of prices, stabilize market prices and facilitate the masses' supervision, the commodities sold at negotiated prices shall be separated from those sold at market quotations and have their prices clearly marked. The commodities purchased at par shall not be sold at negotiated prices. In general, the supply at par of some rationed commodities shall not be stopped or reduced. It shall not be allowed to raise the prices of negotiated sales wantonly or to use the trading in scarce commodities with negotiated prices as a means to make excessive profits or to issue more rewards (the negotiated sales of cereals and oils shall be carried out in accordance with the relevant provisions of the Ministry of Food).

III The Administration of the Prices of Negotiated Purchases and Sales

The principles in the administration of the prices of negotiated purchases and sales of agricultural and sideline products shall be to contribute to the development of agricultural production, increase the supply of commodities in the market and to help maintain the basic stability of market prices; keep them in good order without rigidity and make them live without confusion. In respect of the limits of authority of administration, such principles of unified leadership and administration by levels shall also be put into effect. The State Bureau of Prices and the department concerned of the State Council shall prescribe the pricing principles and pricing procedures for the commodities to be purchased and sold through negotiations and the departments concerned of the State Council shall prescribe the maximum limits of the negotiated purchased prices for the essential commodities. A price synthesizing department and business authorities at the provincial level shall concretely formulate the procedures for the implementation or the detailed rules in the light of local actual conditions on the basis of the pricing principles and procedures stipulated by higher authorities and at the same time administer the prices of negotiated purchases and sales. In order to protect the interests of producers and consumers and avoid rushing to purchase by forcing up prices or forcing prices down to a large extent for purchase which may affect the production, the business authorities of a province, a municipality or an autonomous region shall make suggestions as to the maximum limits of prices and the minimum protective prices for the commodities which are under the administration of the departments concerned of the State Council in accordance with the limits of authority of the administration of prices, the people's government of the province, municipality or autonomous region shall examine and determine them after the opinions of the departments of the State Council are obtained the publicized. The maximum limited prices and the minimum protective prices of some commodities shall be examined and determined by a prefectural or county people's government. The principal management corporations at a city or county level shall have the following pricing powers for the commodities to be purchased and sold through negotiations: (1) To put prices under concrete control within the scope stipulated by higher authorities; (2) to negotiate and determine the prices by themselves in accordance with the stipulated pricing principles and procedures for the commodities without any scope stipulated by the higher authorities; (3) to determine the prices of fresh or live commodities on the principle of fixing the price according to the quality and in accordance with the seasonal price differences and qualitative price difference stipulated by higher authorities; (4) to be entitled to cut prices for their own disposal within the limits of the sums of money stipulated by the higher authorities for dull, unsalable, shopworn or inferior commodities. The enterprises and units concurrently engaged in marketing shall carry out purchases and sales at the levels of prices controlled by the principal management corporations. The pricing powers of independent accounting enterprises shall be considered and determined by the province, municipality or autonomous region in the spirit of the aforesaid and in the light of actual conditions.

In order to check the driving up of the prices of negotiated prices, the related provisions in Document No. 295 of 1980 and Document No, 3 of 1981 of the State Council shall be conscientiously executed and the administration of prices shall be closely combined with that of the market (the administration of cereals and oils shall be executed as stipulated in the notice No. Liang-Ji-Lian 19(81) of the Ministry of Food and the State Bureau of Prices). The agricultural and sideline products in Class 1 and Class 2 shall be prohibited from transactions at negotiated prices before the fulfilment of the state purchasing quotas. The agricultural and sideline products in Class 2 permitted to be purchased through negotiations after the fulfilment of the purchasing quotas and those in Class 3 from the concentrated producing areas shall be distributed in a unified manner by the local business authorities among the purchasing units and the individual petty businessmen and pedlars with licences and they shall be prohibited from driving up prices or rushing to purchase among each other. The prices of negotiated purchases shall not be higher than the maximum limited prices fixed by the people's government of the province, municipality or autonomous region or of the prefecture, city of county. If the prices of negotiated purchases are higher than the maximum limited prices, the offenders shall be punished for driving up prices and violating the discipline of prices.

The activities of negotiated purchases and sales shall be carried out under the direction of the state plans in the spirit of the instruction of the Central Committee of the CPC and the State Council and that contracts shall be signed for the purchase of agricultural and sideline products so as to reduce the blindness in the production and purchase. The state commercial units and the supply and marketing cooperatives shall sign contracts with the producing units as far as possible for large quantities of agricultural and sideline products in Class 3 purchased at negotiated prices. The quantities of commodities, the standards of grades and their prices shall be stipulated in the contracts. If necessary, the signing of a contract shall be witnessed by the administration for industry and commerce which shall also supervise and examine the execution of the contract. If there is no extraordinarily serious natural calamities, any party in breach of the contract shall assume the economic responsibilities.

The business authorities and price departments at each level shall conscientiously carry out the relevant provisions of these Procedures in the light of actual conditions under the leadership of the local people's government.

Appendix: The Current List of Agricultural and Sideline Products in Class 1 and Class 2.

CLASS 1: Grain, cotton, oils, timber.

CLASS 2

1. The Categories under the Administration of the All-China Federation of Supply and Marketing Cooperatives: Jute, bluish dogbane, ramie, fluecured tobacco, sheep wool, cashmere, cattle hide, goat hide, sheep hides, kid, lambskin, feathers, casings, hog bristles, silkworm cocoons, tussah cocoons, tea, famous sun-cured tobacco, straw mats, palm sheets, bamboo, sagebrush, citrus, handmade paper, honey, raw lacquer, apples, edible fungi, star aniseeds, fox hides, goat hair, sheep casings, red jujubes, hot-pickled mustard roots, day lilies, reed mats, charcoal, farm animals, hemp, goat casings.

2. The Categories under the Administration of the Ministry of Commerce: Live pigs, beef cattle, mutton goats, fresh eggs.

3. The Categories under the Administration of the Ministry of Forestry: Rosin, crude rubber.

4. The Categories under the Administration of the State Bureau of Aquatic Products: Large yellow croakers, yellow croakers, hairtails, cuttlefishes, Spanish mackerel, silvery pomfrets, Chinese herring, congers, Pacific herring, slate cod croakers, flatfish, prawns, abalones, shark's fins, fish maw, sea cucumbers, dried scallops, dried shrimps, dried small shrimps, squids, jellyfish.

5. The Categories under the Administration of the Ministry of Food: Tung oil, castor oil, wood oil, Chinese tallow tree oil, Chinese catalpa oil.

6. The Categories under the Administration of the Ministry of Foreign Trade: Peppermint oil, citronella oil.

7. The Categories under the Administration of the Central Administration for Medicines (including Class 2 and precious medicinal materials):

Musk, bezoar, Coptis chinensis, Fritillaria thunbergii, liquorice, Lycium chinense, yams, Corydalis yanhusuo, Eucommia ulmoides, skinned taros, Lonicera japonica, safflower, ginseng (including wild ginseng), Codonopsis pilosula, Angelica sinensis, Ligusticum chuanxiong, Rehmannia glutinosa (dried), Atractylodes macrocephala, Paeonia lactiflora, Poria cocos, Ophiopogon japonicus, Aconitum carmichaela, Aucklandia lappa, Achyranthes bidentata, Scrophularia ningpoensis, Paeonia suffruticosa (root bark), Panax notoginseng, deer's antlers, Astragalus membranaceus, chrysanthemums.

Magnolia officinalis, Gastrodia elata, Amomum villosum, Cordyceps sinensis, pearls, tiger bones, leopard bones, bear gallbladders, dried dead scorpions, Chinese cassia bark, agalloch eaglewood, dried venom of toads, Morinda officinalis, donkey-hide gelatin, rhinoceros horns, Guangdong goat horns, antelope horns, frankincense, myrrh, Daemonorops draco, sandalwood, cloves, western safflower.

8. The Categories under the Administration of the Ministry of Light Industry: sugarcane, beet.

3

FINANCE AND BANKING

Bank/ Currency/ Foreign Exchange/ Loans/ State Bonds

ARTICLES OF ASSOCIATION OF THE BANK OF CHINA

(Approved by the State Council on September 22, 1980)

I. General Provisions

Article 1 The Bank of China is a socialist state enterprise and is the specialized foreign exchange bank of the People's Republic of China.

Article 2 The tasks of the Bank of China shall be: to raise, utilize, accumulate and manage foreign exchange funds, to engage in all kinds of foreign exchange operations and to participate in international financial activities for the purpose of serving socialist modernization.

Article 3 The head office of the Bank of China shall be established in Beijing. To meet the needs of business, the Bank may open branches or representative offices at places of commercial and financial importance both in China and abroad.

II. Capital

Article 4 The authorized capital of the Bank of China shall be Renminbi 1,000 million yuan.

III. Scope of Business

Article 5 The Bank of China shall engage in and be entrusted to handle the following kinds of business:

(1) International settlements in connection with foreign trade and non-trade transactions;

(2) International inter-bank deposits and loans;

(3) Overseas Chinese remittances and other international remittances;

(4) Deposits and loans in foreign currencies and, with the permission of the People's Bank of China, deposits and loans in Renminbi that relate to foreign exchange operations;

(5) Buying and selling of foreign exchange (including foreign currencies);

(6) Buying and selling of gold on international markets;

(7) Organizing and participating in international syndicated loans;

(8) Investing by itself or jointly with others in banks, finance companies and other enterprises in foreign countries and in Hongkong, Macao and other regions;

(9) Issuing bonds and securities in foreign currencies with the authorization of the State;

(10) Providing trust and consulting services; and

(11) Engaging in other kinds of banking business permitted or entrusted by the State.

Article 6 The Bank of China shall participate in international financial meetings with the authorization of the State.

Article 7 Offices of the Bank of China established in foreign countries and in Hongkong, Macao and other regions may engage in all the kinds of banking business permitted by local laws and regulations.

IV. Organization

Article 8 The Bank of China shall have a board of directors consisting of an honorary chairman, a chairman and a number of vice-chairmen, managing directors and directors, all to be appointed by the State Council.

Article 9 The tasks of the board of directors of the Bank of China shall be as follows:

(1) To consider and determine the business policies and plans of the Bank;

(2) To receive and examine the reports of the president on the work of the Bank;

(3) To examine and adopt the Bank's annual financial statements and proposals for the handling of profits;

(4) To appoint and remove high officials of the Bank;

(5) To consider and determine the opening and closing of branches of the Bank in China and abroad; and

(6) To examine and discuss other important matters relating to the Bank.

Article 10 The Bank of China shall have a board of supervisors consisting of a chief supervisor and a number of supervisors, all to be appointed by the State Council.

Article 11 The tasks of the board of supervisors of the Bank of China shall be as follows:

(1) To supervise the Bank's observance of the

policies, laws and decrees of the State as well as the implementation of the Bank's business policies;

(2) To examine the annual financial statements and reports of the Bank; and

(3) To investigate matters of a serious nature and present opinions on ways of dealing with them.

Article 12 The Bank of China shall have a president and a number of vice-presidents, all to be nominated by the chairman of the board of directors who shall, with the approval of the board of directors, submit his nominations to the State Council for appointments.

Article 13 The president of the Bank of China shall be responsible for the overall operation and administration of the Bank and shall submit to the board of directors periodic reports on the work of the Bank. The vice-presidents shall assist the president in his work.

V. Meetings

Article 14 A meeting of the board of directors of the Bank of China shall be held once a year and is to be convened by the chairman.

A meeting of the board of supervisors of the Bank of China shall be held once a year and is to be convened by the chief supervisor.

If necessary, the above-mentioned meetings may be convened ahead of schedule or be postponed; and the chairman of the board of directors may also convene joint meetings of the directors and supervisors.

Article 15 Meetings of the board of directors, meetings of the board of supervisors, and joint meetings of the directors and supervisors of the Bank of China must have a quorum of more than two-thirds of their respective members (including proxies). All resolutions, to be effective, must be passed by more than one-half of the persons attending the meetings.

VI. Supplementary Provisions

Article 16 These Articles of Association shall go into effect upon the approval of the State Council. The same procedure shall apply when amendments are made.

THE PROCEDURES OF THE PEOPLE'S REPUBLIC OF CHINA FOR PROHIBITING THE STATE CURRENCY FROM ENTERING OR LEAVING OUR COUNTRY

Promulgated by the Government Administrative Council
(March 6, 1951)

1. These Procedures are formulated in order to consolidate the value of our state currency, stabilize our finance and safeguard the property of our people.

2. The state currency referred to in these Procedures means the currency issued by the People's Bank of China and also includes the local currencies issued with special permission of the Central People's Government.

3. The People's Republic of China shall prohibit the state currency from entering or leaving the country. The state currency carried or transported without authorization over the borders shall be confiscated.

4. Those who carry or transport the state currency without authorization over the borders under suspicion of damaging the state currency or those who smuggle forged or counterfeit Renminbi into our country shall be handed over together with the evidence by the authorities discovering them to the local judicial authorities to be dealt with according to law.

5. Postal parcels which are found to contain state currency smuggled over the borders shall be confiscated. If the smuggled currency is used for commission of crimes or suspected of being forged or counterfeit, it shall be handed over together with the postal parcels to the local judicial authorities to be dealt with according to law.

6. These Procedures shall be put into effect from the date of issue.

INTERIM REGULATIONS ON PUNISHMENT FOR IMPAIRMENT OF STATE CURRENCY

Promulgated by the Government Administrative Council of the Central People's Government
(April 19, 1951)

Article 1 These Regulations are formulated for the purpose of protecting our state currency and consolidating our state finance.

Article 2 The state currency referred to in these Regulations means the currency issued by the People's Bank of China.

Article 3 If the state currency is forged for counter-revolutionary purposes, the major culprits or those whose cases are serious shall be sentenced to death, those whose cases are less serious shall be sentenced to imprisonment for life or for a term of no more than 15 or less than 7 years and the whole or a part of their properties shall be confiscated.

If the state currency is counterfeited or the forged or counterfeit state currency is circulated for sale or put to use for counter-revolutionary purposes, the major culprits or those whose cases are serious shall be sentenced to death or imprisonment for life; those whose cases are less serious shall be sentenced to imprisonment for a term of no more than 15 or less than 5 years and the whole or a part of their properties shall be confiscated.

Article 4 If the state currency is forged with the intention of seeking profits, the major culprits or those whose cases are serious shall be sentenced to death or imprisonment for life, those whose cases are less serious shall be sentenced to imprisonment for a term of not more than 15 or less than 3 years and the whole or a part of their properties shall be confiscated.

If the state currency is counterfeited or the forged or counterfeit state currency is circulated for sale or put to use with the intention of seeking profits, the major culprits or those whose cases are serious shall be sentenced to imprisonment for life or for a term of not more than 15 or less than 7 years and the whole or a part of their properties shall be confiscated; those whose cases are less serious shall be sentenced to imprisonment for a term of not more than 10 years or less than 1 year and fined as the court thinks fit; those whose cases are not serious shall be sentenced to corvée for a term of not more than 1 year or punished by fines as the court thinks fit.

Article 5 Those who spread rumours or use other means to damage the credit of the state currency shall be sentenced to imprisonment for not more than 5 years or punished by fines.

Those who commit the above crime for counter-revolutionary purposes shall be sentenced to imprisonment for a term of not more than 15 or less than 5 years, the major culprits or those whose cases are serious shall be sentenced to death or imprisonment for life and the whole or a part of their properties shall be confiscated.

PROVISIONAL REGULATIONS OF THE BANK OF CHINA ON FOREIGN EXCHANGE CERTIFICATES

(March 19, 1980)

1 With a view to strengthening exchange control, the State Council has authorized the Bank of China to issue Foreign Exchange Certificates (hereinafter called "Exchange Certificates").

2 Exchange Certificates are in seven denominations, namely, 100 yuan, 50 yuan, 10 yuan, 5 yuan, 1 yuan, 5 jiao and 1 jiao. The yuan expressed in them is equivalent in value to the Renminbi yuan. No refund is allowed in case of loss.

3 Exchange Certificates are usable only in China for specific purposes. They are to be used by short-time visitors (foreigners, overseas Chinese, Hongkong and Macao compatriots), personnel of the diplomatic corps and foreign representative offices in China at the following places or for making the following payments:

a) at travel services dealing exclusively with foreigners, overseas Chinese, Hongkong and Macao compatriots, friendship stores, companies provisioning foreign ships, arts and crafts stores, curio shops, foreign trade centres and special shop counters for selling imported goods;

b) at guest houses, hotels and clubs accommodating exclusively foreigners, overseas Chinese, Hongkong and Macao compatriots;

c) payment of fares for through train or ship to Hongkong or Macao, and charges for transporting luggage or personal effects;

d) payment of fares for domestic or international flights and charges for transporting luggage or personal effects;

e) payment of international telecommunication charges and international parcel post;

f) at places where Exchange Certificates are required for payment as approved by the State General Administration of Exchange Control (or its branches) or according to official regulations.

4 Convertible foreign banknotes, bills of exchange or payment instruments in foreign currency that are immediately cashable or remittances from abroad may be exchanged by the above-mentioned categories of persons for Exchange Certificates at the Bank of China or its designated exchange centres throughout the country. When handing out Exchange Certificates, the Bank of China (or its exchange centres) shall issue to the customer an "exchange memo."

5 Holders of Exchange Certificates may within six months and against the "exchange memo," convert the Exchange Certificates into Renminbi special deposits or foreign currency deposits with the Bank of China, or into foreign currency, or take them out of the country.

6 No private dealings in Exchange Certificates are permitted. Speculation in or counterfeit of Exchange Certificates is strictly prohibited. Violators will be punished for undermining the socialist economic order according to Chapter 3 of the Criminal Law of the People's Republic of China.

PROVISIONAL REGULATIONS FOR EXCHANGE CONTROL OF THE PEOPLE'S REPUBLIC OF CHINA

Promulgated by the State Council

(December 18, 1980)

I General Provisions

Article 1 These provisional regulations are formulated for the purpose of strengthening exchange control, increasing national foreign exchange income and economizing on foreign exchange expenditure so as to expedite national economic growth and safeguard the rights and interests of the country.

All foreign exchange income and expenditure, the issuance and circulation of all kinds of payment instruments in foreign currency, dispatch and carriage into and out of the People's Republic of China of foreign exchange, precious metals and payment instruments in foreign currency shall be governed by these regulations.

Article 2 Foreign exchange herein mentioned refers to:

a. Foreign currencies, including banknotes, coins, etc.

b. Securities in foreign currency, including government bonds, treasury bills, corporate bonds and debentures, shares, interest and dividend coupons, etc.

c. Instruments payable in foreign currency, including bills, drafts, cheques, bank deposit certificates, postal savings certificates, etc.

d. Other foreign exchange funds.

Article 3 The People's Republic of China pursues the policy of centralized control and unified management of foreign exchange by the state.

The administrative organ in charge of exchange control of the People's Republic of China is the State General Administration of Exchange Control (SGAEC) and its branch offices.

The specialized foreign exchange bank of the People's Republic of China is the Bank of China. No other financial institution shall engage in foreign exchange business, unless approved by the SGAEC.

Article 4. All Chinese and foreign organizations and individuals in the People's Republic of China must, unless otherwise stipulated by law or decree or in these regulations, sell their foreign exchange proceeds to the Bank of China. Any foreign exchange required is to be sold to them by the Bank of China in accordance with the quota approved by the state or with relevant regulations.

See Chinese

The circulation, use and mortgage of foreign currency in the People's Republic of China are prohibited. Unauthorized sales and purchases of foreign exchange and unlawful seizure and possession of foreign exchange in whatever ways and by whatever means are prohibited.

II Exchange Control Relating to State Organizations and Collective Economic Units

Article 5 Foreign exchange income and expenditure of state organs, units of the armed forces, non-governmental bodies, educational institutions, state enterprises, government establishments, and urban and rural collective economic units in China (hereinafter referred to as domestic organizations) are all subject to control according to plan.

Domestic organizations are permitted to retain a proportion of their foreign exchange receipts in accordance with relevant regulations.

Article 6 Unless approved by the SGAEC or its branch offices, domestic organizations shall not possess foreign exchange; deposit foreign exchange abroad; offset foreign exchange expenditure against foreign exchange income; or use the foreign exchange belonging to state organs stationed abroad or Chinese enterprises and establishments resident in foreign countries or in the Hong Kong and Macao regions, by way of borrowing or acquisition.

Article 7 Unless approved by the State Council, domestic organizations shall not issue securities with foreign exchange value inside or outside China.

Article 8 Departments under the State Council and people's governments of various provinces, municipalities and autonomous regions shall compile annual overall plans for domestic organizations under their respective jurisdiction whereby loans may be accepted from banks or enterprises in foreign countries or in the Hong

Kong and Macao regions. These plans shall be submitted to the SGAEC and the Foreign Investment Control Commission for examination and forwarding to the State Council for approval.

The procedure for examining and approving individual borrowings shall be prescribed separately.

Article 9 The portion of foreign exchange retained by domestic organizations, non-trade foreign exchange and foreign exchange under compensatory trade received in advance for later payments, funds borrowed in convertible foreign currency, and other foreign exchange held with the approval of the SGAEC or its branch offices, must be placed in foreign currency deposit accounts or foreign currency quota accounts to be opened with the Bank of China, and must be used within the prescribed scope and be subject to the supervision of the Bank of China.

Article 10 When domestic organizations import or export goods, the banks handling the transactions shall check their foreign exchange receipts and payments either against the import or export licences duly verified by the Customs or against the Customs declaration forms for imports or exports.

Article 11 State organs stationed abroad must use foreign exchange according to the plan approved by the state.

The operating profits of enterprises and establishments in foreign countries or in the Hongkong and Macao regions must, except for the portion kept locally as working funds according to the plan approved by the state, be transferred back on schedule and be sold to the Bank of China.

No Chinese organization stationed abroad is permitted to keep foreign exchange for domestic organizations without authorization.

Article 12 Delegations and workgroups sent temporarily to foreign countries or to the Hongkong and Macao regions must use foreign exchange according to their respective specific plans, and must, upon their return, promptly transfer back to China their surplus foreign exchange to be checked by and sold to the Bank of China.

Foreign exchange earned in their various business activities by the delegations and workgroups referred to in the above paragraph and by members thereof, must be promptly transferred back to China and must not be kept abroad without the approval of the SGAEC or its branch offices.

III Exchange Control Relating to Individuals

Article 13 Foreign exchange remitted from foreign countries or from the Hongkong and Macao regions to Chinese or foreign nationals or stateless persons residing in China must be sold to the Bank of China, except the portion retained as permitted by the state.

Article 14 Chinese and foreign nationals and stateless persons residing in China are permitted to keep in their own possession foreign exchange already in China.

The foreign exchange referred to in the above paragraph shall not, without authorization, be carried or sent out of China either in person or by others or by post. If the owners wish to sell the foreign exchange, they must sell it to the Bank of China and are permitted to retain a portion thereof as convertible foreign currency according to the percentage prescribed by the state.

Article 15 When foreign exchange that has been kept in foreign countries or in the Hong Kong and Macao regions by Chinese residents in China prior to the founding of the People's Republic of China, by overseas Chinese prior to their returning to and settling down in China, by Hongkong and Macao compatriots prior to their returning to and settling down in their home places, is transferred to China, the owners are permitted to retain a portion thereof as convertible foreign currency according to the percentage prescribed by the state.

Article 16 When foreign exchange belonging personally to individuals sent to work or study in foreign countries or in the Hong Kong and Macao regions is remitted or brought back to China, the owners returning after completion of their missions are permitted to retain the entire amount as convertible foreign currency.

Article 17 The percentages of foreign exchange retention permitted under Articles 13, 14 and 15 of these regulations shall be prescribed separately.

Foreign exchange retained by individuals as permitted under Articles 13, 14, 15 and 16 of these regulations must be deposited with the Bank of China. These foreign exchange deposits may be sold to the Bank of China or remitted out of China through the Bank of China, or taken out of China against certification by the Bank of China. It is however not permitted, without authorization, to carry or send deposit certificates out of China either in person or by others or by post.

Article 18 Foreign exchange remitted or brought into China from foreign countries or from the Hong Kong and Macao regions by foreign nationals coming to China, by overseas Chinese and Hongkong and Macao compatriots returning for a short stay, by foreign experts, technicians, staff members and workers engaged to work in domestic organizations, and by foreign students and trainees, may be kept in their own possession, or sold to or deposited with the Bank of China, or remitted or taken out of China.

Article 19 Chinese and foreign nationals and stateless persons residing in China may apply to the local branch offices of the SGAEC for the purchase of foreign exchange to be remitted or taken out of China. When approved, the required foreign exchange will be sold to the applicants by the Bank of China.

When foreign experts, technicians, staff members and workers engaged to work in domestic organizations require foreign exchange to be remitted or taken out of China, the Bank of China will deal with their applications in accordance with the stipulations in the contracts or agreements.

IV Exchange Control Relating to Foreign Representatives in China and Their Personnel

Article 20 Foreign exchange remitted or brought into China from foreign countries or from the Hong Kong and Macao regions by foreign diplomatic missions, consulates, official commercial offices, offices of international organizations and nongovernmental bodies resident in China, diplomatic officials and consuls as well as members of the permanent staff of the above units, may be kept in their own possession, or sold to or deposited with the Bank of China, or remitted or taken out of China.

Article 21 The conversion into foreign currency, if required, of visa and certification fees received in Renminbi from Chinese citizens by foreign diplomatic missions and consulates in China, is subject to approval by the SGAEC or its branch offices.

V Exchange Control Relating to Enterprises with Overseas Chinese Capital, Enterprises with Foreign Capital, and Chinese and Foreign Joint Ventures and Their Personnel

Article 22 All foreign exchange receipts of enterprises with overseas Chinese capital, enterprises with foreign capital and Chinese and foreign joint ventures, must be deposited with the Bank of China, and all their foreign exchange disbursements must be paid from their foreign exchange deposit accounts.

The enterprises referred to in the above paragraph must submit periodic reports and statements of their foreign exchange business to the SGAEC or its branch offices, all of which are empowered to inspect their activities in respect to their foreign exchange receipts and payments.

Article 23 Except where otherwise approved by the SGAEC or its branch offices, Renminbi should in all cases be used in the settlement of accounts between enterprises with overseas Chinese capital, enterprises with foreign capital, Chinese and foreign joint ventures and other enterprises and individuals residing in the People's Republic of China.

Article 24 Enterprises with overseas Chinese capital, enterprises with foreign capital and foreign partners in Chinese and foreign joint ventures may apply to the Bank of China for remitting abroad their net profits after tax as well as other legitimate earnings by debiting the foreign exchange deposit accounts of the enterprises concerned.

The enterprises and foreign partners referred to in the above paragraph should apply to the SGAEC or its branch offices for transferring foreign exchange capital abroad by debiting the foreign exchange deposit accounts of the enterprises concerned.

Article 25 An amount not exceeding 50% of their net wages and other legitimate earnings after tax may be remitted or taken out of China in foreign currency by staff members and workers of foreign nationality and those from the Hongkong and Macao regions employed by enterprises with overseas Chinese capital, enterprises with foreign capital and Chinese and foreign joint ventures.

Article 26 Enterprises with overseas Chinese capital, enterprises with foreign capital and Chinese and foreign joint ventures which wind up operations in accordance with legal procedure, should be responsible for the liquidation within the scheduled period of their outstanding liabilities and taxes due in China, under the joint supervision of the relevant departments in charge and the SGAEC or its branch offices.

VI Control Relating to Carrying Foreign Exchange, Precious Metals and Payment Instruments in Foreign Currency into and out of China

Article 27 No restriction as to the amount is imposed on the carrying into China of foreign exchange, precious metals and objects made from them, but declaration to the Customs is required at the place of entry.

To carry foreign exchange out of China or to carry out of China the foreign exchange previously brought in shall be permitted by the Customs against certification by the Bank of China or against the original declaration form at the time of entry.

To carry out of China precious metals and objects made from them or to carry out of China precious metals and objects made from them previously brought in shall be permitted by the Customs according to the specific circumstances as prescribed by government regulations or against the original declaration form at the time of entry.

Article 28 Renminbi traveller's cheques, traveller's letters of credit and other Renminbi payment instruments convertible into foreign currency may be brought into China against declaration to the Customs, and taken out of China against certification by the Bank of China or against the original declaration form at the time of entry.

Article 29 Unless otherwise approved by the SGAEC or its branch offices, the carrying or sending out of China either in person or by others or by post of the following documents and securities held by Chinese residing in China is not permitted:

Bonds, debentures, share certificates issued abroad;

Title deeds for real estate abroad;

Documents or deeds necessary in dealing with creditor's right or owner's right to possession regarding inheritance, real estate and other foreign exchange assets abroad.

Article 30 The carrying or sending out of China of Renminbi cheques, drafts, passbooks, deposit certificates and other Renminbi instruments held by Chinese or foreign nationals or stateless persons residing in China, is not permitted, either in person or by others or by post.

VII Supplementary Provisions

Article 31 All units and individuals have the right to report any violation of these regulations. Reward shall be given to such units or individuals according to the merit of the report. Violators shall be penalized by the SGAEC, its branch offices or by the departments of public security, or by the departments of Administration of Industry and Commerce, or by the Customs. According to the seriousness of the offence, the penalties may take the form of compulsory exchange of the foreign currency for Renminbi, or fine or confiscation of the properties or both, or punishment by judicial authorities according to law.

Article 32 The exchange control regulations for special economic zones, for trade in border areas, and for personal dealings between inhabitants across the border shall be formulated by the people's governments of the provinces, municipalities and autonomous regions concerned in the spirit of these regulations and in the light of specific local conditions, and shall be enforced upon the approval of the State Council.

Article 33 Detailed provisions for the enforcement of these regulations shall be formulated by the SGAEC.

Article 34 These regulations shall come into force on March 1, 1981.

RULES FOR THE IMPLEMENTATION OF FOREIGN EXCHANGE CONTROLS RELATING TO FOREIGN INSTITUTIONS IN CHINA AND THEIR PERSONNEL

Promulgated by the State General Administration of Exchange Control
(August 10, 1981)

Article 1 These Rules are formulated in order to implement the provisions of Articles 20 and 21 of the Provisional Regulations for Exchange Control of the People's Republic of China.

Article 2 Convertible foreign exchange and Renminbi foreign exchange instruments remitted or brought in from foreign countries or from Hongkong, Macao or other regions by foreign diplomatic missions, consular missions and commercial missions in China, by offices of international organizations and non-governmental institutions in China (hereafter referred to as "institutions in China"), and by diplomats, consuls and permanent personnel attached to the various institutions in China, may be kept in their own possession, or sold to or deposited in the Bank of China, or remitted abroad. If they are to be taken abroad, the matter shall be handled according to the Rules for the Implementation of Controls Relating to Carrying Foreign Exchange, Precious Metals and Foreign Exchange Instruments Into and Out of China.

Article 3 In regard to countries that have signed payment agreements with China, their institutions in China and personnel thereof shall only receive payment in Renminbi when foreign exchange remittances to them are effected through a clearing account.

Article 4 If foreign diplomatic missions and consular missions in China request that the visa fees and certification fees that they receive in Renminbi from Chinese citizens be converted into foreign exchange, they must file a written application with the State General Administration of Exchange Control or its branch office in their locality, and the matter shall be handled in accordance with the approval received.

Article 5 If institutions in China and their personnel sell various kinds of articles, equipment and appliances, etc. that they previously brought into China from abroad or from Hongkong, Macao or other regions, or that they bought in China, the Bank of China shall not provide them with foreign exchange for the Renminbi proceeds they receive from the sale.

Article 6 These Rules shall be promulgated and put into effect by the State General Administration of Exchange Control.

RULES FOR THE IMPLEMENTATION OF CONTROLS RELATING TO CARRYING FOREIGN EXCHANGE, PRECIOUS METALS AND FOREIGN EXCHANGE INSTRUMENTS INTO AND OUT OF CHINA

Promulgated by the State General Administration of Exchange Control
(August 10, 1981)

Article 1 These Rules are formulated in order to implement the provisions of Articles 27, 28, 29 and 30 of the Provisional Regulations for Exchange Control of the People's Republic of China.

Article 2 No restriction as to amount shall be imposed when foreign exchange, Renminbi foreign exchange instruments and gold, silver, platinum and other precious metals and objects made from them are brought into China by persons entering the country, but a Customs declaration must be made at the place of entry.

Article 3 When persons who have entered the country take abroad foreign exchange and Renminbi foreign exchange instruments, or gold, silver, platinum or other precious metals and objects made from them that they previously brought in, Customs clearance shall be based on inspection of the original declaration made at the time of entry.

Article 4 The unused portion of the Renminbi that has been converted either from foreign exchange and Renminbi foreign exchange instruments that have been brought in, or from foreign exchange remitted by persons who have entered the country may, in accordance with regulations, be converted back into foreign exchange before they leave the country; and when they leave the country, Customs clearance shall be based on inspection of the exchange memo issued by the Bank of China.

Article 5 When persons who have entered the country take abroad objects made from gold, silver, platinum or other precious metals that have been bought in China, Customs clearance shall, within the limits prescribed by the State, be based on inspection of the certification issued by the selling unit.

Article 6 When persons leaving the country take with them foreign exchange and Renminbi foreign exchange instruments, Customs clearance shall be based on inspection of the certification issued by the Bank of China.

With respect to drafts, traveller's checks or traveller's letters of credit in foreign currency and Renminbi banknotes and passbook custodian certificates issued or sold within the country by the Bank of China, Customs clearance shall be based on inspection, and no separate certification by the Bank of China shall be issued.

Article 7 When Chinese, foreign nationals or stateless persons who reside in China emigrate from the country and take with them gold, silver, platinum or other precious metals and objects made from them, Customs clearance shall be based on inspection within the limits prescribed by the State.

Article 8 Renminbi checks, drafts, passbooks, deposit certificates and other Renminbi payment instruments held by Chinese, foreign nationals or stateless persons residing in China may not be taken abroad in person or sent abroad through others or by mail.

Article 9 Unless otherwise approved by the State General Administration of Exchange Control or its branch offices, Chinese who reside in China may not take abroad in person or send abroad through others or by mail foreign bonds and debentures, shares of stock or real estate title deeds in their possession, as well as any kind of certificate or contract held by them that is related to the handling abroad of creditors' rights, inheritances, real estate and other foreign exchange assets, or any written authorization or letter containing payment orders.

Article 10 Where foreign enterprises that have terminated their business and foreign nationals who have left the country wish to take abroad foreign securities kept in China, they must obtain the approval of the State General Administration of Exchange Control or its branch offices, and Customs clearance shall be based on the certificate of approval; but Chinese securities and shares of stock may not be taken abroad in person or sent abroad through others or by mail.

Article 11 Where bilateral agreements have

been concluded between China and foreign countries on the movement of currencies into and out of each other's territory, matters will be handled in accordance with the provisions of the agreements.

Article 12 These Rules shall also apply where foreign exchange and Renminbi foreign exchange instruments, gold, silver, platinum or other precious metals and objects made from them are taken out of and brought into the country by compatriots from Hongkong and Macao.

Article 13 These Rules shall be promulgated and put into effect by the State General Administration of Exchange Control.

RULES FOR THE IMPLEMENTATION OF THE EXAMINATION AND APPROVAL OF APPLICATIONS BY INDIVIDUALS FOR FOREIGN EXCHANGE

Promulgated by the State General Administration of Exchange Control (December 31, 1981)

Article 1 These Rules are formulated in order to implement the provisions of Article 19 of the Provisional Regulations for Exchange Control of the People's Republic of China.

Article 2 The "individuals" mentioned in these Rules refer to Chinese, foreign nationals and stateless persons residing in China (hereafter referred to as "individuals").

Article 3 The items for which individuals may apply for foreign exchange shall include: incidental remittances to be sent abroad; travelling and miscellaneous expenses needed when leaving China; the transfer abroad of investments and bank deposits of overseas Chinese; and the transfer abroad of funds belonging to persons leaving China and emigrating abroad.

Article 4 In cases of special circumstances (such as serious illness, death or other disaster) involving an individual's lineal relative abroad, the individual may apply for foreign exchange for incidental use, by presenting a certificate issued by his unit and a pertinent certificate issued by the locality where his relative is, and his application may be granted according to the circumstances.

Article 5 An individual who has been given permission to leave China by the department of public security, and who has obtained a valid entry visa from the country of destination (in the case of a Chinese individual, an "exit receipt" must be obtained from the department of public security), may be provided with foreign exchange for travelling and miscellaneous expenses needed for the trip via the shortest route from the port of departure from China to his destination.

With respect to an individual who is leaving the country with a one-way exit visa in his passport, in addition to being provided with foreign exchange for travelling and miscellaneous expenses, his other requirements for foreign exchange shall be dealt with according to the following provisions:

1. Any retirement pay, severance pay, subsidies for leave of absence from work or pensions for the disabled and for survivors that he has received from domestic institutions in accordance with relevant provisions may be permitted to be remitted abroad in tote, provided that he has obtained the certificate of his unit and the approval of the next higher department in charge, and subject to the examination and agreement of the Bank of China.

2. An individual who does not receive any retirement pay, severance pay, subsidies for leave of absence from work or pensions for the disabled and for survivors may be provided with foreign exchange according to the actual circumstances.

Foreign exchange shall not be provided to an individual who has been granted a two-way exit-entry visa and who has applied for permission to remit abroad his retirement pay, severance pay, subsidies for leave of absence from work or pensions for the disabled and for survivors.

Article 6 If an individual who has been granted permission to leave China by the department of public security has received foreign exchange remitted from abroad to use for his travelling and miscellaneous expenses when he leaves China and has made a request to retain the original currency before the bank effects payment to him, he may retain the money in the original currency and remit or take it abroad in person at the time he leaves the country.

Article 7 When Chinese living abroad and Hongkong and Macao compatriots have invested foreign exchange in national or local overseas Chinese investment corporations, they may be permitted to remit abroad the share capital and dividends that they receive as due if, according to the corporation's articles of association, these are to be paid by the investment corporation in foreign exchange; foreign exchange shall not be provided if payment is to be made in Renminbi.

Article 8 When Chinese living abroad or Hongkong and Macao compatriots apply for permission to remit abroad the money that they have deposited in their own names in an Overseas Chinese Renminbi Savings Account in banks within our country, they may be provided with foreign exchange according to the circumstances.

Article 9 When an individual and his entire family have been given permission by the department of public security to emigrate abroad, in accordance with the deposit regulations he shall not be permitted to remit abroad money in his Overseas Chinese Renminbi Savings Account, which he entrusts to a bank in China for safekeeping at the time he leaves the country; if, on account of economic difficulties, the depositor applies for permission to remit his deposits abroad, after he submits evidence he may be provided with foreign exchange according to the circumstances.

Article 10 All types of applications for foreign exchange mentioned above shall be filed with the local branch office of the State General Administration of Exchange Control or with the Bank of China or its branches that have been authorized to handle such matters; after examination and approval, such foreign exchange may be remitted or taken abroad in person.

Article 11 These Rules shall be promulgated and put into effect by the State General Administration of Exchange Control.

RULES FOR THE IMPLEMENTATION OF FOREIGN EXCHANGE CONTROLS RELATING TO INDIVIDUALS

(Approved by the State Council on December 31, 1981 and Promulgated by the State General Administration of Exchange Control on December 31, 1981)

Article 1 These Rules are formulated in order to implement the provisions of Chapter III of the Provisional Regulations for Exchange Control of the People's Republic of China.

Article 2 When Chinese, foreign nationals or stateless persons residing in China receive foreign exchange remitted from foreign countries or from Hongkong, Macao or other regions, they must sell it to the Bank of China; they shall be permitted to retain 10% in foreign exchange of each single large remittance that is equivalent to 3,000 yuan or more in Renminbi.

All owners shall enjoy the relevant preferential treatment for overseas Chinese remittances with respect to the Renminbi that they receive through sales of foreign exchange remittances to the Bank of China as mentioned above.

Article 3 When entrusting the Bank of China to repatriate the foreign exchange that was kept in foreign countries or in Hong Kong, Macao or other regions by Chinese residing in China prior to the founding of the People's Republic of China, by overseas Chinese prior to their returning to take up residence in the country or by Hongkong and Macao compatriots prior to their returning to take up residence in their native places, or to repatriate the foreign exchange received by inheriting property in foreign countries or in Hongkong, Macao or other regions by Chinese residing in China after the founding of the People's Republic of China, by overseas Chinese after their returning to take up residence in the country or by Hongkong and Macao compatriots after their returning to take up residence in their native places, the owners shall be permitted to retain 30% of the foreign exchange; as to the Renminbi received after the remaining 70% is converted, the owners may enjoy the relevant preferential treatment for overseas Chinese remittances.

Foreign nationals and stateless persons residing in China who entrust the Bank of China to repatriate foreign exchange that they have kept abroad or that they have received by inheriting property outside China shall be permitted to retain a portion of the foreign exchange in accordance with the perçentage as stipulated in the preceding paragraph.

Article 4 When overseas Chinese and Hongkong and Macao compatriots, etc. return to take up residence in the country or in their native places, they shall be permitted to retain 30% of any foreign exchange that they remit or bring in, if they apply to the Bank within two months after their entry; as to the Renminbi received after the remaining 70% is converted, the owners may enjoy the relevant preferential treatment for overseas Chinese remittances.

The application for permission to retain a portion of the foreign exchange brought in as mentioned above can be made only after producing the relevant Customs declaration.

Article 5 When personnel sent by the State to work in foreign countries or to Hongkong, Macao or other regions return home after completion of their missions, they must promptly remit or bring back to China the remaining foreign exchange from wages, allowances, etc. that belongs to them, and it may not be kept abroad; they shall be permitted to retain the foreign exchange on the strength of certification by our institutions functioning abroad.

Article 6 Students, trainees, postgraduate students, scholars, teachers, coaches and other personnel who are sent by the State to study in foreign countries or in Hongkong, Macao or other regions must, upon their return, promptly remit or bring back to China what remains of the foreign exchange they have received during their stay abroad, and it may not be kept abroad; they shall be permitted to retain the foreign exchange that they are entitled to receive, on the strength of certification by our institutions functioning abroad.

Article 7 The foreign exchange from fees for publication, copyright royalties, awards, subsidies, author's remuneration, etc. earned by individuals for making public or publishing abroad their inventions, writings and the like, for speeches and lectures made in their own name outside China, for their contributions to foreign newspapers, magazines and specialized journals, etc., must promptly be repatriated and may not be kept abroad; individuals shall be permitted to keep that part of the earnings in foreign exchange which they are entitled to receive according to the relevant provisions approved by the State Council or the ministries or commissions concerned, or with the approval of the State General Administration of Exchange Control.

Article 8 The foreign exchange that individuals are permitted to retain under the preceding articles must be deposited in the Bank of China. Such deposits in foreign currency may be remitted abroad or may be taken abroad on the strength of certification by the Bank of China; if these deposits are converted into Renminbi, the owners may enjoy the relevant preferential treatment for overseas Chinese remittances. However, these deposit certificates may not, without authorization, be taken abroad in person or sent abroad through others or by mail.

The foreign exchange retained by individuals may not be dealt with in violation of the provisions of Article 4, Paragraph 2 of the Provisional Regulations for Exchange Control of the People's Republic of China.

Article 9 Chinese, foreign nationals and stateless persons residing in China shall be permitted to hold in their own possession the foreign exchange that they keep in China. However, such foreign exchange may not, without authorization, be taken abroad in person or sent abroad through others or by mail; if the owners need to sell the foreign exchange they must sell it to the Bank of China, and the matter shall be handled in accordance with the provisions of Article 2 of these Rules.

Article 10 Foreign exchange that is remitted or brought in from foreign countries or from Hongkong, Macao or other regions by foreigners visiting China, by overseas Chinese or Hongkong and Macao compatriots returning for a short stay, by foreign experts, technicians or staff and workers engaged to work in domestic institutions in China, or by foreign students or trainees, etc., may be kept in their own possession, may be sold to or deposited in the Bank of China, or may be remitted or taken abroad on the strength of the original Customs declaration made at the time of entry.

Article 11 When foreign experts, technicians or staff and workers engaged to work in domestic institutions in China need to apply for foreign exchange to be remitted or taken abroad, the Bank of China shall handle the matter in accordance with the relevant provisions of the contracts or agreements.

Article 12 These Rules shall be promulgated and put into effect by the State General Administration of Exchange Control after approval by the State Council.

PROVISIONAL REGULATIONS ON PROVIDING LOANS FOR CAPITAL CONSTRUCTION PROJECTS

Approved for Transmission by the State Council
(August 28, 1979)

For the purpose of speeding up socialist modernization, upgrading the financial management of capital construction and making the most of the investment capital, provisional regulations are hereby issued to provide loans for some capital construction projects.

I The Lending Institution

Article 1 The institution authorized to grant loans for capital construction projects is the People's Construction Bank of China (hereinafter called the Construction Bank).

II The Eligible Borrowers and the Purposes for which the Loans are to be Used

Article 2 The Construction Bank shall grant loans for investment capital to enterprises engaged in industry, transport, land reclamation, animal husbandry, marine products, commerce, tourism, etc. who have instituted an independent accounting system and are able to repay the loans.

Investment capital required by government organizations and non-profit institutions and for construction projects specified in the state plans shall be allocated by the Ministry of Finance.

Article 3 The borrower must be an independent entity who assumes economic responsibility for production. Where loans are to be used for renovations or extension of existing plants, it is the responsibility of the existing enterprise to apply for and repay the loans; in case of establishing a new enterprise, it is the responsibility of the preparatory organ who will be in charge of production after the project is in operation. If the borrower has been incorporated into a specialized or regional enterprise, it is the responsibility of that specialized or regional enterprise.

III Prerequisites for Borrowing

Article 4 Before a project is financed by the Construction Bank, the borrower shall submit a target plan duly approved by the competent authorities and a preliminary design of the project that has been included in the state plans for capital construction for the current year.

The planning commissions at all levels and the departments in charge must invite the Construction Bank to join them in examining and approving the target plan for the project and in deciding on the current-year plan for capital construction. The capital construction commissions at all levels and the departments in charge must do likewise when examining and approving the preliminary design of the project.

When approved, a copy each of the target plan, the preliminary design and the current-year plan for capital construction shall be provided to the head office of the Construction Bank or its branch, whichever is involved in the financing.

Article 5 The projects must meet the following conditions before they are financed:

1) The production technique is up to standard and the products in good demand;

2) Factors of production such as raw materials, fuel, power, water supply, transport are in place and ready to be used;

3) An acceptable estimate of the time it takes to generate enough returns to pay for the investment, and an assurance that repayment of the loan will be made when due;

4) The construction site, equipment, materials and construction manpower have been duly arranged.

IV Application, Examination and Approval of the Loan

Article 6 After the approval of the target plan, the borrower may submit a preliminary application to the Construction Bank who shall, if agreeable, sign an agreement with the borrower. Funds needed for the preparatory stage before the start of the project may be borrowed from the Construction Bank, if the department in charge stands surety for the borrower.

Article 7 After the preliminary design is approved, the borrower will ask the department in charge to include the project in the current-year plan for capital construction and simultaneously submit a formal application to the Construction Bank with supportive documents such as an estimate of the total cost for the preliminary design duly approved by the authorities higher up, a yearly construction plan and an agreement signed with other enterprises to work in cooperation during the construction of the project. When the documents are found in order, the Construction Bank shall sign a loan contract with the borrower.

Article 8 The loan contract shall set forth the term of the loan, the total loan amount, interest rate and the purposes for which the loan is granted. The contract shall also include yearly plans for the drawdown and repayment. The contract specifies the responsibilities of both parties: the borrower undertakes to use the loan for the purposes as stated in the contract, to make repayment when due, and the Construction Bank undertakes to provide loanable funds according to the progress of the project.

The contract is legally binding on both parties. Either party in breach of the contract shall indemnify the other party for the losses incurred.

Article 9 For the project in progress for which a loan contract has been signed, the planning commissions at all levels and the departments in charge shall guarantee the continuity in construction in the subsequent years so that the project will be completed on time or ahead of schedule. The materials and equipment needed for construction shall be provided by the departments in charge of supplies.

Article 10 The Construction Bank may provide loans to finance small-size projects that do not take long to construct with all factors of production in place and ready for use, that will turn out products in urgent demand, and that will yield quick returns and large profits. Such loans are to be provided within the Bank's quota of freely disposable loanable funds.

V Repayment and Supervision of the Loan

Article 11 According to the progress of the project, the borrower shall make out an annual repayment plan up to the total amount of the loan and present it to the Construction Bank who shall, if agreeable, provide the funds according to the plan.

If the amount that needs to be drawn out in any one year exceeds the amount listed in the annual repayment plan, the matter is to be settled between the Bank and the borrower. In case the total repayment exceeds the total loan amount but comes within the estimate of the total cost of the project, a supplementary loan contract may be signed. For drawings in excess of the said estimate, consent must be obtained from the departments who have respectively approved the preliminary design and the target plan for the project.

Article 12 The Construction Bank shall supervise the performance of the borrower and oversee how the loan is being utilized. Upon discovering that the borrower has diverted funds to unauthorized construction work, to aimless purchases of materials and equipment or has violated financial regulations, the Construction Bank shall give warnings and demand such misbehaviour be corrected within a specific period of time. If not heeded, the Bank has the right to suspend the loan before maturity and report to authorities higher up.

The borrower shall provide financial statements and statistics to the Construction Bank. The Bank should be given access to materials it needs for examination.

VI Repayment of the Loan

Article 13 The borrower must repay the loan plus interest on maturity as set out in the loan contract.

The term of the loan is to be counted from the date of the loan contract to the date of full repayment. For enterprises in heavy industry, it shall be not longer than 15 years; for others no longer than 10 years, except those referred to in Article 10 for which the term shall not exceed five years. The term of the loan is to be determined according to the specific case and set out in the loan contract.

Article 14 Interest shall be charged on an annual basis as of the date of the drawdown. Normally, the interest rate is 3% per annum. The specific rate is to be determined by the borrower's line of trade, its importance in the development of the national economy and according to the government economic policies.

Where the loan is not fully repaid on maturity, interest rate on the overdue loan shall be charged at double the rate. In case the loan is diverted to unauthorized projects, the interest rate on the diverted portion shall be tripled.

Article 15 Sources of funds for repayment: During the period of repayment, newly established enterprises may repay the principal and interest out of the depreciation reserves for fixed assets, charges payable to the government for the use of the fixed assets and profits to be turned over to the government after the project is in operation. This shall also supply to existing enterprises that have borrowed from the Bank for renovations or extension of existing plants provided that they have instituted an accounting scheme to assess the economic gains from the borrowings. If not, they must repay out of profits to be turned over to the government corresponding to the proportion of the new fixed assets to the entire fixed assets as well as out of the depreciation reserves for the new fixed assets and charges payable to the government for the use of the new fixed assets.

For enterprises that have difficulty in repaying the loan out of the above-mentioned funds because of heavy tax and low profits, the industrial-commercial tax may be exempted during the period of repayment, if recommended by the provincial internal revenue department and approved by the Ministry of Finance.

Prior to the completion of the project, interest may be paid out of the loan and the portion so used shall be free of interest.

Borrowers that have completed construction on time or ahead of schedule and are thus able to repay the loan before maturity may use the funds set aside for repayment to expand production and improve the welfare of their workers and staff. In case borrowers fail to make repayment when due, they shall repay out of funds earmarked for making technological innovations or from capital accounts. They are not permitted to make repayment by way of including the loan in the cost of products or out of profits previously accumulated.

VII Supplementary Regulations

Article 16 Where a dispute over the implementation of the loan contract cannot be settled between the borrower and the Bank, the case shall be submitted to an economic court for arbitration. If the court has not been established, the matter shall be dealt with by the Capital Construction Commission in their locality.

Article 17 The present regulations are applicable to state-owned enterprises. Loans to collectively owned enterprises may be handled on the principle of these regulations.

Article 18 The head office of the Construction Bank shall formulate and make public detailed rules for implementing these Provisional Regulations.

Article 19 Loans granted by the Construction Bank before these regulations become effective shall continue to be handled according to the provisions previously issued.

Article 20 The present regulations shall come into force on the date of issue.

PROVISIONAL REGULATIONS ON GRANTING LOANS TO AND OPENING ACCOUNTS BY UNEMPLOYED YOUTH IN CITIES AND TOWNS FOR THE PURPOSE OF SETTING UP ENTERPRISES OF COLLECTIVE OWNERSHIP

Issued by the People's Bank of China
(October 12, 1979)

1. Enterprises of collective ownership that are in operation with the approval of the competent authorities at a level not lower than the county or district (part of city) under licences issued by the Administration of Industry and Commerce, that have a certain amount of working capital, that have instituted an independent accounting system and are responsible for their own profits and losses may open accounts with the People's Bank of China (hereinafter called "the Bank").

2. Industrial enterprises of collective ownership who have opened accounts with the Bank, and met the requirements mentioned in (1) above, and provided their products are of fine quality, in good demand and profit-yielding may apply for industrial loans to cover shortage of working capital to pay for the concentrated arrival of raw materials they ordered. The Bank shall extend credit facilities to such enterprises consistent with the regulations for granting loans to collective industrial enterprises in cities and towns.

Enterprises that need to buy machines and equipment to expand production or upgrade the quality of products may apply for loans for purchasing equipment, provided that their investments will bring economic returns and the borrowers are able to repay the loans when due. The Bank shall extend support to such enterprises consistent with the regulations for granting loans to collective industrial enterprises in cities and towns for buying equipment.

3. Commercial enterprises of collective ownership that have opened accounts with the Bank and met the requirements mentioned in (1) above may apply for marketing loans to cover a temporary shortage of funds to stock up for the busy seasons, festivals or for urgent needs. The accounts to be opened thereunder should be kept separate from the deposit accounts they have opened, i.e., transactions of loans and deposits should be passed to the respective loan and deposit accounts.

No loans will be granted by the Bank to commercial enterprises of collective ownership who are subsidiaries of the state commercial enterprises, or who act as sales/purchase agents of the supply and marketing cooperatives, or who have obtained from them initial capital to launch themselves.

4. Collectively owned enterprises engaged in catering, services and repairs who have opened accounts with the Bank and met the requirements mentioned in (1) above, may obtain funds from the Bank to finance the purchases of raw materials they need. In addition, the Bank may provide a temporary credit facility, but once only, to finance the purchases of simple equipment and tools vital to their business operations. Applications for such loans should be submitted by the enterprises with the departments in charge standing surety for them. The term of the loan is to be determined by the specific circumstances but no longer than two years. Repayment is to be made by installments.

5. To provide funds for production and business operations, the enterprises mentioned in (2), (3) and (4) above should improve their business management, make a sound distribution of profits and have an increasing accumulation of surplus. The surplus should be set aside first to repay the loans and replenish their working capital.

6. Collectively owned enterprises failing to meet the requirements mentioned in (1) above, must have their accounts opened en bloc with the Bank in the name of the street administrative office, neighbourhood committee or the business entity with which the enterprises are affiliated. Generally, no loans are to be granted to them.

7. The Bank may provide loans to cooperative shops not only to stock up for the busy seasons or festivals but to cover temporary shortage of funds to keep the shops stocked in order to increase sales.

The Bank and its branches shall give active support to and exercise strict supervision over the collectively owned enterprises run by the unemployed youth in cities and towns. In providing loans, the Bank should stick to the principle of "three assessments" (i.e., to assess the creditworthiness of the borrowers, to assess their applications for loans and to assess the effectiveness of the loans after they are granted); the term of the loan must be set and repayment made when due, so as to ensure the healthy development of the enterprises.

No credit will be granted to those enterprises that operate at a loss. Interest for the loans is to be charged at the prevailing rates for industrial/commercial loans.

The Bank's branches in the provinces, cities and autonomous regions may grant loans within the quotas allocated to them for industrial/commercial loans.

PROVISIONAL REGULATIONS ON PROVIDING SPECIAL SHORT- AND MEDIUM-TERM LOANS FROM THE PEOPLE'S BANK OF CHINA TO THE LIGHT AND TEXTILE INDUSTRIES

(January 14, 1980)

For the purpose of carrying out the policy of "readjustment, restructuring, consolidation and improvement" and taking special measures to boost the light and textile industries so as to meet market demands at home and abroad, provisional regulations are hereby issued for the People's Bank of China and the Bank of China to provide special short- and medium-term loans and foreign-currency loans in the form of buyers' credits to the light and textile industries.

I Eligible Borrowers and the Purposes for Which Loans Are to be Used

Article 1 Loans are to be granted to state-owned and collectively owned enterprises in the light and textile industries (including specialized companies responsible for their own profits and losses). The loans are to be used primarily for the purposes of tapping production potential (including raw material potential), making technological innovations and launching small-scale construction and renovation projects related to such purposes.

Article 2 No loans shall be granted for construction of new factories or for extension of existing factories.

II Prerequisites for Borrowing

Article 3 Applicants must meet the following requirements:

a) They must be able to generate quick returns, more profits and more foreign exchange earnings in proportion to the money borrowed.

b) They must have the necessary materials, equipment, design and construction manpower in place and ready to be used for the project undertaken, and must be assured of the availability of raw materials, power and labour force once the project is in operation. They must be able to find markets to sell their products.

c) Their production techniques must be up to standard.

d) They must promise economic yields and must be able to repay the loan with operating profits when due.

e) They must be able to take effective measures to prevent environmental pollution.

III Term and Repayment of Loans

Article 4 A loan is normally available for one to two years but not longer than three years.

Article 5 A borrower must institute a separate accounting system to monitor the economic gains from the loan. Repayment of the loan plus interest shall be made out of earnings attributed to the loan, not from previous earnings.

State-owned enterprises must repay loans out of the profits from new projects or from the depreciation reserves for fixed assets or from the charges payable to the government for the use of fixed assets. If the above-mentioned funds are not sufficient for repayment, the deficit may be covered by the industrial-commercial tax that would otherwise be collected by the government on the increased output attributed to the loan.

Collectively owned enterprises must repay loans out of the accumulated profits from the new project after tax (during the period of repayment, the department in charge is not allowed to collect profits or other funds from the borrower for tax purposes) or from the depreciation reserves for fixed assets. If these funds are inadequate for repayment, the deficit may be covered by the income tax and industrial-commercial tax that would otherwise be collected by the government on the increased output attributed to the loan.

Article 6 If a loan cannot be repaid when it falls due, owing to suspension of the project in the course of construction or to failure of the borrower to generate the expected returns, repayment must be made out of the depreciation reserves for fixed assets and other reserves.

Article 7 The interest rate to be charged for a loan is 4.2% per month and interest is to be paid as soon as the financed project is in operation.

IV Applications for Loans, Examination and Approval of Applications

Article 8 Plans for borrowing shall be examined and approved as follows:

The Bureau of Light Industry, the Bureau of Light Industry No. 2 (handicrafts) and the Bureau of Textile Industry in the provinces, municipalities and autonomous regions (hereinafter called "local departments in charge") shall submit annual plans for borrowing on the basis of their programmes for tapping production potential and for making technological innovations duly approved by the Economic Commission in their locality. Plans for borrowing are to be examined by the local branches of the People's Bank of China (hereinafter called "bank branches"). They are to be submitted for re-examination by the head office of the People's Bank of China (hereinafter called "bank head office") and the ministries of light and textile industries (hereinafter called the "responsible ministries") who will, after adding their comments, submit the plans for further approval to a joint conference chaired by the State Economic Commission and attended by the bank head office, the State Planning Commission, responsible ministries and the Ministry of Finance. Then, the responsible ministries and the bank head office shall send back to the local departments in charge the approved plans for borrowing involving maximum project financing of over two million yuan for the textile industry and over one million yuan for light industries, with copies sent to the bank branches, the local economic commissions, planning commissions and finance bureaus. As for loans below the said maximum amounts, the bank head office and responsible ministries shall send back the approved plans for borrowing to the bank branches with copies sent to the local departments in charge.

Article 9 Authority to deal with applications for loans: Borrowers shall submit their applications to the bank branch where they keep an account. If a loan is below the said maximum amount, the bank branch has the right to approve the application in consultation with the local departments in charge. A report shall be sent to the responsible ministries and bank head office and a copy sent to the local economic commission, planning commission and finance bureau. For a loan over the maximum amount, the application shall be examined by the bank branch together with the local departments in charge and then, if agreeable, submitted to the bank head office and the responsible ministries for approval. The bank head office and the responsible ministries shall send back the approved application to the bank branches and local departments in charge with copies sent to the State Economic Commission, State Planning Commission and Ministry of Finance and their respective organizations.

Article 10 After approval of the project to be financed, the borrower and the bank shall sign a loan agreement whereby the bank is to provide funds within the approved amount in accordance with the progress of the project.

Article 11 A loan that has not been completely drawn down in the current year may continue to be available in the next year. Repayment received during the current year may be used for lending by the bank within its jurisdiction.

V Supply of Materials for Projects to be Financed

Article 12 The planning commission and supply administration at different levels shall be responsible for the supply of materials such as steel, timber, cement, etc. needed by the projects to be financed. These materials shall first be supplied from the local stockpile. The State Administration of Supplies will provide half of the necessary amount, which is then included in its distribution plans for tapping production potential and technological innovation. The ministries of light and textile industries shall make suggestions on the allocations of materials to be provided by the State Administration of Supplies. Accordingly, the State Administration of Supplies will instruct its local branches to supply the materials on the spot. The remaining supplies are to be provided, in principle, by the local authorities.

Article 13 Special equipment shall be supplied by the ministries of light and textile industries; general equipment by the State Administration of Supplies and its local branches; and optional equipment by the local authorities.

VI Periodic Review and Supervision of Loans

Article 14 The People's Bank of China and the departments in charge shall inquire into each project before financing it and oversee the performance of the borrower after the loan is granted. They must carefully check whether the project conforms to the provisions of Articles 1, 2 and 3 and see to it that all necessary measures have been taken, giving preference to those borrowers who promise good returns and have the ability to repay loans.

Article 15 The loan must be used to finance the project for which it is granted. The bank has the right to suspend the loan before maturity in case the borrower changes its plans and raises its expenditure without the bank's consent or diverts the loan and construction materials to projects other than those agreed upon by the bank.

Article 16 The People's Bank of China and the departments in charge should work in close cooperation to help the borrower run its enterprise and regularly check the progress of the project and how the loan is being utilized so as to urge the enterprise to make the most of the loan with early returns.

Article 17 The borrower must submit to the departments in charge and the bank branch quarterly and annual reports on the progress of the project and how the loan is being used, with supporting statements and statistics. On the basis of these reports, the ministries of light and textile industries shall submit a quarterly consolidated report to the State Economic Commission and State Planning Commission with a copy sent to the bank head office.

VII Loans in Convertible Foreign Currency

Article 18 When light and textile industrial enterprises require loans in foreign currency, such loans shall generally be in the form of buyers' credits. In addition to the funds from buyers' credits, the Bank of China may, if necessary, grant a supplementary loan in convertible foreign currency to cover down payment for imported equipment plus freight and insurance, or to import major components to fit the equipment to be manufactured by the borrower, or to import such things that are not covered by buyers' credits, thereby accelerating the development of light and textile industries.

Article 19 Foreign currency loans are to be applied for and granted according to the regulations issued by the Bank of China.

VIII Supplementary Regulations

Article 20 These regulations are to be formulated and amended by the head office of the People's Bank of China. Branch banks in the provinces, municipalities and autonomous regions may issue supplementary rules to suit local conditions and submit a report to the head office for the record.

These regulatons shall come into force on the date of issue.

REGULATIONS FOR PROVIDING SHORT-TERM LOANS IN FOREIGN CURRENCY BY THE BANK OF CHINA

Approved by Transmission by the State Council

(August 30, 1980)

With the funds it raises from abroad, the Bank of China is ready to provide loans in foreign currency to export-oriented industries and other enterprises in order to boost their foreign exchange earnings on the basis of self-reliance, thereby speeding up the socialist modernization of our country. It is for these purposes that the following regulations are formulated.

I Eligible Borrowers and the Purposes for which Loans are to be Used

Article 1 Loans are to be granted to export-oriented industries and other enterprises earning foreign exchange income directly or indirectly who can meet the prerequisites for borrowing. The loans are primarily for encouraging export-oriented industries to tap production potential and renovate obsolete plants and equipment.

Article 2 The loans are to be used for:

a. financing imports of advanced technology, equipment and materials essential to upgrading the borrower's productivity and the quality, variety and packaging of export goods;

b. financing imports of raw materials and components to be processed for export;

c. developing transportation and tourism and carrying out engineering projects contracted with foreign firms;

d. supporting the processing of raw materials and assembling of parts supplied by foreign buyers, and supporting compensatory trade; and

e. providing short-term working capital to production that earns foreign exchange directly or indirectly.

II Prerequisites for Borrowing

Article 3 Applicants must meet the following requirements:

a. Effective productivity of the loan: Preference is given to borrowers who are able to earn more foreign exchange in proportion to the money invested and repay bank loans sooner. Borrowers should be able to run their enterprises efficiently, make the most of the imported advanced technology, equipment and raw materials, tap their production potential, renovate obsolete plants and equipment, enhance the competitiveness of their export goods in the international markets, thereby earning more foreign exchange for the country.

b. Assurance of repayment: Borrowers must give evidence of a reliable source of foreign exchange income and the ability to repay loans plus interest for which they are required to submit a schedule of repayment.

Where loans are granted to the export-goods industry, the increased output attributed to the loan should be primarily for export and not be included in the state domestic marketing plan. The income from the increased output and the export proceeds in foreign exchange should first be set aside for repayment of the bank loan. In case the goods are to be turned over to a foreign trade corporation for export, the borrower should sign a sales contract with this corporation which commits the latter to repay the bank loan in foreign exchange for the borrower.

Enterprises not directly related to the export trade must submit a document of approval signed by the department in charge committing the latter to repay the loan from its own foreign exchange income. When necessary, the bank may demand that some organization that has a regular foreign exchange income stand surety for the borrower.

c. Readiness of domestic factors of production to make imported materials and equipment operational: Domestic factors of production refer to factory buildings, equipment, steam, water, electricity and fuel, raw materials, labour force, technological expertise and counterpart funds in Renminbi requisite to making the imported equipment and materials operational. These items must be duly arranged and approved by the Planning Commission or the authorities in charge who have to list them in their plans or sign contracts with the borrower.

d. With respect to the items mentioned above, borrowers should obtain prior approval of higher authorities for those items that require allotment of funds for capital construction or technological installations.

III Applications for Loans, Examination and Approval of Applications and Drawdowns of the Loans

Article 4 Applications for loans should be submitted to the Bank of China (or People's Bank of China where the Bank of China does not exist) together with the following supporting documents: a document evidencing the approval of the proposed project by the department in charge; a list of imports the loan is to finance; a schedule proving the domestic factors of production are in readiness or a copy of the relevant contract; a document approved by the department in charge showing that counterpart funds in Renminbi have been earmarked for repayment of the loan (if the borrower is not directly involved in the export trade); a copy of the sales contract signed with a foreign trade corporation which commits itself to repay the loan in foreign exchange for the borrower (if the borrower is to repay the loan with export proceeds).

Article 5 Applications for loans by the departments under the State Council shall be examined item by item against the prerequisites for borrowing by the head office of the Bank of China. Applications by local departments and enterprises shall be reviewed by the Bank of China's regional branches in the provinces, municipalities and autonomous regions within the bounds of their respective loan quotas assigned by the head office. Cases that need to be reviewed by the head office or ministries concerned should be submitted to them for approval. In examining the applications, the bank should keep in touch with the departments in charge and work in cooperation wth them.

Article 6 After the application is approved, the borrower should sign a loan agreement, open a loan account with the Bank of China and place an order for imports. If the borrower fails to sign the loan agreement or submit a list of imports within the specified time, the bank may revoke its approval of the loan. The list of imports must be signed by the bank before the order is placed. Without the approval of the bank, neither the purpose for which the loan is to be used nor the descriptions and quantities of imports should be changed. The borrower should submit to the bank a copy of the contract signed with the foreign trader who provides the goods. The bank should help the borrower to make the most of the loan.

Article 7 For a substantial loan, the borrower should submit a quarterly withdrawal plan according to which the bank will raise the funds. In case the plan needs to be adjusted because of miscalculation or unexpected changes of circumstances, the borrower should apply to the bank for adjustment a month before the end of the quarter. For failure to carry out the plan, the borrower shall bear additional bank charges on the amount of the withdrawal falling short of, or in excess of, the planned amounts so as to compensate the bank for losses in raising funds from abroad.

IV Term of Loans and Rates of Interest

Article 8 The term of the loan is to be counted from the day of the withdrawal to the day of repayment. Loans for importing raw materials and components to be processed for export are normally available for one year. Loans for importing equipment or materials to be used in making equipment, and loans for other purposes shall not exceed three years. Where loans take the form of buyers' credits, the maturity shall not exceed five years.

Article 9 The interest rates for loans are to be determined and made public by the head office of the Bank of China on the basis of the cost of raising funds on the international money markets plus its handling charges.

V Repayment of Loans

Article 10 Full repayment must be made on the due date specified in the loan agreement. If the borrower fails to repay, the surety is responsible for repayment. If necessary, the Bank of China or the People's Bank of China may force repayment by debiting the foreign currency deposit account of the borrower or the surety (or by writing off the foreign exchange quota alloted to the borrower and seizing his counterpart funds in Renminbi earmarked for the purchase of the foreign exchange quota).

Article 11 A borrower who has a regular foreign exchange income should repay the loan from foreign exchange earnings. A borrower who is not directly involved in the export trade should repay the loan from export proceeds received through a foreign trade corporation. This corporation or some other organization which stands surety for the borrower should issue a certificate to "repay foreign exchange quota" against which the borrower may purchase foreign exchange with Renminbi from the Bank of China to repay the loan. Foreign exchange earnings from the processing of raw materials and assembling of parts provided by foreign buyers or earnings from compensatory trade must first be set aside for repayment of the loan.

Article 12 Loans made to finance a construction project by a state-owned enterprise may be repaid out of profits derived from the increased output, out of depreciation reserves for fixed assets, or out of charges payable to the government for the use of fixed assets. Enterprises that are authorized to retain a portion of their profits may make repayment from the retained profits after deductions for the staff's welfare fund and bonus fund. However, deductions for the production development fund and for retention of increased profits are not allowed. Loans to collectively owned urban enterprises may be repaid out of profits derived from the increased output (profits before tax) or from depreciation reserves for fixed assets. The department in charge is not allowed to collect profits or demand payment out of the project financed by the bank loan so long as the loan remains to be repaid.

If the above-mentioned funds are sufficient to repay the loan and a surplus remains, income tax shall be paid on the surplus or a percentage of profits shall be turned over to the government as required. If not, the deficit may, with the consent of the Internal Revenue Bureau, be covered by the industrial and commercial tax on the increased output which would otherwise be collected by the Bureau. When applying for the loan, the borrower should send a copy of the application to the Bureau for its reference.

VI Buyers' Credits

Article 13 When loans are provided in the form of the buyers' credits, the following rules shall apply, apart from other provisions in the regulations:

a. The borrower must abide by the provisions in the buyer's credit agreement that the Bank of China has signed with a foreign bank and must place orders for imports from the country in which the foreign bank is located.

b. The borrower must indicate in the order for imports that the buyer's credit is to be used for payment. The sales contract signed between the Chinese foreign trade corporation and the foreign seller should indicate the name of the bank providing the buyer's credit.

c. At the time the sales contract is signed, the Bank of China shall negotiate with the foreign bank providing the buyer's credit and sign an agreement on the drawdown of the credit. The agreement shall be signed by the Bank of China head office or by one of its branches with its authorization.

VII Bank Supervision

Article 14 The Borrower must maximize the effective productivity of the loan by relying on cost accounting. Preference is given to the borrower who earns more foreign exchange in proportion to the amount of the loan granted and makes repayment sooner. The borrower who performs poorly or who is unable to repay his loan upon maturity, will not receive further loans until he shows improvement in mangement.

Article 15 Both the bank and the borrower shall abide by the loan agreement: the Bank undertakes to provide the loanable funds; the borrower undertakes to draw on the loan and utilize its productive potential effectively. The bank shall raise the interest by 10–50% for overdue loans counting from the maturity date, and by 100% for loans diverted to uses other than those authorized by the bank.

Article 16 The bank shall inquire into each project before financing it, examine the borrower's application before approving it and oversee the performance of the borrower after the loan is granted. The bank has the duty to help the borrower achieve its economic goals. In this way the bank shall fulfil its role of promoting, regulating and supervising the economic activities of the borrower.

For large loans, the bank shall sit in on the negotiations between the borrower and the foreign supplier and make suggestions as to the preferred currency for making payment and the method of payment. The borrower must provide the bank with all necessary information, documents, statistics and a duplicate of the relevant contract.

The borrower shall be held accountable for violation of government decrees and policies; failure to abide by the regulations, the contract or the agreement; dissipation of foreign exchange; or failure to repay the loan when due. At the same time the bank may take such disciplinary actions as suspending or recalling the loan before maturity, raising the interest rate or even suing the borrower in a court of law.

VIII Supplementary Regulations

Article 17 On the date the regulations come into force, "Regulations for Providing Short-term

Loans in Foreign Currency," issued by the Ministry of Finance on September 29, 1978, shall no longer be valid except for loans and loan agreements previously approved and signed.

Detailed rules for the enforcement of the regulations shall be formulated separately by the Bank of China.

PROVISIONAL REGULATIONS FOR PROVIDING LOANS TO JOINT VENTURES USING CHINESE AND FOREIGN INVESTMENTS FROM THE BANK OF CHINA

(Approved by the State Council on March 13, 1981 and promulgated by the Bank of China on March 13, 1981)

Article 1 According to Article 8 of the Law of the People's Republic of China on Joint Ventures Using Chinese and Foreign Investment that a joint venture shall open an account with the Bank of China or a bank approved by the Bank of China, the Provisional Regulations are hereby issued to provide loans for financing business operations of joint ventures using Chinese and foreign investment (hereinafter referred to as joint ventures).

Article 2 The prospective borrower. Any joint venture that has been approved by the Foreign Investment Commission of the PRC according to the Law of the People's Republic of China on Joint Ventures Using Chinese and Foreign Investment, registered with the General Administration for Industry and Commerce of the PRC and granted a business licence is qualified to apply for loans.

Article 3 Types of loans. The Bank of China provides loans of the following types to joint ventures:

a. Self-liquidating loans: to provide short-term circulating funds needed by joint ventures in the process of production and marketing.

b. Accounts receivable financing: to provide funds for production to joint ventures before their accounts receivable are collected in China or abroad.

c. Loans for long-term investment: to finance the purchase of fixed assets for expanding business operations or for technological innovation.

The above-mentioned loans are granted in Renminbi or foreign currency and are to be repaid in the currency in which the loans are denominated. Interest on foreign-currency loans is payable in foreign currency.

Article 4 Prerequisites for borrowing. The applicant must fulfil the following requirements:

a. To abide by the Law of the People's Republic of China on Joint Ventures Using Chinese and Foreign Investment;

b. To have opened a deposit account with the Bank of China or with a bank (hereinafter referred to as bank) duly approved by the Bank of China;

c. Of good credit standing and sound management;

d. To have sufficient means to repay the principal and interest. Loans are granted on collateral security or a surety bond acceptable to the bank.

Article 5 Term of the Loan. The maturity of the loan is to be determined between the borrower and the bank according to the purpose for which the loan is granted and the specific requirements of each case.

Article 6 Rate of Interest. The interest rate for loans in Renminbi is determined by the People's Bank of China. The Bank of China shall fix the interest rate for loans in foreign currency with the approval of the People's Bank of China.

Article 7 Application for, documentation and utilization of the loan:

a. With the approval of its board of directors, the qualified borrower may fill out an application form and submit it to the bank together with the certified documents, supportive materials and a copy of the relevant contract.

b. After the application is approved, the borrower should sign a loan agreement, open a loan account with the bank and complete other formalities as required by the agreement. For credit loans, a letter of guarantee acceptable to the bank should be attached to the loan agreement; for collateral loans, the borrower should attach a collateral security written proof agreed upon by the bank.

Article 8 Repayment of principal and interest of the loan:

a. Full repayment must be made when due as set in the loan agreement. In the event of default the guarantor is responsible for full repayment in the case of a credit loan. The bank has the right to debit the account of the borrower or the guarantor for the repayment of principal and interest. In the case of a collateral loan, the bank has the right to sell the collateral property for the purpose of repayment. Interest on overdue loans shall be charged 20% to 50% over and above the original interest rate as from the maturity date.

b. Successive interest payments shall be made as scheduled by the bank. When overdue, the bank shall take the initiative in debiting the payable interest to the borrower's loan account to be compounded.

Article 9 Loan service and supervision. In pursuance of the government decrees and policies, the bank serves the needs of joint ventures by giving active support to their development, production and business management. The borrowers should accept the supervision and examination by the bank as to how the loans are being utilized. They should submit materials and reports to the bank in respect to their programs for production, marketing, finance and capital construction and how such programs are being carried out. In case of violation of the loan agreement, the bank may, according to the specific circumstances, take such financial measures as suspending or recalling the loan before maturity, so as to safeguard its own interest.

REGULATIONS ON THE TREASURY BILLS OF THE PEOPLE'S REPUBLIC OF CHINA

(Adopted by the Routine Meeting of the State Council on January 16, 1981 and Promulgated by the State Council on January 28, 1981)

Article 1 The Treasury Bills of the People's Republic of China are determined to be issued from the year 1981 in order to regulate and stabilize the national economy, properly centralise financial resources from all quarters, carry out the socialist modernization construction and gradually raise the standards of the material and cultural life of the people.

Article 2 The Treasury Bills shall be mainly distributed and issued to state enterprises, enterprises of collective ownership, competent authorities of enterprises and local governments. They shall be properly subscribed for by Party and government organizations, bodies, units of armed forces, institutions and opulent rural people's communes, production brigades and teams. Individuals shall also be allowed to volunteer to subscribe for them.

Article 3 The number of Treasury Bills to be issued each year shall be determined by the State Council and the issue shall begin as of January 1 of that current year. All payments must be made on or before June 30 and the interest therein shall be calculated from July 1 of that current year.

Article 4 The annual interest shall be fixed at 4% for the Treasury Bills. The interest of the Treasury Bills shall be paid in one lump sum when the principal is repaid and no compound interest shall be calculated.

Article 5 The Treasury Bills shall be calculated in Renminbi. The Treasury Bills are of 8 different denominations: 10 yuan, 50 yuan, 100 yuan, 500 yuan, 1,000 yuan, 10,000 yuan, 100,000 yuan and 1,000,000 yuan.

Article 6 From the sixth year of the issue of the Treasury Bills, lots shall be drawn at a time specified and the principal shall be repaid by 5 different payments in 5 years in accordance with the amount of issue, no less than 20% of the total amount to be repaid each time.

Article 7 The issue of the Treasury Bills, the repayment of the principal and the payment of the interest shall be handled by the People's Bank of China and its subordinate organizations.

Article 8 The funds raised by means of the Treasury Bills shall be used in a unified way by the State Council in accordance with the development and overall balance of the national economy.

Article 9 The Treasury Bills shall not be circulated as money and shall not be freely bought and sold.

Article 10 Those who forge the Treasury Bills or damage their reputation shall be punished according to law.

Article 11 The Ministry of Finance shall be authorized by the State Council to handle the interpretation of the Regulations on the Treasury Bills.

REGULATIONS ON THE 1982 TREASURY BILLS OF THE PEOPLE'S REPUBLIC OF CHINA

Adopted by the Routine Meeting of the State Council
(January 8, 1982)

Article 1 The issue of the 1982 Treasury Bills of the People's Republic of China is determined in order to regulate and develop the national economy, properly centralise financial resources from all quarters, carry out the socialist modernization construction and gradually raise the standards of the material and cultural life of the people.

Article 2 The Treasury Bills shall be issued to: state enterprises, enterprises of collective ownership, competent authorities of enterprises and local governments, Party and government organizations, bodies, units of armed forces, institutions and opulent rural people's communes, production brigades and teams; individuals in urban and rural areas.

Article 3 The number of Treasury Bills to be issued each year shall be determined by the State Council and the issue shall begin from January 1 of that current year. All payments by units must be on or before June 30 and that by individuals on or before September 30.

Article 4 The interest rates of the Treasury Bills: the annual interest shall be fixed at 4% for those purchased by units; the annual interest shall be fixed at 8% for those purchased by individuals.

The interest for all the Treasury Bills shall be calculated from July 1 of that current year and no interest shall be paid for principal before its payments due day.

The interest of the Treasury Bills shall be paid in one lump sum when the principal is repaid and no compound interest shall be calculated.

Article 5 The Treasury Bills shall be calculated in Renminbi. The units purchasing them shall be given the receipts of the Treasury Bills and shall have their names on record or report the loss of the receipts in case of loss; the individuals purchasing them shall be granted the Treasury Bills proper. The Treasury Bills are of 6 different denominations: 1 yuan, 5 yuan, 10 yuan, 50 yuan, 100 yuan and 1,000 yuan.

Article 6 The repayment of the principal and the payment of the interest of the Treasury Bills shall become payable from the sixth year of issue. For those purchased by individuals, lots shall be drawn at a time specified and the money shall be repaid by 5 different payments in 5 years in accordance with the amount of issue, no less than 20% of the total amount to be repaid each time; for those purchased by units, no lots shall be drawn and the money shall be repaid by 5 different payments in 5 years on the average in accordance with the total amount of the purchases by units.

Article 7 The issue of the Treasury Bills, the repayment of the principal and the payment of the interest shall be handled by the People's Bank of China and its subordinate organizations.

Article 8 The funds raised by means of the Treasury Bills shall be used in a unified way by the State Council in accordance with the needs of the development and overall balance of the national economy.

Article 9 The Treasury Bills shall not be circulated as money and shall not be freely bought and sold.

Article 10 Those who forge the Treasury Bills or damage their credit shall be punished according to law.

Article 11 The Ministry of Finance shall be authorized by the State Council to handle the interpretation of the Regulations on Treasury Bills.

REGULATIONS ON THE 1983 TREASURY BILLS OF THE PEOPLE'S REPUBLIC OF CHINA

(Adopted by the Routine Meeting of the State Council on September 21, 1982 and promulgated by the State Council on September 27, 1982)

Article 1 The issue of the 1983 Treasury Bills of the People's Republic of China is determined for the purpose of properly concentrating financial resources from all quarters and carrying out the socialist modernization construction.

Article 2 The Treasury Bills shall be issued to: state enterprises, enterprises of collective ownership, competent authorities of enterprises and local governments; Party and government organizations, bodies, units of armed forces, institutions and opulent rural people's communes, production brigades and teams; individuals in urban and rural areas.

Article 3 The number of Treasury Bills to be issued shall be determined by the State Council and the issue shall begin from January 1 of that current year. The deadlines for payment: all payments by units shall be made on or before June 30 each year and those by individuals shall be made on or before September 30 each year.

Article 4 The interest rates of the Treasury Bills: the annual interest shall be fixed at 4% for those purchased by units; the annual interest shall be fixed at 8% for those purchased by individuals.

The interest for all Treasury Bills shall be calculated from July 1 of that year and interest shall not be allowed for the payments ahead of schedule.

The interest of Treasury Bills shall be paid in one lump sum when the principal is repaid and no compound interest shall be calculated.

Article 5 The Treasury Bills shall be calculated in Renminbi. The units purchasing them shall be granted the receipts of the Treasury Bills and entitled to have their names entered therein or report the loss of the receipts; the individuals purchasing them shall be granted the Treasury Bills. The Treasury Bills are issued in four denominations: 5 yuan, 10 yuan, 50 yuan and 100 yuan.

Article 6 The repayment of the principal and the payment of the interest of the Treasury Bills shall be handled from the sixth year after issue. For those purchased by individuals, lots shall be drawn at a time specified and the money shall be repaid by five different annual payments in five years in accordance with the amount of issue, 20% of the total amount to be repaid each time; for those purchased by units, no lots shall be drawn and the money shall be repaid by 5 different annual payments in five years in equal terms in accordance with the total amount of the purchases by units.

Article 7 The issue of the Treasury Bills, the repayments of the principal and the payment of the interest shall be handled by the People's Bank of China and its subordinate organizations.

Article 8 The funds raised by means of the Treasury Bills shall be used in a unified way by the State Council in accordance with the needs of the development and overall balance of the national economy.

Article 9 The Treasury Bills shall not be circulated as money and shall not be freely bought and sold except in the manner specified above.

Article 10 Those who forge the Treasury Bills or damage their reputation shall be punished according to law.

Article 11 The Ministry of Finance shall be authorized to handle the interpretation of the Regulations on the Treasury Bills.

4

INSURANCE

Air Transport/ Construction & Installation/
Labour/ Land Transport/ Marine/
Motor Vehicles/ Property & Investment

THE PEOPLE'S INSURANCE COMPANY OF CHINA: AIR TRANSPORTATION CARGO INSURANCE CLAUSE

I Scope of Coverage

This insurance is classified into two conditions – Air Transportation Risks and Air Transportation All Risks. Where the insured goods sustain loss or damage, the Company shall undertake to indemnify therefore according to the Insured Condition specified in the policy and the provisions of these Clauses.

1. Air Transportation Risks

This insurance covers:

1) Total or partial loss of the insured goods caused in the course of transportation by lightning, fire, explosion, jettison due to the aircraft encountering bad weather or other perils, collision, overturning, crashing or missing of the aircraft and other accidents.

2) Reasonable cost incurred by the Insured in salvaging the goods or averting or minimizing a loss recoverable under the policy, provided that such cost shall not exceed the value of the consignment so saved.

2. Air Transportation All Risks

Aside from the risks covered under the Air Transportation Risks conditions as above, this insurance also covers all risks of loss of or damage to the insured goods whether partial or total, arising from external causes in the course of transit.

II Exclusions

This insurance does not cover:

1) Loss or damage caused by the intentional act or fault of the Insured.

2) Loss or damage falling under the liability of the consignor.

3) Loss or damage arising from the quality or shortage of the insured goods prior to the attachment of this insurance.

4) Loss or damage arising from normal loss, inherent vice or nature of the insured goods, loss of market and/or delay in transit and any expenses arising therefrom.

5) Risks and liabilities covered and excluded by the Air Transportation War Risks Clause and Strikes, Riots and Civil Commotions Clause of the Company.

III Commencement and Termination of Coverage

1. Warehouse to Warehouse Clause

This insurance attaches from the time the goods hereby insured leave the warehouse or place of storage named in the Policy for the commencement of the transit and continues in force in the ordinary course of transit until the insured goods are delivered to the consignee's final warehouse or place of storage at the destination named in the Policy or to any other place used by the Insured for allocation or distribution of the goods or for storage other than in the ordinary course of transit. This insurance shall, however, be limited to thirty (30) days after completion of discharge of the insured goods from the aircraft at the final airport of discharge before they reach the above mentioned warehouse or place of storage. If prior to the expiration of the above mentioned thirty (30) days, the insured goods are to be forwarded to a destination other than that named in the Policy, this insurance shall terminate at the commencement of such transit.

2. If, owing to delay, deviation forced discharge, reshipment or transhipment beyond the control of the Insured or any change or termination of the voyage arising from the exercise of a liberty granted to the carrier under the contract of carriage, the insured goods arrive at a place other than that named in the Policy, subject to immediate notice being given to the Company by the Insured and an additional premium being paid, if required, this insurance shall remain in force and shall terminate as hereunder:

1) If the insured goods are sold at a place not named in the Policy, this insurance shall terminate on delivery of the goods sold, but in no event shall this insurance extend beyond thirty (30) days after completion of discharge of the insured goods from the carrying aircraft at such place.

2) If the insured goods are to be forwarded to the final destination named in the Policy or any other destination, this insurance shall terminate in accordance with Section 1 above.

IV Duty of the Insured

It is the duty of the Insured to attend to all

matters as specified hereunder, failing which the Company reserves the right to reject his claim for any loss if and when such failure prejudice the rights of the Company:

1. The Insured shall take delivery of the insured goods in good time upon their arrival at the port of destination named in the Policy. In the event of any damage to the goods, the Insured shall immediately apply for survey to the Survey and/or Settling Agent stipulated in the Policy. If the insured goods are found short in entire package or packages or show apparent traces of damage, the Insured shall obtain from the carrier, bailee or other relevant authorities (Customs and Airport Authorities, etc.) a certificate of loss or damage and/or shortlanded memo. Should the carrier, bailee or the other relevant authorities be responsible for such shortage or damage, the Insured shall lodge a claim with them in writing and, if necessary, obtain their confirmation of an extension of the time limit of validity of such claim.

2. The Insured shall, and the Company may also, take reasonable measures immediately in salvaging the goods or preventing or minimizing loss or damage thereto. The measures so taken by the Insured or by the Company shall not be considered respectively, as a waiver of abandonment hereunder or as an acceptance thereof.

3. The following documents should accompany any claim hereunder made against this company: Original Policy, Airway Bill, Invoice, Packing List, Survey Report and Statement of Claim. If any third party is involved, documents relative to pursuing of recovery from such party should also be included.

V The Time of Validity of a Claim

The time of validity of a claim under this insurance shall not exceed a period of two years counting from the time of completion of discharge of the insured goods from the aircraft at the final airport.

AIR TRANSPORTATION CARGO WAR RISK CLAUSES OF THE PEOPLE'S INSURANCE COMPANY OF CHINA

(Revised on January 1, 1976)

I. Scope of Coverage

The Company shall be liable for the compensation of the loss of insured goods owing to the following causes:

(1) Losses caused by war, hostile acts or armed conflicts;

(2) Losses caused by the seizure, restraint, confiscation or blockade resulting from those mentioned in clause (1), but these losses shall only be adjusted six months after the date of occurrence;

(3) Losses caused by various conventional weapons and bombs.

II. Exclusions

The Company shall not be liable for compensation of the losses caused by such nuclear weapons as atom bombs, hydrogen bombs, etc.

III. Commencement and Termination of Coverage

This insurance liability shall commence at the time of the loading of insured goods on board the aircraft at the place of dispatch indicated in the policy and terminate at the time of their unloading from the aircraft at the destination indicated in the policy. If the insured goods are not unloaded from the aircraft, the length of the validity of this insurance liability shall be 15 days from midnight of the date of their arrival at the destination. If the insured goods are transshipped midway, the insurance liability shall terminate at the time of their unloading from the aircraft at the place of transshipment; if the insured goods are not unloaded from the aircraft, the length of the validity of this insurance liability shall be 15 days from the midnight of the date of their arrival at the place of transshipment, but this insurance liability shall remain valid if the insured goods are loaded on the aircraft to carry them on at the midway place of transshipment.

Notes: These clauses are the additional clauses to the Air Transportation Cargo Insurance Clauses. If these clauses go against any articles of the Air Transportation Cargo Insurance Clauses, these clauses shall be taken as standard.

THE PEOPLE'S INSURANCE COMPANY OF CHINA
AIRCRAFT INSURANCE CLAUSES

I. Scope of Coverage

The Company shall be liable, in accordance with the following provisions, during the effective period of this policy, for loss of or damage to the insured aircraft and legal liability assumed by the Insured to any third party and/or passengers, arising from the causes hereunder mentioned:

1. **Aircraft**

The Company shall be liable for accidental loss of or damage to the insured aircraft including equipment or accessories arising from whatsoever cause other than those enumerated in Clause 2 – Exclusions hereunder whilst the aircraft is in flight (including taxiing) or on the ground. The Company shall also be liable for the cost of dismantling, transporting and reassembling the insured aircraft and the cost of removal of the wreck of the insured aircraft resulting from an insured accident.

2. **Third Party Liability**

The Company shall be liable for all sums which the Insured shall become liable to pay in respect of death or bodily injury or damage to property of third parties caused by the insured aircraft or by persons or objects falling therefrom. However, the third party liability risk referred hereto shall not cover death or bodily injury or property damage to representatives of the Insured, his working personnel aboard the insured aircraft or any person on the payroll of the Insured at airports whilst engaged in his duties as such.

3. **Legal Liability to Passengers**

The Company shall be liable for all sums for which the Insured shall become legally liable or by contract to pay in respect of accidental death or of bodily injury to passengers whilst embarking into, being carried in or disembarking from the insured aircraft, or for loss of or damage to the registered baggage and/or property belonging to or being carried by passengers and for damage occasioned by delay in the carriage by air of passengers, baggage and/or property.

The term "Passengers" referred to hereunder shall mean persons flying as fare-paying passengers or being carried gratis otherwise than for the performance of duties for the Insured.

The maximum limits of indemnity under items (1), (2) and (3) above are specified in the schedule of this policy. However, the Company shall in addition pay, notwithstanding the maximum limit in the above-mentioned schedule, legal costs incurred in respect of any claim to the Insured's liability.

II. Exclusions

The Company shall not be liable for any lost expenses and/or liability arising from the following causes:

(1) failure to observe airworthiness requirements of the aircraft at the commencement of flight.

(2) intentional act of the Insured.

(3) wear and tear and structural and mechanical defects in any part of the insured aircraft (but loss of or damage to the aircraft consequent upon such causes is covered under this policy).

(4) those covered by and excluded from Aircraft War, Hijacking and Other Risks Clauses of the Company.

III. Treatment of Losses

(1) In the event of accident to the insured aircraft which falls within the scope of coverage, the Insured shall give notice thereof immediately to the Company and take all possible measures to minimize the loss. The Company shall further defray expenses reasonably incurred as a result thereof, subject however to a maximum of 10% of the insured amount of the aircraft unless prior consent has been obtained from the Company.

(2) In the case of total loss of the insured aircraft, the full amount insured of the aircraft shall be indemnified. In the case of a partial loss of the aircraft, the Company shall be liable for the reasonable costs of replacements and repairs minus the applicable deductibles.

(3) Where no news is received of the whereabouts of the insured aircraft over a period of 15 days after the date of commencement of flight, it shall be regarded as a missing aircraft and the Company shall pay for the full insured amount of the aircraft.

(4) If any third party is to be held responsible for claims covered hereunder, the Insured

shall, when submitting his claim to the Company, subrogate his right of recovery against the third party and transfer the necessary documents to the Company.

IV. Maintenance and Overhaul of the Insured Aircraft

(1) The Insured shall be responsible for periodic maintenance and overhaul of the insured aircraft so as to keep it in a constant serviceable condition.

(2) Where the insured aircraft undergoes repair or is laid up for a period exceeding ten consecutive days, 50% (fifty percent) of the premium, to be calculated pro rata daily, for such period shall be returned to the Insured. But no return of premium shall be made to the Insured during the period the aircraft is undergoing repair as a result of an accident covered under this policy.

V. Treatment of Disputes

All disputes arising between the Insured and the Company shall be settled through negotiation on the principle of seeking truth from facts and of fairness and reasonableness.

THE PEOPLE'S INSURANCE COMPANY OF CHINA: CONTRACTORS ALL RISKS CLAUSES

I. Scope of Coverage

The Company shall undertake to indemnify the Insured in the manner and to the extent stipulated in the Schedule for the loss, damage and expenses in connection with the insured construction work arising from the causes hereunder mentioned:

(1) flood, high seas, inundation, earthquake, seaquake, storm, tempest, avalanche, landslide, rockslide, frost, hailstorm and other natural calamities;

(2) lightning, fire and explosion;

(3) air crashes or articles dropped therefrom or out of other falling objects;

(4) theft and burglary;

(5) lack of skill, negligence, fault or wilful misconduct of workers and technicians;

(6) accident due to defects of original material or bad workmanship;

(7) any other unexpected and accidental events other than those enumerated in Exclusions under Article II hereinafter.

The Company shall also indemnify the Insured for necessary expenses in removing debris from the work-site consequent upon the above mentioned loss or damage subject to sums insured specified in the Schedule.

II. Exclusions

The Company shall not be liable for:

(1) loss, damage, expenses or liability arising from intentional acts or actual fault of the Insured and his representatives;

(2) loss, damage, expenses or liability arising from war, warlike operation, act of hostilities, armed conflict, confiscation, requisition, strike and riot;

(3) loss, damage, expenses or liability arising from nuclear reaction, nuclear radiation or radioactive contamination;

(4) wear and tear, oxidation, rust and corrosion;

(5) loss, damage, expenses or liability arising from faulty design;

(6) cost of replacement, repair or rectification of the defective material and/or workmanship;

(7) mechanical or electrical breakdown or derangement of construction machinery, equipment and installation not caused by exterior influence;

(8) loss, damage, expenses or liability arising from total or partial suspension of work;

(9) consequential loss of any kind or description whatsoever, such as penalties, losses due to delay, loss of contract;

(10) loss or damage to documents, books, notes and instruments, cash, securities, charts and data;

(11) the deductibles stated in the policy to be borne by the Insured;

(12) loss or damage to vehicles, ships or aircraft licensed for general transport use;

(13) shortage discovered at the time of taking an inventory;

(14) risks covered and excluded in Contractors' Third Party Liability Clauses of the Company.

III. Period of Insurance

Subject to the construction period specified herein, this insurance shall go into effect as of the commencement of work or from the time when the insured items are unloaded at the site of the construction work and expire at the time of taking over upon completion of the work but not later than the expiry date stipulated in this policy. Extension of this insurance is subject to the prior consent of the Company in writing.

IV. Sum Insured

The sum insured for construction work shall be the full value of the insured items at the completion of the construction work plus freight, erection cost, customs duty, etc. Construction machinery, equipment and installation shall be covered on their replacement values. Other items shall be covered on the sum agreed upon between the Insured and the Company.

V. Insured's Obligations

(1) The Insured shall take reasonable preventative measures to avoid occurrence of accidents at the site of construction work and pay sufficient attention to and put into practice the justified recommendations for prevention of loss put forward by the representatives of the Company.

(2) In the event of any accident which might give rise to a claim hereunder, the Insured shall notify the Company immediately and furnish full information about the accident to the Company in writing.

(3) To facilitate inspection, the Insured shall preserve the spot affected before survey of loss and damage is carried out.

(4) In order to avoid aggravation of loss, the Insured shall take all necessary measures to minimize loss or damage to the least extent. The Company shall pay for the expenses reasonably incurred in this respect, but in no case shall the aggregate of the amount of indemnity and the amount referred to here exceed the sum insured on the items sustaining loss or damage.

(5) The Insured shall advise the Company in writing of any material change in the risks and request the Company to endorse this policy of such alterations as additions or deletions of the insured items, prolonging or shortening of the construction period, necessary adjustment of insured sums, etc.

(6) The Company shall not be liable for loss or damage had the Insured or his representatives not fulfilled the above mentioned obligations wilfully.

VI. Claim and Indemnity

(1) In submitting a claim, the Insured shall furnish all necessary and valid documents to the Company to substantiate his claim.

(2) The indemnification of the Company shall be limited to the cost necessary to restore the damaged or lost items to their condition immediately before the occurrence of the accident. The value of the scrap or parts of the damaged item shall be deducted from the amount of indemnity.

(3) Claims may be settled either in cash or by way of replacement or repair of the items damaged provided that the total amount of indemnity shall not exceed the sum insured as stipulated in the Policy.

(4) Should the sum insured be lower than the amount required to be insured under Article IV hereinabove, the difference shall be regarded as self-insured by the Insured, and the Company shall be liable to pay only such proportion as the sum insured bears to the amount required to be insured under the above Article IV.

(5) If reinstatement of the sum insured is required after settlement of the loss is effected by the Company, the Insured shall pay an additional premium calculated pro rata daily from the date of the loss to the expiration of the insured period.

(6) Should any loss, expenses or liability recoverable hereunder also be covered by any other insurance, the Company shall only be liable to pay or contribute their proportion of the claim irrespective as to whether the other insurance is arranged by the Insured or not, or whether any indemnification is obtainable under such other insurance.

VII. Dispute

All disputes under this insurance arising between the Insured and the Company shall be settled through friendly negotiations. Where a settlement fails after negotiations, such dispute shall be submitted to arbitration or to a court for legal action. Unless otherwise agreed, arbitration or legal actions shall be carried out in the place where the defendant is domiciled.

CONTRACTORS' THIRD PARTY LIABILITY CLAUSES

Article 1 The Company shall indemnify the Insured against such sums which the Insured shall become legally liable to pay as damages in respect of death of or bodily injury to or illness of third parties, or loss of or damage to property belonging to third parties on or in the vicinity of the construction site consequent upon an accident taking place within the insurance period of the construction project, and also be liable for the relevant legal costs payable by the Insured and other expenses incurred with the written consent of the Company.

Article 2 The indemnifications made by the Company for each and every accident shall be subject to the amounts to be payable by the Insured which are decided in accordance with the law or by the government department concerned, but shall in no case exceed the limits of indemnity specified in this Policy. No admission, offer, promise, payment or indemnity shall be made or given by the Insured or his representatives without the written consent of the Company.

Article 3 The Company shall not be liable in respect of:

(1) the deductibles stated in the Schedule to be borne by the Insured;

(2) death of or bodily injury to or illness of the employees or workmen of the Insured and other contractors engaged in work in connection with construction project on the construction site;

(3) loss of or damage to property belonging to or held in care, custody or control of the Insured, other contractors or their employees or workmen;

(4) damage to any property, land or building caused by vibration or by the removal or weakening of support or injury or damage to any person or property occasioned by or resulting from any such damage;

(5) any accident caused by vehicles, ships or aircraft licensed for general transport use;

(6) indemnification or payment made by the Insured in accordance with any agreement between the Insured and other parties.

These clauses are additional clauses to the Company's Contractors' All Risks Clauses.

THE PEOPLE'S INSURANCE COMPANY OF CHINA: ERECTION ALL RISKS CLAUSES

I. Scope of Coverage

The Company shall undertake to indemnify the Insured in the manner and to the extent stipulated in the Schedule for the loss, damage and expenses in connection with the insured erection work arising from the causes hereunder mentioned:

(1) flood, high sea, inundation, earthquake, seaquake, storm, tempest, avalanche, landslide, rockslide, frost, hailstorm or other natural calamities;

(2) lightning, fire and explosion;

(3) Air crashes or articles dropped therefrom or falling out of other flying objects;

(4) overloading, excess voltage, electric line contact, arcing, leakage of electricity, short-circuiting, electricity discharged from the atmosphere or other electric phenomena;

(5) theft and burglary;

(6) accident due to poor technique in erection;

(7) lack of skill, negligence, fault or wilful misconduct of workers and technicians;

(8) any other unexpected and accidental events except those enumerated in Exclusion under Article II hereinafter.

The Company shall also indemnify the Insured for the necessary expenses for removing debris from the work-site consequent upon the above mentioned loss or damage, subject to sums insured as specified in the Schedule.

II. Exclusions

The Company shall not be liable for:

(1) loss, damage, expenses or liability arising from intentional acts and actual fault of the Insured and his representatives;

(2) loss, damage, expenses or liability arising from war, warlike operation, acts of hostilities, armed conflict, confiscation, requisition, strike and riot;

(3) loss, damage, expenses or liability arising from nuclear reaction, nuclear radiation or radioactive contamination;

(4) wear and tear, oxidation, rust and corrosion;

(5) loss of or damage to the insured items themselves due to faulty design, defective casting or material or bad workmanship and expenses incurred for rectifying such defects or mistakes;

(6) loss of or damage to the electric equipment or apparatus due to overloading, overvoltage, electric line contact, arcing, leakage of electricity, short-circuiting, electricity discharged from atmosphere and other electric phenomena;

(7) loss, damage, expenses or liability arising from total or partial suspension of work;

(8) consequential loss of any kind or description whatsoever such as penalties, losses due to delay and loss of contract;

(9) loss of or damage to documents, books, notes and instruments, cash, securities, charts, data and packing materials;

(10) the deductibles stated in the policy to be borne by the Insured;

(11) shortages discovered at the time of taking an inventory;

(12) risks covered and excluded in Erection Third Party Liability Clauses of the Company.

III. Period of Insurance

Subject to the erection period specified herein, this insurance shall go into effect from the commencement of work or from the time when the insured items are unloaded at the site of the erection work and expire at the time of taking over upon completion of the work. If testing and trial use are provided for in the contract, the periods of such testing and trial use shall not be longer than that specified in this Policy. However, if the insured item is a second-hand one, insurance liability shall terminate as soon as its testing starts. At the latest, the insurance shall expire on the expiry date stipulated in this Policy. Extension of this insurance is subject to the prior consent of the Company in writing.

IV. Sum Insured

The sum insured for erection items shall be the full value of the insured items at the completion of the erection plus freight, erection cost, customs duty, etc. Civil engineering machinery equipment and installations shall be covered on their replacement values. Other items shall be covered on the sums agreed upon between the Insured and the Company.

V. Insured's Obligations

(1) The Insured shall take reasonable preventive measures to avoid occurrence of accidents

at the site of erection work and pay sufficient attention to and put into practice the justified recommendations for prevention of loss put forward by the representatives of the Company.

(2) In the event of any accident which might give rise to a claim hereunder, the Insured shall notify the Company immediately and furnish full information about the accident to the Company in writing.

(3) To facilitate inspection, the Insured shall preserve the spot affected before survey of loss and damage is carried out.

(4) In order to avoid aggravation of loss, the Insured shall take all necessary measures to minimize loss or damage to the least extent. The Company shall pay for the expenses reasonably incurred in this respect, but in no case shall the aggregate of the amount of indemnity and the expenses referred to here exceed the sum insured on the items sustaining loss or damage.

(5) The Insured shall advise the Company in writing of any material change in the risks and request the Company to endorse this Policy with such alterations as additions or deletions of the insured items, prolonging or shortening of the construction period, necessary adjustment of insured sums, etc..

(6) The Company shall not be liable for loss or damage if the Insured or his representatives have not fulfilled the above mentioned obligations wilfully.

VI. Claim and Indemnity

(1) In submitting a claim, the Insured shall furnish all necessary and valid documents to the Company to substantiate his claim.

(2) The indemnification of the Company shall be limited to the cost necessary to restore the damaged or lost items to their original condition immediately before the occurrence of the accident. The value of the scrap or parts of the damaged items shall be deducted from the amount of indemnity.

(3) Claims may be settled either in cash or by way of replacement or repair of the items damaged provided that the total amount of indemnity shall not exceed the sum insured as stipulated in the Policy.

(4) Should the sum insured be lower than that required to be insured under Article IV hereinabove, the difference shall be regarded as self-insured by the Insured, and the Company shall only be liable to pay such proportion as the sum insured bears to the amount required to be insured under the above Article IV.

(5) If reinstatement of sum insured is required after settlement of the loss is effected by the Company, the Insured shall pay an additional premium calculated pro rata daily from the date of the loss to the expiry of the insurance period.

(6) Should any loss, expenses or liability recoverable hereunder be also covered by any other insurance, the Company shall only be liable to pay or contribute their proportion of the claim irrespective as to whether the other insurance is arranged by the Insured or not or whether any indemnification is obtainable under such other insurance.

VII. Disputes

All disputes under this insurance arising between the Insured and the Company shall be settled through friendly negotiations. Where a settlement fails after negotiations, such dispute shall be submitted to arbitration or to a court for legal action. Unless otherwise agreed, arbitration or legal actions shall be carried out in the place where the defendant is domiciled.

ERECTION THIRDPARTY LIABILITY CLAUSES

1. The Company shall indemnify the Insured against such sums which the Insured shall become legally liable to pay as damages in respect of death of or bodily injury to or illness of third parties, or loss of or damage to property belonging to third parties on or in the vicinity of the construction site consequent upon an accident taking place within the insurance period of the erection project, and be also liable for the relevant legal costs payable by the Insured and other expenses incurred with the written consent of the Company.

2. The indemnification made by the Company for each and every accident shall be subject to the amounts to be payable by the Insured which are decided in accordance with the law or by the governmental department concerned, but shall in no case exceed the limits of indemnity specified in this Policy. No admission, offer, promise, payment or indemnity shall be made or given by the Insured or his representatives without the written consent of the Company.

3. The Company shall not be liable in respect of:

(1) the deductibles stated in the Schedule to be borne by the Insured;

(2) death of or bodily injury to or illness of the employees or workmen of the Insured and other contractors engaged in work in connection with erection project on the construction site;

(3) loss of or damage to property belonging to or held in care, custody or control of the Insured, other contractors or their employees or workmen;

(4) any accident caused by vehicles, ships, or aircraft licensed for general transport use;

(5) indemnification or payment made by the Insured in accordance with any agreement between the Insured and other parties.

These clauses are additional clauses to the Company's Erection All Risks Clauses.

LABOUR INSURANCE REGULATIONS OF THE PEOPLE'S REPUBLIC OF CHINA

(Adopted by the 73rd Government Administrative Meeting of the Government Administration Council on February 23, 1951 and promulgated by the Government Administration Council on February 26)

Chapter I General Rules

Article 1 These Regulations are formulated according to present economic conditions for the purpose of protecting the health of paid labourers and easing the special difficulties in their livelihood.

Article 2 In the implementation of these Regulations, the procedures for provisional implementation in key enterprises shall be adopted and the implementation shall be popularized after achievements are made and experience is obtained in the provisional implementation. Their application shall be limited to the following enterprises for the time being:

(1) State-operated, joint state-private, private and cooperative factories, mines and their subsidiary units and business management organizations, each of which employs more than 100 workers and staff members.

(2) Each railway, shipping or postal and telecommunications enterprise and its subsidiary units.

Article 3 With regard to the labour insurance of the enterprise beyond the limits of Clauses (1) and (2) of Article 2 and seasonal enterprises, the administration or capital of each enterprise and its grass-roots trade union committee shall consult with each other and enter into a collective contract to stipulate it on the principles of these Regulations and in accordance with the actual conditions of the enterprise.

Article 4 These Regulations shall be applicable to all the workers and staff members (including apprentices) working in each enterprise which practises labour insurance, making no distinction between nationalities, ages, sexes and citizenship, but those who are deprived of political rights shall be excluded.

Article 5 The labour insurance remuneration to the casual labourers, seasonal workers and personnel on probation working in each enterprise which practises labour insurance shall be separately prescribed in the rules for the implementation of these Regulations.

Article 6 If an enterprise to which these Regulations are applicable is difficult to maintain owing to special economic difficulties or has not officially commenced business, the administration or capital of the enterprise shall consult and reach an agreement with the grass-roots trade union committee and put off implementing these Regulations with the approval of the labour administrative authorities of the local people's government.

Chapter II The Collection and Maintenance of Labour Insurance Funds

Article 7 All the labour insurance payments stipulated in these Regulations shall be borne by the administration or capital of each enterprise which practises labour insurance, part of them to be directly paid by the administration or capital of the enterprise and the other part to be handed over by the administration or capital to the trade union organization for disposal as labour insurance funds.

Article 8 The administration or capital of each enterprise which practises labour insurance in accordance with these Regulations shall, by the month, pay the amount which is equivalent to three percent of the total of the wages of all the workers and staff members of the enterprise for use as labour insurance funds. These labour insurance funds shall not be deducted from the wages of the workers and staff members nor be separately collected from them.

Article 9 The procedures for the collection and care of the labour insurance funds are as follows:

(1) The administration or capital of an enterprise shall calculate the monthly payable labour insurance funds on the basis of the total of the wages in the previous month and pay them once to the state bank appointed by and on behalf of the All-China Federation of Trade Unions to collect labour insurance funds within the limited time of the first to tenth days of each month.

(2) Within the first two months of the beginning of practising labour insurance, all the labour insurance funds paid monthly by the

administration or capital of every enterprise shall be deposited into the account of the All-China Federation of Trade Unions as general labour insurance funds for use to run collective labour insurance facilities. Commencing from the third month of the beginning of practising it, 30 percent of the labour insurance funds paid each month shall be deposited into the account of the All-China Federation of Trade Unions as general labour insurance funds; 70 percent shall be deposited into the account of the grass-roots trade union of each enterprise as labour insurance funds for use as the pensions, subsidies and relief funds which are payable to its deserving workers and staff members in accordance with these Regulations.

Article 10 If the administration or capital of an enterprise does not pay or is in arrears with the labour insurance funds when the time limit is exceeded, the fines for late payment shall be additionally paid, the sums to be one percent of the unpaid parts. If they are not paid 20 days in excess of the time limit, the grass-roots trade union committee shall notify the local state bank to deduct them for payment from the funds of the state, joint state-private or cooperative enterprise; with regard to a private enterprise, the grass-roots trade union committee shall report to the labour administrative authorities of the local people's government so as to investigate and affix the responsibility on the owner of the enterprise.

Article 11 The All-China Federation of Trade Unions shall entrust the People's Bank of China with the care of the labour insurance funds on its behalf.

Chapter III Provisions for Various Types of Labour Insurance Remuneration

Article 12 The provisions for the remuneration for an injury or disability caused while on duty:

(1) If a worker or a staff member is wounded while on duty, he or she shall be treated at the clinic, hospital or special hospital of the enterprise. If the clinic, hospital or special hospital of the enterprise cannot treat him or her, the administration or capital of the enterprise shall transfer him or her for treatment at another hospital and bear all the treating expenses, medicinal charges, hospitalization expenses, board expenses at hospital and travelling expenses for going to doctors. The wages shall be paid as usual during the medical treatment.

(2) If a worker or a staff member is certified to be disabled due to an injury caused while on duty, the pensions or subsidies for the disability caused while on duty shall be paid monthly under the labour insurance funds in accordance with the following conditions:

a. If he or she needs others' assistance in eating and drinking and other aspects of daily life after discharge owing to the complete loss of his or her ability to work, the sums of the pensions for his or her disability caused while on duty shall be 75 per cent of his or her wages, which shall be paid until his or her death.

b. If he or she does not need others' assistance in eating and drinking and other aspects of daily life after discharge owing to the complete loss of his or her ability to work, the sums of the pensions for his or her disability caused while on duty shall be 60 per cent of his or her wages, which shall be paid until the restoration of his or her ability to work or until his or her death.

c. If his or her working ability is partially impaired but he or she can still work, the administration or capital of the enterprise shall assign him or her to a suitable job and pay him or her the subsidies for the disability caused while on duty according to the degrees of the loss of his or her ability until his or her retirement or until his or her death; the sums shall be five to 20 percent of his or her wages before the disability, but the total of them with the addition of his or her wages when he or she returns to work shall not exceed his or her original wages before the disability. The detailed procedures shall be formulated in the rules for the implementation.

d. The determination and change of the condition of disability shall be examined by the disability examination board. The detailed procedures shall be formulated in the rules for the implementation.

Article 13 The provisions for the remuneration for diseases contracted or an injury or disability sustained while off-duty:

(1) If a worker or a staff member is ill or wounded while off-duty, he or she shall be treated at the clinic, hospital or special hospital of the enterprise. If the clinic, hospital or special hospital of the enterprise cannot treat him or her, the administration or capital of the enterprise shall transfer him or her to another hospital for treatment and hospitalize him or her if necessary. His or her treating expenses, hospitalization expenses and ordinary medicinal expenses shall be borne by the administration or capital of the enterprise; costly medicinal expenses, travelling expenses to

go to doctors and board expenses at the hospital shall be borne by himself or herself.

(2) If a worker or a staff member stops working to receive the medical treatment of a disease contracted or injury sustained while off-duty and the period of his or her treatment is continued for less than three months, the administration or capital of the enterprise shall pay him 50 to 100 percent of his or her wages according to the length of his or her standing in the enterprise; if the treatment continues for more than three months, he or she shall be paid the relief funds for the disease contracted or the injury sustained while off-duty instead by the month under the labour insurance funds until he or she is able to work or is certified to be disabled or until he or she dies, the sums to be 30 to 50 percent of his or her wages. But the continued suspension of work for medical treatment shall be limited to six months and handled according to the remuneration for the discharge owing to disability in Clause (3) if it exceeds six months. The detailed procedures shall be formulated in the rules for the implementation.

(3) If a worker or a staff member resigns because of the complete loss of his or her ability to work due to a disease contracted or disability caused by an injury sustained while off-duty, the relief funds for the disability caused while off-duty shall be paid by the month under the labour insurance funds according to the length of his or her standing in the enterprise until the restoration of his or her ability to work or until his or her death, the sums to be 20 to 30 percent of his or her wages. If he or she has other financial sources to maintain his or her livelihood, these relief funds for the disability caused while off-duty shall not be given. The detailed procedures shall be formulated in the rules for the implementation.

(4) If a directly-related family member supported by a worker or a staff member becomes ill, he or she shall be given free treatment at the clinic, hospital or special hospital of the enterprise. He or she shall bear half of the ordinary medicinal expenses, with costly medicinal expenses, travelling expenses for visits to doctors, hospitalization expenses, board expenses at hospital and all other costs to be borne by himself or herself.

Article 14 The provisions for the remuneration for the death of a worker or a staff member or a directly-related family member supported by him or her:

(1) If a worker or a staff member dies while on duty, the administration or capital of the enterprise shall provide funeral expenses, the sums to be two months' average wages of all the workers and staff members of the enterprise. In addition, the pensions shall be paid every month to the directly-related family member(s) according to the number supported by him or her under the labour insurance funds until the supported become(s) disqualified for the support, the sums to be 25 to 50 per cent of the deceased's wages. The detailed procedures shall be formulated in the rules for the implementation.

(2) If a worker or a staff member dies of a disease contracted or an injury sustained while off-duty, the funeral subsidies shall be paid under the labour insurance funds, the sums to be one month's average wages of all the workers and staff members of the enterprise. In addition, relief funds shall be paid to the directly-related family member(s) normally supported by him or her according to the length of his or her standing in the enterprise under the labour insurance funds, the sums to be three to 12 months' wages of the deceased. The detailed procedures shall be formulated in the rules for the implementation.

(3) If a worker or a staff member dies after his or her discharge owing to the complete loss of his or her ability to work because of the disability caused while on duty, funeral subsidies and relief funds for the directly-related family member(s) normally supported by him or her shall be paid according to the remuneration stipulated in Clause (2) of this Article.

(4) If a worker or a staff member dies after his or her retirement, or if he or she dies after his or her discharge because of the complete loss of his or her ability to work owing to the disability caused while off-duty, funeral subsidies shall be paid under the labour insurance funds, the sum to be one month's average wages of all the workers and staff members of the enterprise.

(5) If a directly-related family member supported by a worker or a staff member dies, the funeral subsidies for him or her shall be paid under the labour insurance funds. If the deceased is above the age of 10, the sum shall be one third of one month's average wages of all the workers and staff members of the enterprise, one quarter of one month's average wages for the deceased in the range of ages from one to 10 and no remuneration shall be given for the deceased below the age of one.

Article 15 The provisions for the remuneration to provide for old age:

(1) If a male worker or staff member has reached the age of 60, the general standing of 25 working years and the standing in his own enterprise of 10 working years, old-age pensions shall be

paid according to the length of his standing in the enterprise under the labour insurance funds until his death, the sums to be 35 to 60 percent of his wages. If he continues to work as required by the work of the enterprise with his own consent, in-service old-age pensions shall be paid per month in addition to the deserved wages, the sums to be 10 to 20 percent of his wages. The detailed procedures shall be formulated in the rules for the implementation.

(2) A female worker or staff member who has reached the age of 50, the general standing of 20 working years and the standing in her own enterprise of 10 working years shall enjoy the remuneration of old-age pensions stipulated in Clause (1).

(3) With regard to those who work in underground mines or regularly in a working place at low temperatures below 32°F or at high temperatures above 100°F, a male worker or staff member who has reached the age of 55 or a woman worker or staff member who has reached the age of 45 shall be entitled to enjoy the remuneration of old-age pensions stipulated in Clause (1). But in the calculation of his or her general standing and the standing in his or her own enterprise, one year for working in such a place shall be calculated as one year and three months.

(4) In the case of those who are directly engaged in work which is harmful to health in the refinement or manufacture of lead, mercury, arsenic, phosphorus, acids and in other chemical or ordnance industries, a male worker or staff member who has reached the age of 55 or a female worker or staff member who has reached the age of 45 shall be entitled to enjoy the remuneration of old-age pensions stipulated in Clause (1). But in the calculation of his or her general standing or his or her standing in the enterprise, one year for being engaged in such work shall be calculated as one year and six months.

Article 16 The provisions for childbearing remuneration:

(1) If a female worker or staff member gives birth to a child, she shall have leave of 56 days before and after the childbearing and her wages shall be paid as usual during maternity leave.

(2) A woman worker or staff member who has a miscarriage shall have 15 days' leave if she is pregnant for less than three months; she shall have 30 days' leave if she is pregnant between three and seven months and her wages shall be paid as usual during maternity leave.

(3) If she still is unable to work at the expiration of her maternity leave (whether normal labour or miscarriage), she shall be dealt with in accordance with the provisions for the remuneration for diseases in Article 13 after being certified by a doctor.

(4) When a female worker or staff member or the spouse of a male worker or staff member gives birth to a child, childbearing subsidies shall be paid under the labour insurance funds, the sum to be the local retail price of 5 *chi*(1/3 metre) red cloth.

Article 17 The provisions for collective labour insurance facilities:

(1) All the workers and staff members working in each enterprise which practises labour insurance shall have the rights to enjoy collective labour insurance facilities. Detailed procedures shall be formulated by the All-China Federation of Trade Unions.

(2) Collective labour insurance facilities shall be run by the All-China Federation of Trade Unions in an overall way, but the Federation shall entrust each local trade union organization or each industrial trade union organization with their management, including the following items:

A. Sanatoriums;
B. Asylums for the disabled;
C. Asylums for the aged;
D. Orphan asylums;
E. Rest homes;
F. Others.

Detailed procedures shall be otherwise formulated by the All-China Federation of Trade Unions.

Article 18 The workers and staff members working in an enterprise which practises labour insurance who have not joined any trade unions shall only enjoy half of the stipulated sums for all such payments as wages and relief funds during the medical treatment of diseases or injury for non-duty reasons, relief funds for disability for non-duty reasons, relief funds for supported directly-related family members, old-age pensions, childbearing subsidies, etc.; but the remuneration for injury, disability or death caused on duty or the remuneration for the treatment of diseases or injury for non-duty reasons they shall still enjoy as stipulated in these Regulations.

Article 19 In drawing various pensions, subsidies and relief funds, a worker or a staff member who works in an enterprise which practises labour insurance shall only draw the kind of remuneration with the maximum amount and shall not draw two kinds at the same time.

Chapter IV Provisions for the Granting of Outstanding Labour Insurance Remuneration

Article 20 A model worker who makes special contributions to the enterprise or a combat hero who is transferred to work in the enterprise shall be entitled to be granted more outstanding labour insurance remuneration as follows with the proposal of the grass-roots trade union committee and with the approval of each provincial or municipal trade union organization or of the national committee of each industrial trade union:

(1) All of his or her medical expenses and board expenses at the hospital for diseases contracted or injury sustained while off-duty shall be borne by the administration or capital of the enterprise.

(2) His or her wages during the first three months of the period of the medical treatment of diseases contracted or injury sustained while off-duty shall be paid as usual. All relief funds for diseases contracted or injury sustained while off-duty and those for disability caused while off-duty shall be paid at a rate half of his or her wages. The pensions for disability caused on duty shall be 100 percent of his or her wages. The subsidies for disability caused on duty shall be the balance between his or her wages before the disability and the wages now drawn after the disability. The pensions for directly-related family members of one who died while on duty shall be 30 to 60 percent of his or her wages. Retired old-age pensions shall be 50 to 80 percent of his or her wages. In-service old-age pensions shall be 15 to 30 percent of his or her wages. The detailed procedures shall be formulated in the rules for the implementation.

(3) He or she shall have the priority to enjoy collective labour insurance facilities.

Article 21 In the case of a disabled military man who is transferred to work in the enterprise, his wages during the first three months of the period of the medical treatment of diseases contracted or injury sustained while off-duty shall be paid as usual disregarding the length of his standing in the enterprise. It shall be handled as stipulated in Clause (2) of Article 13 if the stop lasts for more than three months.

Chapter V. The Control of Labour Insurance Funds

Article 22 The procedures for the control of labour insurance funds are as follows:

(1) The general labour insurance funds shall be used by the All-China Federation of Trade Unions to run collective labour insurance facilities.

(2) The labour insurance funds shall be used by the grass-roots trade union committee to pay various pensions, subsidies and relief funds and settled once a month, the surplus to be wholly transferred into the account of the provincial or municipal trade union organization or of the national committee of the industrial trade union for use as labour insurance regulating funds (hereinafter simply referred to as "regulating funds").

(3) The regulating funds shall be used by the provincial or municipal trade union organization or the national committee of the industrial trade union to subsidize each grass-roots trade union committee under it when its labour insurance funds fall short of the expenditure or to run collective labour insurance facilities. The national committee of each industrial trade union shall be entitled to authorize its local organization to take care of the transfer and use of the regulating funds. The All-China Federation of Trade Unions shall be entitled to concentrate the regulating funds from each provincial or municipal trade union organization or the national committee of each industrial trade union under it and entitled to use them to run collective labour insurance facilities. If the regulating funds of a provincial or municipal trade union organization or the national committee of an industrial trade union fall short of the expenditure, an application shall be made to the All-China Federation of Trade Unions for the allotment of the regulating funds as subsidies.

Article 23 Labour insurance funds shall not be transferred for purposes other than labour insurance facilities.

Article 24 The accounting department of each enterprise shall set up the independent accounting for the labour insurance funds and the special accountant shall take charge of the receipts and payments of the labour insurance funds. The accounting regulations on the labour insurance funds shall be formulated by the Ministry of Labour of the Central People's Government jointly with the All-China Federation of Trade Unions.

Article 25 The receipts and payments of the labour insurance regulating funds shall be handled by the financial department of the trade union organization at each level in accordance with the provisions of the All-China Federation of Trade Unions.

Chapter VI The Execution and Supervision of Labour Insurance Transactions

Article 26 Each grass-roots trade union committee is the grass-roots unit which executes labour insurance transactions and its main functions are to: supervise and urge the payment of labour insurance funds; decide on the expenditure of labour insurance funds; supervise the expenditure of various payments directly made by the administration or capital of the enterprise as stipulated in these Regulations; impel the enterprise to improve the business of its clinic or hospital; execute all actual transactions concerning labour insurance; draw up a monthly statement of labour insurance funds every month, work out budgets, final accounts, business plans and business reports every year and submit them to the provincial or municipal trade union organization or the national committee of the industrial trade union and the labour administrative authorities of the local people's government; report to the general meeting or the congress of the trade union on its work.

Article 27 The fund examination committee of each grass-roots trade union committee shall, by the month, examine the receipts and payments of labour insurance funds and various payments directly made by the administration or capital of the enterprise as stipulated in these Regulations and make them public.

Article 28 Each provincial or municipal trade union organization or the national or regional committee of each industrial trade union shall hold itself responsible for directing and supervising the labour insurance transactions of each grass-roots trade union committee under it, to check if there are any mistakes in the monthly statements of the receipts and payments of labour insurance funds, budgets, final accounts and the receipts and payments of labour insurance funds themselves, accept and hear the complaints of workers and staff members on labour insurance matters, draw up a monthly statement of the receipts and payments of labour insurance funds and regulating funds every month, work out budgets, final accounts, business plans and business reports every year and submit them in the following procedure:

(1) Each provincial or municipal trade union organization shall submit the above to the labour administrative authorities of the local people's government and the trade union organization of the large administrative region.

(2) The national committee of each industrial trade union shall submit the above to the All-China Federation of Trade Unions and the Ministry of Labour of the Central People's Government.

Article 29 The trade union organization of each large administrative region shall hold itself responsible for directing and supervising the labour insurance transactions of each provincial or municipal trade union organization under it and each industrial trade union organization within its region, check the provincial and municipal trade union organizations' monthly statements of the receipts and payments of labour insurance funds and regulating funds, budgets, final accounts, business plans and business reports, draw up a report of the receipts and payments of labour insurance funds every three months, work out budgets, final accounts, business plans and business reports every year and submit them to the department of labour of the people's government of the large administrative region where it is located, the Ministry of Labour of the Central People's Government and the All-China Federation of Trade Unions.

Article 30 The All-China Federation of Trade Unions is the supreme leading body of the national labour insurance business which plans the execution of the national labour insurance business in an overall way; supervises and guides each local trade union organization and each industrial trade union organization in the execution of labour insurance business; checks and compiles the report forms of the receipts and payments of labour insurance funds and general funds; works out the budgets and final accounts of labour insurance funds, business plans and business reports every year and submits them to the Ministry of Labour and the Ministry of Finance of the Central People's Government for future reference.

Article 31 The labour administrative authorities of the people's government at each level shall supervise the payment of labour insurance funds, inspect the execution of labour insurance business and handle the complaints on labour insurance matters.

Article 32 The Ministry of Labour of the Central People's Government is the supreme supervisory body of the national labour insurance business which puts the Regulations on Labour Insurance into effect and inspects the execution of the national labour insurance business, the regulations for the inspection of which shall be otherwise formulated.

Chapter VII Supplementary Provisions

Article 33 These Regulations shall be promulgated and put into effect after adoption by the Government Administration Council of the Central People's Government and the same procedure shall be followed if any amendments are made.

Article 34 These Regulations shall be put into effect as of March 1, 1951 and the labour insurance payments payable to deserving workers and staff members in accordance with these Regulations shall be paid as of May 1,1951. In the case of an enterprise which practises labour insurance in accordance with these Regulations, its original procedures for labour insurance shall be annulled as of May 1, 1951. However, if the workers and staff members of the enterprise consider the totals of various kinds of remuneration stipulated in the original procedures to be more than those in these Regulations and are unwilling to change them, the administration or capital of the enterprise shall make an application jointly with the grass-roots trade union committee to the labour administrative authorities of the local people's government and shall be entitled to maintain the original procedures and postpone implementing these Regulations with the approval of the Ministry of Labour of the Central People's Government.

REVISED DRAFT OF THE RULES FOR THE IMPLEMENTATION OF THE REGULATIONS OF THE PEOPLE'S REPUBLIC OF CHINA ON LABOUR INSURANCE

(Promulgated by the Ministry of Labour on January 26,1953)

Chapter I Provisions for the Limits of Implementation

Article 1 The provision for "more than 100 workers and staff members" in Clause A of Article 2 in the Regulations of the People's Republic of China on Labour Insurance (hereinafter simply referred to as "the Regulations on Labour Insurance") refers to the number of workers and staff members in a factory or a mine itself, excluding the numbers of personnel in its business management organization and subsidiary units. In the calculation of the number of persons, the personnel under the wage and supply systems, apprentices, casual labourers (excluding temporary builders and porters) and personnel on probation shall be included.

Article 2 In an enterprise which practises labour insurance, its business management organization and subsidiary units shall implement the Regulations on Labour Insurance simultaneously with the enterprise. "The business management organization" means the one with all its outlays paid out of its business income or its capital construction costs or its operating expenses. "The subsidiary units" refers to the organizations in relations to business and staff and workers' culture, education, welfare, etc. which are attached to the enterprise.

Article 3 The wages during childbearing leave or sick leave or injury leave or the funeral expenses for those who die while on duty shall be paid by the unit which pays the wages to the workers and staff members who work in a subsidiary unit of an enterprise which practises labour insurance and to the working personnel of trade unions if their wages are not directly paid by the administration or the capital of the enterprise; the wage-paying unit shall pay labour insurance premiums at three per cent of the total of the wages of the workers and staff members in the unit (the labour insurance premiums shall be exempted from payment with regard to the members of the grass-roots trade union committee who originally worked in the enterprise and have been released from production) and hand them over to the administration or capital of the enterprise for the payment in one lump sum. The medical expenses for workers, staff members and trade union working personnel during medical treatment shall be borne by the administration or capital of the enterprise as stipulated in the Regulations on Labour Insurance.

Article 4 The personnel within the supply system in an enterprise which practises labour insurance shall still be dealt with in accordance with the provisions in the supply system and the Regulations on Labour Insurance shall not be applicable to them. If the armed guards of an industrial or mining enterprise are servicemen within the establishment of the People's Liberation Army, they shall still enjoy various kinds of remuneration of the PLA and the Regulations on Labour Insurance shall not be applicable to them.

Article 5 When an enterprise which does not implement the Regulations on Labour Insurance is to enter into a collective contract for labour insurance, it shall consult and execute the contract in the spirit of the Regulations on Labour Insurance and in accordance with the actual conditions of the enterprise, the industry or the trade, submit it to the local labour administrative authorities where it is located for approval and put it into effect. Various labour insurance expenses stipulated in the collective contract shall be borne by the administration or capital of the enterprise.

Chapter II Provisions for the Total Amount of Wages

Article 6 When an enterprise which practises labour insurance pays labour insurance premiums as stipulated in Article 8 of the Regulations on Labour Insurance, the calculation of the total of wages shall be handled in accordance with the "Provisions for the Composition of the Total Amount of Wages" of the Financial and Economic Commission of the Government Administration Council of the Central People's Government.

Chapter III Provsions for the Calculating Standards of Labour Insurance Remuneration

Article 7 When a worker or a staff member

whose wages are calculated by the day or by the month enjoys labour insurance remuneration, the wages obtained by him or her per day or per month shall be regarded as the calculating standard if the remuneration is calculated according to his or her wages.

Article 8 When a worker or a staff member whose wages are calculated by piece work enjoys labour insurance remuneration, his or her daily average wages in the last three months shall be regarded as the calculating standard if the remuneration is calculated according to his or her wages. If all his or her working time is less than three months, the daily average wages of his or her actual working days shall be regarded as the calculating standard. But if the period of sick or injury leave is less than seven days, the daily average wages of the last month shall be regarded as the calculating standard.

Article 9 When a worker or a staff member who receives subsidies for disability caused on duty resigns from office or dies, the wages obtained shall be calculated together with the subsidies for the disability caused on duty with regard to his or her wages for calculating the remuneration if the pension, relief fund or subsidy with his or her wages as the calculating standard is received under the labour insurance funds.

Article 10 If the wages of an apprentice whose wages are lower than the minimum of an ordinary worker of the enterprise are used to calculate his or her labour insurance damages, they shall be calculated in accordance with the minimum wages of an ordinary worker of the enterprise, but the labour insurance damages he or she obtains shall not be more than his or her own wages.

Chapter IV Provisions for Remuneration for Injury, Disability or Death Caused on Duty

Article 11 A worker or a staff member shall enjoy remuneration for injury, disability or death caused while on duty if he or she is wounded, disabled or dies under the following conditions:

1. In the execution of routine duties or in the execution of a job provisionally assigned or consented by the administration or capital of the enterprise;

2. Engaged in work which is advantageous to the enterprise in an emergency even without the assignment of the administration or capital of the enterprise;

3. Engaged in invention or technological improvement.

With regard to determining whether the accident is caused on duty, the trade union group shall report as things really are to the labour insurance commission of the grass-roots trade union committee (hereinafter simply referred to as the "labour insurance commission") for examination and determination and ask the grass-roots trade union committee to notify the administration or capital of the enterprise and the worker or staff member himself or herself or the directly related family members supported by him or her. If there is any objection, it shall be submitted to the labour administrative authorities of the local people's government for prompt handling. But before handling, the notice of the grass-roots trade union committee shall be followed.

Article 12 The disability examination committee stipulated in Clause C of Article 12 in the Regulations on Labour Insurance shall be set up under the leadership of the city trade union organization or the local organization of an industrial trade union. The persons selected into the committee shall be composed of three to seven deputies of the above trade union organization, the labour administrative authorities and the public health administrative authorities with the deputy of the city trade union organization or the local organization of the industrial trade union as the convener and the representative(s) of the labour insurance commission of the enterprise which the disabled worker or staff member belongs to and the doctor in charge shall be entitled to attend meetings but does not vote. No disability examination board shall be organized in a place with a very few enterprises implementing the Regulations on Labour Insurance and the labour insurance commission of the enterprise shall exercise its functions and powers on its behalf. The functions and powers of a disability examination board are as follows:

1. To determine the condition of disability of a disabled worker or staff member;

2. To make an examination of the disabled's condition of disability every six months so as to determine whether the condition of disability has changed, but to examine the state of disability at any time on the disabled's request.

Article 13 The subsidies for the disability caused on duty which are receivable as stipulated in Item 3, Clause B, Article 12 of the Regulations on Labour Insurance shall be paid according to the reduced sums of the wages after the disability to a worker or a staff member who has partially lost his or her ability to work because he or she is maimed on duty but is still able to work; the subsidies for the disability caused on duty shall be 10 per cent of his or her wages before the disability if the wages are reduced by 11 to 20 per cent; they shall be 20 per cent of his or her wages before the disability if the wages are reduced by 21 to 30 per cent; the subsidies shall all be 30 per cent of his or her wages before the disability if the wages are reduced by more than 30 per cent.

Article 14 The expenses for an artificial hand or leg fixed for a worker or a staff member who is wounded on duty, or for an artificial tooth inserted or for an artificial eye refitted shall be wholly borne by the administration or capital of the enterprise after the conclusion of his or her medical treatment at the clinic or hospital of the enterprise or at a special hospital or by a special Chinese medical practitioner or a special Western doctor or at the hospital to which he or she was transferred.

Article 15 If a worker or a staff member who continues to work after partially losing his or her ability to work because he or she is maimed on duty is maimed a second time while off duty and is still able to work, he or she shall continue to receive the subsidies for the disability caused on duty which are receivable as stipulated in Item 3, Clause B, Article 12 of the Regulations on Labour Insurance. If he or she is unable to work and has to resign from office because he or she has completely lost his or her ability to work for being maimed a second time while off duty, the remuneration shall be handled as stipulated in Clause C of Article 13 of the Regulations on Labour Insurance.

Chapter V The Provisions for the Remuneration for Diseases Contracted, Injury Sustained while Off Duty or Disability Caused while Off Duty

Article 16 If a worker or a staff member stops working and is under medical treatment for less than six months due to a disease contracted or injury sustained while off-duty, the administration or capital of the enterprise shall pay him or her the wages during sick or injury leave in accordance with the following standards as stipulated in Clause B of Article 13 of the Regulations on Labour Insurance: 60 per cent of his or her wages if he or she has worked in the enterprise for less than two years; 70 per cent of his or her wages if he or she has worked there between two and four years; 80 per cent of his or her wages if he or she has worked there between four and six years; 90 per cent of his or her wages if he or she has worked between six and eight years; 100 per cent of his or her wages if he or she has worked for eight or more than eight years.

Article 17 If a worker or a staff member stops working and is under medical treatment for more than six months due to a disease contracted or injury sustained while off duty, his or her wages shall be suspended during sick or injury leave as stipulated in Clause B of Article 13 of the Regulations on Labour Insurance and the relief funds for a disease contracted or injury sustained while off duty shall be paid him or her by the month instead under the labour insurance funds at the following standards: 40 per cent of his or her wages if he or she has worked in the enterprise for less than one year; 50 per cent of his or her wages if he or she has worked there between one and three years; 60 per cent of his or her wages if he or she has worked there for three or more than three years. These relief funds shall be paid until he or she is able to work or determined to be disabled or dies.

Article 18 If the wages of a worker or a staff member are lower than the average ones of the enterprise, the relief funds shall be paid at 40 per cent of the average funds if the sums of the relief funds he or she obtains are lower then 40 per cent of the average wages of the enterprise when he or she receives the relief funds for a disease contracted or injury sustained while off duty, but they shall not be higher than his or her wages.

Article 19 If a worker or a staff member has completely lost his ability to work due to the disability caused on duty and resigns his office, or resigns his or her office to live in retirement, he or she shall continue to enjoy medical treatment for the disease(s) until he or she dies as stipulated in Clause A of Article 13 of the Regulations on Labour Insurance.

Article 20 After a worker or a staff member has been determined to be disabled, completely lost his or her ability to work and resigned his or her office when the medical treatment of the disease contracted or the injury sustained while off duty has been concluded, he or she shall stop enjoying all other labour insurance damages but shall receive the relief funds for the disability sustained while off-duty, the funeral subidies when he or she dies and the relief funds to support his or her directly-related family members.

Article 21 If a worker or a staff member has to stop working for medical treatment due to a disease contracted or injury sustained while off duty, he or she shall have the certificate put forward by the medical organization in charge or be certified by the head of the trade union group or the group labour insurance officer in charge if he or she cannot obtain the above certificate before enjoying labour insurance remuneration. When he or she returns to work after recovery, he or she shall obtain the certificate of the medical organization in charge to prove he or she is able to work.

Chapter VI Provisions for the Remuneration for Death

Article 22 When a worker or a staff member dies while on duty or dies after resigning his or her job due to the disability caused on duty, the administration or capital of the enterprise shall pay three months' average wages of the enterprise as funeral expenses as stipulated in Clause A of Article 14 of the Regulations on Labour Insurance and pay pensions monthly to support the directly-related family members of the deceased under the labour insurance funds in accordance with the following provisions: 20 per cent of the deceased's wages for supporting one directly-related family member; 40 per cent of the deceased's wages for supporting two persons; 50 per cent of the deceased's wages for supporting three or more than three persons. These pensions shall be paid until the supported lose(s) their (or his or her) qualifications for the support (see the qualifications for support in Chapter XI).

Article 23 When a worker or a staff member dies of a disease or from injury while off duty or when he or she dies after resigning to live in retirement or when he or she dies after completely losing his or her ability to work due to the disability caused while off duty and resigning his or her office, two months' average wages of the enterprise shall be paid under the labour insurance funds as funeral subsidies as stipulated in Clause B of Article 14 of the Regulations on Labour Insurance; in addition, the relief funds to support the directly-related family members of the deceased shall be paid at one go under the labour insurance funds in accordance with the following provisions: six months' wages of the deceased to support one directly-related family member; nine months' wages of the deceased to support two persons; 12 months' wages of the deceased to support three or more than three persons.

Article 24 When a worker or a staff member dies while on duty or has completely lost his or her ability to work due to the disability caused while on duty, the administration or capital shall employ any of his or her directly-related family member as fast as possible if he or she has the ability to work and the enterprise needs anyone to work; the son, daughter, younger brother or younger sister who is originally supported by him or her shall be entitled to be admitted into the schools run by the enterprise.

Article 25 When a directly-related family member is commonly supported by two or more than two members of the family who work in the enterprise(s) that practise(s) labour insurance the funeral subsidies shall be received by either of them and no double drawing shall be allowed.

Chapter VII Provisions for the Remuneration Provided for Old Age

Article 26 When a worker or a staff member lives in retirement, old-age pensions shall be paid by the month under the labour insurance funds: 50 per cent of his or her wages shall be paid if he or she has worked in the enterprise between five and 10 years; 60 per cent of his or her wages shall be paid if he or she has worked there between 10 and 15 years; 70 per cent of his or her wages shall be paid if he or she has worked there for 15 or more than 15 years. The payment shall be made until his or her death.

Article 27 If a worker or a staff member who conforms to the provisions for the remuneration to provide for old age in Article 15 of the Regulations on Labour Insurance is required by the enterprise to continue his or her work there, in-service old-age pensions shall be paid by the month under the labour insurance funds in addition to the usual payment of wages: 10 per cent of his or her wages shall be paid if he or she has worked in the enterprise between five and 10 years; 15 per cent of his or her wages shall be paid if he or she has worked there between 10 and 15 years; 20 per cent of his or her wages shall be paid if he or she has worked there for 15 or more than 15 years.

Article 28 When a worker or a staff member who draws in-service old-age pensions resigns his or her office to live in retirement, his or her in-service old-age pensions shall not be calculated in his or her wages.

Article 29 A worker or a staff member shall still be entitled to enjoy old age pensions as stipulated in Clauses C and D of Article 15 of the Regulations on Labour Insurance if the working time for him or her to be engaged in underground mining work or to work regularly at a place at low temperatures below 32°F or at high temperatures above 100°F amounts to 10 years or if the time for him or her to be directly engaged in the work which is harmful to health in relation to lead, mercury, beryllium, phosphorus or acids or in other chemical or ordinance industry amounts to eight years although at present he or she is not engaged in any of these jobs.

Article 30 The old-age pensions of a worker or a staff member shall be calculated in accordance with the average wages of the enterprise when he or she resigns his or her office to live in retirement if he or she is transferred to another post due to old age and weakness and his or her wages are reduced to less than the average ones of the enterprises after the enterprise practises labour insurance.

Chapter VIII Provisions for Childbearing Remuneration

Article 31 The maternity leave (whether normal labour or miscarriage) stipulated in Article 16 of the Regulations on Labour Insurance shall include Sundays and statutory holidays and no supplementary leave shall be allowed.

Article 32 If a female worker or a female staff member or the wife of a male worker or a male staff member gives birth to two or more children, the childbearing subsidies shall be paid according to the number of the children born, eight yuan per child.

Article 33 If a couple works together in one enterprise or separately in two enterprises which practise labour insurance, the childbearing subsidies shall be drawn by the wife and no double drawing shall be made by the husband.

Article 34 The maternity leave for a female worker or a female staff member who has a miscarriage after less than seven months' pregnancy shall be less than 30 days but more than 20 days.

Article 35 The midwifery expenses of a female worker or a female staff member in her childbearing shall be borne by the administration or capital of the enterprise if its clinic or hospital or its special hospital or special doctor cannot practise midwifery.

Chapter IX The Provisions for the Labour Insurance Remuneration to Casual Labourers, Seasonal Workers and Personnel on Probation

Article 36 The labour insurance remuneration to the casual labourers, seasonal workers and personnel on probation in an enterprise which practises labour insurance is temporarily provided for as follows:

1. Their remuneration during the medical treatment of the injury caused while on duty is the same as for that of general workers and staff members. If he or she has been determined to be disabled and has to resign his or her office due to the complete loss of his or her ability to work after the conclusion of the medical treatment of the injury caused on duty, the pensions for the disability caused on duty shall be paid in one lump sum under the labour insurance funds, the amount being 12 months' of his or her wages; one who has partially lost the ability to work but is still able to work shall be assigned by the administration or capital of the enterprise to another appropriate post.

2. The period for the medical treatment of his or her disease contracted or injury sustained while off duty shall be confined to three months and his or her medical remuneration shall be the same as that of general workers and staff members. During the period of stopping working for medical treatment for less than three months, the administration or capital of the enterprise shall pay him or her the wages during sick or injury leave by the month, the sums being 50 percent of his or her wages; if he or she does not recover at the expiration of three months, the relief funds for the disease contracted or the injury sustained while off duty at three months' of his or her wages shall be paid at one time under the labour insurance funds.

3. If any of them dies while on duty, the administration or capital of the enterprise shall pay funeral expenses, the amount being three months' average wages of the enterprise and pay the pensions to support his or her directly-related family member(s) in one lump sum payment under the labour insurance funds: six months' of his or her wages shall be given to support one

directly-related family member; nine months' wages shall be given to support two persons; 12 months' wages shall be given to support three or more persons.

4. If any of them dies of a disease or from injury while off-duty, funeral subsidies shall be paid under the labour insurance funds, the amount being two months' average wages of the enterprise; in addition, relief funds to support his or her directly-related family member(s) shall be paid in one lump sum payment under the labour insurance funds, the amount being three months' of his or her wages.

5. The remuneration of a female worker or a female staff member who is pregnant or who gives birth to a child shall be the same as that of general female workers and female staff members in respect of pregnancy examination expenses, midwifery charges, childbearing subsidies and period of childbearing leave; during her maternity leave, the administration or capital of the enterprise shall pay 60 per cent of her wages.

Article 37 The labour insurance remuneration shall still be paid in accordance with the original provisions to casual labourers, seasonal workers and personnel on probation if the standards originally stipulated by each enterprise or its subsidiary industry or trade before the promulgation of these Rules are higher than those stipulated in Article 36 of these Rules.

Chapter X Provisions for General Standing

Article 38 General standing means the working years when a worker or a staff member relies upon the income of wages as the whole or major source of his or her means of livelihood. In the calculation of the general standing, the working years in the enterprise shall be included.

Article 39 The standing in an enterprise shall be calculated as the composition of the successive working years of a worker or a staff member in the enterprise. If anyone once leaves the enterprise, the standing shall be calculated as from his or her last return to the enterprise. But any of the following cases shall be excepted:

1. If anyone is transferred to another post by the authorities in charge of the enterprise or by the administration or capital of the enterprise, his or her working years in the enterprise before and after the transfer shall be successively calculated. But there shall be real proof that he or she was transferred to anther post as required by business before the Liberation before his or her working hours can be successively calculated.

2. If there is real proof that a worker or a staff member who had worked in the enterprise returned after being forced to leave it before the Liberation, his or her working years before leaving the enterprise and after returning to it shall be calculated together as his or her standing in the enterprise with the approval of the labour insurance commission after the discussion and adoption of the trade union group.

3. If anyone is transferred and dispatched by the authorities in charge of the enterprise or by the administration or capital of the enterprise to study at home or abroad, his or her standing in the enterprise during the study and before and after the transfer and dispatch shall be successively calculated. If there is real proof that he or she was transferred and dispatched by the authorities in charge of the enterprise or by the administration or capital of the enterprise to study vocational skills at home or abroad before the Liberation, his or her standing in the enterprise before the transfer and dispatch and after returning to the enterprise shall be calculated together with the exception of the period of study which shall not be included in the standing.

4. If the workers and staff members of an enterprise are transferred to work in other enterprises by the authorities in charge of it because the enterprise stops production, ceases business or reduces production after the Liberation, their standing in the enterprise before and after the transfer shall be successively calculated. If the workers and staff members who are sent away return to work in an original enterprise when the enterprise reinstates production, resumes business or expands production, their standing in the enterprise before being sent away and after returning to work shall be calculated together.

5. If an enterprise is transferred, reorganized or merged, the standing in the enterprise of the original workers and staff members who still work in the enterprise before and after the transfer, reorganization or merger shall be successively calculated.

6. The period of stopping work for the medical treatment of an injury caused on duty shall all be calculated into the standing in the enterprise.

7. If the period of stopping work for the medical treatment of a disease contracted or an injury sustained while off duty is less than six months, it shall be successively calculated in the standing in the enterprise; if anyone returns to

work in the original enterprise after recovery if the period of stopping work is more than six months, his or her standing in the enterprise shall be calculated together except for the time in excess of six months.

8. If anyone was forced to leave the enterprise because of the opposition of the rule and oppression under the reactionary rule of the enemy and the puppet regime during the Japanese occupation or of the Kuomintang but continued to struggle even though he or she was put in jail by the enemy and the puppet regime or the Kuomintang government during his or her leave of the enterprise, his or her standing in the enterprise during the imprisonment, before leaving the enterprise and after returning to work there or being transferred to work in another enterprise shall be successively calculated.

Article 40 If one who is specially engaged in revolutionary work or a revolutionary military man is transferred to work in an enterprise, the number of years for him or her to participate in revolutionary work or the length of his military service shall be calculated in the standing in the enterprise.

Article 41 If a worker or a staff member held any of the following posts during the period under the reactionary rule of the enemy and the puppet regime or of the Kuomintang, his or her time when he or she held the post shall not be calculated in his or her standing:

1. The post at which he had committed oppressive and exploiting acts such as a labour contractor, in overseer, a factory guard, a mine guard, etc.

2. An officer or a man from the ranks in the army of the enemy and the puppet or Kuomintang army, an officer or a constable in its police force, an official in the enemy and the puppet or Kuomintang government organ, but the personnel in the former enterprise organizations shall be excluded.

3. A person above the rank of district branch committee member of the Kuomintang, element leader of the China Chingnientuan (the youth organization under the Kuomintang), district head office committee member of the Young China Party or district branch committee member of the Democratic Socialist Party or a major person in charge of a reactionary secret society.

Article 42 In the case of a person who is deprived of political rights, the period when he or she is deprived of political rights shall not be calculated in the standing. The standing on the enterprise of a person who is deprived of political rights because of counterrevolutionary crime(s) shall be calculated as from the restoration of his or her political rights; if a person is deprived of political rights because of other criminal offenses, his or her standing in the enterprise before the deprivation of political rights and after their restoration shall be calculated together.

Article 43 The provisions for the conversion of general standing and the standing in the enterprise in Clause C and D of Article 15 of the Regulations on Labour Insurance are also applicable to the calculation of various kinds of labour insurance remuneration.

Article 44 The period when an apprentice learns in the enterprise shall be calculated in the standing in the enterprise; when a casual labourer or a person on probation becomes a regular worker or staff member, his or her standing in the enterprise shall be calculated as from the date of his or her joining the enterprise.

Chapter XI Provisions for the Support of Directly-Related Family Members

Article 45 The directly-related family member(s) of a worker or a staff member who depend(s) on the worker or the staff member for the supply of their sources of income and conform(s) to any of the following shall be included in the directly-related family members so supported of the worker or staff member and enjoy labour insurance remuneration:

1. Grandfather, father or husband who has reached the age of 60 or who has completely lost his ability to work;

2. Grandmother, mother or wife who is not engaged in paid work;

3. Son or daughter (including adopted son or daughter, son or daughter left by the former wife or husband, illegitimate child) or younger brother or sister (including one with the same father but different mother or with the same mother but different father) who is below the age of 16;

4. Grandson or granddaughter who is below the age of 16, whose father is dead or has completely lost his ability to work and whose mother is not engaged in paid work.

Article 46 If a worker or a staff member has been brought up by other persons since his or her childhood, any of these persons shall be regarded as the directly-related family member so supported if a male one has reached the age of 60 or has completely lost his ability to work or a female one is not engaged in any paid work and if either of them is supported by the worker or staff member and lives together with the latter.

Article 47 After a worker or a staff member dies while on duty, his or her posthumous child shall be included in the directly-related family members so supported.

Article 48 If a directly-related family member supported by a worker or a staff member does not live at the same place with the latter, he or she shall obtain the certificate from the government organ at the place where he or she is residing to prove that he or she is really supported by the worker or staff member before being included in the supported directly-related family members.

Chapter XII Provisions for the Medical Organization

Article 49 An enterprise which practises labour insurance and is provided with any medical organization shall replenish the equipment and establish a perfect system according to the necessary and possible conditions; those without medical organizations shall solely or jointly set up clinics or hospitals; if they cannot be set up due to the limitation of conditions, they shall have special hospitals or special Chinese traditional medical practitioners or western-medicine doctors to take charge of sick and wounded workers and staff members. All expenses in relation to clinics, hospitals, special hospitals or special Chinese traditional medical practitioners or western-medicine doctors shall be borne by the administration or capital of every enterprise.

Chapter XIII Provisions for Sanatoriums, Sparetime Sanatoriums and Nurseries

Article 50 An enterprise which practises labour insurance shall, solely or jointly with other enterprises, set up a sanatorium, a sparetime sanatorium or a nutrition canteen according to the needs of its workers and staff members and economic conditions of the enterprise. The house facilities, the wages of working personnel and all regular expenses of the sanatorium, sparetime sanatorium or nutrition canteen shall be completely borne by the administration or capital of the enterprise. The recuperating or nourished persons shall be subsidized in respect of board expenses if there is surplus of labour insurance funds after the payment of various subsidies, relief funds and pensions, but the subsidies shall not be more than one half of the amount of the board expenses; if someone can not afford the board expenses due to physical weakness or real financial difficulty, his or her subsidies shall be increased as the administration or capital thinks fit, but they shall not be more than two thirds of the amount of the board expenses. The grass-roots trade union committee of each enterprise shall work out the budgets of board subsidies on schedule, submit them to the higher trade union organization in charge of regulating funds for approval and put them into effect.

Article 51 If the female workers and staff members together of an enterprise which practises labour insurance have more than a total of 20 children below the age of four,the grass-roots trade union committee shall consult with the administration or capital of the enterprise and, solely or jointly with other enterprises, set up a nursery (if it is not provided with conditions for setting up a nursery but has more than five breast-fed babies, it shall set up a nursing room). Its house facilities, the wages of working personnel and all regular expenses shall be completely borne by the administration or capital of the enterprise and the food and drink expenses for the children so nursed shall be borne by their parents; if their parents really have financial difficulties, the subsidies shall be given out of the labour insurance funds, but the subsidies to each child shall not be more than one third of the amount of food and drink expenses.

Chapter XIV Provisions for Outstanding Labour Insurance Remuneration

Article 52 If a worker or a staff member who enjoys preferential labour insurance remuneration in conformity with the provisions in Article 19 of the Regulations on Labour Insurance dies while on duty, the pensions for the directly-related family member(s) supported by him or her shall be paid by the month under the labour insurance remuneration in accordance with the following provisions: 30 per cent of the deceased's wages to support one directly-related family member of his or hers; 45 per cent of the deceased's wages for two persons; 60 per cent of the decreased's wages for three or more. These pensions shall be paid until the supported lose(s) the qualifications for the support.

Article 53 If a worker or a staff member enjoys preferential labour insurance remuneration in conformity with the provisions in Article 19 of the Regulations on Labour Insurance, retired old-age pensions shall be paid by the month: 60 per cent of his or her wage if he or she has worked in the enterprise between five and 10 years; 70 per cent of his or her wages if he or she has worked there between 10 and 15 years; 80 per cent of his or her wages if he or she has worked there for 15 or more years. These pensions shall be paid until his or her death. If a worker or a staff member who conforms to the provisions for living in retirement is required to continue to work in the enterprise according to the needs of the work, in-service old-age pensions shall be paid by the month under the labour insurance funds in addition to the usual payment of his or her wages: 20 per cent of his or her wages for one with the standing in the enterprise between five and 10 years; 25 per cent of his or her wages for one with the standing between 10 and 15 years; 30 per cent of his or her wages for one with the standing of 15 or more years. These pensions shall be paid until his or her retirement or until his or her death.

Chapter XV Provisions for the Formalities of the Application for and the Payment of Various Labour Insurance Payments

Article 54 For various pensions, subsidies and relief funds paid under the labour insurance funds, a worker, a staff member or a supported directly-related family member shall apply to the labour insurance commission for drawing in the procedure stipulated as follows:

1. At the beginning of the application, he or she shall fill in an application of his or her actual conditions and submit it together with supporting certificates if required to the trade union group officer in charge of labour insurance or the head of the union trade group who then calls a meeting of the group to discuss it, check if the items filled in are correct, write down the comments of the check in the column "Comments of Trade Union Group" and submit it to the labour insurance commission after signing and sealing.

2. Upon receipt of the application, the labour insurance commission shall check it against the labour insurance registry card and then the head of the commission (who shall call the labour insurance commission together to discuss it if necessary) shall annotate and approve of the labour insurance remuneration payable to the applicant in the application, fill in and sign a payment voucher and hand it over to the applicant together with the application for him or her to draw money at the labour insurance accounting office by them; if the money is drawn by the month, a drawing certificate shall be issued on the approval of the application. Afterwards, the head shall report on it at the regular meeting of the labour insurance commission.

3. According to the needs of the work, the labour insurance commission of the enterprise shall authorize the workshop labour insurance commission to examine and approve of the labour insurance remuneration to the workers and staff members in accordance with the provisions in the Regulations on Labour Insurance and the rules for their implementation.

4. After payment, the labour insurance accountant shall clearly write the amount and date of the payment in the application, sign and seal it and return it to the labour insurance commission for filing.

5. A worker or a staff member who needs a signature for the monthly drawing of the labour insurance remuneration shall send the drawing certificate to the head of the labour insurance commission for signing or sealing and for the issue of a payment voucher and then draw money at the labour insurance accounting office; if the worker or staff member or the supported directly-related family member is not in the locality of the enterprise, he or she shall apply to the labour insurance commission for the remittance by posting the drawing certificate together with the certificate made and signed by the government organ where he or she is located and the remittance fee and postage shall be paid under the labour insurance funds.

Article 55 If the pensions, subsidies and relief funds paid by the labour insurance commission are paid by the month, they shall be paid by the end of each month at the latest; if the payee does not live in the locality, the labour insurance commission shall pay them by the quarter (pay them once every three months). If they are paid in one lump sum, they shall be paid within five days of the approval at the latest.

Article 56 After the wages during sick or injury leave or childbearing leave and the funeral expenses for death while on duty directly paid by the administration or capital of the enterprise are paid each month, a list shall be drawn up in respect of the names of the payees, the standards of payment, the sums of payment, etc., according to the classification of expenses, and submitted to the labour insurance commission for future reference.

Article 57 Applications shall be made by the supported directly-related or other directly-related family members of the deceased for drawing the funeral expenses for death while on duty or the funeral subsidies for death while off-duty; if there is no family member as aforesaid or such a family member is not in the locality, the grass-roots trade union committee shall draw them on their behalf and take charge of the funeral matters.

Article 58 If an enterprise which practises labour insurance moves to another area, the pensions, subsidies and relief funds drawn by the month by the workers and staff members who cannot move along with the enterprise shall continue to be paid by the provincial or municipal trade union or by the national committee of the industrial trade union out of the regulating funds; the workers and staff members who have not recovered from diseases or injuries shall continue to be treated and the administration or capital of the enterprise shall continue to pay medical expenses and wages during medical treatment by remittance as stipulated in Clause A of Article 12 or Clauses A and B of Article 13 of the Regulations of Labour Insurance.

Article 59 If an enterprise which practises labour insurance ceases business, the pensions, subsidies and relief funds drawn monthly by its workers and staff members shall continue to be paid by the provincial or municipal trade union or by the national committee of the industrial trade union out of the regulating funds; if the workers and staff members have not recovered from diseases or injuries, the administration or capital of the enterprise and the grass-roots trade union committee shall consult with each other and deal with them at the time of ceasing business.

Article 60 If an enterprise which practises labour insurance is transferred, reorganized or merged, all its labour insurance business shall be continuously handled by the succeeding enterprise and various labour insurance payments which shall continue to be paid to the workers and staff members shall not be discontinued.

Article 61 If a worker or a staff member or a supported directly-related family member who draws pensions, subsidies or relief funds is deprived of political rights, the payment shall be immediately stopped; if his or her political rights are restored, he or she shall put forward a certificate and be entitled to continue to draw the payments with the approval of the labour insurance commission, but the labour insurance remuneration during the suspension shall not be paid retroactively.

Article 62 If a worker or a staff member who works in one enterprise that practises labour insurance is transferred by the authorities in charge of enterprises to work in another enterprise that also practises labour insurance, the labour insurance commission of the original enterprise shall send his or her labour insurance registry card and other relevant labour insurance documents to the enterprise to which he or she is transferred and the labour insurance commission of the new enterprise shall handle the registry upon the arrival of the worker or staff member who shall continue to enjoy the labour insurance remuneration. If he or she is ill, wounded, disabled or dies in the course of the transfer, the enterprise to which he or she is transferred shall handle the case in accordance with the provisions in the Regulations on Labour Insurance. As for a worker or a staff member who is transferred from one enterprise that has practised labour insurance to another one that is not practising insurance, the matters relating to his or her labour insurance remuneration shall be handled in accordance with the existing provisions of the unit from which he or she is transferred.

Article 63 If a worker or a staff member or a supported directly-related family member of his or hers has any objection to the administration or capital of the enterprise or to the labour insurance commission in respect of the decision, accounting and payment of labour insurance remuneration, he or she shall submit it to the higher trade union organization for handling or make a complaint to the labour administrative authorities of the local people's government.

Article 64 If a worker or a staff member or a supported directly-related family member who draws any kind of pensions, subsidies or relief funds has any change in his or her qualifications for drawing them or has lost the qualifications for drawing them, he or she shall promptly report to the labour insurance commission thereon and the commission shall publicly criticize him or her or suspend his or her right to enjoy various kinds of labour insurance remuneration for one to three months and demand the repayment of the sums drawn by means of concealment from the commission or making a false report if the concealment or the false report is discovered.

Article 65 If the standards for calculating the pensions, subsidies or relief funds drawn by the month change, the labour insurance commission shall make annotations and commentaries in the drawing certificate; if the categories change, the original drawing certificate shall be returned for cancellation and the applicant shall make another application for the new category.

Chapter XVI Provisions for the Care of the Receipt and Payment of Labour Insurance Funds

Article 66 The grass-roots trade union committees under the national committee of the railway, posts and telecommunications, ordnance industry or seamen trade union shall every month transfer the surplus of the labour insurance funds respectively into the account of the national committee of each industrial trade union for use as regulating funds; the grass-roots trade union committees under the national committee of an industrial trade union other than the above-mentioned shall every month transfer the surplus of the labour insurance funds into the account of their higher provincial or municipal trade union organization to which they are subordinate for use as regulating funds. If the textile, coal industry or any other industrial trade union is qualified for taking care of the regulating funds on its own, it shall do so upon the approval of the All-China Federation of Treade Unions.

Article 67 If the national committee of an industrial trade union which takes care of the regulating funds authorizes its local organizations to take care of the transfer and use of the regulating funds, it shall formulate detailed procedures according to the specific conditions of the industry and submit them to the All-China Federation of Trade Unions and the Ministry of Labour of the Central People's Government for record.

Article 68 The fines for late payment shall be transferred by the grass-roots trade union committee into the labour insurance funds and their purposes are the same as those of the labour insurance funds.

Article 69 The accounting department of each enterprise shall set up an independent set of books in accordance with the provisions in the accounting system of the labour insurance funds so as to make entries of the receipts and payments of the labour insurance funds. This work shall be handled by the accounting department of the enterprise which shall hold itself responsible to the labour insurance commission.

Article 70 When an enterprise begins to practise labour insurance, the grass-roots trade union committee shall report to the national committee of the industrial trade union or to the provincial or municipal trade union organization, work out the budget of the printing expenses of the labour insurance registry cards, submit them to the All-China Federation of Trade Unions for verification and approval and then pay them out of the labour insurance funds. With regard to the paper printing expenses of application forms and drawing cards required by a grass-roots trade union organization to handle labour insurance business, an application shall be made to the provincial or municipal trade union organization or the national committee of the industrial trade union which takes care of the regulating funds for verification and approval so as to pay them out of the regulating funds. The paper printing expenses of statistical forms, propaganda expenses, administrative expenses and other expenditures required by the trade union organization at each level shall be paid out of the operating expenses of the trade union. The wages of the accounting personnel in the accounting department of an enterprise who handle the labour insurance funds, vouchers, books, report forms and other regular expenses shall be borne by the administration or capital of the enterprise.

Chapter XVII Provisions for the Supervision and Examination of Labour Insurance Business

Article 71 The trade union organization of each large administrative region shall work out quarterly the report on the receipts and payments of the labour insurance funds which is submitted every three months to the labour administrative authorities of the large administrative region where it is located, the Ministry of Labour of the Central People's Government and the All-China Federation of Trade Unions; the first quarter of each year includes January, February and March, the second quarter includes April, May and June, the third quarter includes July, August and September and the fourth quarter includes October, November and December. If the report is made in the second or third month of a quarter, it shall handle it as stipulated in this Article and shall not draw up the report across quarters or years.

Article 72 The fund examination committee

shall be entitled to examine the accounts relating to the receipts and payments of the labour insurance funds and make suggestions upon finding any error and the accounting department of labour insurance commission of the enterprise shall promptly reply or correct it; if no reply or any improper handling has been made in excess of 10 days and if the error is made by the accounting department of the enterprise, the committee shall ask the administration or capital of the enterprise to handle it or ask the labour administrative authorities of the local people's government to investigate it when necessary; if the error is made by the labour insurance commission, the committee shall ask the grass-roots trade union committee or the higher trade union organization to handle it.

Article 73 If a worker or a staff member finds a doubt or an error in the receipts and payments of the labour insurance funds or in various labour insurance payments directly made by the administration or capital of the enterprise, he or she shall report to the grass-roots trade union committee on it for handling or report to the higher trade union organization or the labour administrative authorities of the local people's government for handling by bypassing the grass-roots trade union committee if the case is serious.

Article 74 The accounting department of each enterprise shall draw up the monthly report form by the month for the labour insurance payments directly made by the administration or capital of the enterprise and submit it to the grass-roots trade union committee for verification after the examination of the fund examination committee and transmission up to the provincial or municipal trade union organization or the national committee of the industrial trade union and to the labour administrative authorities of the local people's government. The monthly report form of the directly-made labour insurance payments shall be provided with the following items:

1. The wages during the medical treatment of an injury caused while on duty;
2. The wages during the medical treatment of diseases contracted and injuries sustained while off-duty;
3. The wages during maternity leave;
4. The funeral expenses for deaths occurring while on duty;
5. Medical expenses and medical funds:
6. Sanatorium outlays;
7. Sparetime sanatorium outlays;
8. Nutrition canteen outlays;
9. Nursery or nursing room outlays;
10. Miscellaneous expenses.

Article 75 The labour administrative authorities of the people's government at each level shall exercise supervision and examination over the labour insurance business of the administration or capital of each enterprise and the trade union organization at each level in the area under their jurisdiction as stipulated in Article 30 of the Regulations on Labour Insurance and be entitled to examine the implementation of labour insurance by each enterprise at any time and demand the submission of various books, report forms and other documents concerning labour insurance; if they find any violation of the Regulations on Labour Insurance, they shall put it right promptly or submit it to the higher labour administrative authorities for handling ot hand it over if necessary to the judicial authorities for handling according to law.

Chapter XVIII Supplementary Provisions

Article 76 In the case of an enterprise which conforms to the provisions in Article 2 of the Regulations on Labour Insurance, its grass-roots trade union committee and administration or capital shall apply jointly to the labour administrative authorities of the local provincial or municipal people's government for the implementation of labour insurance and the grass-roots trade union committee shall report in writing to the higher trade union organization after registration and approval for transmission level by level right up to the All-China Federation of Trade Unions for filing. However, the national committee of the railway, posts and telecommunications or ordnance industry trade union shall be entitled to apply jointly with the administration to the Ministry of Labour of the Central People's Government for the implementation of labour insurance and directly report in writing to the All-China Federation of Trade Unions for filing after registration and approval. Their subsidiary enterprises shall no longer apply to the local labour administrative authorities for registration.

Article 77 The labour administrative authorities of each provincial or municipal people's government shall report to the higher labour administrative authorities on the enterprises in their area which have been approved to practise labour insurance for transmission level by level right up to the Ministry of Labour of the Central People's Government for filing.

Article 78 The municipalities referred to as "provincial or municipal trade unions" in the Regulations on Labour Insurance Mean those directly under the Central People's Government, the Administrative Committee of a large administrative region and a provincial people's government.

Article 79 These Rules shall be promulgated and put into effect by the Ministry of Labour of the Central People's Government. If any matters remain unclear, the Ministry of Labour of the Central People's Government shall supplement or amend them at any time.

RESOLUTION OF THE GOVERNMENT ADMINISTRATION COUNCIL CONCERNING CERTAIN REVISIONS OF REGULATIONS ON LABOUR INSURANCE OF THE PEOPLE'S REPUBLIC OF CHINA

(Adopted by the 165th Government Administrative Meeting of the Government Administration Council on January 2, 1953)

Our Council promulgated the Regulations of the People's Republic of China on Labour Insurance and we have made some achievements and gained some experience in the implementation. They have been supported by the broad masses of workers and staff members and have played a positive role in moderating the difficulties in the livelihood of workers and staff members and encouraging their labour enthusiasm. But as the Regulations on Labour Insurance were formulated in the case that the state finance and economy had not been recovered in an all-round way, some remuneration has been prescribed too low and only the procedures for the trial implementation at key points can be adopted in respect of the limits of implementation. Now as our state financial and economic situations have taken an essential turn for the better and the large-scale economic construction is about to be spread out, it is only natural to properly enlarge the limits of the implementation of the Regulations on Labour Insurance and raise the standards of the remuneration as we think fit, but the present limits of the implementation of the Regulations shall not be excessively enlarged and the standards of remuneration shall not be raised too high because the struggle to resist U.S. aggression and aid Korea is still going on, large funds must be put into the economic construction and the state must first use the financial resources for major undertakings concerning the fundamental interests of the whole nation and meanwhile because the welfare of the working class and the whole people can only be gradually improved on the basis of the development of production. For this reason, our Council has made the following decisions:

1 With regard to the enlargement of the limits of the implementation, in addition to the railway, posts and telecommunications, shipping and the factories and mines with employment of more than 100 workers and staff members which have originally put them into implementation, now the limits of the following enterprises shall be enlarged:

(1) The capital construction units of factories, mines and communications undertakings;

(2) State-operated building corporations.

In general, the administration of a unit within the limits of the enlargement shall pay labour insurance funds as of January 1, 1953 and its workers and staff members shall enjoy various kinds of labour insurance remuneration stipulated in the Regulations on Labour Insurance as of March 1, 1953.

The administration of an enterprise within the limits of the enlargement shall work out the procedures for the implementation of the Regulations jointly with the grass-roots trade union organization, apply to local labour administrative authorities for examination and approval and then put them into effect. If an enterprise cannot implement them for the time being due to special difficulties, it shall postpone the implementation with the approval of the local labour administrative authorities.

2 With regard to the raising of the standards of labour insurance remuneration, the provision for the limitation of the time for the medical treatment by stopping work to six months shall be annulled and we shall properly raise the standards of the remuneration to workers and staff members during the medical treatment of their diseases, prescribe the appropriate subsidies for expensive medicinal expenses, increase old-age pensions, relax the requirements for old-age retirement and appropriately increase such other payments as childbearing allowance, funeral expenses, funeral subsidies, family member relief funds for deaths while off duty, etc. The above standards have been particularly stipulated in the amended Regulations on Labour Insurance. All the enterprises which have implemented the Regulations on Labour Insurance shall pay various labour insurance payments payable to workers and staff members in accordance with the new stipulations as of January 1, 1953.

3 The Ministry of Labour of the Central People's Government shall, jointly with the All-China Federation of Trade Unions, revise the draft rules for the implementation of the Regulations and other relevant decrees in accordance with the amended Regulations of the People's Republic of China as soon as possible and promulgate them.

THE PEOPLE'S INSURANCE COMPANY OF CHINA: OVERLAND TRANSPORTATION CARGO INSURANCE CLAUSES

(TRAIN, TRUCK)

I. Scope of Coverage

This insurance is classified into two conditions–Overland Transportation Risks and Overland Transportation All Risks. Where the goods insured hereunder sustain loss or damage, the Company shall undertake to indemnify therefor according to the Insured condition specified in the Policy and the provisions of these Clauses:

1. Overland Transportation Risks

This insurance covers:

1) Total or partial loss of or damage to the insured goods caused in the course of transportation by natural calamities–windstorm, lightning, earthquake, flood, etc. or by accidents–collision, overturning or derailment of the conveyance, including grounding, stranding, sinking or collision of the craft in case crafts are employed and/or collapse of tunnel, landslide, fire, explosion, etc.

2) Reasonable cost incurred by the Insured in salvaging the goods or averting or minimizing a loss recoverable under the Policy, provided that such cost shall not exceed the sum Insured of the consignment so saved.

2. Overland Transportation All Risks

Aside from the risks covered under the Overland Transportation Risks as above, this insurance also covers all risks of loss of or damage to the Insured goods whether partial or total, arising from external causes in the course of transit.

II. Exclusions

This insurance does not cover:

1. Loss or damage caused by the intentional act or fault of the Insured.

2. Loss or damage falling under the liability of the consignor.

3. Loss or damage arising from the quality or shortage of the insured goods prior to the commencement of this insurance.

4. Loss or damage arising from normal loss, inherent flaw or nature of the insured goods, loss of market and/or delay in transit and any expenses arising therefrom.

5. Risks and liabilities covered and excluded by the ocean marine cargo war risks clauses and strike, riot and civil commotion clauses of this Company.

III. Commencement and Termination of Coverage

Warehouse to warehouse clause:

This insurance commences from the time the goods hereby insured leave the warehouse or place of storage named in the Policy for the commencement of the transit and continues in force in the ordinary course of transit including incidental transit by craft until the insured goods are delivered to the Consignee's final warehouse or place of storage at the destination named in the Policy or to any other place used by the Insured for allocation or distribution of the goods. This insurance shall, however, be limited to sixty (60) days upon arrival of the insured goods at the final station of discharge before the insured goods reach the Consignee's warehouse.

IV. Duty of the Insured

It is the duty of the Insured to attend to all matters as specified hereunder, failing which the Company reserves the right to reject his claim for any loss if and when such failure prejudices the rights of the Company:

1. The Insured shall take delivery of the insured goods in good time upon their arrival at the port of destination named in the Policy. In the event of any damage to the goods, the Insured shall immediately apply for a survey to the Survey and/or Settling Agent stipulated in the Policy. If the insured goods are found to be missing entirely or partially or to show apparent traces of damage, the Insured shall obtain from the carrier, bailee or other relevant authorities a certificate of loss or damage and/or short delivery. Should the carrier, bailee or the other relevant authorities be responsible for such shortage or damage, the Insured shall lodge a claim with them in writing.

2. The Insured shall, and the Company may also, take reasonable measures immediately in salvaging the goods or in preventing or minimizing a loss or damage thereto.

3. The following documents should ac-

company any claim hereunder made against this Company:

Original Policy, Consignment Note, Invoice, Packing List, Weight Memo, Certificate of Loss or Damage and/or Short Delivery, Survey Report, Statement of Claim.

If any third party is involved, documents relating to pursuing of recovery from such party should also be included.

V. The Time of Validity of a Claim

The time of validity of a claim under this insurance shall not exceed a period of two years counting from the time of completion of discharge of the insured goods from the seagoing vessel at the final port of discharge.

DOMESTIC GOODS TRANSPORTATION INSURANCE CLAUSES OF THE PEOPLE'S INSURANCE COMPANY OF CHINA

Chapter I General Rules

Article 1 Domestic cargo transportation insurance is run for the purpose of compensating for the economic loss of goods caused by natural calamities and accidents in the course of transportation, strengthening the safety work and precautions against losses in goods transportation and promoting the economic accounting of enterprises.

Article 2 All enterprises of the people's ownership or those of collective ownership, state organizations, people's bodies, institutions, people's communes and individual citizens shall have the goods in transportation insured by the Company under the domestic goods transportation insurance as stipulated in these Clauses.

Chapter II Insurance Liability

Article 3 The Company shall be liable for the compensation for the losses of insured goods in transportation on account of the following causes:

1. Losses caused by fires, explosions, lightning and thunder, hail, storm winds, torrential rains, floods, tsunamis, earthquakes, cave-ins or landslides.
2. Losses caused by fires, explosions or collisions of the means of transport and losses caused by or reasonable expenses incurred for the unloading of the means of transport in perils.
3. Losses caused by accidents occurring in loading, unloading or transfer.
4. Losses, in cases of transport by vessel, caused by grounding, reef-striking, subsiding or sinking or the collapse of wharves and general average salvage expenses which shall be shared according to state decrees or general practice.
5. Losses caused by the overturning or derailment of vehicles, the collapse of tunnels or the skidding of men or animals when transported by train, motor vehicle, cart or carriage.
6. Losses, in cases of transport by airplane, caused by overturning, falling or disappearance of aircraft and jettisoning occurring in bad climate or in other perils or accidents.
7. Losses caused by theft or in chaos when any of the above-mentioned calamities or accidents happens.

Article 4 The Company shall be liable for the compensation of reasonable expenses incurred for the salvage or protection of insured goods when a calamity or an accident within the limits of the insurance liability happens.

Article 5 The insurance liability shall become effective as from the time of the departure of insured goods from the warehouse or storage at the place of dispatch and terminate at the time of their arrival at the warehouse of storage of the consignee at the destination. If they have not arrived at the warehouse or storage or the consignee, the longest validity of the liability shall be confined to 10 days of the unloading of the insured goods from the final means of transport.

Chapter III Exclusions

Article 6 The Company shall not be liable for the compensation for the losses of insured goods in transportation on account of the following causes:

1. War or military action.
2. Losses or expenses directly caused by the natural wear and tear of goods, drops in their prices or their intrinsic defects and by the delays of transportation.
3. Deliberate acts or faults of the Insured.
4. Other losses which are not within the limits of the insurance liability.

Article 7 The Company shall not be liable for the indemnity of the losses of insured goods directly caused by breakage, seepage, pilferage, failure to take delivery of goods, shortage or mixed packing without the consent and special agreement of the Company.

Chapter IV The Insured's Duties

Article 8 The Insured shall pay off the premiums in one payment as stipulated in the Company's rules and regulations of premium rates when the Company signs and issues the policy. Installments or payments may be arranged if there is a special agreement.

Article 9 In the case of the goods which shall be packed, the Insured shall ensure the conformity of their packages to the standards stipulated by the government departments concerned.

Article 10 The Insured shall observe various

rules and regulations formulated by the government departments concerned for safe transportation, the Company shall make an inspection of insured goods to guard against losses if necessary and the Insured shall provide the Company with assistance.

Article 11 When insured goods meet a calamity or an accident within the limits of the insurance liability, the Insured shall take necessary measures as far as possible to rescue or protect them so as to prevent or reduce losses and promptly inform the Company.

Chapter V Adjustment of Claims

Article 12 When the Insured applies to the Company for indemnity, he or she shall furnish the following documents:

1. The certificates of the determined causes of losses;
2. Insurance policy, bill of lading, or other waybill(s) and dispatch list(s);
3. Bills of the reasonable expenses incurred for the salvage or protection of the insured goods.

Upon receipt of the above application and documents, the Company shall promptly check and determine whether the indemnity shall be made in accordance with the limits of the insurance liability. The insured amount shall be promptly paid after agreement is reached with the Insured.

Article 13 If the loss of insured goods within the limits of the insurance liability shall be compensated for by a third party according to the provisions of law or relevant agreements, the Company shall compensate the Insured first in accordance with the relevant provisions in these Clauses. The Insured shall transfer the right to recover the damages to the Company and assist the Company in recovering the damages from the third party jointly.

Article 14 The remaining part of insured goods after loss shall be put into full use discounted and depreciated for the Insured and deducted from the amount of damages payable.

Article 15 The Insured shall be regarded as having waived his or her rights and interests of his or her own accord if he or she does not apply to the Company for indemnity or put forward necessary documents or certificates or claim the entitled damages within one year after the date of his or her knowledge of the loss of the insured goods.

Article 16 If any dispute occurs between the Insured and the Company, it shall be settled through consultation in the spirit of seeking truth from facts. If both parties cannot reach an agreement, it shall be submitted to the arbitration organization for arbitration or the court for handling.

THE PEOPLE'S INSURANCE COMPANY OF CHINA: HULL CLAUSES

With a view to meeting the requirements for the development of the shipping enterprise and according to the principle of equality and mutual benefit, this Company writes Hull Insurance, the Clauses being as follows:

1. Scope of Coverage

This insurance is classified into Total Loss Coverage (Time and Voyage) and Comprehensive Coverage (Time and Voyage). This Company shall undertake to indemnify the Insured for loss of or damage to the ship insured according to the risks involved and the provisions of these Clauses.

(1) Total Loss Coverage

This Company shall be liable for total loss of the insured ship caused by:

(a) Natural calamities and/or accidents;

(b) Latent defects in Hull and Machinery;

(c) Negligence by the Master, Crew, Pilots or ship repairers.

(2) Comprehensive Coverage

This Company shall be liable for total or partial loss of the insured ship caused by:

(a) Natural calamities and/or accidents;

(b) Latent defects in Hull and Machinery;

(c) Negligence by the Master, Crew, Pilots or ship repairers.

This Company shall further be liable for the following liabilities and expenses arising from the foregoing events:

(i) Contribution to General Average;

(ii) In case of collision, the indemnity assumed by the insured ship towards the loss to the other ship in collision and the goods aboard such other ship, as well as docks, wharves or other fixed structures, and delay to or loss of use of such other ship or fixed structures and salvage expenses incurred in connection therewith, but in no case shall the amount so indemnified exceed the insured amount of the insured ship;

(iii) Salvage expenses;

(iv) Expenses for pursuing recovery from third parties, reasonable expenses for ascertaining the loss or damage within the Scope of Coverage and the expenses for examining the ship's bottom after grounding.

Partial losses caused by the events in subsections (a) to (c) under section (2) hereinabove shall be subject to the deductible franchise stipulated in the Policy for each and every voyage (a voyage is a sailing from port of sailing to port of destination).

Ships may be insured for Total Loss Coverage or Comprehensive Coverage on application and may also be insured against additional risks upon consultation.

2. Exclusions

This Company shall not be liable for:

(1) Loss or damage caused by unseaworthiness of the insured ship;

(2) Loss or damage caused by the negligence of the Shipowner and his representative and by the intentional act of the Shipowner and his representative and Master;

(3) Maintenance repairs to the Hull and Machinery of the insured ship, expenses for painting, wear and tear and corrosion;

(4) Risks covered and excluded in the Hull War Risk Clauses of this Company;

(5) Demurrage of the insured ship and other indirect expenses;

(6) Expenses for removal or disposal of obstructions.

3. Trading Limit

The prior agreement of this Company shall be obtained in case the insured ship sails out of the trading limit stipulated in the Policy, and an additional premium may be charged by this Company when so required.

4. Period of Insurance

(1) Time Insurance

Longest duration is one year, the time of commencement and termination being subject to the stipulation in the Policy.

In the event that the insured ship is sold or transferred during the currency of insurance, the insurance shall become terminated forthwith unless such sale or transfer is agreed to by this Company in writing. Where the insured ship is sold or transferred in the course of a voyage, the insurance may be extended until the completion of such voyage.

(2) Voyage Insurance

To be subject to the voyage stipulated in the Policy. The time of commencement and termination to be dealt with according to the following provisions:

(a) With no cargo on board: To commence from the time of unmooring or weighing anchor at the port of sailing until the completion of casting anchor or mooring at the port of destination.

(b) With cargo on board: To commence from the time of loading at the port of sailing until the completion of discharge at the port of destination, but in no case shall a period of thirty days be exceeded, counting from midnight of the day of arrival of the ship at the port of destination.

5. Cancellation of Insurance and Return of Premium

(1) Time Insurance

(a) Where the insured ship is sold or transferred or the insurance thereon is cancelled during the currency of insurance, a premium to be calculated pro rata daily shall be returned to the Insured.

(b) Where the insured ship undergoes repairs while at a dock or shipyard or is laid up in port for a period exceeding thirty consecutive days, 50% (fifty percent) of the premium, to be calculated pro rara daily, for the period during which the insured ship is under repairs or laid up shall be returned to the Insured.

(2) Voyage Insurance

In no case shall the insurance be cancellable once it commences.

6. Treatment of Loss

(1) In the event of accidents to the insured ship which fall under the Scope of Coverage, the Insured shall notify this Company immediately and take all possible measures to minimize the loss to the insured ship. The prior consent of this Company shall be obtained before repairs are carried out. This Company shall be entitled to make deductions of unreasonable repairing costs and other expenses.

The Insured shall cause the insured ship to undergo periodic overhaul and repairs and be well kept, so as to keep her in good technical condition.

(2) Where the insured ship is in collision with other ships, the Insured shall obtain the prior agreement of this Company on the liability resting with both parties and the amount of recovery which he ascertains with the party concerned.

7. Claim and Subrogation of Rights

(1) In the case of a total loss of the insured ship, the full insured amount of the insured ship shall be indemnified.

(2) Where no news is received of the whereabouts of the insured ship over a period of six months after the date on which she is expected to arrive at the port of destination, it shall constitute an event of missing ship.

Where the insured ship is missing or it is estimated that the aggregate of the amount of loss to the ship, salvage expenses, cost of repairs and other necessary disbursements will exceed the insured value of the insured ship, it may be deemed a total loss, and the full insured amount of the insured ship shall be indemnified.

(3) In the case of a partial loss of the ship, this Company shall be liable for the reasonable costs of replacements and repairs.

(4) In the case of loss of or damage to the insured ship, should the insured amount be lower than the sound value of the ship, the contributions to the general average and the salvage expenses to be paid by this Company shall be calculated in the proportion that the insured amount bears to the sound value.

(5) In submitting his claims for loss, the Insured shall, in case third party liability is involved, subrogate the right of recovery from the third party and transfer the necessary documents to this Company.

8. Treatment of Disputes

All disputes arising between the Insured and this Company shall be settled by friendly negotiations on the principle of seeking truth from facts and of fairness and reasonableness. Where a settlement fails after negotiations and it is necessary to submit to arbitration or take legal actions, such arbitration or legal actions shall be carried out at the place where the defendant is domiciled.

HULL WAR RISK CLAUSES

1. Scope of Coverage

This Company shall be liable for loss of or damage to the insured ship, expenses and liabilities caused by:

(1) War, hostile acts or armed conflicts;

(2) Seizure, detainment, confiscation or blockade arising from the events in (1) hereinabove, but such claim shall be dealt with only upon expiration of six months from the day when such events arise;

(3) Conventional weapons of war, including mines, torpedoes or bombs.

2. Exclusions

This Company shall not be liable for loss of or damage to the insured ship caused by:

(1) Requisition, pre-emption, detainment or confiscation by the government of the country of which the Insured is a national;

(2) Atomic or hydrogen bombs or nuclear weapons of war.

3. Termination of Coverage

With respect to time insurance, this Company shall be entitled to issue to the Insured, at any time, notice of cancellation to terminate such war risk insurance upon expiration of fourteen days from the day on which such notice is issued.

Note: These Clauses are the clauses of an additional insurance to the Hull Clauses of this Company. In case of conflict between any clauses in these Clauses and the Hull Clauses, these Clauses shall prevail.

MARINE CARGO INSURANCE CLAUSES OF THE PEOPLE'S INSURANCE COMPANY OF CHINA

(Revised on January 1, 1981)

I Scope of Coverage

This insurance is classified into three categories, i.e., free of particular average (F.P.A.), with particular average (W.P.A. or W.A.) and all risks. When insured goods sustain a loss, this insurance shall be liable for indemnity as stipulated by the clauses of the cover category stated in the policy.

1. F.P.A. (free of particular average) shall cover:

(1) Total loss or "constructive" total loss of the whole lot of insured goods caused by such natural calamities as adverse climate, lightning and thunder, tsunamis, earthquakes, floods, etc. when in transport. When the Insured claims compensation for the constructive total loss, he or she shall entrust the Insurance Company with the goods sustaining losses and their title. If the insured goods are transported to or from a ship by the lighter, the goods so loaded on each lighter shall be taken as a whole lot.

Constructive total loss means that the actual loss of insured goods has been inevitable or that the expenses for reinstating or repairing the damaged goods and transporting them to the original destination cost more than the value of the goods received at the destination.

(2) Total or partial loss of goods caused by such accidents of the means of transport as grounding, reef-striking, sinking, collisions with icebergs or other objects, catching fire, explosions, etc.

(3) Partial loss of goods caused by such natural calamities as adverse climate, lightning and thunder, tsunamis, etc. on the high seas before or after the occurrence of an accident whereby the means of transport has been grounded, has struck a reef, sunk or has been burnt down.

(4) Total or partial loss caused by one package or several packages of goods being dropped into the sea while being handled or during transshipment.

(5) Reasonable expenses incurred by the Insured for measures taken to rescue, prevent or reduce the loss of goods in cases of the goods sustaining a risk within the liability coverage, such expenses in no case to exceed the insured amount of the rescued goods.

(6) Losses caused by the unloading of goods at a port of refuge after the means of transport meets with a peril of the sea and special expenses incurred in the unloading, warehousing and are transport of the goods at a midway port or at a port of refuge.

(7) Sacrificial, shared and salvage expenses of general average.

(8) If the clause "Ships' Collision Liability" is stipulated in the transport contract, the owner of the goods shall compensate for the losses of the ship as stipulated by the clause.

2 W.P.A. (with particular average):

In addition to the coverage of items of liability of F.P.A. listed above, this insurance shall cover the partial loss of insured goods caused by such natural calamities as bad climate, lightning and thunder, tsunamis, earthquake, floods, etc.

3 All Risks:

In addition to the coverage of items of liability of F.P.A and W.P.A. listed above, this insurance shall cover the total or partial loss of insured goods due to external causes in transport.

II Exclusions

This insurance shall not be liable for compensation of the following losses:

(1) Losses caused by deliberate acts or faults of the Insured.

(2) Losses caused by the liability of the shipper.

(3) Losses caused by intrinsic bad quality or short quantities of insured goods before the commencement of the insurance liability.

(4) Losses and expenses caused by the natural wear and tear, intrinsic defects or properties, drop of prices, delays of transportation of insured goods.

(5) The scope of coverage and exclusions stipulated in the Marine Cargo War Risk Clauses and the Cargo Transportation Strike Risk Clauses of the Company.

III Commencement and Termination of Coverage

1. This insurance shall provide coverage

"from warehouse to warehouse," and becomes effective at the beginning of the transportation of insured goods from the warehouse or storage at the place of dispatch indicated in the policy, including the transport, by sea, land, inland river and lighter in the course of normal transport, and terminating at the arrival of the goods at the final warehouse or storage of the consignee at the destination indicated in the policy or at the other storage point used by the Insured for distribution, assignment or abnormal transportation. If the insured goods have not arrived at the above-mentioned warehouse or storage, the coverage shall terminate 60 days after the goods are completely unloaded from the ship at the final port of unloading. If the insured goods are transshipped to a destination other than that indicated in the policy within the above-mentioned 60 days, the coveraege shall terminate at the beginning of the transshipment of the goods.

2 This insurance shall remain valid so long as the Insured has duly notified the Insurer of the appraised situation and paid additional premiums when necessary if the insured goods are transported to a destination other than that indicated in the policy due to transport, delay, detours, forced unloading, reloading or transshipment beyond the control of the Insured or because of any alteration in the navigation or the termination of the transport contract made by the carrier with the authority conferred under the said contract. Coverage shall terminate in accordance with the following provisions:

(1) If the insured goods are sold at a destination other than that indicated in the policy, the coverage shall terminate at the time of delivery, but it shall terminate 60 days after the complete unloading of the insured goods from a ship at the port of unloading, regardless of any conditions.

(2) The coverage shall still terminate as stipulated in the above clause 1 if the insured goods continue to be transported to the original destination indicated in the policy or to other destination(s) within the above-mentioned period of 60 days.

IV The Duties of the Insured

The Insured shall handle relevant matters in accordance with the duties stipulated as follows and the Company shall refuse to compensate for any losses if the Insured has not fulfilled the following duties, affecting the interests of the Insurer:

1 After the arrival of the insured goods at the port (place) of destination indicated in the policy, the Insured shall duly take delivery of them. If he or she finds any loss sustained in the insured goods, he or she shall promptly apply to the surveyor or adjuster indicated in the policy for inspection. If he or she finds shortage in the whole packages of the insured goods or evident traces of damage to them, he or she shall promptly ask the carrier, consignee or the authorities concerned (Customs, port authorities, etc.) for a certificate of damage to or shortage of goods. If the Insured finds the carrier or consignee or any other party is responsible for the loss or shortage so found, he or she shall lodge a claim thereby in writing and if necessary obtain a certificate for extension of claims.

2 With regard to the goods sustaining a risk under the coverage, the Insured and the Company shall promptly take reasonable rescue measures so as to prevent or reduce the loss or damage of the goods. If the Insured takes these measures, he or she shall not be regarded as having waived the entrustment, while if the Company takes the measures, it shall not be regarded as being obliged for acceptance of the entrustment as well.

3 This insurance shall remain valid only if the Insured notifies the Insurer of the change of the voyage or any omissions or errors found with regard to the goods, name of ship or voyage indicated in the policy upon discovery and pays additional premiums if necessary.

4 The Insured shall furnish the following documents when he or she claims compensation from the Insurer:

The original copy of the policy, bill of lading, invoice, packing list, weight list, damage and shortage certificate, surveyor's report and claims list. If third party liability is involved, he or she shall also furnish the letters and cables concerning the recovery of the damages from the responsible party and other necessary documents or papers.

5 The Insured shall duly notify the Insurer after he or she discovers the actual liability concerning the clause "Ships' Collision Liability" in the transport contract.

V Time Limit for Filing Claims

The prescription for filing claims for this insurance shall be calculated from the complete unloading of the insured goods from a ship at the final port of unloading within two years.

MARINE CARGO WAR RISK CLAUSES OF THE PEOPLE'S INSURANCE COMPANY OF CHINA

(Revised January 1, 1981)

I. Scope of Coverage

This insurance shall cover:

(1) Losses directly caused by war, quasi-war manoeuvres, hostile acts, armed conflicts or piracies.

(2) Losses caused by capture, seizure, detention,, prohibition or restraint resulting from the above clause (1).

(3) Losses caused by use of various conventional weapons, including mines, torpedoes and bombs.

(4) Sacrifice, shared and salvage expenses of general average resulting within the scope of coverage of these clauses.

II. Exclusions

This insurance shall not cover the following:

(1) Losses and expenses caused by those weapons made with atoms or thermal nuclei as a result of hostile acts.

(2) Any claims put in for the loss or setback of cover voyages caused by the restraint or seizure of the ruling persons, persons in power or other armed groups.

III. Commencement and Termination of Coverage

1 This insurance liability shall commence at the time when the insured goods are loaded on board a ship or lighters at the port of dispatch indicated in the policy and terminate at the time of their unloading from the ship or lighters at the port of destination indicated in the policy. If the insured goods are not unloaded from the ship or lighters, the length of the validity of this insurance liability shall be 15 days from the midnight of the date of the ship's arrival at the port of destination. The ship's arrival at the port of destination means that the ship casts anchor, is berthed or moored at a berth or place in the port area or that the ship casts anchor, is berthed or moored for the first time in the original port or place of unloading or its nearest place if there is no such berth or place.

2 If the goods are transshipped in a midway port, the insurance liability shall be suspended 15 days from the midnight of the date of the ship's arrival at the port or the place of unloading and resumed at the time of their loading on board the ship to carry them on.

3 If the transport contract terminates at a place other than the destination indicated in the policy, the place shall be taken as the destination of this insurance and the liability shall terminate as stipulated in above clause (1). If the goods are to be transported to the original destination or another one, the Insured shall notify the Insurer before the continuation of the shipment and pay additional premiums so that the liability shall become effective again from the time when the goods are loaded on board the ship or on lighters to carry them on.

4 This insurance shall remain valid so long as the Insured duly notifies the Insurer of the situation appraised and pays additional premiums if necessary or if a detour or a change of voyage occurs in the transportation or if the carrier makes any change in the navigation by means of the authority conferred under the transport contract.

THE PEOPLE'S INSURANCE COMPANY OF CHINA: MOTOR VEHICLE INSURANCE CLAUSES

(January, 1982)

1. Scope of Coverage

This insurance is classified into Loss or Damage Coverage and Third Party Liability Coverage. The Company shall undertake to indemnify the Insured according to the risks insured and the provisions of the Clauses.

(1) Loss or Damage Covarage

The Company shall be liable for loss of or damage to the insured car including its accessories, spare parts and equipment thereon as arising from the following causes:

(a) Thunder and lightning, flood, earthquake, avalanche, collision, over-turning, fire, explosion, self-ignition, loss and robbery;

(b) Accidents involving a ferryboat whilst maneuvering on condition that the driver of the insured vehicle is on the ferryboat in attendance.

(2) Third Party Liability Coverage

The Company shall indemnify the Insured in the event of accident caused by or arising out of the use of the insured vehicle by the Insured, his employed driver or other person who is driving with his permission against all sums including claimants' legal costs which the Insured shall become legally liable to pay in respect of:

(a) Motor Vehicles for Official Use

Death of or bodily injury to any person other than the Insured's driver and employees; damage to property other than property belonging to the Insured, the Insured's driver and employees or as held in trust by them;

(b) Motor Vehicles for Private Use

Death of or bodily injury to any person other than the Insured, any member of the Insured's household or the Insured's driver and employees; damage to property other than property belonging to the Insured, any member of the Insured's household or the Insured's driver and employees or held in trust by them.

2. General Exclusions

The Company shall not be liable to indemnify the Insured for any loss or damage, expenses and/ or liability caused:

(1) By intentional act and engagement in illegal activities of the driver, the Insured or members of his family or his employees;

(2) Whilst the insured vehicle is being driven by someone without a license issued by the Chinese Public Security Department, or by one who is drunk or intoxicated or under the influence of drugs;

(3) Whilst the insured vehicle is being used for racing, speed testing, giving driving lessons or towing other vehicles;

(4) By war and military actions.

Further, the Company shall be not liable for:

(1) Wear and tear or corrosion of the insured vehicle;

(2) Any indirect loss sustained by the Insured arising from the loss of or damage to the insured vehicle;

(3) Loss or damage caused or aggravated by the use of the damaged vehicle before the necessary repairs are effected.

3. Treatment of Claim

(1) In the event of loss of or damage to the insured vehicle which falls under the Scope of Coverage, the Insured shall take reasonable measures in good time to minimize the loss and notify the Public Security Department and the Company immediately. The Insured shall also assist the Company to survey the damaged vehicle.

(2) When lodging a claim, the Insured shall submit in good time to the Company the Policy, a report on accident, a claim list, statements of account together with supporting vouchers and other necessary documentary evidence. In case third party liability is involved, the amount of indemnity shall be determined in accordance with the decision made by the Public Security Department. The time of validity of a claim shall not exceed a period of six months counting from the date of accident.

(3) When the insured vehicle has sustained loss or damage which falls within the Scope of Coverage, the Company shall pay the reasonable repair expenses but such amount of indemnity shall in no case exceed the insured amount indicated in the Policy. If the value of the vehicle is higher than the insured amount at the time of loss or damage, the difference shall be held as the self-insurance of the Insured who must bear due proportion of the loss or damage. If the value of the insured vehicle is below the insured amount at the time of total loss, the Company shall indemnify the Insured for the amount of its actual value.

(4) If the claim is settled on a total loss basis, the damaged vehicle shall be transferred to the Company, this Policy shall be surrendered and no return premium for the unexpired period shall be refunded to the Insured.

In case of loss of or damage to the insured vehicle recoverable under the Policy, for which any third party should be held responsible, the Insured shall subrogate his right of recovery against such third party to the Company upon settlement of the claim.

(5) Where the insured vehicle cannot run on its own power upon sustaining loss or damage recoverable under this Policy, the Company shall be liable for the expenses incurred for the transportation of the damaged vehicle to the repairing shop subject to a maximum of 20% of the repair expenses in respect of the above loss or damage. This does not apply to the motor vehicle if it is insured against the Third Party Liability Coverage only.

4. No-Claim Discount

In the event of no claim for loss of or damage to the insured vehicle being made during the year preceding the renewal of the Policy, a no-claim discount shall be allowed on the renewal premium for the Loss or Damage Coverage only.

5. Other Matters

(1) The Insured and his employed driver should consistently pay attention to the upkeep of the insured vehicle, make necessary maintenance from time to time to keep the insured vehicle in a constantly good state and safeguard it from loss or damage.

(2) The Policy may be cancelled either at the request of the Insured at any time or by the Company by giving the Insured a fifteen-day's previous notice. The premium for the period the Policy has been in force should be calculated on the short-period rates if the Insured requests the cancellation of the Policy.

(3) The Insured must have the utmost good faith at the time of applying for insurance and claiming for indemnity. If concealment, misrepresentation or fraud is discovered, the Company is entitled to be exempted from all the liabilities provided for in the Policy.

(4) All disputes between the Insured and the Company shall be settled through friendly negotiations. Where the contracting parties fail to arrive at a settlement after negotiations and it is necessary to submit to arbitration or take legal actions, such arbitration or legal actions shall be carried out at the place where the motor vehicle is insured.

DOMESTIC MOTOR VEHICLE INSURANCE CLAUSES OF THE PEOPLE'S INSURANCE COMPANY OF CHINA

(December, 1980)

Chapter I Insurance Liability

Article 1 This insurance is classified into vehicle loss insurance and third party liability insurance. The Insured shall have both of them insured or have either of them insured. The Insurer (namely, the insurance company, the same hereinafter mentioned) shall assume the insurance liability according to the category of the insurance coverage.

1. Vehicle Loss Insurance:

The Insurer shall undertake to compensate for the loss of an insured vehicle, including the accessories, spare parts and equipment with the vehicle, on account of the following causes in parking or driving:

(1) Collision or overturning;

(2) Catching fire, being struck by lightning, explosion, flood, earthquake, cave-in, landslide, tunnel collapse, drop of a flying object from the air;

(3) The whole vehicle lost by theft for more than three months;

(4) The ferry which is carrying the insured vehicle crossing the river meets with an accident, but the vehicle must be with a driver attending;

(5) Reasonable expenses incurred for the insured vehicle for the rescue or protection measures taken due to the above causes (1), (2) and (4) and conveying expenses to a repair shop because it cannot be set in motion after damage.

2. Third Party Liability Insurance:

If an accident occurring due to the Insured's or his or her driver's use of the insured vehicle causes the death or injury of a third party or damage to the property of the third party, the Insurer shall undertake to indemnify him or her for the economic indemnity liability which shall be assumed by the Insured according to law. But all consequential matters shall be dealt with by the Insured.

Article 2 The insurance validity is one year from the time of signing the policy to 12 o'clock at night of the date of expiration of insurance. The procedure shall be otherwise handled if the insurance is renewed at its expiration.

Chapter II Exclusions

Article 3 The Insurer shall not be liable for the loss, the expenses and the economic indemnity liability for a third party of an insured vehicle on account of the following causes:

(1) War or military action;

(2) Natural wear or erosion and the automatic puncture of tire(s);

(3) Deliberate acts of the Insured or his or her driver;

(4) Driving without licence or driving after consuming alcoholic drinks or under drug influence;

(5) Race, speed test, training or trailing another vehicle without an agreement in the insurance coverage;

(6) The enlarged part of loss due to the continuous use of the insured vehicle without necessary repair after damage;

(7) Loss caused by the cessation of business of the insured vehicle due to the loss of its running capacity;

(8) Other loss which is not within the limits of the insurance liability.

Article 4 The death or injury of any of the following personnel or the damage to his or her property caused by the accident of an insured vehicle shall not be taken as the third party liability and the Insurer shall not assume economic indemnity liability:

(1) A public motor vehicle: The death or injury of the Insured, his or her driver or worker or the damage to the property in their own possession or in their custody;

(2) A private motor vehicle: The death or injury of the Insured, his or her driver, family member or worker or the damage to the property in their own possession or in their custody.

Article 5 The Insurer shall not be liable for the death or injury of any passenger in or on the vehicle or the damage to the goods in or on it, including the articles consigned or carried by passenger(s) due to the accident of an insured vehicle, whether the economic indemnity liability shall be assumed by the Insured according to law or not.

Chapter III Amount of Insurance

Article 6 The insured amount of an insured vehicle shall be determined in accordance with the

Insured's book value or determined by the Insured and the Insurer through consultation.

Article 7 The Insured shall apply to the Insurer for the formalities of approval and revision if the insured amount shall be readjusted due to the transfer of the insured vehicle, the change of its uses or other causes during the insurance validity.

Chapter IV Duties of the Insured

Article 8 The Insured shall pay off the insurance premiums in one payment when signing the policy. Installment payments may be arranged if there is a special agreement.

Article 9 The Insured and his or her driver shall strictly observe traffic regulations, drive safely, keep maintenance and servicing well and make examinations and repairs on time so as to keep the insured vehicle in a roadworthy condition.

Article 10 If an insured vehicle sustains a loss within the limits of the insurance liability, the Insured shall take rescue and protection measures to prevent the enlargement of the loss, promptly report to public security, communications and other departments concerned and notify the Insurer.

Chapter V Safety Rewards for No Damages

Article 11 If no damages occur in respect of an insured vehicle within the period of insurance, 10 percent of the premiums originally paid shall be returned as the safety reward when the insurance is renewed. No such reward shall be given to the Insured who does not renew the insurance.

If the Insured has more than one vehicle insured, the safety rewards shall be calculated separately as per vehicle. But no safety rewards shall be given if the total amount of damage paid is more than 80 percent of all the premiums paid when the insurance is renewed.

Chapter VI Adjustments of Claims

Article 12 If an insured vehicle sustains a loss within the limits of the insurance liability and has to be repaired, the Insured shall first make an inspection jointly with the departments concerned, make clear the limits and items of repair, estimate the repair charges required and carry out the repair work after the decision through consultation with the Insurer.

Article 13 When the Insured puts in a claim, he or she shall provide the Insurer with the original of the policy, the proof of the determined cause of accident, the list of losses, the bill(s) of repair charges and other necessary documents. If the documents are not complete or the cause of the accident is unknown, the Insured shall refurnish it or them or fill the deficiency. The Insurer shall pay the damages within 15 days after the damages for vehicle less insurance have been decided through consultation or after those for third party liability insurance have been decided according to law.

Article 14 Regardless of the frequency of the occurrence of the loss within the limits of the insurance liability or the incurring of expenses or the economic indemnity liability for a third party in respect of an insured vehicle within the validity of the insurance, the Insurer shall compensate each and every time in accordance with the following provisions:

1. Vehicle Loss Insurance:

The Insurer shall compensate in accordance with the actual loss of an insured vehicle or the expenses actually paid, but the damages shall not be more than the insured amount within the limit. If the damages at one time are equal to the total of the insured amount, the policy shall become null and void automatically.

2. Third Pary Liability Insurance:

The Insurer shall compensate in one payment and conclude the case in accordance with the decided insured amount. The policy shall remain valid after the compensation until the expiration of the insurance.

Article 15 If the loss of an insured vehicle is caused by a third party and the third party shall be liable for the compensation according to law, the Insured shall claim compensation from the third party. If the responsibility of the accident cannot be determined for the time being, the Insurer shall compensate first. But the Insured shall transfer the right to recover the damages to the Insurer and demand the indemnity from the third party jointly with the Insurer. The damages recovered shall belong to the Insurer.

Article 16 With regard to the remaining part of an insured vehicle sustaining a loss, the Insurer and the Insured shall discuss and determine its value and depreciate it for the Insured and deduct the value from the amount of damages payable.

Article 17 The Insured shall be regarded as

having waived his or her rights and interests of his or her own accord and shall not claim indemnity from the Insurer afterwards if he or she does not claim compensation from the Insurer or put forward the documents required in Article 13 or draw the entitled damages within two years after the date of his or her knowledge of the loss or accident of the insured vehicle.

Article 18 If any dispute occurs between the Insured and the Insurer, they shall settle it through consultation in the spririt of practicability and being fair and reasonable. If both parties fail to reach an agreement, they shall submit it to the arbitration organization for arbitration or to the court for handling and the arbitration or legal costs shall be borne by the party who fails in his claim.

PROPERTY INSURANCE CLAUSES

1. The Insured Property

The property insured hereunder shall refer to all properties specified in the Policy and the Schedule attached hereto either owned by the Insured or held by him in trust or under joint account with others for which he is responsible.

2. Properties Insured by Special Agreement

Unless specially agreed upon between the Insured and the Company and stipulated in the Policy, gold, silver, pearls, diamonds, precious stones, postage stamps, ancient coins, antiques, articles of virtu, ancient books and paintings and work of fine art and computer systems records shall not be covered under the Policy.

Under no circumstances shall securities, bills, banknotes, documents, account books, drawings, guns and ammunition and explosives be covered hereunder.

3. Scope of Coverage

The Company shall be liable for loss of or damage to the insured properties caused by:

(1) Fire, thunder and lightning, explosions or bursting of water pipes;

(2) Storm, hurricane, typhoon, cyclone, flood, seaquake, hailstorm, rockslide, avalanche, earthquake, volcanic explosion, subsidence of ground and subterranean fire;

(3) Air crashes and parts or articles falling from aircraft.

4. Exclusions

The Company shall not be liable for:

(1) Loss of or damage to the insured properties caused by war, warlike operation, acts of hostilities, armed conflicts, confiscation, requisition, strike and riot;

(2) Loss of or damage to the insured properties caused by intentional acts or actual fault of the Insured and his representatives;

(3) Loss of or damage to the insured properties directly or indirectly arising from nuclear reaction, nuclear radiation or radioactive contamination;

(4) Loss of or damage to any electric equipment or apparatus due to overloading, overvoltage, electric line contact, arcing, leakage of electricity, short-circuiting, electricity discharged from the atmosphere and other electric phenomena;

(5) Loss of or damage to the insured property occasioned by its own fermentation, natural heating, spontaneous combustion or by its undergoing any heating or drying process;

(6) Loss or damage arising from the burning of the property by order of any public authority;

(7) Loss or damage caused by or arising from suspension of production or interruption of business and other indirect losses;

(8) Loss of or damage to the insured property caused by storms whilst it is stored in the open or under sheds made of reeds, cloth, straws, or asphalt felt;

(9) Other accidents or natural calamities not covered under Article 3 hereinabove.

5. Treatment of Claims

(1) In the event of any loss or damage which might give rise to a claim hereunder, the Insured shall notify the Company immediately and furnish detailed information about the loss or damage to the Company in writing.

(2) The Insured shall take all necessary measures to minimize loss or damage to the least extent and the Company shall pay for expenses reasonably incurred in this respect up to the sum insured of the items sustaining loss or damage.

(3) In lodging a claim, the Insured shall submit to the Company the Policy, a claim list and all other necessary documents. The time of validity of a claim shall not exceed a period of one year beginning from the date of loss.

(4) In case of a loss of or damage to the insured property falling within the scope of the Policy, the indemnity shall be based upon the market value of the property prevailing at the time of loss. In case the market value of the property so damaged is lower than the sum insured, the claim shall be settled on its market value. In case its market value is in excess of the sum insured hereunder, the difference shall be held as the self-insurance of the Insured and the Company shall be liable to pay only such proportion as the sum insured bears to the market value of the property so lost or damaged. If the property is insured severally in items, the provision of this clause shall be applicable to each of them.

(5) If the insured property sustains a partial loss, the Company may either effect a cash settlement based on the depreciation of the damaged

property, or alternatively pay for the repair costs for restoring the damaged property to the nearest condition existing immediately before the loss.

(6) If the claim for a loss to the insured property is settled on a total loss basis, the salvage value shall be deducted from the indemnity paid by the Company.

(7) When a claim has been settled, the sum insured shall be reduced by the amount so settled and an endorsement to this effect be issued by the Company but no return premium therefor shall be made.

(8) If at the time of any loss or damage to the insured property, there be any other subsisting insurance or insurances, whether effected by the Insured or by any other person or persons covering the same property, the Company shall not be liable to pay or contribute more than its ratable proportion of such loss or damage.

6. Other Matters

(1) The Insured shall take reasonable measures to avoid occurrence of accidents to the insured property and pay sufficient attention to and put into practice the justified recommendations for prevention of loss put forward by the representative of the Company.

(2) The Insured shall advise the Company in time in writing of any material change in the risks such as the removal of the insured property, dismantling, repairing and extending of the buildings, adjustment of sum insured, etc. and request the Company to endorse the Policy accordingly.

(3) This insurance may be either terminated at any time at the request of the Insured or cancelled at any time at the option of the Company by giving a 15-day prior notice to the Insured. In the former case, the Company shall retain a premium calculated on short period basis for the time the Policy has been in force and in the latter case such premium shall be calculated on pro-rata daily basis.

(4) All disputes under this insurance arising between the Insured and the Company shall be settled through friendly negotiation. Where a settlement fails after negotiation, such dispute shall be submitted to arbitration or to court for legal action. Unless otherwise agreed arbitration or legal action shall be carried out in the place where the defendant is domiciled.

ENTERPRISE PROPERTY INSURANCE CLAUSES OF THE PEOPLE'S INSURANCE COMPANY OF CHINA

(January 1, 1981)

Chapter I General Rules

Article 1 Enterprise property insurance is run in order to make economic compensation for the loss of enterprise property caused by natural calamities or accidents and strengthen the safety work on enterprise property to guard against calamities so as to contribute to the normal progress and economic accounting of enterprise production or work.

Article 2 All enterprises of the people's ownership or those of collective ownership shall have the coverage of enterprise property insurance by the Company as stipulated in these clauses. These clauses shall be applicable to the coverage of state organizations, institutions, people's bodies and people's communes.

Chapter II The Scope of Insured Property

Article 3 All the property listed in the policy and the attached list shall be within the scope of insured property whether it is in the possession of the Insured or in his or her custody for another person or in his or her common possession with another person with the Insured in charge.

Article 4 The following property shall also be within the scope of insured property with the special agreement between the Insured and the Company and with the indication in the policy:

1. Gold, silver, jewelry, ornaments, antiques, ancient books, ancient paintings, stamps, works of arts, rare metals and other precious belongings;
2. Livestock, poultry and other domestic animals.

Article 5 The following property shall not be within the scope of insured property:

1. Dykes, weirs, sluices, railways, roads, culverts, land and municipal public water supply lines and sewers outside buildings;
2. Underground structures, equipment and materials of mines or pits;
3. Goods and materials in transport (including the period of transshipment);
4. Crops which have not been harvested;
5. Weapons and ammunition;
6. Currencies, bills and notes, valuable securities, documents, books, charts and tables, technical data and property with no appraisable value.

Chapter III Insurance Liability

Article 6 The Company shall be liable for the compensation of the loss of insured property on account of the following causes:

1. Fires, explosions;
2. Hail, lightning and thunder, floods, tsunamis, earthquakes, cave-ins, landslides;
3. Falling of flying objects from the air;
4. Losses of insured property caused by the collapse of the mainstructures of houses or buildings — walls, roofs and trusses — due to storm winds or torrential rain;
5. Losses of insured property caused by the necessary measures taken to rescue or to prevent the spread of the calamity when any of the above calamities occurs.

Article 7 The Company shall be liable for the compensation of the reasonable expenses incurred for the rescue of insured property when any of the calamities or accidents listed in each of the clauses of Article 6 occurs or for the protection or rearrangement so as to reduce the loss of the insured property after the occurrence of the calamity.

Article 8 The insurance liability shall become effective from midnight of the date agreed on to start the coverage to 12 o'clock at night of the date of expiration of insurance and the validity of insurance shall not exceed one year as the limit. All formalities shall be observed if the insurance is to be renewed at its expiration.

Chapter IV Exclusions

Article 9 The Company shall not be liable for the compensation of the loss of insured property on account of the following causes:

1. War or military action;
2. Nuclear radiation and pollution;
3. Deliberate acts of the Insured;
4. The automatic damage of electrical

machinery, electrical appliances and electrical equipment due to such causes as overuse, over-voltage, line contact, arclight, leakage of electricity, over-heating, etc.

5. Losses of the means of communications and transportation in motion;

6. Losses caused by storm winds or torrential rain of insured property piled in the open or under awnings and of the awnings with reed mats, cloth, grass, asphalt, felt or plastics as roofs;

7. Other losses which are not within the limits of the insurance liability.

Chapter V Insured Amount

Article 10 The insured amount of insured property shall be determined in accordance with the recent book value in the Insured's account books, or agreed on and determined by the Insured and the Company.

Article 11 If any insurance matter changes or the insured amount has to be readjusted within the validity of insurance, the Insured shall apply to the Company for approval and revision.

Chapter VI The Insured's Duties

Article 12 The Insured shall pay off the premiums in one payment as stipulated by the Company in the rules and regulations on premium rates within 15 days of the commencement of the insurance. Installment payments may be arranged if there is a special agreement.

Article 13 The Insured shall observe various provisions of the government for the protection and safety of property, accept the suggestions of the departments concerned and the Company as to the improvement of the state of safety of the property and conscientiously do the safety work well to guard against calamities.

Article 14 When insured property meets a calamity or an accident within the scope of cover, the Insured shall take necessary measures as far as possible to rescue or protect it so as to prevent the aggravation of the loss and promptly notify the Company.

Chapter VII Adjustment of Claims

Article 15 The Insured shall put forward the list of the losses of insured property, the list of rescue and protection expenses, necessary account books, documents and certificates of public security and other departments concerned when he or she applies to the Company for compensation. After the receipt of the above application, the Company shall promptly check and determine whether the compensation shall be made within the scope of coverage. The relevant insured amount shall be paid as soon as an agreement has been reached with the Insured.

Article 16 When insured property sustains a loss within the scope of coverage, the Company shall estimate the damages according to the actual loss of the insured property and the actual value of the loss on that day, but the maximum damages shall not be more than the insured amount as the limit. If there are more than one item of insured property, the damages shall be handled by the item in accordance with the provisions in this Article.

Article 17 The maximum damages paid by the Company for the compensation for rescue, protection and repair expenses as stipulated in Article 7 of these clauses shall not be more than the insured amount as the limit.

Article 18 If the loss of insured property within the scope of coverage shall be compensated for by a third party according to the provisions of law or relevant agreements, the Company shall make compensation first to the Insured in accordance with the relevant provisions of these clauses. The Insured shall transfer the right to recover the damages to the Company and assist the Company in recovering the damages jointly.

Article 19 The remaining part of insured property after a loss shall be put into full use, discounted and depreciated for the Insured and deducted from the amount of damages payable.

Article 20 The Insured shall be regarded as having waived his or her rights and interests of his or her own accord if he or she does not apply to the company for compensation or put forward necessary documents and certificates or draw the entitled damages within two years after the date of the loss of insured property.

Article 21 If any dispute occurs between the Insured and the Company, it shall be settled through consultation in the spirit of practicability. If both parties cannot reach an agreement, it shall be submitted to the arbitration organization for arbitration or to the court for handling.

THE PEOPLE'S INSURANCE COMPANY OF CHINA: INVESTMENT INSURANCE (POLITICAL RISKS) CLAUSES

I Scope of Coverage

The Company shall be liable for loss of the investment specified in the Policy caused by or due to:

a. War, warlike operations, insurrection, strikes and/or riots;

b. Confiscation or expropriation brought about by the government's department concerned;

c. The insured's inability to transfer his remittance laid down in the investment contract in consequence of restrictions on remittances imposed by the government's department concerned.

But the amount of indemnification shall in no case be in excess of the amount of insurance as is stated in the Policy.

II Exclusions

The Company shall not be liable for:

a. Commercial loss resulting from loss of or damage to the Insured's invested object;

b. Loss caused or contributed by the counteract or non-fulfillment of the investment contract by the Insured or his representative, confiscation or expropriation by the government's department concerned as a result of the Insured's intentional act or disorderly conduct;

c. Loss consequent upon failure of the Insured to effect remittance within the period stipulated by the government's department concerned;

d. Loss caused by atomic bomb, hydrogen bomb and nuclear weapons;

e. Loss consequent upon confiscation or expropriation of any other properties not falling within the scope of the investment contract.

III Claims Shall be Payable As Follows:

a. For confiscation or expropriation brought about by the government's department concerned: 6 months after the onset of the confiscatory or expropriatory action;

b. For damage due to war, warlike operations, insurrection, strikes and/or riots: on proof of loss or damage to physical assets or 6 months after the invested object has been put out of action;

c. For restrictions on remittances imposed by the government's department concerned: 3 months after presentation by the Insured of the application for remittance;

d. In case of a loss in investment recoverable under the Policy, the amount of indemnity to be paid by the Company shall be based on the amount of loss to be calculated in the proportion that the amount of insurance bears to the amount of investment.

IV Compensation and Recoveries

Compensation and recoveries from confiscation or expropriation shall be shared between the Insured and the Company in the proportions in which loss is borne.

V Treatment of Dispute

All disputes between the Insured and the Company shall be settled through friendly negotiations according to the principles of seeking truth from facts and of fairness and reasonableness. Where a settlement fails after negotiations and it is necessary to submit to arbitration, such arbitration shall be carried out at the place where the defendant is located.

5

LAND

REGULATIONS ON THE ADMINISTRATION OF THE LAND FOR BUILDING HOUSES IN VILLAGES AND TOWNS

(March 6, 1982)

Chapter I. General Rules

Article 1 These Regulations are formulated in order to defend the socialist public ownership of land, put land to economic and rational use, prevent the arbitrary occupation and abuse of cultivated land in the house building in villages and towns, ensure the development of agricultural production and suit the needs of rural construction.

Article 2 These Regulations shall be applicable to rural villages and market towns but inapplicable to county seats and the towns provided with the town organizational system.

Article 3 As our country has a great population but less land, it is our national policy to treasure and rationally use every inch of land. In the house building in villages and towns, uniform plans shall be made and economy shall be practised on the use of land. No cultivated land shall be occupied wherever there is wasteland available; no flat plots, good fields or garden plots shall be taken up wherever sloping plots or poor plots are available; original house bases and vacant lots in villages and towns shall be fully utilized wherever transformations shall be carried out on the spot.

Article 4 The land of a rural people's commune, a production brigade or a production team shall be collectively owned by the people's commune, production brigade or production team respectively. With regard to house bases, family plots, family hills, forage fields and contracted plots, commune members have only the right of use for the purposes as stipulated without any proprietary rights thereof. They shall not build houses, dig graves or exploit mines on family plots, family hills, forage fields or contracted plots nor destroy fields to make earthen bricks or bake bricks or tiles and so on.

It is forbidden to market or lease or illegally transfer the land used for house building.

Article 5 If an individual is to use a piece of land in a village or a town to build a house or if a commune or brigade enterprise or institution is to use the same for construction, he or it shall go through the formalities of application, examination and approval as stipulated in these Regulations. Any organization, enterprise, institution or individual shall not occupy any land without authorization for house building or for construction nor exceed its or his powers to approve of the occupation of any land.

The land used for construction by a unit of the whole people's ownership, including its joint venture with a people's commune or a production brigade, shall be handled in accordance with the provisions for the requisition of land for state construction. The land used for construction by an enterprise of collective ownership set up by non-agricultural residents shall be handled in the light of the provisions for the requisition of land for state construction.

Chapter II Unified Planning

Article 6 The house building in a village or a town shall be carried on in a planned way under the unified direction of a village or town plan. In order to serve the needs of house building, the plan shall be rough at first and detailed later with the first stress laid on the solution of rational layout and control of land used and then the detailed plan shall be made.

Article 7 To proide for a village or town plan, the results of the agricultural divisions and the land utilization plans shall be turned to full use. Within the definite limits of the land to be used in the village or town, it is necessary to rationally arrange the commune members' house bases and the land used for public buildings, production buildings, public facilities, threshing grounds, roads, tree planting, etc. as required to be in line with local conditions, save on the land to be used, contribute to production, make daily life convenient, conform to public health and make environment green.

A village or a town within the limits of a city plan shall have its plan formulated as required by the city plan.

Article 8 A village plan shall be formulated by the production brigade, a market town plan shall be formulated by the people's commune and then submitted to the administration committee of the commune or the people's government at a county level for approval after being passed by the commune members' congress or the commune members' general meeting. No unit or individual shall alter the approved plan without authorization. If it requires amendments, an application shall be made to the original approving authorities for approval.

Chapter III The Standards of Land Used

Article 9 The limits of the land to be used for commune members' house building shall be prescribed by the people's government at a provincial level separately on the basis of the different conditions of mountain areas, hills, plains, pastoral areas, city outskirts, market towns, etc. and then the standards of the areas of house bases shall be prescribed by the people's government at a county level on the basis of the limits of the land to be used prescribed by the provincial people's government and in the light of the local conditions of cultivated land per capita, household sideline production, national customs, family planning, etc.

Article 10 There shall be rational ratios between the areas of various kinds of land to be used for house bases, public buildings, public facilities, roads, tree planting, etc. in a village or a town. Various ratios shall be considered and prescribed by each province, autonomous region or municipality directly under the Central Government on the basis of the rural characteristics of each area.

Article 11 The land used for construction by rural commune and brigade enterprises shall be strictly controlled. The limits of the land so used shall be respectively prescribed by the authorities in charge of commune and brigade enterprises at a provincial level in accordance with different trades and production scales and put into effect after approval of the provincial people's government.

Article 12 The standards of the areas of the land to be used for house building by non-agricultural residents in a market town shall be prescribed by the county people's government in the light of the average housing standards of the local town residents.

Chapter IV The System of Examination and Approval

Article 13 A village or town plan and the standards of the land to be used form the fundamental basis for the examination and approval of the land to be used for house building in a village or a town.

Article 14 In case a rural commune member, a worker or an armyman who has left his office temporarily or retired or resigned from his office and returned to settle in his native place or an overseas Chinese who has returned to settle down in the native village wants a house base for building a house, he shall make an application to the production team where he lives, which shall be discussed and passed by the commune members' meeting, examined and consented by the production brigade and then submitted to the administration committee of the commune for approval. If it is really necessary to take up cultivated land or a garden plot, it shall be submitted to the county people's government for approval. A certificate for the use of a house base shall be issued by the approving authorities after approval.

Article 15 Those who transfer the right of use of house bases due to any dealings in houses shall go through the formalities of application, examination and approval as stipulated in Article 14.

Those who sell or lease their houses shall not be entitled to apply for any more house bases.

A house base vacated as a result of the commune member's move or the removal of the house shall be recovered by the production team and arranged to be used in a uniform manner.

Article 16 An application of a rural commune or brigade enterprise or institution for land to be used for construction purposes shall be submitted to the people's government above a county level for approval after being discussed and adopted by the commune members' congress. The specific limits of the authority for examination and approval of the province, prefecture or county and the standards of land compensations shall be prescribed by the provincial people's government according to the specific conditions such as the quality and area of the land to be taken up.

If a commune or brigade enterprise or institution applies for land to be used for construction purposes, it shall submit the documents of the construction project and the floor area plan of the project approved by the business administration authorities above a county level. If a people's commune or a production brigade is to take up the land of a production team, a land compensation agreement signed by both parties shall also be submitted. If the construction project may cause pollution, a treatment scheme shall also be submitted.

Article 17 An application for land to be used as a brickyard or a tilery shall be strictly examined and approved. A brickyard or a tilery shall make the best use of the earth from such places as earth hills, hillsides, etc. that are not suitable for planting and shall not take up cultivated land. If it is really necessary to take up a small area of cultivated land to take the earth, practical measures shall be taken for the restoration of planting or to suit other production.

Article 18 A non-agricultural resident in a market town who wants any land for building a house shall make an application to the administration organization of the market town and shall consult with the production team concerned and his application shall be handled in the light of the provisions in Article 14.

Chapter V Rewards and Punishments

Article 19 Any cultivated land which is vacated for agricultural production as a result of the construction of a new village or the transformation of the old village shall be exempt from the agricultural tax for three to seven years from the year with gains as stipulated in the "Regulations of the People's Republic of China on Agricultural Taxes."

Article 20 Those who take up collective land without approval or authorization for house building or for construction shall return the land to the collective within a definite time and shall be fined. They shall be ordered to compensate for the economic losses resulting from such occupation. Administrative punishments shall also be imposed on the commune or brigade cadres and state personnel concerned according to the degrees of the seriousness.

Any land for house building or construction that exceeds the approved quantity or that remains unused after approval shall be returned to the collective within a definite time.

Article 21 Those who sell or lease the land for house building shall return the land to the collective within a definite time, all their proceeds shall be confiscated and fines shall be imposed on them. Administrative punishments shall be imposed on the commune or brigade cadres and the state personnel concerned according to the degrees of the seriousness.

Article 22 If any commune or brigade cadres or state personnel abuse their office to practise graft or retaliate in the examination and approval of the land for house building, their administrative, economic and/or even criminal responsibilities shall be investigated according to the degrees of seriousness.

Chapter VI. Supplementary Provisions

Article 23 The procedures for the land to be used for production by rural specialized residents or non-agricultural self-employed residents in market towns and the land for the construction of marketable houses shall be formulated by the people's government of each province, autonomous region or municipality directly under the Central Government according to local conditions.

Article 24 The people's government of each province, autonomous region or municipality directly under the Central Government shall formulate the procedures for the implementation on the basis of these Regulations and submit them to the State Council for filing.

Article 25 These Regulations shall be put into effect from the date of promulgation.

REGULATIONS ON THE REQUISITION OF LAND FOR STATE CONSTRUCTION

(Promulgated by the State Council on May 14, 1982)

Article 1 These Regulations are formulated in accordance with the Constitution of the People's Republic of China in order to put land resources to rational use, ensure the land necessary for the state construction and make appropriate arrangements for the production and life of the units and the masses with the requisitioned land.

Article 2 The state requisition of the land of collective ownership required to carry out economic, cultural or national defence construction and set up social and public undertakings shall be handled in accordance with these Regulations. Any unit shall be prohibited from directly buying or renting or covertly buying or renting any land from rural people's communes, production brigades or teams. No rural people's commune, production brigade or team shall participate in the management of any enterprise or undertaking by giving its land in exchange for the share(s) thereof.

Article 3 Saving on land is our national policy. All construction projects shall follow the principles of economy and rationalization so as to raise the utilization ratio of land. No cultivated land shall be taken up wherever there is wasteland available; no fertile land shall be taken up wherever there is barren land available. Especially it is not allowed to occupy such land with high economic benefit such as vegetable plots, garden plots, intensive-breeding fish ponds, etc.

Every area, especially the outskirts of a big city or a densely populated area, shall keep strict control of various pieces of land used for construction in accordance with the land utilization plans.

The construction within the limits of the planned areas of a city shall comply with the requirements in the plan of the city and shall be combined with the transformation of old city areas so as to reduce the newly-occupied land.

Article 4 If any land is requisitioned for the state construction in conformity to the provisions in these Regulations, the cadres and the masses of the people's commune, production brigade(s) and team(s) with the land to be requisitioned shall serve the needs of the state and shall not present any obstacle.

Article 5 The requisitioned land is owned by the state and the user unit only has the right of use.

Article 6 In the use of land, each project shall be in conformity to the requirements of the state laws and regulations relating to land administration, environmental protection, water and soil conservation, etc. so as to avoid land sandization, soil erosion, dried-up water sources, mud-rock flows, salinization, floods and waterlogging and environmental pollution. If any loss results from this, the user unit shall carry out renovations or pay renovation expenses and give the victim(s) appropriate compensations. The requirements for the renovations and the standards of the renovation expenses and compensations shall be discussed and resolved by the user unit, the victimized unit and other units concerned under the direction of the local county or city land administration authorities. If no agreements can be reached, they shall be decided upon by the county or city people's government; if the county or city people's government fails to make any decision, they shall be submitted to a higher authority for decision. The land which is no longer suitable for cultivation shall be treated as requisitioned land and arranged for use by the people's government above a county or city level in accordance with the limits of the authority for examination and approval as stipulated in these Regulations.

If there are facilities within the requisitioned land such as water sources, irrigation ditches, culverts and floodgates, pipelines, roads, cables, etc. which are closely related to the industrial and agricultural production and to the life of the masses, the user unit and the construction unit shall handle them carefully and skillfully and jointly with the departments concerned under the organization of the local people's government and shall not block them or damage them without authorization; if any block or damage occurs, repairs shall be done or relevant construction facilities shall be built.

Article 7 The Procedure of the Requisition of Land:

(1) *Making an Application and Selecting the Site:* The user unit shall make an application to the county or city land administration authorities at the location of the land to be requisitioned by means of the approved specifications of the construction project or the relevant papers of the

higher authorities and then select the construction site after the examination and approval of the county or city people's government. If the site is selected within the limits of the planned areas of a city, prior consent of the city planning administration department must be obtained.

(2) *Consulting about the areas of Land to Be Requisitioned and the Compensation and Arrangement Schemes:* After the construction site has been selected, the county or city land administration authorities at the location shall organize the user unit, the unit with land requisitioned and other units concerned to discuss and determine the area of the land estimated to be requisitioned and the compensation and arrangement schemes and sign a preliminary agreement.

(3) *Checking and Ratifying the Area of the Land to Be Used:* After the preliminary plan of the construction project is approved, the user unit shall make an official report of the area of the land to be used for the construction to the county or city land administration authorities at the location by means of relevant papers of approval and the general arrangement plan or the construction map, and after the examination, approval and ratification of the people's government above a county or city level in accordance with the limits of authority as stipulated in these Regulations, the user unit shall sign an agreement with the unit with land requisitioned under the direction of the land administration authorities.

(4) *Transferring the Land:* After the application for the requisition of land is approved, the county or city land administration authorities at the location shall transfer the land once for all or by stages according to the planned progress of the construction and urge the unit with land to be requisitioned to turn over the land on schedule.

Article 8 The Limits of the Authority of Examining and Approving the Requisition of Land:

The requisition of more than 1,000 *mu* of cultivated land and/or garden plots or more than 10,000 *mu* of other land is to be approved by the State Council; that of the land in the suburbs of a municipality directly under the Central Government is to be approved by the municipal people's government; that of the land in the suburbs of a city with a population of more than 500,000 shall be examined by the city people's government at the location and then submitted to the people's government of the province or autonomous region for approval; that of more than 3 *mu* of cultivated land or garden plot or more than 10 *mu* of forest land or grassland or more than 20 *mu* of other land in other areas shall be examined by the county or city people's government at the location and then submitted to the people's government of the province or autonomous region for approval; that of the land less than the above limits is to be approved by the county or city people's government.

The people's government of a province or an autonomous region or a municipality directly under the Central Government shall properly relax or reduce the limits of the authority of a county or city people's government in the examination and approval of the area of the land to be requisitioned in the light of the actual conditions of the locality.

The application for the approval of the land needed by a construction project shall be made once for all on the basis of the overall design and the whole shall not be broken up into pieces. The land shall be requisitioned by stages for a project to be constructed by stages and it shall not be permitted to requisition land earlier than necessary. The applications for the approval and the procedures for the requisition of the land needed by a main railway or highway shall be made and handled by sections.

Article 9 The user unit shall pay compensations for the land requisitioned. The standards of various compensations are as follows:

(1) The standards of the compensations for cultivated land (including vegetable plots) requisitioned shall be three to six times as much as the annual output value of the cultivated land and this value shall be calculated on the basis of the average annual output within the three years before the requisition and the prices as stipulated by the state. The specific standards of the compensations for various kinds of cultivated land shall be prescribed by the people's government of a province, an autonomous region or a municipality directly under the Central Government within these limits. The people's government of a province, an autonomous region or a municipality directly under the Central Government shall prescribe the standards of the compensations for the requisition of garden plots, fish ponds, lotus ponds, reed ponds, house bases, forest land, pastureland, grassland, etc. No compensations shall be given for the land without any gains.

(2) The people's government of a province, an autonomous region or a municipality directly under the Central Government shall prescribe the standards of the compensations for young crops and those for such attachments on the requisitioned land as buildings, water wells, trees and

so on. However, no compensations shall be given for all the crops or trees rush-planted and all the facilities rush-built after the start of the consultation about the land requisition schemes.

Development and construction funds for new vegetable plots shall be paid to the state in accordance with relevant provisions for the requisition of the vegetable plots in the suburbs of a city and the specific procedures shall be separately formulated.

Article 10 In order to make appropriate arrangements for the production of the units and the life of the masses with the land requisitioned, the user unit shall pay settlement allowances in addition to the payment of compensations.

The Standards of Settlement Allowances are as follows:

(1) If any cultivated land is requisitioned, the standard of the settlement allowance per capita of agricultural population is two to three times as much as the annual output value per *mu* of the cultivated land. The agricultural population to be resettled shall be calculated on the basis of the agricultural population of the unit with land requisitioned before the requisition (on the basis of the agricultural residents, excluding those who move in after the start of the consultation about the land requisition schemes), the proportion of the cultivated area and the area of land to be requisitioned. The annual output value shall be calculated on the basis of the average annual output within three years before the requisition and the prices as stipulated by the state. However, the settlement allowance per *mu* of the cultivated land shall not exceed ten times its annual output value.

(2) The people's government of a province, an autonomous region or a municipality directly under the Central Government shall prescribe the standards of the settlement allowances for the requisition of garden plots, fish ponds, lotus ponds, forest land, pastureland, grassland and other land in the light of those for the general cultivated land.

(3) No settlement allowances shall be given for the requisition of residential house bases.

If the above standards of compensations and settlement allowances still fail to keep the original levels of the production and life of the masses in isolated or particular cases, the settlement allowances shall be increased proportionately after the examination and approval of the people's government of the province, autonomous region or municipality directly under the Central Government, but the total amount of the land compensations and settlement allowances shall not exceed twenty times the annual output value of the requisitioned land.

Article 11 All the compensations and settlement allowances paid by the user unit shall be used by the unit with land requisitioned to develop production, arrange for the employment of the surplus labour resulting from the requisition of land and as living allowances for the persons who are unable to obtain employment and shall not be transferred for other purposes, with the exception of a case where the compensations for the attachments on the requisitioned land are payable to the owners themselves and the compensations for the young crops collectively grown on the land shall be brought into the collective gains of the current year for distribution. The leading authorities concerned and other units shall not take them up on any excuse.

Article 12 The unit with land requisitioned, the user unit and other units concerned are separately responsible for the arrangements of the surplus agricultural labour resulting from the requisition of land with the organization of the county or city land administration authorities. The main ways of arrangement include:

(1) *To Develop Agricultural Production:* Ameliorate the soil, build water conservancy projects and improve farming conditions; reclaim wasteland properly to enlarge the cultivated area with the approval of the county or city land administration authorities under potential and rational conditions; the user unit shall also assist in improving farmland in combination with the construction of the project, but the settlement allowances shall be deducted according to the area of farmland improved.

(2) *To Develop the Industrial and Sideline Production of People's Communes, Production Brigades and Teams:* Initiate industries, sideline production and service undertakings which are useful to the national economy and the people's livelihood and suitable to local conditions under the circumstances in conformity with the relevant provisions of the state.

(3) *To Transfer a Team or Merge Teams:* The production teams with their land wholly requisitioned or basically wholly requisitioned shall be organized to move to other locations where the conditions are suitable; they shall also be merged with other production teams in the vicinity on the principles of volunteer participation and mutual benefit.

With regard to the surplus labour which really cannot be accommodated in the above ways, the persons who accord with the requirements shall be earmarked for employment in the units of collective ownership within the limits of the labour plan with the approval of the people's government of the province, autonomous region or municipality directly under the Central Government and the relevant settlement allowances shall be turned over to the units which absorb the labour; if the user unit has worker recruitment targets available, it shall select the recruit those who accord with the requirements to become its workers and accordingly check and deduct the settlement allowances paid to the unit with land requisitioned with the consent of the people's government of the province, autonomous region or municipality directly under the Central Government.

If the land of a production team is wholly requisitioned and the team is not qualified in accordance with the conditions of transfer or merger, the original agricultural residents of the team shall be turned into non-agricultural or town residents after the examination and approval of the people's government of the province, autonomous region or municipality directly under the Central Government. The original property of collective ownership and the compensations and settlement allowances obtained shall be discussed and disposed of by the people's government above a county or city level together with the people's commune, production brigade and team concerned and those used for the organization of production and the living allowances for those who are unable to obtain employment shall not be distributed without authorization.

Article 13 In cases where it is permitted to arrange for the employment of the personnel of the unit with land requisitioned or to turn the agricultural residents into non-agricultural or town ones, the local labour, public security, grain and civil administration departments shall be respectively responsible for handling the relevant grain supply quotas and the living settlement of the persons who are unable to obtain employment.

Article 14 When the collective or commune members' houses have to be pulled down in the requisition of land, the production team or the house owners shall rebuild them in accordance with the unified arrangement of the people's commune, production brigade and team concerned.

Article 15 The people's commune, production brigade and team concerned shall make ready the construction materials needed by the unit with land requisitioned to set up production and living facilities with the compensations and settlement allowances if they are capable of doing so; if the people's commune, production brigade and team are incapable of doing so, the local government shall help them to get the materials ready; with regard to a small number of materials under the unified distribution and administration of the ministries concerned, the land user unit shall make an application for distribution together with its construction project to the department concerned of the state after they have been examined and verified by the county or city land administration authorities. The costs of the materials shall be paid by the unit with land requisitioned.

Article 16 The procedures for the migration and resettlement in case of large or medium water conservancy or hydropower engineering construction projects shall be separately formulated by the state water conservancy and power departments jointly with the state land administration authorities in the light of these Regulations.

Article 17 The units with land requisitioned shall not put forward any extra requirements or additional terms beyond the limits of the compensations and allowances as stipulated in these Regulations.

Article 18 In the course of the construction of a project, the necessary construction of material piling yards, transport passageways and other provisional facilities shall be arranged for within the limits of the requisitioned land as far as possible. If it is necessary to get additional land for provisional use, the construction unit shall make an application of the area of the land and the time limit for provisional use to the original authorities which have approved of the land used for the project, sign an agreement with the production team(s) on the land for provisional use after approval and compensate yearly for it in accordance with the average annual output value of the team's land within three years. No permanent buildings shall be built on the land for provisional use. At the expiration of the term of use, the user unit shall be responsible for restoring the farming conditions of the land and return it to the production team(s) in time or pay expenses to the team(s) on the basis of the amount of the restoration work.

The above principles shall also be followed if the additional and for provisional use is needed to erect power lines above ground, lay underground pipelines or build other underground projects as required by some departments, such as geological prospecting department, to do fieldwork. If the term of use is within one year, the approval shall be granted by the county or city people's government at the location of land.

If the construction unit needs to survey the land for the purpose of selecting the construction site, it shall obtain the consent of the local county or city people's government; it shall compensate for the loss resulting from the survey according to the actual conditions.

Article 19 If any land is urgently required for use in particular cases such as dealing with an emergency or emergent military demand, the land for provisional use shall be used first and then a prompt notice shall be given to the county or city people's government where the land is located; the land for permanent use shall be used first with the consent of the people's government above a county or city level and the requisition formalities shall be made up in conformity to the limits of authority of examination and approval.

Article 20 If there are young crops on the requisitioned land, they shall be left there until they are harvested by the farmers so long as they do not affect the normal progress of the project and shall not be destroyed by shovelling. In the case of the land which is not required for use within one growing and harvesting season of the locality, the construction unit shall sign an agreement with the production team to permit farmers to use it for farming.

Article 21 The local county or city people's government shall be entitled to recover the land which has been requisitioned for two years but remains unused and report the recovery to the original approving authorities for filing with the exception of the land with its use deferred with the consent of the authorities originally approving the requisition. The original user unit shall not dispose of and other units and individuals shall not occupy it without authorisation. The recovered land shall be handled in the following ways: (1) To be assigned to another unit qualified for the requisition of land of its own use, within the limits of the authority of examination and approval. The cost shall be calculated on the basis of all the compensations and settlement allowances actually paid by the original user unit and disposed of by the unit in accordance with the relevant provisions of the state. (2) To be leased to a production team for farming. During the term of farming, the production team shall not set up any buildings or grow perennial crops on the land. When it is required for the use of state construction, the production team shall promptly return it and shall not make any demand for compensation or resettlement; if there are young crops on the land, the user unit shall pay compensations for the young crops at its discretion.

The reserved land along railways or land required for public safety and protection in conformity to the state provisions shall not be regarded as requisitioned but remains unused.

Article 22 In the case of tombs on the requisitioned land, the user unit shall apply to the local people's government for an announcement to inform the owners thereof to move them and pay tomb moving expenses therefor. The tombs without owners shall be moved or reburied by the user unit.

If cultural or historical relics or effects without owners are found within the requisitioned land, the user and construction units shall be responsible for protecting them and report to the people's government above a county or city level for disposition.

Article 23 With regard to a project crossing the boundaries of more than one county, the requisition of land shall be organized in a unified way by the land administration authorities of the people's government of the province, autonomous region or municipality directly under the Central Government.

Article 24 The land administration authorities of the people's governments at various levels and the higher authorities of the user unit shall carry out timely supervision and examination of the use of the requisitioned land and the implementation of the arrangement schemes.

Article 25 Those who contravene these Regulations shall be given economic sanctions or administrative punishments and their criminal responsibilities shall be investigated and dealt with.

(1) If illegal means are adopted to obtain approval fraudulently of the requisition of land or if the limits of the authority of examination and approval are exceeded in the approval of the requisition of land, the agreement of the requisition shall become invalid. If the cases are serious, administrative punishments and/or fines shall be imposed on the persons in charge and those with direct responsibility.

(2) Those who seize collective land or who continue to occupy the land for provisional use and do not return it after the expiration of the term shall be ordered to return the land and compensate for the economic loss resulting from their default. If the cases are serious, administrative punishments and/or fines shall be imposed on the

persons in charge and those with direct responsibility.

(3) If the land is marketed or leased or covertly marketed or leased, or if the land is illegally transferred, the illegal proceeds shall be confiscated and the buildings built there illegally shall be confiscated or pulled down. If the cases are serious, fines and/or administrative punishments shall be imposed on the persons in charge and those with direct responsibility.

(4) In the case of the land where requisition has been approved, if a party persists in making unreasonable demands and refuses to sign the agreement of the requisition of land, the land administration authorities shall make a ruling. Any party in breach of the agreement of the requisition of land which results in the economic loss of the opposite party shall be ordered to make compensations. If the cases are serious, fines shall be imposed on the persons in charge and those with direct responsibility.

(5) Those who misappropriate or seize compensations or settlement allowances shall be ordered to return and compensate for them; if the cases are serious, administrative punishments and/or fines shall be imposed on the persons in charge and those with direct responsibility. Those who seize worker recruitment or residence conversion targets shall have the recruitment or conversion become invalid; if the cases are serious, administrative punishments and/or fines shall be imposed on the persons in charge and those with direct responsibility.

With regard to the above, the suggestions for administrative punishments shall be made by the land administration authorities and submitted to the people's government above a county level for approval so that it shall order the unit where the punished is (are) located or its higher authorities to decide and execute. Economic sanctions shall be decided upon by the land administration authorities and fix a definite period for execution. If the party refuses to accept the decision as final, he or they may appeal to the people's court before the expiration of the term; if the party does not appeal at the expiration nor execute the decision, the land administration shall apply to the people's court for enforcement in civil process.

The judicial authorities shall, according to law, investigate and deal with the criminal responsibilities of the stirring up of trouble among the masses, the obstruction of state construction, the graft and embezzlement of state and collective property, bribery, extortions and blackmail and other violations or offences constituting crimes in the course of the requisition of land. Public order administration penalties, economic sanctions or administrative punishments shall be respectively imposed on those whose cases are less serious and do not institute any crimes.

Article 26 The amount of a fine on an individual is RMB 30 yuan at least and shall not exceed the amount equivalent to six months' income of the individual.

The economic compensations paid by the enterprises and institutions of the whole people's ownership and administrative organizations shall be paid from such funds as enterprise funds, profit reserves, balance after the complete undertaking of outlays, etc. and shall not be included in the production cost or apportioned into the capital construction investment.

Article 27 If the agreements on the requisition of land have been entered into in accordance with the relevant provisions of the state before the promulgation of these Regulations, the original agreements shall still be executed.

Article 28 If any land of collective ownership in a rural people's commune, a production brigade or team is required for use by a construction project as a joint venture of a unit of the whole people's owership and a rural people's commune, a production brigade or team, this shall be regarded to be the same as the requisition of land for state construction and shall be handled as stipulated by these Regulations.

Article 29 If any land of collective ownership of a rural people's commune, a production brigade or team is required for use by a project constructed by a town unit of collective ownership or in a joint venture with a rural people's commune, a production brigade or team, this shall be handled in the light of the provisions in these Regulations.

Article 30 If any land of a production team is required for use by a rural people's commune or a production brigade in its construction, compensations shall be given and the farmers shall be carefully and meticulously resettled and the specific procedures and the standards of compensation and settlement shall be formulated by the people's government of a province, an autonomous region or a municipality directly under the Central Government in the light of these Regulations.

Article 31 If any state-owned barren hills, wasteland, beachland and other state-owned land used by other units are used for state construction, they shall be transferred free in accordance with the procedure and the limits of the authority of examination and approval as stipulated in these Regulations; proper subsidies shall be given to the people's commune, production brigade or team according to specific conditions in case of recovering the state-owned land used by it for farming for a long time. The use of river beaches shall be approved by water conservancy, aquatic production and communications departments.

Article 32 The people's government of each province, autonomous region or municipality directly under the Central Government shall formulate the procedures for the implementation in the light of the local particular conditions and on the basis of these Regulations.

Article 33 These Regulations shall be put into effect from the date of issue. "The Procedures for the Requisition of Land for State Construction" promulgated by the State Council on January 6, 1958 shall be annulled right then.

6 ENERGY

TENTATIVE REGULATIONS (DRAFT) ON BONUSES FOR SAVING SPECIALLY DESIGNATED FUELS AND RAW MATERIALS IN STATE-OWNED INDUSTRIAL AND TRANSPORT ENTERPRISES, ISSUED BY THE MINISTRY OF FINANCE, THE STATE BUREAU OF LABOUR AND THE STATE ADMINISTRATION OF SUPPLIES

(Promulgated on November 10, 1979)

To increase production and practice economy is a common and long-range task in carrying out socialist modernization. With a view to increasing production and practicing economy in a far-reaching and sustained way and encouraging the staff and workers of enterprises to save funds and materials for the state, reduce the cost of production, increase the profits of enterprises and speed up the development of production, we have formulated the following regulations:

Article 1 All enterprises which consume large quantities of fuels, electricity, non-ferrous metals and other much-wanted products and precious materials in production and which have established management systems (including consumption quotas, consumption measurements, keeping original records, making regular inventories, checking product quality and assessing economic results) may, with the approval of the ministries which they are under, introduce a single-item bonus system for saving specially-designed fuels and raw materials on a trial basis in line with the specific requirements of the respective enterprises. Enterprises which do not have the above-mentioned requisites shall not introduce the system. Administrative action shall be taken against anyone who introduces this bonus system in enterprises which do not have the above-mentioned requisites.

Article 2 The fuels and raw materials that are designated for single-item bonuses are the ten categories that are consumed in large quantities, namely: coal, coke, electricity, gasoline, diesel oils, heavy oils, crude oil, timber, rare and precious metals or other non-ferrous metals that cannot be produced at home in large quantities, and high-quality rolled steel. The bonuses will be paid from the amount of value saved and counted as part of the production cost.

The saving of fuels and raw materials other than those mentioned above should be taken into consideration in issuing regular production bonuses, which shall be paid from the regular bonus funds drawn according to the percentages permitted by the state and shall not be paid again from the amount of value saved as a single-item saving bonus.

Article 3 The savings of fuels and raw materials in the enterprises should be counted according to the quotas set by the state. The actual consumption under a set quota is the saved amount.

The consumption quotas for the above-mentioned fuels and raw materials as a whole will be fixed by the respective ministries on the basis of the average best level of consumption ever achieved in the respective industries or trades. If some ministries have difficulties in fixing their quotas, the municipalities, provinces and autonomous regions may fix quotas on the basis of the local average best levels of consumption ever achieved. In principle, quotas should be revised once a year on the basis of the new level of consumption achieved so as to maintain the most advanced and rational levels.

Article 4 The rates of bonuses for the savings, worked out on the basis of the prices of the fuels, electricity and raw materials consumed and the degree of difficulty in reducing the consumption quotas, are defined as follows:

1–3% of the amount of value saved for non-ferrous metals and high-quality rolled steels;

3–8% of the amount of value saved for gasoline, diesel oils, heavy oils, crude oil and coke;

8–15% of the amount of value saved for coal, electricity and timber.

The ministries must obtain approval from the Ministry of Finance, the State Bureau of Labour and the State Administration of Supplies in working out the details of the rates of bonuses for each industry.

Article 5 Savings shall be assessed annually. Bonuses for savings may be given quarterly or monthly according to the actual amount saved. If more fuels, electricity and raw materials are consumed than the quotas permit in a quarter or a month, no bonus will be given for that quarter or that month, and the above-quota amount will be deducted from the amount saved in the next quarter or the next month, and bonuses will be given on the basis of the amount saved after deduction and according to the fixed rates of bonuses.

In the case of a combined operation in which a group of people doing different kinds of work take part, a shift, a group or a section will be taken as a counting unit. In the case of an operation by an individual, the individual will be taken as the counting unit. The collective receiving the award should distribute the bonus to its members according to their contributions: bigger shares for bigger contributions, smaller shares for smaller contributions and no share for no contribution.

Article 6 Enterprises which introduce the single-item saving bonus system must check the quality of products strictly and must not alter the quality of products for the sake of saving fuels or raw materials. Bonuses shall be suspended if frauds are discovered and the quality of products drops. If bonuses are given in this case, the same amount of money shall be deducted from wages. Action shall be taken against those who are responsible for fraud. Disciplinary action shall be taken against individuals involved in serious cases.

Article 7 The departments of supplies and planning should, in accordance with the policy of "savings to factories," leave to the factories the fuels and raw materials saved by reducing the factories' consumption quotas for above-quota production. The increased part of production will be distributed according to the relevant state regulations.

Article 8 The savings and the issued bonuses must be made known to the workers and staff from time to time in the interest of democratic management and mass supervision.

Article 9 Details may be worked out by the ministries under the State Council and the governments of provinces, municipalities and autonomous regions in line with this regulation. They should be sent to the Ministry of Finance, the State Bureau of Labour and the State Administration of Supplies for the records. Regulations previously published by the local governments and ministries which contravene this regulation should be abrogated.

THE ORDER OF THE STATE COUNCIL FOR THE REDUCTION OF OIL BURNING IN VARIOUS BOILERS AND INDUSTRIAL KILNS AND FURNACES

(Energy-saving Order No. 1, October 27, 1980)

Petroleum is an important strategic material. The rational use and the economy of petroleum have become problems followed by the whole world with common interest since the petroleum crisis occurred at the beginning of the seventies. At present, our country burns a large quantity of heavy oil and crude oil every year and a considerable part of them is put to irrational use. In order to save energy, the oil burning shall be reduced with great efforts to enable more petroleum to be used as a raw material in light, textile and chemical industries and to produce more refined oils so as to meet the needs of the four-modernizations construction. The following order is issued for this purpose:

I Reduce Oil Burning in Various Boilers

1. The present oil-burning industrial boilers, domestic boilers and the power station boilers which were originally designed for coal burning but later converted to oil burning shall be promptly converted back to coal burning in the order of the easy ones to the difficult ones by different stages and in batches and the conversion shall be completed before the end of 1985 at the latest.

2. The power stations which were originally designed for oil burning shall be converted to coal burning if they are capable of being converted; those which are really incapable of being converted shall be changed by stages and in batches into power stations in reserve or those used for readjustment before 1990. The annual operating hours of each shall be reduced to 1,500 to 2,000 hours and the oil burning quantity shall be reduced by 60 to 70 per cent. The generator sets changed into reserve or readjustment ones shall be replaced by newly-built coal-burning ones of the same capacity. A new set shall be built before changing an old one.

3. In the course of the transformation of oil-burning boilers into coal-burning ones, attention shall be paid to overall economic effects and the functions of the coal-burning boilers shall be improved so as to raise their thermal efficiency; the transformations shall be arranged as a whole on the basis of technical and economic factors and combined as far as possible with the development of centralized heat supply so as to combine heat with power. Attention shall also be paid to the control of the "three wastes" (waste gas, waste water and industrial residue) and the environmental protection.

II Reduce Oil Burning in Industrial Kilns and Furnaces

1. Oil burning shall be permitted for the oil and chemical tubular heating furnaces with particular requirements in such aspects as the technology of production, quality of products, combustion temperatures, etc., high-temperature kilns and furnaces above 1,500°C, low-speed international combustion engines, gas turbines designed for oil burning, alkali-recovery burning furnaces and other industrial kilns and furnaces which cannot be replaced by coal-burning or gas-burning ones for the time being.

The units permitted to burn oil shall strengthen their administration, carry out technical transformations in a planned way and make great efforts to reduce oil-consuming quotas. It is necessary to reduce the unit product oil consumption by 10 to 15 per cent by 1985 from the actual consumption in 1979.

2. The units which do not conform to the conditions in the preceding clause shall not be permitted to burn oil. Those of them in which the furnaces can be transformed more easily and which have the sources of coal supply shall promptly convert their furnaces over to coal burning and the conversion shall be completed by the end of 1982 at the latest. Those which have great difficulty in transforming their furnaces and whose products do not suit the needs shall promptly be closed, stopped, merged and transferred to the production of other items.

III Reduce the Self-used Oils of Oil Fields and Oil Refineries

1. The oils burned by oil fields, oil refineries and their subsidiary enterprises and institutions shall be included in the state plans by accounts

and in items in the same way as the oils burned by other units.

2. The thermal power plants of oil fields and oil refineries provided for themselves mainly for the purpose of heat supply, which were originally designed for oil burning, shall be permitted to continue to burn oil if they have no grounds for conversion to coal burning. But the power generated shall be fixed on the basis of the heat demand and the units shall strictly carry out the fixed-quantity oil burning.

3. Oil fields' and oil refineries' oil-burning industrial boilers, domestic boilers and other industrial boilers which do not conform to the requirements for oil burning shall be converted to coal burning by stages and in batches so long as they have sources of coal supply.

4. It shall be strictly prohibited to supply oils beyond the plans. Oil fields and oil refineries shall not supply oils to any units whose use of oils is not approved by the state. The oil produced from scattered wells and ground oil shall be supplied to the oil-consuming units approved by the state in the locality and in the neighbourhood.

5. Oil fields and oil refineries shall cut down various types of wastage, reduce self-used oils and increase commodity percentages through the strengthening of administration, the improvement of technology and the execution of technical transformations. By the year 1985, the commodity percentage of the crude oil for uniform distribution shall be more than 96 percent for oil fields and the overall commodity percentage shall be more than 92.5 percent for oil refineries.

IV Execute Oil Burning Plans and the System of Examination and Approval Strictly

1. The State Planning Commission, State Economic Commission and State Energy Commission shall be responsible for formulating and making known to units of lower levels long-term and annual energy-saving plans and each area, each department and each unit shall resolutely execute them.

2. Oil burning shall be examined and approved by the State Planning Commission jointly with the departments concerned. For units permitted to burn oil, the oil-burning quotas and quantities shall be examined and ratified and oil-burning licences shall be granted so as to supply oils in fixed quantity by means of the licences. For those which shall make transformations within a definite period and are temporarily permitted to burn oil, the time limits for the transformation of furnaces shall be appraised and decided and provisional oil-burning licences shall be granted; those which do not transform their furnaces when the time limits are exceeded shall have their provisional oil-burning licences withdrawn and the supply of oil shall be stopped. All those which are not approved or have no oil-burning licences or provisional oil-burning licences shall be prohibited from burning oil.

3. From now on, no area, department or unit shall design, build, construct or introduce oil-burning equipment without examination and approval of the State Planning Commission and shall not enlarge the oil-burning scopes or increase oil-burning consumption without authorization.

4. A small number of oil-burning boilers and other industrial kilns and furnaces shall have their oil-burning periods properly extended with the examination and approval of the State Planning Commission jointly with the departments concerned if it is really very difficult for them to be converted to coal burning or if it is impossible for them to obtain coal supply for the time being.

V The Sources of Funds and the Supply of Materials

1. The transformation funds required for the reduction of oil burning shall first be raised and solved by each area. each department or each unit for itself; the state shall subsidize them for the deficiencies in accordance with the following standards:

(1) A power station which was originally designed for coal burning and later changed into oil burning shall be subsidized at 100 to 150 yuan per kilowatt provided it is to be switched back to coal burning;

(2) A unit which switches an oil-burning industrial boiler or civil boiler over to coal burning shall be subsidized at 150 to 200 yuan per ton decrease of oil-burning amount;

(3) A unit which switches oil-burning industrial kilns and furnaces over to coal burning shall be subsidized at 80 to 100 yuan per ton decrease of oil-burning amount.

The above subsidizing funds shall be settled from the state energy-saving funds.

2. When a newly-built coal-burning generator set replaces the oil-burning one to be switched over for reservation or readjustment, the funds required shall be offered by the state as special loans with the checking and ratification on the basis of the designed standards.

3. Such materials as steel products, timber, cement, etc. required for the conversion of furnaces shall first be provided and solved by each area, each department or each unit for itself; the deficiencies shall be included in plans, arranged for as special items and have the supply ensured through the supply channels of materials.

4. The coal-burning boilers required for the transformation of furnaces shall be arranged for production and distribution as special items and in complete sets by the First Ministry of Machine Building Industry and the State Bureau of Supplies in a uniform manner. They shall be designed in accordance with the advanced types of boilers with high thermal efficiency and in conformity to the requirements for environmental protection, and the quality of products shall be up to the standards prescribed by the First Ministry of Machine Building Industry. The First Ministry of Machine Building Industry shall design and build part of boiling furnaces in a planned way for some oil-burning units to switch over to burning inferior coal.

5. The production and transportation of the coal required after the transformation of furnaces shall be arranged for as special items by the State Planning Commission in long-term plans and annual plans and shall be ensured by the supply and transportation departments.

THE ORDER OF THE STATE COUNCIL FOR THE ECONOMY ON ELECTRICITY

(Energy-saving Order No. 2, April 15, 1981)

At present, the electric energy of our country is both short of supply and very wasteful. The following order is issued for the purpose of strengthening the administration of power consumption, economizing on electricity and increasing the utilization ratios of the electric energy in order to suit the needs of the four-modernizations construction and the life of the people:

1 The controlled power consumption in quantity shall strictly be put into practice. The economic commission of each area shall regularly check and ratify the unit product electric consumption quotas and power consumption norms and supervise the implementation of them jointly with the power department and the authorities in charge of the users. They shall implement the procedures that "those who use power excessively shall be restricted; the excess shall be deducted from subsequent consumption in return; the quantity saved shall belong to the units themselves" for the purpose of restricting the units which consume power above quota and encouraging economy of electricity so as to use the saved electric energy for the increase of the units' production.

Newly-built and extended projects shall go through the formalities of the examination and approval of power consumption before construction, otherwise no power shall be supplied.

2 The use of electrical heating equipment shall strictly be controlled. All equipment originally heated with such primary energy as coal, oil, gas, etc. shall not be switched over to heating with electric energy from now on with the exception of the units approved by the authorities jointly with the power supply departments due to particular needs; the equipment which was irrationally transformed in the past shall be switched back within a definite time and if it is not transformed back when the time limit is exceeded, the power supply shall be discontinued.

3 Preferential power supply shall be put into effect. Production power supply shall be preferred to the products with low energy consumption, good quality and suitable for sale. The enterprises whose product power consumption exceeds the quotas shall reduce it to less than the quotas within a definite time through rectifications and transformations and if some of them still fail to reduce the consumption by the end of 1982, the power supply departments shall restrict the power supply or raise the power charges. The power consumption quotas for various products are as follows:

Technological unit consumption for synthetic ammonia: 1,600 kwh/ton

Technological unit consumption for calcium carbide: 3,650 kwh/ton

Direct current unit consumption for caustic soda: 2,450 kwh/ton

Alternating current unit consumption for electrolytic aluminium 20,000 kwh/ton

Technological unit consumption for silicon iron (containing 75% silicon): 9,500 kwh/ton

Technological unit consumption for electric steel (in metallurgical industry): 700 kwh/ton

Technological unit consumption for electric steel (in machinery industry): 800 kwh/ton

4 Power consumption loads shall be regulated and balanced power consumption shall be put into effect. Non-continuous production shall be urged to keep clear of the peak-load power consumption and low-trough preferential power charges shall be put into practice. In balancing power consumption, the economic commission of each area shall arrange the regular overhauls of large enterprises as far as possible in the peak periods of power consumption. In the places where hydropower is available, products with big power consumption such as iron alloys, electric steel, electrolytic aluminium, calcium carbide, silicon carbide, yellow phosphorus, etc. shall be arranged for more yields by making use of hydropower in the water-abundant periods. Preferential power charges shall be put into effect for the units which only consume power in the water-abundant seasons.

5 Living power consumption shall be saved. Power-undertaking and charge-undertaking systems shall be cancelled for the living power consumption of the residents in the families' dormitories of Party and government organiza-

tions, troops, enterprises and institutions. Annual plans shall be formulated in the light of the specific conditions of each area and they shall require that all users shall have electric meters installed and pay electricity charges according to the actual power consumption. Under the present circumstances, where electric meters still fail to satisfy the needs, the charges shall be settled by the provisional means of the calculation of charges on the basis of the actual wattages of the electrical appliances used.

6 Power-consuming equipment shall be renewed or transformed. The scientific research, designing and building departments of the machinery industry shall speed up the research and manufacture of energy-saving and high-efficiency power-consuming equipment and the replacement of energy-wasting and low-efficiency power-consuming equipment. The State Commission of Machine Building Industry and the State Bureau of Standardization jointly with departments concerned such as the First Ministry of Machine Building Industry, shall prescribe, promulgate and put into effect the efficiency standards for major power-consuming equipment before 1982.

7 Jointly with the departments in charge of enterprises, the Bureau of Standardization and the power department of each province, municipality or autonomous region shall make a general survey of the electric energy utilization efficiency of such existing universal machines and tools as ventilators, blowers, centrifugal pumps, axial flow pumps, rectifiers, electric heaters, etc. Those with actual utilization efficiency lower than the following provisions shall be included in energy-saving plans and replaced or transformed by stages and in groups:

Ventilators, blowers:	70%
Centrifugal pumps, axial flow pumps:	60%
Rectifiers:	90%
Electric heaters:	40%

8 The First Ministry of Machine Building Industry shall be responsible for organizing the production units of mechanical and electrical products in each province, municipality or autonomous region to stop the production of the following old products with high power consumption and low efficiency before the end of 1982 at the latest:

Plug-in salt bath furnaces;

Low-temperature electric heating equipment without the use of remote infrared heating technology;

AC contactors of more than 100 A without the use of noiseless operating technology.

9 Electrical equipment shall be rationally deployed so as to remove the phenomenon of "big horses drawing small carts." The electric motors with normal operating load rates lower than 40% and the transformers with the same lower than 30% shall be regulated or replaced by the power-using units before the end of 1983 at the latest.

10 In order to reduce idle power consumption, all the medium and small electric motors and various arc-welding transformers with idle rates more than 50% shall be additionally fitted with idling restricting devices by the power-using units before the end of 1983.

11 In the places where industries are concentrated, the local economic commissions shall gradually organize and establish heat treatment, electroplating, casting and oxygen-producing centres on the principle of extensive cooperation among specialized departments so as to increase the effect of the utilization of electric energy.

12 The economic management of power networks shall be strengthened. Water energy and high-efficiency coal-burning generator sets shall be put to full use to generate more power. The problems such as the imbalance between power transmission, transformation and generation and the imbalance between the idle and working proportions shall be solved step by step. The transformation of city power networks shall be speeded up so as to ensure the quality of power supply. Power departments shall be required to reduce the average power line damage rates of the whole country to between 8.2% and 8.5% by 1985 on the existing basis.

13. Idle potentialities shall be exploited with great efforts. Power supply and power user departments shall jointly take measures to compensate for idling so as to increase power factors and achieve the on-site balance of idle power and the grading balance of power transmission, transformation and distribution networks. The current system of rewards and punishments for power factors shall continue to be in force.

14. Rural power networks shall be rectified and transformed. In general, the radius of power supply of a rural power network shall not exceed the following provisions:

10 kilovolts – 15 kilometres

35 kilovolts – 40 kilometres.

Power departments shall, jointly with local

departments concerned, be responsible for rectifying and transforming the networks in excess of the above provisions or which supply power in a roundabout way. Iron cables shall be prohibited from use as newly-built rural power lines. The transformation of the original iron cables shall be completed by stages and in groups before 1984. It shall be required to reduce the line damage rates of rural power supply lines to less than 12%.

Power supply departments shall organize people's communes, production brigades and teams to transform the low-voltage power supply lines which endanger safety and incur serious loss of electric energy so as to ensure safe and economic operation.

15 With regard to the army's industrial and living power consumption, specific procedures for the implementation of power-saving shall be formulated in the spirit of power saving in this Order.

THE ORDER OF THE STATE COUNCIL FOR THE SAVING OF REFINED OILS

(Energy-saving Order No. 3
April 17, 1981)

Petroleum is a short supplied product in the economic construction of our country and refined oils are strategic materials of even greater importance; therefore the saving of refined oils shall be put in an important place. At present, refined oils are consumed in large quantities in our country and there is too much waste of them because they are not strictly administered. The following order is issued for the purpose of reducing the consumption of oils conscientiously so as to serve the needs of the four-modernizations construction.

1 The system that refined oils are distributed in a unified manner, supplied in fixed quantity and used within the limits shall strictly be implemented. The economic commission at each level shall regularly examine and ratify the oil consumption of each oil user unit jointly with the departments concerned, ration them for use within the limits, supply them with coupons and shall not supply any excessive quantity.

Refined oils shall be supplied by local oil companies in a unified manner in accordance with the fixed quotas. Oil fields, oil refineries and the like shall not sell refined oils themselves. The refined oils used by oil departments themselves shall also be brought into the state distribution plans by accounts and in items and similarly the oils used shall be provided for in fixed quantity and used within the limits.

2 The oils used by motor vehicles shall conscientiously be controlled and reduced. Oils shall be supplied to specialized transportation companies in accordance with the transportation plans transmitted to lower levels by the state. With regard to the lorries of industrial and mining enterprises, the economic commissions at each level shall, jointly with the departments concerned, re-examine and re-ratify the number of lorries used by each unit in accordance with the current condition where social transport capacity is greater than the transport volume and in the spirit of giving full play to the transport capacity of specialized transport departments and supplying oils in accordance with the newly-fixed number of lorries used. The lorries not in use and in surplus as a result of the regularized production and construction tasks shall be reserved in stock and the supply of oils stopped. A small number more of the lorries of Party and government organizations, bodies and institutions shall be reserved in stock; during reservation, they shall be exempt from road tolls and their licences and oil books returned. Oils shall be supplied for the cars of each unit in accordance with the establishment of cars. The quantity of oils for a special car used by senior cadres shall not exceed 100 kilogrammes a month and that for a public car shall not exceed 70 kilogrammes a month, both of which shall be used within the limits.

3 There shall be standards for the allocation of cars. The cars used by the leading cadres of central organs, state organizations and of each province, municipality and autonomous region shall be allocated in accordance with the document No. 83 (1979) issued by the Central Committee of the CPC, i.e. "A Number of Provisions of the Central Committee of the CPC and the State Council for the Living Remuneration of Senior Cadres."

A car shall be allocated to three to five cadres at the rank of director or vice-director of a department, a bureau or an office under a ministry (including the cadres at the same rank of a prefecture, a city directly under the jurisdiction of a province or an enterprise or an institution at the prefectural level).

Two to three additional cars for communication shall be allocated according to the volume of official business to each department of a central organ or a state organization or to each province, municipality or autonomous region. One to two cars shall be allocated to each bureau under a prefecture or a city directly under the jurisdiction of a province.

Three to six cars shall be allocated to each county for common use by the county Party committee, county people's government and county people's political consultative conference. One to three cars shall be allocated to an independent enterprise or institution at the county level. A certain number of jeeps shall be allocated as required by the work to a geological, oil field, mine or field capital construction unit and the specific numbers shall be checked and ratified by local planning commissions and business authorities. In principle, no cars shall be allocated to a unit below the county level.

All foreign affairs departments shall use taxis whenever possible. A certain number of cars shall be allocated to each foreign affairs department of a central organ or a state organization or to another department with relatively more affairs and duties and the specific numbers shall be examined and ratified by the Bureau of Administration for Organ Affairs. The business cars used by the foreign affairs departments of each province, municipality or autonomous region shall be examined and determined by the people's government of the province, municipality or autonomous region.

The business cars used by procuratorates, courts and banks in every area shall be examined and determined by the people's government of each province, municipality or autonomous region and reported to the State Council for record. With regard to the business cars used by public security departments, the Ministry of Public Security shall formulate the establishment of cars used for public security business, in the spirit of oil saving, submit it to the State Council for approval and then put it into effect.

The allocation of cars to each unit, including those purchased through various channels and with various outlays in the past, shall not exceed the total of the establishment as stipulated above. From now on, the allocation of cars to each administrative unit shall be under the unified administration of the Bureau of Administration for organ affairs at each level, while the planning commission in each area shall, jointly with the financial department and business authorities, be responsible for arranging and examining the allocation of cars to each enterprise or institution. Oils shall be supplied in accordance with the new establishments as of July 1, 1981. The units which do not have enough cars presently shall be gradually provided with more up to the stipulated establishments. The present surplus cars shall first be redistributed in accordance with the establishments within the same organization or the same province, municipality or autonomous region and if there are still surplus ones, they shall be submitted to the State Planning Commission for unified distribution.

4 From now on, the distribution quotas for cars (including sedans, jeeps, pick-up trucks, station wagons) shall be transmitted by the State Planning Commission in a unified manner to lower levels in accordance with the provisions for the establishments of cars and the requirements for the renewal of vehicles. All units shall go through the formalities of examination and approval as stipulated. Financial departments shall not reimburse for the cars purchased without examination and approval; banks shall not pay and transfer accounts for them, public security and communications supervision and administration departments shall not issue licences for them, commercial oil supply departments shall not supply oils for them, the office for the control of social group purchasing power at each level shall be entitled to confiscate them and turn them over to the departments in charge of supplies and then the departments shall otherwise redistribute them in accordance with the state plans.

5 Four-wheel-drive jeeps shall no longer be allocated to the units without tasks in the countryside in the capital of each province or each autonomous region or in a city with a population of more than one million. The original four-wheel-drive jeeps shall gradually be replaced by sedans or two-wheel-drive jeeps and transferred for use by prefectures, counties or fieldwork units.

6 The long-distance transportation of lorries across provinces, municipalities and autonomous regions shall strictly be controlled and the transportation at a distance of more than two hundred kilometres shall be approved by the economic commissions of provinces, municipalities and autonomous regions. The formalities of approval shall be handled quarterly or yearly for the reasonable transportation with long-term fixed cooperative relations. Each communications administration station on the way shall be responsible for the examination.

The cars of local Party and government organizations at each level shall run within the area under their jurisdiction. Each unit along a railway shall go out on official business by train with the exception of urgent cases.

7 Various motor vehicles which have been used for many years and which consume oils for more than 20 per cent above the standards shall be rejected through the appraisal of local public security and communications departments, their fixed assets shall be checked and cancelled and they shall be recovered in a unified manner by the supplies department of each province, municipality or autonomous region for disposal and shall not be transferred for further use.

8 Social vehicles shall be organized for rational transportation. The economic commissions in each area shall be responsible for the organization of cooperative transportation in various forms on the principles of voluntary participation and mutual benefit. The stress ahead of the distribution of lorries shall be laid on communications and transport departments and generally lorries shall no longer be distributed among state organizations, mass bodies and institutions.

9 The supply of diesel oil shall be reduced with great efforts. The oil used by agricultural tractors shall be examined, ratified and supplied in fixed quantity for use within the limits in accordance with the annual volume of operations of the tractors actually started. The oil used for non-agricultural transportation shall be deducted from the fixed quantity. Commercial, agricultural and highway supervision and administration departments shall strictly control the non-agricultural business transportation of tractors.

From now on, the vehicles refitted with diesel engines shall be prohibited from carrying on business transportation. Higher authorities in charge shall make technical appraisals of existing vehicles refitted with diesel engines and stop the use of those which consume oil in excessive quantities and are unsafe. Local public security and communications departments shall put the execution of the aforesaid under their conscientious supervision.

10 In order to save oil for agricultural irrigation and drainage power, the farming machinery departments shall organize the technical tests and appraisals of the water pumps produced by the existing water pump factories, issue production licences to those with their products up to standard and stop the production of and rectify those whose products are not up to the standard. The water conservancy and agricultural departments in each area shall organize people's communes, production brigades and teams to regulate irrigation and drainage machines which do not form complete sets and it shall be required to eliminate the phenomenon of "big horses drawing small carts" in respect of irrigation and drainage power before 1984. In the first half of 1982, the State Agricultural Commission shall, jointly with the Ministries of Water Conservancy and Electric Power Industry, prescribe the rational lift norms for agricultural irrigation and drainage and the cost limits for draught relief and flood drainage and those in excess of the norms or limits shall not be permitted to use oils or electricity.

11 Urban and rural residents shall strictly be prohibited from burning diesel oil for rice cooking or heating. Commercial departments shall control the supply of civil kerosene stoves and generally they shall not supply them, with the exception of the appropriate supply to suit the particular needs of the patients in hospitals and for field operation.

12 The oil used by the existing diesel generators shall be examined by commercial departments jointly with the departments concerned. Generally no oil shall be supplied except that coupons shall be issued and oil shall be supplied in accordance with the rated hours actually required for such operations as mining, exploration, construction, reclamation, pastoral area well drilling, etc. in the border and open country areas without power sources or for power source sets which shall be made ready for hospitals or for broadcasting, posts and telecommunications, scientific research, etc.

13 If the designed oil consumption of the oil-consuming machines and tools now in production exceeds the following limits, they shall be improved before the end of 1982 at the latest so as to reduce the oil consumption to below the limits and their production shall be stopped for reduced at the expiration of the time limit, the execution of which shall be arranged for by the State Commission of Machine Building Industry.
Commission of Machine Building Industry.

The Oil Consumption of a Motor Vehicle:—

4-ton lorry	29 litres/100 kilometres
2-ton lorry	17 litres/100 kilometres
common sedan	12 litres/100 kilometres
4-wheel – drive jeep	17 litres/100 kilometres
2-wheel – drive jeep	15 litres/100 kilometres
station wagon (less than 15 seats)	17 litres/100 kilometres

The Oil Consumption of a Diesel Engine:

1. Swirl-chamber or prechamber

(1) 65 to 85 mm cylinder bore, 2,000 to 3,000 r.p.m. rotation speed 220 g./hp-hr

(2) 90 to 125 mm cylinder bore, 1,400 to 2,000 r.p.m. rotation speed 195 g./hp-hr

(3) more than 130 mm cylinder bore, 400 to 1,500 r.p.m rotation speed 195 g./hp-hr

2. Direct-injection-chamber

(1) 90 to 125 mm cylinder bore, 1,400 to 2,000 r.p.m. rotation speed 185 g./hp-hr

(2) more than 130 mm cylinder bore, 400 to 1,500 r.p.m. rotation speed 175 g./hp-hr

Red Flag brand high-grade sedans consume more oil, so their production shall be stopped as of June 1981.

14 The new increase of oil-consuming machines and tools shall strictly be controlled. The balance of supply and demand of oils shall be used as an important ground for the formulation of the plans to produce and import oil-consuming machines and tools. Production units and import units shall strictly act according to the state plans and strictly control the overfulfilment of production quotas and import plans.

It shall strictly be forbidden to refit, assemble

or process various motor vehicles with supplied materials beyond the state plans. The import of cars shall strictly be controlled and that of various cars with state foreign currencies or with the foreign currencies owned by each unit itself shall be examined and approved by the State Commission of Machine Building Industry.

15 The system that old lubricating oil shall be turned over before supplying new oil shall be put into effect. The industrial and communications authorities and other departments concerned of each province, municipality or autonomous region shall transmit used lubricating oil recovery quotas down to each enterprise or institution and it shall strictly be forbidden to burn off, pour away or wash away used lubricating oil. The equipment which leaks shall be repaired within a definite time and the supply of lubricating oil shall be deferred or periodically stopped if the waste is serious. The supply shall be deferred or stopped until the defects are put right.

16 Commercial departments shall gradually build more oil-filling stations in large and medium cities and vital communications lines and urban construction and public security departments shall give them active support so as to reduce the wastage due to the scattered self-storage and long-distance oil filling of the oil user units.

17 The army shall formulate the specific procedures for the implementation of the establishments of cars and the saving of refined oils in the spirit of oil saving of this Order.

THE ORDER OF THE STATE COUNCIL FOR THE CONSERVATION OF COAL USED BY INDUSTRIAL BOILERS

(Energy-Saving Order No. 4
July 24, 1982)

Industrial boilers constitute heating power equipment which is indispensable to the development of the national economy and the improvement of people's life. Most of the existing boilers in our country are rather backward in equipment and rather low in the levels of management of their operation, resulting not only in much waste of fuel but also in serious pollution of the environment. The following order is issued for the purpose of improving the equipment situation of industrial boilers and strengthening the management of their operation so as to increase their thermal efficiency, save fuel and reduce pollution.

1 The fuel rationing system shall be put into effect for industrial boilers (excluding the boilers of power stations, locomotives and ships). Fuel supply departments shall, jointly with the authorities in charge of the users, regularly examine and ratify the fuel consumption quotas and the quantity of supply for boilers and the fuel supply departments shall issue fuel supply coupons accordingly. The fuel rationing by coupons shall be put into effect as of January 1, 1983, the saved part to be left to the users' disposal, and the excessive part shall not be supplied or shall be supplied at a higher price. Each user shall strengthen the management of the coal used by boilers by means of measurement and assessment.

2 Coal production departments and fuel supply departments shall jointly be responsible for the gradual achievement of the relative stability in respect to the variety and quality of coal supplied to each area. Key enterprises shall be selected in 1983 to begin the experiments of the fixed-point supply of coal. For the large and medium cities with coal supplied in a greater variety, the fuel supply departments shall be responsible for processing and supplying the power coal of sizes less than 15 mm in accordance with the situation of coal resources and the demands of enterprises.

3 The heat energy utilization ratios of heat-generating equipment shall be increased so as to save steam. Each industrial or mining enterprise shall set up a perfect system of the administration of the technological steam-consuming quotas so as to gradually achieve the planned, rated and measured steam consumption. The backward steam-consuming technology and equipment shall be transformed in a planned manner. The management of the heat power networks shall be made more effective and the heat preservation of the equipment piping networks shall fulfill the designed requirements. The total rate of leakage of pipelines, valves, drainages, etc. shall not exceed 0.2 per cent. When the steam is indirectly consumed, the recovery rate of condensation water shall not be lower than 60 to 80 per cent.

4 Heating with steam shall be switched over to heating with hot water. The heating systems to be built in future shall make use of hot water for heating. The existing steam heating systems shall be switched over to hot water heating ones before the heating season of 1984 except for those approved by the energy-saving authorities. The fuel supply departments shall reduce the supply of coal if they are not transformed when the time limit is exceeded.

5 The blind expansion of boiler capacity shall strictly be restricted. If a newly added or renewed or transformed boiler is to have its evaporative capacity expanded, it shall be examined and approved in advance by the local energy-saving department jointly with the fuel supply department and the department in charge of the user to review the procedure of the capacity expansion for the boiler, otherwise no coal shall be supplied.

6 Low-efficiency boilers shall be renewed or transformed within a definite time. The renewal of such old-type boilers as Lancashire ones shall be completed before the end of 1986 at the latest. Other boilers with the operating thermal efficiency lower than the following minimum requirements shall be transformed; if the transformed ones still fall short of the requirements, or if their transformation expenses exceed 65% of the costs of purchase although they can fulfill the requirements, they shall be renewed. The transformation and renewal shall be completed before the end of 1990 at the latest. If they are neither renewed nor transformed when

the time limit is over, the supply of fuel shall be stopped. All boilers not in use as a result of renewal shall be rejected, and sold to the material recovery companies in each area for disposal and strictly prohibited from being transferred for further use.

The minimum requirements (under the conditions of burning bituminous or brown coal Class 2 or 3) for the operating thermal efficiency of industrial boilers are as follows:

50% in the case of boilers with the capacity less than 1 t/h;

55% in the case of boilers with the capacity in the range of 1 t/h to 1.5 t/h;

60% in the case of boilers with the capacity of 2t/h;

65% in the case of boilers with the capacity in the range of 4 t/h to 6.5 t/h;

72% in the case of boilers of 10 t/h and of more than 10 t/h.

The plans and projects of the renewal or transformation of boilers shall be examined and determined by the energy-saving departments of provinces, municipalities and autonomous regions jointly with fuel supply, machine building, labour and environmental protection departments and submitted to the state and then the state shall entrust the State Bureau of Supplies with the verification of them jointly with the departments concerned so as to bring them into the state energy-saving plans. The State Bureau of Supply shall organize their implementation. The boilers required for renewal shall be included in state plans and arranged for their production by the machine-building industrial departments.

The advanced techniques for the transformation of boilers shall go through the technical appraisals of the authorities above the prefectural or city level before being popularized or put to use.

7 Necessary meters and water treatment or other devices shall be installed. Before the end of 1985, heating process monitoring or measuring meters and dust removers shall be fitted in each industrial boiler room which shall be equipped with soot blowing and water treatment devices or in which effective water treatment measures shall be adopted.

8 The renewal and transformation of boilers shall be arranged for in combination with the focused development of centralized heat supply or the combined production of heat and electricity. The planning and economic commissions of each province, municipality or autonomous region shall, jointly with the production, energy-saving, electric power and urban construction departments, do the overall planning well on the basis of city overall plans and combine them with the switching of oil burning and gas burning over to coal burning so as to put energy-saving funds to effective use.

Local people's governments shall be responsible for organizing the departments concerned in the good planning and design of the industrial and residential areas to be built in the future so as to carry out centralized heat supply. Otherwise, urban construction departments shall not start construction and fuel supply departments shall not supply fuels.

9 Users shall select and buy appropriate boilers according to the categories of coal locally supplied, boiler manufacturing enterprises shall produce them according to the needs of users and supplies distribution departments shall supply them according to the users' requirements. The new boilers ordered in the future which do not suit the categories of burned coal shall not be used; they shall be returned to the suppliers or returned for repairs and economic losses shall be compensated for in accordance with the provisions in the purchase contracts. If a boiler manufacturing enterprise does not produce it or them as stipulated in the contract, it shall compensate for the economic losses; if a user does not order an appropriate boiler according to the category of coal locally supplied, he shall compensate for the economic losses.

10 No unit shall build any boilers without the examination and approval of the Ministry of Machine Building Industry and the Ministry of Labour and Personnel and without the issue of boiler manufacture licences by them. The boilers which do not conform to the standards of the product quality stipulated by the state shall not be delivered out of the plants. All hand-operated boilers of 1 t/h or more than 1 t/h shall not be built. Boiler products shall be supplied as stipulated in "The Supply Range of Industrial Boilers in Complete Sets" and equipped with necessary heating process measuring and recording meters.

11 Boiler users shall carry out the technical operation training and examination of their operating personnel. A fireman shall pass an examination and obtain a certificate of qualification from the local safety supervisory organization for boilers and pressure containers before his independent operation. Each user shall strengthen the maintenance and management of boilers and establish a

perfect overhauling system and a routine assessment system so as to ensure the good equipment condition and safe operation of boilers.

12 The funds required for the renewal and transformation of boilers shall mainly be raised and settled by localities and enterprises themselves. If they really have difficulty, they shall apply to banks for seller's loans or be subsidized by the state as it thinks fit.

13 The army shall formulate the specific procedures for the saving of the coal used by boilers in the spirit of this Order.

7

TAXATION

Enterprise Profit Tax/
Foreign & Joint-Venture Enterprises Tax/
General Regulations/
Industrial & Commercial Tax/
Personal Income Tax

CIRCULAR ON IMPROVING THE PAYMENT OF INDUSTRIAL AND COMMERCIAL INCOME TAX BY COOPERATIVE STORES AND INDIVIDUAL ECONOMIC UNITS

(Promulgated by the Ministry of Finance on October 9, 1980)

The existing regulations concerning the levying of income tax on cooperative stores and individual economic units were ratified by the State Council in 1963 for trial implementation. A nine-grade progressive tax rate is imposed upon cooperative stores on their income over and above a specified limit, and a 14-grade one on the gross income of individual economic units. It is also stipulated that a higher tax rate applies to those whose yearly income has exceeded the specified figure. In 1979, the Ministry of Finance abolished the stipulation of imposing a higher income tax rate on cooperative stores whose yearly income has surpassed the specified sum. At the same time, it made it clear that the provinces, municipalities and autonomous regions may allow those stores with difficulties tax reductions or exemptions, provided that they do not pay less tax than the handicraft cooperatives. But no changes have been made with regard to the above-mentioned nine-grade progressive tax, the 14-grade one and the higher tax rate for individual economic units.

At present, the government encourages the development of the collective economy and permits individual economy to expand to a certain extent, so as to promote economic prosperity, enliven the market and create more work opportunities for young people awaiting jobs in cities and towns. Certain departments in charge and local governments, however, have reported that the tax burdens of cooperative stores are still too heavy. Although the stores are no longer required to pay according to a higher tax rate when their yearly income exceeds the specified figure, they are still encountering difficulties in operation. Therefore, the departments and local governments demanded that the eight-grade progressive tax rate that is imposed on incomes in excess of the specified limit of collectively owned handicraft industry be applied to these stores. For individual economic units, they proposed to abrogate the stipulation of collecting a higher rate of tax from them if their annual income is more than the specified sum, and to lower their tax rate.

To appropriately lighten the income tax burden of cooperative stores and individual economic units, the Ministry of Finance, upon approval of the State Council, has decided to take the following interim measures before a new income tax law is enacted:

1. Starting on October 1, 1980, income tax will be levied on cooperative stores in cities, towns and the countryside according to the eight-grade progressive tax rate which has been imposed on the income of the collectively owned handicraft industry in excess of the specified limit. The provinces, municipalities and autonomous regions should act according to the spirit of this regulation and make proper arrangements for implementation in light of their local conditions.

2. For those cooperative stores engaged in catering, services and repair trades which still have difficulties after the aforesaid eight-grade progressive tax rate has applied to them, the provinces, municipalities and autonomous regions may, after examining their cases, allow appropriate tax reductions.

3. The 14-grade progressive taxation on gross income and the current practice of collecting income tax at a higher rate from those units whose yearly income has surpassed the specified limit may not be applied to individual economic units for the time being. The provinces, municipalities and autonomous regions may, with local conditions in mind, determine the actual standard of the tax burden of these units according to the principle that it will correspond to the eight-grade progressive tax rate that has been imposed on the income of handicrafts industry. Regulations concerning the management and collection of taxes shall likewise be formulated for implementation by the various localities.

INTERIM PROVISIONS OF THE MINISTRY OF FINANCE OF THE PEOPLE'S REPUBLIC OF CHINA REGARDING THE REDUCTION AND EXEMPTION OF INCOME TAXES ON FEES FOR THE USE OF PROPRIETARY TECHNOLOGY

(January 1, 1983)

According to the stipulations of Article 11 of the Foreign Enterprise Income Tax Law and Article 27 of the Implementing Regulations of the Foreign Enterprise Income Tax Law, foreign companies, enterprises and other economic organizations which have not set up establishments in China shall pay a 20% income tax (i.e., withheld income tax) on fees obtained for the use of proprietary technology they provide for use in China. In order to better implement the state's policy on the introduction of technology, to encourage foreign companies, enterprises and other economic organizations to provide new technology, new technological processes and advanced scientific and technical achievements to China, preferential treatment of reducing and exempting income tax is to be specially granted to fees for the use of proprietary technology. Following are the detailed stipulations:

I. With regard to fees for the use of the following items of proprietary technology (including fees for blueprints and documentation, fees for technical services and fees for personnel training related to the right of use of the transferred proprietary technology, the same for all below), income tax may be levied at a reduced rate of 10%, and income tax may be exempted for those cases among them where the technology is advanced and the terms are preferential.

(1) Fees received for the use of proprietary technology provided in the areas of development of agricultural, forestry, fishery and animal husbandry production, including among these; proprietary technology provided for the improvement of soil or grasslands, for the exploitation of barren hills and for the full use of natural conditions; proprietary technology provided for new breeds of animals and new strains of plants and for the production of high effectiveness, low toxicity agricultural pesticides; and proprietary technology provided in such areas as conducting scientific production management in agriculture, forestry, fishery and animal husbandry, maintaining ecological balance, and strengthening the ability to resist natural disasters.

(2) Fees received for the use of proprietary technology provided to the Chinese side in the conducting of scientific research or scientific experiments for China's academies of science, institutes of higher learning and other scientific research units or the conducting of scientific research in cooperation with China's scientific research units.

(3) Fees received for the use of proprietary technology provided for China's key construction projects in exploiting energy and developing communications and transport.

(4) Fees received for the use of proprietary technology provided in the areas of energy conservation and prevention and control of environmental pollution.

(5) Fees for the following proprietary technology provided for China's development of important technical areas:

(i) Technology for the production of major, advanced electronic equipment;

(ii) Nuclear technology;

(iii) Technology for the production of large-scale integrated circuits;

(iv) Technology for the production of optical integration, microwave semiconductors, and microwave integrated circuits and technology for the manufacture of microwave electron tubes;

(v) Technology for the manufacture of ultra-high speed computers and microprocessing machines;

(vi) Technology for fibre optics communication;

(vii) Technology for long-distance superhigh pressure direct current electricity transmission;

(viii) Technology for liquefaction, gasification or multiple use of coal.

II Withheld income tax is not to be levied on the following items of income, not involving the transfer of the right to the use of proprietary technology (However, for those who have set up establishments or sites to engage in contracted business and the provision of labor services, income tax shall be calculated and levied on the basis of an enterprise/unit set up to engage in profit-making activity.):

(1) Service fees received for the provision of consulting services for the reform of present production technology, improvements in operations management and choice of technology,

feasibility analyses of investment projects and choice of design proposals and bid proposals, etc. for China's engineering construction or enterprises.

(2) Technology instruction fees, personnel training fees and fees for books or blueprints and documentation obtained from the presentation of technical knowledge seminars regarding such items of business knowledge as enterprise management and application of production technology for China's educational institutions, scientific research institutes and enterprises and institutions.

(3) Technical assistance fees received for the provision of technical assistance for the existing equipment or products of China's enterprises, according to specially fixed technical targets that are presented by the Chinese side on such areas as function, efficiency, quality and reliability and durability, and for the conducting of new designs, debugging or trial manufacture of components or spare parts that require improvements, to attain technical targets stipulated in contracts.

(4) Technical service fees, design fees and fees for related blueprints and documentation received for technical instruction, civil engineering construction design and technological process design and quality inspection and data analysis, etc. provided for the manufacture, installation or assembly of construction sites and equipment.

III With regard to fees for the use of proprietary technology paid for the introduction of technology in any case where in accordance with the stipulations of Article 1 of this Provision the preferential treatment of tax reduction may be granted, the departments in charge of reviewing and approving the technology introduction project shall first raise their opinions and send them together with the relevant documents and materials to the local tax authorities for consideration and confirmation. For those cases among them where the advanced technology or preferential terms necessitate the granting of tax exemption the tax bureau of the province, municipality or autonomous region shall, together with the relevant departments, consider and raise their opinions on the matter and report them to the Ministry of Finance for approval. Without consideration and approval, the units introducing technology may not, of their own accord, fix tax reductions or tax exemptions. To facilitate tax management, copies of all technology introduction contracts signed with foreign parties shall be sent to the local tax authorities for reference.

IV This Provision is to be enforced from January 1, 1983. In all cases where previous regulations are in conflict with this Provision, matters are to be handled according to this Provision. As regards any contracts which were signed and took effect after approval before the implementation of this Provision which already made provisions for handling tax levy, tax reduction or tax exemption in accordance with regulations at that time, no change is to be made during the effective period of the contract (not including extensions of the contract period).

THE INCOME TAX LAW OF THE PEOPLE'S REPUBLIC OF CHINA CONCERNING JOINT VENTURES WITH CHINESE AND FOREIGN INVESTMENT

(Adopted on September 10, 1980 by the Fifth National People's Congress of the People's Republic of China at its Third Session.)

Article 1 Income tax shall be levied in accordance with this Law on the income derived from production, business and other sources by any joint venture with Chinese and foreign investment (hereinafter called joint venture for short) in the People's Republic of China.

Income tax on the income derived from production, business and other sources by branches within or outside the territory of China of such joint ventures shall be paid by their head office.

Article 2 The taxable income of a joint venture shall be the net income in a tax year after deduction of costs, expenses and losses in that year.

Article 3 The income tax rate on joint ventures shall be 30%. In addition, a local surtax of 10% of the assessed income tax shall be levied.

The income tax rate on joint ventures exploiting petroleum, natural gas and other resources shall be stipulated separately.

Article 4 In the case of a foreign participant in a joint venture remitting its share of profit from China, an income tax of 10% shall be levied on the remitted amount.

Article 5 A newly established joint venture scheduled to operate for a period of 10 years or more may, upon approval of the tax authorities for an application filed by the enterprise, be exempted from income tax in the first profit-making year and allowed a 50% reduction in the second and third years.

With the approval of the Ministry of Finance of the People's Republic of China, joint ventures engaged in such low-profit operations as farming and forestry or located in remote, economically underdeveloped outlying areas may be allowed a 15–30% reduction in income tax for a period of 10 years following the expiration of the term for exemptions and reductions mentioned in the preceding paragraph.

Article 6 A participant in a joint venture which reinvests its share of profit in China for a period of not less than five years may, upon approval of the tax authorities for an application filed by the said participant, obtain a refund of 40% of the income tax paid on the reinvested amount. A participant which withdraws its reinvested funds within five years shall pay back the tax amount refunded.

Article 7 Loss incurred in a joint venture in a tax year may be carried over to the next tax year and made up with an equal amount drawn from that year's income. Should the income in the subsequent tax year be insufficient to make up for the said loss, the balance may be made up with further deductions from income year by year over a period not exceeding five years.

Article 8 Income tax on joint ventures shall be levied on an annual basis and paid in quarterly installments. Such provisional payment shall be made within 15 days after the end of each quarter. The final settlement shall be made within three months after the end of a tax year. Excess payments shall be refunded by the tax authorities or deficiencies made good by the taxpayer.

Article 9 Joint ventures shall file their provisional income tax returns with the local tax authorities within the period prescribed for provisional payments. The taxpayer shall file its final annual income tax return together with its final accounts within three months after the end of the tax year.

Article 10 Income tax levied on joint ventures shall be computed in terms of Renminbi (RMB). Income in foreign currency shall be assessed according to the exchange rate quoted by the State General Administration of Exchange Control of the People's Republic of China and shall be taxed in Renminbi.

Article 11 When joint ventures go into operation or when they change the nature of their business, change their address, close down, and change or transfer registered capital, such joint ventures shall register with the General Administrative Bureau for Industry and Commerce of the People's Republic of China, and within 30 days of such registration, present the relevant certificates to the local tax authorities for tax registration.

Article 12 The tax authorities have the right to investigate the financial affairs, account books and tax situation of any joint venture. Such joint venture must make reports according to the facts and provide all relevant information and shall not refuse or conceal the facts.

Article 13 A joint venture must pay its tax within the prescribed time limit. In case of failure to pay within the prescribed time limit, the appropriate tax authorities, in addition to setting a new time limit for tax payment, shall surcharge overdue payments at one half of one percent of the overdue tax for every day in arrears, starting from the first day of default.

Article 14 The tax authorities may, acting at their discretion, impose a penalty on any joint venture which has violated the provisions of Articles 9, 11 and 12 of this Law.

In dealing with any joint venture which has evaded or refused to pay tax, the tax authorities may, in addition to pursuing the tax, impose a penalty of not more than five times the amount of tax underpaid or not paid, acccording to the seriousness of the offence. Cases of gross violation shall be handled by the local people's courts according to law.

Article 15 In case of disputes with tax authorities about tax payment, joint ventures must pay tax according to the relevant regulations first before applying to higher tax authorities for reconsideration. If they do not accept the decisions made after such reconsideration, they can bring the matter before the local people's courts.

Article 16 Income tax paid by a joint venture or its branch in other countries may be credited against the assessed income tax of the head office as foreign tax credit.

Where agreements on avoidance of double taxation have been concluded between the Government of the People's Republic of China and the government of another country, income tax credits shall be handled in accordance with the provisions of the related agreements.

Article 17 Detailed rules and regulations for the implementation of this Law shall be formulated by the Ministry of Finance of the People's Republic of China.

Article 18 This Law shall be put into effect from the date of promulgation.

DETAILED RULES AND REGULATIONS FOR THE IMPLEMENTATION OF THE INCOME TAX LAW OF THE PEOPLE'S REPUBLIC OF CHINA CONCERNING JOINT VENTURES WITH CHINESE AND FOREIGN INVESTMENT

(Approved by the State Council on December 10, 1980)

Article 1 These detailed rules and regulations are formulated in accordance with the provisions of Article 17 of the Income Tax Law of the People's Republic of China concerning Joint Ventures with Chinese and Foreign Investment (hereinafter called Tax Law for short).

Article 2 "Income derived from production and business" mentioned in Article 1 of the Tax Law means income from the production and business operations in industry, mining, communications, transportation, agriculture, forestry, animal husbandry, fisheries, poultry farming, commerce, tourism, food and drink, service and other trades.

"Income from other sources" mentioned in Article 1 of the Tax Law covers dividends, bonuses, interest and income from lease or transfer of property, patent right, ownership of trademarks, proprietary technology, copyright, and other sources.

Article 3 "A local surtax of 10 per cent of the assessed income tax" in Article 3 of the Tax Law means a surtax to be computed and levied according to the actual amount of income tax paid by joint ventures.

Reduction or exemption of local surtax on account of special circumstances shall be decided by the people's government of the province, municipality or autonomous region in which the joint venture is located.

Article 4 A foreign participant in a joint venture, who wants to remit its share of profits from China, shall report to the local tax authorities; the remitting agency shall withhold an income tax of 10% from the remittance. No tax shall be levied on that part of its share of profits which is not remitted from China.

Article 5 "The first profit-making year" mentioned in Article 5 of the Tax Law means the year in which a joint venture has begun making profit after its losses in the initial stage of operation have been made up in accordance with the provisions of Article 7 of the Tax Law.

Article 6 A participant in a joint venture, who reinvests its share of profit in this enterprise or in other joint ventures with Chinese and foreign investment for a period of not less than five years in succession, may receive a refund of 40% of the income tax already paid on the reinvested amount upon the examination and approval of the certificate of the invested enterprise by the tax authorities to which the tax was paid.

Article 7 The tax year for joint ventures starts from January 1 and ends on December 31 on the Gregorian calendar.

Article 8 The amount of taxable income shall be computed by the following formulae:

1. Industry:

A. Cost of production of the year is equal to direct material used in production of the year plus direct wages plus manufacturing expenses.

B. Cost of production of the year is equal to inventory of semi-finished product at the beginning of the year and in-production product plus cost of production of the year minus inventory of semi-finished product at the end of the year and in-production product.

C. Cost of sale of product is equal to cost of product of the year plus inventory of product at the beginning of the year minus inventory of product at the end of the year.

D. Net volume of sale of product is equal to total volume of sale of product minus (sales returns plus sales allowance).

E. Profit from sale of product is equal to net volume of sale of product minus taxes on sales minus cost of sale of product minus (selling expenses plus administrative expenses).

F. Amount of taxable income is equal to profit from sale of product plus profit from other operations plus non-operating income minus non-operating expenditure.

2. Commerce:

A. Net volume of sale is equal to total volume of sale minus (sales returns plus sales allowance).

B. Cost of sales is equal to inventory of merchandise at the beginning of the year plus [purchase of the year minus (purchase returns plus purchase discount) plus purchase expenses] minus inventory of merchandise at the end of the year.

C. Sale profit is equal to net volume of sale minus sale tax minus cost of sales minus (selling expenses plus overhead expenses).

D. Amount of taxable income is equal to sale profit plus profit from other operations plus non-operating income minus non-operating expenditure.

3. Service trades:

A. Net business income is equal to gross business income minus [business tax plus operating expenses plus overhead expenses].

B. Amount of taxable income is equal to net business income plus non-operating income minus non-operating expenditure.

4. Other lines of operation:

For other lines of operation, refer to the above-mentioned formulae for calculation.

Article 9 The following items shall not be counted as cost, expense or loss in computing the amount of taxable income:

1. Expenditure on the purchase or construction of machinery, equipment, buildings, facilities and other fixed assets;
2. Expenditure on the purchase of intangible assets;
3. Interest on capital;
4. Income tax payment and local surtax payment;
5. Penalty for illegal operations and losses in the form of confiscated property;
6. Overdue tax payment and tax penalty;
7. Losses from windstorms, floods and fire risks covered by insurance indemnity;
8. Donations and contributions other than those for public welfare and relief purposes;
9. That part of the entertainment expenses for operating purposes above the quota of three per thousand of the total sale income in the tax year or above the quota of ten per thousand of the total operational income and those entertainment expenses that are not relevant to production and operation.

Article 10 Depreciation of fixed assets in use shall be calculated on an annual basis. Fixed assets of joint ventures cover houses, buildings, machinery and other mechanical apparatus, means of transport and other equipment for the purpose of production with useful life or more than one year. But items with a per-unit value of less than 500 yuan and a short useful life can be itemized as expenses according to the actual number in use.

Article 11 Fixed assets shall be assessed according to the original price.

For fixed assets used as investment, the original price shall be the price agreed upon by the participants at the time of investment.

For purchased fixed assets, the original price shall be the purchase price plus transport fees, installation expenses and other related expenses incurred before they are put to use.

For self-made and self-built fixed assets, the original price shall be the actual expenditures incurred in the course of manufacture or construction.

Article 12 In depreciating fixed assets, the residual value shall be assessed first and deducted from the original price, the principle being making the residual value at 10% of the original price; those requiring to retain a little or no residual value shall be submitted for approval to the local tax authorities.

The depreciation of fixed assets shall generally be computed on average by the straight-line method.

Article 13 The useful life for computing depreciation of fixed assets is as follows:

1. The minimum useful life for houses and buildings is 20 years;
2. The minimum useful life for trains, ships, machines and equipment and other facilities for the purpose of production is 10 years;
3. The minimum useful life for electronic equipment and means of transport other than trains and ships is five years.

For cases where the fixed assets of joint ventures, owing to special reasons, need to accelerate depreciation or where methods of depreciation need to be modified, applications shall be submitted by the said ventures to the local tax authorities for examination and then relayed level by level to the Ministry of Finance of the People's Republic of China for approval.

Article 14 Expenditures arising from the increase of value of fixed assets in use as a result of technical reform shall not be listed as expense.

The fixed assets continuing in use after full depreciation shall no longer be depreciated.

Article 15 The balance of the gain of joint ventures derived from sale of fixed assets at the current price after the net sum of non-depreciated assets or the residual value is deducted shall enter the year's loss and gain account.

Article 16 Intangible assets such as technical know-how, patent right, ownership of trademarks, copyright, ownership of sites and other royalties used as investment shall be assessed by amortization according to the sums provided in the agreements or contracts from the year they begin in use; for intangible assets that are bought in at a fixed price, the actual payment shall be assessed from the year they are put in use.

The above-mentioned intangible assets with provision of time limit for use, shall be assessed by amortization according to the provision of time limit for use; those without the provision shall be assessed by amortization in ten years.

Article 17 Expenses arising during the period of preparation for a joint venture shall be amortized after it goes into production or business, with the amount of amortization not exceeding 20% each year.

Article 18 Inventory of merchandise, raw materials, in-production products, semi-finished products, finished products and by-products shall be computed according to the cost price. For the method of computation, the joint ventures may choose one of the following: First-in first-out, shifting average and weighted average. In those cases where a change in the method of computation is necessary, it shall be submitted for approval to the local tax authorities.

Article 19 Income tax to be paid in quarterly installments as prescribed in Article 8 of the Tax Law may be computed as one-fourth of the planned annual profit or the actual income in the preceding year.

Article 20 Joint ventures shall file their income tax returns and their final accounting statements with the local tax authorities within the prescribed period irrespective of profit or loss in the tax year and send the reports for auditing by the chartered public accountants registered in the People's Republic of China.

The accounting statements submitted by branches of joint ventures within China to their head offices shall be submitted to the local tax authorities at the same time for reference.

Article 21 Joint ventures shall file tax returns within the time limit set by the Tax Law. In case of failure to submit the tax returns within the prescribed time limit owing to special circumstances, application should be submitted in the said time limit, and the time limit may be appropriately extended upon the approval of the local tax authorities.

The final day of the time limit for tax payment and filing tax returns may be extended if it falls upon an official holiday.

Article 22 Income of joint ventures in foreign currency shall be assessed according to the exchange rate quoted by the State General Administration of Exchange Control on the day when the tax payment certificates are made out and shall be taxed in Renminbi.

Article 23 The accounting on the accrual basis shall be practised for revenue and expenditure of joint ventures. All accounting records shall be accurate and perfect and shall have lawful vouchers as the basis for entry account.

Article 24 The method of finance and accounting of joint ventures shall be submitted to local tax authorities for reference.

When the method of finance and accounting of joint ventures contradicts the provisions of the Tax Law, tax payments shall be computed according to the provisions of the Tax Law.

Article 25 Vouchers for accounting, accounting books and reports used for joint ventures shall be recorded in the Chinese language or in both Chinese and foreign language.

Accounting vouchers, accounting books and reports shall be kept for at least 15 years.

Article 26 Sales invoices and business receipts shall be submitted for approval to the local tax authorities before they are used.

Article 27 Officials sent by tax authorities shall produce identification cards when investigating the financial affairs, accounting books and tax situation of a joint venture, and they shall maintain confidentiality.

Article 28 Tax authorities may impose a penalty of not more than 5,000 yuan on a joint venture which has violated the provisions of Articles 9, 11 and 12 of the Tax Law according to the seriousness of the case.

Article 29 Tax authorities may impose a penalty of not more than 5,000 yuan on a joint venture which has violated the provisions of Paragraph 2 of Article 25, and Article 26 of these detailed rules and regulations.

Article 30 Tax authorities shall serve notices on cases involving penalty in accordance with the relevant provisions of the Tax Law and these detailed rules and regulations.

Article 31 When a joint venture applies for reconsideration in accordance with the provisions of Article 15 of the Tax Law, the tax authorities concerned are required to make decisions within three months after receiving the application.

Article 32 Income tax paid abroad by joint ventures or its branches on their income earned outside China may be credited against the amount of income tax to be paid by their head offices upon presenting the foreign tax payment certificate. But the credit amount shall not exceed the payable tax on the income abroad computed according to the tax rate prescribed by China's Tax Law.

Article 33 Income Tax returns and tax payment certificates used by joint ventures are to be printed by the General Tax Bureau of the Ministry of Finance of the People's Republic of China.

Article 34 The right of interpreting the provisions of these detailed rules and regulations resides in the Ministry of Finance of the People's Republic of China.

Article 35 These detailed rules and regulations come into force on the same date as the publication and enforcement of the "Income Tax Law of the People's Republic of China Concerning Joint Ventures with Chinese and Foreign Investment."

CIRCULAR OF THE MINISTRY OF FINANCE CONCERNING SOME QUESTIONS ABOUT THE INCOME TAX OF JOINT VENTURES COMPRISING CHINESE AND FOREIGN INVESTMENT

(June 8, 1981)

To financial departments (bureaus) in the provinces, municipalities and autonomous regions:

Since the Income Tax Law Concerning Joint Ventures with Chinese and Foreign Investment and the Detailed Rules and Regulations for the Implementation of the Law were promulgated and enforced, various localities have raised a number of specific questions concerning policy matters and demanded clarification. These questions were discussed at a recent meeting on tax work involving foreigners, attended by representatives of six provinces (municipalities). Hereby we clarify some of the major questions as follows:

1. Concerning the refund of tax on reinvestment:

a. According to the provisions of Article 6 of the Income Tax Law Concerning Joint Ventures with Chinese and Foreign Investment, partners eligible to apply for a refund of tax paid on reinvestment should include Chinese partners as well as foreign partners. The scope of reinvestment to apply for tax refund should be confined to the reinvestment in the same joint ventures in China or other joint ventures using Chinese and foreign investment as well as the use of the profits shared to set up new joint ventures with Chinese companies or enterprises. Reinvestment in operations with one's sole investment or in cooperative production or cooperative operations is not eligible for tax refund.

b. When a joint venture draws from the reserve fund or enterprise development fund to purchase fixed assets according to the provisions of the Law Concerning Joint Ventures involving Chinese and Foreign Investment, this means using statutory funds to expand reproduction and does not belong to the scope of reinvestment applying for the tax refund.

c. In applying for tax refund on reinvestment, a partner should obtain a certificate written by the enterprise that has accepted the investment. The said certificate must include the source of the investment fund, the amount of investment and the time limit of investment, and enclose a copy of the agreement or contract on the said investment. A partner who gains this share of profit from a joint venture in place A and invests it in a joint venture in place B or uses it to open a new joint venture in place B with a Chinese company or enterprise, may apply, on the strength of the above certificate, for tax refund on the reinvestment with the tax authorities at the place he has paid the tax.

d. The portion of income tax already paid on which a partner applies for refund as reinvestment out of his share of profit, does not include the local surtax levied on the assessed income tax. According to the provisions of Paragraph 2, Article 3 of the Detailed Rules and Regulations for the Implementation of the Income Tax Law Concerning Joint Ventures with Chinese and Foreign Investment, it is up to the people's government of the province, autonomous region or municipality where the joint venture is located to decide whether the local income tax should be reduced or exempted on special grounds.

The following are formulae for calculating the tax amount to be applied for a refund on reinvestment:

$$\text{Formula 1 : [reinvestment amount} + (1 - \frac{33}{100})\,] \times \frac{30}{100} \times \frac{40}{100} = \text{tax refund amount}$$

$$\text{Formula 2: reinvestment amount} \times \frac{17.91}{100} = \text{tax refund amount}$$

e. If a foreign partner remits abroad the amount of tax refund on reinvestment, it shall not be taxed as a remittance of profit.

2. Concerning the taxation on profit remitted abroad:

When a foreign partner is going to remit abroad his share of profit obtained from the joint venture, the remittance handling unit shall, without exception, withhold an income tax of 10% of the amount of profit to be remitted, according to the provisions of the Detailed Rules and Regulations for the Implementation of the Income Tax Law Concerning Joint Ventures with Chinese and Foreign Investment.

3. Concerning the time limit for tax reduction or remission for new joint ventures:

For a new joint venture to run for more than 10 years, if it starts operation in the middle of a tax year and makes a profit the same year, it should be regarded as the first profit-making year and is exempted from income tax. As for isolated, special cases, the enterprise may file a request and the local tax authorities shall deal with it in accordance with the actual circumstances.

4. Concerning the calculation of credit limit:

According to the provisions of Article 16 of the Income Tax Law Concerning Joint Ventures with Chinese and Foreign Investment and Article 32 of the Detailed Rules and Regulations, the income tax paid abroad by a joint venture and its branches can be credited against the amount of tax income the head office is due to pay; but the credit amount must not exceed the amount of tax on the income obtained abroad calculated according to the tax rate stipulated in the Chinese tax law. This credit limit should be calculated on a country-by-country basis, that is, income derived from profits abroad such as interest and royalties can be calculated for credit limit by countries and not by categories; for a tax paid in a given country, the credit limit shall be calculated out of the amount of income earned from that country according to the tax rate stipulated in the Chinese tax law.

5. Concerning the taxation on dividends and bonuses obtained by joint ventures:

The dividends and bonuses obtained outside China by a joint venture should be lumped together by the head office with the incomes from production and operation and be taxed. The tax already paid at the time of receiving the said dividends and bonuses abroad, can be credited against the assessed tax amount in China. For the dividends and bonuses obtained in China, such as those obtained by joint venture A for its investment in joint venture B, if the income tax is already paid at joint venture B according to the regulations of the tax law, then the sum shall not be included in the yearly profit of joint venture A for calculating the income tax.

6. Concerning accelerated depreciation of fixed assets:

The minimum period for depreciation of fixed assets in joint ventures has been listed in three categories in the Detailed Rules and Regulations. These have taken into consideration the fast development of modern production technology and the universal practice of accelerated depreciation in various countries of the world, so they basically suit the actual needs of property renewal and capital recovery. Therefore, it is generally not allowed to be less than the depreciation period prescribed in the Detailed Rules and Regulations. Only in certain special cases is it permissable to apply for accelerated depreciation. In actual implementation, the following points can serve as reference for the time being, but must be strictly controlled:

a. The period of joint operation is shorter than the depreciation period of fixed assets as stipulated in the tax law and the property after the expiration of the joint operation period will become the property of the Chinese side (for instance, the period of the joint operation is generally 10 years for the cooperative construction and operation of a tourist hotel and, when the capital is recouped within this joint operation period, the hotel will be turned over to the Chinese side. In such circumstances, the enterprise can be allowed to apply for accelerated depreciation);

b. Strong acid, alkaline or corrosive equipment and factory buildings and structures subject to vibration and oscillation throughout the year;

c. Machinery or equipment operating around the clock year in and year out with a view to raising the utilization rate and stepping up utilization intensity.

THE INCOME TAX LAW FOR FOREIGN ENTERPRISES OF THE PEOPLE'S REPUBLIC OF CHINA

(Adopted at the Fourth Session of the Fifth National People's Congress on December 13, 1981)

Article 1 Income tax shall be levied in accordance with this law on the income derived from production, business and other sources by all foreign enterprises operating in the People's Republic of China.

"Foreign enterprises" mentioned in this law refer, with the exception of those for whom separate provisions are stipulated in Article 11, to foreign companies, enterprises and other economic organizations which have establishments in the People's Republic of China and are engaged in independent business operation or co-operative production or joint business operation with Chinese enterprises.

Article 2 The taxable income of a foreign enterprise shall be the net income in a tax year after deduction of costs, expenses and losses in that year.

Article 3 Income tax on foreign enterprises shall be assessed at progressive rates for the parts in excess of a specific amount of taxable income. The tax rates are as follows:

Range of income	Tax Rate (percent)
Annual income below 250,000	20%
That part of annual income from 250,000 to 500,000 yuan	25%
That part of annual income from 500,000 to 750,000	30%
That part of annual income from 750,000 to 1 million yuan	35%
That part of annual income over 1 million yuan	40%

Article 4 In addition to the income tax levied on foreign enterprises in accordance with the provisions of the preceding article, a local income tax of 10% of the same taxable income shall be levied.

Where a foreign enterprise needs reduction in or exemption from local income tax on account of the small scale of its production or business, or its rate of profit, this shall be decided by the people's government of the province, municipality or autonomous region in which that enterprise is located.

Article 5 A foreign enterprise scheduled to operate for a period of 10 years or more in farming, forestry, animal husbandry or other low profit occupations may, upon approval by the tax authorities of an application filed by the enterprise, be exempted from income tax in the first profit-making year and allowed a 50 per cent reduction in the second and third years.

With the approval of the Ministry of Finance, a 15-30% reduction in income tax may be allowed for a period of 10 years following the expiration of the term for exemptions and reductions specified in the preceding paragraph.

Article 6 Losses incurred by a foreign enterprise in a tax year may be carried over to the next year and made up with a corresponding amount drawn from that year's income. Should the income in the subsequent tax year be insufficient to make up for the said losses, the balance may be made up with further deductions against income year by year over a period not exceeding five years.

Article 7 Income tax on foreign enterprises shall be levied on an annual basis and paid in quarterly installments. Such provisional payments shall be made within 15 days after the end of each quarter. The final settlement shall be made within five months after the end of a tax year. Excess payments shall be refunded by the tax authorities or deficiencies made good by the taxpayer.

Article 8 Foreign enterprises shall file their provisional income tax returns with the local tax authorities within the period prescribed for provisional payments. The taxpayer shall file its final annual income tax return together with its final accounts within four months after the end of the tax year.

Article 9 The method of financial management and the system of accounting of foreign enterprises shall be submitted to local tax authorities for reference.

Where the method of financial management and the system of accounting of foreign enterprises are in contradiction with the provisions of the tax law, tax payments shall be assessed according to the provisions of the tax law in any event.

Article 10 Foreign enterprises shall present relevant certificates to the local tax authorities for tax registration when they go into operation or close down in accordance with law.

Article 11 A 20% income tax shall be levied on the income derived from dividends, interests, rentals, royalties and other sources in China by foreign companies, enterprises and other economic organizations which have no establishments in China. Such tax shall be deducted by the paying unit in each of its payments of dividends, etc.

For the payment of income tax according to the provisions in the preceding paragraph, the foreign companies, enterprises and other economic organizations earning the income shall be the taxpayer, and the paying unit shall be the deduction agent. Taxes deducted on each payment by a deduction agent shall, within five days, be turned over to the State Treasury and the income tax return submitted to the tax authorities.

Income from interest on loans given to the Chinese Government or China's state banks by international finance organizations shall be exempted from income tax. Income from interest on loans given at a preferential interest rate by foreign banks to China's state banks shall also be exempted from income tax.

Income derived from interest on deposits of foreign banks in China's state banks and on loans given at a normal interest rate by foreign banks to China's state banks shall be taxed. However, exemption from income tax shall be granted to those foreign banks in whose countries income from interest on deposits and loans of China's state banks is exempted from income tax.

Article 12 The tax authorities have the right to investigate the financial affairs, account books and tax situation of all foreign enterprises, and have the right to investigate the deducting situation of any deduction agent. Such foreign enterprises and deduction agents must make reports on facts and provide all relevant information and shall not refuse to cooperate or conceal any facts.

Article 13 Income tax levied on foreign enterprises shall be computed in terms of Renminbi (RMB). Income in foreign currency shall be assessed according to the exchange rate quoted by the State General Administration of Exchange Control of the People's Republic of China and taxed in Renminbi.

Article 14 Foreign enterprises and deduction agents must pay their tax within the prescribed time limit. In case of failure to pay within the prescribed time limit, the appropriate tax authorities, in addition to setting a new time limit for tax payment, shall surcharge overdue payments at one half of one per cent of the overdue tax for every day in arrears, starting from the first day of default.

Article 15 The tax authorities may, acting at their discretion, impose a penalty on any foreign enterprise which has violated the provisions of Articles 8, 9, 10 and 12 of this law.

In dealing with those withholding agents who have violated the provisions of Article 11 of this law, the tax authorities may in addition set a new time limit for the payment of the part of tax that should have been deducted and, at their discretion, impose a penalty of not more than the amount that should have been deducted.

In dealing with foreign enterprises which have evaded or refused to pay income tax, the tax authorities may, in addition to pursuing the tax, impose a fine of not more than five times the amount of tax underpaid or unpaid, according to the seriousness of the offence. Cases of gross violation shall be handled by the local people's courts according to law.

Article 16 In case of disputes with tax authorities about tax payment, foreign enterprises must pay tax according to the relevant regulations first before applying to higher tax authorities for reconsideration. If they do not accept the decisions made after such reconsideration, they can bring the matter before the local people's courts.

Article 17 Where agreements on tax payment have been concluded between the Government of the People's Republic of China and the government of another country, matters concerning tax payment shall be handled in accordance with the provisions of these agreements.

Article 18 Detailed rules and regulations for the implementation of this law shall be formulated by the Ministry of Finance of the People's Republic of China.

Article 19 This law shall be put into effect as of January 1, 1982.

DETAILED RULES AND REGULATIONS OF THE PEOPLE'S REPUBLIC OF CHINA FOR THE IMPLEMENTATION OF THE INCOME TAX LAW CONCERNING FOREIGN ENTERPRISES

(Approved by the State Council on February 17, 1982, and promulgated by the Ministry of Finance on February 21, 1982)

Article 1 The Detailed Rules and Regulations are formulated in accordance with the provisions of Article 18 of the Income Tax Law of the People's Republic of China Concerning Foreign Enterprises (hereinafter called Tax Law for short).

Article 2 "Establishments" mentioned in Article 1 of the Tax Law refers to organizations, places or business agents established in the Chinese territory by foreign enterprises and engaged in production and business operations.

The organizations and places mentioned in the preceding paragraph mainly include management offices, branches, representative offices, factories and places where natural resources are exploited and where contracted projects of building, installation, assembly and exploration are operated.

Article 3 Foreign enterprises and Chinese enterprises engaged in any cooperative production or joint business operation should, unless separate provisions are stipulated, each pay their income taxes respectively.

Article 4 "Income derived from production and business" mentioned in Article 1 of the Tax Law refers to income from the production and business operations by foreign enterprises in industry, mining, communications, transportation, agriculture, forestry, animal husbandry, fisheries, poultry farming, commerce, service and other trades.

Income from other sources as mentioned in Article 1 of the Tax Law covers dividends, interest, income from lease or sale of property, income from transfer of patents, technical know-how, trademark interests, or copyright and other non-business income.

Article 5 The taxable income for assessing the local income tax as mentioned in Article 4 of the Tax Law is the same as the taxable income mentioned in Article 3 of the Tax Law, i.e., it is calculated according, to the formulas given in Article 9 of the Detailed Rules and Regulations.

Article 6 Enterprises engaged in small-scale production and enterprises of low profits, as mentioned in paragraph 2 of Article 4 of the Tax Law, refer to foreign enterprises with an annual income less than one million RMB yuan.

Article 7 Foreign enterprises scheduled to operate in low profit occupations, as mentioned in Article 5 of the Tax Law, include those low-profit enterprises engaged in exploiting coal mineral resources in deep wells.

Article 8 The tax year for foreign enterprises starts from January 1 and ends on December 31 on the Gregorian Calendar.

Where a foreign enterprise finds it difficult to compute its income of the tax year as stipulated in the preceding paragraph, it may apply to the local tax authorities for approval to use its own 12-month fiscal year for tax computation and payment.

Article 9 The taxable income shall be calculated in accordance with the following formulas:

1. Industry:

a) Production costs of the year = Direct materials used in production for the year + direct wages + manufacturing expenses;

b) Cost of the product of the year = Production costs of the year + inventory of products semi-finished and in process of production at the beginning of the year − inventory of products semi-finished and in process of production at the end of the year;

c) Cost of the sales of the product = Cost of the product for the year + inventory of the product at the beginning of the year − inventory of the product at the end of the year;

d) Net sales of the product = Gross sales of the product − (sales return + sales allowance);

e) Profit from sales of the product = Net sales of the product − tax on the sales of the product − cost of the sales of the product − (selling expenses + overhead expenses);

f) Taxable income = Profit from sales of the product + profit from other operations + non-business income − non-business expenditure.

2. Commerce:

a) Net sales = Gross sales – (sales return + sales allowance);

b) Cost of sales = Inventory of merchandise at the beginning of the year + [purchases of the year – (purchase returned + purchase discount) + purchase expenses] – inventory of merchandise at the end of the year;

c) Profit of sales = Net sales – cost of sales – tax on sales – (selling expenses + overhead expenses);

d) Taxable income = Profit of sales + profit from other operations + non-business income – non-business expenditure.

3. Service trades:

a) Net business income = Gross business income – (tax on business + operating expenses + overhead expenses);

b) Taxable income = Net business income + non-business income – non-business expenditure.

4. Other trades:

For other trades, refer to the above-mentioned formulas for calculation.

Article 10 The following items shall not be counted as cost, expense or loss in calculating the taxable income:

1. Expenditure on the purchase or construction of machinery, equipment, building facilities and other fixed assets;

2. Expenditure on the purchase of intangible assets;

3. Interest on equity capital;

4. Income tax payment and local income tax payment;

5. Penalty for illegal operations and losses in the form of confiscated property;

6. Overdue tax payment and tax penalty;

7. Losses from windstorms, floods and fire covered by insurance indemnity;

8. Donations and contributions other than those for public welfare and relief purposes in China;

9. Royalties paid to the head offices;

10. Other expenses that are not relevant to production and business operations.

Article 11 Reasonable overhead expenses that are relevant to production and operation paid by a foreign enterprise to its head office and actual expenses paid to its head office for services directly provided may be listed as expenses on the condition that the said expenses are backed up by certificates and vouchers from the head office, together with a financial report signed by a chartered public accountant, and examined and approved by the local tax authorities.

Where a foreign enterprise is engaged in cooperative production and joint business operation with a Chinese enterprise and an agreement has been reached and included in the signed contract for the sharing of overhead expenses of the head office, such payments may be listed as expenses in accordance with the confirmed method in the contract after being examined and ratified by the local tax authorities.

Article 12 Foreign enterprises are permitted to list as expenses the interest payments on loans at reasonable rates on the condition that the loans and interest payments are backed up by certifying documents and, after being examined by the local tax authorities, are considered as being of normal terms.

Article 13 Reasonable entertainment expenses paid by foreign enterprises that are relevant to production and business operation shall be supported by reliable records or vouchers and documents, and then may be listed as expenses within the following limits respectively:

1. For enterprises with annual net sales less than 15 million RMB yuan, the reasonable entertainment expenses shall not be in excess of 0.3 percent of the net sales; for those with annual net sales more than 15 million RMB yuan, the expenses for that portion above the limit shall not exceed 0.1 percent of the said portion.

2. For enterprises with annual total business income less than 5 million RMB yuan, the reasonable entertainment expenses shall not be in excess of one percent of the total business income; for those with annual total business income more than 5 million RMB yuan, the expenses for that portion above the limit shall not exceed 0.3 percent of the said portion.

Article 14 Depreciation of fixed assets of foreign enterprises in current use shall be calculated on an annual basis. The fixed assets cover houses, buildings, machinery and other mechanical apparatus, means of transport and other equipment for the purpose of production or business operations with useful life span of more than one year. But articles with a per-unit value of less than 500 RMB yuan and a shorter useful life span that are not essential equipment for production or operation can be itemized as expenses according to the actual quantity in current use.

Article 15 Fixed assets shall be assessed according to the original value.

For fixed assets counted as an investment by

foreign enterprises and Chinese enterprises engaged in cooperative production and business operation, the original value shall be the price of the assets agreed upon by all participants at the time of cooperation.

For purchased fixed assets, the original value shall be the purchase price plus freight, installation expenses and other related expenses incurred before they are put into use.

For self-made and self-built fixed assets, the original value shall be the actual expenditures incurred in the course of manufacture or construction.

For self-owned and used fixed assets that are shipped in from abroad, the documents certifying their original value and the number of years in use, together with reference data on their market price, shall be presented and their actual value shall be reassessed according to the quality. For assets without certifying documents, the value shall be assessed by the enterprise and submitted to the local tax authorities for examination and approval in accordance with the quality of the assets.

Article 16 Depreciation of fixed assets shall be calculated starting from the month when the assets are put into use. Depreciation shall no longer be calculated starting from the month following that in which the fixed assets cease to be used.

For enterprises engaged in exploiting offshore petroleum resources, all investments at the stage of development shall be counted as capital expenditure with the oil (gas) field as a unit, and depreciation shall be calculated starting from the month when the oil (gas) field begins to go into production for commercial purposes.

Article 17 In calculating depreciation on fixed assets, the residual value shall be assessed first and deducted from the original value, the principle being to make the residual value about 10 percent of the original value; those assets to retain a lower or no residual value shall be submitted for approval to the local tax authorities. If the depreciation is calculated in accordance with a composite life method, residual value may not be retained.

Depreciation on fixed assets shall generally be computed in average under the straight-line method.

Article 18 The depreciation period for various kinds of fixed assets is set as follows:

1. The minimum depreciation period for houses and buildings is 20 years;

2. The minimum depreciation period for trains, ships, machines and equipment and other apparatus for the purpose of production is 10 years;

3. The minimum depreciation period for electronic equipment, means of transport other than trains and ships, as well as appliances, tools and furniture relevant to production and operation is five years.

For cases where the depreciation on fixed assets of foreign enterprises, owing to special reasons, needs to be accelerated or to be computed under modified methods, applications may be submitted to the local tax authorities for examination and then relayed level by level to the Ministry of Finance for approval.

Depreciation of various kinds of fixed assets resulting from the investments of enterprises engaged in exploiting offshore petroleum resources, during and after the stage of development, may be calculated in accordance with a composite life method. The depreciation period shall not be less than six years.

For enterprises engaged in exploiting coal mineral resources, the provisions of the preceding paragraph may also be applied.

Article 19 Expenditure arising from expansion, replacement, refitting and technical innovation and resulting in the increase of value of the fixed assets in use, should be regarded as capital expenditure, and shall not be listed as expenses.

For the fixed assets remaining in use after the full depreciation period, no depreciation shall be allowed.

Article 20 The balance of the proceeds from the alienation or disposal of fixed assets at the current prices, after the net unamortized value or the residual value of the assets is deducted, shall be entered into the profit and loss account for the current year.

Article 21 For intangible assets such as parents, technical know-how, trademark interests, copyright, right to use sites and other franchises that are assigned to foreign enterprises, the payment made by the enterprises at reasonable prices shall be amortized from the month they come into use.

Intangible assets mentioned in the preceding paragraph and counted as the investment by foreign and Chinese enterprises in co-operative production and business operation, may be amortized on the basis of the assessed value as provided in the agreements or contracts from the month they come into use.

The intangible assets mentioned in the preceding two paragraphs that are earmarked or counted as investment by the foreign enterprises with the provision of time limit for use, shall be assessed and amortized according to the time limit; those without such provision shall be assessed and amortized in a period not less than 10 years.

Article 22 Expenses arising during the period of preparation for a foreign enterprise shall be amortized after it goes into production or business in a period not less than five years.

Reasonable exploration expenses incurred by foreign enterprises engaged in exploiting offshore petroleum resources may be amortized from the revenues derived from the oil (or gas) field that has gone into production for commercial purposes, but the time limit of such amortization shall not be less than one year.

Article 23 Inventory of merchandise, raw materials, products in process of production, semi-finished products, finished products and by-products shall be valued according to the cost price. For the method of computation, the enterprises may choose one out of the following: first-in first-out, shifting average and weighted average. In case a change in the method of computation is necessary, it shall be submitted to the local tax authorities for approval.

Article 24 If a foreign enterprise cannot provide accurate evidence of costs and expenses and cannot correctly work out its taxable income, the local tax authorities shall appraise and determine its profit rate with reference to the profit level of other enterprises of the same or similar trade, and then calculate its taxable income on the basis of its net sales or its gross business income.

The taxable income of a foreign enterprise engaged in contracted projects for exploring and exploiting offshore petroleum resources shall be calculated according to the profit rate appraised and determined in relation to its gross income of the contract.

Article 25 For foreign air and ocean shipping enterprises engaged in international transport business, the taxable income shall be 5 percent of the gross income from transport services for passengers and cargoes loaded within the Chinese territory.

Article 26 Foreign enterprises engaged in cooperative production with Chinese enterprises on the basis of prorating of products are considered as receiving income when such products are distributed, and the amount of their income shall be computed according to the prices at which the products are sold to the third party or with reference to the prevailing market prices of the products.

Foreign enterprises engaged in cooperative exploitation of offshore petroleum resources are considered as receiving income when they receive their share of crude oil, and the amount of their income shall be computed according to the prices which are regularly adjusted with reference to the international market price of crude oil of equal quality.

Article 27 The income of dividends, interest, rentals, royalties and other sources in China as mentioned in Article 11 of the Tax Law is explained as follows:

"Dividends" refers to the dividends or the share of profits obtained from enterprises in China.

"Interest" refers to interest earned from deposits and loans, interest on various bonds purchased and interest earned from payments made for others and from deferred payments in China.

"Rentals" refers to rentals on properties rented to persons in China.

"Royalties" refers to income obtained from the provision of various patents, technical know-how, copyright and trademark interest for use in China.

"Income from other sources" refers to income specified to be taxable by the Ministry of Finance other than those mentioned above.

Article 28 The income from dividends, interest, rentals, royalties and other sources in China as mentioned in the preceding article, with the exception of those for which separate provisions are stipulated, shall be assessed on its full amount, and the tax to be paid shall be withheld by the paying unit from each payment.

Article 29 "International finance organizations" as mentioned in Article 11 of the Tax Law refers to the International Monetary Fund, the International Bank for Reconstruction and Development, the International Development Association, the International Fund for Agricultural Development and other finance organizations of the United Nations.

The "preferential interest rate" mentioned therein refers to a rate that is at least 10% less than the general prevailing interest rate in the international financial market.

Article 30 "China's state banks" mentioned in Article 11 of the Tax Law include the People's Bank of China, the Bank of China, the

Agricultural Bank of China, the People's Construction Bank of China, the Investment Bank of China, and the International Trust and Investment Corporation which has been authorized by the State Council to be engaged in business of foreign exchange deposits, loans and credits with foreign clients.

Article 31 "Income derived from interest on deposits," as mentioned in paragraph 4 of Article 11 of the Tax Law shall not include the interest on deposits of foreign banks in China's state banks at a rate of interest lower than that prevailing in the international financial market. Income from interest on deposits at a rate lower than that prevailing in the international financial market shall be exempted from income tax.

Article 32 Payments of income, as mentioned in Article 11 of the Tax Law, include payments in cash, payments by remittance, payments through transfer accounts, as well as payments made in marketable securities or in kind which are rendered into equivalent amounts of money.

Article 33 Income tax to be paid provisionally in quarterly instalments as stipulated in Article 7 of the Tax Law may be paid according to the actual quarterly profit, or it may be paid on one-fourth of the taxable income calculated on the basis of the planned profit for the current year or the actual income in the preceding year.

Article 34 For foreign enterprises which have operated for less than a year, the income tax shall be assessed on the actual income earned in the operation period at the applicable tax rate prescribed by the Tax Law.

Article 35 When foreign enterprises go into operation or close down, such enterprises shall, within 30 days after starting operation or before closing down, go to the local tax authorities for the relevant tax registration according to Article 10 of the Tax Law.

Article 36 Foreign enterprises shall file their income tax returns and final accounting statements with the local tax authorities within the prescribed period irrespective of making profit or loss in the tax year and, unless otherwise stipulated, shall send in at the same time the audit certificate of the chartered public accountants registered in the People's Republic of China.

Article 37 In case of failure to submit the tax returns within the prescribed time limit owing to special circumstances, the foreign enterprises should submit application to the local tax authorities within the said time limit, and the time limit for filing tax returns and accordingly that for final settlement may be appropriately extended upon the latter's approval.

The final day of the time limit for tax payment and that for filing tax returns may be extended if it falls upon a public holiday.

Article 38 The revenue and expenditure of foreign enterprises shall in principle be accounted on accrual basis. All accounting records shall be accurate and complete, and shall have proper vouchers as the basis for entries.

Article 39 Accounting vouchers, books, statements and reports adopted by foreign enterprises shall be made in the Chinese language or in both Chinese and foreign languages.

Accounting vouchers, books, statements and reports shall be kept for at least 15 years.

Article 40 Forms of sales invoices and business receipts shall be submitted for approval to the local tax authorities before they are put to use.

Article 41 Officials sent by tax authorities to investigate the financial, accounting and tax affairs of a foreign enterprise shall produce identification cards and undertake to maintain secrecy.

Article 42 As foreign enterprises with income in foreign currencies pay income tax in quarterly instalments, the income shall be assessed according to the exchange rate quoted by the State General Administration of Exchange Control on the day when the tax payment certificates are made out and shall be taxed in Renminbi; when the final settlement is made after the end of the tax year, excess payments of the tax shall be refunded or deficiencies made up in Renminbi according to the exchange rate quoted by the State General Administration of Exchange Control on the last day of the tax year.

Article 43 Tax authorities may impose a penalty of 5,000 RMB yuan or less on a foreign enterprise which has violated the provisions of Article 8, paragraph 1 of Article 9, Article 10 or Article 12 of the Tax Law according to the seriousness of the case.

Article 44 Tax authorities may impose a

penalty of 5,000 RMB yuan or less on a foreign enterprise which has violated the provisions of paragraph 2 of Article 39 or Article 40 of the Detailed Rules and Regulations according to the seriousness of the case.

Article 45 "Evade or refuse to pay income tax," as mentioned in paragraph 3 of Article 15 of the Tax Law, shall be interpreted as follows:

"Evade paying income tax" refers to the taxpayer's deliberate violation of the regulations of the Tax Law by forging, altering or destroying account books, papers or vouchers for accounting entries; falsifying and overstating costs and expenses; concealing or understating the amount of taxable income or gross income; evading taxes or recovering paid taxes through or by other illegal activities.

"Refuse to pay income tax" refers to the taxpayer's defiance of the regulations of the Tax Law by refusing to file tax returns and present certificates, papers and vouchers for tax purposes; refusing the investigation of the financial, accounting and tax affairs conducted by tax authorities; refusing to pay tax and penalties according to the Tax Law; or by other illegal activities.

Article 46 Tax authorities shall serve notice on relevant parties for case involving penalty in accordance with the relevant provisions of the Tax Law and the Detailed Rules and Regulations.

Article 47 When a foreign enterprise applies for reconsideration in accordance with the provisions of Article 16 of the Tax Law, the tax authorities concerned are required to make decisions within three months after the application is received.

Article 48 Income tax returns and tax payment certificates for foreign enterprises are to be printed by the General Taxation Bureau of the Ministry of Finance of the People's Republic of China.

Article 49 The right of interpreting the provisions of the Detailed Rules and Regulations rests in the Ministry of Finance of the People's Republic of China.

Article 50 The Detailed Rules and Regulations come into force on the same date as the Income Tax Law of the People's Republic of China Concerning Foreign Enterprises.

PROVISIONS OF THE GENERAL CUSTOMS OFFICE AND THE MINISTRY OF FINANCE FOR THE COLLECTION OR REMISSION OF CUSTOMS DUTIES AND INDUSTRIAL AND COMMERCIAL CONSOLIDATED TAXES ON IMPORTS AND EXPORTS FOR THE CHINESE-FOREIGN COOPERATIVE EXPLOITATION OF OFFSHORE OIL

(Approved by the State Council on February 28, 1982 and promulgated by the General Customs Office and the Ministry of Finance on April 1, 1982)

For the purpose of encouraging the Chinese-foreign cooperative exploitation of offshore oil, the Customs duties and industrial and commercial consolidated taxes on the imports and exports for oil operations are stipulated as follows:

1. The following imports shall be exempt from taxation:

(1) The machines, equipment, spare parts and materials which have been inspected and approved to be directly used in prospecting operations;

(2) The machines, equipment, spare parts and materials which are required and have been inspected and approved to be imported and directly used in exploiting operations in accordance with Article 19 to Article 21 of the "Regulations on the Exploitation of Offshore Petroleum Resources in Cooperation with Foreign Enterprises of the People's Republic of China;"

(3) The parts, components and materials which are required and have been inspected and approved to be imported and used for the manufacture in China of the machines and equipment used in offshore oil exploitation operations (including prospecting, well drilling, well cementation, well survey, well logging, oil recovery, well repair, etc.);

(4) Machinery and other engineering equipment which are temporarily imported by foreign contractors for the exploitation of offshore oil and of which the re-export is guaranteed shall be exempt from duties at the time of import or re-export abroad.

2. The crude oil obtained by foreign contractors as stipulated in contracts shall be exempt from export duties when it is shipped abroad.

3. Customs duties and industrial and commercial consolidated taxes shall be levied on the imports or exports which are not within the ranges stipulated in Article 1 and Article 2 in accordance with the "Import and Export Duty Tariff of the Customs of the People's Republic of China" and the "(Draft) Regulations of the People's Republic of China on Industrial and Commercial Consolidated Taxes."

4. The goods imported free of duties shall not be transferred for other purposes without inspection and approval by the Customs. Those who violate this clause shall be dealt with by the Customs in accordance with the "Interim Law of the People's Republic of China on Customs."

APPENDIX: DETAILED DUTY-FREE LIST OF THE IMPORT MATERIALS FOR THE CHINESE-FOREIGN COOPERATIVE EXPLOITATION OF OFFSHORE OIL

I Goods Which Are Required and Have Been Inspected and Approved for Import and Direct Use in Prospecting Operations:

1. Those for Geophysical Prospecting:

(1) Geophysical prospecting vessels and their integral accessories;

(2) Seismographs and their integral accessories and fittings; heavy magnetometers and their fittings;

(3) Isobuoyant cables and their integral accessories;

(4) Data processing special-purpose electronic computers and their integral accessories;

(5) Seismograph tapes;

(6) Shore platform positioning equipment and its accessory facilities.

2. Those for Well Drilling:

(1) Various offshore drilling units, including

self-elevating or semi-submersible drill ships, floating drilling vessels, drilling platforms, auxiliary vessels and service craft;

(2) Drilling machines and their components, accessories and fittings;

(3) Well cementation equipment and its accessory equipment, including soot-blowing equipment;

(4) Well survey equipment and its accessory equipment, including electrographs, pneumographs, inclinometers and other well loggers;

(5) Oil testing and well repairing equipment and its components, accessories and fittings;

(6) Well drilling special-purpose tools, including drilling bits, drill collars, drilling rods, deflecting tools, deflection preventing tools, fishing tools and other tools;

(7) Drilling mud treating equipment and chemical materials;

(8) Oil well special-purpose materials, including oil pipes, casings, well head assemblies and underwater appliances;

(9) Oil well cement and various additives.

3. Those for Safety and Rescue:

(1) Various oil well blowout preventing devices, spare parts and materials;

(2) Various fire prevention and fighting devices and materials;

(3) Various lifesaving appliances, accessories and tools;

(4) Special labour protection articles of offshore operating personnel;

(5) Equipment and materials for diving operations.

4. Those for Communications and Transportation:

(1) Helicopters and parking apron equipment;

(2) Communications, transportation and escort vessels and their accessory components;

(3) Various wire and wireless communication equipment and its fittings.

5. Oils:

Special fuel oils, lubricating oil, coolant fluids, etc. required for offshore operations.

II Goods Which Are Required and Have Been Inspected and Approved to be Imported and Used in Exploiting Operations, i.e. in the Construction of Oil Fields:

1. Those for Oil Recovery:

(1) Production platforms, including recovery platforms, treating platforms, living platforms and beacon towers;

(2) Offshore oil loading facilities, including single-point moorings, hinged rocking posts, oil storage ships or underwater oil tanks and piled piers;

(3) Offshore engineering operation vessels;

(4) Power plants and their fittings, including internal combustion engines, steam turbines, steam engines, generators and electric motors and their control equipment and devices;

(5) Injection equipment and fittings, including water injection equipment, gas injection equipment and water quality or gas treatment facilities;

(6) Well water packers and underground blowout preventers;

(7) Lifting equipment and tools;

(8) Oil (gas) transportation equipment, pipelines and their gate valves and pipe fittings; intermediate stations and shore terminal equipment and their gate valves and pipe fittings, including various machines and pumps and fluid separation, heat exchange, purifying and pressurizing devices, various measuring, monitoring and parameter indicating meters, various gate valves and pipe fittings; various electrical instruments and meters and cables.

2. Those for Automation Remote Control and Remote Monitoring:

(1) Including various devices and instruments and meters;

(2) Air-conditioning installation.

III Parts, Components and Materials Which Are Required and Have Been Checked and Approved to be Imported and Used for the Manufacture in China of Machinery and Equipment for Offshore Oil Exploitation Operation.

IV The Ministry of Petroleum Industry Shall Be Responsible for Checking and Approving Whether It is Necessary for the Above Materials to be Purchased From Abroad.

NOTICE OF THE STATE COUNCIL CONCERNING THE TAXATION OF CHINESE-FOREIGN JOINT VENTURES AND COOPERATIVE PROJECTS

(September 21, 1982)

On September 10, 1980, the National People's Congress promulgated "The Income Tax Law Concerning Chinese-Foreign Joint Ventures" and "The Individual Income Tax Law;" on December 13, 1981, "The Income Tax Law Concerning Foreign Enterprises" was promulgated. Before the promulgation of these tax laws, some areas, departments or enterprises had entered into the contracts of joint ventures or cooperative projects with foreign or Hong Kong firms with the approval of the state authorities and some of the contracts contain clauses concerning tax liabilities. With this view, the Bureau of Revenue of the Ministry of Finance has given notice that the original clauses stipulated in the contracts concerning tax liabilities shall still be executed. But it is reported that some disputes still exist. For the sake of the proper implementation of policies, a notice is given as follows:

1 The original clauses stipulated in contracts shall be executed in the event that enterprise income tax liabilities under preferential clauses are listed, or when clauses for tax liabilities preferential treatment are clearly indicated for import materials required in the course of the construction of the projects contracted for by joint ventures or cooperative projects with foreign or Hong Kong firms with the approval of the state authorities before the promulgation of "The Income Tax Law Concerning Chinese-Foreign Joint Ventures" and "The Income Tax Law Concerning Foreign Enterprises."

2 The original clauses stipulated in contracts shall also be executed in case the above contracts contain the clauses of tax liabilities preferential treatment given to the income deriving from patent, copyright or other royalties obtained by foreign or Hong Kong firms.

3 The original clauses stipulated in contracts shall be executed in case the clauses of tax liabilities preferential treatment are included for individual income in the contracts approved by the state authorities before the promulgation of "The Individual Income Tax Law."

The above three clauses shall be executed until the expiration of the time limits originally stipulated in the contracts. If the time limits for the contracts are to be extended after the expiration, all taxes shall be paid in accordance with the provisions in "The Income Tax Law Concerning Chinese-Foreign Joint Ventures," "The Income Tax Law Concerning Foreign Enterprises" and "The Individual Income Tax Law." We hope the financial and tax departments shall execute them in accordance with this Notice. The Ministry of Finance shall be responsible for interpreting the specific problems in the course of execution.

INTERIM PROVISIONS OF THE MINISTRY OF FINANCE REGARDING THE REDUCTION AND EXEMPTION OF INCOME TAX ON INTEREST EARNED IN CHINA BY FOREIGN BUSINESSES

(January 1, 1983)

In order to create advantageous circumstances for the greatest possible increase in the use of foreign capital to carry on economic construction, the following stipulations are hereby provisionally made on questions relating to preferential treatment of reducing and exempting income tax on the interest income obtained by foreign companies, enterprises and other economic organizations from China:

1 Income tax on interest obtained from loans, advances and deferred payments provided under credit contracts or trade contracts signed between 1983 and 1985 by foreign companies, enterprises and other economic organizations with China's companies or enterprises may, during the effective period of the contract, be paid at a reduced tax rate of 10%.

2 In addition to those items for which tax exemption is already stipulated under the Foreign Enterprise Income Tax Law and Implementing Regulations, the following items of interest income may also provisionally be exempted from income tax:

(1) Interest income from loans to China's state banks by foreign banks at the interest rate of international interbank loans.

Matters may be handled according to the stipulations of the preceding clause in the case of trust and investment companies approved by the State Council or the State Council's authorized units to engage in foreign exchange business.

(2) Interest income from loans to the China National Offshore Oil Corporation by foreign banks at an interest rate no higher than the interest rate of interbank loans.

(3) In the case of seller's credits provided by the other side's state bank for the import of technology, equipment and commodities by China's companies, enterprises or institutions, interest on deferred payments paid by the Chinese side to be received in turn by the seller at an interest rate no higher than that on the Chinese side's buyer credit.

(4) Interest on deposits of foreign banks and individuals in China's state banks when the interest rate on such deposits is lower than the interest rate on deposits in the country of the depositing bank or depositor.

(5) Cases where equipment and technology are provided to China's companies or enterprises and the Chinese side uses such methods as repayment with the resultant products or the delivery of products to repay the principal and interest of the price, or uses fees paid for processing or assembly to offset the principal and interest of the price.

3 Income tax on leasing fees, after deducting the equipment price, obtained by foreign leasing companies from the supply of equipment and related articles to China's companies or enterprises by the leasing trade method between 1983 and 1985 may, during the effective period of the contract signed, be paid at a reduced tax rate of 10%.

For interest included in leasing fees, if the loan agreement or contract and interest payment documents and vouchers sufficient to prove that the interest rate conforms to the stipulations of Article 2., Paragraph (3) of this Provision can be provided, it may be permited to pay income tax of 10% on the amount remaining after deduction of the interest.

Leasing fees obtained through such methods as repayment with the resultant products or the delivery of products may be exempted from income tax payment.

4 With regard to interest obtained from loans provided under contracts signed directly with China's companies or enterprises by the long-term representative offices of foreign banks which, upon receiving approval, have set up long-term representative offices in China, it is permitted for related costs and expenses to be deducted therefrom. To facilitate calculation, 15% of the amount of interest income may be provisionally taken as the amount of taxable income and income tax paid in accordance with the tax rates stipulated in Articles 3 and 4 of the Foreign Enterprise Income Tax Law.

5 In any cases where it is required according to this Provision to grant exemption from income tax for interest obtained from China on

deposits, loans, advances and deferred payments and on the purchase of bonds, the Chinese company or enterprise taking in the deposit, accepting the loan and advance, taking on the deferred payment or issuing the bond must produce the relevant agreement or contract and provide information on the interest rate, sending these to the local tax authorities for consideration and confirmation. Without having gone through the consideration and confirmation procedures, no unit or individual may, of its own accord, reduce or exempt income tax.

6 This Provision is to be enforced from January 1, 1983. As regards any contracts which were signed and took effect after approval by the departments in charge before the implementation of this Provision for which there were already stipulations at that time for the levy of taxation on the interest under the contract, no change is to be made during the effective period of the contract (not including extensions of the contract period).

PRINCIPAL RULES FOR IMPLEMENTATION OF THE NATIONAL TAX ADMINISTRATION

(Adopted by the 17th Government Administrative Meeting of the Government Administration Council on January 27, 1950; promulgated on January 31, 1950)

In order to centralize the national tax administration, set up a new tax system and strengthen the taxation work, the Central People's Government called the National Taxation Conference in the capital in November of 1949 to formulate the 12 articles of the "Principal Rules for Implementation of the National Tax Administration" in the spirit of the general policy in Article 40 of the Common Programme that "the state tax policy shall be based on the principles of ensuring the supply of the revolutionary war and considering the resumption and development of production and the needs of the state construction, the tax system shall be simplified and reasonable burdens shall be practised."

1 In order to execute the budgetary estimate of 1950, the taxation work shall be strengthened and a unified tax system shall be set up.

2 As the farmers' burdens are far more than those of industrialists and businessmen, the urban and rural burdens shall be properly balanced on the principle of reasonable burdens so as to make the burdens fair and reasonable.

3 The tax administration, categories, items and rates practised in each area of the country are quite inconsistent; they shall be promptly regulated and the regulation shall be gradually implemented in a short time so as to attain the unity of the national tax administration.

4 The National Taxation Conference has temporarily designated the following taxes as the central and local taxes:

(1) Commodity taxes;

(2) Industrial and commercial taxes (including business taxes and income taxes of tradesmen, itinerant traders and street peddlers);

(3) Salt taxes;

(4) Customs duties;

(5) Salary or remuneration taxes;

(6) Deposit interest taxes;

(7) Stamp duties;

(8) Inheritance taxes;

(9) Transaction taxes;

(10) Slaughter taxes;

(11) Property taxes;

(12) Real estate taxes;

(13) Special consumption taxes (feasts, entertainments, cold food, hotels);

(14) Licensing taxes.

5 The provisions for tax legislation:

(1) All tax regulations and decrees concerning the whole country shall be formulated, promulgated and put into effect in a unified way by the Government Administration Council of the Central People's Government, each area shall conscientiously observe and implement them and any objection shall be made to the central authorities for consideration. They shall not be revised or altered before the revision of the central authorities.

(2) The rules for the implementation of various national tax regulations shall be formulated by the central tax authorities in a unified way and put into effect with the approval of the Ministry of Finance. The tax administration of each large administrative region shall formulate the procedures for the collection of taxes in the spirit of the tax laws, rules and regulations promulgated by the central authorities and put them into effect with the approval of the department of finance of the region.

(3) If the legislation of local taxes is within the jurisdiction of a county, the county people's government shall make a proposal to the provincial people's government which shall check and transmit it to the people's government or the military and political committee of the large administrative region for approval and report to the central authorities for filing; if the legislation is within the jurisdiction of a province (municipality), the provincial (municipal) people's government shall submit a proposal to the people's government or the military and political committee of the large administrative region which shall check and transmit it to the central authorities for approval.

6 Each area shall control different tax key points according to different situations of tax sources and the tax leading authorities at each level shall put emphasis on urban taxation and pay attention to the time and seasons for tax payment and the turning-over of cash to the state

treasury on time so as to ensure the payment in and out and stabilize the finance.

7 As tax payment is a glorious duty of the people, the patriotic sense of responsibility to pay taxes according to regulations shall be cultivated among the people. Tax workers shall establish closer relations between the government and the people, enhance revolutionary qualities and keep to the fine style of hard struggle and simple living.

8 All public enterprises shall pay taxes according to regulations and pay the taxes to the local tax authorities with the independent funds of the enterprises as the calculating units. Cooperatives shall also pay taxes to the state in the same way and shall not be exempted.

9 Foreign nationals and the enterprises run by them shall observe the decrees of the People's Republic of China and pay taxes according to regulations.

10 With regard to the cases of violating tax laws and tax administration, the tax authorities shall punish the offenders according to regulations or educate them; it shall strictly be forbidden to mete out punishments or confiscations wantonly.

11 The tax organization at each level of the whole country shall be under the dual leadership of the higher bureau and the government at the same level and the director of the tax bureau shall attend the government administration meetings of the government at the same level.

12 The provisions for several important systems:

(1) The tax authorities at each level shall set up strict systems of asking for instructions and making reports.

(2) The tax authorities at each level shall rigorously implement the systems of turning taxes over to the state treasury on schedule and the system of national treasury shall be implemented in each area provided with banks so as to duly receive the taxes into the treasury.

(3) The tax authorities at each level shall set up accounting, review, submission, audit, rewards and punishments, conference, study and other systems.

(4) The tax authorities at each level shall set up a statistical system and attach great importance to investigations with the stress laid on the situations of industry and commerce, the degrees of tax burdens, the influence of the tax policy on various economies, etc.

NOTICE OF THE MINISTRY OF FINANCE ON CONSCIENTIOUSLY IMPLEMENTING TAXATION PROVISIONS IN THE "DECISION BY THE STATE COUNCIL CONCERNING BALANCING REVENUE AND EXPENDITURE AND ENFORCING FINANCIAL ADMINISTRATION"

(March 11, 1981)

The People's Government of Each Province, Municipality or Autonomous Region:

Recently, the "Decision Concerning Balancing Revenue and Expenditure and Enforcing Financial Administration" promulgated by the State Council points out that the state system of taxation shall be resolutely safeguarded and it shall be forbidden to alter tax categories or tax rates or reduce or remit taxes at will. In order to implement the "Decision" of the State Council better and strengthen the centralized and unified administration of taxation, the following provisions are made:

I Conscientiously strengthen provisions for the reduction and remission of taxes.

1 A check-up shall be made on both national tax-reduced or tax-free items and those submitted by each area and approved by our ministry or the Bureau of Revenue of our ministry and on the provisions for the reduction or remission of taxes determined by each area within the limits of authority stipulated in the administration system of taxation. In the case of those which have expired, the taxes shall be re-levied on them as stipulated and the terms of the reduction or remission shall not be extended at will. Those which do not conform to the spirit of the current policies of the economic regulation even within the terms of the reduction or remission shall be reported to the original approving authorities for consideration and improvement.

2 The tax rates of industrial and commercial taxes and industrial and commercial income taxes or the tax-paying links which have been altered without authorization beyond the limits of authority shall promptly be put right. A conscientious check-up shall be made by each province, municipality or autonomous region or by each prefecture, city or county on the reduction or remission of taxes determined by each area in violation of the limits of authority stipulated in the system and on the expansion of the limits of tax reductions or exemptions or the extension of the terms of the reduction or remission in violation of the unified provisions of the state and they shall promptly be put right so as to execute the unified provisions. If any tax reductions or exemptions are really required, they can only be put into practice after the handling of the formalities of application and approval as stipulated in the system.

3 In April, each area shall conscientiously make an overall check-up of the provisions for the reduction or remission of taxes made by it in the past in strict accordance with the requirements in the State Council's "Decision Concerning Balancing Revenue and Expenditure and Enforcing Financial Administration." The people's government of each province, municipality or autonomous region shall conscientiously summarize the check-ups, the problems discovered, the results of correction and handling and the experience and lessons to be drawn and let us know of them by correspondence at the end of May.

II Properly centralize the authority for administration and strengthen the unified administration of taxation.

1 In the case of the taxes within the limits of authority for administration of the State Council or the Ministry of Finance in accordance with the provisions in the administration system of taxation, no area shall be entitled to make any decision on the reduction or remission of any taxes or the alteration of any tax rates whether the revenue comes under the central finance or under the local finance. In future, any area or department shall be in violation of law and discipline if it decides to reduce or remit any taxes or alter any tax rates without authorization beyond the limits of authority. If less taxes are paid, the taxpayers shall be ordered to pay the balance which shall be turned over to the state treasury and the responsibility shall be investigated and affixed on those whose cases are serious.

2 Strict control shall be exercised in future

in respect of the provision in Item 3 of the administration system of taxation that the authority under the control of a province, a municipality or an autonomous region "shall, in general, not be transferred down level by level." All the authority for the reduction or remission of taxes which was transmitted down to a prefecture, a city or a county in the past, shall be recovered and put under the control of the province, municipality or autonomous region except that it shall still be determined by the province, municipality or autonomous region whether a few tax reductions or exemptions in the case of the individual economy or rural commune and brigade enterprises are transmitted down to a prefecture or a city for examination and approval.

3 In future, each province, municipality or autonomous region shall strictly follow the guiding principles of the regulation of national economy in the approval of tax reductions or exemptions within the limits of authority under its own control and shall not give the preferential treatments of tax reductions or exemptions to the enterprises which vie with big industries for raw materials and are determined to be closed, stopped, merged or transferred.

4 No tax reductions or exemptions shall be given any longer in future to the production operations with losses allowed by policies but subsidized by finance except for those otherwise stipulated and any tax reductions or exemptions shall not be used to compensate for financial subsidies. The price subsidies practised in commercial departments shall not be replaced by tax reductions or exemptions.

III Conscientiously strengthen the administration of taxation.

1 The tax authorities at each level and all tax cadres shall enhance the overall point of view and the sense of policy, conscientiously fulfill their own duties and strengthen the administration of the collection of various taxes so as to "act according to law and calculate and collect taxes according to rates" and enable the taxes collectable to the state to be duly and fully turned over to the state treasury.

2 Taxpaying discipline shall be rigorously enforced. The state's law on taxes clearly stipulates that taxpaying units and individuals shall pay the taxes on schedule and the fines for late payment shall be additionally levied on those which are overdue. In the implementation of the law on taxes, if a dispute occurs between the tax authorities and a taxpaying enterprise with regard to the interpretation of the law, it shall be handled in accordance with the past provisions of the State Council, namely: "The specific provisions and interpretations concerning the law on taxes shall be handled by the financial or tax departments; if an enterprise has any objection, it shall first pay the taxes as stipulated in the law on taxes and then submit the objection to the higher authorities ...." Those who evade taxes, refuse to pay taxes, intercept and retain taxes or divert taxes to another purpose, or those whose cases are serious or those who assault tax cadres or besiege tax authorities so as to obstruct tax work shall be handed over to the judicial authorities for punishment according to law.

INTERPRETATION OF TAX EVASION, REFUSAL TO PAY TAXES, TAX DODGES AND ARREARS IN TAX PAYMENT BY THE GENERAL TAXATION BUREAU OF THE MINISTRY OF FINANCE

(May 15, 1981)

Tax evasion: with reference to illegal acts of taxpaying units or individuals deliberately done to violate tax laws and decrees and by deception, concealment and other means to evade tax payment involving forgery, altering or destroying account books, papers or vouchers for accounting entries;understating or concealing taxable items, sales income and business profit; overstating costs, falsifying expenses, and understating profit; transferring property, income and profit accounts, evading due tax payment, all these are acts of tax evasion.

Instigation, direction and connivance with the above law-breaking acts are also considered acts of tax evasion.

Refusal to pay tax refers to illegal acts of taxpaying units or individuals in refusing to carry out the obligation of paying taxes according to the provisions of tax laws. For instance, refusal to pay taxes according to provisions of the tax law; resorting to various pretexts to ignore the notice to pay tax of tax authorities and refusal to pay the tax; refusal to file tax returns and provide tax payment data according to the legal procedures; resisting checks on tax payment by tax authorities according to law; inciting people to make trouble, threaten or besiege tax offices, and beat up tax workers, etc. all these are acts to refuse payment of tax.

Abetting or habouring the above illegal acts also belong to acts of refusing payment of tax.

Tax dodging refers to unconscious acts by taxpayer units or individuals in failing to pay tax or pay less tax than payable. For instance, ignorance, unfamiliarity with provisions of tax laws or financial administration system or careless work resulting in the wrong application of tax rates, failure to ,declare taxable items, and undercalculation of taxable amounts, sales money, business profit, etc.

Arrears with tax payment refers to acts by taxpaying units or individuals failing to pay taxes on time by the deadline set by tax authorities and falling behind in tax payment schedule.

At present, acts of tax evasion, refusal to pay tax, tax dodging and arrears with tax payment by enterprises, units and individuals involve complex circumstances and varied forms. The above interpretation is only a general explanation. Taxation departments in various places may study and enforce it in the light of actual conditions.

ANNOUNCEMENT OF THE BUREAU OF REVENUE OF THE MINISTRY OF FINANCE OF THE PEOPLE'S REPUBLIC OF CHINA CONCERNING THE HANDLING OF TAX REGISTRATION

(September 1, 1982)

It has been decided to administer tax registration throughout the country with the approval of the State Council in order to maintain laws, protect lawful business, strengthen the administration of the collection of industrial and commercial taxes and guarantee the state revenue. All units (including state and collective enterprises, the same hereinafter) and individuals engaged in industry and commerce shall go through tax registration and be put under the administration and supervision of tax authorities in relation to tax payment. Now the matters relating to tax registration are announced as follows:

1. All the units and individuals engaged in industrial production, communications and transportation, post and telecommunications, construction and installation, commercial business, finance and trust, import and export trade, services and all other business with profit and gain shall pay taxes according to law (hereinafter simply referred to as "tax-paying units and individuals") and declare and go through the tax registration of opening or closing business at local tax authorities within 30 days respectively after the opening of business or before the closing of business.

All the tax-paying units and individuals which have started business before the promulgation of this Announcement shall go again through tax registration within one month of the promulgation of this Announcement whether they went through any tax registration in the past or not.

2. In respect of the matters of tax registration, the units which are directly engaged in production or business and implement independent economic accounting or other units or individuals that directly pay taxes shall be responsible for declaring and going through them. The non-independent economic accounting branches across provinces, cities or counties shall declare and go through tax registration at the local tax authorities in addition to declaring and going through registration in a uniform manner by their higher independent economic accounting units.

3. When tax-paying units and individuals declare and go through tax registration for the opening of business, they shall obtain "Tax Registration Forms" printed in a uniform manner from the local tax authorities, write down the names of enterprises, the names of persons in charge, economic natures, scopes of business, ways of operation and other contents of registration, in triplicate, retain one copy of each on file and submit the other two copies to the local tax authorities.

4. Tax authorities shall examine and ratify the tax-paying units and individuals in declaring and going through tax registration for the opening of business and the city or county tax bureaux shall grant "Tax Registration Certificates" on completion of the examination and registration.

5. If changes of names of enterprises, nature of production or scope of business take place or the removal of business addresses occurs after the tax-paying units and individuals have gone through tax registration for the opening of business, they shall report them in writing to the local tax authorities within 15 days of such changes and go through alteration registration by means of the papers of approval from the authorities concerned; if there are such cases as transfer of trades mergers, branching out, joint ventures, etc., they shall go again through tax registration.

6. When tax-paying units and individuals go through tax registration for the closing of business, they shall report the cause of the closing of business in writing to the local tax authorities, submit for examination the papers of approval relating to the termination of business or the withdrawal of the organization and go through the formalities of cancelling the tax registration with the tax authorities which originally handled the registration after obtaining clearance in the matters of tax payment.

7. If a tax-paying unit or individual does not go through tax registration as stipulated by this Announcement, tax authorities shall make criticisms on it or him or impose a fine of not more than 5,000 yuan on a unit or a fine of not

more than 500 yuan on an individual according to the degrees of seriousness.

8. The tax registration of Chinese-foreign joint ventures or foreign enterprises shall still be executed in accordance with the provisions in relevant tax laws.

REGULATIONS OF THE MINISTRY OF FINANCE CONCERNING THE COLLECTION AND REMISSION OF INDUSTRIAL AND COMMERCIAL TAXES ON IMPORT AND EXPORT COMMODITIES

(Approved and Transmitted by the State Council on December 30, 1980)

It is hereby stipulated as follows on the question of collecting and remitting industrial and commercial taxes on import and export commodities in order to facilitate the protection of domestic production and the development of export trade, to facilitate the import of foreign capital and advanced technology and equipment and to ensure the protection of the country's financial revenues and strengthen tax control:

I Concerning the Collection and Remission of Industrial and Commercial Taxes on Export Commodities

1. An industrial and commercial tax shall be levied on industrial products and dutiable agricultural, forestry, animal husbandry and aquatic products for export according to the provisions of the state tax laws when the industrial products are leaving the factory or when the agricultural, forestry, animal husbandry and aquatic products are being purchased.

2. As for the commodities exported with state approval, the industrial and commercial tax shall be exempted on those whose cost involved in earning foreign exchange, calculated after the tax is deducted, is higher than the internal settlement price for foreign exchange earned through trade in the same year; the industrial and commercial tax can be reduced according to the circumstances on those whose cost is lower than the internal settlement price. Tax reductions or remissions shall be reported to the Ministry of Finance or provincial, municipal and autonomous regional governments for approval in accordance with the provisions of the current tax administration system.

3. Export commodities on which the tax is reduced or exempted upon approval, shall be settled according to the price after deducting the sum of tax reduction or remission when the supply units sell them to the export department (not including the tax reduction or remission at the request of the supply units owing to the big deficit involved in the manufacture of export commodities).

4. When commodities on which the industrial and commercial tax has been levied are transferred to the export department for sales abroad, the industrial and commercial tax already paid shall not be refunded regardless of the deficit involved in the export. When export commodities on which the industrial and commercial tax has been reduced or exempted are switched to sale on the home market, the tax shall be paid as overdue according to the regulations if the tax rate exceeds 20%; the industrial and commercial tax for the industrial link or the purchase link shall not be paid if the tax rate is no more than 19%, except otherwise stipulated.

5. The export department and the manufacturing and managing unit, in requesting tax reduction or remission, must provide the local tax authorities with such data about the export commodity as price, cost, profit or deficit and the cost involved in earning foreign exchange through export.

II Concerning the Collection and Remission of Industrial and Commercial Taxes on Import Commodities

An industrial and commercial tax shall be levied according to the provisions of the state tax laws on the commodities imported from abroad by the foreign trade department and other state-owned enterprises, collective enterprises, joint ventures with Chinese and foreign investment, government organs, mass organizations, institutions, etc. But industrial and commercial tax is exempted on the following commodities:

1. Advanced technology and prototypes imported with state approval;

2. Mechanical equipment, parts and raw or processed materials imported as capital investment by the foreign partner in a joint venture with Chinese and foreign investment according to the provisions of the contract;

3. Equipment, appliances, transport and loading or unloading tools imported with state

approval for the construction of special economic zones, as well as mechanical equipment, parts and raw or processed materials imported by enterprises in the special economic zones for the manufacture of export commodities;

4. Raw or processed materials, parts and equipment imported by foreign firms, overseas Chinese firms and Hong Kong and Macao industrialists and businessmen as required for processing with supplied material, assembly with supplied parts and medium and small compensation trade according to the provisions of the contract;

5. Instruments and equipment directly used in scientific research, scientific experiments and teaching;

6. Commodities with loss owing to policy considerations and imported with financial subsidies upon state approval, such as grain, raw sugar, insecticides and chemical fertilizer.

The industrial and commercial tax is exempted on the raw or processed materials, auxiliary material, packing material and parts imported for use in processing export commodities. But the industrial and commercial tax for import shall be paid as overdue on the imported raw or processed materials, auxiliary material, packing material and parts consumed in processing commodities originally meant for export but later switched to sale on the home market.

As for exhibits at the foreign economic, cultural, scientific and technological exhibitions in China, no tax shall be levied if they are shipped out again within three months after the exhibitions; a tax shall be levied according to the regulations on those left behind for sale.

III Concerning the Collection and Remission of Industrial and Commercial Taxes and Income Taxes on Enterprises Accepting Processing with Supplied Materials and Assembly with Supplied Parts

Where the materials or parts supplied by foreign firms, overseas Chinese firms and Hong Kong and Macao industrialists and businessmen account for less than 20% of the total value of the raw or processed materials, auxiliary materials and parts used on the products, an industrial and commercial tax and an income tax shall be levied according to the regulations on the processed or assembled products and the income from the processing or assembly. Where they account for more than 20% of the total value, the industrial and commercial tax shall be exempted on the products; as for the income from the processing or assembly, the state-owned enterprises shall be exempted from the industrial and commercial tax and the collective enterprises shall be exempted from the industrial and commercial tax and the income tax for three years beginning from the month when the first batch of such income is earned.

When an enterprise accepting processing with supplied materials or assembly with supplied parts asks other factories to do the processing or assembly, the case can be dealt with according to the above-mentioned principle if this matter is included in the contract signed by the foreign client on the processing with supplied materials or the assembly with supplied parts.

When the above-mentioned duty-free imported raw or processed materials, auxiliary materials and parts and the manufactured commodities are switched to sale on the home market, taxes shall be paid as overdue according to regulations.

Tobacco, cigarettes and alcoholic drinks are highly taxable products, and taxes shall be levied on them according to the general regulations.

IV Concerning the Collection and Remission of Industrial and Commercial Taxes and Income Taxes on Certain Enterprises Involved in Construction Items with Loans

An industrial and commercial tax shall be levied according to regulations on the products manufactured by the construction items imported by enterprises with foreign exchange loans (including the loans for domestic auxiliary capital construction), the medium and small compensation trade items and the capital construction items built with loans for the special plants or workshops manufacturing export commodities.

In each of the years during the period of repayment of the loans, state-owned enterprises can repay the loans, principal and interest, with the profit made from the newly added products of the loan items, the fixed asset depreciation fund and the due charges for using the fixed funds; enterprises which institute the system of retaining a share of profits can draw the workers' welfare fund and the reward fund according to the ratio based on the state-approved base figure before repaying the loans, but they must not draw the production development fund nor the above-quota profit retention fund. Urban collective enterprises can repay the loans, principal and interest with the profit made from the newly added products of the loan items (that is, the profit before the income tax is paid) and the fixed asset depreciation fund; during the period when the loans are being repaid, the departments in charge of enterprises must not draw profit and various funds from the loan items in the enterprises under them.

If there is a surplus after an enterprise has used the above sums of money in repaying the loan, principal and interest repayable that current year, an income tax shall be levied on the surplus or the profit shall be turned in according to regulations; if the sums so used are not enough, the deficit can be made up by the due amount of the industrial and commercial tax on the newly added products of the loan items after the case has been examined and approved by the tax authorities.

Having paid off the loans, principal and interest, enterprises shall immediately resume paying the taxes or turn in profits according to regulations.

Enterprises applying for use of special loans must send copies of the relevant documents to the local tax authorities for reference.

The present regulations come into force as of January 1, 1981. In case past regulations contradict the present, the latter shall prevail.

PROVISIONS OF THE STATE COUNCIL FOR THE REGULATION OF INDUSTRIAL AND COMMERCIAL TAX BURDENS OF RURAL COMMUNES AND BRIGADE ENTERPRISES

(January 30, 1981)

The following provisions are made for the problems of the industrial and commercial tax liabilities of rural communes and brigade enterprises in order to implement the guiding principles of promoting regulations vigorously and stabilizing the economy, balance the tax liabilities properly among various economic sectors and embody the encouraging and restricting functions of taxation.

Article 1 In order to foster the normal development of the production of communes and brigade enterprises, taxes shall continue to be reduced or remitted in the following cases with the approval of the people's governments of provinces, municipalities and autonomous regions:

(1) With regard to the products produced by communes and brigade enterprises to serve agricultural production directly and the business income of brigade- or team-run enterprises from their services for the life of the commune members in the same brigades or teams, the proceeds shall be exempt from industrial and commercial taxes by listing the specific products and services;

(2) If it is really necessary to be taken into account, the proceeds shall be exempt from industrial and commercial income taxes by listing specific products or services for the profits obtained from the chemical fertilizers and pesticides produced by communes and brigade enterprises and the repair and making of farming machines and tools to serve agricultural production directly and for the profits obtained by brigade- or team-run enterprises from their trades which serve commune members' life directly such as beancurd mills, flour mills, oil mills, soy sauce mills, grain and cotton processing, hairdressing, tailoring, etc.;

(3) The communes and brigade enterprises in border counties and national autonomous counties (Mongolian banners – divisions at the county level) shall continue to be exempt from industrial and commercial income taxes from 1979 till 1983;

(4) To be engaged in production and provide self-help, the people's communes, production brigades and teams in a disaster area shall be given the preferential treatment of the reduction or remission of industrial and commercial taxes and industrial and commercial income taxes within a definite time.

Article 2 In order to restrict their vying with larger advanced industrial enterprises for raw materials and avoid the blind or repeated establishment of factories, the current provisions for the exemption of communes and brigade enterprises from industrial and commercial taxes and industrial and commercial income taxes for two to three years immediately after their opening shall be cancelled and replaced by the procedures to deal with different cases in different ways.

(1) In respect of industrial and commercial taxes, these taxes shall be collected according to regulations from those which produce such high-tariff-rate products as cigarettes, wine, sugar, cotton yarn, watches, etc., and they shall not be reduced or remitted. If the people's government of a province, a municipality or an autonomous region deems it necessary to increase high-tariff-rate products in the list, it shall list the items and levy industrial and commercial taxes on them. Preferential treatment of the reduction or remission of industrial and commercial taxes within one year shall be given for the proceeds from the production of other products and from other business, for the sugar produced by the areas with insufficient processing capacity and to those who have difficulty in paying taxes according to provisions.

(2) In respect of income taxes, industrial and commercial income taxes shall be levied according to regulations on all communes and brigade enterprises which vie with large advanced industrial enterprises for raw materials and which make more profits, whether they are newly-built or existing (in the case of other newly-built enterprises which need to be fostered, the preferential treatment of exemption from taxes for one to two years according to different cases). A few enterprises among them which still have difficulty in paying the taxes after the expiration of the exemption period shall be given the preferential treatment of exemption from taxes for one year more.

(3) An enterprise shall apply to the local tax authorities for the above preferential treatment of the reduction or remission of taxes and the authorities shall submit it level by level to the people's government of the province, municipality or autonomous region after examination and verification.

Article 3 In order to save grain and improve the quality of wine, industrial and commercial taxes shall be levied again at 40 per cent of the tariff rate on the rural people's communes, production brigades and teams which are approved by the county people's government to fix places to make wine with the preserved forage grain, which is to be purchased by the commercial departments. For very few of them which have difficulty in paying the taxes, the preferential treatment of the reduction of 10 to 20 per cent from the payable taxes shall be given if the people's government of the province, municipality or autonomous region thinks it necessary to do so. Industrial and commercial taxes at 60% of the tariff rate for grain wine shall be levied on the wine which is not made and sold in conformity to the requirements as stipulated.

Article 4 Taxes shall continue to be levied at the links of purchase on such agricultural and sideline products purchased by the state as native sugar, native paper, native silk, handwoven cloth, etc. It shall be strictly prohibited from altering the tax-paying links without authorization, from giving people's communes and production brigades and teams the taxes which shall be paid by the commercial purchasing units or from increasing the income of communes and brigades but reducing the income of the state by means of tax reduction or exemption.

Article 5 Industrial and commercial taxes shall be levied on agricultural-industrial-commercial combined enterprises; industrial and commercial income taxes shall also be levied on part of the collective ownership. Industrial and commercial income taxes shall be levied at 8-grade super-profit progressive rates on the profits earned by the original town collective enterprises which participate in agricultural-industrial-commercial combined enterprises on the principle of sharing the unit economic ownership without any change of financial relations. Industrial and commercial income taxes shall be levied at the tax rate of 39% on the grassroots supply and marketing cooperatives which participate in agricultural-industrial-commercial combined enterprises.

Article 6 Industrial and commercial taxes and industrial and commercial income taxes shall be paid according to regulations by educated urban and town youths working in the countryside and mountain areas for such high-tariff-rate products as cigarettes, wine, sugar, cotton yarn, watches, etc., produced from the workshops (factories) and teams they set up in the countryside or in the suburbs of cities and towns and for the business and services they establish in cities and towns. Industrial and commercial taxes and industrial and commercial income taxes shall also be levied according to regulations on such taxable commodities as tobacco leaves, tea, etc. produced by them and sold by themselves without being sold to the commercial purchasing units. Besides, other products produced by them and income from their other lines of business shall continue to be exempt from industrial and commercial taxes and industrial and commercial income taxes up to the end of 1985 as originally stipulated. They shall be handled in accordance with the provisions of tax payments for rural communes and brigade enterprises as of January 1, 1986 and no special preferential treatment shall be given.

The above provisions shall be put into effect as of April 1, 1981. These Provisions shall prevail if there is anything in conflict against these Provisions.

CIRCULAR OF THE GENERAL TAXATION BUREAU OF THE MINISTRY OF FINANCE OF THE PEOPLE'S REPUBLIC OF CHINA

(May 5, 1981)

Industrial and commercial tax revenues are an important financial source for the country's socialist construction. It is the duty of all enterprises, establishments and individuals to truthfully file their tax returns and pay the tax in full without delay in accordance with the state tax laws and decrees. In implementing the state industrial and commercial tax policy correctly, preserving the seriousness of the tax laws and decrees and ensuring the country's tax revenues, the State Council has decided to conduct a thorough check of the evasion, dodge and arrears on payment of industrial and commercial taxes by taxpayer units and individuals. It is hereby declared as follows:

1. Within two months of the promulgation of this Circular, the taxpayer units and individuals should make a conscientious check of tax payment themselves, and report the results of the self-check to the local tax authorities.

2. The period for the check of tax evasion, dodge and arrears in tax payment is: tax evasion and dodge, from January 1, 1980 onward; tax payments in arrears, any time.

3. Taxpayer units or individuals who take the initiative to solve their own problems in the self-check drive, and promptly make up the tax amount in arrears, evaded or dodged, can be dealt with leniently and excused from the overdue defaulter's charges and penalty upon the verification and consent of the tax authorities. Taxpayer units or individuals who refuse to conduct the self-check and make up the delayed tax, or employ trickery to cover up the tax evasion or dodge, shall be dealt with according to tax laws as follows upon the examination and verification of the tax authorities:

a. The delayed tax on the part of taxpayer units or individuals must be paid within a time limit and a defaulter's charge shall be surcharged for every day in arrears, starting from the first day of default.

b. Where the delayed tax is not paid off despite repeated demands, the tax authorities shall notify the bank to withhold the sum together with the defaulter's charge and turn it over to the state treasury.

c. The tax evaded or dodged by taxpayer units or individuals must be paid within a time limit, and a penalty of not more than five times the evaded or dodged amount shall be imposed according to the provisions of state tax laws.

d. In serious cases of tax evasion or refusal to pay taxes, the tax must be paid and a penalty shall be imposed. In addition, those held directly responsible shall be referred to the judicial organs for investigations of their criminal liability.

4. Taxpayer units or individuals who disagree with the verification and treatment of the tax authorities shall first make up the tax and pay the penalty or defaulter's charges according to regulations before reporting their objection to the next higher tax authorities. They must not refuse to pay the sum on any excuse. The higher tax authorities shall study the case and deal with it without delay.

5. In both starting and closing down operation, taxpayer units and individuals must register on tax matters with local tax authorities, accept the latter's tax check and financial supervision, send in final accounts on time, and truthfully provide relevant data about tax payment.

6. No unit or individual is allowed to obstruct or create difficulties for tax cadres carrying tax authority identity documents in performing their duties of tax collection and control.

Tax cadres shall give more publicity to the tax policy and laws and decrees, be practical, collect taxes according to law, persuade people with patience, treat others as equals, and avoid acting in a rude or crude manner. In case of such incidents as causing trouble, assaulting tax workers, besieging the tax office, or resorting to other intimidating means to obstruct tax workers in performing their duties, the troublemakers shall be referred to local judicial organs for punishment according to law.

7. In case of collecting tax money fraudulently by forging identity documents and impersonating tax workers, the taxpayer units and individuals should promptly report to local tax authorities which shall refer the matter to judicial organs for dealing according to law.

8. Everybody is duty bound to safeguard the state tax laws and decrees. All units and their

staff members have the right to expose or prosecute tax evasion and dodge by taxpayer units or individuals and graft practised by tax cadres. Having verified and dealt with the case, tax authorities may, according to state regulations, give appropriate reward to the exposer or informer and keep their identities secret so as to protect their legitimate rights. When the exposer or informer is under retaliation, tax authorities shall promptly raise a protest against the retaliator and request the relevant department to deal with it sternly.

REGULATIONS OF THE MINISTRY OF FINANCE CONCERNING THE COLLECTION OF INDUSTRIAL AND COMMERCIAL TAXES ON PRODUCTS MARKETED BY INDUSTRIAL ENTERPRISES THEMSELVES AND THE HANDLING OF PROFITS THEREFROM

(Approved and Transmitted by the State Council on August 12, 1981)

In recent years, with the restructuring of the country's economic system, the products marketed by industrial enterprises have been increased rapidly. They have occupied a considerable portion of total production in some enterprises. This has not only resulted in changes in the channels of commodity circulation and the distribution of industrial and commercial incomes, but has also reduced the tax revenues of the country as a result of a lighter tax on the marketing of products by industrial enterprises themselves than on the marketing by commercial enterprises. To suit the restructuring of the economic system and ensure the financial revenues of the country, it is hereby stipulated as follows regarding the collection of the industrial and commercial tax on the products marketed by industrial enterprises themselves and the handling of the profits therefrom:

1. Where industrial enterprises set up sales departments (including sales exhibition, trial sales and other outlets) to market their own products, in addition to the industrial and commercial tax collected for the industrial link when the products are transferred to the sales departments, an industrial and commercial tax for the commercial retail link shall be levied according to the actual sales income at the sales departments, the same as in the commercial enterprises.

2. Where products are marketed by industrial enterprises without sales departments, in addition to the industrial and commercial tax collected for the industrial link, an industrial and commercial tax for the commercial retail link shall also be levied, the same as commercial retail, in order to prevent willful attempts to market products at lower prices, disrupt commercial operations and reduce tax revenue of the country.

3. For products marketed by industrial enterprises themselves of which the industrial and commercial tax for the industrial link is reduced or exempted according to regulations (including new products put on trial sale after examination and approval), an industrial and commercial tax for the commercial retail link shall be levied according to the actual sales income. After this is enforced, if loss or no-profit occurs in the case of some self-marketed products, the industrial and commercial tax for the retail link can be reduced or remitted on the merit of each case upon the approval of the tax authorities.

4. Where industrial enterprises market their own products according to regulations, whether via their own sales departments or not, the profit realized through the self-marketed products shall be added into the total profits of the enterprises, and the enterprise fund or profit sharing fund shall be assessed and retained according to state regulations while the balance shall be turned over to the state treasury.

5. The regulations concerning the collection of the industrial and commercial tax on the products marketed by industrial enterprises themselves come into force as of August 1, 1981.

NOTICE OF THE MINISTRY OF FINANCE TO ADJUST THE INDUSTRIAL AND COMMERCIAL TAX RATES FOR A NUMBER OF PRODUCTS AND TO EXTEND TAXABLE ITEMS

(June 10, 1982)

It has been approved by the State Council to make necessary adjustments in the industrial and commercial taxes for a number of products for the purpose of putting taxation, the lever of economy, to better use so as to regulate the profits of industrial products and the revenues of enterprises, promote the regulation and development of the national economy and help stabilize the state revenue. Now this Notice is given as follows:

1. The following five items shall have their tax rates lowered:—

(1) Soap: the tax rate will be lowered from 12% to 5%.

(2) Canvas rubber shoes: the tax rate will be lowered from 18% to 5%.

(3) Condensed milk and powdered milk: the tax rate will be lowered from 10% to 5%.

(4) Earthenware: the tax rate will be lowered from 12% to 5%.

(5) Washing powder: the tax rate will be lowered from 12% to 5%.

2. The following two items shall have their tax rates raised:

(1) Crude oil (an enterprise with annual yield of more than 1.5 million tons): the tax rate will be raised from 5% to 12%.

(2) Tires and tubes: motor vehicle tires — the tax rate will be raised from 10% to 15%; other tires and tubes — the tax rate will be raised from 10% to 12%.

3. The following item shall be included in the taxable items as an extended one:

A bank shall pay a tax rate of 10% for the balance of its business income after deducting the expenditure of deposit interest. The taxation on credit cooperatives shall be deferred.

The tax shall be paid in the locality by the accounting unit of each bank earning the business income, namely, in a county or a district of a city, the tax shall be paid by the county branch or the district office; if the banks at various levels above the county one carry on business directly, the banks shall respectively pay taxes in their own locations.

4. The adjustment of tax rates and the extension of taxable items this time are mainly for the purpose of regulating the levels of the profits of industrial products and the revenues of enterprises. It relates only to the changes between taxes and profits and should not affect the changes of market prices. In the course of implementation, each area or each department shall pay attention to the solution of the following problems:

(1) Each area, department or enterprise shall not raise market prices with the excuse of the adjustment of product tax rates leading to price fluctuation and increase the burden of the masses. Those who violate this clause shall strictly be dealt with.

(2) After the adjustment of product tax rates, the enterprises which really have difficulty in business due to objective factors shall be given preferential treatment of tax reduction or tax exemption as the authorities think fit after approval in accordance with the limits of authority stipulated in the system of taxation administration. However, those which have various difficulties resulting from subjective factors or those which shall be closed, suspended or transferred to the production of other products in policy shall not have their taxes deducted or be exempt from taxation.

(3) If the adjustment of product tax rates makes a greater change in the revenues of an enterprise which reserves part of profits or assumes profits or losses within the limits, the proportion of profit reserves and the quota of profit or loss assumption shall be readjusted as stipulated.

(4) The financial assumption basis shall be readjusted for the part of local revenue increased or reduced as a result of the adjustment of product tax rates and the extension of taxable items in an area implementing the financial system of "dividing revenue and expenditure and having profits or losses assumed by levels."

The above provisions for the adjustment of industrial and commercial tax rates and the extension of taxable items shall be put into effect as of July 1, 1982.

The adjustment of tax rates and the extension of taxable items this time are an important measure to promote the regulation of the national economy and the development of production. It touches upon the interests of some departments and enterprises and bears much on policies. The

people's government at each level shall be requested to strengthen leadership, organize the departments concerned into close cooperation, pay attention to the knowledge of the developments and sum up experience so as to make a good job of it.

INDIVIDUAL INCOME TAX LAW OF THE PEOPLE'S REPUBLIC OF CHINA

(Adopted by the Fifth National People's Congress of the People's Republic of China at its Third Session on September 10, 1980)

Article 1 An individual income tax shall be levied in accordance with the provisions of this Law on the incomes gained within or outside China by any individual residing for one year or more in the People's Republic of China.

For individuals not residing in the People's Republic of China or individuals residing in China less than one year, individual income tax shall be levied only on that income gained within China.

Article 2 Individual income tax shall be levied on the following categories of income:

1. Wages and salaries;
2. Remuneration for personal services;
3. Royalties;
4. Interest, dividends and bonuses;
5. Income from lease of property; and
6. Other kinds of income specified as taxable by the Ministry of Finance of the People's Republic of China.

Article 3 Individual income tax rates:

1. Income from wages and salaries in excess of specific amounts shall be taxed at progressive rates ranging from 5% to 45% (see appended tax rate table).
2. Income from remuneration for personal services, royalties, interest, dividends, bonuses and lease of property, and other kinds of income shall be taxed at a flat rate of 20%.

Article 4 The following categories of income shall be exempted from individual income tax:

1. Prizes and awards for scientific, technological or cultural achievements;
2. Interest on savings deposits in the state banks and credit co-operatives of the People's Republic of China;
3. Welfare benefits, survivors' pensions and relief payments;
4. Insurance indemnities;
5. Military severance pay, decommission or demobilization pay for cadres and fighters of the armed forces;
6. Severance pay or retirement pay for cadres, staff members and workers;
7. Salaries of diplomatic officials of foreign embassies and consulates in China;
8. Tax-free incomes as stipulated in international conventions to which China is a party or as stipulated in agreements China has signed;
9. Incomes approved as tax-free by the Ministry of Finance of the People's Republic of China.

Article 5 The amount of taxable income shall be computed as follows:

1. For income from wages or salaries, a monthly deduction of 800 yuan shall be allowed; that part in excess of 800 yuan shall be taxed.
2. For income from remuneration for personal services, royalties or lease of property, a deduction of 800 yuan shall be allowed for expenses if the amount in a single payment is less than 4,000 yuan; for single payments in excess of 4,000 yuan a deduction of 20% shall be allowed. The balance remaining after deduction shall be taxed.
3. Interest, dividends, bonuses or other kinds of income shall be taxed on the full amount received in each payment.

Article 6 For individual income tax, the income earner shall be the taxpayer and the paying unit shall be the withholding agent. Taxpayers not covered by withholding are required personally to file declarations of their income and pay tax themselves.

Article 7 Taxes withheld each month by a withholding agent and those to be paid each month by taxpayers filing personal returns shall be turned in to the state treasury and the tax return submitted to the tax authorities within the first seven days of the following month.

Any taxpayer who earns income outside China shall pay the tax due to the state treasury and submit a tax return to the tax authorities within 30 days of the end of each year.

Article 8 All incomes shall be computed in terms of Renminbi (RMB). Income in foreign currency shall be assessed according to the exchange rate quoted by the State General Administration of Exchange Control of the People's Republic of Chna, and shall be taxed in Renminbi.

Article 9 The tax authorities have the right to conduct investigations concerning the payment of tax. Withholding agents and taxpayers filing personal returns must report according to the facts and provide all relevant information and shall not refute or conceal the facts.

Article 10 A commission of 1% of the tax amount withheld shall be paid to the withholding agents.

Article 11 A withholding agent or a taxpayer filing personal returns must pay the tax due within the prescribed time limits. In case of failure to pay within the prescribed time limits, the appropriate tax authorities, in addition to setting a new time limit for tax payment, shall surcharge overdue payments at one half of 1% of the overdue tax for every day in arrears, starting from the first day of default.

Article 12 The tax authorities may, acting at their discretion, impose a penalty on a withholding agent or on a taxpayer filing personal returns who has violated the provisions of Article 9 of this Law.

In dealing with those who have concealed income or evaded or refused to pay tax, the tax authorities may, in addition to pursuing the tax, impose a penalty not more than five times the amount of tax underpaid or not paid, according to the seriousness of the offence. Cases of gross violation shall be handled by the local people's courts according to law.

Article 13 In case of disputes with the tax authorities on the payment of taxes, the withholding agent or taxpayer filing personal returns must pay taxes according to the relevant regulations first before applying to higher tax authorities for reconsideration. If they do not accept the decisions made after such reconsideration, they can bring the matter before the local people's courts.

Article 14 Detailed rules and regulations for the implementation of this Law shall be formulated by the Ministry of Finance of the People's Republic of China.

Article 15 This law shall be put into effect from the date of promulgation.

Individual Income Tax Rates
(Applicable to wages and salaries)

Grade	Range of Income	Tax Rate (%)
1	Monthly income of 800 yuan and less	Exempt
2	That part of monthly income from 801 yuan to 1,500 yuan	5
3	That part of monthly income from 1,501 yuan to 3,000 yuan	10
4	That part of monthly income from 3,001 yuan to 6,000 yuan	20
5	That part of monthly income from 6,001 yuan to 9,000 yuan	30
6	That part of monthly income from 9,001 yuan to 12,000 yuan	40
7	That part of monthly income above 12,001 yuan	45

CIRCULAR OF THE MINISTRY OF FINANCE CONCERNING THE PAYMENT OF THE INDIVIDUAL INCOME TAX BY FOREIGNERS WORKING IN CHINA

(October 24, 1980)

Financial departments (bureaus) in the provinces, municipalities and autonomous regions:

Since the Individual Income Tax Law of the People's Republic of China was promulgated for implementation, some units have raised questions about the payment of individual income tax by foreigners working in China. After deliberation, it is provisionally stipulated as follows:

1. Staff members sent by aid countries specifically to work on the construction projects given gratis to China are exempted from individual income tax on the wages and allowance for living expenses so earned, be they paid by China or foreign countries.

2 Foreign experts in cultural and educational fields, during the period of working for China, are paid wages and salaries by the Chinese side, and are given free accommodation, car service and medical treatment. The individual income tax can be levied only on their income of wages and salaries according to the provisions of the tax law; the free accommodation, car service and medical treatment provided them by the Chinese side are exempted from tax.

3 The wages and salaries earned by foreigners serving in China, whether paid by the Chinese side, foreign countries or jointly, all are considered as income derived from China. With the exception of preferential tax exemption as stipulated in Item 1 of this Circular, individual income tax shall be levied on all individuals according to regulations. But, for those residing in China not more than 90 days at a stretch, the tax can be calculated and levied on the part of their wages and salaries paid by the Chinese side, and the part paid by foreign countries can be exempted from tax.

4 The allowance for living expenses and scholarship obtained by foreign students studying in China do not belong to the category of wages and salaries, and are therefore exempted from the individual income tax.

5 As for foreigners working in China who are given a lump sum by foreign dispatch units, including personal wages, public expenses (postal and telegraphic charges, office expenses, advertisement fees, and entertainment costs necessitated by business intercourse) and allowance for living expenses (lodging and travelling expenses), if the above items can be clearly divided, the individual tax can be levied only on the part of the income from wages and salaries according to regulations.

The aforegoing shall be studied and implemented.

DETAILED RULES AND REGULATIONS FOR THE IMPLEMENTATION OF THE INDIVIDUAL INCOME TAX LAW OF THE PEOPLE'S REPUBLIC OF CHINA

Approved by the State Council
(December 10, 1980)

Article 1 These detailed rules and regulations are drawn up in accordance with the provisions of Article 14 of the Individual Income Tax Law of the People's Republic of China (hereinafter called Tax Law for short).

Article 2 "Any individual residing for one year or more in the People's Republic of China" mentioned in Article 1 of the Tax Law means any individual who resides in China for a full 365 days within a tax year. No subtractions shall be made of the number of days of temporary absence from Chinese territory within the tax year.

A tax year starts from January 1 and ends on December 31 on the Gregorian calendar.

Article 3 Individuals residing in the People's Republic of China for one year or more but less than five years shall pay tax only on that part of their income gained abroad which is remitted to China; individuals whose period of residence in China exceeds five years shall pay tax on all their income gained outside China beginning from the sixth year of residence.

Article 4 The range of the various categories of income mentioned in Article 2 of the Tax Law is as follows:

a) "Wages and salaries" means wages, salaries, bonuses and year-end extras gained from work in offices, organizations, schools, enterprises, and other units.

Bonuses mentioned in the preceding paragraph do not include prizes and awards for scientific, technological or cultural achievements.

b) "Compensation for personal services" means earnings from personal services in designing, installation, drafting, medical treatment, practising law, accounting, consultation, lecturing, news reporting, radio and television broadcasting, contributions to publications, translation, calligraphy and painting, sculpture, cinema, drama and opera, music, dancing, acrobatics, ballad singing and comic talk, sports and technical services.

c) "Royalties" means income from the provision and transfer of patent right, copyright, the right to use proprietary technology and other rights.

d) "Interest, dividends and bonuses" means interest on deposits, loans and various kinds of securities and dividends and bonuses from investments.

e) "Income from lease of property" means income from lease of houses, warehouses, machinery and equipment, motor vehicles and boats, and other kinds of property.

f) "Other kinds of income" means income specified as taxable by the Ministry of Finance of the People's Republic of China other than that provided in the preceding items.

Article 5 The following categories of income from sources in China, regardless of whether the place of payment is in China or not, shall be taxed according to the Tax Law:

a) Individual income from work and compensation for services within China. But, for individuals whose period of residence in China does not exceed 90 days, the above compensation paid by employers outside China shall be exempted from taxation.

b) Dividends and bonuses gained by any individual within China. But dividends and bonuses derived from joint ventures and from urban and rural cooperative organizations shall be exempted from taxation.

c) Remuneration for staff members sent to work abroad by government offices at all levels of the People's Republic of China.

d) Royalties and interest derived by any individual within China and income from lease of property within China as well as other kinds of income specified as taxable by the Ministry of Finance of the People's Republic of China.

Article 6 For a taxpayer who has two or more categories of taxable income as provided in Article 2 of the Tax Law, income tax shall be computed and levied separately.

Article 7 If a taxpayer's taxable income is paid in kind or in marketable securities, that part of the income thus paid shall be computed in terms of money according to the market price at the time of its acquirement.

Article 8 "Prizes and awards for scientific,

technological or cultural achievements" mentioned in item 1, Article 4 of the Tax Law means prizes and awards given to individuals by the Chinese Government or Chinese or foreign scientific, technological or cultural organizations for inventions or creations in the fields of science, technology and culture.

Article 9 "Interest on savings deposits in the state banks and credit cooperatives of the People's Republic of China" mentioned in Item 2, Article 4 of the Tax Law includes interest on savings deposits in Renminbi and foreign currency and interest on savings deposits in other banks entrusted by the state banks.

Dividends from investments by individuals in local construction (investment) companies in China, which pay no bonuses and whose dividends are not higher than the interest on savings deposits in state banks and credit cooperatives, are also exempt from tax.

Article 10 "Salaries of diplomatic officials of foreign embassies and consulates in China" mentioned in Item 7, Article 4 refers to salaries of diplomats in foreign embassies, consuls and other persons enjoying the same treatment as diplomats.

Tax exemption for salaries earned by other persons in foreign embassies and consulates in China shall be kept at the same level as the tax exemption for persons of similar status in Chinese embassies and consulates granted by the relevant countries.

Article 11 Compensation for personal services, royalties and income from lease of property gained in China by individuals not residing in China shall be taxed on the full amount received in such payment.

Article 12 "Income from compensation for personal services, royalties or lease of property" "in a single payment" mentioned in Article 5 of the Tax Law means income gained on one single occasion or income from performance of only one task or matter, and the amount so paid is counted as a single payment. For succeeding income from the same item that cannot be obviously divided into separate payments, such income received within a month is combined and counted as a single payment.

Article 13 For the same item of income gained by two or more persons in collaboration, deduction for expenses, if eligible according to the Tax Law, may be made from each share separately.

Article 14 The withholding agents in making various kinds of taxable payment shall withhold the taxes according to the Tax Law, turn them in to the state treasury in time and put them in itemized records for future reference.

The various kinds of taxable payment referred to in the preceding paragraph includes payment in cash, payment by remittance, payment by the transfer of accounts and payment in marketable securities or in kind, the value of which is computed in terms of money.

Article 15 Withholding agents and taxpayers filing personal returns shall submit tax returns within the time limit prescribed by the Tax Law. In cases of failure to submit the returns within the prescribed time limit on account of special circumstances, applications for extension shall be submitted within the prescribed time limit for approval to the local tax authorities.

The final day for tax payment and submission of tax returns may be extended if it falls on an official holiday.

Article 16 For individuals residing in China for one year or more, the income gained outside China shall be computed and taxed separately from the taxable income earned within China. The amount of taxable income shall be computed after deducting expenses for different categories as provided in Article 5 of the Tax Law.

Income tax paid by taxpayers outside China for income earned abroad may be credited against the amount of income tax computed according to the tax rate prescribed by the Tax Law of China through applications by presenting a tax payment certificate.

Article 17 Individual income in foreign currency shall be assessed according to the exchange rate quoted by the State General Administration of Exchange Control on the day when the tax payment certificate is made out and shall be taxed in Renminbi.

Article 18 Individuals liable to the tax in China who desire to leave the country are required to pay off the tax to the local tax authorities seven days before departure from China and only then can they go through exit formalities.

Article 19 In conducting investigations concerning the payment of tax by withholding agents or taxpayers filing personal returns, the tax officials sent by tax authorities are required to produce identification cards and maintain confidentiality.

Article 20 For a commission of 1% of the tax amount paid to the withholding agents provided in Article 10 of the Tax Law, the local tax authorities shall make out refund notices for the withholding agents on a monthly basis in accordance with the actual amount of tax withheld and the withholding agents may go through refunding formalities at the designated banks.

Article 21 A withholding agent or taxpayer filing personal returns who has violated the provisions of Article 9 of the Tax Law shall be penalized 500 yuan or less by the tax authorities according to the seriousness of the case.

Article 22 A withholding agent or a taxpayer filing personal returns who has violated the provisions of Articles 14 and 15 of these detailed rules and regulations shall be penalized 500 yuan or less by the tax authorities.

Article 23 The tax authorities shall serve notice on cases involving penalty in accordance with the relevant provisions of the Tax Law and these detailed rules and regulations.

Article 24 For cases of applying for reconsideration by a withholding agent or a taxpayer filing personal returns according to the provisions of Article 13 of the Tax Law, the tax authorities concerned are required to make decisions within three months after the application is received.

Article 25 Tax returns and tax payment certificates for individual income tax are to be printed by the General Tax Bureau of the Ministry of Finance of the People's Republic of China.

Article 26 The right of explanation of the present detailed rules and regulations resides in the Ministry of Finance of the People's Republic of China.

Article 27 These detailed rules and regulations come into force on the same date as the publication and enforcement of the "Individual Income Tax Law of the People's Republic of China."

CIRCULAR OF THE MINISTRY OF FINANCE ON CERTAIN QUESTIONS CONCERNING ABOUT INDIVIDUAL INCOME TAX

(June 2, 1982)

Financial departments (bureaus) in the provinces, municipalities and autonomous regions:

Since the Individual Income Tax Law of the People's Republic of China and the Detailed Rules and Regulations for its Implementation were made public and put into effect, various localities have raised a number of specific questions concerning policy matters and demanded clarification. These questions were discussed at a recent meeting on tax work involving foreigners, attended by representatives of six provinces (municipalities). Hereby we clarify some of the major questions as follows:

1 The Taxing of Allowances.

a. In the case of various allowances given by foreign enterprises to their staffs in China, those belonging to the category of personal wages and salaries should be calculated and taxed as income from wages and salaries. Those belonging to the public expenses given by foreign firms or enterprises to their staffs in China, such as allowances for travelling and business expenses (lodging expense, travelling expense and postal and telecommunications charges), public expenses (office expense, advertisement fees, and entertainment costs necessitated by business intercourse), etc., may not be calculated and taxed as income from wages and salaries if a certificate is issued by the dispatch firm or enterprise and verified by local tax authorities.

b. The various allowances or pocket money obtained in China by foreign experts or service workers sent to China owing to gratuitous aid or assistance are exempted from the individual income tax according to the provision of Item 1 in the Cai Shui No. 189 Document (80) issued by the Ministry of Finance.

2 The Taxing of Bonus and Year-end Additional Pay.

As for the bonuses or additional pays of several months obtained by the taxpayer in one payment, generally the whole sum of bonuses and/or additional pay should be calculated together with the wages or salaries of that month for the individual income tax. However, if this calculation results in a higher tax rate, the principle of relief and simplicity can be applied, an appropriate tax rate can be found with the monthly bonus (or additional pay) plus that month's wages or salaries as the base figure, and that rate can be used to calculalte the individual income tax by timing the whole sum of rewards (or bonuses) as well as that month's wages or salaries.

3 The Taxation of Incomes Obtained Outside and in China by Senior Intellectual Foreigners of Chinese Origin Who Have Retired and Settled Down in China.

The question of how to tax the pensions obtained abroad and the living allowances and wages obtained in China by senior intellectual foreigners of Chinese origin who have retired and settled down in China can be dealt with according to different circumstances in line with "The Suggestions Concerning Senior Intellectual Foreigners of Chinese Origin Who Have Come to Settle Down in China After Retirement" by the Department of Approval and Transfer of Overseas Chinese of the State Council and the Ministry of Foreign Affairs and other departments, and in accordance with the spirit of the provisions of the Individual Income Tax Law of our country:

a. Pensions and annual bonuses obtained from abroad owing to past employment are exempted from individual income tax.

b. Remunerations obtained from abroad for work in foreign institutions in China after retirement shall be dealt with according to the provisions of Article 5 of the Detailed Rules and Regulations for the Implementation of the Individual Income Tax Law. Other incomes obtained outside China (excluding pensions and annual bonuses) shall be dealt with according to the provisions of Article 3 of the Detailed Rules and Regulations for the Implementation of the Individual Income Tax Law.

c. For those whose work is arranged by China and who gain wages from China, the individual income tax shall be levied on the part of the monthy income in excess of 800 yuan. But the monthly allowance for such posts as technical adviser is tax-free.

4 Tax Exemption on the Income of Salaries of Other Persons in the Embassies and Consulates of Various Countries in China.

Article 10 of the Detailed Rules and Regulations for the Implementation of the Individual Income Tax Law of the People's Republic of China stipulates that tax exemption on the income of salaries of the other persons in the embassies and consulates of various countries in China should be limited to the same treatment as given by the said country to other persons in China's embassy and consulate in that country. Our country is a party to the Vienna Convention on Diplomatic Relations and the Vienna Convention on Consular Relations. According to the provisions of Articles 34 and 37 of the Vienna Convention on Diplomatic Relations and Article 49 of the Vienna Convention on Consular Relations, other persons in the embassies (administrative and technical personnel, service workers and dependants) are all exempted from personal income tax, except those employed by the dispatch country in the recipient country.

In view of this, the income of wages and salaries obtained by other persons (administrative and technical personnel, service workers and depandants) in the embassies and consulates of various countries in China can be exempted from the individual income tax, except persons employed in China.

5 Taxation of Wages and Salaries for Less than One Month.

For a foreigner residing in China for more than 90 days, if his period of stay in the month of entry or exit does not add up to a full month, taxation on individual income tax can be levied on the wages or salaries he obtained during the actual days of his residence in China.

6 The Calculation in Respect of a Foreigner Residing in China for not More than 90 Consecutive Days.

Article 5 of the Detailed Rules and Regulations for the Implementation of the Individual Income Tax Law stipulates that for individuals providing labor-services in China but residing for not more than 90 consecutive days, their incomes received from their employers outside China are exempted from tax. As for the limits of "90 days," four questions should be clarified: First, is the tax levied from the 91st day on while no tax is levied for the preceding 90 days? Second, if somebody resides in China for more than 90 consecutive days, but the days are spread over two tax years, is he taxable since his residence is less than 90 days when calculated on a yearly basis? Third, if someone originally plans to reside in China for less than 90 days but his stay is later extended for business to exceed 90 days, how is he taxed? Fourth, if the passport visa is valid for more than 90 days and the passport bearer leaves China temporarily during this period, is his residence counted as being consecutive?

The following is decided after research:

a. For taxpayers residing in China for more than 90 days, their incomes obtained in and outside China in the previous 90 days are taxable.

b. Taxpayers residing in China for more than 90 consecutive days shall be taxed according to the provisions of the tax law no matter whether their stay runs across one tax year or not.

c. If someone originally plans to reside in China for less than 90 days, he may not file a declaration in China of the income of the wages paid by his employer outside China during this period. But if his stay is extended to exceed 90 days, the case can be dealt with according to different circumstances as far as tax collection is concerned: If he cannot predetermine that his stay will exceed 90 days, he may wait until after 90 days to file personal returns and pay tax; if he can predetermine that his stay will exceed 90 days, he should file personal returns and pay tax according to the provisions of the tax law.

d. If the taxpayer's passport visa is valid for more than 90 days and he returns after a temporary exit from China during this period, it should still be regarded as a consecutive stay. However, in special circumstances, various localities may deal with the case under the principle of allowance for tax relief.

7 "Temporary Exit" from China of Taxpayers.

Article 2 of the Detailed Rules and Regulations for the Implementation of the Individual Income Tax Law stipulates that if a taxpayer temporarily exits from China in the tax year, the days shall not be deducted. Here, the "temporary exit" shall mean:

a. If a foreigner in China has obtained the permit of residence issued by the Chinese public security department, left China in the period approved and returned, his case should be regarded as temporary exit and the days of his absence are not to be deducted from his days of stay in China. If a foreigner hasn't obtained the permit of residence, but has left China and returned within the permitted period of entry and exit as stipulated in the visa of his passport (including the extended permitted period approved by the Chinese public security department after entry), his case shall belong to temporary exit and the days of his absence are not to be deducted. The days of residence are counted from the very day of entry.

b. If a foreigner in China leaves at the end of the valid period as stipulated in the entry visa of his passport and then enters for residence again after obtaining another entry visa, his days of residence in China, in principle, should be counted anew. However, for a foreigner who obtains the entry visa continuously and subsequently extends his stay, if the period of his exit and re-entry does not exceed 30 days, his case should be regarded as temporary exit.

8 The Determination of the Time of Commencement for Levying Tax on Labour and Services Remuneration.

The Cai Shui No. 179 Circular (80) of the Ministry of Finance stipulates that the incomes from labour and service remuneration that are collected in different payments after September 10 should be taxed according to regulations. According to reflection, the determination of the time of commencement is not clear enough. For instance, it takes a writer several years to finish a book from writing to publication. Should the time of occurrence refer to the time from writing to publication or to the collection of the payment for the book? According to the provisions of the Individual Income Tax Law, the income tax should be levied at the time of realizing the income. And the condition for realizing the income refers to the occurrence of the legal obligation of paying tax. Therefore, the time of realizing the income from labour and services remuneration should be the time when the taxpayer receives the income, or the time when the paying unit pays the sum, which is the time of commencement of the income.

9 How to Tax a Taxpayer Who Has Worked at Several Places in China.

For a foreigner working or providing personal services in China, his income obtained from his employer abroad should be taxed at the place of his work or services according to the provisions of the tax law. As to a taxpayer who works at several places, how is the taxation determined? It is decided after deliberation that for a taxpayer who works or provides personal services in China for more than 90 days, his income obtained from his employer abroad should be taxed at the place of his work or services according to regulations. If he works or provides personal services at more than one place, he can file his personal returns and pay tax with the tax authorities at the place of his work within the period of filing declarations of income and paying taxes as stipulated by the tax law, or he can apply with the tax authorities at the place of work for permission to pay the tax every month at that place. The relevant tax authorities should strengthen contacts and exchange information about the above-mentioned situations so as to prevent tax evasion.

10 The Refund of Tax.

In order to correctly implement the tax policy and strictly carry out the principle of refunding excess payments and making good deficiencies, in case a tax on an untaxable item has been paid by mistake and the taxpayer or the withholding agent files an application or it is found by the tax authorities on their own, the tax authorities at the place of the tax collection shall allow the taxpayer to go through the procedure of tax refund after the case has been examined as true.

11 Individual Income Tax Credits.

Article 16 of the Detailed Rules and Regulations for the Implementation of the Individual Income Tax Law stipulates that for the income tax already paid abroad on a taxpayer's income obtained outside China, the taxpayer can, by producing tax payment receipts, apply for credit against the income tax calculated in accordance to the tax rate stipulated in Chinese tax law. The principle of credits follows:

a. The credit of the income tax paid by a taxpayer abroad to be applied for in China refers to the income tax already paid abroad on the income obtained outside China. The income derived from sources in China does not belong to income obtained outside China and should be taxed by China. Even if a taxpayer has paid the tax abroad on the income derived from sources in China, he cannot apply for credit in China.

b. When a taxpayer applies for credit in China of the tax he has paid in his own country, the sum can only be credited against the income tax calculated according to the tax rate stipulated in Chinese tax law. If the income tax paid abroad exceeds the credit quota, it shall not be credited nor calculated in other ways.

c. If the income tax the taxpayer has paid abroad is lower than the credit quota calculated according to the tax rate stipulated in Chinese tax law, he shall pay the deficiency to China. However, if the above deficiency is the result of calculating too many living expenses or other special causes and the taxpayer really has difficulty making up the tax deficiency to China, he may, together with proofs, apply to the local tax authorities for tax reduction or exemption, but the reduced or exempted amount of tax must not exceed the tax deficiency he is due to make up.

12 The Withholding Unit and Handling Charges.

Article 10 of the Individual Income Tax Law stipulates that a handling charge of 10 percent of the tax amount withheld shall be paid to the withholding agents. Now that foreign enterprises have established permanent offices in China, can they withhold the tax paid by their staff members? If they are acknowledged as withholding agents, are they given handling charges for the tax they have withheld? As stipulated by the tax law, income paying units are withholding agents, and such agents, once approved by the local tax authorities, bear the responsibility for withholding taxes. For permanent foreign offices in China with the conditions, the local tax authorities can entrust them to act to withhold taxes and give them the 10 percent handling charges according to regulations. As for the certificates for tax paid, the withholding agent should make out the list to the tax authorities for examination before filling out the same one by one, and pay the taxes to the bank.

The present regulations shall come into force from the date of arrival of this Circular.

8

FINANCIAL MANAGEMENT

Control System/ Personnel/ Profits

CIRCULAR OF THE STATE COUNCIL ON THE INTRODUCTION OF A FINANCIAL MANAGEMENT SYSTEM BY WHICH THE SCOPE OF REVENUES AND EXPENDITURES WILL BE DEFINED FOR CENTRAL AND LOCAL GOVERNMENTS RESPECTIVELY AND WHEREBY EACH WILL BE RESPONSIBLE FOR THE BALANCE OF ITS OWN BUDGET

(February 1, 1980)

In order to carry out the policy of "readjustment, restructuring, consolidation and improvement" of our economy, to bring the initiative of both the central and the local governments into full play, and to meet the need of gradually realizing the modernization programme, the State Council has decided to introduce from 1980 a system of financial management by which the scope of revenues and expenditures will be defined for the central and local governments respectively and each will be responsible for the balancing of its own budget. The recently held national planning conference has discussed and decided on the basic norms of revenue and expenditure fixed for local governments, the ratio between that part of revenues to be handed over to the central government and the part to be used locally, and the fixed amounts of subsidies for areas entitled to such help. Herewith, we are transmitting a copy of the "Provisional Regulations Concerning the Introduction of a Financial Management System by Which the Scope of Revenues and Expenditures Will Be Defined for Central and Local Governments Respectively and Whereby Each Will Be Responsible for Balancing Its Own Budget," hoping you will abide by them.

To define the scope of revenues and expenditures for central and local governments and to make each responsible for the balance of its own budget is an important reform of the system of financial management by the state, a reform which will not only affect the structure of revenues and expenditures, the division of financial powers and the readjustment and improvement of the distribution of financial resources, but will also affect the readjustment and improvement of the system of management of planning, capital construction, materials supply, enterprises and public undertakings. To make this reform a success is of great significance to promoting the development of the national economy and the gradual realization of the Four Modernizations. All localities and departments must pay great attention to this question, give better guidance and ask the cadres to take the overall situation into consideration and correctly handle the relationship between the whole and the part and between national and regional interests. In combination with this reform, they should properly readjust and improve relevant systems and regulations concerning economic management so as to facilitate our work in all fields. In the course of introducing the new financial system, they must promptly grasp the current situation, sum up experiences and study and solve any new problems that may crop up in order to make a success of the work of reforming the system of financial management.

Appendix

Provisional Regulations Concerning the Introduction of a Financial System by Which the Scope of Revenues and Expenditures Will Be Defined for Central and Local Governments Respectively and Whereby Each Will Be Responsible for Balancing Its Own Budget.

In order to carry out the policy of "readjustment, restructuring, consolidation and improvement" of our economy, and meet the need of gradually realizing our modernization programme, beginning in 1980 the state will introduce for the provinces, municipalities and autonomous regions a system of financial management by which the scope of revenues and expenditures will be defined for central and local governments respectively and whereby each will be responsible for balancing its own budget. The basic principle is that under the condition that the unified leadership and planning by the central government is consolidated and that the indispensable expenditure of the central government is ensured, the power and responsibility of governments at various levels in financial affairs should be made clear, so that each will exercise its function and shoulder its responsibility, and the initiative of both central and local governments will be brought into full play.

1. Clearly divide the different kinds of revenue and expenditure between the central and local governments according to their relationship of subordination as specified under the system of economic management.

Revenues: Income of the enterprises under the administration of the central government, Customs duties and other income of the central government belong to the Ministry of Finance, as its regular sources of revenue. Income of enterprises under local administration, salt tax, agricultural and animal breeding taxes, industrial and commercial income tax; local taxes and other income of the local governments belong to the local financial departments as their regular sources of revenue. The income of those local enterprises which have been placed under the direct administration of the central ministries, with the approval of the State Council, will be divided according to a fixed ratio: 80% will be handed over to the Ministry of Finance and 20% to the local financial departments. Industrial and commercial taxes will be used to supplement the revenue of the central and local governments.

Expenditures: Capital investments handled by the central government, the circulating funds of the enterprises under central administration, expenses for the tapping of potential and the technological transformation of the enterprises and trial manufacture of new products for geological prospecting, national defence, foreign aid, material reserve of the state, operating expenses for cultural, educational, health and scientific undertakings at the central level, those for agriculture, forestry, irrigation and meteorology and those for the industrial, communications and commercial departments will be disbursed from state revenues. The capital investment handled by the localities, the circulating funds of the local enterprises (including those of the projects built by the central government for them), funds for the tapping of potential and the technological transformation of enterprises, funds for the trial manufacture of new products, financial aid to rural people's communes, operating expenses for agriculture, forestry, irrigation, meteorology, etc., operating expenses for industrial, communications and commercial departments, maintenance fees for the cities, funds for building anti-air-raid defence works, funds for moving people from the cities into the countryside, operating expenses for cultural, educational, health and scientific undertakings, social relief funds; pensions for the disabled and for families of the deceased, administrative expenses, etc. will be disbursed from the revenue of the local governments.

Expenditures on a few particular items, such as relief fees for extraordinary natural disasters, subsidies for campaigns against extraordinary droughts and floods and developing funds in support of underdeveloped regions will be earmarked by the central government and will not be included in the budgets of the local governments.

2. The basic norms fixed for the revenue and expenditure of a local government will be calculated and worked out on the basis of estimated revenues and expenditures for 1979, with suitable readjustments made according to the aforesaid division of the scope of revenues and expenditures. Where local revenues are larger than expenditures, a part of the surplus will be handed over to the central government according to a fixed ratio. Where revenues are not enough to cover expenditures, the deficiency will be made by allowing the local government to keep a portion of the industrial and commercial tax. In places where revenues are still insufficient to cover expenditures even if income from the industrial and commercial taxes has been left entirely with the local government, the Ministry of Finance will give the local government a fixed amount of subsidies. Once the ratio by which the local government divides its revenues with the central government and the amount of the subsidies are fixed, they will, as a rule, remain unchanged for five years; should the local government earn more, it may spend more.

After the introduction of the system by which the scope of revenues and expenditures is defined for central and local governments and each is responsible for the balance of its own budget, if an enterprise or public undertaking originally administered by the central government is placed under local leadership, if a large enterprise which has been newly put into operation is put under local administration, or if a new kind of tax is levied and, as a result, the revenues and expenditures of the central and local governments are seriously affected, the division of local revenues and the amount of subsidies granted by the central authorities should be readjusted. Or, as an alternative, the central financial authorities will settle accounts will the local authorities. When other economic measures are adopted in accordance with decisions of the central government, including the readjustment of prices, increases of wages for factory and office workers, readjustments of tax rates, and tax reductions and exemptions, the aforesaid division of local revenues and expenditures and the amount of subsidies shall not be changed, unless otherwise stipulated. In the case of an exceptional natural disaster, the central government will give aid to the affected areas according to the consequences of the disaster.

3. In order to help step up production in remote border areas, the autonomous areas of minority nationalities, former revolutionary

bases and other economically underdeveloped areas, the central government will, as far as its financial capacity permits, establish development funds for the economically underdeveloped areas. Such funds will gradually increase to account for 2% of state expenditures; these funds will be allocated by the Ministry of Finance. They will be earmarked for special purposes and used on more important projects.

4. The autonomous regions of the nationalities will continue to adopt the system of financial management that has been stipulated for the nationalities' autonomous areas. The special provisions laid down for their finances will remain unchanged. But the amount of subsidies granted to them by the central government will remain unchanged for a period of five years once it is fixed, instead of being changed every year. Within the five years, their increased income will be entirely retained for local use. In the meantime, to give special consideration to the needs of the nationalities' autonomous areas in developing their production, construction and culture and education, the central government will increase the amount of subsidies to the autonomous areas at a rate of 10% each year.

5. After the reform of the system of financial management has been effected, all provinces, municipalities and autonomous regions should make overall arrangements for the production, construction and expenditure of their respective areas according to the guidelines, policies and plans of the state. In working out its budget, the local government must act cautiously and not overextend itself, see to it that revenues and expenditures are balanced, with a small surplus on the credit side. They must not make a budget with a deficit, issue local bonds, or appropriate the funds of and apportion expenses to enterprises under them. The budgets of the localities shall be compiled by the local governments and, after being collected and examined by the Ministry of Finance, submitted to the State Council for approval.

The central departments in charge of the enterprises and public undertakings will no longer make overall arrangements for expenses of enterprises of the same trade, or allocate expenditure targets to the localities as before. However, the various central departments shall continue to formulate guidelines and point to the orientation of work, adopt policies and measures and check up on the economic effects so as to help the local governments to do their work well. The provinces, muncipalities and autonomous regions should take the interests of the whole into account, and respect the opinions of the central departments. Those expenses which have been assigned to a local government and which serve the production and construction of the whole country or of the area concerned must be included in the local budget. The local government must guarantee the transfer from its own area of materials and commodities as required by the state.

6. In executing both the central and the local budgets, all income must be collected according to government policies, all expenses paid must conform to the budgets, and all additional expenses must be made through proper procedures. All income that should be included in the budgets must be treated accordingly. On important questions that concern the whole country such as the taxation system, price policy, the issuance of public bonds, wages and bonus standards, the scope of payment of the costs of enterprises, the proportions of the profit to be used as special funds and the standards of important expenditures, all localities and departments must follow the provisions that apply to the whole country. No changes shall be allowed unless they are approved by the proper authorities. Discipline in economic and financial affairs must be enforced. To grant tax reductions or exemptions, or to encroach on state revenues by going beyond the limits of one's authority as prescribed by the state, is strictly prohibited. All localities and departments must strive to increase production, practise economy, increase their income and cut down expenses, so as to fulfill their tasks with regard to revenues and expenditures and to make greater contributions to the state.

7. The specific kind of system of financial management which a province, municipality or autonomous region adopts in relation to counties and cities under its administration shall be decided by the province, municipality or autonomous region concerned in conformity with the spirit of the present regulations.

REGULATIONS CONCERNING THE WORK OF FINANCIAL SUPERVISION

Promulgated by the Ministry of Finance
(Approved for Transmission by the State Council on July 2, 1980)

To strengthen supervision over financial affairs is an important guarantee for upholding financial discipline, for promoting the increase of revenues and the economy of expenditure and for accelerating the socialist modernization of our country. With a view to combatting graft, embezzlement, extravagance, waste and all violations against financial discipline, to correctly carrying out the financial policies, laws and regulations of the state, and to successfully realizing the state budget, the following regulations have been worked out:

1. The Setting Up of Financial Supervisory Organizations.

A financial supervisory department will be set up under the Ministry of Finance. Financial supervisory offices will also be set up under the financial department (bureau) of each province, autonomous region and municipality directly under the central government. A financial supervisory section will be set up under the financial bureau of each prefectural office, city directly under the province and autonomous zhou. Under the financial section of each county (city) and autonomous county there will be a sub-section or persons in charge of financial supervision.

The financial departments of the ministries, commissions and departments directly under the State Council and of the provinces, autonomous regions, and municipalities directly under the central government may set up financial supervisory offices or sections or may appoint persons in charge of such work according to the requirements of the work.

Where the required conditions exist, the financial departments may engage financial supervisory correspondents from among the accountants in enterprises, public undertakings and government organizations.

2. The Tasks of the Financial Supervisory Organizations.

The tasks of the financial supervisory organizations are as follows:

a) To supervise and check up on government organizations, public bodies, enterprises and public undertakings in their carrying out of the financial policies, laws and regulations, and to discover existing problems;

b) To supervise and check up on the financial departments and related personnel to see whether they are abiding by financial policies, laws and regulations, and to discover the existing problems;

c) To take up and investigate cases of disruption of financial regulations and of violations against financial discipline as well as cases in which people suffered from retaliation for having persisted in following financial regulations;

d) To make proposals for the improvement of financial management and administration on the basis of the problems discovered;

e) To conduct education in socialist legality and financial discipline.

3. Leadership Of the Financial Supervisory Organizations.

Administratively, the financial supervisory organizations are under the leadership of the financial departments at their corresponding levels. In professional matters, they are guided by higher financial supervisory organizations. The lower financial supervisory organizations should periodically report their work to the higher financial supervisory organizations. If necessary, they may bypass their immediate leadership and report to the higher authorities. The financial supervisory organizations at a higher level have the right to check up on the work of the financial supervisory organizations at lower levels.

The appointment, dismissal and transfer of the chief responsible personnel of a financial supervisory organization should be reported for the record to the financial department at the next higher level.

4. Rights of the Personnel in Charge of Financial Supervision.

The personnel in charge of financial supervision have the right:

a) To ask the leaders and other persons concerned in the unit under investigation to provide the necessary information and to attend the relevant meetings;

b) To examine the budget and final accounts, and to plan for revenues and expenditures, reports and forms of statistics, account books, original vouchers, and other related records and files of the unit being investigated; and, if necessary, to xerox or duplicate some of the important material;

c) To check up on the cash, materials and bank deposits of the unit under investigation, and go to the building-sites, workshops and storehouses concerned to investigate;

d) To make investigations and collect materials from units involved in the case;

e) To inquire about any person who is involved in the case and ask him to give an answer on the spot or write down his answer.

When a person in charge of financial supervision performs the above functions, the units under investigation and the people concerned should cooperate voluntarily and give a truthful account of the facts, and should not obstruct the process in any way.

5. The Handling of Cases Under Financial Supervision.

In handling a case it has accepted, the financial supervisory organization concerned should carefully determine the facts and promptly write a report on the result of its investigations. And, according to the specific nature and circumstances of the case, it should make a proposal for its settlement and submit it to the unit under investigation or the department in charge of the unit so as to settle the case. If the case being handled calls for disciplinary action against the offenders, the case should be handed over to the relevant authorities which are in charge of these cadres. If the case is a serious one that calls for punishment by law, it should be handed over to judicial organs to be judged according to law. The financial supervisory organizations should propose to the units concerned the commendation of people who adhere to financial regulations, or provide awards to those who protect state property and dare to combat violations against financial discipline.

The investigation report must be shown to the unit and persons under investigation to ask for their opinions. If they do not agree with the report they are allowed to state their reasons and to present a written statement, which should be appended to the report.

After a case has been dealt with, the unit under investigation or the department in charge should send a copy of its decisions on the case to the financial supervisory organization concerned. If the latter has differing views regarding the handling of the case, it may present its views to the department which has made decision on the case or report to the higher authorities.

6. Requirements for Personnel in Charge of Financial Supervision.

a) They must conscientiously study the financial and economic policies, laws and regulations of the state, be knowledgeable about financial affairs and accounting, and love their work;

b) They must closely rely on the masses, intimately cooperate with the relevant departments, combine their own work with supervision by the masses;

c) They must adhere to principle, abide by law and discipline, be unintimidated by the powerful and the influential, be not swayed by personal considerations, and dare to combat all violations against financial discipline;

d) They must seek truth from facts, pay serious attention to evidence and investigation, be scrupulous about every detail and heed the opinion of everyone concerned, including the units and people who are being investigated.

DECISIONS OF THE STATE COUNCIL TO BALANCE REVENUES AND EXPENDITURES AND RIGOROUSLY ENFORCE FINANCIAL ADMINISTRATION

(January 26, 1981)

For the last period, deficits have continuously occurred in our state finance, banks have additionally over-issued notes and the prices in the market have risen. These problems will certainly affect the situation as a whole and influence stability and unity if they are not solved. In order to ensure the balance between the revenue and expenditure of 1981 and eliminate deficits, the State Council thinks it imperative to adopt the principle of centralization for the distribution and utilization of financial resources, rigorously enforce financial administration and financial and economic discipline, strive to regain the initiative promptly and achieve the stability of the economy. For this reason, the following decisions are made:

1 To endeavour to increase income and be determined to cut down expenditure so as to ensure the balance between revenue and expenditure at both central and local levels. In 1981, it is imperative to make great efforts to tap potentialities, increase the production of the products which are salable and satisfy the needs and increase the revenue. All measures that are advantageous to regulation, to production and to the increase of revenue shall be energetically supported in finance. Meanwhile, expenditure shall be energetically reduced so as to resolutely cut the expenditure down to the limits permitted by our financial resources. In order to make up the deficits in this and next years, each area or each department shall ensure the fulfilment and shall not fall short of the tasks set to issue state treasury bills and have the loan of local financial resources. The regulated revenue and expenditure plan of 1981 shall be fulfilled level by level down to grass-roots units so as to strive to obtain more revenue than planned and make every effort to spend less than the planned expenditure. Without the approval of the Central Committee of the Party and the State Council, no area or department shall make openings wantonly to reduce revenue and increase expenditure and the irrational openings made in the past shall be examined and redressed. The previous year's surpluses of all Party and government organs, bodies, armed forces, enterprises and institutions shall not be put to use without approval except for the purchase of treasury bills. The procedures for their control have been separately transmitted to lower levels.

2 To resolutely defend the state taxation system and not alter tax categories or tax rates or reduce or remit taxation at will. The opening and closing of state tax categories, the addition and deduction of tax items, the raising and lowering of tax rates or the additions, reductions and remissions of taxation shall be administered in a uniform manner and the provisions in this regard shall all be transmitted down by the Ministry of Finance or submitted by the Ministry of Finance to the State Council for approval and then transmitted to lower levels. From now on, all provisions concerning taxation transmitted down by each department itself shall be null and void. The State Council hereby instructs the Ministry of Finance to make a check of some provisions for taxation made by various departments themselves; those which are irrational are to be annulled and those in excess of the limits of authority are to be put right. A small number of enterprises and a few cities that have made the experiments of "taxes in lieu of profits, independent accounting and assuming sole responsibility for profits or losses" shall sum up experience and carry on the experiments; if new units must be added for experiments, applications shall be made to the Ministry of Finance for approval. When tax rates are determined for experimental units, the financial resources left to the enterprises shall not exceed the levels of the original profit reserves and those in excess of these levels shall be readjusted. All the taxes that must be collected by the state shall be duly and fully handed over to the state treasury and no one shall intercept them for use, divert them to other purposes or be in arrears with them; the money recovered by enterprises for selling goods shall first be used to pay taxes. Those who evade tax payment or refuse to pay taxes shall be punished according to law. The tax department at each level shall strengthen the administration of taxation and fight against the activities in violation of tax laws.

3 To endeavour to raise the levels of enterprises' profits and guarantee due and full turnover of enterprises' profits to the state. All industrial and commercial enterprises shall conscientiously make production costs and expenses and strengthen the administration of quotas. If the consumption of raw materials, fuel and power is higher than the best level in the history of an

enterprise itself, measures shall be taken to reduce it within a definite time. With regard to the enterprises which have been ordered by authorities in charge to close or stop production because their products do not satisfy the needs, they consume too much, they are of poor quality or they cause great losses, the supply of the electricity used for production, the supply of raw materials and fuel, financial subsidies and bank loans shall be stopped. In the case of the experiments of the system of profits reserved by enterprises, stress shall be laid on their consolidation and improvement and the scope of experiments shall not be enlarged. In giving rewards, enterprises shall give consideration to their neighbours and shall work strictly in accordance with "Several Provisions for the Correct Implementation of Rewarding Regulations and the Resolute Checking of the Reckless Issue of Rewards" issued on January 16, 1981. The profits and depreciation which must be turned over by enterprises shall be duly turned over to the state treasury as stipulated and no unit or individual shall intercept and retain them without authorization or apportion or take shares in them, or cause the withdrawal of revenue from the state treasury without authorization. To repay technological measure loans or capital construction loans, enterprises shall repay them out of the earnings newly increased after the loan projects are put into production or out of the depreciation funds drawn by them; no enterprise shall make unauthorized use of the profits which originally have to be turned over and no bank shall accept the loans as paid by deducting them from the original profits of the enterprise; meanwhile, no enterprise shall repay the loans out of its tax payments as well. If this principle is violated, the sums shall be recovered in full.

4 To rigorously enforce the administration and supervision of capital construction appropriations and be determined to shorten capital construction fronts. All capital construction funds shall be brought into the state unified capital construction plans and allocated under the supervision of the Construction Bank. All large or medium capital construction projects shall follow the fixed procedures of examination and approval and finally be submitted to the State Council for approval. If they are not approved, financial departments shall not allocate funds and banks shall not offer loans. All capital construction projects shall strictly follow procedures of capital construction. The projects which have been determined by the departments in charge to stop or delay shall resolutely be stopped. Those which have to be stopped but are not stopped shall not be given materials by the material departments nor be built by the construction departments. With regard to stopped or delayed projects, financial and banking departments shall stop all appropriations and loans except necessary engineering maintenance expenses and personnel's wages. In the case of the projects which are built with approval, if there is found to be any arbitrary alteration of designs or any willful addition of the contents of construction or any improper use of funds, which has resulted in losses, waste, etc., the Construction Bank shall be entitled to check it and freeze funds or stop appropriations if necessary.

5 To conscientiously reduce overstocked goods and materials and save current funds. It shall be determined to change the current irrational state of affairs in which too many materials or funds are taken up or lying idle in the fields of circulation. With the exception of the enterprises newly opened, additional current funds, in general, shall no longer be allocated to the existing enterprises by financial departments and the funds required for the increase of their production shall be settled by means of speeding up the turnover of funds and tapping the potentialities of funds. In order to prevent any new overstocking of goods and materials, material and commercial departments shall refuse to purchase the really unsalable products produced by industrial enterprises in future; financial and banking departments shall refuse to offer appropriations or loans for them. Commercial, foreign trade and material departments shall promptly check the stock and put part of the commodities into the market so as to withdraw currency from circulation. Close attention shall be paid to the disposition of such materials as steel or mechanical and electrical products overstocked by enterprises or departments in charge and marketing shall be organized so as to make the best use of everything.

6 To make great efforts to save or reduce operating expenses and administrative outlay. The establishment of personnel shall strictly be controlled. Each department of the Central Government or each province, municipality or autonomous region shall submit its establishment to the State Council for approval and no persons shall be added and no establishments shall be enlarged without approval. Various business expenses and administrative outlays shall be used by means of careful calculation, strict budgeting and economy within the expenditure budgets approved by the state. All institutions with regular incomes shall strengthen the administration of the expenses so as to achieve their self-sufficiency in greater part or in full step by step. Social group

purchasing power shall strictly be controlled and strict regulations of examination and approval shall be enforced in respect of "specially-controlled commodities." The management expenses of enterprises shall also be strictly controlled and reduced by 20 per cent on the basis of the actual expenditure of 1980 with the exception of the staff's wages. An enterprise shall work out an expenditure plan of management expenses and submit it to the department in charge and the financial department for examination and approval. Frequencies and numbers of persons shall conscientiously be controlled in respect of overseas inspections, visits, exhibitions, performances, shows, competitions, matches or attendance at international conferences; participation in international organizations and invitation of foreign guests to our country shall strictly be examined so as to contribute to the economy on the expenditure of foreign currencies. It shall strictly be prohibited to use public funds to entertain guests, send gifts or go on trips.

7 To strictly execute the state budget administration regulations. The budgets of the government at each level and each department shall strictly be implemented. If any additions are really required in the course of the implementation, the additions of each department of the Central Government shall be reported by the Ministry of Finance to the State Council for examination and approval; those of each province, municipality or autonomous region shall be reported by the department (or bureau) of finance to the people's government of the province, municipality or autonomous region for examination and approval. From now on, no leaders shall sign any notes for expenditure by bypassing the financial department. The expenditure of which the financial department applies for the supplement shall not exceed the total of the reserve funds at its level. When each department is formulating policies or measures, those concerning the reduction of revenue and the increase of expenditure shall first obtain the consent of the financial department and then be submitted for examination and approval. They shall not be mixed up with other documents.

8 To enforce financial and economic discipline. The leading cadres at each level and the cadres of enterprises and institutions shall be educated in financial and economic discipline. Various prohibitions concerning financial and economic discipline which were stipulated by the Party Central Committee and the State Council in the past shall remain in force and continue to be implemented, for example, the prohibitions against the diversion of the tax payments and profits which shall be turned over to other purpose, those against the forcible inclusion of any expenditure beyond the cost of production in the selling price, those against the arbitrary or covert raising of prices, those against the diversion of current funds to capital construction, those against the unauthorized raising of the standards of various expenses or the drawing proportions of enterprise special-purpose funds, etc. It shall never be permitted to disrupt the state financial and economic discipline out of selfish departmentalism or personal interest. The units and personnel that violate financial and economic discipline shall strictly be dealt with, and such economic sanctions as ordering them to return what they have unlawfully taken, imposing fines on them or deducting parts of their pay and necessary disciplinary sanctions shall be taken against them. Those whose cases are serious shall be handed over to judicial authorities for punishment according to law.

The above eight articles are quite necessary to overcome current financial difficulties and carry out economic regulation smoothly. Each area or each department shall conduct thoroughgoing and painstaking ideological work well to enable the broad masses of cadres to fully realize that the measures taken by the state fully accord with the long-term and essential interests of the whole nation. The present state of affairs is very good and the difficulty is transient. The State Council requests that each area or each department shall conscientiously strengthen the leadership over revenue and financial work, adopt necessary measures in the light of the specific conditions of its own area or department and conscientiously carry out various provisions. With regard to the question of how the army shall carry out these provisions, the procedures shall be formulated by the Military Commission of the Party Central Committee. We hope each area or each department shall report the situations of its disposition and implementation to the State Council at any time.

INTERIM PROVISIONS OF THE MINISTRY OF FINANCE FOR THE REDUCTION OF THE MANAGEMENT EXPENSES OF STATE ENTERPRISES

(Annotated and passed on by the State Council on January 29, 1981)

At present, the expenditure of such public outlays of the industrial, communications and commercial enterprises throughout the country as administrative, travelling, and meeting expenses, furniture purchases, and labour protection necessities is equivalent to about four times the public outlays of administrative organs. The waste is quite serious in respect of these public outlays for lack of strict administration. It is necessary to reduce the management expenses of enterprises in order to further implement the "Notice of Saving in Non-productive Expenditure and Fighting Against Waste" of the Central Committee of the CPC and the State Council on January 24, 1980, to hold on to diligence and thrift, reduce costs and expenses and increase the profits turned over so as to eliminate financial deficits and ensure the stability of the economy. For this reason, the following provisions are made:

1. Special accounting and administration shall be practised in respect of the management expenses of enterprises. Every enterprise shall independently work out the expenditure plan for its management expenses in accordance with the limits, standards and specific items of expenditure stipulated by the state and execute it with the approval of a higher department in charge and the financial department so as to be used to examine and appraise the management result of the enterprise. The execution of this expenditure shall be included in quarterly and annual accounting report forms for independent report and submitted to the higher department in charge and the financial department for examination.

2. The saving targets of public outlays shall be assigned to enterprises. The enterprises' public outlays of 1981 shall be reduced by 20 per cent from the actual expenditure of 1980. The proportion of the reduction for each enterprise shall be checked and ratified by the department in charge separately according to the general requirements and the specific conditions of the enterprise, which shall only allow reduction and shall not permit excess.

3. Administrative expenses shall be saved. Rated administration shall be practised with regard to the administrative expenses of enterprises in accordance with the standards of expenditure stipulated. All usable old and used articles, stationary, paper, etc. shall be put into use as far as possible. Except for those which are normally required by and indispensable to libraries, reference rooms, newspaper reading boards, etc., the books, newspapers and magazines read by the staff and workers shall be bought and subscribed to by them at their own expense.

4. The expenditure of travelling and meeting expenses shall be saved. When an enterprise dispatches any persons to purchase materials, promote the sale of products, carry out such activities as trial sale, exhibition fairs, services, etc. or attend relevant meetings, the standards and stipulations of the local administrative authorities in relation to travelling and meeting expenses shall strictly be implemented and every effort shall be made to save them. It shall strictly be forbidden to go on trips to visit scenic spots, indulge in food and drink or give dinner parties and send gifts with public funds. Anyone who violates this provision shall have part of his own wages deducted for repayment.

With the exception of the specialized ordering, fittings, material distribution, product acceptance, appraisal or comparison and assessment meetings and small fact-finding meetings which shall be at the enterprises' expense in accordance with the provisions for travelling expenses, the hotel charges, food allowances, etc. for the personnel of enterprises to attend the meetings convened by higher authorities shall be at the expense of the convening units which shall not allow the attendants to apply for reimbursements from their own units upon their return nor apportion them to enterprises under any pretences. Higher authorities shall pay various expenses alone for the meetings held in enterprises which are not required to bear them.

5. The number of non-productive motor vehicles shall be reduced. The non-productive vehicles of an enterprise shall be allocated with approval of the department in charge of the enterprise. Surplus vehicles shall be turned over to the department in charge for disposal. The vehicles additionally required by newly-established units shall be redistributed by the department in charge.

The vehicle-using regulations shall be rigorously enforced and the leaders and other personnel of an enterprise shall not use public motor vehicles for private purposes; if they use vehicles on private business, they shall be charged as stipulated.

6. The administration of labour protection necessities shall be strengthened. The distribution standards and use time limits stipulated by the labour department shall strictly be implemented with regard to labour protection necessities. The replacement of old ones by new ones and the repair and utilization of old and used ones shall be effected. It shall strictly be forbidden to buy or make high-grade clothing materials, garments, etc. for distribtuion without authorization or reckless issue on the excuse of labour protection, nor shall it be allowed to turn the issue of labour protection necessities into staff and workers' welfare or rewards.

7. Practical results shall be emphasized in civilized production. The trees shall be planted in the factory areas on the principles of diligence and thrift and the masses shall be mobilized to do the work on their own. Potted flowers and potted landscapes shall not be bought under the pretence of greening.

8. The expenditure for entertaining foreign guests shall strictly be controlled. An enterprise shall implement the state provisions for the expenses to entertain foreign guests and extravagance and waste shall not be allowed. It shall strictly be forbidden to buy such high-quality articles as sofas and carpets for use by taking advantage of the opportunity to entertain foreign guests.

In the entertainment of the personnel of higher authorities and brotherly units at dinner, cinema, theatre, accommodation, etc., the money shall be collected at established rates and any enterprise shall not be allowed to expend entertaining expenses under any pretences.

9. The management expenses of a corporation shall be controlled. In the case of a corporation in the nature of an enterprise which has been set up, it shall be consolidated on the principle of simplification so as to reduce its personnel and expenditure as far as possible. If it is an administrative organization, its expenditure shall come from the administrative expenses instead. A corporation which is not necessary to be set up shall be dissolved. The new set-up of specialized corporations shall be approved by the economic commission of the province, municipality or autonomous region. If the outlays of a corporation are borne by the enterprises under it, the budgets of the management expenses for the corporation shall be worked out annually and submitted to the financial department at the same level for approval. The corporation shall make the budgets approved by the financial department and the sums apportioned to the enterprises under it known to the enterprises. The enterprises under it shall be entitled to refuse to turn over the management expenses of the corporation without approval or in excess of the approved sums.

10. The mass supervision shall be strengthened. After the enterprise's plan of management expenses is determined, it shall be conscientiously implemented and its implementation shall be reported quarterly to the staff and workers' congress so as to carry out the mass supervision. The saving of the expenditure of management expenses shall be regarded as one of the requirements for the appraisal and issue of rewards to the personnel concerned. The parts of the annual expenditure of the enterprise's management expenses in excess of the approved plan shall be drawn out of the enterprise funds or its profit reserves and shall not be included into the cost of production.

11. Financial regulations shall strictly be followed. The financial and accounting personnel of an enterprise shall be entitled to refuse to pay or reimburse the expenses spent in violation of financial regulations and financial and economic discipline. The leaders of the enterprise shall support the financial and accounting personnel to exercise their powers.

The coal, electricity, oils, etc. for daily use by an enterprise shall be strictly and clearly differentiated from those needed for the production of the enterprise and separate accounting shall be carried out for them. Living expenses shall not be reimbursed as those for production.

The expenses which shall be drawn from such special funds as welfare funds, trade union outlays, etc. and which shall be borne by the staff and workers themselves shall not be included in the management expenses and other productive operation expenses.

12. Jointly with the departments in charge of the enterprises concerned, the department (or bureau) of finance of each province, municipality or autonomous region shall formulate the expenditure standards and management procedures for management expenses, promulgate them and put them into effect in accordance with the above provisions and the local specific conditions.

INTERIM PROVISIONS FOR THE PROFESSIONAL TITLES OF ECONOMIC PROFESSIONAL CADRES

(Annotated and Passed On by the State Council on December 24, 1980)

These Provisions are made for the purpose of the better training and rational employment of economic professional cadres and of the accomplishment of their appraisal and promotion so as to give full play to their initiative, encourage them to endeavour to gain professional proficiency, improve the standards of the scientific management of economic work and speed up the socialist four-modernizations construction.

Article 1 The professional titles of economic professional cadres shall be defined as: Senior Economists, Economists, Assistant Economists and Economic Clerks.

Article 2 An economic professional cadre who will be determined to have a professional title or promoted to it shall support the leadership of the Communist Party of China, be devoted to the socialist motherland, make great efforts to study Marxism, Leninism and Mao Zedong Thought, conscientiously carry out the Party's line, guiding principles and policies, endeavour to obtain proficiency in economic theory and vocational work and diligently serve the socialist construction.

Article 3 The determination or promotion of the professional titles of economic professional cadres shall mainly be based on the degrees of their learning, their professional competence and their working achievements, and proper consideration shall also be given to their records of education and their qualifications at economic professional service.

Article 4 A graduate from a polytechnic school who has undergone one year's probation at the post of economic professional cadre or a person who has the same educational level shall be defined as an economic clerk if he or she has the following qualifications:

(1) Possessing the general basic theoretical and vocational knowledge of the profession;

(2) Being familiar with relevant rules and regulations and able to execute them accordingly;

(3) Being able to make preliminary analysis and sorting of the special economic activities and accomplish his or her own job.

Article 5 A graduate from the regular course of an institution of higher learning who has undergone one year's probation, an economic clerk or a person who has the same educational level shall be defined as or promoted to the position of an assistant economist if he or she has the following qualifications:

(1) Possessing a good command of the basic theoretical and vocational knowledge of the profession;

(2) Being familiar with relevant guiding principles, policies, rules and regulations and able to implement them;

(3) Being familiar with his or her own job, able to handle the work within the jurisdiction of his or her position and accomplish tasks better;

(4) Possessing a preliminary command of a foreign language.

Article 6 An assistant economist or a person who has the same professional level shall be defined as or promoted to the position of an economist if he or she has the following qualifications:

(1) Possessing a rather systematic command of the basic theoretical and vocational knowledge of the profession;

(2) Possessing a certain understanding of policies and being able to properly implement relevant guiding principles, policies, rules and regulations;

(3) Possessing relatively rich experience in actual work, being familiar with his or her own position, being able to work independently, properly handle rather sophisticated problems in service and achieve good economic results;

(4) Possessing a good command of a foreign language.

Article 7 An economist or a person who has the same professional level shall be defined as or promoted to a senior economist if he or she has the following qualifications:

(1) Possessing the systematic and substantial theory and knowledge of the branch of learning, having made a more profound study of and attainments in a certain economic profession or field, having made greater achievements and written scientific writings or service reports on a higher level;

(2) Possessing a higher understanding of policies and being able to make valuable suggestions as to policies in relation to economy according to actual conditions;

(3) Possessing very rich experience in actual work and the ability to direct an area, a department or a large enterprise in a certain aspect of economic work, being able to solve the major problems in relevant economic business and having made remarkable achievements in the improvement of business management and the training of economic qualified personnel;

(4) Possessing a very good command of a foreign language.

Article 8 To be determined or promoted to the professional title of an economic professional cadre, he or she shall undergo examinations. An examination shall be arranged every one to three years on the basis of the usual tests of achievements. Those with outstanding achievements shall be examined at any time and promoted out of turn. Those without the records of education as stipulated shall be examined in the basic theory and vocational knowledge necessary for the profession and in the degrees of their command of any foreign language(s) in addition to the appraisal of their achievements in their service.

Article 9 The determination or promotion of the professional titles of economic professional cadres shall be assessed and decided upon by a corresponding appraising and examining organization within the limits of authority in the administration of cadres. The composition of the appraising and examining organization shall be approved by the authorities at the same level.

Article 10 To be defined as or promoted to a professional title of an economic cadre, the person concerned shall make a personal application or shall be recommended by his organization, file his or her resume and submit his or her service reports or academic writings and the professional title shall be conferred by the authorities after the appraisal of the corresponding appraising and examining organization.

A title of senior economist shall be conferred by each ministry or commission of the State Council or by the people's government of each province, autonomous region or municipality directly under the Central Government; an economist shall be conferred by the authorities at the same level as a prefectural administrative office; an assistant economist or an economic clerk shall be conferred by the authorities equivalent to the county level. Certificates shall be issued to the cadres who obtain the professional titles above the rank of economist.

Article 11 The determination or promotion of the professional titles of economic professional cadres shall be practical and realistic as well as serious and conscientious. Those who practise graft or suppress economic professional cadres shall sternly be dealt with according to the degrees of seriousness. Those who forge the records of education or qualifications, make false reports of achievements or obtain professional titles by fraud shall have their professional titles withdrawn and be severely dealt with according to the degrees of seriousness.

Article 12 These Provisions are applicable to the professional cadres engaged in economic service in economic and other departments.

Article 13 Each ministry or commission of the State Council and the people's government of each province, autonomous region or municipality directly under the Central Government shall formulate the detailed rules for the implementation of these Provisions in the light of actual conditions.

STIPULATIONS CONCERNING PROCEDURES FOR THE IMPLEMENTATION OF PROFIT RESERVES AND PROFIT OR LOSS UNDERTAKINGS BY STATE INDUSTRIAL AND COMMUNICATIONS ENTERPRISES

(December 26, 1981)

In order to urge enterprises to improve their business management, tap their internal potentialities and enable their system of economic responsibility to develop healthily, the following specific stipulations are now made in respect of the matters concerning procedures for the implementation of profit reserves and profit or loss undertakings by state industrial and communications enterprises on the principles stipulated in Documents No. 159 and 166 (1981) of the State Council:

1 The state implements many types and styles of profit reserves and profit or loss undertaking methods according to different conditions over enterprises and departments in charge, i.e., "base profit reserves plus growth profit reserves," "full-amount profit reserves," "undertaking profits turned over and sharing out or reserving excessive profits," "undertaking loss subsidies and sharing out or reserving the subsidies for reduced loss" and "plan-overfulfilled profit reserves."

In case there are conditions for the implementation by the department (including corporations) of the procedures for profit reserves or profit or loss undertakings, the financial department at each level shall adopt one method out of the above five types for trial implementation with the consent of the department in charge. The department in charge shall implement different types of methods for profit reserves or profit or loss undertakings over the enterprises (including losing enterprises) under it within the limits of reserve proportions or undertaking quotas checked and ratified by the financial department. In case there are no conditions for the time being for the trial implementation by the department, the method for profit reserves or profit or loss undertakings shall be implemented by the enterprise after agreement is reached through consultation between the financial department and the department in charge. However, whether they are implemented by the department or by the enterprise, a department or an enterprise shall only adopt one method and shall not adopt two methods concurrently to draw reserves in a repeated way. The units that implement profit or loss undertakings shall not draw profit reserves or enterprise funds. Those who have drawn them repeatedly shall resolutely be checked and return the overdrawn profit reserves and enterprise funds.

In a county (or city) with the industrial bureau dissolved through the reform of the management system, it shall be adopted that the financial department puts the methods for profit reserves or profit or loss undertakings into trial implementation over the economic commission at the same level.

2 The departments and enterprises with normal production and rather stable profits shall implement the method of base profit reserves plus growth profit reserves or that of full-amount profit reserves. The method of full-amount profit reserves can better embody the interests of the state, the enterprise and the staff and workers, is easy to implement and shall be put into energetic practice.

The departments and enterprises that practise the method of base profit reserves plus growth profit reserves shall strictly implement the limits of base profit reserves and the proportions of growth profit reserves as stipulated in Document No. 23 (1980) of the State Council. However, in order to determine the base rather rationally, the originally stipulated determination of the base on the basis of the profit of the previous year (meaning the balance of the total profit after the deduction of the technological measure loans repaid and the profits left with the enterprise as stipulated for the control of the Three Wastes (gas waste, water waste and industrial residue), the same hereinafter mentioned) shall be changed into the revolving calculation on the basis of the average profit of the last three years. If the enterprise's profit of that year is higher than the average profit of the last three years, the base profit reserves shall be drawn according to the checked and ratified proportion out of the part which is equal to the average profit of the last three years; the growth profit reserves shall be drawn according to the proportion stipulated by the state out of the part in excess of the average profit of the last three years. If the enterprise's profit of that year is lower than the average profit of the last three years, the base profit reserves shall be drawn according to the profit of that year and the checked and ratified proportion. In future the departments and enterprises with new approval shall put the method of base profit reserves plus growth profit reserves into trial implementation, the proportions of their base profit reserves shall be calculated on the basis of several funds which have been brought into the profit reserves for the last three years and the total profits of the same period.

In the case of the departments and enterprises implementing the method of full-amount profit reserves, the proportions of their full-amount profit reserves shall be examined and determined in accordance with the proportions of the reserved sums of base profit reserves and growth for the last three years and the total profits of the last three years.

3 Some departments and enterprises that, due to special conditions, have difficulty in implementing the above two procedures for profit reserves shall respectively implement the following methods according to different conditions:

(1) The departments and enterprises with insufficient production tasks assigned and greatly reduced profits during the period of readjustment shall implement the method of plan-overfulfilled profit reserves. The annual profit plan of a department or an enterprise shall be particularly checked and ratified by the financial department in accordance with the income tasks assigned by the state and in the light of the production plan and the requirements for increasing production and tapping potentialities. The profits fulfilled in excess of the plan shall be regarded as increased profits, with a major part of them to be turned over to the state and a minor part to be left with the departments and enterprises. The profits left with the departments and enterprises shall be controlled within the limits of the proportions of growth profit reserves as stipulated in Document No. 23 (1980) of the State Council.

(2) The departments and enterprises with small profits but rather great potentialities shall implement the method of undertaking profits turned over or sharing out or reserving excessive profits. Among them, some shall implement the method of "undertaking base profits and sharing out excessive ones;" some others shall implement that of "undertaking base profits with increments and sharing out or reserving excessive ones." The undertaken base profits to be turned over shall be higher than those of the previous year and out of the excessive parts, in general, those obtained by the state shall not be lower than 60 per cent and those obtained by the departments and enterprises shall not be higher than 40 per cent. In the case of individual enterprises with small profits and small potentialities in the increase of production and income, the method of "undertaking base profits, reserving excessive ones or assuming short ones for themselves" shall also be implemented.

(3) The departments and enterprises whose losses are really due to objective causes shall implement the method of undertaking rated subsidies for the losses. Among them, some shall implement the method of "undertaking base losses, giving no subsidies for excessive losses and sharing out the subsidies for the reduced losses;" some others shall implement that of "undertaking losses with decrements, giving no subsidies for excessive losses and reserving or sharing out the subsidies for the reduced losses," some others shall implement that of "undertaking rated subsidies, giving no subsidies for excess losses and sharing out or reserving those for the reduced losses." In general, the undertaken base loss subsidies shall be lower than those of the previous year and out of the subsidies for the reduced losses, in general, the proportions obtained by the state shall not be lower than 60 percent and those obtained by the departments and enterprises shall not be higher than 40 per cent. Very few enterprises which have greater difficulty in reducing losses or which have reduced losses by small amount shall reserve some more or the whole of the subsidies for the reduced losses for use with the approval of the financial department at the same level.

4 The power-expanded enterprises and departments which have originally been approved to put profit reserves into trial implementation shall, in principle, still continue to implement the original method if the trial has not expired. Even if the trial has expired, they shall continue to implement the original method or use other proper ones instead on the approval of the financial department.

5 In the case of each department of the Central Government, the proportion of profit reserves and the base and share-out proportions of profit or loss undertakings shall be checked and ratified by the Ministry of Finance. With regard to the proportions of profit reserves and the base and share-out proportions of profit or loss undertakings for the local departments at each level in charge of enterprises, those for the three municipalities of Beijing, Tianjin and Shanghai and for the provinces and autonomous regions which implement the method of the proportional shares of totals between the central and local authorities in the financial system shall be examined and gathered by local financial departments and then submitted to the Ministry of Finance for checking and ratification; those for other areas shall be checked and ratified by the province, municipality or autonomous region itself.

The unreasonable bases of profit or loss undertakings which are already fixed by each area shall be properly readjusted; too high share-out proportions of undertakings shall be reduced.

6 The proportions of profit reserves and the bases of profit or loss undertakings shall remain unchanged for three or four years after their determination so as to facilitate the departments and enterprises to make long-term arrangements except for the enterprises which implement the method of plan-overfulfilled profit reserves. In the case of a small number of departments and enterprises with unstable production and profits, the bases of their profit or loss undertakings shall also be fixed once a year.

7 In the case of the enterprises which implement the method of base profit reserves plus growth profit reserves and full-amount profit reserves, the staff and workers' welfare funds and staff and workers' rewards shall be paid out of the profits reserved and shall not be included in the costs of products; the excessive piece rate wages payable as stipulated could be calculated into the costs of products and the totals of these wages shall be deleted from calculation in the checking and ratification of the reserve proportions of rewarding funds.

In the case of the enterprises which implement the method of profit or loss undertakings and plan-overfulfilled profit reserves, the staff and workers' welfare funds and bonuses expanded as stipulated could be calculated into the costs of products, but the bonuses included into the costs of products shall only be restricted to the parts drawn at 10 to 12 percent of the totals of the standard wages. The amount of bonuses checked, ratified and issued but higher than 10 to 12 percent of the standard wages shall be paid out of the shares of the excessive profits.

8 In order to give play to the role of prices or taxes as an economic lever, all the total profits, reserve proportions or undertaking bases shall not be readjusted after the implementation of the method for profit reserves and profit or loss undertakings except for the case that the readjustment of the prices of products and the reform of tax system as stipulated by the state and the new increase of production capacity with state investments cause the profits of enterprises to increase or decrease to a larger extent.

9 Rewards and punishments shall be upheld in the implementation of the methods for profit reserves and profit or loss undertakings. A department or an enterprise shall be examined in the quantities, qualities, categories, costs and other targets of its products in addition to the examination of its target of profits. Those who fulfill the above targets in an all-round way shall draw profit reserves or share out excessive profits as stipulated. If an enterprise fulfills less of the five targets, its drawable profit reserves or excessive shares shall be deducted by eight percent per target. In a very few particular cases, the examined targets shall be increased or decreased; the proportions of the deductions shall also be reduced according to the different degrees of importance of each target. If an enterprise does not fulfill all of the examined targets, its drawable profit reserves or excessive shares shall be deducted by 40 percent. If a profit or loss undertaking task is not fulfilled, it shall be made up for with various special-purpose funds of the department or enterprise. If those of that year are insufficient to make good the deficiency, it shall be made good the next year.

The examined targets for railway, communications and transportation, postal service and telecommunications, civil aviation and other departments and enterprises shall be otherwise determined by each department in charge and the Ministry of Finance through consultation.

10 An enterprise shall use the drawn profit reserves and undertaking and excessive shares to separately establish production development funds, the staff and workers' welfare funds and their rewarding funds. A trade with more trial-production tasks of new products shall also use the profit reserves or undertaking and excessive shares to establish the trial- producing funds for new products alone. The major part of an enterprise's growth profit reserves or excessive profit shares shall be used to develop production and the minor part shall be used for the staff and workers' welfare and rewards. The extent of the increase on rewards shall be lower than that of profits. The granting of rewards shall strictly be executed in accordance with the provisions in Documents No. Guo-Fa 10 and 94 (1981) of the State Council and the "Notice of the Control of the Rewards Given" of October 2 of the same year. The specific proportions of various funds shall be stipulated by each area or each department itself.

In principle, the staff and workers' welfare funds and their rewarding funds shall be arranged for use by an enterprise itself. If necessary, the department in charge shall properly centralize parts of the staff and workers' welfare funds for the unified building of the staff and workers' dormitories or other collective welfare facilities and labour protection facilities for enterprises, but shall not use them for the rewards and welfare of the department in charge for itself. The department in charge of enterprises shall control parts of production development funds for key measures and projects and the technological transformation of the whole trade in accordance with the features of the trade.

The department in charge shall gather the use plans of various funds and report them to the financial department at the same level for record. The situations of use shall be submitted together with final accounts at the end of a year.

11 In order to urge enterprises to economize on the use of state funds and improve the efficiency of funds used, all industrial and communications enterprises shall pay fixed-capital take-up charges and circulated-capitals as from 1982 as stipulated by the state. The payment of take-up charges and circulated-capital as of 1982 as stipulated by the state. The payment of take-up the proportions of profit reserves shall not be re-adjusted for the time being. In checking and ratifying the proportions of profit reserves in the case of the enterprises which are newly approved to make experiments, the calculation shall, in principle, include the fund take-up charges. The profits of an enterprise which are increased with the take-up charges saved due to the reduction of fixed capital and circulated capital shall have 30 percent of the shares drawn in accordance with the provisions in Document No. Cai-Qi 49 (81) of the Ministry of Finance.

12 The departments and enterprises that implement the methods for profit reserves and profit or loss undertakings shall conscientiously carry out the Party's and the state directions and policies, abide by financial and economic discipline and various financial regulations, ensure fulfillment of the state revenue tasks, various planned targets, economic and technical targets and report to the financial departments at the same levels the utilization and economic results of profit reserves and excessive profit shares. It shall strictly be forbidden to apportion costs confusingly, intercept and retain profits, practise fraud, shift burdens onto others or damage state interests. The financial department at each level shall enforce its supervision and examination. In the case of those who violate state provisions, it shall deduct parts of or stop the drawable profit reserves and excessive profit shares according to the degrees of seriousness.

9

COMMERCIAL MANAGEMENT

Business Registration/ Import & Export/ Market Control/ Prices/ Warehousing

INTERIM PROCEDURES FOR THE ADMINISTRATION SYSTEMS OF NATIONAL SPECIALIZED CORPORATIONS

(Adopted by the Routine Meeting of the State Council on March 12, 1982 and promulgated by the State Council on March 16, 1982)

With the progress in economic combination and reorganization and organizational reform, the number of various national specialized corporations is constantly increasing. A national specialized corporation is an organizational form of enterprises, an economic entity of production and management and different from an administrative organization. However, before the tremendous reform of our current economic administration systems, it is necessary to proceed from actual conditions, guide the process according to circumstances and gradually achieve the division of labour between the government administration and enterprises so as to enable a corporation to become a relatively independent economic unit. For this reason, the following interim provisions are made for the matters of leading systems and treatments of different levels concerning the establishment of national specialized corporations:

1 In the establishment of various types of national specialized corporations, their positions shall be determined according to their functions in the national economy and the ranges of their business and no administrative levels shall indiscriminately be adopted for them. But seeing that there shall be appropriate provisions for such aspects as the appointment or dismissal of cadres, the rights to peruse documents, attend meetings or listen to superiors' speeches, etc., various national specialized corporations shall have their levels determined, i.e. to be equivalent to a ministry of the administrative organization, or to a bureau directly under the State Council or to an office or a bureau under a ministry so as to determine their treatments according to appropriate levels.

2 No national specialized corporations shall be included in the administrative organization of the State Council but shall be put separately under the leadership of the departments concerned. Among them, (1) all specialized corporations within the range of business under the administration of a ministry shall be put under the leadership of that ministry; (2) the specialized corporations across departments shall be put under the leadership of one of the departments and under the direction of the other departments concerned in business; (3) a small number of specialized corporations which play important parts in the national economy and which integrate industry, agriculture, commerce and foreign trade shall be put directly under the leadership of the State Council and certain corporations shall be put under the leadership of the ministries or commissions concerned entrusted by the State Council.

3 The State Council and all ministries or commissions shall exercise leadership over national specialized corporations by laying stress on guiding principles, policies and plans and be responsible for such jobs concerning the corporations as the appointment or dismissal of cadres, the transmission of documents and political and ideological work as provided by the Central Committee of the Chinese Communist Party and the State Council. The corporations shall have the right to act on their own in business management.

4 The establishment of national specialized corporations shall be submitted for approval after the examination of the composite economic departments concerned.

(1) The establishment of production or commercial specialized corporations or those with production and marketing combined shall be submitted to the State Council for approval after the examination of the State Economic Commissions; (2) that of specialized corporations for foreign economic relations or foreign trade shall be submitted to the State Council for approval after the examination of the department in charge of foreign economic relations and trade; (3) that of financial specialized banks or corporations shall be submitted to the State Council for approval after the examination of the People's Bank of China.

The establishment of national specialized corporations by scientific, educational, cultural, public health and other departments shall be submitted to the State Council for approval after the examination of the departments in charge.

5 The authorized sizes of national specialized corporations shall strictly be controlled and checked and determined by examina-

tion departments jointly with the department in charge of establishments.

6 The stamps of the corporation shall not bear the national emblem. They shall be made and issued in accordance with the State Council's "Provisions for the Stamps of State Administrative Organs and Enterprises and Institutions."

7 Some of the national specialized corporations which have been set up actually have administrative nature to a considerable extent, so each organization of them has two signs (i.e. names) and the funds and expenses are shared by the administrative part and the enterprise one. In the reform of organizations and systems, the duties shall clearly be distinguished between their administration and production management so that the specialized corporations shall truly become economic entities in the nature of enterprises.

8. Some departments are deliberating on the establishment of national specialized corporations from upper to lower level and the ranges of production business of these corporations and their relations with other corporations shall be arranged in a unified manner so as to avoid their conflict of interest.

9 Each specialized corporation shall formulate the constitution of corporation.

REGULATIONS FOR THE ADMINISTRATION OF REGISTRATION OF INDUSTRIAL AND COMMERCIAL ENTERPRISES

(Adopted by the Routine Meeting of the State Council on July 7, 1982)

Article 1 These Regulations are formulated in order to strengthen the administration of industrial and commercial enterprises, ensure legal operation, ban illicit activities, maintain the socialist economic order and promote the socialist construction.

Article 2 The producing or dealing units of the following industrial, communications and transportation, building, commercial, foreign trade, catering, service, tourist, handicraft and repairing trades (hereinafter generally referred to as "industrial and commercial enterprises") shall register themselves in accordance with the provisions in these Regulations:

(1) State-operated industrial and commercial enterprises;

(2) Cooperative and other industrial and commercial enterprises of collective owner ship;

(3) Combined or joint industrial and commercial enterprises;

(4) Industrial and commercial enterprises under railway, civil aviation, post and telecommunication departments and other public utilities.

Other industrial and commercial enterprises which the people's government of the province, autonomous region or municipality directly under the Central Government thinks necessary to register themselves.

Article 3 The authorities in charge of the registration of industrial and commercial enterprises are the General Administration for Industry and Commerce in the Central Government and the administrations for industry and commerce in such localities as provinces, autonomous regions, municipalities directly under the Central Government, cities and counties.

Except for national corporations, all industrial and commercial enterprises shall register themselves with the administrations for industry and commerce in the cities or counties where they are located.

Article 4 The industrial and commercial enterprises which apply for registration shall be the units which are directly engaged in production or business and practise independent accounting. The branches without independent accounting under industrial and commercial enterprises shall have their registration applied for by the industrial and commercial enterprises in a uniform manner.

Article 5 The main items which an industrial or commercial enterprise shall register are: the name of the enterprise, address, the name of the person in charge, date of establishment or commencement, economic nature, the scope of production or business, the mode of production or business, total capital, the number of staff and workers or the number of employees.

Article 6 An industrial or commercial enterprise shall only register and use one name. It shall not use the name of another industrial or commercial enterprise in the same trade, which has been registered within the same city or county.

Article 7 If capital construction is required for setting up an industrial or commercial enterprise, an application for preparation registration shall be made to the city or county administration for industry and commerce within 30 days after the approval of the project. After the establishment of the industrial or commercial enterprise is completed, an application for opening registration shall be made to the city or county administration for industry and commerce within 30 days before it is put into production or before it starts business.

Article 8 If no capital construction is required for setting up an industrial or commercial enterprise, no preparation registration shall be needed and an application shall be directly made for opening registration. An application for opening registration shall be made to the city or county administration for industry and commerce within 30 days after the approval of setting up the enterprise.

Article 9 When an industrial or commercial enterprise applies for preparation or opening registration, it shall submit the copies of the following documents according to different conditions in accordance with the procedures for the examination and approval of the opening of industrial and commercial enterprises stipulated by the state and other relevant provisions:

(1) The application for opening the enter-

prise and the document of approval of the department in charge;

(2) The document of approval from the planning department or the people's government above the county level;

(3) Other relevant documents.

In the application for preparation or opening registration, foreign trade enterprises, combined or joint industrial and commercial enterprises, cooperative and other industrial and commercial enterprises of collective ownership shall also submit the memorandums and articles of association of the enterprises in addition to the copies of the documents stipulated in the previous clause.

Article 10 With regard to the application of an industrial or commercial enterprise for preparation or opening registration, the city or county administration for industry and commerce shall approve of its registration if it deems the application has conformed to the provisions in these Regulations through examination and it shall issue a preparation permit or a business licence. The industrial or commercial enterprise shall open an account with a bank and carry out preparation for establishment or production or business by means of the preparation permit or the business licence.

An industrial or commercial enterprise without the approval of registration shall not prepare its establishment or start its business nor make an official seal or sign contracts or register trade marks or publish advertisements and the bank shall not allow it to open any account.

Article 11 If an industrial or commercial enterprise is to alter its name, economic nature, scope of production or business or mode of production or business, it shall register the alteration with the city or county administration for industry and commerce within 30 days after approval in accordance with relevant provisions.

If other items of registration are altered, a written report shall be made to the city or county administration for industry and commerce at the end of a year.

Article 12 When an industrial or commercial enterprise is closed, it shall go through the formalities of dissolution at the city or county administration for industry and commerce and hand in the business licence for cancellation within 30 days after approval in accordance with relevant provisions.

If an industrial or commercial enterprise ceases production or business for more than one year, it shall be regarded as having been closed and therefore shall go through the formalities of dissolution and hand in the business licence for cancellation.

Article 13 If an industrial or commercial enterprise is merged, branched out, transferred to another trade or moved, it shall go through the formalities of opening registration, alteration registration or closing cancellation according to different conditions within 30 days after approval in accordance with relevant provisions.

Article 14 If an industrial or commercial enterprise registers, it shall pay the registration fee. The amount of the registration fee shall be fixed by the General Administration for Industry and Commerce.

Article 15 The administration for industry and commerce at each level shall duly handle the applications for registration from industrial and commercial enterprises and shall not delay without cause or reason if they are proved to conform to the provisions in these Regulations through examination.

Article 16 An administration for industry and commerce shall set up enterprise registration files for the registration data of industrial and commercial enterprises and other related data and administer them as specialized files.

Article 17 An industrial or commercial enterprise shall be engaged in production or business in accordance with state policies and decrees and the items of registration checked and ratified. The administration for industry and commerce at each level shall be entitled to exercise the supervision and examination of the industrial and commercial enterprises within the area under its jurisdiction and the industrial and commercial enterprises shall supply the documents, books, statistical tables and reports and other related materials required for the examination.

Article 18 If an industrial or commercial enterprise has one of the following violations of the provisions in these Regulations, the administration for industry and commerce shall, according to different conditions, criticize it; or impose such punishments upon it if its case is serious as giving warning, fining it, notifying the bank to freeze its deposit or cancel its bank account, ordering it to close or cancelling its preparation permit or business licence:

(1) Preparing its establishment or starting its

business without registration and authorization;

(2) Carrying out production or business in violation of the items of registration checked and ratified and not accepting advice or not correcting it within the stipulated time;

(3) Concealing the true conditions or practising fraud in the registration;

(4) Forging, altering or transferring the preparation permit or the business licence.

If an industrial or commercial enterprise uses the business licence as a legal form to carry out illicit operation, its illicit proceeds shall be confiscated.

Article 19 The procedures for the administration of the registration of Chinese-foreign joint ventures and the resident representative offices of foreign enterprises in China shall be implemented in accordance with relevant provisions.

The procedures for the administration of the registration of foreign enterprises within the territory of the People's Republic of China shall be implemented in the light of relevant provisions.

Article 20 The procedures for the administration of the registration of individual dealers shall be implemented in accordance with relevant provisions.

Article 21 The detailed rules for the implementation of these Regulations shall be formulated by the General Administration for Industry and Commerce.

Article 22 These Regulations shall be put into effect as from the date of promulgation. The "Provisional Procedures for the Administration of the Registration of Industrial and Commercial Enterprises" promulgated by the State Council on December 30, 1962 shall be annulled at the same time.

PROVISIONAL REGULATIONS CONCERNING THE EXPORT LICENCE SYSTEM

Issued by the Import and Export Commission and the Ministry of Foreign Trade

(June 3, 1980)

The following regulations have been formulated with a view to strengthening the control of foreign trade:

Article 1 The introduction of the export licensing system by the People's Republic of China is a necessary measure to strengthen the control of export commodities and to coordinate foreign trade transactions and exports of different localities and departments, so as to achieve unity in dealing with foreign countries. The Ministry of Foreign Trade of the People's Republic of China (hereinafter referred to as the "Ministry of Foreign Trade") and the foreign trade bureaus of provinces, municipalities and autonomous regions that have been authorized by the Ministry are designated by the state as the organizations which shall carry out the export licensing system.

Article 2 The general import and export corporations under the Ministry of Foreign Trade and their branches, as well as the corporations authorized by the Import and Export Commission to engage in export business, have the right to conduct export business within a prescribed sphere. Any corporation that wishes to export certain commodities must first make an application and can start business only after it has received approval from the Import and Export Commission and has registered with the Ministry of Foreign Trade or the foreign trade bureau of the province, municipality or autonomous region and with the customs office concerned, while presenting to it its document of authorization.

Article 3 According to the provisions of Article 2, a corporation which has been authorized to engage in export business, when exporting commodities within the prescribed sphere, is generally regarded as having obtained authorization to export, and Customs give clearance to the export commodities according to the "export declaration" filled in by the corporation. It is not necessary for the corporation to apply for an export licence. But an export licence should be applied for in any of the following cases:

a) When commodities are limited by the countries and regions to which they are exported (specific rules shall be worked out separately by the Ministry of Foreign Trade);

b) In case of commodities to which the Ministry of Foreign Trade thinks it necessary to apply the export licence system and of which the Ministry has fixed the amounts to be exported by different localities and departments, so as to ensure that the total amount of such commodities exported by different localities and departments will not exceed the marketing capacity of the countries and regions to which the commodities are exported;

c) In the case of commodities to which the Ministry of Foreign Trade thinks it necessary to apply the export licence system and for which minimum export prices must be fixed in order to prevent the export prices from being set too low;

d) In the case of commodities which are to be exported under control or which are forbidden for export as explicitly declared by the relevant departments of the State Council;

e) In the case of export commodities which the Ministry of Foreign Trade thinks should be suitably controlled within a certain period of time because of changes in the world market or because of the need to carry out policies towards some specific countries.

Article 4 Export licences are necessary in the cases as follows:

a) Goods to be sent abroad by enterprises, state organs, public organizations, schools or individuals who are not authorized to conduct export business;

b) Goods for sale at exhibitions organized by Chinese departments, enterprises or public organizations in foreign countries;

c) Commodities which are produced by various enterprises, factories or mines on the basis of contracts signed with foreign countries with regard to compensatory trade, the processing of goods with materials supplied by clients and loan grants and which are to be exported directly without going through the foreign trade corporations;

d) Goods sent abroad by foreign diplomatic missions, business representatives, citizens and tourists;

e) Goods in excess of the reasonable amount to be taken out of China by foreign citizens and tourists for their own use.

Article 5 In the following cases, the Ministry of Foreign Trade may notify any enterprise at any time to stop, postpone or reduce its export of any commodity to any country or region:

a) If the exports do not conform to the policies of China towards the countries or regions to which the exports are directed;

b) If the exports do not conform to the content and spirit of bilateral trade agreements or payment agreements between China and the countries or regions to which the exports are directed;

c) If the exports have to be postponed or reduced in order to achieve a balance of foreign exchange in bilateral trade;

d) If inspection by the General Bureau for Imports and Exports Inspection has shown that the quality of the export commodities is not up to the standard fixed by the state, or does not conform to the provisions of the contract.

Article 6 Export licences should be applied for, respectively, by enterprises, governments organizations, public bodies, schools, people's communes and individuals. Entries in the application include the names of the commodities (or goods), specifications, the countries and regions to which they are to be exported, quantity, unit price, total value of the exports, date of delivery and method of payment (i.e., how foreign currency is to be collected for the exports. Export licence application forms will be issued separately). Application must be submitted for examination and approval by the Ministry of Foreign Trade or the authorized foreign trade bureau of the province, municipality or autonomous region concerned before the dispatch of the goods.

In applying for export licences, the applicants shall not try to obtain the licences through deception or by making false entries in the application form. Those who do so must be investigated and held responsible. Serious cases must be dealt with according to law.

Article 7 After the application has been examined and approved by the department concerned, the applicant will be issued a "licence for the exportation of goods" (hereinafter referred to as "export licence") in triplicate copies. One copy will be kept by the applying unit or individual. The other two will be handed over, together with the "export declaration," to Customs, which will examine it and give clearance accordingly. Customs will keep one of these two copies, while the third one, after being signed by Customs, will be sent to the local branch of the Bank of China, which will check it, settle the account and collect foreign currency accordingly.

Article 8 The Customs of the People's Republic of China at various levels should exercise supervision and control over export commodities and goods in accordance with these provisional regulations and other relevant provisions. When passing commodities and goods that require an export licence through the Customs, the exporter must present the export licence to Customs for inspection. If Customs find that the export commodities do not tally with the export licence, they should urge the unit concerned to apply for a new export licence or correct the errors before they give clearance. Those commodities which require an export licence shall not be passed until the licence is granted for them.

Article 9 The term of validity of an export licence should be fixed on the basis of the time goods are to be delivered as prescribed in the contract and according to other factors. The term of a licence should not exceed six months starting from the date the licence is issued, and the licence will become invalid after the specified date. If the applicant cannot deliver the goods within the period of validity he may apply for an extension, unless the export licence has stipulated otherwise. The licence may be extended only once, and for a period of two months. If the applicant still cannot send the goods abroad within the extended period but still needs to export them, he should apply for a new licence. The authorities responsible for its approval should examine the application again in the light of the conditions then prevailing.

Article 10 The list of commodities which require an export licence as stipulated in these regulations will be drawn up by the Ministry of Foreign Trade and will be readjusted from time to time according to the actual situation and distributed to units concerned for them to abide by.

INTERIM PROVISIONS OF THE STATE PLANNING COMMISSION, THE STATE ECONOMIC COMMISSION AND THE STATE COMMISSION OF MACHINE BUILDING INDUSTRY FOR THE CONTROL OF THE PRODUCTION AND IMPORT OF MOTOR VEHICLES AND THE IMPROVEMENT OF THEIR DISTRIBUTION

(April 4, 1981)

Owing to the imbalance of recovery and storage and the failure to reserve resources, it is very difficult in the near future for the present oil production of our country to maintain its existing level of production, which shall be further reduced to a proper extent. Under these circumstances, the production and import of various oil-consuming machines and tools shall strictly be controlled so as to reduce the consumption of oil products. Motor vehicles are one of the power machines and tools which consume more oil products. On the one hand, 150,000 trucks had been reserved in stock by the end of 1980 due to the decrease of the transport volume caused by the reduction of the scale of capital construction; and on the other hand, the production of motor vehicles overfulfilled the plan with the actual completion of 220,000, 77.4 per cent more than the planned 124,000. Various areas and departments also imported more than 20,000 motor vehicles beyond the plans. In order to effectively control the production and import of motor vehicles so as to be advantageous to the regulation of the auto industry and to the improvement of their distribution, the following measures shall be taken:

Article 1 Planned administration shall be strengthened. From 1981 on, each enterprise shall strictly organize the production of motor vehicles and refitted vehicles in accordance with state plans and no enterprise shall produce them in excess of the plans without the approval of the State Planning Commission. The existing motor production works shall be divided into three classes according to such conditions as oil consumption, quality, price, etc. in the spirit of regulation, Class 1 being the key motor works with more favourable conditions in every aspect to which priority shall be given for the arrangement for production. Class 2 are those which, from a long-term point of view, are not provided with the conditions of production and the quality of their motor types is not so good, but there shall be one or two years' transition period for them to become qualified for continuing their production through such measures as regulation, reorganization and specialized cooperation. Class 3 are those with poor quality, high oil consumption and serious losses and without prospects of development and they shall be closed, stopped, merged or transferred to the production of other things. The specific schemes shall be formulated by the State Commission of Machine Building Industry.

In order to effectively control the production and import of motor vehicles, the system of motor supply certificates in triplicate shall be put into effect from 1981 on, the original for payment, the duplicate for obtaining the licence and the triplicate for the supply of oils. Motor vehicles shall be distributed to the particular using units as far as possible so as to reduce transfer links. If a motor vehicle must be transferred through the dealing unit, it shall be delivered to the dealing unit by means of a contract with a copy of the original attached so as to be used as a payment voucher, but only one transfer shall be allowed. Motor supply certificates shall be formulated by the State Planning Commission which shall entrust the State Bureau of Supplies with uniform printing and then separately distribute them to the departments concerned. Without motor supply certificates, banks shall not make payments and commercial departments shall not issue oil supply tickets; public security and communications departments shall not issue licences. The above-mentioned units concerned shall check the motor supply certificates, oil supply tickets and licences issued every year. If the number is found to be inconsistent, examinations shall be made and with regard to the unit or individual in breach of the above provisions, the causes shall be found out and disciplinary punishments shall be imposed.

Article 2 The regulation of the market shall be subject to the direction of the state plans and the implementation of the relevant provisions of the state. The processing with supplied materials and the cooperative production shall be organized by the First Ministry of Machine Building Industry according to the number stipulated by the state. The goods shall be chosen and arranged so as to contribute to competition. The standards of the materials and charges collected shall be rational and the specific procedures shall be formulated by the First Ministry of Machine Building Industry and put into effect with the approval of the State Commission of Machine Building Industry.

Article 3 Cars (including sedans, jeeps, station wagons, vans, etc. hereinafter mentioned) and buses are special controlled commodities under the unified administration of the state and all Party and government organs, bodies and enterprises can buy cars and buses only if they hold social group purchasing certificates as stipulated by the state in addition to motor supply certificates.

Article 4 The import of motor vehicles shall strictly be controlled. In order to protect the domestic auto industry, each department or each area shall go through the formalities of examination and approval in accordance with Document No. Guo-Fa 6 (1981) of the State Council if it will import motor vehicles. The import of cars shall be more strictly controlled and applications shall be made to the State Commission of Machine Building Industry for examination and approval if there are special needs. No motor supply certificates shall be issued without approval.

Article 5 The administration of the distribution, allocation and transfer of motor vehicles shall be improved. The motor vehicles included in the state distribution plans shall still be distributed by the State Bureau of Supplies. The procedures for the distribution shall be readjusted according to the new conditions after finance is administered by different levels and, in principle, the distribution shall be made according to the channels of supply. The past practice of the transmission to lower levels with trivial additions shall be cancelled and the contradiction between the distribution of motor vehicles and the sources of funds shall be overcome.

The trucks which will be distributed to various departments and areas by the state in future shall mainly be used to replace or eliminate the old ones with high oil consumption. The procedures for the replacement of motor vehicles (including cars) shall be handled by means of "Motor Replacement Technical Appraisal Forms" in accordance with the provisions in Document No. Ji-Zong 666 (1980) and the state shall not issue motor supply certificates separately.

Article 6 Various exhibition fairs or commodity fairs, cooperations of the material system at each level or the supply and marketing organizations of each department shall not resell motor vehicles at negotiated prices nor collect management expenses repeatedly.

APPENDIX: PROCEDURES FOR THE ISSUANCE OF MOTOR SUPPLY CERTIFICATES.

1. Motor supply certificates shall be worked out by the State Planning Commission which shall entrust the State Bureau of Supplies with the uniform printing and separately issue them to the departments and areas concerned according to the provisions for the division of labour. Motor supply certificates shall be printed according to the types of motor vehicles and numbered in a uniform manner, one certificate for each vehicle.

2. Motor supply certificates shall be issued according to the number in the contract signed and no supply certificates shall be issued for those without purchase contracts signed. Each unit concerned shall surely implement this provision strictly.

3. The motor supply certificates distributed in the state plans shall be issued by the State Bureau of Supplies to the departments or areas in charge of the using units. If the numbers in purchase contracts are less than the production quotas, the State Bureau of Supplies shall transfer the motor supply certificates to the First Ministry of Machine Building Industry one month after the closing of the annual orders-placing meeting and then organize the enterprises to sell them by themselves. In the case of the motor vehicles additionally produced with approval as a result of the regulation of the market under the direction of state plans, the motor supply certificates shall be issued to the First Ministry of Machine Building Industry, the National Defence Industry Office and localities. With the consent of both supplying and demanding parties, the motor vehicles involved in a contract which cannot be implemented shall be duly cleared by the producing works and separately reported to the First Ministry of Machine Building Industry and the State Bureau of Supplies. In the case of those distributed within the state plans, the demanding party shall return the motor supply certificates to the State Bureau of Supplies; those as a result of the market regulation shall be returned to the First Ministry of Machine Building Industry and those within the local quotas shall be returned to the planning

commission of the province, municipality or autonomous region concerned.

4. In the case of the motor vehicles included in the local quotas of the state plans, the motor supply certificates shall be issued to the planning commission of the province, municipality or autonomous region concerned according to the categories arranged by the plans.

5. The procedures for the issue of motor supply certificates of various refitted motor vehicles shall be the same as the aforesaid. As the chassis used for refitted motor vehicles are not end products, no motor supply certificates shall be issued for them.

6. If each department or each area still has any motor vehicles in stock at the end of 1980 (including the stock of finished products of producing works and imported motor vehicles) before these "Interim Provisions" become effective, the motor supply certificates shall be issued to the departments in charge of the stocking units.

7. With regard to the motor vehicles imported with the approval of the state, the motor supply certificates shall be issued to the import units.

8. No motor supply certificates shall be issued for the motor vehicles distributed by the state for export or foreign aid. When an export or foreign aid plan is altered and the motor vehicles are transferred for home sale, the motor supply certificates shall be issued by the State Bureau of Supplies according to the procedures for home distribution.

9. These "Interim Provisions" shall become effective as of May 1. In principle, no motor supply certificates shall be reissued for the motor vehicles produced before this date. If the reissue is really required due to various causes, the situation and the reasons shall be clearly given and certified by the unit in charge. Those within the part distributed by the state shall be reissued by the State Bureau of Supplies; those as a result of the market regulation shall be reissued by the First Ministry of Machine Building Industry or the National Defence Industry Office.

10. Each unit shall strictly administer the motor supply certificates and shall not reproduce or forge them. It shall be strictly forbidden to make use of motor supply certificates for illegal activities and those in violation of this provision shall be punished according to law.

11. If no sufficient details are given in the implementation of these procedures, they shall be reported to the State Bureau of Supplies and the First Ministry of Machine Building Industry at any time so as to duly report them to the unit concerned for supplements or amendments.

REGULATIONS ON CONTROL OF THE PURCHASING POWER OF SOCIAL GROUPS

(Revised by the Financial and Trade Group of the State Council, the State Planning Commission, the State Commission, the Ministry of Finance, the People's Bank of China, the Ministry of Commerce, the All-China Federation of Supply and Marketing Cooperatives and the State Statistical Bureau on November 17, 1980)

Economizing on non-production expenses by limiting the purchasing power of social groups is an important measure for the implementation of the policy of "building the country industriously and thriftily" and speeding up the process of the Four Modernizations. This measure should be enforced over a long period of time. In light of the development and changes of the economic situation, we have revised the "Regulations on Control of the Purchasing Power of Social Groups" adopted in 1977 as follows:

I The Scope of Control

The purchasing power of social groups refers to the public funds spent by social groups in the market for non-production commodities. Its scope is defined in the "Provisions on the Scope of the Purchasing Power of Social Groups," an appendix to the "Regulations on Control of the Purchasing Power of Social Groups" issued by the the State Planning Commission and three other departments in 1977.

Except for some specially controlled commodities, no control quotas are imposed on neighbourhood offices in the cities, on districts, towns and people's communes of the counties and their affiliated enterprises and establishments, or on units of the People's Liberation Army below battalion level. The provinces, municipalities and autonomous regions, the General Logistics Department and the General Bureau of Frontiers can work out their own regulations on control of the purchasing power of social groups.

II Control Measures

The purchasing power of social groups shall be controlled through planning, quotas, authorization for specially controlled commodities and supply quotas. Concrete measures are as follows:

A. **Control through Planning.** The state will fix annually the purchasing power quotas of social groups and decide on the extent of their increase or decrease as part of the national economic plan in accordance with the needs of developing the national economy and of maintaining balance in the market. The quotas should be implemented at all levels.

When making plans for the production, importation and distribution of commodities, the departments of planning, materials, commerce and foreign trade at various level should keep an overall balance between production, supply and marketing. With regard to those commodities specially produced for social groups, the departments should decide on the quotas after consultations with relevant departments at the same levels.

B. **Control Through Quotas.** All provinces, municipalities and autonomous regions should allocate the quotas distributed by the higher authorities to the independent accounting units at the grass-roots level before the beginning of a new fiscal year with reference to the actual fulfilment of the quotas of the previous year, in proportion to the number of workers and staff members and with the expansion of the units in mind. The quotas can be allocated at one time or at several times; when the base figure is not available, it is better to allocate the quotas quarterly. In allocating the quotas it is necessary to deal with each case on its own merit. Efforts should be made to control the quotas in the spirit of practising strict economy while not interfering in the work of the units concerned. Purchasing power quotas should be closely integrated with financial quotas.

The purchasing power quotas of social groups are completely controlled. However, quotas for such commodities as medicines, medical apparatus and instruments, labour safety supplies, coal for drinking water, bathing and heating, and fuel for cars used for non-production purposes can be allocated to grass-roots units or kept at the provincial, municipal or autonomous regional level. The purchasing power of local enterprises and establishments located outside the capital belonging to the central government departments and the standing organs of the central government departments should be controlled by the local department concerned.

All units should deal properly with the quotas allocated by the higher authorities in accordance with the actual situation and distribute them to those departments in need of the commodities. The departments in need of the commodities should regularly work out plans for purchasing non-production commodities and purchase the commodities within the framework of the quotas. The accounting section of the units that purchase commodities under the purchasing power of social groups should enter the purchased items according to the invoice in the subsidiary account book for the purchasing power of social groups. Commodities purchased by the enterprises and establishments as production commodities but later used for non-production purposes should also be entered in the subsidiary account book. The finance section should strictly check and supervise non-production expenses and see that they do not exceed the quotas. Meanwhile, it should submit the precise statistical figures to the higher authorities as required.

C. **Authorization for Specially Controlled Commodities.** The purchase of specially controlled commodities should be authorized on the basis of the "Regulations on the Purchase of Specially Controlled Commodities by Social Groups" issued by the Ministry of Finance and four other central government departments in 1980, and related documents. All units which purchase commodities under special control should go through the necessary procedures and refrain from fraudulently purchasing these commodities without the authorization of the department concerned. A unit which purchases specially controlled commodities in other provinces should have an "authorization paper" issued by the authorities of the province in which the unit is located.

D. **Supply by Quota.** All units supplying commodities under the purchasing power of social groups should supply those items strictly on the basis of the quota and relevant regulations. Supply in excess of the quota and plan is not allowed. The supply unit should submit the marketing plan for these commodities and the actual marketing situation to the local office in charge of controlling the purchasing power of social groups.

All regions and departments should establish step by step the quota system for the commodities and expenses which can be put under quota control.

III Relying on the Masses

The method of combining professional management with mass administration shall be put into effect. The significance of controlling the purchasing power of social groups should be repeatedly made known to the masses. It is necessary to rely on the masses to work out thrift measures, draw up warehouse inventories, tap the latent potential of enterprises, repair and utilize old or discarded articles, use substitute materials to practise thrift and actively further the movement to increase production and practise economy.

When planning its expenses related to the purchasing power of social groups and reporting specially controlled commodities to the higher authorities, each unit shall consult democratic management and supervisory setups, regularly publicize the implementation of the regulations on the purchasing power of social groups, solicit opinions and suggestions from the broad masses and place itself under the surveillance of the masses.

IV Strict Discipline

All government and mass organizations, PLA units, schools, enterprises and institutions must observe the financial and economic discipline of the state, act according to the present regulations and various other provisions. In case of statutory violations, financial departments have the power to reject accounts to be rendered, banks have the power to refuse to pay and transfer accounts, commodity supply units have the power to refuse to supply goods, departments of public security and traffic supervision and control have the power to refuse to issue car licences, and the office of controlling purchasing power of social groups and financial organs has the power to confiscate the indiscriminately purchased commodities. In serious cases, reports will go to the leadership for taking disciplinary actions against the violators.

A regular inspection system shall be set up with one or two general and special inspections organized by each province, municipality and autonomous region per year. Various units and departments shall undertake regular book-keeping activities and carry out joint auditing and mutual inspections so as to learn from and supervise each other.

V Strengthening the Leadership

Leading groups and offices of controlling

purchasing power of social groups shall be established by the people's governments above the county level. Leading groups shall consist of leading comrades from the State Council Financial Office, the State Planning Commission, the State Economic Commission, financial, banking, commercial, supply and marketing, statistical and other departments. Each group leader is to be selected from among the leading comrades by the people's government. The leading group is to hold regular meetings, review its work and strengthen the leadership in earnest. The offices of controlling purchasing power of social groups are standing executive organs of the said leading groups. Each office must have a regular authorized size and enough staff members to suit the needs of its work.

All responsible departments, enterprises, institutions and administrative units must appoint special persons to take charge of the work of controlling the purchasing power of social groups.

All departments of planning, finance, banking, commerce, supply and marketing, materials, statistics, public security, transportation and communications at various levels shall adopt a clear-cut division of labour, work in close coordination, support and cooperate with each other. The implementation of the present regulations must be included in the system of personal responsibility for checking on and appraising through comparison cadres in charge of finance and taxes, financial accountants, employees of commodity supply units, bank bookkeepers, cashiers, public security personnel, and workers of traffic supervision and control.

The regulations on control of the purchasing power of social groups for the Chinese People's Liberation Army and the People's Armed Frontiers Police of China shall be prepared separately, in the light of the present regulations, by the General Logistics Department of the Military Commission of the Central Committee of the Chinese Communist Party and the General Bureau of Frontiers of the Ministry of Public Security.

The present regulations shall come into force as of January 1, 1981. In case of any contravention between the present regulations and previous regulations, the present regulations shall hold.

INSTRUCTIONS OF THE STATE COUNCIL TO STRENGTHEN MARKET ADMINISTRATION AND CRACK DOWN ON SPECULATION, PROFITEERING AND SMUGGLING

(January 7, 1981)

With the regulation of the national economy, the reform of the economic administrative system and the implementation of various economic policies since the Third Plenary Session of the 11th Central Committee of the Communist Party of China, our industrial and agricultural production has made greater advances, the supply of commodities in the market has been improved and the whole national economy has been enlivened, so the situation is good. However, as the economic legislation and the administration of the market fall short of the demands of the times, the markets in some areas are rather confused and speculation, profiteering and smuggling are rampant there, which directly endanger stability and unity and disrupt the regulation and steadiness of the economy. In order to further develop production, invigorate the economy and effectively maintain the socialist economic order, the following instructions are given in respect of the issue to crack down on speculation, profiteering and smuggling:

1 State-operated commercial enterprises, supply and marketing cooperative commercial enterprises and other units which are engaged in purchasing and selling activities shall energetically expand the channels for the circulation of commodities and buy and sell industrial and agricultural products according to state plans and the demands in the market. The development of production shall be fostered and the prices in the market shall be stabilized. Those who violate the provisions in buying and selling and price policies shall strictly be dealt with. State-operated and collective commercial enterprises shall trade within the limits stipulated in business licences. It shall not be allowed to force up commodity prices or rush to purchase goods and materials.

After the fulfillment of the allocating and transferring tasks, provinces, municipalities and autonomous regions shall be entitled to organize the exchange of goods and materials among them and the departments concerned shall allow them to transport the goods and materials.

Industrial and mining enterprises shall ensure the fulfillment of the state planned purchasing tasks and the implementation of the provisions in contracts. With the prerequisites of these, they shall be entitled to sell their own products by themselves. The administration for industry and commerce shall strengthen the guidance and administration of the sale of the products of industrial and mining enterprises, people's commune and production brigade enterprises and urban neighbouring enterprises.

Without the approval of the administration for industry and commerce, individuals (including private partnerships) shall not be allowed to sell industrial products. Licensed small retailers and peddlers shall deal in small daily necessities as stipulated.

2. Urban and rural fairs play a good supplementary role in the enlivening of the urban and rural economy, so they shall continue to be invigorated and well administered so as to conscientiously keep them in good order without rigidity and liven them up without confusion.

With the prerequisites of ensuring the fulfillment of the state purchasing tasks and the implementation of contracts, state farms, forestry centres, pastures and fishing grounds shall be entitled to sell their own products by themselves.

Party and government organs, bodies, armed forces, schools, enterprises and institutions shall obtain the approval of the administration for industry and commerce before they buy agricultural and sideline products from rural people's communes, production brigades, production teams or country fairs.

Rural people's communes, production brigades, production teams and other collective units shall be allowed to transport for sale Class 2 and Class 3 agricultural and sideline products of their own communes, brigades or teams or those in the neighbourhood, which have not been purchased by the state or which are surplus after the fulfillment of the state purchasing tasks and the execution of the negotiated purchase contracts. They shall not be allowed to sell Class 1 agricultural products.

With the prerequisite not to affect the fulfillment of the state purchasing tasks, commune members shall be allowed, with the consent of the production teams, to engage in transporting wthin their power (for example, by carrying the goods on the shoulder with a pole, carrying them in the hand, drawing them in a cart or carrying them on a bicycle) the agricultural and sideline products which are permitted to go on the market.

Individuals shall not be permitted to buy motor vehicles, tractors, power-driven vessels and other large means of transport for the purpose of engaging in transport for sale.

Cooperative stores, cooperative groups and licenced individual small retailers and peddlers shall engage in the transport of agricultural and sideline products for sale within the limits stipulated in business licences.

3. The following activities fall under speculation and profiteering:

Illegally reselling the means of industrial and agricultural production at profits; forcing up the prices to rush to purchase the state planned purchasing goods and materials and disrupting the state purchasing plans; illegally buying up commodities from state and supply and marketing cooperative retail stores and selling them at raised prices; individuals' taking shares in the wholesale prices of commodities bought by others; black-market brokers' seeking exorbitant profits; speculating or subcontracting to reap unfair gains; bullying and tyrannizing the weak in the same trade and market or hoarding and cornering so as to drive up prices; reselling the tickets of planned supplies or bank negotiable securities at profits; reselling at profits gold and silver, foreign currencies, jewelry, cultural relics, foreign goods or precious medicinal materials; doing shoddy work and using inferior materials, intermingling and adulteration or passing the spurious off as the genuine so as to cheat others out of their money or seek profits; under the pretences of handling business for enterprises, institutions or other units, concocting various pretexts, or swindling and bluffing so as to plunder others' belongings; selling certificates, invoices or contracts, issuing certificates, making out invoices or entering into contracts for others or offering bank accounts, checks or cash so as to seek illicit income out of them.

Any units or individuals that are engaged in speculation and profiteering activities shall be fined or have their belongings confiscated as stipulated by the government and in addition to this, those whose cases are serious shall be handed over to judicial authorities for punishment according to law.

4. All units and individuals that ought to pay taxes shall pay taxes (including Customs duties) according to regulations. Those who evade taxes or refuse to pay them shall strictly be dealt with.

Industrial and commercial taxes shall be levied on the taxable self-produced products sold in the market by rural people's communes, production brigades, production teams or commune members in accordance with proper tax rates. Those who hold the self-production and self-sale certificates shall be given the preferential treatment of tax exemption within the fixed quantities (in accordance with the provisions of each province, municipality or autonomous region).

Taxes shall be levied on individual industrial and commercial dealers without licences according to "provisional business" tax rates. Additional taxes shall be levied on those as stipulated whose profits exceed the permissible limits.

5. Various articles which are carried or mailed in by overseas Chinese, Hong Kong, Macao and Taiwan compatriots as permitted by the provisions of policies shall be confined to their own use or their presentation to their relatives and friends and shall not be allowed to be sold without authorization for the purpose of seeking profits; if they are required to be sold, they shall only be sold to the commercial purchasing units examined and approved to run the business by the administration for industry and commerce above the county level at the prices stipulated by the state. The commercial units which are examined and approved to sell the aforesaid articles shall only be permitted to purchase them from the assigned commercial purchasing units and no negotiated purchases or sales shall be permitted in this respect. No units or individuals shall purchase or sell them and they shall further be prohibited from buying or selling smuggled goods.

Measures against smuggling activities shall be strengthened, and particularly the marine cases. All vessels, including fishing boats, which evade the administration of the Customs and illegally sell and buy commodities, shall be dealt with as smuggling. Public security departments and coastal defence or frontier forces shall assist the Customs in the investigation and seizing of smuggling activities. Anti-smuggling joint defence shall be organized on the Southeast Sea.

Each coastal or border province, municipality or autonomous region, especially Guangdong, Fujian, Zhejiang, Shanghai, Guangxi, Yunnan, etc., shall take powerful measures to resolutely ban black-market transactions and crack down on smuggling activities.

State cadres or servicemen who participate in smuggling or who make use of their powers to practise favouritism or accept bribes shall be severely dealt with.

6. All Party and government organs, bodies, armed forces, state and collective enterprises and institutions, such departments as civil aviation,

railway, communications, posts, banks and people's communes, production brigades and production teams shall take measures to prevent smugglers, speculators and profiteers from making use of state or collective means of transport and financial circulating channels to transport for sale smuggled, speculative and profiteering articles and to remit illicit money.

7. The people's government at each level shall strengthen the leadership over the market administration and the work to crack down on speculation, profiteering and smuggling. The functionary roles of such departments concerned as the administration for industry and commerce, customs, tax, public security and other authorities shall be brought into full play so as to cooperate closely and act in concert. Meanwhile, the people's government shall give wide publicity, mobilize the people to denounce and expose the illicit activities and strengthen supervision.

Severe punishments shall be imposed according to law on the offenders and criminals who obstruct or resist examinations, attack the administration for industry and commerce, Customs, tax and public security authorities or besiege, hurl insults upon or beat up inspecting officers.

The people's government of each province, municipality or autonomous region shall consider the dispositions upon receipt of these Instructions and formulate the specific procedures for the implementation in the light of the local actual conditions.

PROVISIONS OF THE MINISTRY OF COMMERCE FOR STRICT PROHIBITION AGAINST THE UNNECESSARY SUPPLY OF UNWANTED COMMODITIES

(December 14, 1981)

Of late, the newspapers, magazines, grass-roots cooperatives and other units in various places have continuously reported and criticized the unnecessary addition of commodities forced into the regular supply by commercial enterprises. This practice is an unhealthy tendency which goes against policies, affects the reputation of the state-operated commerce and impairs the interests of enterprises and the masses. For the purpose of banning the supply of a commodity unwanted in regular supply, our ministry has issued the 'Notice of the Strict Prohibition against the Addition of an Unnecessary Commodity into Regular Supply" as Document No. Shang-Ji 40 in 1980 and has later reiterated this problem time and again in relevant documents and at relevant meetings. However, unnecessary additions in any form into regular supplies have not been eliminated completely and the commercial departments at each level shall pay close attention to this problem. For this reason, the following provisions are made:

1 The wholesale and retail enterprises at each level shall start with supporting the production, expanding circulation and improving business management, strengthen market surveys and forecasts, organize sources of commodities in a planned manner according to the demand of the market, expand the sales energetically, endeavour to provide consumers with good, salable and inexpensive commodities and prevent blind purchase which may result in the overstocking of commodities. The commercial enterprises at each level shall be entitled to refuse to purchase the products which do not meet the requirements of the market or which are of poor quality (those with some value for use shall be purchased at the prices fixed according to quality or sold by the commercial departments on commission).

2 When a wholesale enterprise distributes commodities to grass-roots supply and marketing cooperatives or retail shops (including collective and individual retail units) or when a retail enterprise sells them to consumers, it shall be strictly forbidden to add unsalable commodities to the supply of those in great demand or add those of inferior quality to the supply of those of good quality or use those of inferior quality or the unsalable ones as "free rewarding supplements" to the supply of those of good quality or those selling well.

With regard to some unsalable commodities or those of inferior quality with high prices, grass-roots cooperatives or retail shops shall be entrusted with their sale on commission or by means of settlements after sale.

3 The wholesale and retail enterprises at each level shall take the prohibition against unnecessary additions in any form as an operational rule of the enterprises and announce it so as to be convenient for the masses' supervision and examination.

4 If there are any more unnecessary additions in any form of commodities, grass-roots supply and marketing cooperatives, grass-roots wholesale or retail enterprises or consumers shall be entitled to refuse to accept them and report them to higher authorities.

5 The commercial departments at each level shall adopt a serious attitude towards the letters and visits of the exposure of unnecessary additions of commodities and duly investigate and handle them. Criticisms shall be given or necessary disciplinary punishments shall be imposed according to the degrees of seriousness on the enterprises or members of staff or workers contravening these provisions by continuing to add unnecessary commodities to the regular supply.

We request the commercial departments and enterprises at each level to conscientiously implement the above-mentioned provisions.

INTERIM PROVISIONS FOR THE MARKET ADMINISTRATION OF THE MEANS OF PRODUCTION OF INDUSTRIAL PRODUCTS

(Annotated and Passed On by the State Council on August 8, 1981)

While the planned economy has been practised in the national economy since the Third Plenary Session of the 11th Central Committee of the Party, the supplementary role of the market regulation has been brought into play. As a result, a considerable part of the means of the production of industrial products has entered the market, which has played a positive role in increasing the channels of circulation, reducing the links of circulation, building closer relations between production and demand and expanding the interchange of goods and materials. The following provisions are provisionally made for the market administration of the means of the production of industrial products in order to further stimulate the circulation of goods and materials, protect legal deals and check illegal operation:

I The Scopes of the Means of Production of Industrial Products Entering the Market:

1. The means of the production of industrial products which are permitted to enter the market for free purchase and sale include:

A. The part of the means of the production of industrial products distributed as planned, which the producing enterprises shall be allowed to sell by themselves according to relevant provisions of the state with the prerequisite that the enterprises shall ensure the fulfillment of the production or distribution plans assigned by the state and the fulfillment of supply contracts;

B. The part of the means of the production of industrial products which the department in charge of goods and materials has priority in placing orders for and which is surplus with the prerequisite that the producing enterprises shall ensure the fulfillment of purchase contracts (or agreements);

C. Other means of the production of industrial products beyond the planned distribution and the priority purchase;

D. The products produced with the main raw materials and fuel organized by the producing enterprises themselves and the new products provisionally produced;

E. The part of the means of the production of industrial products which is managed by the dealing units of the department in charge of goods and materials and which is open to supply to the market with the prerequisite of ensuring the fulfillment of distribution, allotment or transfer plans.

2. The means of the production of industrial products entering the market shall be provided with the certificates of quality. In the case of products without certificates of quality and the inferior products with some value for use, the users shall be told of the situation of their qualities as things actually are and prices shall be fixed according to their qualities.

3. Gold and silver or the means of the production of industrial products which are prohibited by the state from free purchase or sale shall not enter the market.

II Dealing Units and the Division of Labour in Dealing:

1. The dealing units under the department in charge of goods and materials at each level shall deal in the means of the production of industrial products in accordance with the division of labour stipulated by the state and the local government.

2. The sales units of the department in charge of production, various producing corporations in combination and producing enterprises shall only be allowed to sell the products which are produced by the departments, corporations and enterprises themselves and which are allowed to be sold by themselves in accordance with the relevant provisions of the state.

3. The supply organization of each department in charge shall only be responsible for supplying the means of the production of industrial products to the enterprises and institutions directly under the department or directly supplied by it and be responsible for the appropriate supply to its own organizational system.

4. Commercial departments shall deal in the means of the production of industrial products in across organizational systems as stipulated.

5. Except for the dealing units of the people's ownership and collective ownership as afore-

said, other units and individuals shall not deal in the means of the production of industrial products.

6. With regard to the opening or commencement of business of a unit dealing in the means of the production of industrial products, an application shall be made in accordance with the subordinate relation and examined by the material department in coordination with the administration for industry and commerce, then the administration shall approve of its registration and issue a business licence accordingly. If such a unit has been opened or started business but has not registered and obtained a business licence, it must register with and obtain a business licence from the administration for industry and commerce in accordance with the above provisions.

III In the case of the means of the production of industrial products overstocked by each unit and the idle and surplus ones which can only be disposed of by the stopped or delayed projects themselves or by the closed, stopped, merged or transferred enterprises themselves, each unit shall dispose of them by itself or entrust a dealing department with the disposal in accordance with the relevant provisions of the state without any subjection to the above-mentioned dealing ranges or the provisions for registration and obtaining business licences, etc.

IV The economic contracts concerning the means of the production of industrial products which are signed in the market activities shall be handled in accordance with the provisions in the "Interim Regulations on the Contracts of Industrial and Mining Products" promulgated by the State Economic Commission in 1981.

V With regard to the means of the production of industrial products entering the market, a dealing unit shall strictly implement the state provisions for prices and taxation.

VI Illicit operation or speculation and profiteering shall be banned.

The following activities fall under illicit operation or speculation and profiteering: Dealing without a licence or dealing in the means of the production of industrial products other than those stipulated in the business licence; illicitly reselling the means of the production of industrial products at profits; driving up prices for rushing purchase of, illegally buying up or unlawfully selling by themselves the means of the production of industrial products allotted or transferred by the state as planned so as to disrupt the state allotment and transfer plans; acting as black-market brokers in order to seek exorbitant profits; speculating or subcontracting to gain profits; reselling planned supply tickets or certificates at profits; swindling and bluffing to plunder belongings of others; selling certificates, invoices or contracts, issuing certificates or making invoices for others and offering bank accounts, checks or cash so as to gain illicit income.

The units and individuals engaged in illicit operation or speculation and profiteering shall be dealt with in accordance with state laws, decrees and other provisions according to the degrees of seriousness in the cases.

NOTICE OF THE STATE COUNCIL ON THE STRICT CONTROL OF PRICES AND THE CONSOLIDATION OF NEGOTIATED PRICES

(December 7, 1980)

For a certain time recently, it has been rather serious that prices are wilfully or covertly raised and negotiated prices are driven up in the market and discontent of the broad masses has been aroused because of that. The following notice is given in order to further implement the spirit of the "Notice of Strengthening the Administration of Prices and Resolutely Checking the Wanton or Covert Raising of Prices" of the Central Committee of the CPC and the State Council in April of this year, stabilize the economy, maintain the livelihood of the people and ensure the smooth advance of the socialist construction:

1. As from the date of the promulgation of this Notice, the state provisions against raising prices shall be executed for all retail prices throughout the country with regard to industrial and agricultural products. Those with the notices of readjusting prices issued by the departments concerned in accordance with the provisions for the limits of authority for the administration of prices before December 1 shall continue to be readjusted in accordance with the original notices.

2. Various commodities with negotiated prices shall be sold at the retail prices as on December 7, 1980 in every big city, medium city, small city, industrial area, mining area, county seat or town below the county level all over the country. These prices shall only be reduced and not raised.

3. The above two provisions shall be applicable to all state commercial enterprises, cooperative commercial enterprises, commune and brigade enterprises, agricultural-industrial-commercial combined enterprises, trust corporations, trade houses, state or collective self-selling salesrooms, exhibition fairs, trial-sale special counters, urban production service cooperatives, service centres for soldiers, commission sales points and other people's or collective selling units and to individuals distributing state commodities. All the above units and individuals shall strictly execute these provisions and shall not contravene them.

4. The purchase and sales through negotiations shall be executed on the principles stipulated by the State Council and within the limits of categories stipulated by the people's government of each province, municipality or autonomous region.

The state fixed prices shall be executed for the means of production allotted or transferred by the state as planned, including the overproduced and self-selling parts and no negotiated prices shall be allowed for them. If the prices are permitted to float down as stipulated by the state, they shall float down.

No negotiated prices shall be allowed for Class 1 and Class 2 industrial products for daily use. The prices of Class 3 industrial products shall be determined between industrial and commercial enterprises and the limits of categories shall be strictly controlled.

Before the fulfillment of the state purchasing tasks, Class 1 and Class 2 agricultural and sideline products shall be prohibited from deals at negotiated prices or from sales in country fairs and it shall also be forbidden to distribute collective products to individuals for sale. The units which make purchases in the mass producing areas of Class 3 agricultural and sideline products shall register with the local administrations for industry and commerce, subject themselves to the unified administration and the unified distribution of goods. They shall not drive up prices mutually. The maximum limits of the prices of the commodities purchased at negotiated prices shall be prescribed by the people's government of the province, municipality or autonomous region and shall be announced.

5. There shall be certain seasonal price differences for fresh and live commodities (such as vegetables, eggs, fishes, fruits, etc.). In the execution of this Notice, those with seasonal price differences stipulated shall still be readjusted according to different seasons. In the case of those with the unified stipulations of the state, they shall be executed in accordance with the stipulations; if there are no unified stipulations, the people's government of the province, municipality or autonomous region shall make and announce the stipulations.

6. All Party or government organs, bodies, armed forces and institutions shall be prohibited

from being engaged in the activities of reselling at profits.

7. The tax authorities at each level shall strictly collect taxes according to regulations and shall promptly demand the payment from those who fail to pay the taxes.

The people's bank at each level shall strengthen credit administration and cash administration and control the currency in circulation. It shall exercise supervision over buying and selling activities. Those who are found to contravene the provisions in this Notice shall be restricted in credit, settlement and payment.

8. Railway and communications departments shall strictly execute the limits of the luggage carried by passengers and shall not permit any excess.

9. Country fair trade is a supplement to the socialist commerce. The administration shall be strengthened according to state policies and good jobs shall be made of it so as to continue to invigorate it and give play to its positive role.

10. After the promulgation of this Notice, the people's government at each level shall organize several large-scale inspections of prices in succession and mobilize the broad masses of the people to reveal and denounce the activities in violation of this Notice. Such measures as imposing fines, suspending rewards, deducting parts of the pay of the personnel who shall be held responsible, imposing disciplinary punishments, etc. shall be taken against the units that really contravene this Notice. The administration for industry and commerce shall order those whose cases are serious to cease business and lodge charges with the judicial department. The examinations on large scale of prices shall be regularly made in future and shall not be loosened.

The political and ideological work shall be strengthened towards all producing units and the departments engaged in buying and selling activities so as to make them realize the serious harmfulness of the present wanton or covert raising of prices and the driving-up of negotiated prices. Cadres and staff shall be taught to take the interests of the whole into account, observe discipline and serve the people wholeheartedly. It shall be opposed to simply take the local interests of one's own unit or one's own area into account or to go one's own way without regard for others. Such illegal and discipline-violating activities as driving up prices for the purpose of obtaining more rewards shall strictly be forbidden. All enterprises shall endeavour to make good jobs of production, increase the supply of commodities and earnestly and conscientiously make due contributions to the stabilization of economy, prices and the life of the people.

Upon receipt of this Notice, the people's government at each level shall organize the departments concerned to discuss it, take specific measures and conscientiously implement them.

INTERIM PROVISIONS FOR THE PRICES OF HEAVY INDUSTRIAL PRODUCTS

(Promulgated by the State Bureau of Prices on June 18, 1981)

For the purpose of stabilizing market prices and enlivening the economy, the following provisions for the prices of heavy industrial products are made in the spirit of the "Notice of the Strict Control of Prices and the Consolidation of Negotiated Prices" as Document No. 295 (1980) of the State Council (hereinafter simply referred to as the 'Notice"):

Article 1 The meanings of "the means of production allotted and transferred by the state as planned" and "the state fixed prices" in the "Notice" of the State Council:

The "Notice" of the State Council clearly stipulates that the means of production allotted and transferred by the state as planned, including the overproduced or self-selling parts, shall follow the state fixed prices and no negotiated prices shall be allowed. 'The means of production allotted and transferred by the state as planned" mainly refers to the heavy industrial products (excluding the means of the production of agricultural products) administered or distributed by the material departments or business departments in charge at or above the county level. "The state fixed prices" mean those fixed by the price or business departments in charge at or above the county level within the limits of authority in the division of labour for the administration of prices.

Article 2 The provisions for the prescription of temporary prices and coordinated prices by each province, municipality or autonomous region:

In the case of the products with state uniform prices put into practice, such as steel products, major mechanical products, etc., if some enterprises have difficulty in setting the prices and these products are short supplied goods and materials much needed for production, the province, municipality or autonomous region shall prescribe temporary ex-factory prices within the scope of not more than 20 per cent of the state uniform prices on the principles of recovering the costs and obtaining small profits, and execute them inside and outside the province, municipality or autonomous region.

The goods and materials coordinated between provinces, municipalities and autonomous regions and between enterprises shall still follow the state uniform fixed prices. But in the case of a small number of goods and materials, where their low prices will result in losses for the enterprises under the circumstances of normal production and rational management, they shall be coordinated at the temporary prices checked and determined by the province(s), municipality (-ies) and/or autonomous region(s). If there are no temporary prices, both supplying and demanding parties shall consult about the coordinated prices on the principles of recovering the costs and obtaining small profits and coordinate the materials with the checking and determination of the prices by the price department of the province, municipality or autonomous region at the place of production. When they are externally supplied through material departments, they shall be supplied on the principle of recovering the costs. The prices of the products produced with coordinated goods and materials shall not be raised.

Article 3 The prices of coal, cement, plate glass, acids, alkalis and other products and the products of large and medium enterprises (or the enterprises assigned by the ministries in charge in the State Council) shall be prescribed by the department in charge in the State Council; with regard to these products of local small enterprises (or non-assigned enterprises) the province, municipality or autonomous region shall prescribe regional prices for them and they shall be transferred out of the province (or muncipality or autonomous region) at the regional prices. No temporary prices or coordinated prices shall be prescribed for these products from now on.

Article 4 The provisions for floating prices:

Floating prices have played a positive role in the coordination with the regulation of the national economy and the experiments of the system reform since the beginning of their trial implementation. In order to put them into better trial implementation under leadership, the following provisions are required to be made for the categories, scopes and times for the products with floating prices.

(1) In the case of the products whose prices are stipulated to float by the department in charge

within the limits of its authority in the division of labour for the administration of prices, each enterprise shall set the prices strictly according to the stipulated categories and scopes. Those beyond the stipulated categories or ranges shall be approved by the department in charge. After the ex-factory prices have been floated, the prices of the commercial or material department shall also float according to conditions.

(2) An enterprise shall determine the prices within the approved floating scopes according to the production and demand of specific products. In principle, they shall not float at a loss. No floating prices shall be allowed for the products with price subsidies from the financial or commercial department.

(3) After determining prices within the stipulated floating scopes, the enterprise shall submit them to a higher level department in charge for record and keep them relatively stable within a definite time so as to be advantageous to production and circulation.

(4) If some products have the conditions for reducing their prices, their prices shall be reduced within the limits of authority in the division of labour for the administration of prices; if they are still required to float after reduction, they shall be permitted to remain floating within the scopes newly stipulated.

Article 5 The heavy industrial products which can be sold by an enterprise itself as stipulated by the state policies and which are sold to the material department or the commercial wholesale department shall follow the fixed ex-factory prices and those which are sold to production, capital construction or commercial retail units shall follow the ex-factory prices or supply prices; those sold in the salesroom established by the enterprise itself shall, in principle, be sold at the supply prices or retail prices fixed in a uniform manner by the material or commercial department.

Article 6 Coal and timber and their means of transportation organized by the material department itself shall, in principle, follow the fixed supply prices; but if following the fixed supply prices will result in losses, they shall be supplied for recovering the costs by adding the freight or carriage, or sundry expenses and the fixed management expenses to the ex-factory prices and shall be supplied as far as possible to the producing, capital construction, servicing and other units for use. The prices of the products produced with the materials transported by the enterprise itself as the raw materials or fuel shall not be raised.

Article 7 In order to solve the problems of too many links (including the material supply and marketing organization of the business department in charge) of the dealing in some materials, expense collection at every level, etc., the following principled provisions are made for the collection of the expenses of goods and materials:

(1) The goods and materials supplied directly shall be supplied in a direct manner and accounts directly settled by both supplying and demanding parties and the material department shall not collect any expenses. The material department shall only collect management expenses and interest therein and shall not collect stocking or storage charges for the goods and materials managed by it, of which it is responsible for the allocation, transfer, dispatch, paying the funds in advance and handling the settlement, but which do not go through the warehouses of the material department and therefore are not charged for stocking or storage. If the user raises any objection to the quality or quantity of a product managed by the material department, the department shall be responsible for the contact and investigation.

The goods and materials purchased, sold, processed or transported by the material department on commission for an enterprise shall follow the state fixed prices in accordance with the provisions in the "Notice" of the State Council and the material department shall collect the stipulated service charges.

(2) In order to prevent the pressured purchase or resale for profit of short means of production, the material, commercial and other departments shall set the prices stipulated by the state in a uniform manner when they sell the means of production. When the surplus materials of the material department or an enterprise are used to make up others' deficiencies, it shall only be allowed to add one amount for all the transportation, sundry and management expenses stipulated according to the normal direction of circulation to the ex-factory prices no matter how many links they will go through.

Article 8 The ex-factory prices already readjusted before the promulgation of the "Notice" of the State Council or those which received the notices of the readjustment of the ex-factory prices for heavy industrial products with specific categories, specific prices and specific dates for execution, which had been transmitted down by various areas or departments within the limits of authority in the division of labour for the administration of prices before December 1, 1980, shall generally continue to be readjusted in accordance with original notices of readjustment. The allotment or transfer prices, supply prices, wholesale prices and retail prices shall also be readjusted accordingly with the exception of those which will cause serious influences on the market.

Article 9 Each province, municipality or autonomous region shall formulate concrete procedures for implementation in the light of the local specific conditions on the basis of these Provisions.

NOTICE OF THE STATE COUNCIL FOR RESOLUTELY STABILIZING MARKET PRICES

(January 8, 1982)

The Fourth Session of the Fifth National People's Congress has instructed the State Council, in the economic work of this year, "to take care to further strengthen the administration of revenue, credit and prices, maintain the basic balance between revenue and expenditure and ensure the basic stability of market prices on the basis of the development of production and the energetic saving." For this reason, the following Notice is made for the stabilization of market prices.

1. In the case of industrial and agricultural products with the state stipulated list prices, the state provisions shall be implemented for their retail prices in every part of the country, which shall not be raised.

2. In the case of various commodities with negotiated prices, their retail prices shall only be lowered and not raised in each large, medium and small city, industrial area, mining area, county town or town below the county level.

3. The above two provisions shall be applicable to all such people's and collective selling units as state-operated commerce, cooperative commerce, commune and brigade enterprises, agricultural-industrial-commercial combined enterprises, trust corporations, trade houses, state or collective self-selling salesrooms, exhibition fairs, trial-sale special counters, urban production service cooperatives, military services and commission sales points and to individual dealers who deal in state commodities. The above units and individuals shall strictly implement these provisions and shall not violate them.

4. No negotiated prices shall be allowed for Class 1 and Class 2 industrial products for daily use. The ranges of categories shall strictly be controlled for Class 3 industrial products with prices to be fixed through negotiations between industrial and commercial enterprises.

5. The guiding principle of basic stabilization shall be implemented for the purchasing prices of agricultural products. Without the approval of the State Council, no area or department shall raise or covertly raise the prices of Class 1 and Class 2 agricultural and sideline products on their own initiative. Before the fulfillment of the state purchasing tasks, they shall not be sold or bought at negotiated prices nor be sold in country fairs. The units that make purchases in the concentrated producing areas of Class 3 agricultural and sideline products shall register themselves with the local administrations for industry and commerce, subject themselves to the unified administration and unified distribution of sources of goods and shall not drive up prices mutually.

6. The commodities with seasonal price differences stipulated shall still have their prices readjusted according to different seasons. If they have the uniform provisions of the state, they shall be implemented in accordance with these provisions. If there are no uniform provisions of the state, the people's government of a province, a municipality or an autonomous region shall make provisions for them and announce these provisions.

7. The tax authority at each level shall strictly collect taxes according to regulations and promptly demand payments from those who fail to pay taxes.

The people's bank at each level shall strengthen credit administration and control the currency put into circulation. It shall exercise the supervision of buying and selling activities and restrict in credit, settlement or payment for those who are found to violate the provisions of this Notice.

8. No Party and government organs, bodies, armed forces and institutions shall engage themselves in the activities of reselling at profits.

9. Country fair trade is the supplement to the socialist commerce. Its administration shall be strengthened and good jobs shall be made in accordance with state policies to continue to invigorate it and give play to its positive role. Strong and resolute measures shall be taken against such illegal activities as speculation, profiteering, driving up prices, etc. With regard to a small number of persons who deliberately fabricate rumours to mislead the people and

disrupt the market, such cases shall seriously be detected and sternly be dealt with.

10. After the issue of this Notice, the people's government at each level shall organize the departments concerned to make several large-scale inspections of prices and mobilize the broad masses of the people to expose and denounce the acts in violation of this Notice. In the case of the units that actually violate this Notice, such measures shall be taken as fining them, suspension of rewards, deducting parts of the wages of the persons who are held responsible, imposing disciplinary punishments, etc. With regard to the units and individuals that refuse to pay fines and turn over illicit proceeds, the departments of prices are empowered to notify banks or credit cooperatives to force transfers out of their deposits. With regard to those who are in serious violation of pricing discipline, the administrations for industry and commerce shall order them to cease business and lodge charges against them with judicial departments. The large scale inspections shall regularly be made in future and shall not be slackened.

The people's government at each level shall strengthen its leadership over pricing service, strengthen the pricing personnels of cities, counties, industrial and commercial enterprises and organize the forces of all the departments concerned to resolutely implement the provisions in this Notice.

INTERIM REGULATIONS ON THE ADMINISTRATION OF PRICES

(Adopted by Ordinary Meeting of the State Council on July 7, 1982)

Chapter I General Rules

Article 1 These Regulations are formulated to implement the guiding principle of maintaining the basic stability of market prices, readjust prices rationally step by step in a planned way, strengthen the administration of prices, promote the development of production, expand the circulation of commodities, stabilize the livelihood of the people and guarantee smooth advance of the cause of the socialist construction.

Article 2 In the administration of prices, consideration shall be given to the economic interests of producers, dealers and consumers with the prerequisite of safeguarding the overall interests of the state and a proper balance shall be maintained in the relationship between the central and local authorities or between areas or between departments.

Article 3 By following the principles of practising the planned economy on the basis of the socialist public ownership and simultaneously giving play to the auxiliary role of the market regulation, state fixed prices and enterprise fixed prices or country fair trade prices within the limits stipulated by the state shall be adopted separately according to the different degrees of the influence of different commodities on the national economy and the people's livelihood. The state fixed prices are the principal form.

Article 4 The State Council shall establish a State Bureau of Pricing which shall administer and supervise the pricing work all over the country. The local people's government at each level is provided with the department of prices which administers and supervises the pricing work in its own area. The business department concerned in charge at each level or an enterprise or an institution shall be provided with a pricing organization or pricing personnel suited to its working tasks to take charge of the administration and supervision of prices in its own organizational system or unit.

Article 5 The state implements the principles of unified leadership and administration by levels over the pricing work.

The state's pricing directions, policies, laws, regulations and plans shall be formulated and approved by the State Council.

Prices of important industrial and agricultural products, important communications and transportation rates, important non-commercial commodity charges and material management expenses shall be administered by the State Bureau of Pricing and the business departments of the State Council concerned in charge.

Relatively important industrial and agricultural product prices, communications and transportation rates and non-commercial commodity charges shall be administered by the department of prices of the local people's government at each level and the business departments concerned in charge.

With regard to other prices of industrial and agricultural products and non-commercial commodity charges, an industrial or commercial enterprise shall have the price-fixing power within the limits stipulated by state policies.

On the above principles, the department of pricing at each level shall, jointly with other departments concerned, formulate or revise the list of the division of labour in the administration of the prices of industrial and agricultural products, communications and transportation rates and non-commercial commodity charges so as to be used as the specific ground for the division of labour in the administration of prices.

Article 6 In the formulation and readjustment of the prices of industrial and agricultural products, communications and transportation rates, the standards of non-commercial commodity charges and those of material management expenses, each area, department, enterprise or institution shall handle them within their authorities as stipulated and regard the official documents as the standard.

Article 7 In the formulation and readjustment of the prices of commodities, each area, department, enterprise or institution shall implement the principles of fixing the prices according to quality or grades, good price for good quality and low price for low quality, and shall maintain rational price differences between the commodities of different qualities and specifications.

Necessary rational regional price differences shall be maintained between areas and there shall be rational seasonal price differences for some commodities.

Article 8 Except for those particularly stipulated by the state, all areas, departments, enterprises, institutions, communes, production teams and individual labourers shall abide by these Regulations.

Chapter II The Division of Powers in the Administration of Prices

Article 9 The powers of the State Bureau of Prices are:

1. To be responsible for making suggestions and schemes in the course of the formulation of the state's pricing guiding principles, policies, laws, regulations and plans. It shall be responsible for nationwide implementation and supervision after they are approved and promulgated by the State Council.

2. To take charge of the administration and overall balance of prices throughout the country. Jointly with other departments concerned, it shall draft the long-term, medium-term and annual plans of prices which shall be brought into the state plans of the national economy and the social development after the overall balance by the State Planning Commission. It shall, within the limits of authority in the administration of prices, stipulate pricing principles and procedures and prescribe and readjust the prices of industrial and agricultural products, the standards of material management expenses, the rates of communications and transportation and the standards of non-commercial commodity charges. The prescription and readjustment of the commodity prices, transportation rates and charges which have a significant influence on the national economy and the people's livelihood shall be approved by the State Council.

3. Within the limits of authority in the administration of prices, to check and determine the pricing principles for important commodities put forward by the business departments in charge in the State Council with regard to the price differences between purchase and sale, those between wholesale and retail, those between areas, those between specifications or qualities, those between seasons, allotting and transferring prices, supply prices, etc.

4. To be responsible for directing the pricing work of the business departments in charge in the State Council, and provinces, autonomous regions and municipalities directly under the Central Government. It shall supervise and examine the implementation of pricing policies and provisions, be entitled to check the activities in violation of pricing directions, policies and discipline and deal with or help the departments concerned to deal with them according to laws and relevant provisions.

5. To handle the disputes on prices between the business departments in charge in the State Council, between provinces, autonomous regions and municipalities directly under the Central Government and between the business departments in charge in the State Council and provinces, autonomous regions or municipalities directly under the Central Government.

6. To wield other powers granted by the State Council.

Article 10 The powers of the department of prices of a province, an autonomous region or a municipality directly under the Central Government are:

1. To be responsible for the implementation and supervision of the state pricing directives, policies, laws and regulations in its own area. It shall also be responsible for arranging the implementation of the price-fixing or price-readjusting schemes transmitted down by the State Council and the State Bureau of Prices. It shall urge the departments concerned to implement the price-fixing or price-readjusting schemes transmitted down by the business departments in charge in the State Council.

2. To be responsible for the administration and overall balance of prices in its own area. It shall, jointly with the departments concerned, make and draft long-term, medium-term or annual planning in respect of pricing and include the same in the plans of the national economy and the social development after the overall balance by the planning commission. It shall, within the limits of authority in the administration of prices, stipulate the pricing principles and procedures and prescribe and readjust the prices of industrial and agricultural products, the rates of communications and transportation and the standards of non-commercial commodity charges. The prescription and readjustment of the commodity prices, transportation rates and charges with rather great influences shall be approved by the people's government of the province, autonomous region or municipality directly under the Central Government. The price-fixing and price-readjusting documents shall be submitted to the State Bureau of Prices and the business departments concerned in charge in the State Council for filing.

3. In accordance with the pricing principles and procedures, and within the limits of authority in the administration of prices, to arrange or check and determine the price differences of commodities between purchase and sale, those between whole-

sale and retail, those between areas, those between specifications or qualities and those between seasons and the allotting or transferring and supply prices of major commodities.

4. To take charge of directing the pricing work of the business departments in charge at the same level and the lower departments of prices. It shall supervise and examine the implementation of pricing policies and provisions, and be entitled to check the activities in violation of pricing directions, policies and discipline and deal with them according to laws and relevant provisions.

5. To handle the disputes on prices between the business departments in charge at the same level or between areas or between the business departments in charge at the same level and areas.

6. To wield other powers granted by the people's government of the province, autonomous region or municipality directly under the Central Government.

Article 11 The powers in the administration of prices of a business department in charge in the State Council, a province, an autonomous region or a municipality directly under the Central Government are:

1. To be responsible for the implementation and examination of the state pricing directions, policies, laws and regulations in the same organizational system. It shall also be responsible for arranging the implementation of the price-fixing or price-readjusting schemes transmitted down by the department of prices at a higher level or at the same level.

2. To take charge of the administration of prices in its own organizational system. It shall, within the limits of authority in the administration of prices, regulate pricing directions and procedures, balance and coordinate the levels of the prices for the commodities of the same categories between areas and prescribe and revise the prices of industrial and agricultural products, the rates of communications and transportation and the standards of non-commercial commodity charges. The price-fixing and price-readjusting documents shall be submitted to the department of prices at the same level for filing. If these shall be examined and approved by the department of pricing at a higher level or at the same level, it shall be responsible for putting forward the suggestions as to the formulation of plans and price-fixing in price-readjusting schemes.

3. In accordance with the stipulated pricing principles and procedures, it shall, within the limits of authority in the administration of prices, arrange various price differences of commodities and their allotting or transferring prices or supply prices.

4. To take charge of directing the pricing work of its own organizational system. It shall supervise and examine the implementation of pricing policies and provisions, be responsible for checking the activities in violation of pricing directions, policies and discipline and deal with them according to laws and relevant provisions.

5. To wield other powers granted by higher authorities.

Article 12 The powers in the administration of prices for the department of pricing and the business departments in charge in each prefecture, autonomous prefecture, city, county, autonomous county or district under a city shall be stipulated by the people's government of the province, autonomous region or municipality directly under the Central Government with reference to these Regulations.

Article 13 The duties of an enterprise or an institution in the administration of prices are: To implement pricing directions and policies and compliance of pricing discipline; to implement accurately the price-fixing and price-readjusting notices of the department of pricing and the business department in charge according to the fixed time and prices; to provide the department of prices and the business department in charge with the costs of production, circulation costs, the production and sales of commodities, profits or losses and other relevant information, and to report the situations of the implementation of prices.

Article 14 The price-fixing competence of an industrial or commercial enterprise is:

1. To prescribe the specific prices of the commodities with floating prices according to the stipulated categories and floating ranges.

2. To negotiate and determine the prices of the agricultural and sideline products purchased or sold through negotiations in accordance with the procedures for the administration approved by the State Council.

3. To consult and set the prices of the small commodities among Class 3 light industrial and textile products and those among handicraft products in accordance with the stipulated categories and pricing principles.

4. To prescribe the prices of new products for test marketing within the limits of authority stipulated by the department of prices.

5. To prescribe the coordinated prices inside the enterprise for the specialized coordinated products as stipulated.

6. To prescribe commodity prices, non-

commercial commodity charges and technological cooperation expenses without the prices fixed by the state.

7. To determine the disposal prices of broken, damaged, used and inferior commodities within its authority as stipulated by the business department in charge.

8. To prescribe the prices of food without unified prices according to the rates of gross profits for the catering trade stipulated by the business department in charge.

Chapter III The Administration of the Prices of Industrial and Agricultural Products

Article 15 The selling and buying prices stipulated by the state shall be implemented for Class 1 and Class 2 agricultural and sideline products. The provisions of the State Council shall be implemented for the categories and ranges with the additional prices for over-purchase and the extraprice subsidies and each area or each department shall not alter them without authorization.

The limits of categories, pricing principles and the procedures for the administration of prices of the agricultural and sideline products to be purchased or sold through negotiations shall be implemented in accordance with the procedures for the administration approved by the State Council and each area, department or enterprise shall not expand the ranges of categories with negotiated prices or mark up negotiated prices without authorization.

Article 16 If the purchasing prices of agricultural and sideline products are inconsistent in the contiguous areas between provinces, autonomous regions and municipalities directly under the Central Government, both parties shall consult with each other so as to equalize the purchasing prices on the whole.

The grades and specifications of the same agricultural or sideline product in the contiguous areas shall follow unified standards. If the standards of grades and specifications cannot be unified, both parties shall consult with each other and rationally prescribe the specification or qualitative price differences on the principles of comparing the prices according to qualities.

The department of pricing and the business departments concerned in charge at or above the county level in a contiguous area shall regularly convene price dovetailing meetings to balance the purchasing prices of agricultural and sideline products between neighbouring areas through consultation.

Article 17 The prices of agricultural and sideline products in urban and rural country fair trade shall be negotiated and determined by both buying and selling parties within the limits permitted by the state policies and decrees. Commercial departments shall take in and send out goods and materials in a planned way so as to keep the country fair prices down. The administrations for industry and commerce shall strengthen the administration of the prices in urban and rural country fair trade.

Article 18 The state fixed prices shall be implemented and no negotiation of prices shall be allowed for the heavy industrial products with stated fixed prices, no matter whether they are produced within the plans or beyond the plans or over-produced. If some categories require the prescription of temporary ex-factory prices, regional ex-factory prices or coordinated prices or if a very few categories require the implementation of over-produced additional prices, all these shall be done in accordance with the provisions approved by the State Council.

Article 19 The state fixed prices shall be implemented and no negotiation of prices shall be allowed for the light and textile industrial products and handicraft with state fixed prices, no matter whether they are produced within the plans or beyond the plans or over-produced. With regard to the small commodities among Class 3 light and textile industrial products and those among handicraft products, the people's government of the province, autonomous region or municipality directly under the Central Government shall stipulate the list of the categories which are permitted to have the prices fixed through consultation, and industrial and commercial enterprises shall set the prices through consultation in accordance with the stipulated categories and pricing principles.

Article 20 When adopting floating prices in industrial products, the department of prices or the business department in charge shall, within their authority in the administration of prices, stipulate the categories with prices permitted to float and the floating ranges, and enterprises shall implement them as stipulated. The required increase or decrease of categories or the alteration of floating ranges shall be approved by the department of prices or the business department in charge within their authority in the administration of prices.

Article 21 The prices of new products shall be advantageous to the development in their production and to popularizing the use of them. During the test-marketing of a new product, the enterprise shall prescribe the price for trial sale according to the costs and in the light of the prices of the product of the same kind and report it to the department of prices and the business department in charge for record. An important new product trial-selling price shall be approved by the department of prices of the province, autonomous region or municipality directly under the Central Government. In general, the period of test marketing shall be one year or two years at most. At the expiration of the test marketing, the department of prices or the business department in charge shall, within the limits of authority in the administration of prices, prescribe the official price in accordance with the normal cost of production and in the light of the prices of the product of the same kind.

New products shall be appraised and confirmed separately by such departments as the economic commission, the scientific and technological commission and/or the Central Government ministry or bureau in charge or the province, autonomous region or municipality directly under the Central Government on the principle of administration by levels and according to the degrees of their importance, the levels of their technology, etc. If any products have not been appraised and confirmed by the departments aforesaid, their prices shall not be fixed as though they are new products.

Article 22 If the commodities, in accordance with the regulation, which could be sold by industrial enterprises themselves have the prices affixed by the state, different prospective buyers shall be differentiated so as to separately implement the ex-factory prices, wholesale prices, supply prices or retail prices stipulated by the state.

Article 23 The department of pricing or the business department in charge shall, within the limits of authority in the administration of prices, prescribe minimum protective prices for the purchasing prices of some agricultural and sideline products in the outlying districts, mountain areas and minority nationality areas; it shall also prescribe the maximum limit for the selling prices of some industrial products.

Article 24 The commodities purchased by individual labourers from state industrial and commercial enterprises and collective enterprises shall be sold at the retail prices stipulated by the state. The products produced with the raw materials supplied by the material department shall be sold at the prices affixed according to quality and in the light of the prices of the same products of state enterprises. If they deal in agricultural and sideline products with negotiated prices, the small commodities among Class 3 light and textile industrial products and those among handicraft products they shall sell them at the prices fixed by themselves in accordance with the relevant provisions of the state.

Article 25 A business department in charge shall exercise the appropriate administration of the pricing of industrial and agricultural products in accordance with the list of the division of labour in the administration of the prices of commodities. In the case of the commodities produced and managed by industrial and commercial enterprises outside their trades, the business department in charge shall be responsible for the administration of prices and the concurrent dealing units shall execute the prices prescribed by the principal dealing units. The material supply and marketing units of each department shall execute the material supply prices and the standards of management expenses of the department of prices.

The department of pricing shall exercise the unified leadership of the administration of prices with regard to units of trade houses, trust corporations, agricultural-industrial-commercial combined enterprise, intellectual and youth stores, neighbourhood stores, factory-operated stores, soldier services and individual labourers, and the state specialized corporations shall exercise the administration over them.

Without any distinction of their subordinate relations, all industrial and commercial enterprises and institutions shall obey the administration and supervision of prices by the local departments of pricing and the appropriate business departments in charge.

Article 26 Except for those otherwise stipulated by the state, all administration of the prices in respect of import and export commodities, the commodities of Chinese-foreign joint ventures and foreign enterprises, the commodities supplied to foreigners, overseas Chinese and Hong Kong and Macao compatriots shall be implemented according to these Regulations.

Chapter IV The Administration of Communications and Transportation Rates and Non-commercial commodity Charges

Article 27 The provisions of the State Council, the State Bureau of Prices or the business departments in charge in the State Council shall be implemented within the limits of authority in the administration of prices for railway and civil aviation passenger and goods transportation charges, pipeline transportation charges, the marine-transport passenger and goods transportation charges and port dues of the enterprises directly under the Ministry of Communications and postage or telephone or telegram charges, and each area, department, enterprise or institution shall not alter the prices and charging standards without authorization nor collect additional charges.

The external rates of the above transportation charges, postage and telegram or telephone charges shall, within the limits of authority in the administration of prices, be duly and properly readjusted by the State Bureau of Prices or the business departments of the State Council in charge in accordance with state policies and in the light of the changes of international rates.

The provisions of the department of prices or the business departments in charge in the province, autonomous region or municipality directly under the Central Government shall be implemented for local railway and local water-transport passenger and goods transportation charges, motor passenger and goods transportation charges, urban tram, bus and taxi fares, handling and transport charges and rural telephone basic charges. In the prescription or readjustment of local transportation charges, each area shall maintain rational parity with those charges stipulated by the State Council, the State Bureau of Prices or the business departments of the State Council in charge and those in neighbouring areas.

Article 28 The charging standards shall be prescribed within the limits of authority in the administration of prices for travelling charges, civil housing rentals, guest room charges of hotels, guesthouses and hostels, medical expenses, tuition and sundry fees of primary and secondary schools, park and movie ticket fees, bathing, hairdressing and photo charges and other repair or service charges relating to the people's living. Each area, department, enterprise or institution shall execute the stipulated charging standards and shall not alter the charging standards or add charging items otherwise by exceeding its power nor lower the quality of services.

Article 29 Charging standards shall be appraised and prescribed through discussion by the individual labourers' association in the business of servicing, repairing and transport trades by non-motorized means run by individual labourers or shall be negotiated and determined by both suppliers and demanding parties.

Chapter V The Supervision of Prices

Article 30 The department of pricing at each level shall take the inspection of prices as a principal task. The department of pricing at each level above the county one (exclusive of the county one) shall be provided with a price inspection organization.

Article 31 The inspection of prices shall also be taken as a principal task by each business department at each level in charge of industry, commerce, foreign trade, supply of goods and materials, communications, posts and telecommunications, culture, education and health, tourism, etc. and by enterprises and institutions.

If an enterprise supplies goods short of the stipulated quantity or passes off the inferior as the good, the business department in charge and the administration for industry and commerce shall strengthen education and inspection and be responsible for correcting and dealing with it.

State specialized corporations shall be entitled to exercise the inspection and supervision of prices over trade houses, trust corporations, agricultural-industrial-commercial combined enterprises, intellectual and youth stores, neighbourhood stores, factory-operated stores, soldier services and other units and over individual labourers on the principle of the appropriate administration of prices and deal with the cases in violation of pricing directives, policies and pricing discipline according to laws and relevant provisions.

Enterprises and institutions shall regularly make inspections of prices. A pricing clerk of an enterprise or an institution shall be responsible for supervising his own unit's implementation of pricing policies and provisions and be entitled to resist or inform and accuse, by bypassing the immediate leadership, the activities in violation of pricing directives, policies and pricing discipline.

Article 32 The people's government of a city or a county shall invite cadres, workers, retired persons, neighbourhood activists and commune members to be voluntary pricing inspectors. A voluntary pricing inspector shall inspect the implementation of the policies and provisions of commodity prices and non-commercial commodity charges by enterprises, institutions and individual labourers within the designated area. A local people's government and department of pricing shall also adopt other forms and rely on the masses of the people to supervise prices.

Article 33 The people's government at each level shall organize the forces of the parties concerned regularly or irregularly to carry out price inspections and consolidations, several times a year. It shall invite the deputies to the people's congress, the members of the political consultative conference and the representatives of the trade union, the women's federation, etc. to participate in price inspections and conscientiously heed their opinions.

Article 34 Pricing inspectors and voluntary pricing inspectors shall implement policies, abide strictly by discipline, implement laws impartially and shall not act wrongly out of personal consideration. The inspected units shall subject themselves to the inspections and make the situations known and supply information as things really are.

Article 35 The department of prices or the business department in charge at each level or each enterprise or institution shall establish perfect systems for the administration of prices and strictly implement them, such as the system of personal responsibility, system of inspections, system of statistical reports, system of bench or counter accounts, system of marked prices, system of security, system of rewards and punishments, and system of register on file for dealing with discipline-violating cases, etc.

Chapter VI Rewards and Punishments

Article 36 A unit or an individual with one of the following achievements shall be rewarded:

1. Having made outstanding deeds in implementing these Regulations conscientiously;
2. Being energetically engaged in pricing work, endeavouring to gain professional proficiency and having fulfilled the tasks remarkably;
3. Resolutely resisting, energetically informing of and exposing, being bold in the struggle with the activities in violation of pricing directives, policies and pricing discipline and having achieved remarkable merits in this respect.

Each area, department, enterprise or institution shall take the ways in which the units and personnel under it observe pricing directives, policies and pricing discipline as an important factor for appraising their achievements and rewarding them.

Article 37 Necessary disciplinary punishments and economic sanctions shall be imposed on a unit or an individual with one of the following acts:

1. Prescribing or readjusting commodity prices, transportation charges or charging standards by exceeding its or his powers;
2. Refusing to implement the commodity prices, transportation charges and charging standards stipulated by the state, raising grades and prices, reducing grades and prices or collecting charges recklessly without authorization.
3. Extending the categories of agricultural and sideline products to be purchased or sold through negotiations or marking up negotiated prices without authorization;
4. Willfully moving up or postponing or being in breach of price-readjusting notices, increasing users' burdens or causing great losses to the state;
5. Contravening provisions, cutting prices to dispose of commodities without authorization, or distributing commodities among the staff without authorization at prices less than the retail ones;
6. Raising prices covertly to seek illegal profits by such means as passing off the inferior as the good, reducing the quality of services, etc.;
7. The leading cadres at each level refusing to implement pricing policies and provisions and the limits of authority in the administration of prices and deciding without authorization to raise or lower prices;
8. Shielding or conniving with the units or individuals contravening pricing directives, policies and pricing discipline;
9. Retaliating upon the personnel who conscientiously implement pricing directives and policies or who inform of and expose the violations of pricing discipline;
10. Divulging the secrets of prices, resulting in losses.

If a unit or an individual commits one of the above acts, the illicit income shall be fully returned to the user, that which cannot be returned shall be confiscated and fines shall be imposed on some of such units or individuals. Those whose cases are serious shall be ordered by the administration for industry and commerce to cease business for reform or have their business licences suspended or cancelled.

Article 38 The specific procedures for rewards, disciplinary punishments and economic sanctions shall be handled in accordance with the

"Regulations on the Rewards and Punishments of the Staff Members and Workers of Enterprises" promulgated by the State Council and other relevant provisions of the state.

Article 39 Disciplinary punishments and economic sanctions shall be increased for the person who has committed one of the following acts; if the act constitutes a crime, the judicial authorities shall investigate and affix his criminal responsibility:

1. Divulging the secrets of prices, resulting in serious losses;

2. Adopting such illicit means as marking up prices, forcing prices down, raising prices covertly, etc. and collecting graft from these acts;

3. Violating pricing discipline and retaliating upon or framing the persons who resist or expose or accuse of his discipline-violating acts, causing serious results.

Chapter VII Supplementary Provisions

Article 40 The departments concerned of the State Council and the people's government of each province, autonomous region or municipality directly under the Central Government shall formulate supplementary provisions or detailed rules for implementation in accordance with the provisions in these Regulations.

If the current provisions for the administration of prices of the people's government at each level, each department, enterprise or institution go against these Regulations, these Regulations shall be taken as the standard.

Article 41 These Regulations shall be put into effect from the date of promulgation.

PROVISIONAL PROCEDURES FOR THE ADMINISTRATION OF THE TRADE HOUSES OF SUPPLY AND MARKETING COOPERATIVES

(Published and Distributed by the National Federation of Supply and Marketing Cooperatives on June 20, 1981)

The following Provisional Procedures for the Administration are formulated in order to act better in the spirit of the Third Plenary Session of the Party's 11th Central Committee, promote industrial and agricultural production, invigorate the economy, expand the flow of goods and materials between city and country and between areas and further run the trade houses of supply and marketing cooperatives well.

I Nature and Tasks

A supply and marketing cooperative trade house is a commercial enterprise of intermediate and servicing nature and socialist charity under the people's ownership and is mainly engaged in commercial services.

A trade house is the product of the development of the commodity economy and has a long history in our country. In the socialist society, trade houses still play a positive role in the circulation of commodities. It is an indispensable auxiliary channel for the circulation of commodities in our country, a necessary supplement to the planned economy, a better organizational form for the regulation of the market and a component part of the whole business of supply and marketing cooperatives.

The main functions of a trade house are: promoting the mutual knowledge of quotations in the market and clearing channels; acting as go-betweens and organizing transactions; making good omissions and deficiencies and helping supply each other's needs; making good jobs of taking in and sending out and keeping down prices; coordinating production and sale and stimulating the economy.

A trade house shall put itself under the direction of state policies and plans so as to make good jobs of market regulation, gear itself to the needs of the countryside, of the production and of the market by upholding political, production and mass viewpoints and serve industrial and agricultural production, the life of the people and the grass-roots supply and marketing cooperatives.

A trade house shall give full play to its specialties such as wide connections, quick access to information, flexible dealings and convenient purchase and sale. It shall use its major strength to stimulate the exchange of Class 3 agricultural and sideline products and at the same time energetically replenish the supply of goods to the rural market so as to promote the exchange of industrial and agricultural products. It shall attend to commercial reputation and improve its service. It shall act in mutual coordination and close cooperation with specialized corporations. It shall take care to prevent unhealthy tendencies caused by making use of the trade house under the guise of "cooperation."

The specific tasks of a trade house are:

1. Give energetic help to grass-roots supply and marketing cooperatives and specialized corporations to promote the sale of Class 3 agricultural and sideline products and make good jobs of the dealing in other agricultural and sideline products according to policies so as to promote industrial and agricultural production and urban and rural economic prosperity.

2. Energetically organize for grass-roots supply and marketing cooperatives extra-planned daily industrial products, means of agricultural production, farmers' building materials and commune members' articles for daily use so as to make good the deficiencies in the supply of commodities in the rural market.

3. Help rural people's communes, production brigades and teams and urban neighbouring collective enterprises and other departments to promote the sale of commodities.

4. Make good jobs of the circulation of notices of quotations and forecast the developments in the market.

5. Participate in the administration of countryside trade fairs and keep down market prices by economic means.

II Ranges of Dealing

A multiple-dealing trade house has the following major scopes of dealing:

1. Class 3 agricultural and sideline products falling under the administration of supply and marketing cooperatives, namely, Class 3 native products, dried and fresh fruits, dried vegetables and seasonings, daily groceries, used and old materials, small farm tools and other Class 3 agricultural, sideline, native and special products.

2. Class 2 agricultural and sideline products which are permitted by the State Council and the people's government of the province, municipality or autonomous region to be purchased or sold through negotiations after the fulfilment of state plans.

3. Cereals and oils at negotiated prices for which a trade house shall be entrusted by the grain department with the commission purchase or sale. With the approval of the local government, it shall properly deal in petty cereals other than rice and wheat and certain raw materials for roasted seeds and nuts.

4. Extra-planned daily industrial products, including commodities which are permitted by state policies to be sold by industrial departments themselves, those remaining after the selection of commercial departments and overstocked by industrial departments, the products of rural commune and brigade and urban neighbouring collective enterprises which are not brought into state plans nor purchased by the specialized corporations, the foreign trade export commodities turned for home sale and the commodities imported by the Federation or the locality and distributed for sale.

5. The commercial, basic material, military and industrial commodities with which a trade house is entrusted for the commission purchase or sale by other departments.

6. The articles permitted by policies to be carried or mailed in by overseas Chinese or Hong Kong and Macao compatriots and those distributed for sale after the investigation and seizure or confiscation by the local government. However, both selling and buying trade houses shall be examined and approved by the administration for industry and commerce above the county level before dealing in them. Purchase from smugglers is strictly prohibited.

The scopes of dealing for the trade houses in Guangdong and Fujian special zones, minority regions and outlying districts shall be more flexible to a proper extent. Particulars shall be decided by the supply and marketing cooperative at the level of the province, municipality or autonomous region by asking the local government for instructions.

The trust section or the trust service (or the trade house) set up by a specialized corporation deals mainly in the commodities falling under the administration of the specialized corporation.

III Pricing Principles

A trade house shall conscientiously implement the guiding principle of stabilizing prices, strictly carry out the state price policies and be prohibited from raising prices covertly or wantonly or from driving up prices. The pricing principles shall be: fixing prices according to quality in keeping with the trade and the market, achieving frequent turnover at small profits and aiming at rational profits at final accounting even though there have been gains and losses on the basis of the situations of supply and demand in the market and on the principles of contributing to the promotion of production, keeping down prices, and stimulating the market and giving consideration concurrently to the interests of the state, the producers and the consumers. At present, they shall conscientiously implement the relevant provisions in the "Notice of the Strict Control of Prices and the Consolidation of Negotiated Prices" of the State Council on December 7, 1980.

1. The retail prices for the industrial and agricultural commodities with state stipulated list prices shall all accord with the stipulations of the state and shall not be raised.

2. The prices of the Class 1 and Class 2 agricultural and sideline products permitted to be purchased or sold through negotiations after the fulfilment of plans shall accord with the ranges of negotiated prices stipulated by the departments in charge, to be as low as possible.

3. The negotiated prices of Class 3 commodities permitted to be purchased or sold through negotiations shall be consulted about by both purchasing and selling parties in accordance with the above pricing principles, and the levels of the negotiated prices shall be lower than the country fair prices at that time and in that locality. At present, they shall be sold at the negotiated selling prices of December 7, 1980, which can only be reduced and shall not be raised. If they have no negotiated selling prices on

December 7, 1980, their prices shall be rationally fixed in the light of the actual levels of negotiated prices in 1980 and the too high negotiated prices of a small number of understocked commodities shall be reduced. The prices of different enterprises shall be permitted to be different for the same market and the same category so as to be helpful to competition.

4. No Class 1 and Class 2 industrial products for daily use shall be involved in the purchase or sale at negotiated prices.

5. The standards of commission for the commodities sold on commission shall be controlled as low as possible. Different standards of commission shall be prescribed according to different commodities and the difficulty or ease of their sales and specific standards shall be worked out by the supply and marketing cooperative at the level of the province, municipality or autonomous region; the differences between the purchase and the sale of the commodities sold for themselves shall be a little lower than or equal to those of specialized corporations.

6. Qualitative, regional and seasonal price differences shall be put into practice.

A trade house shall observe the state limits of authority in the administration of prices and subject itself to the supervision and examination by senior supply and marketing cooperative and price department.

IV Operating Modes

A trade house shall center its business on four operations on commission with proper development of self-managing business.

The operating modes of a trade house shall be flexible and multi-purpose. For example, to organize the direct dealings between the producing and selling parties or between the supply and demanding parties so as to conclude transactions directly; make the best possible use of letters and telegrams to entrust to others or to act as the agent for the purchase or sale; energetically create favourable conditions for handling the storage, transportation and processing on commission so as to facilitate the circulation of commodities; make a good job of the display of samples so as to be convenient for the comparison of quality and prices and for the conclusion of transactions according to the samples; hold commodity exchanges and commodity fairs well so as to stimulate the interchange of goods and materials; set up retail commodity salesrooms or special counters (mainly selling agricultural, sideline, native and special products) so as to expand purchase and sale; develop necessary self-managing buying and selling business so as to enrich the supplies in the market and keep down prices on the principles of voluntary participation and mutual benefit; energetically develop the joint operations between trade houses, between a trade house and a corporation, between a trade house and a grass-roots supply and marketing cooperative or between a trade house and an industrial enterprise; and organize commodities for grass-roots supply and marketing cooperatives in the form of joint purchase and separate sales.

V Administrative Structure

1. The limits of administrative divisions shall be broken down and trade houses shall be set up in large or medium cities, at the hubs of communications and at the collecting and distributing centres of agricultural and sideline products in accordance with economic regions and actual needs and on the principles of economy and rationality.

2. It is generally suitable for a trade house to engage itself in multi-dealing. If several setups are repeatedly established in the same city with the same scopes of dealing, they shall be properly regulated or a joint operation between them shall be put into practice.

3. In a large or medium city, a trust section or a trust service shall be set up in a specialized corporation; a specialized trade house shall also be set up if it is really necessary. In order to organize the direct meetings between the producing and selling parties of dried and fresh fruits, fruit exchange markets or fruit trade houses shall be set up according to local conditions.

4. In a county where establishing a trade house is necessary, it is better to set it up in a multiple-dealing character. Its setup shall be independent and its accounting shall also be independent in accordance with the conditions of each place; it may also combine with a certain specialized corporation, but its accounting shall be separate. No trade house shall be set up in a county with small volume of business.

5. In general, a grass-roots supply and marketing cooperative shall not set up a trade

house. If trade houses must be set up in a very small number of larger collecting and distributing centres of goods and materials, their setups must be approved by the provincial supply and marketing cooperatives.

6. A trade house in each area or of each type shall be approved by the provincial supply and marketing cooperative and obtain a business licence issued by the local administration for industry and commerce before commencing business.

VI Leadership and Administration

1. The supply and marketing cooperative at each level shall strengthen its leadership over trade houses. Each supply and marketing cooperative of the province, municipality or autonomous region shall have a deputy director to be put in charge of the work of trade houses and there shall be appropriate setup and personnel to take charge of routine work, mainly to investigate and find out the situations, have a good grasp of guiding principles and policies, sum up and exchange experience and direct the trade of trade houses.

2. A multi-dealing trade house shall be treated equally to a specialized corporation of the same level. All documents concerning policy matters shall be issued to trade houses; trade houses shall be represented at meetings which require their attendance.

3. The establishment of trade houses shall be done well. The leading group of a trade house shall be well provided, staff members shall be strengthened, serving personnel shall be trained, the political and ideological work of trade house cadres and staff shall be done well and the trade house shall be helped to settle such actual difficulties as insufficient housing, equipment or funds. Various necessary rules and regulations shall be established and perfected.

4. The business of trade houses shall be included in financial accounting and statistical systems. Accounting headings and statistical report forms shall be prescribed for the business of trade houses through investigations and studies so as to duly and accurately reflect the operating results of trade houses.

VII Supplementary Provisions

The supply and marketing cooperative of each province, muncipality or autonomous region shall act accordingly in the light of the local actual conditions in accordance with these Provisional Procedures for the Administration. If the relevant provisions of the Federation in the past go against these Procedures, these Procedures shall be implemented. If the State Council transmits any relevant provisions in future, the provisions of the State Council shall be regarded as standard.

10 TRADE MARKS AND ADVERTISEMENT CONTROL

PROVISIONAL REGULATIONS FOR ADVERTISEMENT CONTROL

(Promulgated by the State Council on February 6, 1982)

Article 1 The present Regulations are formulated with a view to strengthening advertisement control, correctly bringing into play the media role of advertisements in promoting production, expanding circulation, directing consumption, enlightening the economy, offering conveniences to the life of the people and developing international economic relations and trade, so as better to serve the socialist material civilization and spirit.

Article 2 Advertisements by all enterprises and institutions for marketing commodities or offering paid labour and services that appear in newspapers, journals and films or are broadcast over the radio or television or erected or posted in public places, all come under the control of these Regulations.

Article 3 The advertisment control organizations are the General Administration for Industry and Commerce and the directors of administration for industry and commerce at all levels in local districts.

Article 4 Specialized advertising companies, enterprises and institutions which handle advertisements or serve as advertising agents (hereinafter called "advertising units") must apply for registration and business licences according to the Regulation for the Registration and Control of Industrial and Commercial Enterprises. No one is allowed to handle advertisements without going through the registration procedure or without approval of the application for registration.

Units that handle advertisements for foreign enterprises must be examined and approved by the commission for import and export affairs at the level of the province, autonomous region or municipality under the direct jurisdiction of the Central Government or their superior.

Individuals are not allowed to engage in advertising business.

Article 5 Units that apply for the publishing, broadcasting, erecting or posting of their advertisements (hereinafter called "advertisers") must be enterprises having business licences or units established with government approval.

Article 6 Advertisements must be clearly understood and truthful. No falsehood whatsoever is permitted to cheat or deceive the users and consumers.

Disposal of defective products, trial-manufactured or test-marketing products must be clearly stated in the advertisements to avoid confusion.

Article 7 Advertisers shall present their certificates when applying for publishing, broadcasting, erecting or posting of their advertisements:

(1) Advertisements on medicines and food products must have certification of public health authorities;

(2) Advertisements on weights and measuring instruments must have certification of metrological organs;

(3) Advertisements on prize-winning commodities must have certification of prize-giving institutions;

(4) Advertisements on commodities with trademarks must have certification of trademark registration;

(5) Advertisements stating passing of quality standards must have certification of quality control and inspection authorities.

Advertising units are required to examine the above-mentioned certification papers conscientiously and explain it in the advertisements.

Article 8 Advertisements containing any of the following contents are prohibited from publishing, broadcasting, erecting or posting:

(1) Violating government policies or orders;

(2) Damaging the dignity of the nationalities in China;

(3) Containing reactionary, obscene, unsightly or superstitious content;

(4) Libelous publicity;

(5) Violating government security regulations:

Article 9 The advertising units must see to it that the arrangement for the layout, position, time, place and form of the advertisements to be published, broadcast, erected or posted conform with the government regulations concerning publicity and economic policies.

Monopoly or inproper competition in advertising is prohibited.

Article 10 The posting of advertisements

outdoors must abide by the regulations of the city administration authorities and advertisement control organs, and must not hinder traffic or impair the appearance of a city or the picturesque environment of scenic spots. The erecting of huge billboards must be approved by the city administration authorities.

No advertisement is allowed to be posted or erected on government buildings, memorial buildings or key sites of relics under state protection.

Article 11 The standards of advertisement charges shall be unified if such standards have been set by the local administrations for industry and commerce; the standards shall be decided upon by the advertising units for the time being where there are no unified standards, but they should be reported to the local administrations for industry and commerce for record.

Article 12 The advertising units and the advertisers shall sign contracts defining their respective responsibilities in respect of the publishing, broadcasting, and posting of advertisements.

Article 13 Where the provisions of the present regulations are violated, liabilities shall be held by the implicated party as follows:

The advertising unit is liable for the violation of Article 5;

The advertiser is liable for the violation of Article 6, and the advertising unit is also liable if it is aware of the falsehood contained in the advertisement;

The advertising unit and the advertiser are jointly liable for the violation of Articles 7 and 8.

Article 14 A warning shall be given or a fine imposed by the administration for industry and commerce on the advertiser who has violated the provisions of these regulations according to the facts and circumstances of the case; a penalty – warning, fine, suspension of business or revocation of the business license – shall be imposed on the advertising unit that has violated the provisions of these regulations, according to the gravity of the case.

Advertisers who have violated the provisions of these regulations and caused losses to users and consumers shall be obliged to compensate for the losses.

Serious violations of the provisions of these regulations with grave consequences shall be dealt with by the people's court according to law.

Article 15 All advertising units must pay taxes on time in line with the relevant state regulations.

Article 16 The masses have the right to supervise and the right to report or expose to the administrations for industry and commerce those advertisers and advertising units that have violated the provisions of these regulations.

Article 17 Applications by foreign enterprises for publishing, broadcasting, posting of advertisements on the territory of the People's Republic of China shall be controlled with reference to the provisions of these regulations.

Article 18 Detailed rules for the implementation of these regulations shall be formulated by the General Administration for Industry and Commerce.

Article 19 These regulations shall go into effect on May 1, 1982.

THE TRADEMARK LAW OF THE PEOPLE'S REPUBLIC OF CHINA

(Adopted at the 24th session of the Standing Committee of the Fifth National People's Congress on August 23, 1982)

Chapter I General Provisions

Article 1 This law is enacted for the purposes of improving the administration of trademarks, of protecting the exclusive right to use a trademark, and of encouraging producers to guarantee the quality of their goods and maintain the reputation of their trademarks, with a view to protecting consumer interests and to promoting the development of socialist commodity economy.

Article 2 The Trademark Office of the Administrative Authority of Industry and Commerce under the State Council shall be responsible for the registration and administrative control of trademarks throughout the country.

Article 3 Registered trademark means a trademark which has been approved and registered by the Trademark Office. The trademark registrant shall enjoy an exclusive right to use the trademark, (which right shall be) protected by law.

Article 4 Any enterprise, institution, or individual producer or trader intending to acquire the exclusive right to use a trademark for the goods produced, manufactured, processed, selected or marketed by it or him shall file an application for the registration of the trademark with the Trademark Office.

Article 5 Where the State prescribes that certain kinds of goods must bear a registered trademark, registration of a trademark must be applied for in respect of such goods. Where no trademark registration has been granted, such goods shall not be sold in the market.

Article 6 Any user of a trademark shall be responsible for the quality of the goods in respect of which the trademark is used. The administrative authorities for industry and commerce at all levels shall, through the administrative control of trademarks, exercise supervision over the quality of the goods and shall stop any practice that deceives consumers.

Article 7 Any word, design, or their combination used as a trademark, must be distinctive in character so that it will be distinguishable. Where a registered trademark is used, it should carry the indication "Registered Trademark" or a sign indicating that it is registered.

Article 8 In trademarks, the following words or designs shall not be used:

(1) those identical with or similar to the state name, national flag, national emblem, military flag, or decorations of the People's Republic of China;

(2) those identical with or similar to the state names, national flags, national emblems, or military flags of foreign countries;

(3) those identical with or similar to the flags, emblems, or names of international intergovernmental organizations;

(4) those identical with or similar to the symbols, or names of the Red Cross or the Red Crescent;

(5) those relating to generic names or designs of the goods in respect of which the trademark is used;

(6) those having direct reference to the quality, main raw materials, function, use, weight, quantity or other features of the goods in respect of which the trademark is used;

(7) those having the nature of race discrimination;

(8) those having the nature of exaggeration and deceit in advertising goods;

(9) those detrimental to socialist morals or customs, or having other undesirable influences.

Article 9 Any foreigner or foreign enterprise applying for the registration of a trademark in China shall file an application in accordance with any agreement concluded between the People's Republic of China and the country to which the applicant belongs, or according to the international treaty to which both countries are parties, or on the basis of the principle of reciprocity.

Article 10 Any foreigner or foreign enterprise applying for the registration of a trademark, or dealing with other matters concerning a trademark in China, shall entrust the organization designated by the state to act on his or its behalf.

Chapter II Application for Trademark Registration

Article 11 Any application for the registration of a trademark shall, indicate in a form, in accordance with the prescribed classification of goods, the class of the goods and the designation of the goods in respect of which the trademark is intended to be used.

Article 12 Where any applicant intends to use the same trademark for goods in different classes, a separate application for registration shall be filed in respect of each class of the prescribed classification of goods.

Article 13 Where a registered trademark is intended to be used in respect of other goods of the same class, a new application for registration shall be filed.

Article 14 Where any word and/or design of a registered trademark is to be altered, a new registration shall be applied for.

Article 15 Where, after the registration of a trademark, the name, address or other registered matters concerning the registrant change, an application regarding the change shall be filed.

Chapter III Examination for and Approval of Trademark Registration

Article 16 Where the trademark for which registration has been applied for is in conformity with the relevant provisions of this law, the Trademark Office shall, after examination, preliminarily approve the trademark and publish (it).

Article 17 Where the trademark for which registration has been applied for is not in conformity with the relevant provisions of this law, or where it is identical with or similar to the trademark of another person which, in respect of the same or similar goods, has been registered or preliminarily approved after examination, the Trademark Office shall refuse the application and shall not publish (the said trademark).

Article 18 Where two or more applicants apply for the registration of identical or similar trademarks for the same or similar goods, the preliminary approval, after examination, and the publication shall be made for the trademark which was first filed. Where applications are filed on the same day, the preliminary approval, after examination, and the publication shall be made for the trademark which was the earliest used, and the application of the others shall be refused and (their trademarks) shall not be published.

Article 19 Any person may, within three months from the date of the publication, file an opposition against the trademark which, after examination, has been preliminarily approved. If no opposition is filed, or if it is decided that the opposition is not justified, registration shall be approved, a trademark registration certificate shall be issued and (the trademark) shall be published. If it is decided that the opposition is justified, no registration shall be approved.

Article 20 The Trademark Review and Adjudication Board, established under the administrative authorities for industry and commerce under the State Council, shall be responsible for handling trademark disputes.

Article 21 Where the application for registration of a trademark is refused and no publication of the trademark is made, the Trademark Office shall notify the applicant in writing. Where the applicant is dissatisfied, he may, within fifteen days from the receipt of the notification, apply for a review. The Trademark Review and Adjudication Board shall make a final decision and notify the applicant in writing.

Article 22 Where an opposition is filed against the trademark which, after examination, has been preliminarily approved and published, the Trademark Office shall hear the opponent and the applicant state facts and grounds and shall, after investigation and verification, make a decision. Where any party is dissatisfied, it may, within fifteen days from the receipt of the notification, apply for review, and the Trademark Review and Adjudication Board shall make a final decision, and notify the opponent and the applicant in writing.

Chapter IV Renewal, Assignment and Licensing of Registered Trademarks

Article 23 The period of validity of a registered trademark shall be ten years beginning from the date of the approval of the registration.

Article 24 Where (the registrant) intends to continue to use the registered trademark beyond the expiration of the period of validity, an application for renewal of the registration shall be made within six months before the said expiration. Where no such application could be filed within the said period, an extension period of six months may be allowed. If no application is filed by the expiration of the extended period, the registered trademark shall be cancelled.

The period of validity of each renewal of registration shall be ten years.

Any renewal of registration shall be published after approval.

Article 25 Where a registered trademark is assigned, the assignor and assignee shall jointly file an application with the Trademark Office. The assignee shall guarantee the quality of the goods in respect of which the registered trademark is used.

The assignment of the registered trademark shall be published after approval.

Article 26 Any trademark registrant may, by signing a trademark license-contract, authorize other persons to use his registered trademark. The licensor shall supervise the quality of the goods in respect of which the licensee uses his registered trademark, and the licensee shall guarantee the quality of the goods in respect of which the registered trademark is used.

The trademark license contract shall be submitted to the Trademark Office for filing.

Chapter V Adjudication of Disputes Concerning Registered Trademarks

Article 27 Any person disputing a registered trademark may, within one year from the date of approval of the trademark registration, apply to the Trademark Review and Adjudication Board for adjudication.

The Trademark Review and Adjudication Board shall, after the receipt of the application for adjudication, notify the interested parties and request them to lodge their replies within a specified period.

Article 28 Where the trademark, before being approved for registration, has been opposed and adjudicated, no application for adjudication, based on the same facts and grounds, may be made.

Article 29 After the Trademark Review and Adjudication Board has made the final decision maintaining or cancelling the disputed registered trademark, it shall notify the interested parties in writing.

Chapter VI Administrative Control of the Use of Trademarks

Article 30 Where any person who uses the registered trademark commits any of the following, the Trademark Office shall order him to rectify (the situation) within a specified period or shall cancel his registered trademark:

(1) where any word, design, or their combination, of the registered trademark is altered unilaterally;

(2) where the name, address or other registered matters concerning the registrant of a registered trademark are changed unilaterally;

(3) where the registered trademark is assigned unilaterally;

(4) where the registered trademark has ceased to be used for three consecutive years.

Article 31 Where the registered trademark is used in respect of goods which have been roughly or poorly manufactured, or where inferior goods are substituted for superior goods to deceive consumers, the administrative authorities for industry and commerce at all levels shall, according to the circumstances, order the rectification (of the situation) within a specified period, and may, in addition, circulate a notice of criticism or impose a fine, or the Trademark Office may cancel the registered trademark.

Article 32 Where the registered trademark is cancelled or has expired and not been renewed, the Trademark Office shall not approve, during one year from the date of the cancellation or the removal (on account of expiration), applications for registration of trademarks identical with or similar to the said trademark.

Article 33 In the case of any person violating the provisions of Article 5 of this law, the local administrative authorities for industry and commerce shall order him to file an application for registration within a specified period and may, in addition, impose a fine.

Article 34 Where any person who uses an unregistered trademark commits any of the following, the local administrative authorities for industry and commerce shall stop the use of the trademark, order him to rectify (the situation) within a specified period, and may, in addition, circulate a notice of criticism or impose a fine:

(1) where the trademark is falsely represented as registered;

(2) where any provision of Article 8 of this law is violated;

(3) where the manufacture is rough or poor, or where inferior goods are substituted for superior goods to deceive the consumers.

Article 35 Any party dissatisfied with the decision of the Trademark Office to cancel the registered trademark may apply for review within fifteen days from the receipt of the (corresponding) notice. The Trademark Review and Adjudication Board shall make a final decision and notify the applicant in writing.

Article 36 Any party dissatisfied with the decision of an administrative authority for industry and commerce imposing a fine under the provisions of Article 31, Article 33 or Article 34 may institute proceedings with the people's court within fifteen days from the receipt of the (corresponding) notice. If no proceedings are instituted (and compliance with the decision is not made) by the expiration of the said period, the administrative authority for industry and commerce concerned may ask the people's court to enforce execution.

Chapter VII Protection of the Exclusive Right to Use Registered Trademarks

Article 37 The exclusive right to use a registered trademark is limited to the trademark which has been approved for registration and to the goods in respect of which the use of the trademark has been approved.

Article 38 Any of the following acts shall be an infringement of the exclusive right to use a registered trademark:

(1) to use a trademark which is identical with or similar to the registered trademark in respect of the same or similar goods without the authorization of the proprietor of the registered trademark;

(2) to make or sell, without authorization, representations of the registered trademark of another person;

(3) to cause other damages to the exclusive right to use the registered trademark of another person.

Article 39 In the case of any of the acts infringing the exclusive right to use a registered trademark as provided for in Article 38 of this law, the party whose right was infringed may request the administrative authorities for industry and commerce, at or above the county level, of the location (domicile or establishment) of the infringer to handle (the matter). The administrative authority for industry and commerce concerned shall have the power to order the infringer to stop the infringing act immediately and to compensate the party whose right was infringed for the damages suffered. The amount of compensation shall be the profit which the infringer has earned through the infringement during the period of the infringement or the damages that the party whose right was infringed has suffered through the infringement during the period of the infringement. If the circumstances are serious, the said authority may, in addition, impose a fine. Any dissatisfied party may institute proceedings with the people's court within fifteen days from the receipt of the notice. If no proceedings are instituted and compliance with the decision is not made by the expiration of the said period, the administrative authority for industry and commerce concerned may ask the people's court to enforce execution.

Where the exclusive right to use the registered trademark was infringed, the party whose right was infringed may institute proceedings directly with the people's court.

Article 40 Any party who passes off (a trademark as) a registered trademark of another person – including any party that makes or sells, without authorization, representations of the registered trademark of another person – shall compensate for the damages suffered by the party whose right was infringed and additionally shall be imposed a fine; furthermore, any person directly responsible (for the passing off) shall be prosecuted, according to law, by the judicial organs in respect of criminal responsibilities.

Chapter VIII Supplementary Provisions

Article 41 Any application for trademark registration and any other proceeding in trademark matters shall be subject to the payment of a fee. The rate of the fees shall be prescribed separately.

Article 42 The implementing regulations of this law shall be drawn up by the Administrative Authority for Industry and Commerce under the State Council. They shall enter into force after they have been submitted to and approved by the State Council.

Article 43 This law shall enter into force on March 1, 1983. The "Regulations Governing Trademarks" promulgated by the State Council on April 10, 1963, shall be abrogated on the same date, and any other provisions concerning trademarks contrary to this law shall cease to be effective at the same time.

Trademarks registered before this law enters into force shall continue to be valid.

11 ECONOMIC CONTRACT

A JOINT CIRCULAR OF THE STATE ECONOMIC COMMISSION, THE GENERAL ADMINISTRATION OF INDUSTRY AND COMMERCE AND THE PEOPLE'S BANK OF CHINA ON A NUMBER OF QUESTIONS REGARDING THE SUPERVISION OF ECONOMIC CONTRACTS

(August 8, 1979)

To the Administrations of Industry and Commerce, the Economic Commissions and Branches of the People's Bank of All Provinces, Municipalities and Autonomous Regions:

To practise the contract system, i.e., to stipulate in the form of a contract the details of contact and coordination between enterprises in the production, supply, shipment and marketing of goods, to stipulate each other's economic commitments and responsibilities and to seriously carry out these stipulations, is an important measure for raising the level of management of enterprises, strengthening business accounting, guaranteeing the fulfilment of the state plan and managing the economy by economic measures. This system should be actively pursued in the realization of the Four Modernizations in socialist construction. In order to strengthen the supervision of contracts, to urge the enterprises to execute their contracts strictly and to defend the just interests of both sides, the following circular on a number of major questions regarding the supervision of economic contracts is made in the light of the documents concerned as issued by the Central Committee of the Chinese Communist Party and the State Council:

1. In accordance with the State Council Document No. 102 (1979), the economic contracts on goods supply, production and sales, processing, shipment, etc. are to be supervised by the following authorities on the basis of division of work:

The economic contracts between units belonging to the same department or economic sector, such as industry, agriculture, material administration, communications and transport, commerce (which includes foreign trade, grain and supply and marketing cooperatives, here and below), are to be supervised by the authorities in charge of that department or sector.

Economic contracts between different industrial departments; between industrial enterprises and material administration, building industry and agricultural departments; between industrial, agricultural, commercial, material administration and building units and communications and transport departments; as well as those between industrial, communications and transport departments and government organs, mass organizations, army units and institutions, are to be supervised by economic commissions at various levels or by other corresponding authorities.

Economic contracts between different commercial departments, between commercial units and units of industrial and agricultural departments as well as government organs, mass organizations, army units and institutions are to be supervised by the administrations of industry and commerce at various levels.

2. Before signing a contract, the enterprises or units concerned must conduct realistic and full consultations on an equal footing on the basis of the policies, decrees and laws and plans of the state and in the spirit of the principles of producing according to needs, ensuring supplies and promoting development of the national economy. A contract must have specific details, clear commitments and responsibilities of each side and unequivocal wording.

The main contents of a contract should include: name of the product, its model, specification, quality, quantity, measuring unit, the technical specification of industrial products, package requirements and the supply and retrieval of packing materials, means of delivery and destination, shipment, date of delivery (and taking delivery) of the goods, the price of the product, modes of settlement of accounts, settling bank, the bank account number of the units, economic commitments and responsibilities, etc.

3. For the guarantee of contracts, we do not make any unified stipulations for the time being. The contract supervisory authorities of each province, municipality and autonomous region can make their own decisions in this connection in accordance with actual conditions. But if both the supplier and buyer sides of a contract demand a guarantee, the contract should be guaranteed.

For all the guaranteed contracts, the guarantor authorities should be responsible for the check-up of the contracts' legality and their main contents, and those which do not conform to the policies or stipulations of the state should be corrected.

The guarantor authorities should be the contract supervisory authorities of the region where the supplier side of the contract is located.

4. Once a contract is signed, it has a legal effect. Both sides must scrupulously keep their word and strictly execute the contract. If any side does not execute the contract seriously and causes losses to the other side, it should bear the economic and legal responsibilities.

5. Once a contract is signed, neither side can change it or terminate it on its own authority. If it is necessary to make any changes or terminate the contract, it should be agreed on by both sides through consultations and an agreement should be signed on the amendment to the contract or on its termination. If an important product controlled by the state plan is involved, such an agreement should be reported for the record to the authorities in charge of the product; if a guaranteed contract is involved, it should be reported for the record without exception to the guarantor authorities. Before such an agreement is signed, the original contract remains valid and neither side can refuse to execute it on any excuse. Any losses incurred by the amendment or termination of the contract should be compensated on a fair and reasonable basis by the side which asked for the change or termination.

6. If any disputes arise during the execution of the contract, the two contracting sides should actively consult each other and do their best to find out a reasonable solution. If they fail to agree with each other, any side may apply for arbitration to the Economic Commission (or corresponding authorities) or the Administration of Industry and Commerce of the county or the district, in the case of a big or medium-sized city, where the other side is located, in accordance with the division of work among the contract supervisory authorities. If any side refuses to accept the ruling, it may apply to the next higher supervisory authorities for reconsideration within ten days after the day the notice on the ruling is received. If it still remains unconvinced by the reconsidered ruling, it may sue at the people's court within ten days after the day the notice on the reconsidered ruling is received. In case one side concerned does not apply for reconsideration or does not sue at the court within the ten-day period while refusing to execute the ruling, the People's Bank should transfer the sum of money and the contract-breaking side should pay for the goods or compensate for the losses to the other side's account in accordance with the ruling notice.

For disputes on economic contracts between units belonging to the same department or sector, the mediation and arbitration procedure can be decided by the authorities in charge of that department or sector.

During the period of mediation and arbitration, the arbitrating authorities, in the light of the actual situation, may notify both contractors to stop executing the contract for the time being.

7. The People's Bank is to supervise all enterprises' execution of their economic contracts by means of credit and settlement management. The People's Bank will gradually take the measure of granting loans to enterprises in accordance with their economic contracts, on the basis of the state plan. The rules of settlement must be conscientiously followed and settlement discipline strictly adhered to. Both contractors must settle the account in accordance with the mode of settlement specified in the economic contract, and the bank should handle acceptance or refusal of payments, or deduct the required sum of money from the account of the enterprise which delays payment for the goods or payment of compensation, in accordance with the specific regulations of the rules of settlement.

8. The money paid in compensation caused by an enterprise's own errors should not be included in the cost of production of the goods, but should be paid out of the enterprise's share of the profits or out of its own funds. If a serious violation of this rule occurs, a fine will be deducted from the wages of those who are responsible for it, and an investigation into their administrative or legal responsibilities should be made.

For any failure in executing the contract caused by force majeure or other reasons which are really not brought about by the enterprise itself, the enterprise can be freed from economic responsibilities when the above causes are proved through investigation by the arbitrating authorities. The authorities in charge can take other measures to recoup as much of those economic losses as possible.

9. In order to supervise enterprises and to encourage them to execute their contracts conscientiously, the supervisory authorities have the right to verify both the statistics and data concerned and the actual execution of the contract. If problems that hamper the execution of the contract are discovered, the departments concerned should be asked to take effective steps to solve the problem in time. Any violations of the

law – such as performing shoddy work or using inferior materials, making profits by acting as a broker, selling a contract at a profit, or purposely avoiding supervision – should be put to the Administration of Industry and Commerce for investigation and punishment. If it is a serious case, it should be handed over to the judiciary for punishment by law.

10. Economic contracts are major business documents. All enterprises should establish files, compile ledgers and keep them properly. For a guaranteed contract, the enterprise should give a copy to the guarantor authorities for special filing.

11. In their work, the contract supervisory authorities should closely cooperate with judicial, planning and other business departments concerned. Necessary liaison systems should be established for exchanging information, coordinating actions and strengthening collaboration.

12. All parts of the country are asked to adopt the above points as experiments, to sum up their experiences and to offer suggestions for further amendments.

THE ECONOMIC CONTRACTS LAW OF THE PEOPLE'S REPUBLIC OF CHINA

(Adopted at the Fourth Session of the Fifth National People's Congress on December 13, 1981)

Chapter I General Principles

Article 1 This Law is formulated to protect the legal rights and interests of the parties to the economic contracts, safeguard the socioeconomic order, improve economic results, guarantee the implementation of the state plans and promote the progress of the socialist modernization program.

Article 2 The economic contract is an agreement between legal persons specifying their mutual relations, rights and obligations in order to realize certain economic aims.

Article 3 Economic contracts shall be in writing except those completed instantly. Documents, telegrams and charts concerning amendments to the contract and agreed thereon between the parties form part of the contract.

Article 4 Economic contracts must be made in accordance with state laws and in conformity with the requirements of state policies and plans. No units or individuals are allowed to use contracts for illegal activities, disrupt economic order, undermine state plans, or damage national and social public interest to gain illegal income.

Article 5 Economic contracts must be made in the principle of equality and mutual benefit, agreement through consultation and compensation of equal value. Neither party is allowed to impose its will on the other, and no unit or individual is allowed to interfere illegally.

Article 6 An economic contract, made according to law, is legally binding. The parties must perform the obligations in the contract, and neither party is allowed to alter or rescind the contract unilaterally.

Article 7 The following economic contracts are null and void:

a) Contracts in violation of laws, government policies and plans;

b) Contracts signed by means of deception and coercion;

c) Contracts signed by agents exceeding their authority or contracts signed in the name of the represented with themselves or with others they represent;

d) Economic contracts infringing on national interests or social public interests.

Invalid contracts are void from the time of their creation. If the nullified part of an economic contract does not affect the validity of remaining parts, the latter is still valid.

The right to nullify an economic contract rests with the contract control organs and the people's courts.

Article 8 Provisions of this Law apply to contracts on purchasing and marketing, subcontracting for construction projects, undertaking processing, goods transport, power supply and use, storage, property lease, loan, property insurance, scientific and technological cooperation and other economic contracts.

Chapter II The Establishment and Performance of Economic Contracts

Article 9 An economic contract is made when both parties reach agreement through consultation on the principal clauses of the contract.

Article 10 An agent signing a contract on behalf of his principal must obtain in advance the proof of appointment and sign the contract in the name of his principal within the limits of his appointment so as to bind his principal with the rights and obligations of the contract.

Article 11 For economic dealings involving products and items included in the state mandatory plan, the economic contracts must be signed according to the quotas set by the state; if no agreement is reached at the time of the signing, the matter shall be dealt with by the planning organ superior to both parties. As for economic dealings involving products and items included in the state guidance plan, the economic contracts shall be signed according to the actual conditions of the units concerned in reference to the quotas set by the state.

Article 12 An economic contract shall include the following:

a) Objectives (such as goods, labour service, engineering project, etc.);
b) Quantity and quality;
c) Cost of remuneration;
d) Time limit, place and form of compliance;
e) Liability for breach of the contract.

Clauses which must be included according to provisions of law or the character of the economic contract and mandatory clauses of one party are also the main clauses of an economic contract.

Article 13 Where the fulfillment of an economic contract is by payment of money, it shall be calculated and paid in Renminbi, except otherwise governed by law.

Unless authorized by the state to offer payment by cash, all settlements must be effected through the bank.

Article 14 One party may pay deposit money to the other party. The deposit money should be refunded or offset when the economic contract is carried out.

When the party paying the deposit money fails to fulfill the contract, he shall not be entitled to demand the refund of the deposit money. If the recipient of the deposit money fails to fulfill the contract, he shall return the same twice as much.

Article 15 Where one party to the economic contract demands guaranty, it may be guaranteed by a guarantor unit. The guarantor unit is the one who guarantees one party to the contract in fulfilling the contract. When the guaranteed party fails to fulfill the contract, the guarantor unit shall be held liable to compensate for the loss.

Article 16 After the economic contract is nullified, the party shall return to the other party the property he has obtained under the said contract. The defaulting party shall compensate for the loss incurred therefrom to the other party; if both parties are in the wrong, each shall bear his due responsibility.

Where a contract infringes on national or social public interests, if both parties thereto are intentional, the property they have obtained or are going to obtain shall be turned over to the state treasury. If only one party is intentional, he shall return the property he has gotten from the other party to the latter; the property which the innocent party has obtained or is going to obtain from his counterpart shall be turned over to the state treasury.

Article 17 The quantity and quality of product, the quality of packing, the price of the product and the time limit for delivery in a purchasing and marketing contract (including contracts of supply, purchasing, forward purchase, combination of purchasing and marketing, cooperation, regulation, etc.), shall be performed under the following provisions:

a) The quantity of product shall be agreed in accordance with the plan approved by the state and the superior department in charge; if there is no such approved plan, it shall be consulted, agreed and signed by the supplier and the buyer. The quantity of product shall be measured in accordance with state regulations or the regulations of the department in charge; if there are no such regulations, the quantity can be measured in ways agreed on between the supplier and the buyer.

b) The quality of product and the quality of packing shall be agreed in accordance with state standards or professional standards if there are such standards; if there are no state standards or professional standards, they can be agreed in accordance with the standards of the department in charge; where the parties have special demands, they shall be agreed by the two parties through consultation.

The supplier shall be responsible for the quality of product and its packaging and shall provide the necessary technical data or sample for examination and approval.

The methods of examination and quarantine of product quality shall be carried out in accordance with the relevant regulations approved by the State Council; if there are no such regulations, they can be determined by the parties through consultation.

c) The price of the product shall be agreed in accordance with the price fixed by the price control departments at various levels (including the state-set price and floating price). If policy allows the price to be negotiated, it can be decided upon by the parties through consultation.

Where the state-set price is adopted and if the state price is adjusted within the time limit for delivery as stipulated in the contract, the price so calculated shall be in accordance with the price at the time of delivery. Where the delivery is overdue, the original price shall stand if the price rises; and the new price shall stand if the price drops. Where the pick-up of goods or the payment is overdue, the new price shall stand if the price rises; and the original price shall stand if the price drops. Where floating price or negotiated price is adopted, the price set in the contract shall stand.

d) The time limit for delivery (pick-up) of goods shall be performed as stipulated in the contract. If any party wishes to deliver (pick up) goods ahead of time or postpone it, agreement should be reached in advance and carried out accordingly.

Article 18 Contracts on undertaking construction projects must be agreed in accordance with the procedure set by the state and the state-approved investment plan, planned work quotas and other documents.

As for the undertaking of a construction project, including surveying, designing, building and erection, an overall contract can be agreed by a general contractor with the construction unit, or separate contracts can be agreed respectively by several contractors with the construction unit.

Surveying and designing contracts shall include such clauses as the time when the parties submit the survey report, basic data on the designs and design documents (including cost estimates), the quality requirements for the designs and other conditions for cooperation.

Building and construction contracts shall explicitly include such clauses as the outline of the project, the construction period, the time during intervals to hand over the project for commencement of construction, the quality and cost of construction, the time to hand over the technical data, the responsibility for supplying the materials and equipment, appropriations and settlement, the inspection and approval of the completed project, and the mutual cooperation between the parties.

The inspection and approval of the completed project shall be based on the contract drawings and instructions, the inspection and approval standards and quality control standards issued by the state.

Article 19 A contract on contracted processing shall be agreed in accordance with the description of the article, the item and quality requirement of the principal and the contractor's capacity to process, manufacture and repair. Unless otherwise stipulated in the contract, the contractor must use his own equipment, technology and labor to complete the processing, manufacturing and repairing tasks, and shall not transfer the accepted task to a third party without the consent of the principal. The principal shall accept the finished article or work result by the contractor and pay the remuneration.

The contractor shall promptly examine the raw materials provided by the principal. If anything is found to be not in accord with the provisions of the contract, he shall immediately notify the principal to change or remedy it. The contractor shall not without authorization change the raw and processed materials supplied by the principal, nor secretly change the spare parts of the article to the repaired. Whoever is in breach thereof shall be responsible for compensation.

The contractor, when repairing houses or processing non-standard articles in batches, shall accept the necessary check and supervision by the principal, but the latter shall not impede the contractor's normal work. When the contractor undertakes reproduction, designing, translation and the testing or checking of the property of an article, he shall strictly keep if confidential if the principal so demands.

Where the principal fails to pick up the article made to order six months beyond the time limit, the contractor has the right to sell the article, and the proceeds thereof shall be deposited in the bank in the name of the principal after deducting the remuneration and the storage fee.

Article 20 Contracts on goods transport shall be signed according to the plan for goods transfer, the carrying capacity and the transportation plan. Contracts on the carriage of individual lots shall be signed according to the relevant state transport regulations.

Contracts involving mixed transport shall explicitly set out the responsibility of the two or more parties and the hand-over methods.

Where the consignment is required to be packed, the consignor must pack it according to the standards set by the state organization in charge; if there is no unified standard of packing, the consignor shall pack it according to the principle of ensuring the safety of the goods transport. Otherwise, the carrier may refuse to transport it.

Article 21 Contracts on the supply and use of electricity shall be signed according to the need of the user and the possible power supply. The contract shall include clauses to define the capacity and the volume of electricity, the time of use and responsibility for breach of contract, etc.

Article 22 Contracts for storage shall be signed by the parties through consultation according to the goods owner's storage plan and the keeper's storage capacity. The contract on storing an individual lot shall be signed according to the relevant storage regulations.

A storage contract shall include clauses to define the name, specifications, qualities and storage methods of the goods to be stored, the items and methods of inspection and acceptance, the check-in and check-out procedures, the spoilage standard and the handling of the spoilage, the cost and the method of settlement, responsibility for breach of contract, etc.

The keeper shall in accordance with the provisions of the contract inspect and accept the goods to be stored as to the exterior of the package, the type, quantity and quality of the goods. If anything is found to be not in accord with the provisions of the contract, he shall notify the goods owner in good time. After inspection and acceptance, the keeper shall be liable for compensation should the type, quantity or quality of the goods not conform with the contract provisions.

The goods owner shall provide the keeper with necessary data for the inspection of the goods. Otherwise, the keeper is not liable to compensate if the type, quantity or quality of the goods does not conform with the contract provisions.

Article 23 Contracts on property lease shall include clauses to define the name, quantity and use of the property leased, the lease period, the rent and the time limit for payment of the rent, the responsibility for maintaining the property during the lease period and responsibility for breach of contract, etc.

The owner shall hand over the leased property to the lessee for use according to the time and standards set in the contract. If the owner transfers the property right to a third party, the lease contract shall continue to be valid with the new owner of the property.

The lessee may, if the job requires, sublease the leased property to a third party, but he must obtain the consent of the owner in advance.

The rent shall be signed according to the unified state standards if there are such standards; if there are no such unified standards, it can be decided upon by the parties through consultation.

Article 24 Loan contracts shall be signed according to the credit plan approved by the state and the relevant regulations. The contract shall include clauses to define the sum of the loan, its use, time limit, interest rate, method of repayment, responsibility for breach of contract, etc.

The rate of interest on the loans is set by the state and is under the unified control of the People's Bank of China.

Article 25 Contracts on property insurance shall be signed in the form of insurance policy or certificate.

The insurance contract shall include clauses to define the insurance objective, the site (or the means of transport and voyage), the insured amount, the insurance liability, the exempted liability, the method of compensation, the method of payment of the premium and the insured period, etc.

The insured shall maintain the safety of the insured property. The insurer may inspect the safety of the insured property and, if any unsafe factor is found to be present, he shall promptly notify the insured to remove it.

Where a third party is liable to compensate for the loss of the insured property, should the insured demand it with the insurer, the latter may advance the compensation according to the contract provisions. But the insured must assign the right of claim to the insurer and assist the latter in claiming compensation from the third party.

Article 26 Contracts on scientific and technological cooperation (including scientific research, trial test, the marketing of the results, technological transfer, technical consultant services, etc.) shall be signed according to the plan of the superior department in charge or the relevant department. Where there is no such plan, they can be signed by the parties through consultation.

The contract on scientific and technological cooperation shall include clauses to define object of scientific and technological cooperation, technical and economic requirements, rate of progress, form of cooperation, cost and material estimates, remuneration and responsibility for breach of contract, etc.

Chapter III Alteration and Termination of Economic Contracts

Article 27 Economic contracts are permitted to be amended or terminated in any of the following circumstances:

a) Where both parties agreed through consultation, and it would not harm the national interest nor affect the implementation of the state plan;

b) Where the state plan on which the economic contract is based has been revised or cancelled;

c) Where one party is truly incapable of fulfilling the economic contract owing to closure, suspension of production or switch to another line of production;

d) Where the economic contract cannot be fulfilled owing to force majeure or because of outside unavoidable factors on one party not due to his error;

e) Where the breach of contract by one party makes it unnecessary to fulfill the economic contract.

When one party requests to alter or terminate

the economic contract, he shall promptly notify the other party. If the alteration or termination of an economic contract results in loss to the other party, the responsible party shall compensate for it except where the responsibility can be excused by law.

When one party merges or splits up, the party after the change shall undertake wholly or separately the obligation of fulfilling the contract and enjoy the due rights.

Article 28 The notice or agreement on the alteration or termination of an economic contract shall be in writing (including document, telegram, etc.). Before agreement is reached, the original economic contract continues to be valid.

Article 29 If the alteration or termination of an economic contract involves products or items covered by the state mandatory plan, it shall be reported to the relevant business department handing down the plan for approval before the signing of the agreement.

Article 30 Proposals for and replies to alteration or termination of economic contracts shall be made within the time limit agreed upon by the parties or within the time limit set by the relevant business department in charge.

Article 31 Economic contracts, once agreed, shall not be altered or terminated owing to a change in the principal or legal representative.

Chapter IV Responsibility for breach of Economic Contracts

Article 32 Where the fault of one party renders it impossible to carry out the economic contract entirely or partially, the defaulting party is liable for breach of contract. If it is due to faults of both parties, they shall respectively be responsible for breach of contract according to the actual circumstances.

Those directly responsible for major accidents or serious losses resulting from negligence, malfeasance or other illegal acts, shall be liable economically, administratively or even criminally.

Article 33 Where the economic contract is impossible to carry out entirely or partially owing to the fault of the superior leading organ or the competent business department, the organ or the department is responsible for breach of contract. The wrongful party shall first pay the money for breach of contract or the compensation money to the other party according to regulations, and then the responsible organ or department shall deal with the case.

Article 34 When one party cannot fulfill the economic contract due to force majeure, he shall promptly notify the other party of the reasons for failure to fulfill the economic contract or for the need to postpone its fulfillment or to carry out parts of the contract. Having obtained the certificate of the relevant department in charge, he may be allowed to postpone the fulfillment of the contract or carry out parts of it or not to fulfill it, and may be partially or entirely relieved of the responsibility for breach of contract according to the circumstances.

Article 35 When one party is in breach of the economic contract, he shall pay the money for breach of contract to the other party. If the loss to the other party due to the breach exceeds the amount of the damages for breach of contract, the breaching party shall also compensate for the deficit. The contract shall continue to be fulfilled if the other party so demands.

Article 36 The damages for breach of contract compensation money paid by an enterprise shall be covered by the enterprise fund, the retained share of profit or the apportioned part of profit or loss, and cannot be counted as cost; damages paid by an administrative or institutional unit shall be paid by the surplus from its apportioned budgetary expense.

Article 37 The damages for breach of contract or compensation money shall be paid within ten days after the responsibility is determined. Otherwise, it shall be dealt with as payment overdue. Neither party is allowed unilaterally to withhold goods or payment for goods to offset the money.

Article 38 Responsibility for breach of a contract on purchasing and marketing:

a) The supplier's responsibility:

1. The damages for breach of contract or compensation money shall be paid if the type, specifications, quantity and quality of the products and the quality of packing fail to meet the contract provisions or the goods are not delivered against the deadline set in the contract.

2. If the products are delivered to a wrong destination or consignee, the supplier shall pay the excess transportation and incidental expenses

therefrom in addition to shipping the products to the destination or consignee as provided for in the contract; if the delivery of goods is thus overdue, he shall pay damages for breach of contract for overdue delivery.

b) The buyer's responsibility:

1. Damages for breach of contract or compensation money shall be paid if goods are returned midway.

2. The damages for breach of contract shall be paid if the payment or the pick-up of goods is not carried out against the deadline set in the contract.

3. He shall pay the excess expenses resulting from his giving the wrong destination or changing the destination at the last moment.

Article 39 Responsibility for breach of contracts on undertaking construction projects.

a) The contractor's responsibility:

1. If a loss is caused by a prolonged building time due to the inferior quality of surveying and designing or the failure to present the survey and design documents against the deadline, the surveying and designing unit shall continue to complete the designs and reduce or remit the surveying and designing fees until the loss is compensated.

2. If the quality of the project does not conform with the contract provisions, the builder has the right to demand repairs or to do the work over again or rebuild it gratis within a definite limit. If the hand-over of the project is overdue because of the repairs or re-doing of the work or rebuilding, the contractor shall pay damages for breach of contract for exceeding the time limit.

3. The damages for breach of contract for exceeding the time limit shall be paid if the time to hand over the project does not meet the contract provisions.

b) The builder's responsibility:

1. If the raw and processed materials, equipment, grounds, funds and technical data are not provided according to the time and requirements set in the contract, the builder shall, in addition to extending the building time, compensate for the contractor's actual loss resulting from work stoppage or holdup.

2. If the project is stopped halfway or deferred, the builder shall take measures to make up for or reduce the loss, and at the same time compensate for the contractor's loss and actual expenses resulting from work stoppage or holdup, re-transportation, re-allocation of mechanical equipment, and the overstocking of materials and structural parts.

3. If surveying and designing is done over again or stopped or the designs are revised owing to changes in the plan or inaccurate data provided or failure to provide the necessary working conditions for surveying and designing, an additional sum shall be paid to the contractor according to the actual amount of work involved.

4. The builder shall bear the responsibility himself if the quality of the construction is found unsatisfactory after the project has been put to use ahead of time without inspection and acceptance.

5. The damages for breach of contract shall be paid for exceeding the time limit if the work is inspected and accepted or the construction fees are paid later than the date set in the contract.

Article 40 Responsibility for breach of contracts on undertaking processing:

a) The contractor's responsibility:

1. The contractor shall compensate for the damage or loss of materials and articles provided by the principal owing to poor storage.

2. In case of failure to finish the work of the principal according to the quality and quantity set in the contract, the contractor shall do the repairs or make up for the deficit gratis or reduce the remuneration. If there are major defects in the work done, he shall be liable to compensation.

b) The principal's responsibility:

1. If the work is delayed owing to the failure to provide the contractor with the raw and processed materials according to the prescribed time, quality and quantity, the principal shall compensate for the loss.

2. If the articles made to order or repaired are picked up beyond the prescribed time, the principal shall pay the contractor the storage fee for exceeding the time limit.

3. If the payment is made beyond the time set in the contract, the principal shall pay the damages for breach of contract for exceeding the time limit.

Article 41 Responsibility for breach of goods transport contracts:

a) The carrier's responsibility:

1. Damages for breach of contract shall be paid to the consignor if the train or truck (ship) is not dispatched according to the time and requirements set in the transport contract.

2. If the goods are delivered to the wrong destination or consignee, the carrier shall ship the goods gratis to the destination or consignee

prescribed in the contract. If the delivery is overdue, he shall pay the damages for breach of contract for overdue delivery.

3. Loss, shortage, deterioration, contamination or damage of the goods in the course of transport shall be compensated for according to the actual loss of the goods (including the packing fee, and the transportation and incidental expenses).

4. Where the carrier is liable to compensation for the loss, shortage, deterioration, contamination or damage of the goods contracted for through transport, the compensation shall be made by the carrier in the final phase according to regulations. The latter can claim the sum from the other responsible carrier.

5. When the goods are transported in accordance with law and under the conditions prescribed in the contract, the carrier shall not be held responsible for breach of contract if loss, shortage, deterioration, contamination or damage of goods is caused by the following:

a. Force majeure;
b. Natural properties of the goods;
c. Reasonable spoilage of goods;
d. Fault on the part of the consignor or consignee.

b) The consignor's responsibility:

1. The damages for breach of contract shall be paid to the carrier if the consignment is not provided in accordance with the time and requirements set in the transport contract.

2. The consignor is liable to compensate for such accidents as break of hoisting tools, fall and damage of goods, overturn of the hoist, explosion and corrosion resulting from mixing or concealing dangerous goods among ordinary goods or understating the weight of heavy goods.

3. The consignor is liable to compensate for the contamination and damage of other goods or transportation equipment and even casualties caused by the break-up of the consignment due to faulty packaging.

4. As for the goods loaded by the consignor on his special line or on the special public line or railway in ports or stations, if goods are found to be damaged or missing at the destination when the vehicle is properly sealed or there are no abnormalities, the consignor shall compensate for the loss of the consignee.

5. In the case of goods carried by container, if unloading is not possible due to the absence of the accompanying specification and quality certificate or laboratory test report, the consignor shall pay the carrier the fee for delayed unloading and the damages for breach of contract.

Article 42 Responsibility for breach of contracts on the supply and use of electricity:

a) The supplier's responsibility:

The supplier shall supply the electricity safely according to the state-set power supply standards and the contract terms. In case of limited supply of power with reasons, the user shall be notified in advance. In case of limited supply of power without proper reasons or power failure caused by the supplier, the supplier shall compensate the user for the loss resulting therefrom.

b) The user's responsibility:

The user shall consume electricity according to the contract terms. In special circumstances when electricity is over-consumed or electricity cannot be consumed according to the prescribed time, the supplier shall be notified in advance. If electricity is over-consumed or not according to the prescribed time without proper reasons, the user shall pay the damages for breach of contract.

Responsibility for breach of contracts on the supply and use of water or gas can be handled with reference to the provisions of this Article.

Article 43 Responsibility for breach of storage contracts:

a) The keeper's responsibility:

1. He shall compensate for the loss if the goods, during the period of storage, are lost, missing, deteriorated, contaminated or damaged owing to poor storage. He is not liable to compensation for the damage or deterioration of the goods due to packaging which is not in conformity with the contract terms or because the goods are kept beyond the effective storage period.

2. He shall compensate for the loss if dangerous articles and corruptible goods are damaged owing to his failure to handle or keep them as prescribed.

3. If the storage space is returned or the goods cannot enter the warehouse owing to the keeper's responsibility, he shall compensate the goods owner for the freight and pay the damages for breach of contract according to the contract terms.

4. If the goods to be sent out by the keeper fail to be dispatched on schedule, he shall compensate the goods owner for the loss of overdue delivery; if the goods are sent to a wrong destination, he shall, in addition to shipping the goods to the prescribed destination gratis in accordance with the contract terms, compensate the goods owner for the actual loss resulting therefrom.

b) The goods owner's responsibility:

1. Combustibles, explosives and dangerous articles which are poisonous and corruptible goods must be stated in the contract, and necessary data shall be provided. Otherwise, he shall bear liability in compensation and even criminal liability in case of damage of goods or casualties.

2. If the goods put in storage exceed the agreed amount or are not picked up beyond the prescribed time, he shall pay the damages for breach of contract in addition to the storage fee.

Article 44 Responsibility for breach of property lease contracts:

a) The renter's responsibility:

1. He shall be responsible for the repair or compensation if the leased property is damaged or lost owing to improper use and upkeep or poor maintenance.

2. He shall compensate for the loss resulting from unauthorized acts to dismantle or alter the house, equipment, machinery or other property.

3. The owner has the right to rescind the contract if the lessee subleases the leased property without authorization or engages in illegal activities.

4. If the leased property is not returned on schedule, the lessee shall pay the damages for breach of contract in addition to the rent.

b) The owner's responsibility:

1. He shall pay the damages for breach of contract if he fails to provide the leased property according to the time prescribed in the contract.

2. He shall compensate for the loss resulting from his failure to provide the leased property according to the quality prescribed in the contract.

3. If his failure to provide the relevant equipment or attachments according to the contract terms makes it impossible for the lessee to use the leased property normally on schedule, the owner shall pay the damages for breach of contract in addition to making up the deficiency as prescribed.

4. In case of leasing boats, vehicles and other big tools, if improper operation on the part of the owner or fault on the part of the attendants result in overdue lease, the owner shall pay the damages for breach of contract to the hirer according to the contract terms or related regulations.

Article 45 Responsibility for breach of loan contracts:

a) The creditor's responsibility:

The People's Bank, specialized banks and credit unions shall pay the damages for breach of contract if the loan is not extended on schedule prescribed by the contract.

b) The debtor's responsibility:

If he uses the loan in ways not prescribed by the contract, he shall pay an additional interest according to relevant regulations, and the creditor has the right to recall part or all of the loan ahead of time.

Article 46 Responsibility for breach of property insurance contracts:

a) The insurer's responsibility:

As to loss and expenses resulting from the accidents insured, he is liable to compensate within the insured amount. The reasonable expenses paid for rescue, protection, sorting-out and litigation as a result of the insurer's avoidance of or reducing the insurance liability, shall be paid according to the contract terms. If the expenses are not paid in good time, the insurer is liable for breach of contract.

b) The insured's responsibility:

If the insured conceals the truth about the insured property, the insurer has the right to rescind the contract or is not liable in compensation.

If the insured finds the insured property in danger and does not adopt measures to remove the danger, he shall be responsible for the loss caused by the resultant accident, and the insurer is not liable in compensation.

Article 47 Responsibility for breach of contracts on scientific and technological co-operation.

a) The responsibility of the trustee or the technological transferer:

In case of failure to carry out the contract, the trustee or the technological transferer shall, according to the specific circumstances, return part or the whole of the commission or transfer fees paid by the entrustor or the technological recipient; for delayed progress, the resultant extra expenses shall be paid.

b) The responsibility of the entrustor or the technological recipient:

In case of failure to carry out the contract, the entrustor or the technological recipient shall not claim the commission or transfer fees already paid, and pay all costs paid by the trustee or the technological transferer to deal with the problems resulting therefrom.

Chapter V Mediation and Arbitration of Disputes Over Economic Contracts

Article 48 In case of disputes over economic contracts, the parties shall resolve them through consultation without delay. If consultation is not possible either party can request mediation or arbitration with the contract control organization designated by the state or bring a suit directly at the people's court.

Article 49 Where agreement is reached through mediation, the parties shall perform it. Where a ruling is made, an arbitration award shall be made out by the state-designated contract control organization. If one party or both parties contest the ruling, they can bring a suit at the people's court within 15 days of receiving the arbitration ruling; if no suit is filed upon the expiration of the period, the ruling is legally effective.

Article 50 A party to an economic contract requesting mediation or arbitration with the contract control organization, shall request the same within one year from the date when he learns or should have learned of his rights being encroached upon. Cases presented beyond this period shall generally not be accepted.

Chapter VI Control of Economic Contracts

Article 51 Competent business departments and administration departments for industry and commerce at various levels shall supervise and inspect the relevant economic contracts, and establish the necessary control system. All business departments at various levels should also examine the performing condition of the economic contracts by the enterprises as an economic aim.

Article 52 The People's Bank, specialized banks and credit unions shall supervise the performance of economic contracts through credit control and settlement control.

The People's Bank, specialized banks and credit unions shall handle settlements according to the provisions of the settlement system, and make payment, refuse payment and withhold the deferred sum.

Where a party to an economic contract fails to perform automatically the mediated agreement, arbitration award or court decision within the prescribed time, the People's Bank, a specialized bank or credit union shall, upon receiving the notice of the people's court for assistance in execution, withhold or transfer the desired sum from the account of the said litigant.

Article 53 As to making of fake economic contracts, or resale of economic contracts, or the use of economic contracts to speculate for profit, illegal transfers, offer and/or accept bribes, and other illegal acts to the detriment of national interests and social public interests, these shall be dealt with by the administration departments for industry and commerce; the cases shall be referred to the judicial organization if they carry criminal liability.

Chapter VII Addenda

Article 54 Economic contracts signed by individual businesses or rural commune members with legal persons shall be carried out with reference to this Law.

Article 55 Regulations for economic and trade contracts involving foreigners shall be formulated separately with reference to the principles of this Law and international practices.

Article 56 Relevant departments under the State Council and the provincial, municipal and autonomous regional people's governments may work out rules for implementation in the light of this Law and report to the State Council for approval.

Article 57 This Law shall come into force on July 1, 1982.

12

FOREIGN INVESTMENT AND JOINT-VENTURE

Foreign Representatives/ Investment & Enquiry/ Joint-Venture Enterprises/ Oil Drilling

INTERIM REGULATIONS OF THE PEOPLE'S REPUBLIC OF CHINA CONCERNING THE CONTROL OF RESIDENT OFFICES OF FOREIGN ENTERPRISES

(Promulgated by the State Council on October 30, 1980)

Article 1 The regulations hereunder are formulated with a view to facilitating the development of international economic and trade contacts and the control of resident offices in China of foreign companies, enterprises and other economic organizations (hereinafter referred to as "foreign enterprises").

Article 2 Any foreign enterprise desiring to establish a resident office in China should first apply for permission and then, after securing approval, go through the registration procedure.

No foreign enterprise is allowed to start business activities in the nature of those of a resident office before approval is granted and the registration procedure completed.

Article 3 When applying for permission to establish a resident office in China, a foreign enterprise should produce the following documents and reference materials:

a) An application form signed by the chairman of the board of directors or the general manager of the enterprise. The application form should include such details as the name of the resident office to be established, the name(s) of the responsible member(s), the scope of activity, duration and site of the office;

b) The legal document sanctioning the operation of that enterprise issued by the authorities of the country or the region in which that enterprise operates;

c) The capital creditability document issued by the banking institution(s) having business contacts with that enterprise; and

d) The credentials and brief biographies of the members of the resident office appointed by that enterprise.

A banking or insurance institution which desires to open a resident office should, apart from producing the documents and reference materials as specified in Paragraphs a, b and d above, produce at the same time an annual report showing the assets and liabilities and losses and profits of the head office of that enterprise, its constitution and the composition of its board of directors.

Article 4 Applications of foreign enterprises for permission to establish resident offices are to be submitted to one of the following organizations for approval:

a) A trader, manufacturer or a shipping agent should apply to the Ministry of Foreign Trade of the People's Republic of China;

b) A banking or insurance institution should apply to the People's Bank of China;

c) A maritime shipping operator or a maritime shipping agent should apply to the Ministry of Communications of the People's Republic of China;

d) An air transport enterprise should apply to the General Administration of Civil Aviation of China;

e) Enterprises outside these lines of activity should, according to the nature of their operations, apply to the proper commissions, ministries or bureaus under the Government of the People's Republic of China.

Article 5 When granted approval to establish a resident office, a foreign enterprise should, within 30 days of the date of approval, go to the General Administration for Industry and Commerce of the People's Republic of China on the strength of the approval document and go through the registration procedure. The enterprise must fill in a registration form and pay registration fees before it is issued a registration certificate. The original approval document should be recalled in case of failure to register within the deadline.

Article 6 After approval for the establishment of a resident office is granted in accordance with the stipulations in Article 4, the members of that office and their families should, on the strength of the approval document, apply to the local public security organ for residence permission before they are issued residence permits.

Article 7 When a resident office desires to change its name, its responsible member(s), scope of operation, or duration or site, it should apply to the original approval-issuing organization and, after securing approval, go to the General Administration for Industry and Commerce of the People's Republic of China on the strength of the approval document and go through the procedure for effecting a change in registration and pay the fees. It should also go through the procedure with the local public security organ for changing the residence permits.

Article 8 A resident office should, on the strength of the registration certificate and in accordance with the relevant stipulations of the Bank of China, open an account at the Bank of China or at any bank which the Bank of China may designate.

Article 9 A resident office and its members should, in accordance with the stipulations of Chinese tax laws, go through the tax registration procedure with the local tax office and pay taxes in accordance with the regulations.

Article 10 A resident office and its members should declare to China's House of Customs the imported office articles, articles for daily use and means of transport and pay customs duties and the unified industrial and commercial tax as stipulated.

Imported vehicles and ships should be registered with the local public security organ before the licence plates and permits are issued. Fees should be paid to the local tax office for the use of the vehicles and ships. Unauthorized transfer or sale of the above-mentioned imported goods is not permitted. In the event of a necessary transfer or sale, an application should be put forward to the House of Customs and approval obtained before such a transfer or sale can be effected. Imported goods can be sold only to designated shops.

Article 11 A resident office should entrust local service units for foreigners or other such units as may be designated by the Chinese Government with such matters as renting a house or engaging the service of Chinese personnel.

Article 12 The Government of the People's Republic of China undertakes to protect, in accordance with law, the legitimate rights and interests of resident offices and their members and facilitate their normal business activities.

Article 13 Resident offices are not allowed to set up radio stations on Chinese territory. They should apply to the local telecommunications bureaus for the renting of such commercial communications lines or communications equipment as may be necessary for their business operations.

Article 14 The members of a resident office and their families should abide by Chinese laws, decrees and relevant regulations in all their activities in China and in entering and leaving China.

Article 15 In case a resident office and its members violate the "Interim Regulations" or engage in other law-breaking activities, the proper Chinese authorities have the power to look into the cases and deal with them in accordance with law.

Article 16 A resident office, when the duration of its operation expires, or if it decides to end its business activities before the due date, should notify in writing the original approval-granting organization 30 days in advance of the termination of its operation. After clearing up its debts, paying its taxes and winding up other related matters, the resident office should go through the formalities with the original registration certificate-issuing organization for cancelling the registration and turn in the certificate.

The foreign enterprise which the said resident office represented, should continue to be held responsible for any matter that the said resident office may leave unfinished at the time of its termination.

Article 17 Those resident offices that have already been established with approval should, within 30 days of the promulgation of the "Interim Regulations," go through the procedure of registration with the General Administration for Industry and Commerce of the People's Republic of China on the strength of the documents of approval.

Article 18 Any other matter that may not be covered in the "Interim Regulations" should be handled in accordance with the relevant Chinese laws, decrees and regulations.

Article 19 The "Interim Regulations" should apply to all foreign enterprises which desire to appoint a resident representative or representatives as well as to those desiring to establish resident offices.

Article 20 The "Interim Regulations" enter into effect on the day of promulgation.

ANNOUNCEMENT OF THE GENERAL ADMINISTRATION FOR INDUSTRY AND COMMERCE OF THE PEOPLE'S REPUBLIC OF CHINA CONCERNING THE REGISTRATION OF RESIDENT OFFICES OF FOREIGN ENTERPRISES

(December 8, 1980)

The Interim Regulations of the State Council of the People's Republic of China Concerning the Control of Resident Offices of Foreign Enterprises (hereinafter called "Interim Regulations") have been promulgated for implementation. The present announcement concerns matters relating to registration:

1. As stipulated in the Interim Regulations, resident offices or representatives of foreign enterprises, having secured the approval of the departments in charge under the State Council, should register at this Administration. To enable resident offices or representatives of foreign enterprises to go through the registration procedure at convenient and nearby places, this Administration, upon approval of the State Council, entrusts the administrations for industry and commerce in various provinces, municipalities and autonomous regions to take up this work on its behalf.

2. Resident offices or representatives of foreign enterprises, approved by the departments in charge under the State Council before the promulgation of the Interim Regulations, must go through the registration procedure before December 20, 1980, at the administrations for industry and commerce in the provinces, municipalities and autonomous regions where they are located, on the strength of the approval documents of the departments concerned and copies or duplicates of the documents listed in Article 3 of the Interim Regulations, and obtain a Registration Certificate for Resident Offices of Foreign Enterprises issued by the General Administration for Industry and Commerce of the People's Republic of China.

3. Resident Offices or representatives of overseas Chinese, Hong Kong and Macao enterprises that have been granted approval by the departments in charge under the State Council before and after this announcement is made, must also register in accordance with the Interim Regulations and obtain a Registration Certificate for Resident Offices of Overseas Chinese, Hong Kong and Macao Enterprises issued by the General Administration for Industry and Commerce of the People's Republic of China.

4. Resident offices or representatives of foreign enterprises approved by people's governments of various provinces, municipalities and autonomous regions or departments under them, must go through the registration procedure with the administrations for industry and commerce in the relevant provinces, municipalities or autonomous regions in accordance with the regulations of the respective provinces, municipalities or autonomous regions, and obtain a Registration Certificate for Resident Offices of Foreign Enterprises issued by the administrations of industry and commerce of the provinces, municipalities or autonomous regions.

5. When going through the registration procedure, the resident office or representative of a foreign enterprise, upon approval, should pay a registration fee of 600 yuan. When going through the procedure for changing the registration certificate, it should pay a registration fee of 300 yuan. When going through the procedure for effecting a change in name, responsible member, scope of operation, duration or site, it should pay a fee of 100 yuan.

6. The period of validity of a Registration Certificate for Resident Offices of Foreign Enterprises is the same as the approved duration of operation, beyond which the registration should be renewed. Offices approved to operate for more than one year should go through the registration procedure once every year.

INTERIM REGULATIONS OF THE STATE COUNCIL OF THE PEOPLE'S REPUBLIC OF CHINA CONCERNING THE CONTROL OF RESIDENT CORRESPONDENTS OF FOREIGN NEWS AGENCIES

(Promulgated by the State Council on March 9, 1981)

Article 1 Foreign news agencies intending to have resident correspondents in China for news gathering and coverage should apply to the Ministry of Foreign Affairs of the People's Republic of China for permission and, upon approval, register at the Information Department of the Ministry.

Article 2 Resident correspondents shall not send manuscripts to news agencies other than the one(s) they represent.

Two or more than two news agencies requesting to have one and the same resident correspondent should go through the application and registration procedures as stipulated in Article 1 respectively.

Article 3 The Information Department of the Ministry of Foreign Affairs will issue press cards valid for one year to the approved resident correspondents. The resident correspondents and their relatives should apply to the local public security organs for residence permission on the strength of their press cards before receiving their residence permits.

Article 4 Foreign news agencies desiring to change their resident correspondents should apply to the Ministry of Foreign Affairs of the People's Republic of China for approval 45 days in advance. After approval, the original correspondent should stop the activities of news gathering and coverage as soon as the new correspondent begins to work.

To effect any change in either the resident correspondents, their family members or the addresses of the concerned parties, they should apply for correspondent changes in the residence permits.

Article 5 Resident correspondents desiring to continue their activities of news gathering and coverage upon and after expiration of their press cards should apply, ten days before expiration, to the Information Department of the Ministry of Foreign Affairs of the People's Republic of China for extension.

Resident correspondents desiring to terminate their professional activities in China should notify, 30 days in advance, the Information Department of the Ministry of Foreign Affairs of the People's Republic of China in writing and go through the cancellation of registration procedure after paying their taxes and winding up other related matters.

Article 6 The government of the People's Republic of China duly protects the just rights and interests of the resident correspondents according to law and facilitates their activities in news gathering and coverage.

Article 7 Resident correspondents should entrust local foreign affairs services with the renting of houses and recruitment of staff.

Article 8 Resident correspondents are not allowed to set up radio stations inside Chinese territory. Such facilities as telecommunication lines and communication equipment deemed necessary in their profession should be hired from local telecommunication and TV institutions.

Article 9 Resident correspondents should apply for permission to related authorities as required by the Information Department of the Ministry of Foreign Affairs before gathering news in government offices, organizations, enterprises, institutions and other units.

Article 10 Resident correspondents should register with the local tax bureaus for tax payment according to the stipulations of the tax laws of China.

Article 11 Resident correspondents should declare to the Customs of China any articles for office or daily use or means of transport imported and pay Customs duties as stipulated.

The above-mentioned articles are not to be sold or transferred privately unless approved by the Customs.

Article 12 The professional activities of

resident correspondents should not go beyond the normal scope of news gathering and coverage.

In all their activities in China and in entering and leaving China, resident correspondents and their family members should abide by the relevant laws, decrees and regulations of China. Any unlawful activities will be duly punished by the related responsible organs of China according to law.

Article 13 Matters that are not included in the Interim Regulations will be handled in accordance with the relevant laws, decrees and regulations of China.

Article 14 These Regulations shall be put into effect on the day of promulgation.

PROVISIONAL REGULATIONS FOR THE ESTABLISHMENT OF REPRESENTATIVE OFFICES IN CHINA BY OVERSEAS CHINESE AND FOREIGN FINANCIAL INSTITUTIONS

Issued by the People's Bank of China
(February 1, 1983)

Article 1 In accordance with the Interim Provisions of the State Council of the People's Republic of China for the Control of Resident Representative Offices of Foreign Enterprises, the following regulations are formulated with a view to exercising more effective control over the establishment of representative offices of overseas Chinese and foreign financial institutions in the People's Republic of China.

Article 2 Any overseas Chinese or foreign financial institution, if it deems it necessary, may apply for permission to establish a representative office(s) in Beijing and/or in any of the special economic zones in China.

After a representative office is set up in Beijing with due approval, the represented institution may, if necessary, secure further permission to open a subordinate representative office(s) in other designated cities.

Article 3 Representative offices set up by overseas Chinese and foreign financial institutions in Beijing and the special economic zones shall bear names in immediate conjunction with the description "representative office;" such offices set up by overseas Chinese or foreign insurance companies shall bear names in immediate conjunction with the description "Liaison office;" Additional offices set up in other designated cities shall bear names in immediate conjunction with the description "subordinate representative office," or "sub-rep office" for short.

Article 4 Overseas Chinese or foreign financial institutions desiring to establish representative offices and subordinate representative offices in China shall apply to the People's Bank of China (hereinafter referred to as the Bank) in conformity with the following procedure:

a) For the purpose of establishing a representative office in Beijing, the head office of the applying institution shall address to the governor of the Bank a letter of application duly signed by the chairman of the board or the chief executive of the general management. The application may be sent directly to the Bank or forwarded through a relevant Chinese financial institution.

b) For the purpose of establishing a representative office in a special economic zone or a subordinate representative office in other designated cities, the head office of the applying institution shall address to the governor of the Bank a letter of application duly signed by the chairman of the board or the chief exeuctive of the general management. The application may be sent directly to the Bank or forwarded through the provincial, municipal or autonomous regional branch of the Bank (hereinafter referred to as PBC local branch).

following documents and reference materials:

1. An Application Form for Overseas Chinese or Foreign Financial Institutions Establishing Representative Offices in the People's Republic of China, which is obtainable from the Bank, filled out by the applying institution;

2. A photostat copy of the charter or business licence granted by the authorities of the country or region in which the institution operates;

3. Articles of association and by-laws, a name list of the board of directors or a similar organization controlling the institution, the latest balance sheet and statement of profit and loss of the applying institution;

4. Power of attorney given to the chief representative and signed by the chairman of the board or the chief executive of the general management and curricula vitae of the chief representative and other representative(s).

Chinese or English translations shall be submitted with the documents and materials if they are in other languages.

The applying institution shall inform the Bank in writing of any changes in the submitted documents and materials required in Points 2 and 3.

Article 5 The overseas Chinese or foreign financial institution, when granted permission to establish a representative office or subordinate representative office in China, shall in accordance with the relevant regulations present the approval certificate to the local Administrative Bureau for Industry and Commerce and the Public Security Bureau and go through the formalities for registration and residence.

Article 6 Each of the approved representative offices and subordinate representative offices of overseas Chinese and foreign financial institutions shall on the strength of the registration certificate open an account with the Bank of China and observe exchange control regulations of the People's Republic of China.

Article 7 The representative offices and subordinate representative offices are approved by the Bank for a term of three years. If an extension is desired, the representative shall submit to the Bank thirty days before the term expires a letter of application signed by the chairman of the board or the chief executive of the general management. There is no limit on the number of extensions.

Article 8 The representative offices and subordinate representative offices set up by overseas Chinese and foreign financial institutions shall operate within the scope of non-profit activities such as carrying on business negotiations, acting as liaison, providing consultancy and other services. They shall not engage in any direct profit-making business activities.

The representative offices in a special economic zone shall only engage in such non-profit activities as mentioned above within the confines of the special economic zone.

Article 9 Chief representatives and other representatives shall be approved by the Bank before assuming their duties in China. Their total number shall not be more than:

a) four in a representative office in Beijing,

b) three in a representative office in a special economic zone, and

c) two in a subordinate representative office in other designated cities.

In a particular case where more are needed than the prescribed number, an application shall be sent to the Bank for approval.

Article 10 There is no limit on the number of local Chinese citizens that a representative office or subordinate representative office may decide to employ on the recommendation of local service units for foreigners and other units designated by the Chinese Government; or is the Bank's approval required for such employment.

However, for the purpose of record, a name list of the local Chinese employees:

a) of a representative office in Beijing shall be filed with the Bank and

b) of a representative office in a special economic zone and a subordinate representative office in other cities shall be filed with the PBC local branch.

Article 11 Reports shall be filed with the Bank for approval in cases:

a) where a representative office in Beijing desires to change its name, address or to replace its chief representative(s); or

b) where a subordinate representative office desires to change its name or replace its representative(s); or

c) where a representative office in a special economic zone desires to change its name or replace its chief representative.

Reports shall be filed with the PBC local branch for approval in cases:

a) where a representative office in a special economic zone desires to change its address or representative(s); or

b) where a subordinate representative office desires to change its address.

Article 12 When the chief representative of a representative office is absent from office for a period longer than a month, someone else shall be designated to assume responsibilities during his absence. A copy of the designation document shall be sent to the Bank for record.

Article 13 Members of representative offices and subordinate representative offices of overseas Chinese and foreign financial institutions must observe Chinese laws, decrees, rules and regulations in all their activities within China and in entering and leaving China.

Article 14 The Bank and its local branches have the rights to supervise, regulate and examine the work of the representative offices and subordinate representative offices of overseas Chinese and foreign financial institutions.

Article 15 Each of the representative offices of overseas Chinese and foreign financial institutions in Beijing shall before the fifteenth of January every year submit to the Bank a report in Chinese or in English giving a faithful account of its work in China in the previous year.

Subordinate representative offices in other cities and representative offices in special economic zones shall file such reports with the PBC local branches, copies of which shall be sent to the Bank for record.

Article 16 If an overseas Chinese or foreign financial institution decides to close its representative office or subordinate representative office in China, it shall notify the Bank in writing thirty days before the date of closing. After paying off its debts and taxes and clearing off other obligations, the representative office or subordinate representative office shall go through the formalities of cancelling its registration and turning in the certificate at the registration agency with which it has registered.

The head office of the represented institution shall be held responsible for any obligations its representative office(s) or subordinate representative office(s) leaves unsettled.

Article 17 The Bank and its local branches exercise the rights of examination and penalty in case of violation of these regulations by any representative offices, subordinate representative offices or their members.

Article 18 The "Provisional Regulations" shall be put into effect on the date of issue.

PROCEDURES FOR THE REGISTRATION AND ADMINISTRATION OF RESIDENT OFFICES OF FOREIGN ENTERPRISES IN CHINA

(Promulgated by the State Administration for Industry and Commerce, March 15, 1983)

Article 1 In accordance with the "Interim Provisions of the State Council of the People's Republic of China Concerning the Control of Resident Offices of Foreign Enterprises in China" (hereinafter referred to as "the Interim Provisions"), the present Procedures are formulated to carry out the registration and administration of resident representative offices in China of foreign enterprises and other economic organizations and to protect their legitimate business activities.

Article 2 Resident representative offices of foreign enterprises in China and other economic organizations (hereinafter referred to as "resident offices of foreign enterprises"), which have been approved in accordance with Article 4 of the Interim Provisions, shall go through the registration procedures prescribed in the present Procedures.

Article 3 Resident offices of foreign enterprises shall be understood as those engaging in non-direct-profit-making operations. But, for those provided for in inter-government agreements, they shall be dealt with in accordance with those agreements.

Article 4 The State Administration for Industry and Commerce of the People's Republic of China is the organized authority for the registration of resident offices of foreign enterprises. It shall empower the administrations for industry and commerce in various provinces, municipalities and autonomous regions to handle registration procedures.

Article 5 The main items to be registered for the resident office of a foreign enterprise are: name of the office, address of residence, number of representatives and their names, business scope and duration of residence.

Article 6 Foreign enterprises and other economic organizations shall go through the prescribed registration procedures at the administrations for industry and commerce in the provinces, municipalities and autonomous regions where the said offices are to be located within 30 days from the date when their applications for setting up resident offices within the territory of the People's Republic of China is approved.

Article 7 A foreign enterprise or economic organization shall submit the following documents in applying for the registration of a resident office:

1. The approval document issued by the competent authorities of the People's Republic of China;
2. The documents and materials as listed in Article 3 of the Interim Provisions.

Article 8 If the documents submitted by a foreign enterprise or economic organization for registration are established, through examination, to meet the requirements set forth in the present procedures, the registration office shall grant permission to register and issue a certificate of registration and certificates for the representatives after a registration fee is paid.

The resident office of a foreign enterprise shall, upon the strength of the document of approval, certificate of registration and certificates for the representatives, register with the public security bureau, the bank and the customs and tax authorities and other departments for residence permits and other related matters.

Article 9 The resident office of a foreign enterprise is deemed as officially established from the date of its registration and the legitimate activities of the said office and its representatives shall therefrom be protected by the laws of the People's Republic of China.

A resident office that has not been approved and registered shall not proceed with its business activities.

Article 10 In engaging the service of Chinese personnel, the resident office of a foreign enterprise must follow the provisions prescribed in Article 11 of the Interim Provisions and in due time report this to the registration authorities for the record.

Article 11 The registration certificate for the resident office of a foreign enterprise is valid for a period of one year. The said office shall, upon expiration of the period, have to renew the aforesaid document if it wishes to continue its residence.

To renew its registration, the resident office of a foreign enterprise must, within 30 days before the date of expiration, submit to the registration authorities an annual report of its business operations (in Chinese) and an application for renewal. In cases where the term of residence approved for a resident office expires, the document of approval for renewal issued by the same authorities must also be submitted at the time of renewing the registration and a form for renewal shall be filled out. After examination by the registration office, the original certificate shall be turned in and a new certificate of registration shall be issued.

Article 12 When the resident office of a foreign enterprise wishes to make alterations with regard to the name of the office, the number of representatives and their names, the scope of business and the address of the resident office, an application for alteration shall be filed with the registration office together with the document of approval issued by the competent authorities before going through the prescribed procedure for alterations in the register.

In cases where there is a change of representatives, a power of attorney issued by the foreign enterprise or economic organization shall be submitted together with the resumes of the new representatives.

Article 13 If the resident office of a foreign enterprise desires to terminate its business operations upon or before the expiration of the term of residence, or the enterprise represented by the office declares bankruptcy, it shall go through the deregistration procedures at the registration office. In going through the deregistration procedure, documents issued by tax authorities, banks and Customs to certify the clearing up of taxes, debts and other related matters shall be produced before approval is granted for cancellation and the certificate of registration is revoked.

Should the aforesaid office leave any matter unsettled, the foreign enterprise or economic organization the office represents shall be held responsible for the settlement of that matter.

Article 14 The State Administration for Industry and Commerce of the People's Republic of China and the administrations for industry and commerce in the provinces, municipalities and autonomous regions are entitled to supervise and inspect the business activities of the resident offices of foreign enterprises within the jurisdiction of the present procedures.

In carrying out inspection and supervision, staff members of the aforesaid administrations should present identification cards specially issued for that purpose. The resident offices must report honestly and provide such information and materials as required. Refusal to report or holding back information is not allowed.

Article 15 Any one of the following cases in violation of the provisions in the present procedures shall be punished by the State Administration for Industry and Commerce according to the seriousness of the case:

1. The resident office of a foreign enterprise proven to have engaged in direct profit-making operations in violation of the provisions of Article 3 of the present procedures shall be ordered to stop its business operations, with a fine of less than 20,000 yuan (RMB).

2. The resident office of a foreign enterprise proven to have altered any item in the register without going through the required procedures or failed to deregister when it should have shall be given a notice of warning for circulation. For more serious cases, a fine of less than 5,000 yuan (RMB) shall be imposed or even the cancellation of the registration certificate.

When the resident office of a foreign enterprise is found to have engaged in speculation, swindling and other unlawful activities, all proceeds and properties thus obtained shall be confiscated in addition to a fine or even the cancellation of the registration certificate as the case may be. Cases that violate the criminal code of the People's Republic of China shall be brought before the court and punished according to that law.

Article 16 A foreign enterprise or other economic organization engaging, without authorization, in business operations only allowed for resident offices shall be ordered to stop such activities and a fine of less than 10,000 yuan (RMB) shall be imposed.

Article 17 The present procedures also apply to foreign enterprises and other economic organizations applying to post their resident representatives within the boundaries of the People's Republic of China.

Article 18 Companies and other enterprises run by overseas Chinese or by compatriots from Hong Kong and Macao, when applying for the establishment of resident offices, shall go through registration procedures in reference to the present regulations to obtain registration certificates for the resident offices of overseas Chinese enterprises and enterprises in Hong Kong and Macao.

Article 19 Chinese-foreign joint ventures operating outside China which have been approved to establish resident offices in China shall also go

through registration procedures in reference to the present procedures.

Article 20 The present procedures go into effect as of March 15, 1983.

STATUTES OF THE CHINA INTERNATIONAL TRUST AND INVESTMENT CORPORATION

(Promulgated and enforced on October 4, 1979)

Chapter I General Principles

Article 1 The China International Trust and Investment Corporation (CITIC) (hereinafter called the Corporation) is a state-owned socialist enterprise operating under the direct leadership of the State Council of the People's Republic of China.

Article 2 The function of the Corporation is to introduce, absorb and apply foreign investment, to bring in advanced technology and to import advanced equipment for purposes of China's national construction and promotion of socialist modernization of our country pursuant to the provisions of the Law of the People's Republic of China on Joint Ventures Using Chinese and Foreign Investment and other relevant laws and regulations.

Article 3 The capital of the Corporation shall be 200,000,000 yuan (Renminbi).

Article 4 The Corporation shall resolutely abide by socialist principles, observe economic laws in its operations, and employ modern and scientific methods of management.

Article 5 The head office of the Corporation shall be in Beijing, with a branch office in Xianggang (Hong Kong). Other branch offices, subsidiaries, sub-branch offices or agencies shall be set up inside and outside of China when the need arises.

Chapter II Scope of Operation

Article 6 The Corporation shall undertake under commission of foreign corporations, enterprises, other economic entities or individuals to negotiate and enter into short-term or long-term joint venture agreements and related contracts with the various local administrations and departments in China, and the corporations, enterprises and other economic entities thereunder; and shall render them services by way of making introductions, giving consultation and providing information for the purposes of setting up joint ventures and short-term or long-term technological cooperation.

Article 7 The Corporation shall undertake under commission of the different ministries and local administrations and departments in China, and the corporations, enterprises and other economic entities thereunder to negotiate and enter into short-term or long-term joint venture agreements and related contracts with foreign corporations, enterprises, other economic entities or individuals; and shall render them services by way of making introductions, giving consultation, and providing information for the purposes of setting up joint ventures and short-term or long-term technological cooperation.

Article 8 The Corporation shall accept funds from foreign corporations, enterprises, other economic entities or individuals, or shall raise funds abroad for investment in China by issuing debentures of the Corporation or by serving as agents in the issue of the shares related to investment in China, and shall handle trustee businesses of short-term or long-term investments in China.

Article 9 The Corporation shall render services to foreign corporations, foreign enterprises, other foreign economic entities or individuals, and to the different ministries, local administrations and departments in China, and the corporations, enterprises and other economic entities thereunder by way of providing introduction to and information on the relevant laws and regulations, taxation provisions, foreign exchange control, wages for labour, accounting, and auditing on joint venture enterprises.

Article 10 The Corporation may act as agents under contract with foreign manufacturers and merchants in business activities relating to advanced technology and equipment.

Article 11 The Corporation may out of business necessity engage in joint ventures inside and outside of China, or make investments single-handed by itself.

Chapter III Organization

Article 12 The highest organ of authority

of the Corporation is the Board of Directors.

The Board of Directors consists of a Chairman, Vice-Chairmen, Executive Directors and Directors nominated by the State Council.

The functions of the Board are:

a) To lay down the short-term and long-term business policies and operational programmes of the Corporation pursuant to the spirit of directives from the State Council.

b) To appoint the President and Vice-Presidents, subject to the State Council's approval of such appointments.

c) To examine and approve the infrastructure of the Corporation and the setting-up and closing-down of its branches and subsidiaries inside and outside of China as proposed by the President.

d) To examine and approve the above-norm investment projects as submitted by the President.

e) To examine and approve the Corporation's annual financial reports and proposals for distribution of profits as submitted by the President.

f) To receive and examine the reports of the President on the work of the Corporation.

g) To make reports to the State Council on the major business activities of the Corporation.

Article 13 The President shall be responsible for the overall operation and administration of the Corporation. The Vice-Presidents shall assist him in his work.

The functions of the President shall be:

a) To carry out effectively the business policies and operational programmes of the Corporation as laid down by the Board of Directors.

b) To be responsible for organizing the infrastructure of the Corporation and its branches and subsidiaries inside and outside of China, to appoint and dismiss the key officers and foreign specialists of the Corporation, and to make reports to the Board of Directors for record on file.

c) To examine and make decisions on investment projects, to submit reports to the Board of Directors on the above-norm investment projects for approval.

d) To submit to the Board of Directors the annual financial reports and proposals for distribution of profits.

e) To make periodic reports to the Board of Directors regularly on the work of the Corporation.

Chapter IV Management

Article 14 The Corporation shall establish its own independent business operation with an independent financial and accounting system.

Article 15 The Corporation shall devise and adopt appropriate operational plans and measures to suit its short-term and long-term business policies and operational programmes in order to carry on the business of the Corporation in a planned and effective manner.

Article 16 The entrusted investment projects undertaken by the Corporation must possess the ability to redeem foreign exchange; the Corporation shall be under an obligation to examine, supervise, and promote the work of such projects.

Article 17 The Corporation shall conduct individual audits of accounts of the entrusted investment projects and review their economic performance.

Article 18 The Corporation shall employ its personnel according to their merits, and shall try out a contract system in employing its staff members. The Corporation shall effectively adopt a wage system on the principle of distribution in proportion to work done to each according to his work and shall promote and censure them according to performance gradings.

Chapter V Others

Article 19 These articles of Statute shall become effective as of the date of approval by the State Council. The same applies in the event of alterations.

STATUTE OF THE CHINA INTERNATIONAL ECONOMIC CONSULTANTS INC.

(Adopted at the First Meeting of the Board of Directors of the China International Economic Consultants Inc. on October 30, 1981)

Chapter I General Principles

Article 1 The China International Economic Consultants Inc. (hereinafter referred to as CIEC) is a subsidiary of the China International Trust and Investment Corporation and provides economic and legal consulting services for investment activities.

Article 2 CIEC shall, on commission from domestic and foreign institutions, enterprises, other economic organizations and individuals (hereinafter referred to as the client), provide consulting services in respect of the orientation, modes, feasibility analysis, production, management, financial, accounting and legal matters of investment projects.

Article 3 The capital of CIEC is 10 million yuan.

Article 4 CIEC is based in Beijing.

Chapter II Scope of Business

Article 5 CIEC shall, on commission from the client, make investigations, inquiries and studies of matters and issues related to investment activities and projects both at home and abroad and provide relevant information and data.

Article 6 CIEC shall, on commission from the client, look for suitable domestic or foreign partners for coopeation and make business contacts.

Article 7 CIEC shall, on commission from the client, make feasibility analyses of investment projects both at home and abroad and submit reports on such studies.

Article 8 CIEC shall, on commission from the client, provide legal consulting services for domestic and foreign investments, draft or revise such related documents as contracts and agreements on investment and articles of association of companies, examine and attest other legal documents.

Article 9 CIEC shall, on commission from the client, advise on the financial, accounting, banking and taxation issues related to joint ventures using Chinese and foreign investment, foreign independent enterprises or other cooperation projects in China, devise financial and accounting systems, audit and certify financial reports, and prepare accounting statements.

Article 10 CIEC shall, on commission from the client, provide consulting services in respect of the operation and management of enterprises and carry out management system planning.

Article 11 CIEC shall, on commission from the client, serve as his legal or accounting consultant on an annual retainer basis.

Article 12 CIEC shall, on commission from the client, train personnel for international economic work, trust and investment undertakings and consulting services.

Article 13 CIEC shall edit and publish regular and irregular publications.

Chapter III Organization

Article 14 The highest organ of authority of CIEC is the Board of Directors, which consists of the Chairman, Vice-Chairmen, Executive Directors and Directors. The functions of the Board are:

a) To formulate the operational policies and plans of CIEC;

b) To appoint the General Manager, Deputy General Managers and department heads;

c) To examine and approve the organizational infrastructure of CIEC proposed by the General Manager;

d) To examine and approve the business plans, financial reports and work reports of CIEC; and

e) To report the work of CIEC to the China International Trust and Investment Corporation.

Article 15 The functions of the General Manager shall be:

a) To implement the operational policies and plans formulated by the Board;

b) To organize the infrastructure of CIEC, appoint and dismiss its staff members;

c) To take charge of the overall management of CIEC; and

d) To submit annual financial reports and regular work reports to the Board.

The Deputy General Manager shall assist him in his work.

Article 16 CIEC shall set up, under the Board of Directors, an advisory committee which will assist in the consulting services. The Committee consists of experts from related fields who shall be appointed by the Board upon recommendation of the General Manager.

Chapter IV Management

Article 17 CIEC shall adhere to the principles of socialism, practise democratic centralism and follow the mass line, adopt modern and scientific managerial methods, pay attention to economic effects and efficiency in its operations.

Article 18 CIEC shall, in providing consulting and other services, follow the laws of China and give due consideration to the generally accepted practices in international economic activities, abide by contracts on commissioned assignments and keep information of the client confidential.

Article 19 CIEC shall maintain extensive contacts and close relations of cooperation with related business institutions and consulting organizations both at home and abroad.

Article 20 CIEC shall charge reasonable fees for its services rendered to the client.

Chapter V Appendix

Article 21 The present statute shall take effect upon its approval by the China International Trust and Investment Corporation and be submitted to the State Administrative Commission on Import and Export Affairs of the People's Republic of China for the record. The same procedure shall apply in case of amendment.

THE LAW OF THE PEOPLE'S REPUBLIC OF CHINA ON JOINT VENTURES USING CHINESE AND FOREIGN INVESTMENT

Approved on July 1, 1979 by the Fifth National People's Congress of the People's Republic of China at its Second Session

Article 1 With a view to expanding international economic cooperation and technological exchange, the People's Republic of China permits foreign companies, enterprises, other economic entities or individuals (hereinafter referred to as "foreign participants") to incorporate themselves, within the territory of the People's Republic of China, into joint ventures with Chinese companies, enterprises or other economic entities (hereinafter referred to as "Chinese participants") on the principle of equality and mutual benefit and subject to authorization by the Chinese Government.

Article 2 The Chinese Government protects, by the legislation in force, the resources invested by a foreign participant in a joint venture and the profits due him pursuant to the agreements, contracts and articles of association authorized by the Chinese Government as well as his other lawful rights and interests.

All the activities of a joint venture shall be governed by the laws, decrees and pertinent rules and regulations of the People's Republic of China.

Article 3 A joint venture shall apply to the Foreign Investment Commission of the People's Republic of China for authorization of the agreements and contracts concluded between the parties to the venture and the articles of association of the venture formulated by them, and the commission shall authorize or reject these documents within three months. When authorized, the joint venture shall register with the General Administration for Industry and Commerce of the People's Republic of China and start operations under licence.

Article 4 A joint venture shall take the form of a limited liability company.

In the registered capital of a joint venture, the proportion of the investment contributed by the foreign participant(s) shall in general not be less than 25 per cent.

The profits, risks and losses of a joint venture shall be shared by the parties to the venture in proportion to their contributions to the registered capital.

The transfer of one party's share in the registered capital shall be effected only with the consent of the other parties to the venture.

Article 5 Each party to a joint venture may contribute cash, capital goods, industrial property rights, etc., as its investment in the venture.

The technology or equipment contributed by any foreign participant as investment shall be truly advanced and appropriate to China's needs. In cases of losses caused by deception through the international provision of outdated equipment or technology, compensation shall be paid for the losses.

The investment contributed by a Chinese participant may include the right to the use of a site provided for the joint venture during the period of its operation. In case such a contribution does not constitute a part of the investment from the Chinese participant, the joint venture shall pay the Chinese Government for its use.

The various contributions referred to in the present article shall be specified in the contracts concerning the joint venture or in its articles of association, and the value of each contribution (excluding that of the site) shall be ascertained by the parties to the venture through joint assessment.

Article 6 A joint venture shall have a board of directors with a composition stipulated in the contracts and the articles of association after consultation between the parties to the venture, and each director shall be appointed or removed by his own side. The board of directors shall have a chairman appointed by the Chinese participant and one or two vice-chairmen appointed by the foreign participant(s). In handling an important problem, the board of directors shall reach decision through consultation by the participants on the principle of equality and mutual benefit.

The board of directors is empowered to discuss and take action on, pursuant to the provisions of the articles of association of the joint venture, all fundamental issues concerning the venture, namely, expansion projects, production and business programmes, the budget, distribution of profits, plans concerning manpower and pay scales, the termination of business, the appointment or hiring of the president, the vice-president(s), the chief engineer, the treasurer and the auditors as well as their functions and powers and their remuneration, etc.

The president and vice-president(s) (or the general manager and assistant general manager(s) in a factory) shall be chosen from the various parties to the joint venture.

Procedures covering the employment and discharge of the workers and staff members of a joint venture shall be stipulated according to law in the agreement or contract concluded between the parties to the venture.

Article 7 The net profit of a joint venture shall be distributed between the parties to the venture in proportion to their respective shares in the registered capital after the payment of a joint venture income tax on its gross profit pursuant to the tax laws of the People's Republic of China and after the deductions therefrom as stipulated in the articles of association of the venture for the reserve funds, the bonus and welfare funds for the workers and staff members and the expansion funds of the venture.

A joint venture equipped with up-to-date technology by world standards may apply for a reduction of or exemption from income tax for the first two to three profit making years.

A foreign participant who reinvests any part of his share of the net profit within Chinese territory may apply for the restitution of a part of the income taxes paid.

Article 8 A joint venture shall open an account with the Bank of China or a bank approved by the Bank of China.

A joint venture shall conduct its foreign exchange transactions in accordance with the Foreign Exchange Regulations of the People's Republic of China.

A joint venture may, in its business operations, obtain funds from foreign banks directly.

The insurances appropriate to a joint venture shall be furnished by Chinese insurance companies.

Article 9 The production and business programmes of a joint venture shall be filed with the authorities concerned and shall be implemented through business contracts.

In its purchase of required raw and semi-processed materials, fuels, auxiliary equipment, etc., a joint venture should give first priority to Chinese sources, but may also acquire them directly from the world market with its own foreign exchange funds.

A joint venture is encouraged to market its products outside China. It may distribute its export products on foreign markets through direct channels or its associated agencies or China's foreign trade establishments. Its products may also be distributed on the Chinese market.

Wherever necessary, a joint venture may set up affiliated agencies outside China.

Article 10 The net profit which a foreign participant receives as his share after executing his obligations under the pertinent laws and agreements and contracts, the funds he receives at the time when the joint venture terminates or winds up its operations, and his other funds may be remitted abroad through the Bank of China in accordance with the foreign exchange regulations and in the currency or currencies specified in the contracts concerning the joint venture.

A foreign participant shall receive encouragements for depositing in the Bank of China any part of the foreign exchange which he is entitled to remit abroad.

Article 11 The wages, salaries or other legitimate income earned by a foreign worker or staff member of a joint venture, after payment of the personal income tax under the tax laws of the People's Republic of China, may be remitted abroad through the Bank of China in accordance with the foreign exchange regulations.

Article 12 The contract period of a joint venture may be agreed upon between the parties to the venture according to its particular line of business and circumstances. The period may be extended upon expiration through agreement between the parties, subject to authorization by the Foreign Investment Commission of the People's Republic of China. Any application for such extension shall be made six months before the expiration of the contract.

Article 13 In cases of heavy losses, the failure of any party to a joint venture to execute its obligations under the contracts or the articles of association of the venture, force majeure, etc., prior to the expiration of the contract period of a joint venture, may result in termination of the contract before the date of expiration by consultation and agreement between the parties and through authorization by the Foreign Investment Commission of the People's Republic of China and registration with the General Administration for Industry and Commerce. In cases of losses caused by breach of the contract(s) by a party to the venture, the financial responsibility shall be borne by the said party.

Article 14 Disputes arising between the parties to a joint venture which the board of

directors fails to settle through consultation may be settled through conciliation or arbitration by an arbitration body of China or one agreed upon by the parties.

Article 15 The present law comes into force on the date of its promulgation. The power of amendment is vested in the National People's Congress.

REGULATIONS ON THE REGISTRATION OF JOINT VENTURES USING CHINESE AND FOREIGN INVESTMENT

Approved by the State Council of the People's Republic of China
(July 26, 1980)

Article 1 The present regulations are worked out in accordance with stipulations laid down in the "Law of the People's Republic of China on Joint Ventures Using Chinese and Foreign Investment" and for the purpose of registering such ventures to protect their legitimate operations.

Article 2 A joint venture using Chinese and foreign investment should, within one month after approval by the Foreign Investment Commission of the People's Republic of China, register with the General Administration for Industry and Commerce of the People's Republic of China.

The General Administration for Industry and Commerce authorizes the administrative bureaus for industry and commerce in the provinces, municipalities and autonomous regions to register joint ventures using Chinese and foreign investment in their localities. Licenses for operations shall be issued to the said joint ventures after examination by the General Administration for Industry and Commerce of the People's Republic of China.

Article 3 In applying for registration, a joint venture using Chinese and foreign investment should produce the following documents:

a) The document of approval issued by the Foreign Investment Commission of the People's Republic of China;

b) The agreement on the joint venture reached by the various parties involved, the contract and the articles of association of the venture, in both Chinese and foreign language and each in triplicate;

c) A duplicate of the licence and other documents issued by the departments concerned under the government of the country (or region) from which the foreign participants in the joint venture come.

Article 4 In applying for registration of a joint venture using Chinese and foreign investment, a registration form, in triplicate, shall be completed in Chinese and the relevant foreign language. Items to be registered include the name of the venture, its address, scope of production and business, forms of production and business, registered capital of the parties concerned, chairman and vice-chairmen of the board of directors, general manager and deputy general managers or general director and deputy directors of the plant, the number and date of approval on the document, the size of the entire staff, and the number of foreign workers and staff members.

Article 5 A joint venture using Chinese and foreign investment is regarded as having officially been established the day when the license for its operation is issued, and the legitimate production and business shall be protected by the law of the People's Republic of China.

An unregistered enterprise shall not be permitted to begin operation.

Article 6 A joint venture using Chinese and foreign investment shall, by producing the licence for its operation, open an account with the Bank of China or another bank approved by the Bank of China, and register with the local tax bureau for payment of taxes.

Article 7 In cases where a joint venture using Chinese and foreign investment desires to move to a new site, shift its production, increase or cut or transfer the registered capital, or extend the contract period, the said venture shall, within one month after approval by the Foreign Investment Commission of the People's Republic of China, register the changes with the Administrative Bureau for Industry and Commerce in the province, municipality or autonomous region where it is located.

In cases where changes to other items are effected, the said venture shall have to forward at the end of the year a written report about these changes to the Administrative Bureau for Industry and Commerce in the province, municipality or autonomous region where it is located.

Article 8 In registering or getting its changes registered, a joint venture using Chinese and foreign investment shall pay the registration fee or the fee for getting its changes registered, the sum of which is to be fixed by the General Administration for Industry and Commerce of the People's Republic of China.

Article 9 A joint venture using Chinese

and foreign investment, upon the expiration of the contract period of the venture or desirous of terminating the contract before its expiration date, shall upon production of the document of approval issued by the Foreign Investment Commission of the People's Republic of China register for the nullification of the contract with the Administrative Bureau for Industry and Commerce in the province, municipality or autonomous region where it is located. The licence of the said venture shall be handed in for cancellation after examination by the General Administration for Industry and Commerce of the People's Republic of China.

Article 10 The General Administration for Industry and Commerce of the People's Republic of China and the Administrative Bureaus for Industry and Commerce in the provinces, municipalities and autonomous regions are authorized to supervise and inspect the joint ventures using Chinese and foreign investment in the areas they govern. In cases of violations of the present regulations the violator shall be given a warning or be fined in accordance with the varying degrees of seriousness in each specific case.

Article 11 The present regulations come into force on the date of their promulgation.

REGULATIONS ON LABOUR MANAGEMENT IN JOINT VENTURES USING CHINESE AND FOREIGN INVESTMENT

(Approved by the State Council of the People's Republic of China on July 26, 1980)

Article 1 Labour management problems concerning joint ventures using Chinese and foreign investment (hereinafter referred to as "joint ventures") should be handled in accordance with the regulations, in addition to the pertinent stipulations in Article 6 of the "Law of the People's Republic of China on Joint Ventures Using Chinese and Foreign Investment."

Article 2 Matters pertaining to employment, dismissal and resignation of the workers and staff members, tasks of production and other work, wages and awards and punishment, working time and vacation, labour insurance and welfare, labour protection and labour discipline in joint ventures shall be stipulated in the labour contracts signed.

A labour contract is to be signed collectively by a joint venture and the trade union organization formed in the joint venture. A relatively small joint venture may sign contracts with the workers and staff members individually.

A signed labour contract must be submitted to the labour management department of the provincial, autonomous regional or municipal people's government for approval.

Article 3 The workers and staff members of a joint venture either recommended by the authorities in the locality in charge of the joint venture or the labour management department, or recruited by the joint venture itself with the consent of the labour management department, should all be selected by the joint venture through examination for their qualification.

Joint ventures may run workers' schools and training courses for the training of managerial personnel and skilled workers.

Article 4 With regard to the surplus workers and staff members as a result of changes in production and technical conditions of the joint venture, those who fail to meet the requirements after training and are not suitable for other work can be discharged. However, this must be done in line with the stipulations in the labour contract and the enterprise must give compensation to these workers.

The dismissed workers and staff members will receive assignments for other work from the authorities in charge of the joint venture or the labour management department.

Article 5 The joint venture may, according to the degree of seriousness of the case, take action against those workers or staff members who have violated rules and regulations of the enterprise that result in certain bad consequences. Punishment by discharge must be reported to the authorities in charge of the joint venture and the labour management department for approval.

Article 6 With regard to the dismissal and punishment of workers and staff members by the joint venture, the trade union has the right to raise an objection if it considers them unreasonable, and send representatives to seek a solution through consultation with the board of directors. Should the consultation fail to arrive at a solution, the matter will be handled in accordance with the procedures set forth in Article 14 of the present regulations.

Article 7 When workers and staff members of a joint venture, on account of special conditions, submit their resignation to the enterprise through the trade union in accordance with the labour contract, the enterprise should give its consent.

Article 8 The wage levels of workers and staff members in a joint venture will be determined at 120 to 150% of the real wages of workers and staff members of state-owned enterprises of the same trade in the locality.

Article 9 The wage standards, the forms of wages paid, and bonus and subsidy systems are to be discussed and decided upon by the board of directors.

Article 10 The bonuses and welfare funds drawn by the joint venture from the profits must be used as bonuses, awards and collective welfare and should not be misappropriated.

Article 11 A joint venture must pay for the Chinese workers' and staff members' labour insurance, cover their medical expenses and various kinds of government subsidies in line with the standards prevailing in state-owned enterprises.

Article 12 The employment of foreign workers and staff members and their dismissal, resignation, pay, welfare and social insurance and other relevant matters should all be stipulated in the employment contracts.

Article 13 Joint ventures must implement the relevant rules and regulations of the Chinese Government on labour protection and ensure safety in production and civilized production. The labour management department of the Chinese Government is authorized to supervise and inspect their implementation.

Article 14 Labour disputes occurring in a joint venture should first of all be solved through consultation by both parties. If consultation fails to arrive at a solution, either party or both parties may request arbitration by the labour management department of the people's government of the province, autonomous region or municipality where the joint venture is located. Either party that disagrees to the arbitration may file a suit at the people's court.

Article 15 The right of interpretation of the present regulations belongs to the State Bureau of Labour of the People's Republic of China.

Article 16 The regulations come into force on the date of their promulgation.

PROCEDURES FOR REGISTRATION, EXAMINATION AND APPROVAL OF JOINT VENTURES BETWEEN CHINESE AND FOREIGN INVESTORS

(Printed and Distributed by the State Administration for Industry and Commerce on April 24, 1981)

1. This Procedure for registration, examination and approval is formulated in accordance with "The Measures of Registration and Control of Joint Ventures Between Chinese and Foreign Investment" promulgated by the State Council of the People's Republic of China.

2. Joint ventures between Chinese and foreign investors (hereinafter called joint ventures) must apply for registration with the administrations for industry and commerce in the provinces, municipalities or autonomous regions where they are located within 30 days of the approval by the Foreign Investment Control Commission of the People's Republic of China (hereinafter called the State Foreign Investment Control Commission) or the provincial, municipal and autonomous regional governments it entrusts.

3. A joint venture, when applying for registration, must present the following certificates and materials:

a. A request for registration signed by the chairman and vice-chairman of the board of directors or the general manager and deputy general manager (one each from the Chinese and foreign sides).

b. The certificate of approval issued by the State Foreign Investment Control Commission. Those approved by the provinces, municipalities and autonomous regions as entrusted by the State Foreign Investment Control Commission must present the certificates of approval issued by the provinces, municipalities and autonomous regions where the joint ventures are located.

c. The agreement, contract and regulations of the joint venture (both in Chinese and foreign languages in triplicate).

d. A feasibility study report of the joint ventures.

e. The legitimate business certificate issued by the competent government department in the country (or region) where the foreign partner resides.

f. Verified documents concerning construction conditions such as environmental protection, urban construction, water and power supply, etc. issued by the relevant departments of the people's government in the city or county where the joint venture is located.

4. A joint venture applying for registration must fill out the application form in triplicate. The forms shall be printed and distributed in a unified way by the State Administration for Industry and Commerce. The joint venture must truthfully fill out the items listed in the form. The chairman and vice-chairman of the board of directors or the general manager and deputy general manager shall be held fully responsible for the contents filled therein.

5. The State Administration for Industry and Commerce shall reply within one month of receiving the registration application form of the joint venture and the related documents. Its procedure of examination and approval is as follows:

a. The provincial, municipal or autonomous regional administration for industry and commerce that handles the application shall examine the above-mentioned certificates and application form presented by the joint venture, and write an examination report. Where anything is found not in accordance with the stipulations, the applicant shall be promptly notified to make alterations.

b. The provincial, municipal or autonomous regional administration for industry and commerce that handles the application shall send to the State Administration for Industry and Commerce for approval all the documents and application forms together with the examination report, apart from keeping a copy of the agreement, contract and regulations of the joint venture and sending another copy to the administration for industry and commerce in the city or county where the joint venture is located.

c. The State Administration for Industry and Commerce, having approved the above documents, shall reply to the related provincial, municipal or autonomous regional administration for industry and commerce, instructing the latter to issue on its behalf "Notice of Approved Registration" and "Business License of the People's Republic of China."

d. The items "Examination, Approval and Comments by the State Administration for Industry and Commerce of the People's Republic of China" in the application form shall be signed by the General Director or the Deputy General Director-in-charge. Where the General Director authorizes the director of the provincial, municipal or autonomous regional administration for industry and commerce to sign on his behalf, he shall issue the certificate of authorization.

6. Where a joint venture moves site, switches to another line of production, adds or reduces or transfers its registered capital, or extends the term of the contract, it must, within one month of approval by the State Foreign Investment Control Commission, bring along the approval certificate to the administration for industry and commerce in the province, municipality or autonomous region where the joint venture is located, to change the registration. Where the chairman of the board of directors or the general manager of a joint venture is changed, it must immediately change the registration, fill out the registration change form and change the business license.

Where there is any change in respect of the contents of the registration, it must be reported at the end of the year to the administration for industry and commerce in the province, municipality or autonomous region where the said joint venture is located.

7. Where a joint venture wishes to conduct business abroad and requests to obtain a "Business Cerificate of the People's Republic of China," it must apply to the administration for industry and commerce in the province, municipality or autonomous region where it is located, and send a draft business certificate in duplicate to the State Administration for Industry and Commerce. The business certificate shall be issued by the department that handles the application on behalf of the State Administration for Industry and Commerce upon the latter's approval.

8. A joint venture, during registration or when amending the registration, shall pay fees according to "The Temporary Regulations on the Standards of the Registration Fees Paid by the Joint Ventures Between Chinese and Foreign Investment" prepared by the State Administration for Industry and Commerce.

9. A joint venture whose contract term expires or terminates ahead of time, must bring the approval documents of the State Foreign Investment Control Commission and the certificates of the Ministry of Finance and the Bank of China concerning the clearance of property to the department that handled its registration and go through the procedure to cancel the registration and hand in the business license.

10. Upon the termination of the joint venture contract, if the Chinese party wishes to continue the business, it must register anew and obtain another business license.

11. The procedure of applying for registration and its examination and approval regarding enterprises jointly run by overseas Chinese, compatriots in Hong Kong and Macao or their firms or enterprises together with other economic organizations in various localities or departments shall be handled with reference to this Procedure.

12. Matters not included in this Procedure shall be amended or revised by the State Administration for Industry and Commerce.

REGULATIONS OF THE PEOPLE'S REPUBLIC OF CHINA ON THE EXPLOITATION OF OFFSHORE PETROLEUM RESOURCES IN COOPERATION WITH FOREIGN ENTERPRISES

(Adopted by the Standing Meeting of the State Council on January 12, 1982 and promulgated and enforced on January 30, 1982 by the State Council)

Chapter I General Principles

Article 1 In the interest of developing the national economy, expanding international economic and technological cooperation and safeguarding national sovereignty and economic interests, these regulations are formulated to permit foreign enterprises to participate in the cooperative exploitation of offshore petroleum resources of the People's Republic of China.

Article 2 All petroleum resources in the internal waters, territorial waters and continental shelf of the People's Republic of China and the maritime resources in all waters within the limits of national jurisdiction of the People's Republic of China are owned by the People's Republic of China.

All buildings and structures installed in the aforementioned sea areas to exploit petroleum and vessels serving the petroleum operations, as well as the corresponding onshore oil and/or gas terminals and bases are under the jurisdiction of the People's Republic of China.

Article 3 The Government of the People's Republic of China protects, in accordance with the legislations in force, investments by foreign enterprises participating in the exploitation of offshore petroleum resources, their share of profit and other legitimate rights and interests, and their activities in cooperative exploitation.

All cooperative activities to exploit offshore petroleum resources within the scope of the regulations shall comply with the laws and decrees of the People's Republic of China and relevant state stipulations. All persons and enterprises taking part in the petroleum operations shall be bound by the laws of China and shall accept inspection and surpervision by the competent authorities of the Chinese Government.

Article 4 The Ministry of Petroleum Industry of the People's Republic of China is the competent authority in charge of the exploitation of offshore petroleum resources in cooperation with foreign enterprises. The ministry determines forms of cooperation and demarcates areas for cooperative exploitation in accordance with the zones and surface area designated by the state. It works out plans for the exploitation of offshore petroleum resources in cooperation with foreign enterprises in accordance with the long-term state economic programme, formulates operational and management policies, examines and approves the overall development programme for offshore oil and/or gas fields.

Article 5 The China National Offshore Oil Corporation (CNOOC) is in full charge of the work of exploiting offshore petroleum resources in the People's Repulic of China in cooperation with foreign enterprises.

CNOOC is a state corporation with the qualification of a juridical person which has the exclusive right to explore for petroleum within the areas of cooperation and to develop, produce and market it.

CNOOC may establish regional subsidiaries, specialized companies and overseas offices to carry out the tasks entrusted by the head office as the work requires.

Article 6 CNOOC shall, by calling for bids and entering into petroleum contracts with foreign enterprises, exploit offshore petroleum resources in cooperation with foreign enterprises in accordance with the zones, surface area and areas demarcated for cooperative exploitation.

Petroleum contracts referred to in the preceding paragraph shall come into force after approval by the Foreign Investment Commission of the People's Republic of China.

All documents signed by CNOOC in other forms of cooperative exploitation of petroleum resources utilizing technology and funds provided by foreign enterprises shall also be subject to approval by the Foreign Investment Commission of the People's Republic of China.

Chapter II Rights and Obligations of the Parties to Petroleum Contracts

Article 7 CNOOC shall exploit offshore petroleum resources in cooperation with foreign enterprises by entering into petroleum contracts. Unless otherwise specified by the Ministry of Petroleum Industry or in the petroleum contract, the foreign enterprise that is one party to the contract (hereinafter referred to as foreign contractor) shall provide exploration investment, undertake exploration operations and bear all exploration risks. After a commercial oil and/or gas field is discovered, both the foreign contractor and CNOOC shall make investment in the cooperative development. The foreign contractor shall be responsible for the development and production operations until CNOOC takes over the production operations when conditions permit under the petroleum contract.The foreign contractor may recover its investment and expenses and receive remuneration out of the petroleum produced according to the provisions of the petroleum contract.

Article 8 The foreign contractor may export the petroleum it receives as its share and/or purchases and remit abroad the investment it recovers, its profit and other legitimate income according to law.

Article 9 All Chinese and foreign enterprises involved in the exploitation of offshore petroleum resources shall pay taxes in accordance with the tax laws of the People's Republic of China and pay royalties.

Any employee of the said enterprises in the preceding paragraph shall pay individual income tax according to law.

Article 10 The equipment and materials imported for the implementation of the petroleum contract shall be exempted from customs, or levied customs at a reduced rate, or given other preferential treatment in accordance with state regulations.

Article 11 The foreign contractor shall open a bank account in accordance with the stipulations of the Provisional Regulations for Exchange Control of the People's Republic of China.

Article 12 In implementing the petroleum contract, the foreign contractor shall use appropriate and advanced technology and managerial experience and is obliged to transfer the technology and pass on the experience to the personnel of the Chinese side involved in the implementation (hereinafter referred to as Chinese personnel). In the course of petroleum operations, the foreign contractor must give preference to the Chinese personnel in employment, keep the percentage of Chinese steadily rising, and train the Chinese personnel in a planned way.

Article 13 In the course of implementing the petroleum contract, the foreign contractor must accurately report the petroleum operations to CNOOC in due time; and during the operations it must acquire complete and accurate data, records, samples, vouchers and other original data, and regularly submit to CNOOC the necessary data and samples as well as technological, economic, financing and accounting and administrative reports.

Article 14 For the implementation of the petroleum contract, the foreign contractor shall establish its subsidiary or branch or representative office within the territory of the People's Republic of China and fulfill the registration formalities according to law.

The domiciles of the subsidiaries, branches and representative offices mentioned in the preceding paragraph shall be determined through consultation with CNOOC.

Article 15 The provisions of Articles 3, 8, 9, 10 and 14 of the Regulations shall apply to foreign subcontractors which render services to the pertroleum operations.

Chapter III Petroleum Operations

Article 16 In order to achieve the highest practicable ultimate oil recovery, the operator shall work out an overall development plan for each oil and/or gas field and conduct the production operations in accordance with these regulations and the relevant rules promulgated by the Ministry of Petroleum Industry on exploitation of petroleum resources and with reference to international practice.

Article 17 For the implementation of the petroleum contract, the foreign contractor shall use the existing bases within the territory of the People's Republic of China. If a new base is needed, it shall be established within the territory of the People's Republic of China.

The location of the new base and such arrangements as may be necessary in special circumstances shall be subject to prior written approval from CNOOC.

Article 18 CNOOC has the right to send personnel to join the foreign operator in making master designs and engineering designs for the implementation of the petroleum contract. Design corporations within the territory of the People's Republic of China shall have priority in entering into subcontracts for the master designs and engineering designs, provided that the terms offered by these design corporations are competitive.

Article 19 The operator must give preference to manufacturers and engineering companies within the territory of the People's Republic of China in concluding subcontracts for all facilities to be built in implementing the petroleum contract, including artificial islands, platforms, buildings and structures, provided that they are competitive in quality, price, term of delivery and services.

Article 20 As for the equipment and materials required to implement the petroleum contract, the operator and subcontractors shall give preference to procuring and using equipment and materials manufactured and supplied by the People's Republic of China, provided that these are competitive.

Article 21 As for the services required to implement the petroleum contract, including services for geophysical prospecting, well drilling, diving, helicopter, vessels and onshore bases, the operator and subcontractors shall enter into subcontracts and service contracts with relevant enterprises within the territory of the People's Republic of China, provided that these services are competitive in price, efficiency and service quality.

Article 22 All assets purchased and built by the foreign contractor for implementation of the petroleum contract in accordance with the plan and budget shall be owned entirely by CNOOC when the foreign contractor has fully recovered its investment for those assets (but the rental equipment from any third party is excluded). Within the term of the petroleum contract, the foreign contractor may continue to use those assets in accordance with the provisions of the contract.

Article 23 CNOOC is the owner of all the data, records, samples, vouchers and other original data obtained in the course of the petroleum operations, as provided in Article 13 of the regulations.

The utilization, transfer, donation, exchange, sale and publication of the aforementioned data, records, samples, vouchers and other original data and their delivery and transmission to outside the People's Republic of China shall be conducted in accordance with the Rules on the Control of Data and Information formulated by the Ministry of Petroleum Industry.

Article 24 The operator and subcontractors shall carry out the petroleum operations in compliance with the laws and rules on environmental protection and safety of the People's Republic of China, and with reference to international practice to protect fishery and other natural resources and prevent the air, seas, rivers, lakes and the land from being polluted or damaged.

Article 25 The petroleum produced within the petroleum contract area shall be landed in the territory of the People's Republic of China or may be exported from oil and/or gas metering points of offshore terminals. In case such petroleum has to be landed outside the territory of the People's Republic of China, the approval of the Ministry of Petroleum Industry must be obtained.

Article 26 In case of war, threat of war or other emergency circumstances, the government of the People's Republic of China shall have the right to requisition a portion or all of the petroleum obtained and/or purchased by the foreign contractor.

Chapter IV Supplementary Provisions

Article 27 Any dispute arising between foreign and Chinese enterprises during the cooperative exploitation of offshore petroleum resources shall be settled amicably through consultations. If the parties to the dispute fail to arrive at a solution through consultation, the dispute may be settled through mediation or arbitration by an arbitration body of the People's Republic of China, or through arbitration by another arbitration body agreed upon by both parties.

Article 28 In case an operator or a subcontractor violates the regulations in conducting petroleum operations, the Ministry of Petroleum Industry is authorized to warn the operator or subcontractor and demand remedy within a limited time. Should the operator or subcontractor fail to remedy the violation within the specified time, the ministry shall have the right to take necessary steps, even to the extent of suspending its right to conduct the petroleum operations. All economic losses so incurred shall be borne by the party responsible.

The party responsible for serious violation of the regulations shall be fined or even be sued before juridical authorities by the Ministry of Petroleum Industry.

Article 29 The terms used in the Regulations shall be defined as follows:

a. "Petroleum" means crude oil or natural gas deposited underground and produced or being produced therefrom.

b. "Exploitation" means, in general, activities related to exploration, development, production and marketing of petroleum as well as other related activities.

c. "Petroleum contract" means the contract for the exploration for, and development and production of petroleum signed, under the legislation in force, between CNOOC and foreign enterprises for the cooperative exploitation of offshore petroleum resources of the People's Republic of China.

d. "Contract area" means an offshore area demarcated by geographical coordinates for the cooperative exploitation of petroleum resources under the petroleum contract.

e. "Petroleum operations" means all exploration, development, production operations and other related activities carried out in the implementation of the petroleum contract.

f. "Exploration operations" means all the work done in locating the petroleum-bearing traps by means of geological, geophysical and geochemical methods and exploratory drilling, and all work to determine the commerciality of the discovered petroleum traps, including appraisal drilling, feasibility studies and preparation for the overall development plan of any oil and/or gas field.

g. "Development operations" means all the work of designing, construction, installation, drilling and other relevant research work carried out for petroleum production from the date of the approval of the overall development plan of oil and/or gas field by the Ministry of Petroleum Industry, including production activities carried out before the commencement of commercial production.

h. "Production operations" means all the operations carried out after the date of commencement of the commercial production of an oil and/or gas field for producing petroleum and related activities, such as extraction, injection, stimulation, processing, storage, transportation and lifting of petroleum, etc.

i. "Foreign contractor" refers to a foreign enterprise which may be a company or consortium entering into the petroleum contract with CNOOC.

j. "Operator" refers to an entity which is responsible for performing the operations under the petroleum contract.

k. "Subcontractor" refers to an entity which renders services to the operator.

Article 30 The detailed rules and regulations for the implementation of the regulations shall be worked out by the Ministry of Petroleum Industry.

Article 31 The Regulations shall be put into effect on the date of its promulgation.

13 SPECIAL ECONOMIC ZONES

REGULATIONS ON SPECIAL ECONOMIC ZONES IN GUANGDONG PROVINCE

(Approved by the 15th Session of the Standing Committee of the Fifth National People's Congress on August 26, 1980)

Capter I General Principles

Article 1 Certain areas are delineated from the three cities of Shenzhen, Zhuhai and Shantou in Guangdong Province to form special economic zones (hereinafter referred to as "special zones") in order to develop external economic cooperation and technical exchanges and promote the socialist modernization programme. In the special zones, foreign citizens, overseas Chinese, compatriots in Hong Kong and Macao and their companies and enterprises (hereinafter referred to as "investors") are encouraged to open factories or set up enterprises and other establishments with their own investment or undertake joint ventures with Chinese investment, and their assets, due profits and other legitimate rights and interests are legally protected.

Article 2 Enterprises and individuals in the special zones must abide by the laws, decrees and related regulations of the People's Republic of China. Where there are specific provisions contained in the present regulations, they have to be observed as stipulated herewith.

Article 3 A Guangdong Provincial Administration of Special Economic Zones is set up to exercise unified management of the special zones on behalf of the Guangdong Provincial People's Government.

Article 4 In the special zones investors are offered a wide scope of operation, favourable conditions for such operation are created, and stable business sites are guaranteed. All items of industry, agriculture, livestock breeding, fish breeding and poultry farming, tourism, housing and construction, research and manufacture involving high technologies and techniques that have positive significance in international economic cooperation and technical exchanges, as well as other trades of common interest to investors and the Chinese side, can be established with foreign investment or in joint venture with Chinese investment.

Article 5 Land-levelling projects and various public utilities in the special zones, such as water supply, drainage, power supply, roads, wharves, communications and warehouses, are undertaken by the Guangdong Provincial Administration of Special Economic Zones. When necessary, foreign capital participation in their development can be considered.

Article 6 Specialists at home and abroad and persons who are enthusiastic about China's modernization programme will be invited by each of the special zones to form an advisory board as a consultative body for that special zone.

Chapter II Registration and Operation

Article 7 Investors wishing to open factories or take up various economic undertakings with their investment should apply to the Guangdong Provincial Administration of the Special Economic Zones, and will be issued licences of registry and use of land after examination and approval.

Article 8 Investors can open accounts and deal with matters related to foreign exchange at the Bank of China in the special zones or other banks set up in the special zones with China's approval.

Investors can apply for insurance policies at the People's Insurance Company of China in the special zones and other insurance companies set up in the special zones with China's approval.

Article 9 Products of the enterprises in the special zones are to be sold on the international market. If an enterprise wants to sell its products in the domestic market in China,it must have the approval of the Guangdong Provincial Administration of Special Economic Zones and pay Customs duties.

Article 10 Investors can operate their enterprises independently in the special zones and employ foreign personnel for technical and administrative work.

Article 11 If investors want to terminate their business in the special zones, they should submit the reasons for termination to the Guangdong Provincial Administration of Special Economic Zones, go through related procedures and clear all debts. The assets of the closed enterprises can be transferred and the funds can be remitted out of China.

Chapter III Preferential Treatment

Article 12 The land in the special zones remains the property of the People's Republic of China. Land to be used by investors will be provided according to actual needs, and the length of tenure, rent and method of payment will be given favourable consideration according to different trades and uses. Concrete methods will be specified separately.

Article 13 Machinery, spare parts, raw materials, vehicles and other means of production for the enterprises in the special zones are exempted from import duties. The necessary consumer goods shall be subjected to full or lower import duties or exempted, depending on the merits of each case. Imports of the above-mentioned goods and exports of products of the special zones must go through existing Customs procedures.

Article 14 The rate of income tax levied on the enterprises in the special zones is to be 15%. Special preferential treatment will be given to enterprises established within two years of the promulgation of these regulations, enterprises with an investment of US$5 million or more, and enterprises involving higher technologies or having a longer cycle of capital turnover.

Article 15 Legitimate after-tax profits of the investors, salaries and other proper earnings of the foreign, overseas Chinese and Hong Kong and Macao workers and staff members of the enterprises in the special zones after deduction of personal income tax can be remitted out of China through the Bank of China or other banks in the special zones in line with the zone's foreign exchange control measures.

Article 16 Investors who reinvest their profits in the special zones for five years and longer may apply for exemption of income tax on profits from such reinvestment.

Article 17 Enterprises in the special zones are encouraged to use China-made machinery, raw materials and other goods. Preferential prices will be offered on the basis of the export prices of China's similar commodities and settled in foreign exchange. These products and materials can be shipped directly to the special zones with the vouchers of the selling units.

Article 18 Entry and exit procedures will be simplified and convenience offered to foreigners, overseas Chinese and compatriots in Hong Kong and Macao going in and out of the special zones.

Chapter IV Labour Management

Article 19 Labour service companies are to be set up in each of the special zones. Chinese staff members and workers to be employed by enterprises in the special zones are to be recommended by the local labour service companies or recruited by the investors with the consent of the Guangdong Provincial Administration of Special Economic Zones. Enterprises can test them before employment and sign labour contracts with them.

Article 20 Employees of the enterprises in the special zones are to be managed by the enterprises according to their business requirements, and, if necessary, can be dismissed in line with the provisions of the labour contracts.

Employees of enterprises in the special zones can submit resignation to their enterprises according to the provisions of the labour contracts.

Article 21 Wage scales and forms of wages, award methods, labour insurance and various state subsidies for Chinese staff members and workers in the enterprises are to be included in the contracts signed between the enterprises and the employees in accordance with the stipulations of the Guangdong Provincial Administration of Special Economic Zones.

Article 22 Enterprises in the special zones should take the necessary measures for labour protection to ensure that the staff members and workers work in safe and hygienic conditions.

Chapter V Administration

Article 23 The Guangdong Provincial Administration of Special Economic Zones is to exercise the following functions:

a) Draw up development plans for the special zones and organize their implementation;

b) Examine and approve investment projects of investors in the special zones;

c) Handle the registration of industrial and commercial enterprises in the special zones and land allotment;

d) Coordinate the working relations among the banking, insurance, taxation, Customs, frontier inspection, postal and telecommunications and other organizations in the special zones;

e) Provide staff members and workers needed by the enterprises in the special zones and protect the legitimate rights and interests of these staff members and workers;

f) Run education, cultural, health and other public welfare facilities in the special zones;

g) Maintain law and order in the special zones and protect according to law the persons and properties in the special zones from encroachment.

Article 24 The Shenzhen Special Zone is under the direct jurisdiction of the Guangdong Provincial Administration of Special Economic Zones. Necessary agencies are to be set up in the Zhuhai and Shantou Special Zones.

Article 25 A Guangdong Provincial Special Economic Zones Development Company is to be set up to cope with the economic activities in the special zones. Its scope of business includes fund-raising and trust investment, operating enterprises or joint ventures with investors in the special zones, acting as agents for the investors in the special zones in matters related to sales and purchases with other parts of China outside the special zones, and providing services for business talks.

Chapter VI Appendix

Article 26 These regulations shall be enforced after their adoption by the Guangdong Provincial People's Congress and after they have been submitted to and approved by the Standing Committee of the National People's Congress of the People's Republic of China.

INTERIM PROVISIONS FOR LABOUR AND WAGE MANAGEMENT IN ENTERPRISES IN THE SPECIAL ECONOMIC ZONES OF GUANGDONG PROVINCE

(Adopted by the 13th Session of the Standing Committee of the Fifth People's Congress of Guangdong Province on November 17, 1981 and Promulgated on December 24, 1981)

Article 1 These Interim Provisions are formulated in accordance with the pertinent laws and decrees of the People's Republic of China and the Regulations on Special Economic Zones in Guangdong Province.

Article 2 In employing staff and workers, foreign enterprises, Chinese-foreign joint ventures and cooperative enterprises in the special zones (hereafter referred to as "special zone enterprises") shall implement the contract system, and labour contracts shall be signed by the enterprises and their staff and workers. The labour contracts shall include the following terms: the employment, dismissal and resignation of the staff and workers; their production and work tasks; labour service charges and provisions for awards and punishments; work schedules and holidays and paid leaves of absence; labour insurance and welfare benefits; labour protection; and labour discipline.

The labour contracts shall be submitted to the relevant special zone (municipal) labour bureau for appproval.

Article 3 In the Shenzhen Special Zone and the two municipalities of Zhuhai and Shantou, labour service companies shall be established, under the guidance of the special zone (municipal) labour bureau, to aid the special zone enterprises in recruiting and training staff and workers, to guide staff and workers seeking employment and to direct them in signing labour contracts with the enterprises.

Article 4 The staff and workers to be employed by a special zone enterprise may, after the approval of the special zone (municipal) labour bureau, be recommended by the labour service company or recruited by the enterprise itself, and shall be tested and accepted for employment in accordance with the principle of selecting the best qualified. The staff and workers accepted for employment may be given a three to six month probation period.

Article 5 The staff and workers employed by special zone enterprises shall be 16 years of age or older.

Article 6 A special zone enterprise shall manage the staff and workers it has employed in accordance with the provisions of the contracts and the business requirements of the enterprise. The enterprise may establish skilled workers' schools and training courses for the training of managerial personnel and skilled workers.

Article 7 Special zone enterprises shall pay a labour service charge for each of the staff and workers they employ. The standards for the labour service charge shall be decided through discussion at the time the labour contracts are signed, according to the different types of enterprises and the different kinds of work, and the charge shall be increased at a rate of 5 to 15% per year, according to the degrees of technical proficiency of the staff and workers.

Article 8 The labour service charge paid by the enterprises shall be apportioned as follows:

70% shall go to the staff and workers as wages (including basic and floating wages), to be paid directly to the staff and workers themselves;

5% shall be kept by the enterprises to subsidize the welfare fund for the staff and workers; and

25% shall be used for social labour insurance and as compensation for the various kinds of subsidies which the State provides to the staff and workers.

Article 9 The types of wages and systems of bonuses, subsidies, etc. for staff and workers of a special zone enterprise shall be decided upon by the enterprise itself. As to the types of wages, depending on the business requirements of the enterprise, it may adopt a piece-wage system or a system of wages calculated by the hour, the day or the month.

Article 10 Special zone enterprises shall implement a system of a six working-day week and an eight working-hour day. (The work schedule for special types of work shall be stipulated separately.) Overtime shall be paid accordingly.

Article 11 Staff and workers of special zone enterprises shall enjoy the rest days provided for by our country, official holidays and leaves to visit relatives, for marriage and funerals, etc., as well as other rights and interests clearly stipulated in the labour contracts.

Article 12 Special zone enterprises must implement the rules and regulations of the Government of the People's Republic of China concerning labour protection and environmental protection, and ensure safety in production and civilized production. The competent department concerned in the special zones shall have the right to carry out inspection and supervision.

Article 13 Special zone enterprises shall implement special health protection for women workers in accordance with provisions of the People's Republic of China concerning the protection of women workers.

Article 14 When staff and workers of special zone enterprises suffer work-related injuries, including those causing disability or death, the enterprises shall handle the matter in accordance with the pertinent provisions on labour insurance of the People's Republic of China.

Article 15 Staff and workers of a special zone enterprise, due to special circumstances, may submit their resignations to the enterprise and the enterprise shall permit such resignations. Those staff and workers who have received more than three months' training provided by the enterprise shall not be allowed to resign within one year after the completion of the training; if they insist on resigning or resign without permission, they shall make compensation for the expenses the enterprise has incurred for their training.

Article 16 A special zone enterprise may dismiss staff and workers who become superfluous as a result of changes in production and technical conditions, if after training, they cannot meet its requirements and they are not suitable for transfer to other work within such enterprise. The enterprise shall pay the dismissed staff and workers who have worked for one year or more, according to the length of work in the enterprise, one month's basic wage for each full year's work; it shall pay one month's basic wage to those who have worked for less than a year and one half of one month's basic wage to probationary staff and workers.

Article 17 A special zone enterprise may, in accordance with the seriousness of the case, impose the sanctions of warnings, demerits, wage reductions or even discharge against staff and workers who violate the rules and regulations of the enterprise and thereby cause harmful consequences. The decision to impose the sanction of discharge against personnel shall be reported to the special zone (municipal) labour bureau for examination and reference.

Article 18 If staff or workers who have been dismissed or given other sanctions by a special zone enterprise object to the said sanction, they may propose to the enterprise that the matter be resolved through consultation; if the matter cannot be resolved through consultation, they may request arbitration by the special zone (municipal) labour bureau; if either of the parties considers the arbitration by the labour bureau to be unreasonable, it may file a suit in the local people's court in the special zone.

Article 19 Matters such as the employment, dismissal, resignation, pay, awards and punishment, welfare and social insurance for foreign staff and workers of a special zone enterprise, and for staff and workers from Hongkong, Macao and Taiwan, shall be decided by the board of directors of the enterprise and shall be separately provided for in the employment contracts.

Article 20 These Interim Provisions shall be put into effect on January 1, 1982.

INTERIM PROVISIONS FOR THE REGISTRATION AND ADMINISTRATION OF ENTERPRISES IN THE SPECIAL ECONOMIC ZONES OF GUANGDONG PROVINCE

(Adopted by the 13th Session of the Standing Committee of the Fifth People's Congress of Guangdong Province on November 17, 1981 and Promulgated on December 24, 1981)

Article 1 These Interim Provisions are formulated in accordance with the pertinent laws and decrees of the People's Republic of China and the Regulations on Special Economic Zones in Guangdong Province.

Article 2 Before going into operation, all foreign enterprises, Chinese-foreign joint ventures and cooperative enterprises in the special zones (hereafter referred to as "special zone enterprises") shall apply for registration with the relevant special zone administrative office for industry and commerce and obtain a registration certificate or a business licence; if they intend to engage in any of the special lines of business designated by the People's Republic of China, they shall obtain a special registration certificate or business licence. Those enterprises that have not registered and obtained a registration certificate or a business licence shall not be permitted to go into operation.

Procedures for the application for registration of foreign banks and other financial institutions shall be stipulated separately.

Article 3 A special zone enterprise that applies for registration shall present the following documents:

(1) The document of approval issued by the relevant special zone (municipal) people's government or the special zone administrative committee of the place where the enterprise is located;

(2) One copy each of the Chinese and foreign language texts of the agreement and contract signed by the parties to the enterprise, the enterprise's articles of association and a list of the members of its board of directors; and

(3) A copy of the registration certificate or other credit certificate issued by the competent authorities of the government of the country (or region) where the investor* is located.

Article 4 When a special zone enterprise applies for registration, it shall fill out three copies each of a registration form in Chinese and a foreign language. The main items of registration shall be: the name of the enterprise, the address, the scope of production and operation, the form of production and operation, the registered capital and the proportion to be provided by each party to the joint venture or cooperative enterprise, the members of the board of directors, the president and vice-presidents or the factory manager and deputy factory managers, the institution that has issued the document of approval and the number and date of the document, the total number of staff and workers and the number of staff and workers of foreign nationality.

Article 5 To establish resident offices in the special zones, foreign enterprises and overseas Chinese, Hong Kong, Macao and Taiwan enterprises shall each go through the registration procedures at the relevant special zone administrative office for industry and commerce within 30 days after approval, by presenting an application for the establishment of a resident office and a copy of the registration certificate or other credit certificate issued by the competent authorities of the government of the country (or region) where the said enterprise is located.

Article 6 The enterprise or resident office shall be regarded as formally established from the date it is issued its registration certificate, and its legitimate production and operating activities shall be protected by the laws of the People's Republic of China.

Article 7 A special zone enterprise or a resident office shall, upon presenting its registration certificate, open an account with the Bank of China or another bank established with the approval of our side and register with the local tax authorities for the payment of taxes.

Article 8 When a special zone enterprise desires to move to a new site, change its line of production, increase, decrease or assign the registered capital, extend the contract period or make changes in the registered items, it shall obtain the approval of the relevant special zone (municipal) people's government or the special zone administrative committee and go through procedures for registering the changes with the special zone administrative office for industry and commerce and with the tax authorities.

Article 9 The registration certificate that

an enterprise or resident office in the special zones receives after completing the registration procedures shall be renewed once every year.

Article 10 When a special zone enterprise applies for registration or modifying its registration or for obtaining or renewing its registration certificate, and when an enterprise registers for the establishment of a resident office, it shall pay a registration fee or a fee for modification of registration, the amount of which shall be stipulated by the special zone (municipal) people's government and the special zone administrative committee.

Article 11 A special zone enterprise, upon the expiration of the contract period or upon termination of the contract before the date of expiration, shall go through procedures for nullifying its registration by presenting to the special zone administrative office for industry and commerce and to the tax authorities the document of approval issued by the special zone (municipal) people's government, the special zone administrative committee or other authorized institutions, and hand in its registration certificate or business licence for cancellation.

Article 12 The special zone administrative offices for industry and commerce shall have the right to supervise and inspect the special zone enterprises in the regions under their jurisdiction. Violators of these Provisions shall be given a warning or a fine or ordered to stop business in accordance with the seriousness of each case.

Article 13 These Provisions shall go into effect on January 1, 1982.

---

*Here, as elsewhere in this book, "investors" refers to foreign citizens, overseas Chinese, Hong Kong and Macao compatriots and their companies and enterprises. —*Tr.*

INTERIM PROVISIONS OF THE SPECIAL ECONOMIC ZONES OF GUANGDONG PROVINCE FOR THE CONTROL OF PERSONNEL ENTERING AND LEAVING CHINA

(Adopted by the 13th Session of the Standing Committee of the Fifth People's Congress of Guangdong Province on November 17, 1981 and Promulgated on December 24, 1981)

Article 1 These Interim Provisions are formulated in accordance with the pertinent laws and decrees of the People's Republic of China and the Regulations on Special Economic Zones in Guangdong Province.

Article 2 All foreign nationals, overseas Chinese and compatriots from Hongkong, Macao and Taiwan who enter the special economic zones at the national open ports located in the special zones or at the open ports for special use by such zones and who leave the country via the special zones are subject to control in accordance with these Interim Provisions. Those who enter the country at such national open ports and proceed to other parts of China, and those who come from other parts of China and leave the country via the special zones, shall continue to be subject to already existing provisions.

All personnel who enter and leave China shall accept inspection by the inspection offices at the ports.

Article 3 Depending on their differing circumstances, personnel entering the special zones from Hongkong and Macao shall go through the entry procedures in accordance with the following provisions:

(1) Foreign nationals and overseas Chinese shall go through the procedures for applying for entry and exit by presenting their passports through the tourist agencies or other agencies in Hongkong and Macao that have been authorized by our side to handle such matters, and they shall be granted visas by our visa-granting offiices. The border inspection stations shall give clearance after inspection of the visas.

Foreign nationals and overseas Chinese who set up factories or establish other undertakings in the special zones with their own investment and those who have bought houses or live there for extended periods, and therefore need to enter and leave the special zones frequently, may apply for multiple entry-exit visas, by presenting a certificate issued by the relevant special zone development company.

(2) Clearance shall be given to compatriots from Hongkong and Macao after inspection of their Home Visit Certificates for Hongkong and Macao Compatriots and the attached sheets or cards. Those Hongkong and Macao compatriots who set up factories or establish other undertakings in the special zones and those who have bought houses or live there for extended periods, and therefore frequently need to enter and leave the special zones in the same day, may apply by presenting a certificate issued by the relevant special zone development company or their Residence Permits for Hongkong and Macao Compatriots, which shall be signed by the special zone (municipal) public security bureau, without having to fill in the attached sheets or cards. The Customs office may issue to those who are permitted not to fill in the attached sheets or cards a long-term registration booklet for articles for personal use, which shall be filled in by the owners, and Customs clearance shall be given after verification.

(3) Taiwan compatriots who wish to enter the special zones via Hongkong or Macao may go through the procedures for applying for entry and exit by presenting their personal identification papers through the tourist agencies or other agencies in Hongkong or Macao that have been authorized by our side to handle such matters, and they shall be issued entry and exit papers by our visa-granting offices.

Article 4 Foreign nationals who apply directly for entry into the special zones from other countries or regions (not including Hongkong and Macao) must have visas issued by our visa-granting offices, and clearance shall be given after inspection of the visas.

Article 5 Group visas may be issued to tourist groups of foreign nationals and overseas Chinese who wish to make tourist trips to the special zones from Hongkong or Macao, and clearance shall be given after inspection of the visas.

Article 6 Those foreign nationals, overseas Chinese and compatriots from Hongkong, Macao and Taiwan who have bought houses in the special zones or live there for extended periods shall be issued, respectively, Temporary Residence Permits for Foreigners or Temporary Residence Permits for Overseas Chinese and Compatriots from Hongkong, Macao and Taiwan by the relevant special zone (municipal) public security bureau, if their period of residence in the zones is between six months and one year; Foreigners' Residence Permits or Residence Permits for Overseas Chinese and Compatriots from Hongkong, Macao and Taiwan shall be issued to them, respectively, if their period of residence is more than one year. The permits shall be examined once every year.

Article 7 The luggage and articles belonging to personnel entering the special zones from Hongkong or Macao or from foreign countries shall be handled in accordance with relevant control provisions of the Customs Administration of the People's Republic of China for the special economic zones.

Article 8 Upon entering the country, all personnel and articles from epidemic areas and all objects subject to quarantine under the Regulations of the People's Republic of China on Health Quarantine and the Regulations of the People's Republic of China on the Quarantine of Animals and Plants shall be subject to inspection by the port authorities in charge of health quarantine and the quarantine of animals and plants.

Article 9 Foreign nationals who enter other parts of China from the special zones or enter the special zones from other parts of China shall go through the relevant procedures in accordance with already existing provisions.

Article 10 All means of transport and communication that run between the special economic zones and Hongkong and Macao must be approved by the relevant special zone (municipal) people's government and issued a traffic permit by the special zone (municipal) public security bureau; clearance shall be given after inspection.

Article 11 The entry and exit procedures for cadres, staff and workers and other personnel from our side who work in the special zones shall continue to be handled in accordance with already existing provisions.

Article 12 These Interim Provisions shall be put into effect on January 1, 1982.

INTERIM PROVISIONS OF THE SHENZHEN SPECIAL ECONOMIC ZONE FOR LAND MANAGEMENT

(Adopted by the 13th Session of the Standing Committee of the Fifth People's Congress of Guangdong Province on November 17, 1981 and Promulgated on December 24, 1981)

Chapter I General Provisions

Article 1 These Interim Provisions are formulated in accordance with the pertinent laws and decrees of the People's Republic of China and the Regulations on Special Economic Zones in Guangdong Province.

Article 2 All the mineral resources, waters, wasteland, arable land, hills and forests and other sea and land resources within the limits of this special zone that have been exploited or are yet to be exploited shall be put under the centralized management of the Shenzhen Municipal People's Government in Guangdong Province; the Municipal People's Government may purchase, requisition or nationalize the land according to developmental requirements and in compliance with the provisions of the relevant laws and decrees.

Articles 3 The overall development plan of the special zone that has been determined must be complied with and carried out by all units and individuals. Without approval, no one may arbitrarily alter the topography of or landforms on the land within the limits of the special zone, or privately encroach upon the land or construct any type of structure.

Article 4 Any unit or individual requiring the use of land shall file an application with the Shenzhen Municipal People's Government, and may use land only after obtaining approval and completing the required procedures; if any person who has not been granted permission negotiates directly for the use of land with the unit or individual that has been using it, the agreement that they have signed shall be entirely null and void.

Article 5 The units and individuals that have been approved to use land shall have only the right to the use of the land and shall have no right of ownership. Overt and covert sales and purchases of land, as well as the renting out and unauthorized transfer of land, are forbidden; the development, use and destruction of underground and other resources shall not be allowed.

Article 6 Compensation for land to be requisitioned and for civilian houses and other structures to be dismantled and rebuilt elsewhere to meet the requirements of development shall be handled in accordance with the pertinent provisions of the People's Republic of China and of the People's Government of Guangdong Province.

Article 7 Land development projects in this special zone shall be established with the investment of the Shenzhen Special Economic Zone Development Company, and foreign investment may also be absorbed for participation in such establishment. The income and expenditures involved in land development and utilization shall be arranged by the Special Economic Zone Development Company as part of a comprehensive plan.

Chapter II The Management of Land

Article 8 Investors that require use of land for the purpose of setting up factories or establishing other undertakings with their investment in this special zone, may fill out land use application forms, by presenting the documents of approval issued by the Shenzhen Municipal People's Government and the contracts, agreements and other relevant data concerning their investment in establishing these undertakings. After approval by the municipal planning department and going through the procedures for paying the land use fee, land shall be allocated and delineated, and a Land Use Certificate shall be issued to them.

Article 9 Within six months after the Land Use Certificate becomes effective, the investor shall produce an overall blueprint for the construction of the project, the construction plan and the plan for putting it into operation; and within nine months, the ground shall be broken for construction according to the overall project plan. Otherwise, the Land Use Certificate shall be withdrawn and the funds already paid out shall not be refunded. The plan for putting the project into operation shall be completed as scheduled. If it cannot be completed on schedule, the plan can be appropriately postponed only after the investor has submitted relevant documentation and the original approving authorities have examined the case and confirmed that there are proper reasons for delay. The Land Use Certificate may also be withdrawn in case of a delay without good reason.

Article 10 After the investor has fulfilled the requirements for construction as stipulated in the contract and agreement, the project shall undergo final inspection and approval by the competent authorities before it is officially put into operation. Investors may not demolish, alter or rebuild any existing structure within the confines of the land they use without the permission of the municipal planning department.

Article 11 Investors shall build structures within the confines of the land they use in accordance with the ratio of space allotted to buildings and parks and greenery stipulated by the municipal planning department; they may not arbitrarily enlarge or reduce such space.

Article 12 All structures built by investors within the confines of the land they use shall conform to our country's construction standards and fire prevention and safety requirements. Any structures that violate those provisions shall not be allowed to be put into operation or use. Anyone who puts a structure into operation or use without authorization and thus causes an accident shall make compensation for the losses incurred and bear the legal liability.

Article 13 Investors shall, within the confines of the land they use, carry out construction for the purposes stipulated in the contract or agreement, and they may not arbitrarily use the land for other purposes.

Article 14 Investors may not for any reason encroach upon land outside the confines stipulated in the Land Use Certificate. If they need to enlarge the confines of the land in use, they shall go through the procedures as stipulated in Article 8.

Chapter III The Term of Land Use and Land Use Fees

Article 15 The term of land use by investors shall be determined through consultation, based on the amount of the investment in the project they undertake to build and on actual needs. The maximum term shall be:

(1) For industrial use, 30 years;

(2) For commercial use (including restaurants), 20 years;

(3) For commercial residential buildings, 50 years;

(4) For educational, scientific and technological, and medical and health use, 50 years;

(5) For tourist industries, 30 years;

(6) For crop planting, animal husbandry and aquaculture, 20 years.

If an investor wants to continue to operate on the land which it has used for the operation of its project after the expiration of the term stipulated, the agreement for land use may be renewed upon obtaining the approval of the competent authorities in the special zone.

Article 16 Land use fees shall be computed and collected for all land used by enterprises financed exclusively by investors or by joint ventures with our side, whether it is newly requisitioned land or whether the site of an existing enterprise is used. The rates for the land use fee shall be determined by classification based on the conditions of different regions, the different lines of business and the term of use. The rates per annum per square metre shall be (in Renminbi):

Land for industrial use, 10 to 30 yuan;

Land for commercial use, 70 to 200 yuan;

Land for commercial residential buildings, 30 to 60 yuan;

Land for buildings for tourism, 60 to 100 yuan; and

Rates for land for crop growing, animal husbandry and aquaculture shall be negotiated separately.

The rates shall be subject to adjustment once every three years, beginning from the day these Interim Provisions are promulgated, and the margin of fluctuation shall not exceed 30%.

Article 17 Those who establish educational, cultural, scientific and technological, medical and health or public welfare institutions in the special zone shall receive special preferential treatment in respect of land use fees. Projects involving exceptionally advanced technology and non-profit projects may be exempted from payment of the land use fee.

Article 18 Procedures for payment of the land use fee: it may be paid in full in one lump sum within two years, free of interest; or it may be paid in annual installments at an interest rate of 8% per annum. In the event of price adjustments, the fee shall be paid according to the new rates.

Article 19 The above-mentioned provisions

for the collection of land use fees shall apply to all the units that establish enterprises or other undertakings in the special zone.

Chapter IV Public Utilities

Article 20 The public utilities that investors undertake to construct within the confines of the land they use, as stipulated in the contract or agreement, shall be built in accordance with the requirements of urban planning.

Article 21 Investors shall be responsible for building, within the confines of the land they use, facilities for the supply of electricity and water, drainage, sewage, gas pipes and telecommunications equipment; the investors shall pay installation and extension fees for their connections with all types of mainlines outside the confines of their land.

Article 22 The discharge and disposal of residual substances, fumes and waste water within the confines of the land used by investors shall conform to the standards for discharge and requirements for disposal stipulated by the People's Republic of China, and they shall be subject to the inspection and supervision of the municipal environmental protection department and shall pay disposal fees as required.

Article 23 These Interim Provisions shall be put into effect on January 1, 1982.

RESOLUTION ON THE AUTHORIZATION OF THE GUANGDONG AND FUJIAN PROVINCIAL PEOPLE'S CONGRESSES AND THEIR STANDING COMMITTEES TO FORMULATE VARIOUS SPECIFIC ECONOMIC REGULATIONS FOR THEIR SPECIAL ECONOMIC ZONES

(Adopted on November 26, 1981)

The 21st meeting of the Standing Committee of the 5th National People's Congress had examined and discussed the proposal on the authorization of the Guangdong and Fujian Provincial People's Congresses and their Standing Committees to formulate various specific economic regulations for their Special Economic Zones put forward by the State Council. The meeting held that in order to ensure the smooth progress of the construction of their Special Economic Zones and to suit the economic administration of these Special Economic Zones to the needs of the work so as to make the role of the Special Economic Zones more effective, it decided to authorize the Guangdong and Fujian Provincial People's Congresses and their Standing Committees to formulate various specific economic regulations for their Special Economic Zones according to the principles laid down in the related laws, decrees and policies and in line with the actual conditions and practical needs of the Special Economic Zones of these provinces, and to submit them to the Standing Committee of the National People's Congress and the State Council for the record.

14

CUSTOMS AND TARIFF

Customs' Laws/
Custom Duties/ Health & Quarantine/
Immigration & Emmigration/ Port Control/
Public Security/ Transit Cargo Control

THE INTERIM LAW OF THE PEOPLE'S REPUBLIC OF CHINA ON CUSTOMS

(Adopted by the 77th Government Administration Session of the Administrative Council of the Central People's Government on March 23, 1951, promulgated on April 18 and effective as May 1)

PART I THE ORGANIZATION, TASKS AND POWERS OF CUSTOMS

Chapter I General Provisions

Article 1 All Customs organs of the People's Republic of China and their affairs are governed by the unified administration of the General Customs Office of the Central People's Government.

Article 2 In accordance with this Law and the decrees and resolutions of the Central People's Government concerning the control of foreign trade, the Customs of the People's Republic of China performs the actual supervision over the goods, currencies, gold and silver, postal items, travellers' luggage and the articles carried by means of transport and their attendants which and who cross the borders; checks and collects Customs duties and other taxes, levies and fees which shall legally be collected by the Customs; prevents smuggling; handles other customs affairs.

Article 3 In exercising its duties. as provided in Article 2 of this Law, the Customs is entitled to exercise the following authority:

(1) To check the goods, currencies, gold and silver, postal items, travellers' luggage and the articles carried by the attendants on means of transport over the borders; and to detain those in violation of this Law for disposal.

(2) To search vessels, vehicles, aircrafts or other means of transport which cross the borders or which are suspected of smuggling and detain those in violation of this Law for disposal; and to arrest those who resist and abscond against lawful orders.

(3) To interrogate persons involved in or suspected of violation of this Law; to search them if necessary, detain those whose cases are serious and hand them over to people's courts for trial.

(4) To search all storage places within the jurisdiction of the Customs and to search jointly with local or public security authorities or people's governments the places which are suspected of concealment of smuggled goods, gold, silver or foreign currencies.

(5) To investigate or make copies of invoices, quotations, price lists, bills, books, letters, cables and other documents in relation to import and export trade; to detain those in possession, or custody of the persons involved in or suspected of violation of this Law.

(6) To use force in the event of violent threats or armed resistance, or where means of transport is absconding in defiance of orders in the exercise of all the above authorities.

Article 4 To exercise the authority as provided for in Article 3 of this Law, the Customs shall enforce them with the assistance of public security, military and government authorities concerned if necessary.

Article 5 The Customs shall be responsible for the prohibition of smuggling at the ports, border passes, stations, international airports and international parcel and postal exchanges where they are located as well as other places within the jurisdiction of the Customs; the prevention of smuggling in other places is performed by public security authorities, but they shall notify the Customs of or hand over to the Customs for treatment the cases ferreted out or they shall be entrusted with the treatment by the Customs, the specific procedures for which shall be determined by the General Customs Office jointly with the Ministries of Public Security and Finance of the Central People's Government.

Article 6 All Customs vessels shall hoist Customs flags. In carrying out field duties, Customs officers shall carry credentials, wear uniforms and carry weapons along with them as required by the jobs; the rules of using weapons shall be formulated by the General Customs Office jointly with the Mnistry of Public Security of the Central People's Government.

Chapter II The Organization and Powers of Customs

Article 7 The General Customs Office is a state administrative organ of the People's Republic of China under the leadership of the Administrative Council of the Central People's Government and under the direction of the Financial and Economic Committee of the Government Administrative Council; it keeps in close contact with the Ministry of Trade of the Central People's Government.

Article 8 The General Customs Office is provided with a commissioner who is responsible for the entire affairs of the office and with a number of deputy commissioners who assist the commissioner with his duties. All the commissioners and deputy commissioner shall be appointed or dismissed by the committee in charge of Customs of the Central People's Government.

Article 9 The General Customs Office has the following powers.

(1) To organize and administer the Customs organs and their affairs throughout the country;

(2) Solely or jointly with the departments concerned of the Central People's Government to enforce all rules and regulations relating to the business of the Customs and issue resolutions, instructions and orders;

(3) To formulate the plans and schemes for the execution of the decrees of the Government and the tasks of the Customs;

(4) To study the problems of Customs policies;

(5) To participate in the drafting of international treaties and agreements relating to Customs;

(6) To participate in the enactment of Customs tariffs; draft the plans to modify Customs tariffs and rates of duties; interpret Customs tariffs, hear and handle the appeals against the problems of assessments and the application of Customs tariffs;

(7) To superintend and examine the execution at the Customs house in every part of the country of state policies, laws, decrees, instructions on Customs affairs and regulations;

(8) To examine and verify the treatment at every Customs house of smuggling cases and offences and hear and handle the appeals from the parties to the cases to the Customs;

(9) To draw up the financial budgets and final accounts of all the Customs houses throughout the country and instruct each Customs house in financial affairs;

(10) To check and cancel bad debts in the Customs payments and other income of each Customs house within the limits stipulated by the Administrative Council of the Central People's Government;

(11) To administer such jobs as the selection, provision, inspecting, rewards and punishments of Customs officers throughout the country, foster and train cadres and improve their political and vocational standards;

(12) To work out the Customs statistics of foreign trade and instruct the Customs houses throughout the country in statistics;

(13) To manage and protect all Customs Property.

Article 10 The organic rules of the General Customs Office shall be formulated and approved by the committee in charge of Customs of the Central People's Government.

Article 11 Customs organs shall be set up in the following places:

(1) The ports determined by the Central People's Government to be open to foreign trade;

(2) Border and major international combined transport railway stations;

(3) The places on the land borders and border rivers where goods and travellers are permitted to pass in and out;

(4) International airports where goods and passengers are permitted to land;

(5) The places for exchange of international mailbags and postal matters;

(6) The places where the import or export procedure of goods can be handled by special permission of the Central People's Government.

Article 12 The local organs of the Customs of the People's Republic of China are provided for as follows:

(1) Customs houses;

(2) Sub-Customs houses;

(3) Branch Customs houses.

Article 13 The establishment, modification or dissolution of a local organ of the Customs shall be decided upon by the General Customs Office jointly with the Ministries of Trade, Finance and Public Security as well as with other departments concerned of the Central People's Government.

Article 14 The organization of a local organ of the Customs is stipulated by the General Customs Office.

Article 15 Each Customs house is under the direct command and unified leadership of the General Customs Office, in close working contact with the local foreign trade administration authorities and under the direction of the people's government of the big administrative area where it is located.

Article 16 The leading or subordinate relations between sub-Customs house and branch Customs houses are prescribed by the General Customs Office.

Article 17 A Customs house is provided with a chief and/or with a deputy chief if necessary, whose appointment or dismissal shall be requested by the General Customs Office to the Administrative Council of the Central People's Government. A sub-Customs house or a branch Customs house is provided with a chief officer and/or with a deputy if necessary, both of whom shall be appointed or dismissed by the director of the General Customs Office.

Article 18 The appointment or dismissal of the officers in the rank of section chief in each Customs House and all transfers of personnel between Customs houses shall be determined by the General Customs Office. The appointment or dismissal of other officers in each Customs house and its internal deployment shall be determined by the chief of the Customs house and reported to the General Customs Office for verification and record.

PART II THE SUPERVISION OF FREIGHT TRANSPORT OVER THE BORDERS

Chapter III General Provisions

Article 19 The goods crossing the borders shall be examined and cleared by the Customs in accordance with this Law.

Article 20 The goods and means of transport passing over the borders shall go through the places provided with Customs organs, be declared at the Customs and put under the supervision of the Customs houses concerned. The wharves, godowns, places and other means of transport relating to the above goods shall be under the supervision of the Customs.

Article 21 The time for the Customs to supervise the handling of goods shall be fixed by local Customs houses and the places for handling shall be fixed jointly by the communications authorities concerned. If the Customs' supervision is required beyond the fixed places or time or due to other particular conditions, fees shall be levied in accordance with the procedures stipulated by the General Customs Office.

Article 22 When the Customs executes its duties at stations, post offices, airports and other places, all authorities concerned shall furnish assistance and necessary office space.

Chapter IV Marine Freight Transport

Article 23 A vessel engaged in international sailing and the transshipment or lightering of incoming or outgoing goods and passengers shall be under the supervision of the Customs and searched by Customs officers when it sails by or berths in a port with a Customs organ.

Article 24 An international sailing vessel shall handle goods and/or passengers from or to foreign countries in the ports with Customs organs and the limitation of the types of such vessels shall be prescribed by the Ministry of Communications of the Central People's Government jointly with the General Customs Office.

The vessel shall not, without authorization, sail straight from a foreign country to a port without a Customs house or from such a port to a foreign country.

Article 25 An international sailing vessel shall report to the Customs house near its incoming or outgoing place in an inland river when it sails from a foreign country to an inland port with a Customs house or from such a port to a foreign country and shall be examined by the Customs house before sailing on.

When the vessel is sailing in an inland river, it shall have its holds sealed or be escorted by officers of the Customs house.

Article 26 The agent of an international sailing vessel shall be responsible to the Customs house for the vessel he manages and the goods it carries in accordance with the provisions in this Law.

Article 27 The captain or agent of an international sailing vessel shall make a declaration for import by submitting to the Customs the documents as listed in Article 28 of this Law for examination within 24 hours of import or within 48 hours of berthing outside the port (Sundays and Customs holidays excepted).

The vessel is not required to declare at the Customs for import or go through Customs clearance if it leaves the port or does not handle any goods or passengers within 24 hours of import or within 48 hours of berthing outside the port, but the captain shall report to the Customs house in writing upon arrival in the port the reasons for its arrival in the port, the estimated time of stay and its next destination.

Article 28 When an international sailing vessel declares at the Customs for import, the captain shall submit the following documents for examination:

(1) Ship's import report;

(2) Ship's import manifest;

(3) Passenger manifest;

(4) Crew list;

(5) List of ship's stores;

(6) List of currencies, gold and silver on board;

(7) Sailing register (confined only to vessels under the Chinese flag);

(8) Other papers required by the Customs.

An incoming vessel's certificate of registry shall be submitted to the Customs for examination and record in a port without shipping authorities, while in a port with shipping authorities, the certificate shall be submitted to the authorities and the receipt shall be obtained and submitted to the Customs house for vertification.

The Customs is entitled if necessary to demand submission of the incoming vessel's sea log and other records relating to its sailing, etc. for reading and the captain shall submit them for examination.

Article 29 A ship's import report shall include the following items and be signed and certifies by the captain and agent.

(1) Vessel name, nationality, type, tonnage, captain's name and agent's name;

(2) The ports of departure and those it passes on the voyage;

(3) The date and time of arrival in the port;

(4) The list of the documents submitted.

Article 30 A ship's import manifest shall include the following:

(1) Vessel name, nationality, type, tonnage, date of arrival in the port and captain's name;

(2) The marks, numbers, numbers of packages, types of packages and descriptions of the goods;

(3) Numbers of bill of lading;

(4) The weight or volume of each lot of goods;

(5) The holds and/or tanks and parts where the goods are loaded;

(6) Consignee's name;

(7) The ports of departure and destination of the goods.

Arms, ammunition, combustibles and explosives shall be indicated in the manifest.

Such a list shall be signed by the captain to certify the contents are true. The original for the Customs shall be signed jointly by the agent and the duplicate shall be handed over by the captain to the Customs officer on duty for verification upon his embarkation on the vessel on its arrival.

Article 31 The captain shall be responsible for the entry of the goods and packages carried by the international sailing vessel in the import loading list and neither the captain nor the seamen are allowed to carry any of the goods or packages without permission.

Article 32 If an international sailing vessel carries transit goods and packages to be transported on to a foreign country or another port in our country, they shall be indicated in the import manifest and another manifest of the transit goods shall be made out and submitted to the Customs house for reference.

Article 33 On the arrival of an international sailing vessel at a port, the captain shall enter the necessary materials, foodstuffs, drinks and personal dutiable articles on board which the captain and seamen will not bring to land in a list of ship's stores and the captain's and seamen's personal effects in the form prescribed by the Customs and submit it to the Customs house for verification.

These ship's stores and the like shall be stored in storage and sealed by the Customs house except for the part of them which is permitted by the Customs house to be taken out for use druing the stay, and they can only be unsealed after the vessel leaves the port. If these sealed materials must be taken out for use for some reason during the vessel's stay in the port, an application shall be made to the Customs for unsealing them and picking them up for use.

Article 34 On the arrival of an international sailing vessel at a port, the captain shall, according to law, enter the currencies, gold and silver on board and in the hands of the captain and seamen in a list and put them together under care. None of them shall be brought to land, used or exchanged without authorization.

Article 35 On the arrival at a foreign port, an international sailing vessel under the Chinese flag shall submit the sailing register issued by shipping authorities to the local Chinese consul for the entry of the incoming and outgoing circumstances. If there is not a Chinese consul, a document sufficient to testify the same shall be obtained from the local Customs or port authority. When it returns to a home port, the document shall be submitted to the Customs for verification and record.

Article 36 When the Customs is searching a vessel, it is entitled to notify the captain to open any of the passenger cabins, cargo holds, coal holds, steering room, engine room, seamen's dormitories and so on; if necessary, it is also entitled to notify the captain to open up the parts which can probably be used to conceal smuggled goods and the captain shall furnish assistance upon request.

Article 37 During the Customs' supervision of an international sailing vessel, no one can embark on the vessel without authorization but the officers of Customs, quarantine, public security, port and other authorities who execute official duties and those permitted by the Customs or public security authorities.

Article 38 The area for an international sailing vessel to handle goods in a port shall be jointly fixed by the Customs and shipping authorities.

Article 39 The specified berth of an international sailing vessel and its change of berths shall be determined by shipping authorities with the consent of the Customs.

Article 40 An international sailing vessel shall first apply to the Customs for approval of the handling of goods, passengers, luggage and articles and do the jobs under the surveillance of the Customs. If the Customs believes the vessel to have contravened Customs regulations or hindered its supervision, the handling shall be ceased at any time.

Article 41 The imports carried by an international sailing vessel shall directly be unloaded into the storage place(s) registered with or permitted by the Customs or shall be transported and unloaded by the lighter(s) approved by the Customs into the storage place(s). They shall be sealed or escorted by the Customs in transit.

The manager in charge of the storage place(s) shall be responsible for signing receipt of the goods.

Article 42 The imports damaged in transit or landing shall be unloaded into a specified place with approval of the Customs house. The captain or shipping agent shall make a list upon completion of landing and submit it to the Customs officer(s) on duty for verification with the signed certification of the trustee of the goods.

Article 43 If short-landing or mislanding is found upon completion of unloading an international sailing vessel, the captain shall forthwith write the actual number of the landed packages on the loading list and sign it jointly with the Customs officer on duty. The captain or agent shall report the details of the discrepancy in writing to the Customs house for vertification within a fixed time, and if necessary, the Customs house shall notify the captain or agent to supply certificates.

Article 44 Export goods, packages and ship's fuel and materials shall be loaded on the basis of the shipping orders or permits signed and sealed by the Customs.

Article 45 The captain or agent shall make a report to Customs of goods on drawback upon completion of loading the vessel for exports which have gone through Customs clearance but have not been loaded on board and submit it to the Customs house for verification.

Article 46 When an outgoing vessel applies for clearance, the captain or agent shall make an export loading list and a passenger list in the forms prescribed by the Customs and submit them to the Customs house for vertification.

An export loading list shall, in the order of the destinations of the goods and the numbers of the shipping orders, include marks, numbers, numbers of packages, descriptions of goods, weight or volume, shippers' names, etc. and shall be signed by the captain or agent for certification.

Article 47 After receipt of the documents listed in the preceding article and the report to Customs of goods on drawback, the Customs shall certify that the outgoing vessel has settled all payable taxes and fines or its agent has signed an undertaking to settle as required before issuing a clearance permit.

Article 48 Shipping authorities shall receive and examine the Customs' clearance permit before letting the vessel go out of the port, but if the vessel is discovered to have committed smuggling or serious offences, the Customs shall notify the shipping authorities to prohibit it from going out and it shall not be permitted to leave the port without the consent of the Customs house.

In a port without shipping authorities, the vessel shall go out with approval of the Customs and the Customs house shall return such documents as the certificate of registry it keeps.

Article 49 An international sailing vessel shall stay in a port within the limit of 24 hours after going through Customs clearance (Sundays and Customs holidays excepted), but shall not be allowed to handle goods. If it shall stay in excess of 24 hours due to some reason or shall be required to handle goods within the 24 hours, it shall first apply to the Customs for approval.

Article 50 When an international sailing vessel is forced by a disaster or another force majeure to enter a port without a Customs house or shipping authority, the captain shall forthwith work out a report of the details in duplicate and submit it to local public security authorities and the authorities shall transmit one copy to the Customs house nearby for reference. The vessel shall leave the port upon the elimination of the cause to enter.

If the above vessel has to replenish fuel, fresh water, food and materials for ship repair or has to land the goods and/or passengers temporarily for the purpose of repair, it shall apply to the public security authority for approval and dispatch of officers to supervise the work. After the vessel leaves the port, the public security authorities shall notify the Customs house nearby of the details for reference.

The goods and/or passengers previously temporarily landed shall be transported on to a port with a Customs house or abroad and shall not enter the locality without special permission of the Customs.

Article 51 The goods abandoned and left on shore by an international sailing vessel in distress or having sunk or those salvaged from the sea shall be declared to the Customs house nearby by the captain or holder(s) or trustee(s) concerned and the procedures for the disposal of them shall be prescribed by the General Customs Office.

Article 52 The procedures for the supervision of the small vessels under the stipulated register tonnage which are permitted to handle international transport shall separately be prescribed by the General Customs Office.

The limits of the tonnages for such vessels shall be fixed by the General Customs Office jointly with the Ministry of Communications of the Central People's Government.

Article 53 When a vessel assigned by the army for military service or provisionally commandeered handles general passengers and/or goods from or to abroad, the captain shall inform the Customs house in advance so that it can dispatch officers for supervision.

Article 54 The government official vessels coming from and going abroad shall go through import or export formalities at the Customs like ordinary vessels and be put under the supervision of the Customs houses.

Article 55 Such formalities for an international sailing vessel as the import or export reports, examinations, handling, etc. shall jointly be stipulated by the General Customs Office and the Ministries of Communications, Public Security and Public Health of the Central People's Government.

Article 56 The vessels handling coastal transportation are only confined to those under the Chinese flag.

Article 57 A coastal transport vessel equipped with sealed holds shall carry the transshipped goods as stipulated in Article 97 of this Law with approval of the Customs, but it shall not enter a port without a Customs house and without approval.

Article 58 A coastal transport vessel shall be under the supervision of the Customs in any of the following cases and the procedures shall be prescribed by the General Customs Office jointly with the Ministries of Public Security and Communications of the Central People's Government:

(1) Carrying the transshipped goods as stipulated in Article 97 of this Law;

(2) Having to sail through a foreign country or its neighbouring areas on the voyage;

(3) Sailing from or to a neighbouring foreign area.

Article 59 A coastal transport vessel shall be examined by the Customs when it deems it necessary to do so when the vessel enters or leaves a port with a Customs house.

Chapter V Railway Freight Transport Across Borders

Article 60 A train crossing the border shall stop at a border station in order that the Customs house can execute their duties of examination and supervision, and the time for its stop, examination and supervision shall be fixed by the General Customs Office jointly with the Ministry of Railway of the Central People's Government.

The train referred to in this Law includes the locomotive, coal and water cars, passenger cars, freight cars, luggage cars, postal cars, etc.

Article 61 When a train arrives at a border station from a foreign country, the station shall forthwith submit the necessary documents of train composition, the goods carried and the checked luggage to the local Customs house.

The above documents shall include the items required by the Customs' execution of its duties.

Article 62 Import goods shall go through Customs formalities at the border station and those which are exempt from Customs examination or which can easily be examined on the train are exempt from being unloaded from the train. The import goods which are destined for a home station with a Customs house shall be loaded as far as possible in the cars which can be sealed with prior permit of the Customs and under the surveillance of the Customs house at the border station and go through Customs formalities after they arrive at the destined station.

For the import goods which are destined for a home international combined transport station without a Customs house, a prior application shall be made for the Customs' permit to unload them at the destined station. The procedures for their supervision and Customs formalities shall be prescribed by the General Customs Office jointly with the Ministries of Railway and Trade of the Central People's Government.

Article 63 When import goods are unloaded from a train, the station master or his agent shall inform the Customs in advance and store them in a storage place permitted by the Customs under the surveillance of the Customs. If there are any discrepancies between the unloaded goods and the documents, the railway officer shall make out reports jointly with the Customs officer upon completion of unloading and submit them separately to the Customs house and the station for reference.

Article 64 The Customs shall, upon completion of unloading goods, sign and issue car clearance permits for the cars entering the country.

Article 65 The train's materials and the supplies to be consumed by passengers and crew on the train, which are carried by a train crossing the border, shall be examined by the Customs house at the border station. The procedures for the declaration, examination and supervision shall be prescribed by the General Customs Office jointly with the Ministry of Railway of the Central People's Government.

Article 66 The Customs shall dispatch officers to carry out duties on trains entering the country and the railway party shall provide them with assistance.

Article 67 Before a train bound for a foreign country leaves a border station, the station master shall submit the necessary documents of train composition, the goods carried and the checked luggage to the Customs house at the border station and the train can only leave the border station after Customs clearance.

The above documents shall include the items required by the Customs' execution of its duties.

Article 68 Exports shall go through Customs formalities at an inland station with a Customs house or a border station before they are shipped. The station shall give the Customs a prior notice before loading the train and do the work under the surveillance of the Customs.

A prior application shall be made for the Customs' permit for the exports to be loaded at an international combined transport station without a Customs house and the procedures for their supervision and Customs formalities shall be prescribed by the General Customs Office jointly with the Ministries of Railway and Trade of the Central People's Government.

The export goods shipped at a home station shall be loaded as far as possible in the cars which can be sealed and they shall be checked and cleared by the Customs house at a border station.

Article 69 Checked import luggage shall be unloaded at a border station under the surveillance of the Customs, or the railway party shall apply to the Customs house at the border station for sealing it, be responsible for the transportation of it to the destined home station with a Customs house and notify the Customs to examine and clear it.

If there is a Customs organ at the station of shipment, the railway party shall apply to the Customs for the examination and sealing of checked export luggage, be responsible for the transportation of it to a border station and notify the Customs to examine and clear it; if there is not a Customs organ at the station of shipment, it shall be checked and cleared at a border station.

Article 70 The formalities for the declaration, handling, examination, sealing, submission of documents for examination and clearance for the trains carrying incoming and outgoing passengers and goods and various trains passing over the borders shall be stipulated by the General Customs Office jointly with the Ministries of Railway and Trade of the Central people's Government.

Chapter VI Highway and River Freight Transport Across Borders

Article 71 All motor vehicles and vessels coming and going on border highways and rivers and the transport of goods by manpower and animal-power shall follow the assigned routes and cross the borders at the places fixed by the Customs. The routes shall be fixed by the local communications and public security authorities jointly with the Customs houses.

Article 72 With the exception of the cases specially permitted by the Customs, the freight transport crossing the borders referred to in the preceding article shall be effected between sunrise and sunset.

Article 73 A motor vehicle crossing the border shall stop at a specified place after entering the country or before leaving the country, report to the border Customshouse, make the lists of the incoming or outgoing goods and/or passengers in the forms prescribed by the Customs and submit them to the Customs house for verification. It can only leave the place after clearance by the Customs house.

Article74 A motor vehicle permitted by communications authorities concerned to cross the border and drive on within the country shall report to a border Customs house at the time of its first entry, pay an advance deposit of not less than the import duty and guarantee against the sale or the disassembly for sale of the motor vehicle within the country. The motor vehicle shall go through the formalities of guarantee and obtaining a register from the Customs house before driving on into the country.

The above motor vehicle shall submit the register to the Customs house for verification in its subsequent passage over the border. It shall apply for the refund of the deposit at the time it eventually leaves the country.

Article 75 A motor vehicle engaged originally in domestic runs which has been authorized by the communications authorities concerned to cross the border and concurrently handle passenger and goods transport within the country shall obtain a register from a border Customs house at the time of its first exit and guarantee return to China within the fixed period. It shall submit the register to the Customs house for verification in its subsequent passage over the border.

Article 76 Except for those permitted by the Customs, all import goods and passengers' luggage carried by motor vehicles shall forthwith be declared at border Customs houses after entering our country and go through such formalities as examination and levies; for those which fail to go directly through import formalities, an application shall be made to the Customs for the dispatch of officers to supervise the unloading of them into a storage place registered with or permitted by the Customs.

Article 77 The export goods and passengers' luggage carried by motor vehicles shall be declared at border Customs houses for their examination and clearance.

Article 78 The transport of goods by manpower or animal-power over the borders or the carts which move within the stipulated border areas shall follow the specified routes in the passage over the borders or in the movements. The carts passing over the borders shall report to the Customs houses.

Article 79 The procedures for the administration of such small-quantity trade as vending and peddlingcarried on by the residents within the stipulated border areas by crossing the borders shall be examined and determined by the Ministry of Trade of the Central People's Government jointly with the General Customs Office and the Ministry of Public Security.

Article 80 The vessels coming and going in the border rivers shall sail in the specified river courses. When they handle international sailing, they shall report to the Customs and handle goods and passengers at the places with Customs houses and the procedures for the administration of them shall be prescribed by the General Customs Office jointly with the Ministries of Communications and Public Security of the Central People's Government.

Chapter VII Airfreight over the Borders

Article 81 Except those approved by the General Customs Office, the civil aircraft passing over the borders shall land or take off at the international airports with Customs houses. The airline companies shall give the Customs prior notice of the time for landing or take-off for its supervision.

The procedures for the supervision of the civil aircraft which have been permitted by the General Customs Office to land or take off at the airports without Customs houses shall be prescribed by the General Customs Office.

The civil aircraft referred to in this Law include all non-military airplanes, airships, balloons and other means which can fly in the sky. When a military aircraft crossing the borders is loaded with general goods and/or passengers, the local airforce commander shall give the Customs a prior notice for its examination.

Article 82 After an incoming civil aircraft lands at an airport, the aircraft commander or the airline company shall forthwith report to the Customs, work out an import manifest and a passenger manifest for the goods, passengers and luggage carried in the forms prescribed by the Customs, and submit them to the Customs house for verification. When the Customs thinks it necessary, it is entitled to ask for the certificate of border crossing flight, flight log, load report and certificate of nationality and the aircraft commander shall forthwith submit them for verification.

Article 83 The import goods carried by an incoming civil aircraft shall be unloaded and stored in a storage place registered with or permitted by the Customs under the surveillance of the Customs.

Article 84 The export goods carried by an outgoing civil aircraft shall be confined to those which have been cleared by the Customs and shall be loaded on the aircraft under the surveillance of the Customs.

Article 85 When an outgoing civil aircraft applies for clearance, the aircraft commander or airline company shall work out an export manifest and a passenger manifest in the forms prescribed by the Customs for the goods, passengers and luggage carried, submit them to the Customs house for verification , and it can only be cleared and take off after it has gone through all formalities.

Article 86 The aircraft commander shall work out a list of the aircraft's necessities carried by an incoming civil aircraft, declare them to the Customs house and put them under its supervision.

The loading or replenishment of fuel and materials into an outgoing civil aircraft shall be approved of by the Customs.

Article 87 If an incoming civil aircraft carries the transit goods destined for other international airports in our country or those abroad, the aircraft commander or airline company shall submit the import manifest or the transit list for each destination to the Customs for verification and the Customs is entitled to seal the goods in order to clear them when they arrive at the destination or when they are to lave the last international airport before they leave our country.

Article 88 The Customs is entitled to search a civil aircraft passing over the border, and when it thinks it necessary to open up the parts of the aircraft which can probably be used to conceal smuggled goods, it shall notify the aircraft commander or airline company to handle it.

Article 89 If a civil aircraft passing over the border is forced by special reason to land within our country, the aircraft commander or airline company shall as soon as possible notify the Customs house at the destination or at the place of take-off of the details of the forced landing. If there is a Customs organ at the place of landing, it shall apply for its approval before taking off; if there is not a Customs organ at the place of landing, it shall obtain a testimonial from the local airport authority or people's government to prove no handling of goods or passengers has occurred and submit it to the Customs for reference.

When the aircraft fails to go on flying or has to reduce its load, the aircraft commander shall apply to the local airport authority or people's government for the custody of the goods left by it and they shall only be transshipped with approval of the Customs.

Article 90 If a civil aircraft crossing the border has to cast out goods within our country due to the troubles of the engine parts or other special accidents, the aircraft commander or airline company shall forthwith report the case to the airport nearby so as to be transmitted to the Customs house at the destination or at the place of take-off.

PART III THE SUPERVISION OF TRANSIT AND TRANSHIPPED GOODS

Chapter VIII Transit Goods

Article 91 No matter whether the means of transport have been changed on the border or not, all the goods which are shipped from one foreign country via our land to the other are counted as transit goods.

Article 92 Transit goods shall be declared at a border Customs house of our country on the basis of the permit issued by the Ministry of Trade of the Central People's Government and they can only enter our country after Customs clearance.

If the goods are from a country that has entered into a commercial treaty or agreement with our country relating to transit goods, they shall be exempt from permit formalities on the basis of the treaty or agreement.

Article 93 When transit goods are declared at the Customs on entering our country, the owner or carrier of the goods shall make a list of the transit goods in the form stipulated, submit it to the Customs for verification and guarantee transport of them out of our country within the fixed period.

Article 94 Transit goods shall be carried by the means of transport permitted by the Customs along the specified route. The means of transport shall be sealed by the Customs and escorted by Customs officers.

Article 95 If transit goods are to change means of transport on the border, an application shall be made to the Customs for approval and the Customs shall dispatch officers to supervise the change. If they fail to go on right then, they shall be unloaded into a storage place registered with or permitted by the Customs.

Article 96 When transit goods are transported out of the border, they shall be checked and cleared by a border Customs house.

Chapter IX Transshipped Goods

Article 97 Transshipped goods mean those which have not gone through import formalities of the Customs, are changing means of transport at a place of our country with a Customs house and are to be transported to another place with a Customs house or to a foreign country without going by way of the land of our country, and those which have gone through export formalities and are transported to another place of our country with a Customs house to change means of transport for a foreign country.

Article 98 If transshipped goods are to change means of transport, an application shall be made to the Customs for approval and the Customs house shall dispatch officers to supervise the change and be entitled to seal the means of transport. Those which fail to go on right then shall be unloaded into a storage place registered with or permitted by the Customs.

Article 99 Transshipped goods shall be included in the import and export loading lists.

Article 100 Foreign goods which conform with any of the following can be transshipped:

(1) Bearing a through or combined transport bill of landing;

(2) Indicated for transshipment in the import loading list;

(3) Bearing an ordinary bill of lading but a statement of transshipment shall be made to the Customs before being unloaded;

(4) Mislanded import goods, but the agent of the means of transport can furnish a certified document;

(5) With an application for transshipment due to special reasons and approved by the Customs.

Article 101 If an application for the transshipment of foreign goods has not been made within 28 days of the date when the original means of transport made the declaration for import, the Customs is entitled to levy a fine for late declaration; if they are not transshipped within three months, the Customs is entitled to dispose of them as stipulated in Article 129 of this Law.

Article 102 When an application has been made for the transshipment of foreign goods to a place in our country with a Customs house, the carrier shall be responsible for the transport of them to the destination within the fixed period and no such things are allowed as opening packages, repacking, illegal unloading or replacement. They shall not be delivered to the consignee without the clearance of the Customs.

If the transshipped goods are not declared to the Customs and the duties and not paid within three months of the date when they arrive at the destination and the means of transport make the declaration for import, they shall be disposed of as stipulated in Article 129 of this Law.

Article 103 The procedures for the supervision of Chinese goods which are transshipped by way of a foreign area for home sale shall be prescribed by the General Customs Office jointly with the Ministry of Trade of the Central People's Government.

PART IV. DECLARATIONS FOR EXAMINATION, TAXATION, CUSTODY AND CLEARANCE OF IMPORTS AND EXPORTS

Chapter X Customs Declaration and Examination of Goods

Article 104 Import and export goods shall be declared to the Customs by submitting the permit of the foreign trade administrative authorities for examination according to law.

Article 105 The consignee or his agent shall declare import goods to the Customs within the fixed period after the means of transport makes the declaration for import and shall pay a fine for late declaration beyond the time limit. The time limit and procedures shall be prescribed by the General Customs Office.

Article 106 The consignee or his agent shall make an import declaration in the form stipulated by the Customs for declaration and submit the following papers for examination:-

(1) Bills of lading;
(2) Invoice and its copies;
(3) Packing list.

He shall, if necessary, also submit order note, manufacturer's invoice, certificate(s) of origin and/or place(s) of purchase and/or shipment and other documents for examination.

The import declaration and the attached invoice(s), contract or note, etc. shall be signed and sealed by the consignee or his agent to prove that they are true and correct.

Article 107 Before loading export goods onto the means of transport, the shipper or his agent shall work out an export declaration in the form stipulated by the Customs for declaration and submit shipping or consignment notes, invoice(s) and packing list for examination and, if necessary, also submit order note, commodity inspection certificate and other papers for examination. The export declaration and the attached invoice(s), contract or note, etc. shall be signed and sealed by the shipper or his agent to prove that they are true and correct.

Article 108 Imports and exports shall be examined by the Customs and the Customs house is entitled to pick up samples for examination. In examination, the consignee (or shipper) or his agent shall be present to take charge of such formalities as moving the goods, opening the packages or cases and so on. Those which have been approved of by the Customs are exempt from examination.

Article 109 Imports and exports shall be examined at the time and places fixed by the Customs. If the consignee (or shipper) or his agent has special reason for his goods to be examined beyond the fixed time and places with approval of the Customs house, he shall pay the fees in accordance with the procedures stipulated by the General Customs Office.

Article 110 With approval of the Customs, the examination of perishable goods or livestock is not limited to time and places as stipulated in the preceding article.

Article 111 The consignee of imports or his agent shall be present to go through the examination procedure within the period fixed by the Customs. If the time limit is exceeded, it shall be regarded as a breach of declaration.

Article 112 After imports or exports are examined, they shall be checked again if the Customs deems it necessary to do so or if the consignee (or shipper) or his agent makes such a request.

Chapter XI The Levy of and Exemption from Customs Duties

Article 113 Customs duties shall be levied on imports and exports in accordance with the customs tariff promulgated by the Central People's Government.

Article 114 Duties shall be levied on imports and exports in accordance with the Customs tariff and duty rates in force at the date of declaration.

If imports have been approved by the Customs to be declared in advance of their arrival, duties shall be levied in accordance with the Customs tariff and duty rates in force at the date of the declaration of the means of transport for import.

Article 115 C.I.F. prices shall be regarded as the dutiable values for the goods with import duties paid according to their values. So-called "C.I.F. prices" mean the normal wholesale prices of the goods at the place of purchase, export duties and all the expenses incurred before their unloading at the place of import in our country, such as packing expenses, freights, premiums, service charges, etc., which have been checked and ascertained by the Customs.

If the aforesaid normal wholesale prices cannot be ascertained, the dutiable values shall be otherwise evaluated by the Customs.

Article 116 F.O.B. prices shall be regarded as the basis of the calculation of dutiable values for the goods with export duties paid according to their values. If F.O.B. prices cannot be determined, their dutiable values shall be otherwise evaluated by the Customs.

Article 117 In case the dutiable values of import or export goods are calculated on the basis of a foreign currency but there is no foreign exchange market quotation for reference, the Customs is entitled to convert and calculate them according to the exchange rate fixed by the People's Bank of China.

Article 118 Besides those stipulated by this Law and the Customs tariff, the reduction or remission of import or export duties shall be handled in accordance with the Customs Reduction and Remission Procedures for Import and Export Goods specially stipulated by the Administrative Council of the Central People's Government.

The interim reduction or remission beyond the above range shall be verified and determined by the General Customs Office.

Article 119 Exemptions are provided for the import or export duties below the minimum levied amount fixed by the General Customs Office.

Article 120 The import goods in one of the following cases, which has been proved to be true by the Customs after investigation, shall have their import duties reduced or remitted as the Customs thinks fit:-

(1) Having sustained damage or losses in transit or landing abroad;

(2) Having sustained damage or losses due to force majeure between landing and clearance by the Customs;

(3) Found broken, leaking, damaged or rotten in the examination of the Customs, which has been proved not to have resulted from the careless custody of the warehouse keeper or any relevant party to the goods.

Article 121 Free advertising gifts and samples without any other purposes or commercial values shall be exempt from duties.

Article 122 The Customs levy or remission procedures of the goods for cost-free compensation shall be stipulated by the General Customs Office.

Article 123 Dutiable import samples, engineering equipment, exhibits, troupes' custumes and property, etc. for temporary import and those scheduled to be re-transported abroad within six months shall be allowed to be imported without payment of any duties, but advance deposits shall be paid and re-transporting abroad within the fixed period shall be guaranteed If they are checked and proved to be the original goods by the Customs when they are re-transported abroad, they shall be exempt from export duties and the deposits paid shall be repaid.

The period of six months provided for in this article shall be extended if the Customs thinks it fit according to specific conditions.

When the samples, engineering equipment, exhibits, troupes' costumes and property, etc. temporarily exported and to be re-transported home within a fixed period are transported abroad, they shall be handled in the light of the preceding provision.

Article 124 Such goods as machinery and apparatus transported home or abroad for repair or assembly of parts and to be re-transported abroad or home within the fixed period shall be handled in the light of the provision in Article 123 of this Law, but duties shall be levied on the service charges and costs of materials for the repair or assembly of parts.

Article 125 When a means of international transport changes to or concurrently handles home transport, the customs levy and remission procedures for the fuel and materials stored for its own use shall be prescribed by the General Customs Office.

Article 126 No export duties shall be levied on the fuel and materials carried by means of transport bound abroad for use on the way and the foodstuffs, drinks and other necessities for attendants and passengers.

The categories and quantities of the fuel, materials, foodstuffs, drinks and other necessities shall be checked and ratified by the Customs in the light of the standards stipulated by relevant competent authorities.

Article 127 If Chinese export goods are returned for some reason, the original shipper shall make a declaration for import and furnish all papers of their export. If they are checked and proved to be the original goods, they shall be exempt from import duties, but the export duties already levied shall not be returned.

Article 128 Import duties shall be paid within the period fixed by the Customs and fines for overdue tax payments shall be paid if the duties are not paid within the time limit. The period of payment and the procedures for the collection of fines for overdue tax payments shall be prescribed by the General Customs Office jointly with the Ministry of Finance of the Central People's Government.

Article 129 If import goods have not been declared at the Customs or duties have not been paid at the expiration of three months since the date when the means of transport made the declaration for import, the Customs shall take delivery of them and sell them off. Besides the deduction of the expenses for the sale of goods, the proceeds shall be used to compensate for such expenses as taxes, fees and so on in the following order:

(1) Customs duties;

(2) Other taxes and levies collected by the Customs;

(3) Customs fines, including those for late declaration or for late payment;

(4) Freight and sundry expenses;

(5) Warehouse sundry expenses.

If there is a remaining sum and an application has been made by the owner of the goods within a period of six months, it shall be repaid if the Customs has checked and found no offences against the control of trade. If no one makes such an application within the time limit, it shall be turned over to the state treasury.

The mortgage and other disputes of the goods shall be settled by the relevant parties themselves.

Article 130 If an application has been made by the consignee or his agent for the waiver of import goods, the Customs is entitled to take delivery of them and sell them off. Besides the compensation for the taxes, levies and fines listed in the preceding article, the balance of the proceeds shall directly be turned over to the state treasury.

Article 131 The bonded goods specially permitted are not within the limits of the date stipulated in Article 129 of this Law. The categories and the procedures for the supervison of these goods shall be prescribed by the General Customs Office jointly with the Ministries of Trade and Finance of the Central People's Government.

Article 132 Except for those otherwise stipulated by the Administrative Council of the Central People's Government, the Customs shall calculate and collect Customs duties and other taxes, levies, fees, fines, etc. on the basis of Renminbi.

Article 133 The Customs shall make and issue receipts for the collection of Customs duties and other taxes, levies, fees, fines, etc.; the forms shall be fixed by the General Customs Office jointly with the Ministry of Finance of the Central People's Government.

Article 134 The procedures for national import and export corporations to pay Customs duties shall be otherwise stipulated by the General Customs Office jointly with the Ministries of Finance and Trade of the Central People's Government.

Article 135 The Customs have jurisdiction with regard to the interpretation of Customs tariff, the classification of goods in the Customs tariff and the examination and approval of dutiable values. If the consignee (or shipper) or his agent has any objections, he is entitled to lodge an appeal in writing to the Customs within 14 days from the following day of the Customs' making and issuing the duty receipt.

Article 136 Before the settlement of the appeal, the consignee (or shipper) or his agent shall, with approval of the Customs, pay advance deposits so as to get the goods cleared first. The deposit shall not be less than the payable duties and other sums examined and ratified by the Customs.

Article 137 Upon receipt of the appeal, the

Customs shall examine and verify the case again within the period fixed by the General Customs Office and be entitled to alter the original decision. If the original decision is maintained, the Customs shall write down its suggestions and turn the case over to the General Customs Office for examination and settlement.

If the consignee (or shipper) or his agent still refuses to accept the decision of alteration as final, he shall re-appeal within seven days of receipt of the notice and the Customs shall convey the case to the General Customs Office for consideration.

The decision of the General Customs Office shall be final.

Article 138 An application shall be made for drawback in any of the following cases:-

(1) The drawback is specially permitted under an order after the payment of duties for the import or export goods;

(2) The duties are overpaid for the import or export goods due to the mistake of the Customs in the collection.

(3) In case of import goods which are exempt from examination with approval of the Customs, short-landing is found and recognized by the Customs after investigation and after all duties have been paid.

(4) Between the tax payment and the clearance of the import goods, the cases as described in Article 120 of this Law are discovered.

(5) An application for drawback has been made for the export goods which have been cleared by paying duties but have not been shipped for some reasons that have been proved to be true by the Customs after investigation.

Article 139 Those who apply for drawback in accordance with the provision in Article 138 of this Law shall state the details in writing and submit the statement together with the duty receipt to the Customs for verification and settlement. The application is limited to a period of one year from the date of the payment of duties and shall be dismissed if it exceeds the time limit.

Article 140 For a special commodity for export made of or from duty-paid import raw materials, the import duties on its major raw materials shall be returned after its export and the categories of such goods and the procedures for the return of the duties shall be prescribed by the General Customs Office jointly with the Ministries of Trade and Finance of the Central People's Government.

Article 141 If short levy is found after payment of duties for imports or exports, the Customs shall pursue payment of the short paid duties from the consignee (or shipper) or his agent within one year of the date of the original payment,but for the duties short paid against regulations, the Customs shall be entitled to pursue payment within three years.

If such a demand is refused, or if no payment is made at the expiration of three months of the date of the Customs' shall be entitled to pursue payment by means of legal procedures.

Article 142 The re-export of foreign goods shall be handled in accordance with the export formalities for Chinese goods.

Article 143 The Customs' examination, evaluation and collection of duties shall be completed within the fixed period and such a period shall be separately prescribed by the General Customs Office in the light of the specific conditions of each Customs house.

Chapter XII The Custody and Clearance of Goods

Article 144 Imports or exports shall be stored in the storage places registered witn or permitted by the Customs and the procedures for the supervision of them shall be prescribed by the General Customs Office with the consent of the departments concerned of the Central People's Government.

The above storage places shall be provided with safety facilities for the custody of goods and the warehouses shall also be provided with all necessary equipment for handling, weighing and examining goods.

Article 145 The manager of the storage place referred to in the preceding article shall abide by the Customs' supervision procedures and assume the following responsibilities:-

(1) Only receiving and keeping the imports or exports permitted by the Customs;

(2) Receiving and keeping combustibles and explosives in specified storage places;

(3) Receiving and keeping damaged goods in specified areas of storage places;

(4) Making and signing a receiving note within 48 hours upon receiving and keeping imports (Sundays and Customs holidays excepted) and submitting it to the Customs for verification;

(5) Delivering all goods received and kept only with the clearance of the Customs;

(6) Making detailed records of all the receipts

and deliveries of imports or exports for the Customs' verifications;

(7) Being responsible for payment of duties and/or fines if shortage is found during the custody of goods, but if the packages keep intact with the goods contained falling short, the Customs shall handle it as it thinks fit;

(8) Being responsible for handing over, item by item, the goods to be confiscated or picked up by the Customs as stipulated in Articles 129 and 164 of this Law.

Article 146 After going through Customs formalities, imports shall be cleared by means of the bills of lading or permits signed and sealed by the Customs.

Article 147 After going through Customs formalities, exports shall be cleared by means of the shipping orders or permits signed and sealed by the Customs.

Artucle 148 Except for those specially permitted by the General Customs Office, dutiable imports or exports shall only be cleared after payment of Customs duties and other taxes and levies collected by the Customs or payment of an advance deposit of not less than the total of the above taxes and levies.

Article 149 Imports shall be cleared in whole packages. If part of them is prohibited from import or shall go through special permit formalities, the Customs shall detain them temporarily and dispose of them separately; the remaining shall be cleared.

PART V INTERNATIONAL POSTAL MATTER

Chapter XIII The Supervision, Declaration, Examination, Levy and Clearance of International Postal Matter

Article 150 All international postal matter shall be declared at the Customs and go through import or export formalities.

The international postal matter referred to in this Law means parcels, postal packets, samples and commercial printed matter.

Article 151 The handling and transshipment of international mailbags shall be under the supervision of the Customs and the procedures shall be prescribed by the General Customs Office jointly with the Ministry of Posts and Telecommunications of the Central People's Government.

Article 152 The post office shall give the Customs house a prior notice of the time for sealing, dispatching and opening international mailbags and the Customs shall dispatch officers for supervision. The post office shall only seal, dispatch or deliver international postal matter after examination and clearance by the Customs.

Article 153 After opening the mailbags with import parcels, the post office shall submit a list of parcels to the Customs for verification and the Customs shall demand submission of other documents concerned from the post office for reading if it deems it necessary to do so.

Article 154 Incoming or outgoing letters or printed matter shall not be smuggled with articles, currencies, gold or silver. When the post office find smuggling or suspicion of smuggling, it shall hand the case over to the Customs for treatment, the procedures for which shall be prescribed by the General Customs Office jointly with the Ministry of Posts and Telecommunications of the Central People's Government and the People's Bank of China.

Article 155 If postal matter is destined for a place of our country with a Customs house from a foreign country, the post office with Customs officer(s) stationed shall notify the receiver to come to the office and open the matter in the presence of the Customs officer for examination, but the Customs shall notify the post office directly to open the matter jointly if it considers it necessary to do so.

The postal matter mailed abroad from a place with a Customs house shall be brought by the sender to a post office with a Customs officer so as to go through export formalities.

Article 156 If the General Customs Office and the Ministry of Posts and Telecommunications of the Central People's Government agree, the post office shall go through Customs import or export formalities on behalf of a receiver or sender of international postal matter and collect duties by means of duty receipts issued by the Customs.

Article 157 If import postal matter is in any of the following cases, it shall be handled in accordance with the procedures jointly stipulated by the General Customs Office and the Ministries of Posts and Telecommunications and of Trade of the Central People's Government:-

(1) To be returned to the original place or to be remailed to another foreign place;

(2) Broken or damaged;

(3) Having been waived by receiver or sender.

Article 158 The provisions in Articles 105, 128, 129 and 130 of this Law are not applicable to import postal matter.

When such formalities as supervision, declaration, examination and import or export permits provided for in various chapters of Part IV are not quite applicable to international postal matter, the General Customs Office shall otherwise stipulate them jointly with the Ministries of Posts and Telecommunications and of Trade of the Central People's Government.

PART VI THE CLEARANCE OF PERSONNEL AND THEIR LUGGAGE AND EFFECTS OVER THE BORDERS

Article 159 All travellers and their luggage and personal effects intending to cross the border must pass the places provided with Customs organs.

The procedures for the administration of the articles carried by the residents in the zones of land borders and border rivers who pass over the borders shall be prescribed by the General Customs Office jointly with the Ministry of Public Security of the Central People's Government.

Article 160 The travellers over the borders shall declare their luggage, personal effects, currencies, gold, silver and others at the Customs for examination and clearance in accordance with the law.

Article 161 The luggage of a traveller crossing the border shall be opened by himself or his agent at the time and place fixed by the Customs for examination. The Customs is entitled to open it directly if necessary.

Article 162 The luggage and personal effects of a traveller crossing the border shall be confined to those to be used by himself or his family and not for sale or not carried on behalf of another person or persons, and the limits of categories and quantities for those which are exempt from import or export formalities or which are duty-free shall be fixed by the General Customs Office jointly with the Ministries of Trade and Finance of the Central People's Government.

Article 163 Unaccompanied luggage shall be registered with the Customs by the traveller when he is crossing the border and an application shall be made for examination and clearance within the fixed period. Thus they shall be handled as stipulated in the preceding article.

Article 164 The incoming traveller's luggage which remains unclaimed at the expiration of six months from the date of his arrival when the means of transport makes a declaration for import shall be disposed of as provided for in Article 129 of this Law.

Article 165 The provisions in Articles 105 and 128 are not applicable to import travellers' luggage.

Article 166 With regard to the luggage and personal effects carried by a transit traveller except for those required for use on the journey, an application shall be made to the Customs for sealing or for carrying them by himself after being permitted to do so by signing a guarantee or paying advance deposits, and they shall go through Customs formalities of examination and clearance when they are leaving our country.

The dutiable effects carried by a traveller who is to make a temporary stay in our country for less than six months shall be handled in the light of the above provision.

Article 167 The procedures for the administration of the currencies, gold, silver and the like carried by the travellers who are in transit or to make a short stay of less than six months in our country shall be prescribed by the People's Bank of China jointly with the General Customs Office.

Article 168 The attendants on the means of transport crossing the borders shall not carry goods or effects on others' behalf and the procedures for the examination and clearance of the effects they carry for their own use shall be stipulated by the General Customs Office.

Article 169 The preferential procedures for the luggage and effects of returned overseas Chinese shall be prescribed by the General Customs Office jointly with the Ministry of Trade of the Central People's Government and the Council for Overseas Chinese Affairs.

Article 170 The preferential procedures for the luggage and effects of people's organizations and delegates crossing the borders shall be stipulated by the General Customs Office jointly with the Ministries of Foreign Affairs and Trade.

Article 171 The currencies, gold, silver and other controllable effects carried by travellers crossing the borders shall be handled in the light of various relevant rules and regulations of control.

Chapter XV Preferential Procedures for the Luggage and Effects of Government Senior Officials and Diplomatic Personnel

Article 172 The procedures for the examination and clearance of the luggage and effects of the personnel of the Central People's Government, above the rank of minister, embassy and consulate personnel resident abroad and the delegates attending overseas meetings who cross the borders on official business shall be prescribed by the General Customs Office jointly with the Ministries of Foreign Affairs, Personnel Affairs, Trade and Finance of the Central People's Government.

Article 173 When the public effects of our embassy, consulate or diplomatic delegation accredited abroad cross the border, they shall be exempt from examination or duties or import or export permits but the Customs is entitled to examine them if necessary.

Article 174 The preferential procedures for the levy, remission, examination and clearance of the luggage and public or personal effects of the personnel of foreign embassies and consulates in China, who cross the borders, shall be prescribed by the General Customs Office jointly with the Ministry of Foreign Affairs of the Central People's Government.

PART VII SMUGGLING OFFENCES AND THEIR TREATMENT

Chapter XVI Smuggling Acts and Rules for Punishment

Article 175 A smuggling act means one of the following:

(1) Transporting or carrying goods, currencies, gold, silver and other articles by bypassing the place on the border with a Customs house or going through such a place but evading supervision and control;

(2) Making a false report of the quantities of the goods carried over the border;

(3) Making a false report of the description and specifications of the goods for the purpose of transporting the goods which are prohibited or restricted from import or export;

(4) Mailing international letters or printed matter concealing currencies, gold or silver;

(5) Without permission from the Customs, selling duty-free or duty-reduced goods or selling duty-paid goods without prior approval;

(6) Selling articles transported home from abroad and declared as personal effects for the purpose of gain;

(7) In a designated area along the border, possessing or in custody of foreign currencies, gold and silver, foreign goods exceeding the quantities allowed for personal use or Chinese goods beyond the stipulated categories and quantities without lawful papers;

(8) A coastal transport vessel, in a designated area, carrying foreign goods or Chinese goods beyond the stipulated categories and quantities allowed without lawful papers;

(9) A coastal transport vessel which has passed or come from a neighbouring foreign area carrying foreign goods without lawful papers;

(10) The preparatory act of any of the aforesaid.

The "designated area" referred to in clauses (7) and (8) of this Article shall be fixed by the General Customs Office jointly with the Ministry of Public Security of the Central People's Government.

Article 176 A serious smuggling act means one of the following:

(1) Transporting smuggled goods, currencies, gold, silver and other articles under the cover of specially designed smuggling devices or with the means of transport specializing in smuggling;

(2) A smuggling act done by an organization specializing in smuggling;

(3) The smuggler resisting by violence when

the smuggled goods are being examined or detained;

(4) Secretly transporting narcotic drugs, military supplies or other contrabands;

(5) Forging or fraudulently use government papers to cover for the smugglers;

(6) Habitually collecting, handling, transshipping or marketing smuggled goods;

(7) A government functionary taking advantage of his position for smuggling;

(8) Colluding with a government functionary or functionaries in smuggling;

(9) Swapping or replacing import or export, bonded, transshipped or transit goods;

(10) The preparatory act of any of the aforesaid.

Article 177 For the person who has committed any of the acts listed in Article 175 of this Law, the Customs shall confiscate his smuggled goods and impose on the smuggler a fine not exceeding the total value of the smuggled goods. For those with less seriousness, the Customs shall only impose a fine on them or excuse them from punishment.

Article 178 For the person who has committed any of the acts listed in Article 176 of this Law, the Customs shall confiscate his smuggled goods and impose on the smuggler a fine not exceeding the total value of the smuggled goods. Those with gross seriousness shall be handed over to judicial authorities for investigation and punishment. Those who transport military supplies secretly shall be handed over to public security authorities for trial and punishment.

Article 179 If it has been established through investigation that the secret transport over the border of goods, currencies, gold, silver and other articles actually relates to the means of transport, the Customs shall confiscate the means of transport in addition to notifying the local communications authorities and impose on the person in charge of the means of transport a fine not exceeding the total value of the smuggled goods or hand him over to judicial or public security authorities for investigation and punishment. But for those with less seriousness, the Customs shall only impose a fine on them or excuse them from punishment.

Article 180 The Customs is entitled to confiscate or demolish the articles used to cover smuggling, specially made devices for such purpose, and the buildings exclusively for concealment of smuggled goods.

Article 181 A person who assists in any of the acts listed in Article 175 shall have imposed a fine not exceeding the total value of the smuggled goods. Those with less seriousness shall be excused from punishment.

A person who assists in any of the acts listed in Article 176 shall be handed over to the judicial or public security authorities for investigation and punishment.

Article 182 The smuggler who commits again any of the acts listed in Article 175 of this Law within one year of the date when the punishment of the smuggling case is decided upon shall be punished in accordance with the provision in Article 178 of this Law.

Article 183 If a smuggling act is discovered three years later, the smuggler shall have the punishment reduced or remitted.

Article 184 If a smuggling act is beyond the specific provisions in this Law, it shall be dealt with in the light of the clause(s) of the greatest similarity in this Law.

Chapter XVII Treatment of Smuggling Cases

Article 185 The power of the handling of smuggling cases belongs to the Customs.

Article 186 The punishment of smuggling cases shall be decided upon by the chief of a Customs House. But the chief is entitled to authorize the chief officer of a sub-Customs House or a branch customshouse to do so.

Article 187 In the punishment of a smuggling case, the Customs House shall give the punished a notice of punishment and if it cannot be delivered, the Customs shall make an announcement of it.

Article 188 When the punished refuses to accept the Customs house's punishment as final, he shall make an appeal to the Customs within 14 days on receipt of the notice or announcement of punishment and the chief shall verify the case again and alter the original punishment after review. If the original punishment is maintained, he shall write down his suggestions and hand the case over to the General Customs Office for investigation and treatment.

If the punished still refuses to accept the alteration of punishment as final, he shall reappeal within seven days on receipt of the notice of the alteration of punishment, which shall be handed over by the Customs house to the General Customs Office for investigation and treatment.

If no appeals have been made within the aforesaid periods, the punishment shall be final.

Article 189 The General Customs Office shall make a letter of its decision on the appeals and deliver it to the appellant through the original Customs house and if it cannot be delivered, it shall make an announcement of it.

The decision of the General Customs Office shall be final.

Article 190 When the Customs detains the articles or means of transport, it shall issue a notice of detention.

Article 191 The Customs shall demand payment or an offer from the smuggler or the person in charge of the means of transport cash or other reliable security in an equal value to the smuggled goods or means of transport which cannot be detained.

Article 192 If the Customs thinks the detained goods have the risk of perishing or loss of effectiveness through detention, it shall sell them off before the settlement of the punishment, retain the proceeds and give a notice to the original holder of the goods.

Article 193 Except for the articles and special conditions referred to in Article 192 of this Law, the Customs shall not dispose of the smuggled goods and means of transport detained through investigation before the decision of punishment.

Article 194 The fine in a smuggling case shall be paid off within 14 days of the date of decision of punishment or delivery of the letter of decision or announcement and the Customs shall confiscate the detained articles, means of transport or advance deposits if the time limit is exceeded.

If a fine is inposed on the above detained articles, means of transport or earnest money in addition to confiscation, the procedures for the payment of the fine are the same and if the time limit is exceeded, the Customs shall hand the case over to the judicial authorities so as to demand payment from the punished.

If more than two persons take part in a smuggling case and are punished in the same way, they shall hold themselves jointly responsible for the payment of all the fines.

Article 195 Confiscated articles and means of transport and the articles disposed of by the Customs in accordance with the provisions in Articles 129, 130 and 164 shall be sold off in the light of the procedures prescribed by the General Customs Office. Those which shall not be sold off shall be handed over to the authorities concerned in charge of them and the procedures shall be prescribed by the General Customs Office jointly with the authorities concerned.

The confiscated articles which shall be destroyed as stipulated by the General Customs Office shall be directly destroyed by the Customs house.

Article 196 The procedures for the disposal, reward and report for delivery of the fines from smuggling cases and the proceeds from the sale of confiscated articles shall be prescribed by the General Customs Office jointly with the Ministry of Finance of the Central People's Government.

Chapter XVIII The Punishment and Treatment of Offences

Article 197 In any of the following cases, the person in charge or manager of the means of transport concerned shall be fined no more than the total value of the means of transport concerned:

(1) A vessel sails directly abroad from a port without a Customs house or directly from a foreign country to a port without a Customs house and without approval of the Customs.

(2) A vessel which is prohibited from engaging in international transportation sails to and from foreign countries without authorization.

(3) A means of transport does not report to the Customs upon entering our country or goes to a foreign place without approval of the Customs.

Article 198 In any of the following cases, a fine of less than Renminbi one thousand yuan shall be imposed on the person in charge or shipping agent of the vessel:

(1) A vessel carrying the transshipped goods referred to in Article 97 enters a port without a Customs house and without approval of the Customs.

(2) When an international sailing vessel enters a port in an inland river with a Customs house from a foreign country or sails abroad from the port, it does not report to the Customs house nearest the place of import or export.

Article 199 In any of the following cases, a fine of less than Renminbi five hundred yuan shall be imposed on the person in charge or manager of the means of transport concerned:

(1) A means of transport engaged in international transportation handles goods, passengers, luggage and articles without approval of the Customs or without conforming to the formalities set by the Customs.

(2) Goods or necessities carried by a means of transport crossing the border are not included in the manifest for declaration at the Customs or cannot be found even though they are listed in the manifest.

(3) Contravening the provision in Article 35 of this Law.

(4) A lighter handles import or export, transit or transshipped goods without permit of the Customs or moves without authorization.

(5) As referred to in Article 58 of this Law, a vessel does not go through formalities in accordance with the provisions of the Customs.

(6) There is false information written in the documents submitted to the Customs for examination.

(7) Not acting in accordance with the routes or time provided in Articles 71, 72, 78 and 80 of this Law.

(8) A vessel or an aircraft engaged in international transportation does not report as stipulated when it enters a port without a Customs house due to a disaster or lands at an airport without a Customs house.

(9) The above vessel or aircraft throws out or handles goods within the territory of China due to a disaster but does not report as stipulated.

Article 200 In any of the following cases, a fine of less than Reminbi one hundred yuan shall be imposed on the person in charge or manager of the means of transport concerned:

(1) A means of international transport does not go through Customs import or exports formalities in accordance with the prescribed time or procedure.

(2) A means of international transport fails to submit the prescribed documents to the Customs for examination within the fixed period after completion of handling goods.

(3) An international sailing vessel stays in the port in excess of 24 hours after going through Customs clearance and does not report to the Customs.

Article 201 If transit or transshipped goods are transported abroad or to the destination in excess of the time limit but no proper reason is supplied, a fine of less than Renminbi one hundred yuan shall be imposed on the owner or carrier of the goods.

Article 202 If there is a discrepancy in the quantities of the goods stored in the storage place registered with or permitted by the Customs or delivery takes place without the Customs' clearance and no proper reason is supplied, the manager of the storage place shall be fined sum not exceeding value of the goods.

Article 203 In anyone of the following cases, a fine of less than Renminbi five hundred yuan shall be imposed on the manager of the storage place concerned:

(1) A storage place registered with or permitted by the Customs to receive and keep the goods which have not been permitted by the Customs to be unloaded.

(2) A storage place registered with or permitted by the Customs, without authorization, receives and keeps the goods which should be put under the supervision of the Customs.

Article 204 In any of the following cases, a fine of less than Renminbi one hundred yuan shall be imposed on the manager of the storage place concerned.

(1) A receiving note has not been signed and submitted to the Customs for verification within 48 hours after receiving and storing import goods.

(2) There is a false record with regard to the receipt, delivery and storage of the goods.

Article 205 In any one of the following cases, the owner or agent of the goods shall be fined no more than three times the tax evaded or no more than the equal value of the goods:

(1) Giving false reports of the descriptions, specifications or prices of import or export goods;

(2) Submitting false documents concerning import or export goods, such as invoice(s), contract or note, documents, books, etc., or failing to submit such documents for examination.

Article 206 In any of the following cases, a fine of no more than Renminbi five hundred yuan shall be imposed on the offender or the responsible person:

(1) Without authorization, altering, removing or tearing down the sealing marks of the Customs or opening or entering the place sealed by the Customs;

(2) Without authorization, opening the packages, repacking or altering marks and numbers of

the goods which have not been cleared by the Customs;

(3) Hindering or obstructing customs officers in their execution of duties;

(4) Taking delivery of goods or luggage without authorization and clearance of the Customs.

Article 207 If a person mails, carries or holds blank documents which can be used to make foreign invoices of the import goods, a fine of no more than Renminbi one thousand yuan shall be imposed on him and the documents shall be confiscated and destroyed.

Article 208 All parties concerned who are fined in accordance with Articles 197 and 207 of this Law shall separately be fined by the Customs.

Article 209 If an offence in the same article and clause of this Law is committed again within one year of the date of the decision of punishment, the maximum fine shall be increased by half.

Article 210 If there are no specific provisions in this Law for an offence, it shall be treated as the case may be in the light of the article(s) and/or clause(s) stipulated in this Law of the greatest similarity.

Article 211 If an offence is discovered three years later, the punishment shall be excused.

Article 212 Before the punished in an offence pays or guarantees to pay the fine, the Customs shall detain the means of transport or goods concerned and treat them in accordance with the provisions in Articles 190, 192 and 193 of this Law.

Article 213 The provisions in Article 185 to Article 189 and Article 193 to Article 195 are applicable to the treatment and appeal of an offence.

Article 214 The provision in Article 196 of this Law is applicable to the procedures for the disposal, reward and report for delivery of the fines from offences and the proceeds from confiscated articles.

Article 215 Besides those provided for in this Law, the cases in violation of the control of foreign trade and finance of the Central People's Government shall be treated in accordance with the decrees of the control concerned.

PART VIII SUPPLEMENTARY ARTICLES

Chapter XIX Supplementary Articles

Article 216 In particular areas where this Law is not applicable, the General Customs Office shall work out another ordinance in the light of the principles of this Law and the local specific conditions and apply to the Administrative Council of the Central People's Government for the approval and enactment of the ordinance.

Article 217 This Law has been adopted, promulgated and put in force by the Government Administration Session of the Administrative Council of the Central People's Government.

INTERIM PROCEDURES FOR VESSEL TONNAGE DUTIES

(Approved by the Financial and Economic Committee of the Government Administrative Council on September 16, 1952 and promulgated and put into effect by the General Customs Office on September 29 of the same year)

(The amendements to Articles 2 and 3 were approved by the Financial and Economic Committee of the Government Administrative Council on November 11, 1954 and were notified to become effective by the General Customs Office of the Ministry of Foreign Trade on November 30 of the same year)

Article 1 Vessel tonnage duties (hereinafter simply referred to as tonnages) shall be levied by the Customs in accordance with these Procedures on foreign registered vessels and Chinese registered vessels chartered by foreign firms and Chinese or foreign registered vessels used by Chinese-foreign joint ventures (including vessels exclusively sailing within the ports) sailing in the ports of the People's Republic of China.

It is not necessary for the said vessels paying tonnages to pay additional vehicle and vessel service licence fees to the tax authorities.

Article 2 Tonnages are divided into two types: one to be paid once every three months and the other to be paid once every 30 days, which shall be chosen by the payers themselves when they apply for the payment of the tonnages. The scale and rate of the tonnages are as follows:

(1) Those to be paid once every three months:

Category of Vessel		Ton	Tonnage per Ton	Remarks
		below 50 tons	3 jiao	Tonnages to be calculated
		51 tons to 150 tons	3 jiao 5 fen	and levied by net weight. The
		151 tons to 300 tons	4 jiao	odd amount less than ½
		301 tons to 500 tons	4 jiao 5 fen	ton is exempted from
Power-	Steamships	501 tons to 1,000 tons	6 jiao	taxation; ½ ton or more
Driven	Motorboats	1,001 tons to 1,500 tons	7 jiao 5 fen	than ½ ton is considered
Vessel	Tugboats	1,501 tons to 2,000 tons	9 jiao	as 1 ton. Small vessels
		2,001 tons to 3,000 tons	1 yuan 1 jiao	less than 1 ton shall be
		3,001 tons to 4,000 tons	1 yuan 3 jiao	taxed as 1 ton except for
		4,001 tons to 5,000 tons	1 yuan 5 jiao	those authorized by the
		more than 5,001 tons	1 yuan 8 jiao	General Customs Office to
				be exempted from taxation.
		below 10 tons	1 jiao 5 fen	
Non-	Various Man-driven	11 tons to 50 tons	2 jiao	
powered	Boats, Lighters	51 tons to 150 tons	2 jiao 5 fen	
Driver	and Junks	151 tons to 300 tons	3 jiao	
Vessels		more than 301 tons	3 jiao 5 fen	

(2) Those to be paid once every 30 days shall be levied by half of the rates in the above list.

The tonnage shall be levied on an incoming vessel as from the date of its declaration for import. If the vessel does not leave China at the expiration of the tonnage licence obtained, the levy shall be continued as from the second day of the expiration.

Article 3 The Tonnage for a vessel which is registered in or belong to a foreign country which has entered into treaty or agreement with the

People's Republic of China for mutual preferential treatment in tonnages or fees levied on vessels shall be levied at a preferential rate. The rates of tonnages to be levied once every three months are as follows: (Note: This article has been amended according to Notice No. MGH-221(74) of the Ministry of Foreign Trade.)

Category of Vessel	Ton	Tonnage per Ton	Remarks
	below 50 tons	3 jiao	The procedures for calculation and levy are the same as in the preceding list.
	51 tons to 150 tons	3 jiao 5 fen	
	151 tons to 300 tons	4 jiao	
Power-driven Vessels (Steamships, Motorboats, Tugboats)	301 tons to 500 tons	4 jiao 5 fen	
	501 tons to 1,000 tons	5 jiao 5 fen	
	1,001 tons to 1,500 tons	6 jiao 5 fen	
	1,501 tons to 2,000 tons	8 jiao	
	2,001 tons to 3,000 tons	9 jiao 5 fen	
	more than 3,001 tons	1 yuan 1 jiao	
	below 10 tons	1 jiao 5 fen	
Nonpowered Driven Vessels (Various Man-driven Boats, Lighters and Junks)	11 tons to 50 tons	2 jiao	
	51 tons to 150 tons	2 jiao 5 fen	
	151 tons to 300 tons	3 jiao	
	more than 301 tons	3 jiao 5 fen	

If a vessel paying the tonnage as stipulated by this article applies for the payment once every 30 days in accordance with the procedures in the preceding article, the tonnage shall be levied at half of the rates of the above list.

Article 4 A foreign registered vessel or a Chinese registered vessel chartered by a foreign firm shall submit the vessel tonnage licence and the declaration at the Customs house for examination and import or clearance purposes as stipulated by the Customs when it arrives at or leaves a port with a Customs house. If the original licence has expired at the time of import of the tonnage has not been paid before, it shall file a declaration at the time of import, make the declaration at the Customs house and pay the tonnage by submitting (1) the certificate of the vessel's registry (or the testimonial signed and issued by the port authorities to testify that this certifiate has been kept in their custody) and (2) the proof of the vessel's tonnage for examination.

Article 5 If the term of validity of the tonnage licence of the above vessel is expired after its declaration for import or if it sails exclusively within the port, it shall make a declaration at the Customs house, pay the tonnage and obtain a new licence as stipulated in the preceding article at the expiration of the original licence. If it fails to make a declaration and pay the tonnage within five days of the second day of the expiration, it shall be fined as stipulated in Article 14 of these Procedures.

Article 6 A foreign registered vessel specially permitted to sail to or from a place with no Customs house shall submit the vessel tonnage licence to the local port authorities for examination (it shall be submitted to the local frontier public security authorities or troops for examination in a place without port authorities) as stipulated in Article 4 of these Procedures when it arrives at or leaves the port. At the expiration of the original licence, it shall also make a declaration at the local tax bureau as stipulated in Article 4 and Article 5 of these Procedures and the bureau shall collect the tonnage and issue a new licence in lieu of the Customs according to these Procedures. If it fails to make a declaration within the time limit, it shall be fined in accordance with Article 14.

Article 7 The payer shall pay the tonnage within five days (Sunday and the statutory holidays excepted) from the second day of the issue of the Notice of Tonnage Payment by the Customs house (or the tax bureau) and the Customs house (or the bureau) shall issue the vessel tonnage licence. If the time limit is exceeded, the Customs house (or bureau) shall collect the fine for late payment of 1/1000 of the payable tonnage amount daily from the sixth day to the date of the full payment of the tonnage and pay it into the treasury as the Customs' fines.

Article 8 In the case of a Chinese registered vessel chartered by a foreign firm or a foreign registered vessel chartered by a Chinese public or private enterprise, the vehicle and vessel serivce licence tax or the vessel tonnage already paid shall remain valid if it has not expired at the beginning or termination of the charter. However, the vessel shall make a declaration at the Customs house and pay the tonnage or make the declaration at the tax bureau and pay the vehicle and vessel service licence tax upon its expiration on the basis of its usage at that time.

Article 9 The tonnage amount shall not be readjusted within the term of validity of the tonnage licence already obtained even if the net weight of a vessel is increased or reduced due to repair. However, at the time of the next payment of tonnage, an application shall be made for the adjustment of the tonnage amount on the basis of the certificate of tonnage after the change of its weight. If the increase of weight is not disclosed and declared with intention of evading tonnage payment, the vessel shall be fined as stipulated in Article 14 of these Procedures.

Article 10 If a vessel which has paid tonnage is in any of the following cases, the Customs shall annotate and comment on the extension of the term of the licence validity according to the actual number of days after examining the papers of the port authorities submitted:

(1) A vessel sailing into a port of our country for the purpose of refuge or repair;

(2) A vessel unable to handle goods or passengers as a result of an epidemic prevention isolation;

(3) A vessel having been commandeered or chartered by the central or a local people's government.

Article 11 The following foreign registered vessels shall be exempt from tonnages:

(1) The vessels engaged by the embassies, legations and consulates of the countries having established diplomatic relations with our country;

(2) The vessels with the papers of local port authorities to take refuge, undergo repairs, suspend service or be disassembled and not to carry goods or passengers for the time being;

(3) The mooring pontoons, floating-bridge pontoons and floating boats used exclusively to carry goods and passengers and store goods;

(4) The vessels commandeered or chartered by the central or local people's governments;

(5) The international sailing vessels which are exempt from making declarations at the Customs for import as stipulated in Article 27 of the Interim Law on Customs.

Article 12 If a charter-party goes through Customs formalities before the vessel arrives at the port, he shall submit a written guarantee to the Customs house to assure submission of the tonnage licence for examination or payment of the tonnage and application for licence according to regulations after the vessel has entered the port. The term of validity of the licence shall be calculated as from the date of the vessel's declaration for import.

Article 13 If the tonnage licence obtained by a charter-party is damaged or lost during the term of validity, he shall make a written application to the original licence-issuing Customs house (or tax bureau) for a copy of the tonnage licence. No further payment is required.

Article 14 All formalities have to be observed within the time limit set. A charter-party who fails to make a declaration, pay the tonnage and obtain the licence shall be fined not more than three times the payable tonnage amount and the fine shall be paid into the treasury as the Customs' fine.

Article 15 These Procedures shall be put into force from the date of promulgation.

RULES OF THE PEOPLE'S REPUBLIC OF CHINA GOVERNING THE LEVYING OF IMPORT DUTIES ON ARTICLES OF PASSENGERS' BAGGAGE AND PERSONAL POSTAL PARCELS

(June 16, 1978)

Article 1 These rules have been drawn up with a view to implementing the policy of State control of foreign trade, protecting the country's socialist economy, and simplifying the procedures for the collection of Customs duties so as to facilitate regular traffic.

Article 2 Import duties on dutiable articles carried by inbound passengers, imported by means of personal parcels, carried by crew members of inbound means of conveyance for personal use or imported by any other means for personal use (all hereunder referred to as "imported articles") are to be levied by Customs according to these rules.

The import duties referred to in these rules include both Customs duties and the industrial and commercial consolidated taxes.

Article 3 The schedule of import duty rates is as follows:

Tariff No.	Description of Articles	Rate of Import Duty
1.	Cereals, cereal flours	20%
2.	Medical equipment, scientific instruments and electronic computers	20%
3.	Pharmaceutical products and preparations, medicinal and aromatic substances of animal or vegetable origin	50%
4.	Office or household machines, recorders, cutting tools, hand tools, hand farm implements, and parts or accessories thereof	50%
	Television sets and parts or accessories thereof	50%
	Sports equipment, musical instruments	50%
5.	Foodstuffs and beverages	100%
6.	Deer antlers, musk, ginseng	100%
7.	Cotton cloth, linen, clothing and other articles for personal wear made of cotton or linen, cotton or linen fabrics and other cotton products	100%
8.	Radio sets, record-players and parts or accessories thereof	100%
	Bicycles and other vehicles, and parts or accessories thereof	100%
9.	Fabrics of woollen, silk, artificial and synthetic fibres and clothing and other articles for personal wear made thereof, clothing and articles for personal wear made of other materials (such as leather, fur, plastics, etc.)	150%
	Cameras, photographic supplies or materials, video recorders, and parts or accessories thereof	150%
10.	Birds' nests, sharks' fins, beche-de-mer, awabi, compoy, fish maws, fish lips	200%
	Tobacco and products thereof, wine and spirits	200%
	Cosmetics and perfumes	200%
11.	Wrist-watches, pocket-watches and parts or accessories thereof	200%
12.	Duty-free articles: 1. Books, newspapers, periodicals, educational films and lantern-slides, and language records which are allowed to be imported; 2. Contraceptive devices and medications; 3. Gold and silver, and articles made thereof.	
13.	Articles not otherwise provided for in the above tariff numbers	100%

Article 4 Articles not enumerated in the above schedule shall be classified by Customs under the most appropriate tariff number.

Import duty on an article is to be levied at the tariff rate in force on the date of issue of the Customs Duty Memorandum.

Article 5 Imported articles are liable to ad valorem duties. An article's duty-paying value shall be assessed by Customs on the basis of its c.i.f. value. If the c.i.f. value cannot be ascertained, the duty-paying value shall be assessed by Customs in light of domestic prices.

Article 6 Should a duty-payer be dissatisfied with the tariff classification and/or the duty-paying values of the imported articles as determined by Customs, he shall first pay the import duty in full and then file an appeal in writing with Customs within 14 days of the date on which the duty is paid. On receipt of the written appeal, Customs shall reconsider the case within seven days. If the original decision is maintained, Customs shall, within 14 days of the date of receipt of the original appeal, transmit the appeal, together with its comments, to the Customs Administration of the People's Republic of China for consideration. If the original decision is modified, the duty-payer is to be duly notified and the duty adjusted accordingly. Should the duty-payer still be dissatisfied with the modified decision, he may file another appeal within seven days of the date of receipt of the notification of the modified decision. Customs shall, within seven days of the date of receipt of the second appeal, forward the case to the Customs Administration of the People's Republic of China for consideration. The decision of the Customs Administration of the People's Republic of China shall be final.

Article 7 After approval by the State Council, these rules shall be promulgated and put into force by the Ministry of Foreign Trade.

CUSTOMS PROCEDURES FOR THE SUPERVISION, TAXATION AND TAX EXEMPTION OF IMPORT AND EXPORT SAMPLES AND ADVERTISING MATERIALS

(October 1, 1981)

Article 1 With regard to all samples imported or exported exclusively for reference in placing orders, for analysis and examination, for quality tests and all advertising materials for commercial publicity, the samples shall be supervised, taxed or exempted from duties by the Customs as stipulated in these Procedures whether they are bought at current prices or supplied free.

Article 2 For samples or advertising materials imported or exported, the receiving or sending unit or its agent (or the carrier) shall go through import or export formalities at the Customs.

Article 3 If a sample bought from or sold abroad has a value of more than Renminbi 200 yuan, an import or export licence shall be obtained in accordance with the related provisions of the state administration authorities of foreign trade; a sample with a value of less than RMB 200 yuan shall be examined and approved by the Customs. Samples or advertising materials to be presented are exempt from obtaining a licence. No import or export licences are required for the import and export of samples on advertising matters.

Article 4 All samples and advertising materials which have no commercial value or only analytical purposes and are to be disposed of subsequently shall not be subject to Customs duties and Industrial and Commercial (Consolidated) Tax. All other samples and advertising materials, whether they are bought or supplied free, shall be subject to Customs duties and Industrial and Commercial (Consolidated) Tax as are other imported goods.

Article 5 If dutiable import samples or advertising materials are scheduled to be re-transported out of our country within six months, they shall be declared at the Customs house at the place of entry and the Customs shall collect a sum equal to the amount of the duties as security, which shall be refunded when they are transported out; if they are not re-exported within the time limit, the Customs shall take the said security for duties and pay it into the state treasury.

Article 6 Those acts in violation of these provisions shall be handled in accordance with the Interim Law on Customs and related provisions.

Article 7 These Procedures shall become effective as of October 1, 1980.

INTERIM CUSTOMS PROCEDURES FOR THE SUPERVISION OF BONDED GOODS AND BONDED WAREHOUSES

(March 1, 1981)

Article 1 These Procedures are formulated on the basis of the spirit of the provisions in Article 131 of the Interim Law of the People's Republic of China on Customs and in the light of current conditions for the purpose of meeting the needs of the development of foreign economic relations and trade and facilitating production and socialist modernization.

Article 2 The bonded goods referred to in these Procedures mean those imported with their import taxation formalities suspended by the Customs or those stored for later re-export. Those warehouses specially used for storing the bonded goods permitted by the Customs are known as bonded warehouses.

Article 3 To trade in import bonded goods and manage bonded warehouses, the units registered and permitted to run import and export businesses shall make applications to the local Customs houses and go through related formalities. After the Customs' examination, the independent special-purpose warehouses shall be approved by the Customs before commencing business if the warehouses accord with the provisions of relevant decrees, are provided with the requirements for the close supervision of the Customs and ensure the observation of the provisions of the Customs.

A manager of bonded goods and a bonded warehouse shall be responsible to the Customs for the bonded goods stored in the warehouses in accordance with the related provisions of the Customs and the Customs shall lock them up jointly with the manager of the bonded warehouse.

Article 4 Bonded goods and bonded warehouses shall be put under the supervision of the Customs and the Customs shall be entitled to dispatch officers to enter the warehouses at any time for the purpose of examining the state of goods and related accounts. If necessary, the Customs shall put officers at warehouses for supervision and the managers of the warehouses shall provide them with offices and facilities for board and lodging.

Article 5 When bonded goods enter our country, the consignees or their agents shall file an import goods manifest in triplicate, affix the stamps of "Bonded Goods" on them and state that they shall be stored in designated bonded warehouses in certain places and then declare them at the Customs houses at the places of entry. The Customs shall keep one copy of each declaration on file after examining and proving the declaration to tally with the actual goods and the other two copies shall be carried to the bonded warehouse together with the goods. The manager of the warehouse shall sign the above declaration after the goods are put inside the warehouse, keep one copy on file and return the other to the Customs for filing and reference.

If a bonded warehouse is within the boundary of another Customs house other than the Customs house at the place of entry, the consignees or their agent(s) shall go through Customs formalities at the Customs house at the place of entry in accordance with the Customs' provisions relating to transhipment goods. When the goods arrive at the bonded warehouse, they shall go through the declaration formalities for entering the warehouse at the local Customs house in accordance with the above-mentioned provisions.

No bonded warehouses shall be set up in places without Customs houses.

Article 6 The managers of bonded warehouses shall set up detailed stock account books for the bonded goods stored and submit lists of the receipt, delivery and stock of bonded goods brought forward from the preceding month to the local Customs house(s) for verification within the first five days of each month.

Article 7 When bonded goods are turned for import, the original consignees or their agents shall submit import licences, import goods declarations and other documents required by the Customs to the Customs houses and pay customs duties and industrial and commercial (consolidated) taxes; then the Customs shall sign and seal the same for clearance and cancel the original import bonded goods declarations.

Customs duties and industrial and commercial (consolidated) taxes shall be exempted for the bonded fuel, parts and spares to be used by Chinese or foreign international sailing vessels and bonded parts and spares to be used to repair and maintain related foreign products during the periods of warranty.

Article 8 The managers of the bonded

warehouses shall be responsible to pay Customs duties and industrial and commercial (consolidated) taxes for the shelves, stationery, management appliances, vehicles for transport, transporting, lifting and packing equipment and the machines used for repacking imported for their own use, whether they are bought at current prices or supplied free by foreign businessmen. However, if the articles shall be re-transported abroad within six months, all taxes collected shall be returned.

Article 9 The term of the storage of bonded goods is one year. An applicaton shall be made for its extension if there is any particular reason and such an extension shall not be more than one year. They shall be re-transported abroad at the expiration of the term. If they are not re-transported abroad at the expiration, they shall go through import licence and import taxation formalities, otherwise they shall be sold off or disposed of by the Customs.

Article 10 When bonded goods are re-transported out, the original consignees or their agents shall file an export goods declaration in triplicate, submit the declarations signed and sealed by the Customs at the time when the bonded goods are imported and go through re-export formalities at the local Customs house. The Customs shall sign and seal the declarations after examining and proving the declarations to tally with the goods, keep one copy on file, return a second copy and send the remaining copy together with the goods to the Customs house at the place of exit so as to have the goods cleared.

Article 11 Bonded goods shall not be processed in bonded warehouses. If their packages have to be changed, a prior application shall be made to the Customs for approval and the repacking shall be carried out under the supervision of the Customs officers. The trading unit concerned shall pay fees in accordance with the relevant regulations. When the repacked goods are permitted to be imported, duties shall be levied on them in accordance with the regulations.

Article 12 If shortages occur during the storage of bonded goods, the manager of the warehouse shall pay tax and deal with the situation according to related provisions except those resulting from force majeure, for which the manager shall not be responsible.

Article 13 Those acts in violation of the provisions of these Procedures and resistance to pay, refusal to pay and evasion of taxes and related fees shall be handled in accordance with the relevant laws and regulations of the Customs.

Article 14 These Procedures shall become effective as of March, 1, 1981.

INTERIM CUSTOMS PROCEDURES FOR THE COLLECTION OF FEES

(May 1, 1981)

Article 1 These Procedures are formulated in the light of current conditions and in accordance with the provisions in Article 21 of the Interim Law of the People's Republic of China on Customs in order to meet the needs of the development of foreign economic and trade relations and tourism, facilitate the enterprises or personnel concerned to go through Customs formalities, and strengthen the Customs' supervision.

Article 2 The Customs shall delineate the areas under its supervision according to the actual conditions of import or export of goods, the volume of travellers' luggage, postal matter and means of transport at the ports, stations, international airports, border passes and international postal matter exchange offices (or stations) where it is located. No fees shall be collected for the duties carried out within the supervised areas of the Customs.

Article 3 When an enterprise, unit or person concerned requests Customs officers to handle Customs formalities and carry out supervision duties outside the supervised areas, a prior application shall be made to the Customshouse concerned for approval and fees paid in accordance with the following provisions:

(1) Renminbi 10 yuan shall be paid for each officer for each working day. A working day shall be eight hours; less than four hours are calculated as half a working day, while the required time between four and eight hours is counted as one working day.

(2) The fees shall be doubled on festivals and holidays stipulated by the state.

On duty outside the supervised areas, the applicants shall supply means of transport to and from the working area, board and lodging and pay all the expenses involved.

Article 4 Receipts shall be given by the Customs upon payment of the fees.

Article 5 All fees collected by the Customs are regarded as central revenue and shall be paid into the state treasury under the heading of "Income of Fees" in accordance with relevant provisions.

Article 6 These Procedures shall be put into effect as of May 1, 1981.

ANNOUNCEMENT OF CHINESE CUSTOMS ON THE IMPOSITION OF EXPORT TARIFF ON 34 COMMODITIES

(June 1, 1982)

The Chinese Customs shall impose export tariff on 34 kinds of commodities.

The following is a list of these commodities and their export duty rates:

Tariff No.	Description of goods	Export duty rate
1	Paddy, rice:	
	B) Rice	20%
10	Soybeans:	
	A) Yellow beans	20%
31	Chestnuts	10%
80	Sugar:	
	A) Machine-made sugar	
	1. Not over 98 degree of polarization	20%
	2. Over 98 degree of polarization, and refined Sugar with more than 2% of invest sugar	20%
	B) Non-machine-made sugar:	
	1. Brown sugar, green sugar	20%
	2. White sugar	20%
114	Fish fry:	
	A) Common eel fry	60%
115	Fresh fish (including frozen fish):	
	A) Fresh fish	20%
121	Fresh crustaceans and mollusks (including frozen crustaceans and mollusks):	
	A) Fresh prawn	30%
132	Sea blubber	20%
133	Roe, caviar:	
	A) Roe	40%
143	Cinnamon, cassia bark, cassia twigs, and cassia beds:	
	A) Cinnamon	50%
	B) Cassia bark	50%
154	*Tang-kuei* oryptetaecia canadensia	50%
161	Lycium, nutmegs:	
	A) Lycium	40%
	B) Nutmegs	60%
174	Apricot kernels	20%
202	Crude lacquer	30%
206	Resin:	
	A) White resin	30%
	B) Others	30%
337	Hides (horse, donkey, goat and mule):	
	A) Goat skins	20%
348	Tungsten ore	30%
352	Coal:	
	A) Anthracite	40 yuan/ton
	B) Others	40 yuan/ton
402	Tung oil	20%
427	Turpentine, vegetable	20%
601	Animal hair or wood for textile use, N.O.P.F.	
	A) Angora	20%
680	Pig iron	20%
736	Tin ingots, slabs	40%
750	Crude antimony	30%
751	Antimony regulus	30%
756	Iron alloys:	
	A) Ferromanganese	10%
	B) Ferrotungsten	20%
	C) Ferrochromium	10%
	D) Ferrosilicon	30%
	E) Ferrovanadium	10%
	F) Ferromolybdenum	20%
	G) Others	10%
757	Cobalt, tantalum, cadmium, titanium:	
	A) Titanium	10%
924	Pearls:	
	A) Real pearls	30%

PROCEDURES FOR CUSTOMS REWARDS IN THE PROHIBITION OF SMUGGLING

Promulgated by the General Customs Office

(September 24, 1982)

Article 1 These Procedures are formulated for the purpose of encouraging individuals and units (or organizations) to assist in preventing smuggling so as to contribute to the safeguard of the socialist economic order.

Article 2 In addition to political encouragements, rewards shall be given to the informants in smuggling cases and such units of collective ownership as rural people's communes and production brigades and teams helping to solve such cases after the cases concerned are dealt with according to law.

Article 3 The rewards for the informants shall not exceed 10 per cent of the total proceeds from the fines and confiscations in each case; the maximum amount in each case shall not exceed Renminbi 1,000 yuan.

Article 4 Reward shall be given to such units of collective ownership as rural people's communes and production brigades and teams assisting to solve smuggling cases in amounts not exceeding 10 per cent of the total proceeds from the fines and confiscations in each case. But the maximum amount in each case shall not exceed Renminbi 10,000 yuan.

Article 5 The rewards for the informants with special contributions shall not be limited to the maximum amount aforesaid if special approval of the General Customs Office is obtained.

Article 6 Political encouragement shall be given to the informants in the smuggling cases in which the offenders are acquitted from conviction but only required to pay the evaded duties; and if necessary, a reward of not more than Renminbi 100 yuan shall be given to an informant or a unit of collective ownership assisting in solving such cases.

Article 7 A reward of not more than Renminbi 500 yuan shall be given, if necessary, in addition to political encouragement, to an informant or a unit of collective ownership assisting to solve the smuggling case in which the articles shall be destroyed or forfeited to the government authorities as stipulated and the offender(s) is (are) free from fines.

Article 8 Rewards in foreign currency will be given to informants residing outside our territory in appropriate cases.

Article 9 If a rewarded informant or unit fails to collect the reward within 6 months from the date of the Customs' issue of the Notice of Reward, the right of entitlement shall be regarded as forfeited and the reward shall be paid into the Treasury.

Article 10 The identities of informants in smuggling cases should be kept strictly confidential by Customs.

Article 11 These Procedures shall be implemented by the tax authorities handling smuggling cases on behalf of Customs in the places without customs houses.

Article 12 These Procedures shall be put into effect as of October 1, 1982. "Procedures For Customs' Rewards in the Prohibition of Smuggling" issued by the original Ministry of Foreign Trade shall then be annulled.

TRIAL PROCEDURES FOR MONITORING INFECTIOUS DISEASES IN BORDER PORTS

Issued by the Ministry of Public Health
(June 18, 1980)

To prevent epidemic diseases from spreading in and out of our country, to safeguard the health of travellers and communications staff passing over the borders and the health of our people and to promote international friendly intercourse, we shall, in our health quarantine, strengthen the monitoring of diseases, pay attention to the collection and accumulation of both domestic and overseas information on epidemic situations, sum up and analyse these data conscientiously and identify the patterns of the spreading of diseases so as to put forward countermeasures to prevent them. Hence these Procedures are formulated.

I General Rules

Article 1 The infectious diseases monitored by health quarantine authorities include influenza, malaria, poliomyelitis, dengue fever, typhus and relapsing fever (hereinafter referred to as "monitored diseases") or other types of diseases designated by the Ministry of Public Health.

Article 2 The incubation periods of the monitored diseases referred to in these Procedures are prescribed as follows:

(1) 3 days for influenza;

(2) Malaria: 12 days for malignant malaria; 14 days for intermittent or ovale malaria; 30 days for tertian malaria;

(3) 12 days for poliomyelitis;

(4) 6 days for dengue fever;

(5) 14 days for typhus;

(6) 8 days for relapsing fever.

Article 3 The means of communications referred to in these Procedures include vessels, aircraft and vehicles; the examination ports stated include seaports, airports, stations and border crossings; the meaning of days is the same as in Article 2 of the Rules for the Implementation of the Regulations on Border Health Quarantine.

Article 4 Health quarantine authorities implement the monitoring of infectious diseases in ports, airports, stations and crossings which are open to international navigation, traffic or air traffic and the means of transport stationed in these places.

Article 5 The monitored subjects include personnel (including transit personnel) and means of transport entering or leaving the territory of our country, the people in ports, airports, stations and border crossings and the insect vectors, animals, food and drinking water which can spread the monitored diseases.

Article 6 The monitoring shall cover the following:

(1) The gathering and report of epidemic situations;

(2) The individual investigation of primary cases;

(3) The epidemiological investigation of sudden spreading;

(4) The separation and identification of pathogens;

(5) The investigation of insect vectors;

(6) The observation of the use of vaccines and the evaluation of their effectiveness as well as the investigation of the levels of immunity of people;

(7) The gathering and investigation of the local incidence and mortality of each monitored disease and other information relating to epidemiology;

(8) The supervision of the patients, suspected patients and close contacts of monitored diseases;

(9) The necessary hygienic treatment of the means of communications and luggage contaminated or suspected of being contaminated and the animals and insects infected or suspected of being infected.

Article 7 The monitoring shall be centrally coordinated and administered. Quarantine sections shall be in charge of the monitoring of diseases; Health sections shall be in charge of the monitoring of mass communications and its hygienic treatment; examination sections (or laboratories) shall be in charge of the separation and identification of pathogens.

Article 8 The control of the epidemic situations of the monitored diseases shall be handled by quarantine authorities in accordance with the "Regulations of the People's Republic of China for the Administration of Acute Infectious Diseases". The quarantine authorities shall collect standard fees, which are fixed by the state, for supplying medicines for prevention and treatment or applying hygienic treatment in the monitoring of diseases.

II The Transmission of Epidemics

Article 9 In case a monitored disease or a suspected monitored disease is found on the means of transport in a port, an airport, a station or a border crossing, the person(s) in charge of the said means of transport shall make a report to the quarantine authorities.

After the above report of the epidemic situation is received, the quarantine authorities shall in turn report it to the local health epidemic prevention authorities.

Article 10 In case a monitored disease or a suspected monitored disease is found among the crowds of people in a port, an airport, a station or a border crossing, or found in the personnel entering our country, the epidemic prevention or host or medical organization in the said place shall report the situation to the local health epidemic prevention authorities and notify the local quarantine authorities or those that provide clinic facilities cards.

Article 11 In case the primary or incident case(s) of a monitored disease is (are) identified by the health epidemic prevention authorities in their subordinate areas, they shall promptly give a notice to local health quarantine authorities and supply the information on local epidemic situations at regular intervals.

Article 12 The quarantine authorities shall, on their own initiative, get in touch with the epidemic prevention authorities in the districts where they are located, such as the epidemic prevention departments and other units concerned in seaports, airports, stations and border crossings in order to collect and find out the information on the epidemic situations of monitored diseases.

Article 13 Upon the discovery of any sudden spreading of a monitored disease within the limits of its monitoring area, the quarantine authorities shall report it as soon as possible to the public health authorities of the province, municipality or autonomous region and also report it to the Ministry of Public Health.

Article 14 The overseas epidemic situations of monitored diseases shall be gathered, translated, printed and distributed by the units assigned by the Ministry of Public Health; with regard to domestic epidemic situations, the Ministry of Public Health shall notify the units concerned to supply the information to the quarantine authorities.

Article 15 All reports of monitored diseases shall be filed and submitted in Infectious Diseases Report Cards.

III General Provisions for Monitoring

Article 16 Quarantine authorities shall conduct regular search and analyse both domestic and overseas epidemic situations of monitored diseases and know the epidemic areas and trends well.

Article 17 Quarantine authorities shall strengthen the epidemiological inquiries about monitored diseases in the examination of the means of transport and the personnel passing over the borders.

Article 18 Quarantine authorities shall try to discover patients contracted of monitored diseases or suspected monitored diseases in their exercise of sanitary supervision and their rounds of visits.

Article 19 Quarantine authorities shall carry out pathogenic examination and individual investigation of the patients contracted of monitored diseases or suspected monitored diseases so as to locate the infectious sources.

Article 20 If they deem it necessary, quarantine authorities shall require incoming travellers to file health declaration cards. The way to provide the cards is to distribute them in advance among incoming personnel on the way or before they arrive at their destination with the help of travel service agencies, airline companies or other units concerned so as to save the time of examination upon entering our country.

Article 21 Quarantine authorities shall individually or selectively provide the one with close contacts of any monitored disease or the personnel coming from the epidemic area of any monitored disease with clinic facilities cards.

Article 22 Quarantine authorities shall distribute the knowledge of prevention and treatment of monitored diseases among the travellers and communications staff passing over the borders and provide them with necessary medicines for prevention and treatment.

Article 23 Quarantine authorities shall carry out investigation of insect vectors and animal hosts and that of the immunity levels of crowds at regular intervals in cooperation with epidemic prevention departments in ports, airports, stations and border crossings at any time. When there is a tendency of the sudden spread of an epidemic disease in any of the said places, they shall report it to higher epidemic prevention departments so as to take necessary precautions.

IV The Administration of Monitored Diseases

I. INFLUENZA

Article 24 Quarantine authorities shall take the following measures if any patients or suspected patients of influenza are found in their sanitary supervision or rounds of examinations:

(1) Collect throat gargle or pituitary membrane imprint specimens so as to separate viruses;

(2) According to the patients' conditions, suggest to the patients that they be treated separately from other patients or provide them with medicines for prevention and treatment;

(3) Carry out necessary sterilization or ventilation of the rooms where the patients or suspected patients stay;

(4) Those with close contacts with patients should be kept under medical observation or provided with clinic facilities cards according to conditions.

Article 25 Quarantine authorities shall, jointly with animal and plant quarantines, carry out the epidemiological investigation of the poultry, birds, livestock and monkeys, etc. on the means of transport where influenza occurs and take appropriate and preventive action.

Article 26 During the period when the means of transport from an epidemic area of influenza or from where influenza has occurred within 3 days before its arrival stays in a port, an airport, a station or a border crossing, quarantine authorities shall keep constant sanitary supervision over said vehicle and inquire into the health condition of the personnel on it in a timely manner so as to begin their rounds of treatment.

II. MALARIA

Article 27 When quarantine authorities discover suspected malaria patients during their routine examination, sanitary supervision or rounds of treatment, they shall extract blood from them in good time in order to examine malaria protozoa and make enquiries into the following:

(1) The history of contact with a malaria epidemic area within one month before arrival;

(2) Whether there is any occurrence of malaria within 2 years before arrival;

(3) Whether there are such typical clinical symptoms as feeling cold and hot at the time;

(4) Whether the liver or spleen is swollen.

Article 28 When any malaria patients are discovered aboard any means of transport or among the personnel passing over the borders, quarantine authorities shall:

(1) Make blood smears in time for the patients and separate malaria protozoa;

(2) Provide the patients with cures for malaria or send them to hospital for isolation treatment;

(3) Provide malignant malaria patients coming from a malaria affected area with cures especially for malaria caused by drugfast protozoa.

Article 29 When any mosquitos are found aboard means of transport coming from a malaria epidemic area or carrying any malaria patient(s), quarantine authorities shall:

(1) Examine the sanitary condition of the means of transport and exterminate the mosquitos in time if they are found hiding themselves in some parts of the same;

(2) Collect specimens so as to identify the types of the mosquitos and to test their sensibility to drugs;

(3) Urge the persons in charge of the means of transport to exterminate mosquitos thoroughly and direct them technically; and after exterminating mosquitos, examine the effects carefully.

Article 30 Quarantine authorities shall supply preventive cures for malaria to the personnel travelling from or to a serious epidemic area of malaria.

III. POLIOMYELITIS

Article 31 If suspected poliomyelitis patients are discovered in the course of routine examinations, sanitary supervision or rounds of treatment, quarantine authorities shall gather the specimens of excrement, urine and blood of the patients for virus separation and serologic examination.

Article 32 When poliomyelitis patients are found in the course of routine examinations, sanitary supervision or rounds of treatment, quarantine authorities shall take the following measures:

(1) Gather the specimens of patients' excrement, urine and blood in time for virus identification and serum classification;

(2) Advise the patients to be treated separately from other patients or send them to a hospital especially equipped for infectious diseases;

(3) Sterilize the environment, articles and patients' excrement suspected of being contaminated;

(4) Provide those in close contact with the affected patients with clinic facilities cards or carry out medical observation not exceeding 14 days after leaving the affected environment.

Article 33 Quarantine authorities shall take samples from drinking water and food from the means of transport for examination on which a poliomyelitis case or a suspected poliomyelitis case has occurred within 3 weeks before its arrival and sterilize them if necessary; samples from the drinking water and food from a means of transport coming from the epidemic area of poliomyelitis shall also be examined or sterilized if necessary.

IV. DENGUE FEVER

Article 34 If quarantine authorities find any dengue fever patient(s) or any patient(s) suspected of contracting dengue fever in their examination, sanitary supervision or rounds of treatments, they shall take the following measures:

(1) Send the patient(s) to hospital for isolation treatment and gather blood specimens for virus separation and serologic examination;

(2) Gather the specimens of dengue-fever mosquitos for virus separation from the places where the patient(s) has (have) stayed;

(3) Arrange the patients in a mosquito-free room to be separately treated for not less than 5 days from the date in which the disease was contracted;

(4) Provide those in close contact with the disease with clinic facilities cards or carry out 14 days' health observation;

(5) Promptly exterminate the mosquitos in ports, airports, stations or border crossings or aboard means of transport where dengue fever patient(s) is (are) found.

Article 35 If quarantine authorities find any live mosquitos aboard means of transport from an epidemic area of dengue fever, they shall:

(1) Examine the sanitary state of the means of transport and exterminate mosquitos which are found to conceal themselves in some parts of the means of transport;

(2) Gather specimens of mosquitos for identification and separation of viruses;

(3) Urge the person(s) in charge of the means of transport to exterminate mosquitos thoroughly and direct him (them) technically, and after eliminating them, check the results carefully.

Article 36 Quarantine authorities shall exercise proper administration of animals such as monkeys from the epidemic area of dengue fever jointly with animal and plant quarantines.

V. TYPHUS AND RELAPSING FEVER

Article 37 When quarantine authorities discover any patient(s) suffering from typhus or relapsing fever in their examination, sanitary supervision or rounds of treatments, they shall take the following measures:

(1) Eliminate lice from the patient(s), isolate him (them) and gather specimens for pathogenic separation;

(2) Eliminate insects from suspected patients and carry out medical observation for 14 days or 8 days;

(3) Provide those with contact of the patient with clinic facilities cards after the elimination of lice, or carry out health observation for 14 days or 8 days after the elimination of insects;

(4) Eliminate lice from patients', suspected patients' and contacted's clothes, luggage and other articles and places which are prone to concealment of lice and sterilize them if necessary;

(5) Gather blood specimens from the patient(s) or suspected patients for laboratory examination;

(6) Gather lice specimens from the bodies of the patient(s), suspected patients and contacted for pathogenic separation and drug sensibility tests.

Article 38 When quarantine authorities find lice on the means of transport from the epidemic area of typhus or relapsing fever, they shall gather specimens for examination and eliminate the insects.

Article 39 These Procedures shall be put into effect from the date of issue.

PROCEDURES OF THE PEOPLE'S REPUBLIC OF CHINA FOR SUPERVISION OF SANITATION AT BORDER PORTS OF THE PEOPLE'S REPUBLIC OF CHINA

(Approved by the State Council on December 30, 1981 and issued by the Ministry of Public Health, Ministry of Communications, General Administration of Civil Aviation of China and the Ministry of Railways on February, 4, 1982)

WF-9(82)

I General Rules

Article 1 These Procedures are formulated as required under Article 3 of "The Regulations of the People's Republic of China on Border Health Quarantine." The purposes are to strengthen the supervision of sanitation at border ports and aboard international means of transport, to improve their sanitary conditions and to extinguish infectious sources, cut off channels of spreading, prevent infectious diseases from spreading into or out of our country and safeguard the health of the people.

Article 2 These Procedures are applicable to ports, airports, stations and passages open to foreigners (hereinafter generally designated as "border ports") and to international going vessels, aircraft and vehicles staying in these places (hereinafter referred to as "means of transport").

II Sanitary Requirements for Border Ports

Article 3 A sanitary cleaning system shall be established in border ports to eliminate the breeding places of flies and mosquitos, install litter bins and their regular cleansing so as to keep the environment clean and tidy.

Article 4 Daily refuse in border ports shall be removed every day and fixed refuse dumps provided for that purpose shall be regularly cleared; daily sewage shall not be drained off indiscriminately and shall go through disinfecting treatment so as to prevent the environment and water sources from contamination.

Article 5 The departments concerned shall adopt feasible measures to reduce the quantity of insect vectors and rodents to a harmless level in the buildings of border ports.

Article 6 All floors of waiting rooms in piers, airports, stations and customs houses shall be kept neat and clean, their walls dust-free and their windows and tables bright and clean. They shall be well ventilated and equipped with necessary sanitary facilities.

Article 7 A perfect sanitary system shall be established in restaurants, cafes, canteens, dining rooms, kitchens, buffets and small shops in border ports so as to regularly keep them clean and tidy and make their walls, ceilings, tables and chairs clean and dustfree. The areas shall be provided with equipment to ward off mosquitos, flies, rats and mice and with refrigeration equipment so as to eliminate these pests.

Article 8 Attendants shall be put in charge of the toilets and bathrooms in border ports, cleaning them regularly and keeping them clean and tidy so as to free them from flies and bad odours.

Article 9 The warehouses, godowns and goods yards in border ports shall be kept clean and tidy. When abnormal quantities of dead mice or rats are found, immediate reports shall be given to health quarantine authorities or local public health and epidemic prevention departments.

Article 10 The water sources for border ports shall be well protected and toilets, seepage wells, etc. which will pollute the water sources shall not be built within a distance of 30 meters in diameter from a water source.

III Sanitary Requirements for Means of Transport

Article 11 Means of transport shall be equipped with first-aid medicines and equipment as well as disinfectants, insecticides and rodenticides. If necessary, provisional quarantine rooms shall be arranged aboard ships.

Article 12 The prevention and elimination

of insect vectors and rodents from means of transport shall be as follows:

(1) Ships, aircraft and trains shall be provided with adequate preventive measures against rodents so as to free them from rodents or to keep their quantity at a harmless level.

(2) The means of transport shall be kept free from mosquitos, flies or other injurious insects, which shall be eliminated upon discovery.

Article 13 The toilets and bathrooms on means of transport shall be kept clean, tidy and free from unpleasant odours.

Article 14 The sanitary requirements for the disposition of excrement, urine, refuse and sewage on means of transport are as follows:

(1) Daily refuse shall be put in containers with covers, prohibited from being dumped indiscriminately into port areas, airports or station areas and must be removed by means of special refuse vehicles (or vessels) to designated places for treatments. If necessary, excrement, urine and sewage shall go through sanitary treatment before being disposed.

(2) The refuse in solid form on means of transport from epidemic areas of plague shall be disposed of by incineration, while the excrement, urine, ballast water and sewage on means of transport from the epidemic areas of cholera shall be sterilized if necessary.

Article 15 The sanitary requirements for cargo holds, luggage cars, postal cars and freight cars of means of transport as well as trucks are as follows:

(1) Such insect vectors and harmful animals as mosquitos, flies, cockroaches and mice and their breeding conditions shall be eliminated from cargo holds, luggage cars, postal cars, freight cars and trucks which shall be thoroughly cleaned before goods are being loaded or unloaded so as to be free of excrement, urine and refuse.

(2) The freight cars or trucks carrying poisonous articles and food shall be placed separately in different designated places for decontamination and shall be thoroughly cleaned after goods are completely unloaded.

(3) The luggage and goods from epidemic areas shall be carefully examined to prevent the carrying of insect vectors and rodents.

Article 16 The sanitary requirements for passenger cabins, lodging cabins and passenger cars of means of transport as well as other passenger vehicles are as follows:

(1) Passenger cabins, lodging cabins, passenger cars and other passenger vehicles shall be cleaned whenever necessary, kept free of refuse and dust and well ventilated.

(2) Bedding shall be replaced and washed after use each time and be free from lice, fleas, bedbugs or other insect vectors.

IV Sanitary Requirements for Food, Drinking Water and Personnel Engaged in These Industries

Article 17 The food supplied to border ports and on means of transport shall conform to the provisions in "The Regulations of People's Republic of China on Food Hygienic Administration" and food hygienic standards.

Article 18 The drinking water supplied to border ports and on means of transport shall conform to "Hygienic Standards of Drinking Water" stipulated by our country. The drinking water supplied by means of transport as well as storage containers and water pipelines shall be cleaned regularly and kept clean.

Article 19 The sanitary requirements for personnel engaged in the supply of food and drinking water are as follows:

(1) The patients or carriers of infectious intestinal diseases or sufferers from active tuberculosis or suppurative exudative dermatosis shall not be engaged in work in the supply of food and drinking water.

(2) Each of the personnel engaged in the supply of food and drinking water shall go through a medical check-up every year. Those newly engaged in this work shall first have a medical check-up and those proved up to standard shall be granted health certificates.

(3) The personnel engaged in the supply of food and drinking water shall cultivate good hygienic habits, dress neatly and cleanly at work and strictly abide by the hygienic operation system.

V The Duties of Persons in Charge of Border Ports and Means of Communications

Article 20 The duties of the officers in charge of border ports and means of transport in the field of hygienic work are as follows:

(1) To complete the hygienic work well and regularly subject themselves to the supervision and examination of the sanitary supervision personnel and provide them with facilities for their work.

(2) To abide by these Procedures and other sanitary decrees, regulations and provisions.

(3) To adopt immediate measures to improve the unsanitary conditions of border ports and the means of transport in accordance with the advice of the sanitary supervision personnel.

(4) To report the situation when a quarantine infectious disease or a monitored one is found to the border health quarantine authorities or local epidemic prevention department and immediately adopt epidemic prevention measures.

VI The Responsibilities of Sanitation Supervision Authorities

Article 21 The health quarantine authorities in border ports shall exercise sanitary supervision over border ports and means of transport under the administration of local people's governments. Their major responsibilities are to:

(1) Supervise and direct the officers in charge of the departments concerned in border ports and on means of transport in the prevention and elimination of insect vectors and rodents;

(2) Examine the food and drinking water on the means of transport in border ports or crossings over the borders and exercise sanitary supervision over systems of transport, supply and storage facilities;

(3) Carry out examination, supervision and hygienic treatment of persons who have died from causes other than accidents in border ports and on means of transport;

(4) Supervise the officers in charge of the departments concerned in border ports and means of transport in the removal and treatment of excrement, urine, refuse and sewage;

(5) Exercise sanitary supervision over environmental factors which are of epidemiological significance to quarantine and monitored infectious diseases;

(6) Adopt measures to prevent mosquitoes from breeding in the vicinity of border ports;

(7) Conduct hygienic propaganda and education, spread hygienic knowledge among people and heighten the consciousness of the personnel in border ports and on means of transport to abide by and implement these Procedures.

Article 22 A border port health quarantine organ shall be provided with 1 to 5 border port sanitary supervisors to carry out the tasks of sanitary supervision and such posts shall be concurrently held by the professional personnel above the rank of leading cadre or quarantine doctor of the border port health quarantine organ, who are of good character and conscientious in their work. Border port sanitary supervisors shall be recommended by health quarantine authorities, certified by the public health administration authorities of provinces, municipalities and autonomous regions, and appointed by the Ministry of Public Health of the People's Republic of China and granted "Certificates of Border Port Sanitary Supervisors".

Article 23 With their certificates, border port sanitary supervisors shall be entitled to exercise sanitary supervision, examination and technical control over the officers in charge of border ports and means of transport; they could jointly with the departments concerned put forward proposals of improvement to the units or individuals concerned with unsatisfactory sanitary work and which resulted in the spread of infectious disease and to take necessary measures to deal with them in coordination with the departments concerned.

VII Rewards and Punishments

Article 24 Border port qurantine authorities shall encourage and reward units and individuals that have made remarkable achievements towards the implementation of these Procedures and the state decrees, regulations and provisions relating to public health.

Article 25 Border port health quarantine authorities shall, according to different conditions, warn or fine the units and individuals that have contravened these Procedures and the decrees, regulations and provisions relating to public health and may submit the cases to judicial authorities for punishment according to law.

VIII Supplementary Provisions

Article 26 These Procedures shall go into effect as of the date of issue.

REGULATIONS OF THE PEOPLE'S REPUBLIC OF CHINA ON THE QUARANTINE OF IMPORTED AND EXPORTED ANIMALS AND PLANTS

Issued by the State Council
(June 4, 1982)

I. General Rules

Article 1 These Regulations are formulated in order to protect the agriculture, forestry, animal husbandry and fishery of our country and the health of our people, safeguard our reputation in foreign trade, fulfil our international obligations, prevent diseases, insects, weeds and other harmful organisms which harm animals and plants from spreading into or out of our country and strengthen the quarantine of import and export animals and plants.

Article 2 All commercial or non-commercial animals, plants, animal products, vegetable products and their means of transport which enter, leave or pass through territories of the People's Republic of China are within the quarantine range under these Regulations and particularly include the following:

(1) Animals: Livestock, poultry, wild animals, bees, fish, silkworms, etc.

(2) Animal products: Raw hides, hair, meat, viscera, fat, blood, eggs, semen, bones, hoofs, horns, etc.

(3) Plants: Cultivated plants, wild plants and their seeds, nursery stock, propagating materials, etc.

(4) Vegetable products: Grains, beans, peas, cotton, oils, hemp, flax, tobacco, kernels, dried fruits, fresh fruits, vegetables, raw medicinal materials, logs, fodder, etc.

(5) Vehicles, vessels and aircraft carrying animals, plants, animal products and vegetable products as well as packing, bedding and padding materials, breeding tools, etc.

The other goods and means of transport which may carry the objects of quarantine shall also be put in quarantine.

Article 3 Animal infectious diseases and parasites, insects and weeds which are dangerous to plants as well as other harmful organisms (generally designated as insect vectors) shall be put in quarantine and divided into the objects of quarantine and quarantinable insect vectors.

(1) The objects of quarantine mean the insect vectors which are prohibited from entering our country as stipulated by the state. The list of the objects of quarantine shall be promulgated by the Ministry of Agriculture, Animal Husbandry and Fishery of the People's Republic of China.

(2) Quarantinable insect vectors include those put in quarantine as stipulated in relevant agreements and trade contracts with foreign countries and those for which the export units have applied for quarantine.

Article 4 The animal and plant quarantines set up in the ports and airports of the People's Republic of China which are open to international navigation or air traffic as well as on land borders and border rivers, and the animal and plant quarantine stations set up in the capitals of provinces and autonomous regions concerned (hereinafter generally referred to as port animal and plant quarantine authorities) are the authorities concerned which conduct quarantine duties of import and export animals and plants on behalf of the state.

Article 5 All animals, plants, animal products, vegetable products and their means of transport shall only be permitted to be imported or exported after passing the standard upheld by quarantine.

II. Import Quarantine

Article 6 An application shall be made in advance to the Ministry of Agriculture, Animal Husbandry and Fishery for approval to import animals and animal products. However, an application shall be made in advance to the Ministry of Forestry for approval where the import of wild animals and their products are concerned.

To import seeds, nursery stock and propagating materials, import departments shall fill in "Examination and Approval Lists for Quarantine of Seeds and Nursery Stock Imported" for submission. For those to be imported by the departments concerned of the State Council, such lists shall be submitted separately according to the professional distribution works to the Ministry of Agriculture, Animal Husbandry and Fishery or the Ministry of Forestry respectively for examination and approval; for those to be imported by the departments of provinces, autonomous regions and municipalities directly under the Central Government, they shall be submitted to the Departments (or Bureaux) of Agriculture (Forestry or State Farm and Land Reclamation) of respective areas for examination and approval.

Article 7 Any quarantine regulations which our country stipulated or agreed between governments should be indicated on the agreement for trade, technical co-operation, gift, exchange or assistance for the importation of animals, plants and their products. Also the said agreement shall contain the requirement of a quarantine certificate from the country of origin.

Article 8 Animals, plants, animal products and vegetable products imported shall be quarantined by port animal and plant quarantine authorities.

(1) Before or after the arrival of goods in a port, the consignee unit or its agent shall fill in the declaration for quarantine and submit it (or the waybill) together with such documents as the quarantine certificate from the export country to the port animal and plant quarantine authorities for quarantine.

(2) For trains or motor vehicles entering our country, the port animal and plant quarantine authorities shall carry out quarantine duties and inspection together with the border authorities concerned; for incoming vessels, quarantine duties shall be carried out on board after the joint inspection; for incoming aircraft, quarantine shall be implemented on the spot where goods are unloaded.

Article 9 A "Quarantine Clearance Notice" shall be signed and issued for all animals, plants, animal products or vegetable products imported in which no objects of quarantine or quarantinable insect vectors are found through quarantine, or such clearance shall be stamped on the waybill so as to permit them to be imported.

Article 10 For all imported animals or animal products in which the objects of quarantine and quarantinable insect vectors are found through quarantine, a "Quarantine Disposal Notice" shall be signed and issued according to different circumstances and the declarer(s) shall be notified to dispose of them separately as follows:

(1) The animal(s) which has(have) contracted a serious infectious disease and all others in the same flock shall be wholly returned or killed and its (their) remains shall be destroyed.

(2) The animal(s) which has(have) contracted a general infectious disease shall be returned or killed and its (their) remains shall be destroyed; the other animals in the same group shall be isolated and put under observation in the animal quarantine isolation yard or a designated place.

(3) The animal(s) which has(have) contracted a non-infectious disease shall be treated medically.

(4) Animal products shall be sterilized, returned or destroyed. If the animals which are isolated and observed as mentioned in Item (2) above and which are treated as mentioned in Item (3) do not have any disease found through quarantine, and if the animal products as mentioned in Item (4) passed the examination of quarantine after sterilization, they shall be allowed to be imported.

Article 11 For the import plants or vegetable products in which the objects of quarantine and quarantinable insect vectors are found through quarantine, a "Quarantine Disposal Notice" shall be signed and issued according to different circumstances and the declarer(s) shall be notified to dispose of the same separately in ways such as fumigation, sterlization, controlled use, return or destruction. They shall be allowed to be imported if they passed the examinations after such neutralizing treatments as fumigation, sterilization, etc.

Article 12 The quarantine and disposition of imported animals, plants, animal products and vegetable products shall be carried out in the ports of import.

All application shall be made to the Ministry of Agriculture, Animal Husbandry and Fishery for approval if they shall be transported to a designated inland place for disposition due to the limitation of the conditions in the port or other causes. In the course of transportation and handling, strict measures shall be adopted to prevent the epidemic situation from proliferating and a notice shall be given to the local quarantine department for supervision.

Article 13 The declarer(s) or consignee unit shall deal with the places, warehouses, means of transport, bedding and padding materials, breeding tools, etc. which are contaminated by the objects of quarantine and quarantinable insect vectors as required by the port animal and plant quarantine authorities.

Article 14 If any object of quarantine or quarantinable insect vector is found in imported animals, plants, animal products or vegetable products through quarantine, the port animal and plant quarantine authorities shall issue and sign quarantine certificates according to different circumstances.

Article 15 The following shall be prohibited from import:

(1) Daily injurious insects, animal or plant pathogenic micro-organisms (including cultures of bacteria, cultures of viruses, biological products) and other harmful organisms;

(2) The animals, seeds, nursery stock and propagating materials relating to a country or area in a serious epidemic situation as well as susceptible animal products and vegetable products;

(3) Soil.

The list of the aforesaid which are prohibited from import shall be promulgated by the Ministry of Agriculture, Animal Husbandry and Fishery. If it is necessary to import any of them for scientific research, an application shall be made in advance for the special approval of the Ministry of Agriculture, Animal Husbandry and Fishery.

III. Export Quarantine

Article 16 If export animals, plants, vegetable products or non-commercial animal products are required to be quarantined, the export unit or its agent shall file a declaration for quarantine in advance, submit the quarantine certificate from the place of production and declare the same at the port animal and plant quarantine authorities for quarantine. They shall be cleared by a quarantine certificate signed and issued by the authorities concerned after passing the requisite examination.

The export quarantine of commercial animal products shall be handled by the import and export commodity inspection authorities.

Article 17 The animals, plants, animal products or vegetable products in which quarantinable insect vectors are found through quarantine shall be prohibited from export or shall go through neutralizing treatments before export.

Article 18 The contaminated areas, warehouses, means of transport, bedding and padding materials, breeding tools, etc. shall be dealt with as stipulated in Article 13 of these Regulations.

IV. The Quarantine of Articles Carried by Travellers

Article 19 The animals, plants, animal products or vegetable products carried or consigned by the travellers or communications staff entering our country shall be put in quarantine on the spot in port. They shall be cleared if no objects of quarantine are found through quarantine; those in which the objects of quarantine are found shall be prohibited from entering our country or released only after sterilization. If no quarantine results can be obtained, such articles shall be kept in custody pending further quarantine and the owner shall be informed of the final disposition of the articles after the quarantine results are obtained.

Article 20 The raw meat carried or consigned by the travellers or communications staff shall go through epidemic prevention check before being permitted to enter our country.

Article 21 The animals, plants, animal products or vegetable products carried or consigned by the travellers or communications staff leaving our country shall be put in quarantine and clearance certificates granted in appropriate cases.

V. The Quarantine of International Mail Parcels

Article 22 The plants and vegetable products mailed into our country shall be quarantined by the port animal and plant quarantine authorities. A parcel without any objects of quarantine found through quarantine shall be cleared by putting a mailing clearance stamp on the parcel. A "Quarantine Disposal Notice" shall be signed and issued after the quarantine of a parcel in which the objects of quarantine are found and sent together with the parcel to the receiver by post. A parcel failing to go through quarantine shall be returned with a parcel return label to the sender by post. A "Quarantine Disposal Notice" shall be signed and issued for a parcel to be destroyed and the notice shall be sent to the sender by post.

Raw animal products shall be prohibited from entering our country by post (a small number of samples excepted).

Article 23 The plants, animal products or vegetable products mailed out of our country shall be put in quarantine and clearance certificates shall be granted in appropriate cases.

Article 24 Permits shall be signed and issued by the Ministry of Agriculture, Animal Husbandry and Fishery for the importation of daily harmful injurious insects, animal or plant pathogenic micro-organisms (including the cultures of bacteria, the cultures of viruses, biological products) and other harmful organisms as well as the natural enemies of diseases and insect pests.

VI. Transit Quarantine

Article 25 For the animals, plants, animal products or vegetable products in transit through our country, the carrier shall file a declaration or a waybill for quarantine and declare them at the port animal and plant quarantine authorities for quarantine at the port of entry. This shall be presented together with the quarantine certificate from the country of origin. They shall not be quarantined again at the port of exit.

Article 26 If the plants, animal products or vegetable products carried by a train, truck or aircraft through our territory change means of transport in one of our ports, the exteriors of their packages shall be examined; if they pass through our territory in the original vehicle, the exterior of the vehicle shall be examined. If no objects of quarantine are found through quarantine, a "Quarantine Clearance Notice" shall be signed and issued or a quarantine clearance stamp shall be affixed on the waybill so as to permit them to go through. If any objects of quarantine are found, the articles shall be wholly returned. The contaminated places, tools, etc. shall be dealt with as stipulated under Article 13 of these Regulations.

Article 27 If animals in transit have no objects of quarantine found through quarantine, they shall be permitted to pass through our territory. If any objects of quarantine are found in them, they shall be wholly returned. The contaminated places, tools, etc. shall be dealt with as stipulated under Article 13 of these Regulations.

The fodder, excrement, urine, padding grass, dirt, remains, etc. of the animals in transit shall be treated in designated places and shall not be abandoned indiscriminately.

If any objects of quarantine are found in the fodder of the animals in transit, the carrier shall be notified to replace the fodder and the original fodder shall be sterilized at the spot.

VII. Punishments

Article 28 Those found in violation of these Regulations shall be criticized, disciplined or fined according to different circumstances. Serious cases shall be punished by judicial authorities according to law.

VIII. Supplementary Provisions

Article 29 The units concerned shall render necessary assistance to the port animal and plant quarantine authorities when they are executing their duties in ports, airports, stations, post offices, warehouses, etc.

When the port animal and plant quarantine authorities execute field quarantine, the declarer(s) shall be present to render such assistance as moving, opening and repacking packages, etc.

A sampling certificate shall be issued and signed if the port animal and plant quarantine authorities take samples.

Article 30 The departments in charge shall notify the port animal and plant quarantine authorities concerned in time of the quarantine clauses in any agreements or trade contracts entered into and signed with foreign countries.

Article 31 When port animal and plant quarantine officers are on quarantine duties, they shall wear quarantine uniform and insignia.

Article 32 The port animal and plant quarantine authorities shall collect quarantine fees in the execution of quarantine and the procedures for such collection shall be formulated by the Ministry of Agriculture, Animal Husbandry and Fishery.

Article 33 The detailed rules for the implementation of these Regulations shall be prescribed by the Ministry of Agriculture, Animal Husbandry and Fishery jointly with the Ministry of Forestry.

Article 34 These Regulations shall be put into effect from the date of issue.

CUSTOMS PROCEDURES FOR THE SUPERVISION OF LUGGAGE AND OTHER ARTICLES BELONGING TO TRAVELLERS CROSSING THE BORDERS

(Revised and Promulgated as Order No. GH-Lin-985(58) of the Ministry of Foreign Trade on September 29, 1958)

Chapter I General Rules

Article 1 These Procedures are formulated for the purpose of ensuring the effective implementation of the foreign trade control system and in proper consideration of the needs of travellers crossing the borders.

Article 2 Except for those specially permitted by the General Customs Office of this Ministry, travellers crossing the borders and their luggage and articles shall go through the places with Customs stations.

Article 3 Travellers crossing the borders shall have their luggage and articles examined by the Customs officers and shall make a "Declaration of Traveller's Luggage and Articles" at the Customs stations before being examined.

The personnel of postal or transport organizations, who cross the borders frequently on duty, and those who are entitled to cross the borders frequently may make oral declarations only.

Article 4 The time and places for the examination of travellers' luggage and articles shall be fixed by the Customs. When the Customs examines the luggage and articles, a traveller or his agent shall be present, but the Customs shall be entitled to examine them without their presence if necessary.

Article 5 The Customs shall proceed in accordance with relevant provisions with the clearance of the luggage and articles of senior officials of the Government of the People's Republic of China, diplomats, consuls and diplomatic messengers accredited by China to foreign countries or by foreign countries to China, experts invited to work in China, the delegates of Chinese and foreign governments and people's representatives, etc.

In addition to the supervision under these Procedures, the luggage and articles of returned overseas Chinese shall be handled in accordance with "The Interim Provisions of the Customs for the Supervision of the Luggage and Articles of Such Travellers as Overseas Chinese Crossing the Borders."

(Note: This sentence has been revised in accordance with the Provisions of 1978.)

Article 6 The supervision of the luggage and articles of the travellers coming from or going to Hong Kong or Macao shall be handled in accordance with "The Procedures of the Customs for the Supervision of the Luggage and Articles of Travellers from or to Hong Kong or Macao."

Article 7 The articles declared by a traveller which are prohibited from import or export shall be detained by the Customs and the traveller or his agent shall be responsible for returning the articles abroad or to any place in China within six months respectively. If the articles are not returned before the time limit, they shall be confiscated by the Customs. The articles detained by reason of their harmful effect to politics, culture, morality and public health shall not be returned and shall be disposed of by the Customs in accordance with the relevant provisions of the state.

Article 8 With regard to gold, silver (including gold, platinum, silver and their products), jewelry, diamond jewelry, currencies, negotiable money orders, securities, stamps and other articles which are subject to examination or quarantine as stipulated by the state in addition to those provided for in these Procedures, they shall be handled in accordance with the relevant provisions of the state.

Article 9 A traveller who uses his luggage and articles for the purpose of illegal foreign exchange or sells them without authorization after the luggage and articles have been cleared by the Customs in accordance with these Procedures shall be treated by the Customs as having committed an act of smuggling.

Chapter II Incoming Travellers

Article 10 An incoming traveller's luggage and articles for his personal or family use in reasonable quantity shall be cleared with the exemption from an import licence, Customs duties and industrial and commercial consolidated taxes. However, the articles listed in Appendix (2) of these Procedures shall be limited to the numbers stipulated in the appendix. If the number of articles exceeds the limits stipulated in the appendix but remains within the limits of his personal or family use and in reasonable quantity, the excess shall be cleared after payment of Customs duties and industrial and commercial consolidated taxes.

Article 11 Presents of clothes, food, toys, native or special products in small quantities carried by an incoming traveller and odd numbers of his articles of daily use, provided the total amount is not more than RMB 50 yuan, shall be cleared after payment of Customs duties and industrial and commercial consolidated taxes.

Article 12 The luggage and articles in excess of the limits of his personal or family use and of reasonable quantity or the presents in excess of the limits stipulated in Article 11 of these Procedures shall be prohibited from import and returned abroad by a traveller or his agent within six months (perishable items shall be limited to five days); if they are not returned within the time limit, they shall be sold by the Customs and the proceeds shall be paid into the state treasury.

Article 13 All incoming travellers' luggage and articles shall be examined at the Customs house in the place of entry. However, if there is a Customs house at the destination, all articles carried by means of railway combined transport or aircraft could be examined at the destination.

If an incoming traveller has unaccompanied baggage, he shall indicate them in his declaration and make another declaration for the Customs' examination when the unaccompanied baggage arrives. The luggage and unaccompanied articles must arrive within six months after the traveller's entry so that they can be calculated together with those cleared and examined as stipulated in Article 10 of these Procedures.

Article 14 The luggage articles which are not claimed at the Customs within six months of the date of declaration by the means of transport for import (perishables shall be limited to five days) shall be sold by the Customs and the traveller(s) can claim, within six months, the balance of the proceeds of sales after the deduction of various taxes and fees. The Customs shall return the said balance after proving that there are no violations of law. If the balance of the sales proceeds is not claimed within the time limit, it shall be paid into the state treasury.

Chapter III. Outgoing Travellers

Article 15 An outgoing traveller's luggage and articles which are for his personal or family use and of reasonable quantity shall be exempted from obtaining an export licence, but the articles listed in Appendix (3) of these Procedures shall be limited to the numbers as stipulated in the appendix.

Article 16 Presents consisting of small numbers of cloths, food, toys, native or special products carried by an outgoing traveller and odd numbers of his articles of daily use valued at not more than RMB 50 yuan are not required to go through Customs formalities.

Article 17 Articles in excess of the limits of the traveller's personal or family use and of unreasonable quantity or in excess of the limits stipulated in Appendix (3) or the presents in excess of the limit as stipulated in Article 16 shall be prohibited from export and shall be returned by the traveller or his agent within six months (perishables shall be limited to five days). Those which are not returned within the time limit shall be sold by the Customs and the proceeds shall be paid into the state treasury.

Article 18 An outgoing traveller's luggage and articles shall be examined at the Customs house in the place of exit, but those carried by means of railway combined transport or aircraft shall be examined at the Customs house, if any, in the place of shipment. The declaration and examination formalities for unaccompanied luggage and articles shall be handled according to the provisions in Article 13 of these Procedures.

Chapter IV. Short-term Travellers

Article 19 With regard to the luggage and articles of a traveller who comes to China for a temporary stay of not more than six months or who goes abroad for a temporary period of not more than six months, and used by the traveller on the journey and during his stay and which are of reasonable quantity, they shall be exempted from import or export licence and cleared with the exemption from Customs duties and industrial and commercial consolidated taxes; small numbers of clothes, food, toys, native or special products carried for presentation and odd numbers of articles for daily use with the total value of not more than RMB 50 yuan shall be cleared after the collection of Customs duties and industrial and commercial consolidated taxes in accordance with the regulations.

The articles beyond the limits as stipulated in the above clause shall be prohibited from import or export and returned by the traveller or his agent abroad or to any place in our country within six months (within five days in the case of perishable items); if they are not returned within the time limit, they shall be sold by the Customs and the proceeds shall be paid into the state treasury.

Article 20 In the case of the articles listed in Appendix (2) of these Procedures and those required by the Customs to be re-transported abroad, which are carried by a traveller who comes to China for a temporary stay of not more than six months, they shall be cleared after register by the Customs at the time of entry and shall be taken abroad again by the traveller at the time of exit. If the traveller contravenes this provision, he shall be treated by the Customs as having committed an act of smuggling.

A traveller who intends to take abroad again the gold and silver (including gold, platinum, silver and their products), jewelry and diamond jewelry imported by him shall have them registered with the Customs when they are imported. The Customs shall issue a certificate to him and examine and clear them on the basis of the certificate at the time of the traveller's exit.

Article 21 The articles listed in Appendix (2) of these Procedures and other similar articles which are carried by a traveller who returns from a temporary stay of not more than six months abroad shall be prohibited from import with the exception of those taken abroad from home and registered with the Customs at the time of exit, and shall be disposed of as stipulated in the second clause of Article 19 of these Procedures.

Article 22 Except for those otherwise stipulated, the working personnel of postal or transport organizations, who cross the borders frequently on duty, and others entitled to cross the borders frequently shall only be permitted to carry the articles necessary for use on the journey, which shall be cleared with the exemption of an import or export licence and taxes. The articles beyond the above limits shall be prohibited from import or export and disposed of as stipulated in the second clause of Article 19 of these Procedures.

Chapter V. Travellers in Transit

Article 23 With the exception of those articles necessary for use on the journey, an application shall be made to the Customs for sealing a transit traveller's luggage and articles. The Customs house in the place of exit shall clear them by checking the sealing marks. Those not sealed shall be examined and cleared on the basis of the declaration filled in by the traveller at the time of entry.

Article 24 If a transit traveller leaves behind in our country the luggage and articles brought in at the time of entry without authorization of the Customs, the Customs shall, according to the particular degree of seriousness, treat him as having committed an act of smuggling or instruct the owner of the articles to return them abroad within a fixed period; those which are not returned within the time limit shall be sold by the Customs and the proceeds shall be paid into the state treasury.

Chapter VI. Supplementary Provisions

Article 25 These Procedures shall be interpreted by the General Customs Office of this Ministry.

Article 26 The appendices of these Procedures shall be revised and promulgated at any time by the General Customs Office of this Ministry according to concrete conditions.

Article 27 These Procedures shall be put into effect as of October 15, 1958.

APPENDICES:

THE PROCEDURES OF THE CUSTOMS FOR THE SUPERVISION OF THE LUGGAGE AND ARTICLES OF TRAVELLERS PASSING OVER THE BORDERS

Appendix (1)

THE LIST OF THE ARTICLES PROHIBITED FROM IMPORT AND EXPORT BY THE CUSTOMS OF THE PEOPLE'S REPUBLIC OF CHINA

Articles Prohibited from Import

(1) Various arms, ammunition and explosives;
(2) Radio transmitters, receivers and their main equipment;
(3) Renminbi;
(4) Manuscripts, printed matter, films, photos, discs, movies, sound recording tapes, video recording tapes, etc. which are harmful to the politics, economy, culture and morality of China;
(5) Deadly poisons as well as narcotics, opium, morphine and heroin which can result in human addiction;
(6) Animals, plants and their products or by-products carrying dangerous germs and pests;
(7) Food which is a hindrance to sanitation and which comes from an epidemic area and can spread a disease;
(8) Other articles prohibited from import as stipulated by the state.

Articles Prohibited from Export

(1) Various arms, ammunition and explosives;
(2) Radio transmitters, receivers and their main equipment;
(3) Renminbi and Renminbi negotiable securities;
(4) Foreign currencies, documents and negotiable securities which have not been examined and approved;
(5) Manuscripts, printed matter, films, photos, discs, movies, sound recording tapes, video recording tapes, etc. which touch upon state secrets or which are prohibited from export;
(6) Precious historical relics and books relating to the Chinese revolution, history, culture and art;
(7) Valuable animals, plants and their seeds;
(8) Precious metals and their products and jewelry (except for those carried by outgoing travellers in accordance with the limits as stipulated);
(9) Other articles prohibited from export as stipulated by the state.

(Note: This list has been revised in accordance with the Provisions of 1978.)

Appendix (2)

THE LIST OF THE LIMITS OF IMPORT ARTICLES EXEMPTED FROM LICENCES, CUSTOMS DUTIES AND INDUSTRIAL AND COMMERCIAL CONSOLIDATED TAXES

Watch and Pocket Watch	1 piece per person
Camera	1 piece per family
Radio	1 unit per family
Sewing Machine	1 unit per family
Bicycle	1 unit per person

Appendix (3)

THE LIST OF THE LIMITS OF EXPORT ARTICLES EXEMPTED FROM LICENCES

Jewelry, Diamond Jewelry	Value + RMB 500 yuan per person
Platinum Jewelry	1 commemorative ring of 3 qian per person
Gold Jewelry	1 liang per person
Silver Jewelry	10 liang per person
Silver Utensils	20 liang per person

REGULATIONS GOVERNING THE CONTROL OF THE ENTRY, EXIT, TRANSIT, RESIDENCE, AND TRAVEL OF FOREIGNERS

(Adopted at the 141st plenary meeting of the State Council on February 12, 1964 and approved at the 114th meeting of the Standing Committee of the 2nd National People's Congress on March 13, 1964 and promulgated and enforced on April 13, 1964)

I General Principles

Article 1 The entry into, exit from, transit through the national boundary of the People's Republic of China and residence and travel in China shall be dealt with in accordance with the provisions contained in these regulations.

These regulations are also applicable to stateless nationals.

Article 2 Foreigners in China shall abide by the laws and decrees of China.

Article 3 The entry, exit, transit, residence, and travel of foreigners shall be approved by the competent offices of the Chinese government.

Article 4 Offices of the Chinese government abroad which handle applications of foreigners for entry, exit, and transit are offices of diplomatic representatives and consular offices of China.

Offices at home of the Chinese government which handle applications for entry, exit, transit, residence, and travel of foreigners are the public security bureaus in the areas concerned. Applications by foreign diplomatic envoys, consular officers, and the staff of foreign diplomatic representative organs and consular organs of foreign countries to China shall be handled by the Ministry of Foreign Affairs and by foreign affairs offices in the areas concerned; applications by those foreigners holding diplomatic or official passports shall be handled by the Ministry of Foreign Affairs, the foreign affairs offices or public security bureaus in the areas concerned.

Article 5 Offices handling applications for entry, exit, transit, residence and travel of foreigners have the authority to reject the issuance of visas and certifying documents, and the authority to cancel or declare null and void the visas or certifying documents already issued.

Article 6 Residence and travel of foreigners in important national defence and military localities and restricted areas are prohibited.

II Entry, Exit, and Transit

Article 7 Foreigners shall apply for a visa governing entry, exit, or transit.

Article 8 With regard to entry, exit, or transit, foreigners shall abide by ports of entry and exit, means of transport, and routes prescribed in the visas within the valid period as indicated. Foreigners entering the country may proceed only to the place of destination noted in the visas. In the course of entry, exit, or transit, no stays on the way shall be permitted without authorization.

Article 9 Foreigners who come under the scope of an agreement signed between the Chinese government and a foreign government concerned, which mutually exempts visa arrangements, shall proceed through ports open to the foreign countries designated by the Chinese government. Upon entering the country, such foreigners should explain at national border checkpoints their places of destination and proceed via the route and by means of transport as designated at the national border checkpoints. In the course of entry, exit, or transit, no stay on the way shall be permitted without authorization.

III Residence

Article 10 Foreigners residing in China shall apply for residence registration within the stipulated period of time.

Article 11 Foreigners residing in China shall abide by the residence control system and register the inhabitants in the household as required by the provisions in these regulations.

Organs, schools, enterprises, organizations, hotels, and private residents accommodating foreigners shall register the inhabitants as required by the provisions of the residence control system.

Article 12 Foreigners residing in China shall proceed to public security organs within a specified period of time designated by public security organs to present documents for examination.

Article 13 Foreigners residing in China who change places of residence should apply for certified documents of moving.

IV Travel

Article 14 Foreigners who are to travel in areas out of the travel bounds set forth by municipal or county people's committees shall apply for documents authorizing travel within the specified period of time.

Article 15 Foreigners who travel shall proceed within the valid period noted in the travel documents, and only to the approved places of travel, by the means of transport and along the routes of travel as authorized, which shall not be altered by oneself. In the course of travel, no stay shall be permitted on the way without authorization.

Article 16 Public security organs may set up checkpoints in necessary localities of passage to check on foreigners, or dispatch people's police to check on foreigners with regard to their compliance of the provisions in these regulations. Foreigners should accept such checks.

V Punishment

Article 17 Local public security organs shall, according to the seriousness of the cases, give foreigners who violate the provisions of these regulations punishment respectively in the form of warning, fine, detention, deportation within a time limit, expulsion, and so forth; or investigate the criminal liabilities according to law.

Cases of violation of the provisions of these regulations involving foreigners who enjoy diplomatic immunity shall be handled through diplomatic channels.

VI Supplementary Rules

Article 18 Concrete measures governing the control of entry, exit, transit, residence, and travel of foreigners shall be formulated by the Ministry of Public Security and the Ministry of Foreign Affairs.

Article 19 These regulations shall be in force from the day of promulgation. The Provisional Rules Governing the Entry, Exit, and Residence of Foreign Nationals promulgated by the Administrative Council of the Central People's Government on November 28, 1951; and the Provisional Measures Governing Residence Registration and Issuance of Residence Certificates for Foreign Nationals, Provisional Measures Governing Travel of Foreign Nationals, and the Provisional Measures Governing Exit of Foreign Nationals promulgated by the Ministry of Public Security on August 10, 1954 shall be abrogated simultaneously.

REGULATIONS ON BORDER INSPECTION PROCEDURES

(Adopted at the 155th Plenary Meeting of the State Council on April 30, 1965 and promulgated and enforced on the same day)

Article 1 With a view to safeguarding the sovereignty and national security of the People's Republic of China and facilitating the entry and exit of people and means of communication and transportation, border inspection stations shall be set up at harbours, airports, boundary railway stations and other outlets open to foreign countries and at ports specially authorized for entry and exit.

Article 2 Border inspection stations shall be responsible for inspecting people entering and leaving the country, their passports and other entry and exit documents and baggage, and means of communication and transportation entering and leaving the country and the commodities carried therein.

Article 3 People and means of communication and transportation entering and leaving the country shall pass through harbours, airports, boundary railway stations and other outlets open to foreign countries and through ports specially authorized for entry and exit.

People entering and leaving the country shall comply with the laws and decrees of the People's Republic of China and with the border inspection system.

Article 4 People entering and leaving the country shall produce their passports or other entry and exit documents to the border inspection stations for inspection.

Border inspection stations shall prohibit the entry and exit of those who refuse to produce their passports or other entry and exit documents for inspection. Those whose passports or other entry and exit documents are not in accordance with the entry and exit regulations of our country shall be prohibited from entering or leaving the country and ordered to apply for proper entry and exit documents.

Article 5 People entering and leaving the country shall allow the border inspection stations to inspect their baggage.

The border inspection stations shall handle the baggage of foreign diplomats, consular officers and other personnel entitled to preferential treatment in accordance with the relevant stipulations laid down by the People's Republic of China.

Article 6 Captains of ships entering or leaving the country shall submit to the border inspection stations a list of their crew members and passengers and shall accept inspection by the inspection stations.

Crew members and other personnel when embarking on or disembarking from their ships shall produce valid documents to the border inspection stations for inspection. They shall not embark on or disembark from their ships without the permission of the border inspection stations.

Ships entering or leaving the country, when sailing within the territorial sea, harbours or rivers of the People's Republic of China, shall not drop off or take on people, or load or unload goods midway.

[Chinese] ships and ships of other nationalities in distress, on being allowed to sail into harbours not open to foreign countries in the People's Republic of China, shall accept inspection by the local border defence forces or the public security organs. They shall leave the harbours immediately when the causes of their distress no longer exist.

Article 7 Captains of airplanes entering or leaving the country shall submit to the border inspection stations a list of their crew members and passengers and shall accept inspection by the border inspection stations.

Planes entering the country, before landing at the designated airports, and planes leaving the country, from the time they take off from the designated airports until they leave the border, shall not land midway or air-drop personnel and goods. If, in the event of distress or accident they are compelled to land or air-drop personnel and goods midway, the captains should immediately report the details and the causes to the border inspection stations or local public security organs through civil aeronautic stations.

Article 8 Chief conductors of train crews or conductors of cargo trains entering and leaving the country shall report to the border inspection stations the number of crew members and passengers and the marshalling activity of the train and shall accept inspection by the border inspection stations.

Trains entering or leaving the country, when running from the border to a railway station inside the People's Republic of China, shall not drop off or take on people, load or unload goods, or stop without reason midway.

Article 9 Responsible persons of automobiles or other motor vehicles entering or leaving the country shall report to the border inspection stations the number of crew members and passengers with a description of the goods carried therein. They shall accept inspection by the border inspection stations.

Non-mechanical vehicles or horse-drawn carts entering or leaving the country shall accept inspection by the border inspection stations.

Article 10 If ships, airplanes, trains, automobiles and other means of communication and transportation carry people entering or leaving the country illegally or goods endangering the security of our country, the responsible persons of the means of communication and transportation must report to the border inspection stations immediately and await their action.

Article 11 People violating these regulations shall be dealt with by the border inspection stations according to the circumstances of the cases and in accordance with the law.

Article 12 These regulations shall take effect from the date of promulgation.

PROVISIONAL CUSTOMS REGULATIONS FOR INWARD AND OUTWARD BAGGAGE OF OVERSEAS CHINESE AND OTHER PASSENGERS

(Promulgated by the Ministry of Foreign Trade on March 23, 1978)

1 To effectively implement foreign trade control policy as well as serve the needs of those passengers having relatives in China or abroad, viz. overseas Chinese, foreigners of Chinese origin, permanent alien residents in China and Chinese nationals on visits to relatives abroad, Customs shall deal with their inward and outward baggage according to the present regulation, subject to the "Rules for Customs Supervision and Control over Inward and Outward Passengers' Baggage."

2 Baggage carried by the above-mentioned passengers, if within the prescribed limit set on the attached table, shall be released on entry or departure either free of duty or on payment of duty. In case the imported articles listed as items Nos. 1 to 14 of the table exceed the import duty-free limit, they may still be released on payment of duty, provided they are in reasonable quantities for personal use and their total value does not exceed 200 yuan.

Table of Import/Export Limits for Duty-free or Dutiable Articles

Category	Item	Import Limit	Export Limit
	1. Overcoats	3	3
	2. Underwear	20 pcs.	20 pcs.
	3. Other clothes	20 pcs.	20 pcs.
	4. Bedding	1 pc. of each kind	1 pc. of each kind
	5. Woollen yarn and manufactures made thereof	4 kg.	4 kg.
	6. Scarves	6 pcs.	6 pcs.
	7. Shoes/Socks	12 prs. for each	12 prs. for each
	8. Dress material	30 m. (single width)	15 m (single width)
Duty-free	Woollen piece goods	5 m. (double width)	–
	9. Foodstuffs*	50 kg	25 kg
	10. Cigarettes	600	600
	11. Wine/spirits	4 bottles	4 bottles
	12. Pharmaceutical products	50 yuan	25 yuan
	13. Ginseng/deer antlers	50 g.	50 g.
	14. Daily necessities	100 yuan	50 yuan
	15. Watches	1	
	16. Bicycles	1	
	17. Radios**	1	any 2 of
	18. Sewing machines	1	these 6 items
	19. Electric fans	1	
	20. Pocket calculators	1	
	1. Watches	1	
	2. Recorders (including combinations)	1	
Dutiable	3. TV sets	1	
	4. Cameras	1	
	5. Musical instruments (accordions or violins)	1	
	6. Ginseng/deer antlers	150 g.	

* Luxuries are dutiable ** Without recording facility

Articles exceeding duty-free and dutiable limits shall be returned abroad or to places in China as the case may be, except watches, radios, cameras and other items necessary for the journey, which shall be registered with Customs and taken out of or brought back to China by the passengers at the time of exit or entry.

The provisions of this Article also apply to baggage carried by the accompanying spouse and children of passengers. For children under 16 years of age, not half of the quantities specified under items Nos. 1 to 14 shall be duty-free. For children between the ages of 12 and 15, one watch per person may also be released duty free.

3 The above-mentioned passengers shall be subject to the Customs Rules for Short-term Visitors from the second time of entry or departure if they enter or leave China more than once within a year.

4 The limits prescribed in the table attached to the present regulation do not apply to baggage carried by the above-mentioned passengers who are coming to China or going abroad for resettlement. Their baggage may be released free of duty on entry or departure provided it is in reasonable quantities for personal use.

5 New handicrafts bought at state-owned shops, cultural relics (ascertained by the authorities in charge of cultural relics as permissible for export), old handicrafts, jewelry, gold and silver ornaments, etc., bought at Friendship Stores or Relics Stores by overseas Chinese or foreigners of Chinese origin with Renminbi obtained by the exchanging of foreign currencies, shall be presented on departure to Customs together with the relevant invoices and foreign exchange certificates, on the strength of which Customs shall release the articles concerned.

6 The present regulation came into force on April 5, 1978.

REGULATIONS FOR CUSTOMS CONTROL OVER BAGGAGE OF PASSENGERS COMING FROM OR GOING TO HONG KONG AND MACAO

(Promulgated by the Ministry of Foreign Trade on July 1, 1979)

Article 1 Baggage carried by passengers coming from or going to Hong Kong and Macao (hereinafter referred to as "passengers"), if in reasonable quantities for personal use and within the limit specified in the "Table of Duty-free and Dutiable Articles Carried by Passengers" (see Appendix 1), shall be released either free of duty or on payment of duty after Customs inspection.

Article 2 Inward passengers carrying baggage which is within the import duty-free limit as specified in the attached table may pass through "Green Channel" where it is so provided by Customs. Should articles carried by such a "Green Channel" passenger be found exceeding the import duty-free limit, which is deemed a violation of Customs regulations, Customs shall inflict on

Appendix 1:

Table of Limits for Duty-free and Dutiable Articles Carried by Passengers

Category	Item	Import Limit	Export Limit
Duty-free	Total weight in which:	30 kg.	30 kg.
	1. Clothes of all kinds	35 pcs. (in reasonable quantities)	Total value not exceeding 15 yuan for traditional Chinese medicines, in which the total weight of Chinese medicinal herbs shall not exceed 1 kg.; each kind of medicine 250g.; Yunnanbaiyao 12 g.
	2. Shoes/socks/scarves	10 prs./pcs. of each	
	3. Bedding	1 pc. or pr. of each kind, but 3 pcs. or prs. in all	
	4. Dress material (single width)	10 m.	
	5. Foodstuffs	15 kg.	
	6. Wine and spirits (including medicated wine)	2 bottles (not exceeding 750 g. each)	
	7. Cigarettes	400 pcs.	
	8. Therapeutic medicines and home remedies	in reasonable quantities for personal use only	
	9. Daily necessities	RMB20 yuan (in reasonable quantities for each kind)	
Dutiable	1. Pocket calculators	1 pc.	
	2. Watches, radios, TV sets, recorders (including combinations), cameras, electric fans, bicycles, sewing machines, and accessories thereof	1 pc. per person a year with a reasonable quantity of accessories.	
	3. Ginseng/Deer antlers	100 g. of each	
Remarks	1. For children under 16 years of age, only articles necessary for personal use shall be released free of duty. 2. Furniture or unsanitary old clothes shall not be allowed to be brought into China. 3. Musks, toad cake, cinnabar, eucommia, gastrodia elata, Chinese caterpillar fungus, Pianzihuang, Angongnuihuang pills, Liushen pills and unappraised cultural relics shall not be allowed to be taken out of China. 4. Articles bought with Renminbi obtained through the exchanging of foreign currencies may be taken out on the strength of the relevant commercial invoices.		

the offender a fine not greater than 500 yuan according to the nature of the case. In addition, the articles exceeding the import duty-free limit shall be returned to Hong Kong or Macao. Should dutiable articles be found in such a case, it shall be deemed an act of smuggling and dealt with accordingly.

Article 3 Inward passengers carrying articles which are dutiable and/or over the import duty-free limit as specified in the table shall pass through "Red Channel," where it is so provided by Customs, and declare their articles to Customs, who shall release the articles after inspection according to the present regulation.

Article 4 Baggage carried by outward passengers may be released at the time of exit provided it does not exceed the limit as specified in the attached table.

Article 5 For passengers who will return within 24 hours, only items necessary for their personal use on the journey shall be released.

Article 6 For passengers coming in or going out for resettlement in China or Hongkong or Macao, Customs shall, on the strength of the relevant papers, deal with their baggage according to the provisions of the "Rules for Customs Supervision and Control over Inward and Outward Passengers' Baggage."

Article 7 Articles carried by outward passengers, if found to be in excess of the prescribed export limit, shall not be permitted to be taken out whereas articles carried by inward passengers, if found to be in excess of the prescribed import limit, shall be detained by Customs. In the latter case, the detained articles may be reclaimed and returned to Hong Kong or Macao within a month. On expiration of the time limit, the Customs shall dispose of the articles and remit to the national treasury the proceeds realized from their disposal. However, passengers may make a request to bring along articles necessary for the journey guaranteeing the re-importation or re-exportation of such articles. With Customs approval and registration, such articles shall be released but must be brought back to or taken out of China at the time of re-entry or exit.

Article 8 Passengers shall be forbidden to bring into or take out of China certain prohibited articles (see Appendix 2). However, jewelry and gold and silver ornaments brought in by passengers at the time of entry and registered with Customs may be taken out at the time of exit.

Article 9 Selling for profit the articles released by Customs for inward passengers' personal use shall be strictly forbidden.

Article 10 Offenders of the present regulation shall be dealt with according to the relevant provisions of the regulations.

Appendix 2:

List of Prohibited Import/Export Articles of the People's Republic of China

Prohibited Import Articles

(1) Arms, ammunition and explosives of all kinds;
(2) Radio transmitter-receivers and principal parts;
(3) Renminbi;
(4) Manuscripts, printed matter, films, photographs, phonograph records, cinematographic films, loaded recording tapes and video-tapes, etc. detrimental to Chinese political, economic, cultural and moral interests;
(5) Deadly poison, addictive narcotics, opium, morphia, heroin, etc.;
(6) Animals, plants, and products thereof infected with or carrying harmful germs and insect pests;
(7) Unsanitary foodstuffs and germ-carrying foodstuffs from infected areas;
(8) Other articles the importation of which is prohibited by national regulations.

Prohibited Export Articles

(1) Arms, ammunition and explosives of all kinds;
(2) Radio transmitter-receivers and principal parts;
(3) Renminbi and securities in Renminbi;
(4) Foreign currencies, bills and securities in foreign currencies (with the exception of those allowed to be taken out);
(5) Manuscripts, printed matter, films, photographs, phonograph records, cinematographic films, loaded recording tapes and video-tapes, etc. which contain state secrets or otherwise not permissible for export;
(6) Valuable cultural relics and rare books relating to China's revolution, Chinese history, culture and art;
(7) Rare animals, rare plants and their seeds;
(8) Precious metals and articles made thereof, jewelry and ornaments made thereof (with the exception of those within the quantity allowed to be taken out by outward passengers);
(9) Other articles the exportation of which is prohibited by national regulations.

INTERIM REGULATIONS OF THE PEOPLE'S REPUBLIC OF CHINA FOR THE ADMINISTRATION OF PORTS

Adopted by the 203rd Government Administration Session of the Government Administrative Council on January 21, 1954 and ordered to be promulgated and put into effect by the Government Administrative Council (January 23, 1954)

I General Rules

Article 1 All the ports along the coasts of the People's Republic of China shall be provided respectively with port administration bureaux, sub-bureaux and offices (hereinafter simply referred to as "port central office(s)") by the Ministry of Communications of the Central People's Government (hereinafter abbreviated to the "MOC of the CPG") according to the demands of trade and transport and in light of the handling duties and equipment capacity of each port. With regard to the establishment or withdrawal of a port office, an application shall be made by the MOC of the CPG to the Government Administrative Council of the Central People's Government (hereinafter abbreviated to the GAC) for approval and promulgation.

Article 2 Port offices shall be responsible for the management of port and other affairs as required by these Regulations and each one shall be a business accounting unit in our enterprise economy.

Article 3 Port office shall be under the direct jurisdiction and be centrally coordinated by the Headquarters of Marine Transportation of the MOC of the CPG in administration, business, technology and finance. Port offices shall also be subject to the supervision and direction of local people's government.

Article 4 The director or chief of a port office shall be charged with the fulfillment of the port production and financial plans, the utilization and safeguard of the port property and equipment and the maintenance of the port safety, order and staff discipline. To carry out the above tasks smoothly, he shall maintain close contact and cooperation with the Navy, public security, public health, customs and other departments concerned.

Article 5 The orders and instructions issued by the director or chief of a port office, provided these are within the limits of his statutory authority, shall be strictly observed and executed by the organizations, enterprises, vessels and by all personnel concerned.

Article 6 All port equipment within the boundary of a port shall be under the unified management of the port office. The wharves, warehouses, subsidiary office builings, etc. which are still in the possession of other organizations and enterprises within the port boundary shall be handed over to the port office gradually for its unified management and administration as required under Article 13 of these Regulations.

Article 7 Whenever any other organization or enterprise of the state has to carry out any engineering construction within the boundary of a port, application shall be made to the port office for approval.

Article 8 In compliance with other decrees and regulations, a port office shall be charged with the supervision and direction of the private shipping companies' affairs which include the vessels, wharves and warehouses within the jurisdiction of the port.

II The Delimitation of Port Boundary

Article 9 The land boundary of a port includes the land occupied by the port and the coastline, wharves, warehouses, machinery, equipment, dangerous goods storage areas, fuel and material storage areas and oil-filling equipment, dockyard, docks, related port engineering structures, fresh water supply base, beacons, etc.

Article 10 The water boundary of a port includes the surface and underwater areas occupied by the port, courses for vessels to enter or leave the port, all anchorages and berths, river branches connected with and needed by the port and adjacent waters with potentialities for the future development of the port.

Article 11 To delimit the boundary of a

port, each port office shall work out a scheme of the port boundary according to concrete conditions, draw a plan of the land and water boundaries and submit them together with the manual to the local people's government so that the units concerned can be called together to discuss them and make a decision, which shall be submitted to the MOC of the CPG for verification and then passed on to the GAC for approval before their execution.

Article 12 The railway line within a port boundary used for the transfer of goods and passengers between the railway and a steamship is the business line of the railway authorities. The one used for the transfer of goods within the port itself is the exclusive line of the port office. The system of the division of labour between the railway and the port and the rules for the operation of trains and cars within the port area shall be handled on the basis of agreements or contracts signed by the railway administration office and the port office.

Article 13 Other state organizations and enterprises shall continue to hold and use the wharves, warehouses, subsidiary office buildings, etc. in their present possession within the port boundary; their property rights should not be changed for the time being. They shall also continue to rent the wharves and warehouses they are renting within the port area, but these places shall be placed under the unified management of the port office. To meet the needs for the development of internal and foreign trade, the port office shall, wherever appropriate, make applications to the local people's government for decision so that these premises should be regulated and regained and their leases terminated.

The Ministry of Agriculture and the Ministry of Commerce of the Central People's Government shall still enjoy the property rights of the fishing wharves, petroleum wharves and their special-use warehouses in their present possession within the port boundary and the stevedores assigned to these places shall also be under the leadership and administration of them respectively.

III Authority of Port Offices

Article 14 The duties of the port offices shall be to:

(1) Supervise each party concerned in the observation of the state decrees relating to shipping and port affairs and take effective measures to prevent and stop all acts in violation of the aforesaid decrees;

(2) Be charged with the safeguard of all equipment in port boundaries and waterways, maintain the depths and widths of courses and waterways, and guarantee the safety of vessels in entering or leaving ports and the improvement of their navigation efficiency;

(3) Carry out various items of construction in ports in order to ensure the development of national economy;

(4) Supervise stevedores, coordinate the handling, custody, receipt and delivery of goods, supervise goods and passenger transportation, coordinate such means of land and water communications as motor vehicles, carts, lighters, etc. and handle such business as the receipt, delivery or re-export of goods;

(5) Manage and supply ships' fuel, materials and fresh water and other services for vessels;

(6) Organize pilotage, administer and supervise the entries and exits of vessels;

(7) Establish and supervise port radio stations to circulate meteorological information among sailing vessels and consult with them about maritime affairs;

(8) Rescue vessels, lives, goods, etc. from distress and keep the salvaged property in good custody; investigate and handle all maritime affairs and average cases;

(9) Administer examination of seamen and pilots; grant them certificates; handle the registry of vessels;

(10) Assist ship registry offices in survey and measurement of vessels;

(11) Supervise all projects, machinery and building equipment in ports and carry out technical examination and maintenance of them;

(12) Supervise hygienic and fire prevention equipment in ports and carry out epidemic prevention examination and the jobs of safety and public health;

(13) Supervise and maintain lighting, signal and security equipment which is under the jurisdiction of the ports;

(14) Collect port charges and various fees as stipulated;

(15) Supervise and direct all the affairs of private shipping companies, vessels, wharves, warehouses and holders of port tools which are under the jurisdiction of ports.

Article 15 The limits of the authority of port offices are as follows:

(1) To be entitled to sign various relevant business contracts in the name of port offices in accordance with the laws, regulations, orders and instructions issued by the MOC of the CPG;

(2) To promulgate various necessary rules, regulations and procedures as stipulated by the

decrees after approval from the MOC of the CPG;

(3) To investigate, charge or fine the organizations, enterprises, vessels and individuals who are found contravening the state decrees and regulations relating to shipping and port affairs;

(4) To inflict such punishments as warning, demerit record, demotion or withdrawal of certificates from seamen, pilots, etc. who have violated technical safety provisions;

(5) To be entitled to take effective measures if necessary and to require the vessels staying in ports and the organizations, enterprises or individuals within the port boundaries to supply all first-aid tools or equipment immediately so as to prevent injury to human bodies, lives, vessels, goods and other property and to maintain unobstructed courses;

(6) To be entitled to demand owners of sunken ships and things in port water or its vicinity to salvage the same within a specified time, and to salvage or remove the same without the consent of the owners if they obstruct waterways and are not disposed of within the specified time upon the issue of the announcements or written notices; the expenses required and other payable taxes according to regulations shall be compensated for with the proceeds from selling off the salvaged ships and things, the deficiency to be borne by the original owners or the surplus to be refunded to them;

(7) For the sake of the safety of port boundaries and the needs of operation, the port office is entitled to require the owner(s) to remove or move out any properties or goods in port boundaries within a specified time; with regard to the removal of fixed structures, applications shall be made to local people's governments for disposition;

(8) For goods not taken within the time limit, the port offices shall be entitled to dispose of the same in accordance with relevant decrees and regulations.

Article 16 When a vessel is involved in any of the following cases, the port office shall be entitled to prohibit it from leaving the port:

(1) Contravening the provisions for the safety specifications relating to ship's certificates, ship's current state, supplies, equipment, etc. or the provisions of other decrees and regulations;

(2) Failing to pay the following sums:

1. Various port charges;

2. Fines for contravening decrees and regulations;

3. Reparations for the damage of port engineering structures, course marks and other property in the port.

Article 17 The port office shall clear the vessel which is prohibited from leaving the port due to the failure to pay the sums as stipulated in the preceding Article if it supplies sufficient guaranties to compensate for the sums.

Article 18 If the vessel damages any port project(s), structure(s), course mark(s) or other property in the port, but the responsibility has not been established, the port office shall be entitled to prohibit the vessel from leaving the port for not more than 3 days (to be counted from the time when the order reaches the opposite party until a full 72 hours have elapsed), and if the responsibility has not been established within the said time, the vessel shall be cleared.

Article 19 All expenses of the vessel during the time when it is prohibited from leaving the port (including examination, verification and other fees) shall be borne by the vessel.

Article 20 If a port office without authorization or any decrees prohibits a vessel from leaving the port, the vessel shall be entitled to claim compensation by the port office for the direct loss it has incurred due to the prohibition from leaving the port and has the right to sue the port office.

Article 21 The port office shall be entitled to sue the original claimant(s) if the office has prohibited a vessel from leaving the port upon request by any other organization, enterprise or individual but such a prohibiton has been held by the court to be illegal.

Article 22 The affairs relating to wharves, warehouses and their subsidiary equipment within port areas which are not run by the state shall be dealt with in accordance with the current government decrees and they shall be under the unified administration and control of port offices.

IV Supplementary Provisions

Article 23 With regard to the corporate economic status and fixed capital of a port office, separate regulations shall be formulated and put into effect by the MOC of the CPG.

Article 24 The procedures for the Navy to use ports shall be separately formulated by the GAC.

Article 25 These Regulations shall be put into effect as from the date of approval of promulgation by the GAC.

GENERAL RULES GOVERNING JOINT INSPECTION OF INCOMING AND OUTGOING SHIPS

(Approved by the State Council on September 8, 1961 and jointly promulgated by the Ministry of Communications, Ministry of Foreign Trade, Ministry of Public Security and Ministry of Public Health on October 24, 1961)

1. These General Rules are enacted for the purpose of strengthening joint inspection of incoming and outgoing ships, crews of ships, passengers, baggage and cargo so as to insure safety of navigation, safeguard the security of the frontiers, stop smuggling, prevent epidemics from being brought into or out of the country, and facilitate the movement of ships entering into and leaving the harbours and foreign trade and transportation.

2. The organs which shall take part in the joint inspection and the different spheres of inspection to be carried out on their responsibility are as follows:

a. Harbour Bureau: to assume responsibility for examining the ship's documents and matters concerning the safety of navigation of ships.

b. Customs: to assume responsibility for inspecting the ships, cargo, and the baggage and articles carried by crews of ships and passengers to see whether there is breaching of laws and smuggling.

c. Frontier inspection organ: to assume responsibility for carrying out frontier inspection of the ships as well as the passports, related documents, baggage and articles of ships' crew and passengers.

d. Frontier health and quarantine organ: to assume responsibility for carrying out medical inspection and health inspection and for giving the necessary health treatment to the ships, crews of ships, passengers, luggage and cargo.

Except with the special approval of the State Council, no other organ may carry out inspection.

3. Permits for ships' entry into and departure from ports shall be handled by the Harbour Bureau, and no other organ may obstruct or detain the ships under any pretext. In case it is necessary to prohibit or delay a ship's entry into or departure from the port, the action must be taken through the Harbour Bureau.

4. The Harbour Bureau shall assume responsibility for organizing the joint inspection and shall notify the relevant inspection organs in advance of the time at which a ship enters into and departs from the port and the place of its berth.

5. When the ship is, according to regulations, subject to quarantine inspection at the time of entry into the port, all personnel taking part in joint inspection, except for the pilot and personnel approved by the frontier and quarantine personnel, should board the ship to carry out inspection after the ship is being examined by the quarantine personnel.

6. Inspection of the baggage and personal effects of foreign diplomats and consular officials and other personnel entitled to preferential treatment shall be handled in accordance with the relevant regulations of the People's Republic of China.

7. Unless otherwise provided for by the State, Chinese ships navigating in inland rivers and along the coast shall, in principle, not be subject to inspection. If necessary, inspection may be carried out by the relevant inspection organs through the Harbour Bureau.

8. Inspection of ships, crews of ships, passengers, baggage and cargo shall be limited to the port of departure, port of arrival and port of call. Unless under special circumstances, a ship may not be stopped for inspection while on its way.

9. The Harbour Bureau at each port shall periodically call and chair a joint inspection conference attended by representatives of the Customs, frontier inspection organ and frontier health and quarantine organ and, if necessary, may invite representatives from other organs concerned to attend the conference to discuss matters concerning joint inspection.

The joint inspection conference shall appoint a secretary to handle the routine affairs under the leadership of the Harbour Bureau.

10. The term "inspection" in these General Rules refers to the items listed under Article 2. Where provisions have been made, other matters, such as control exercised by the harbour bureaus over ships, supervision and collection of duties by the Customs in respect of ships and cargo, and

health supervision exercised by the frontier health and quarantine organs in respect of ships shall still be handled by the competent organs in accordance with the relevant provisions.

11. These General Rules shall be put into effect from the date of their promulgation.

CUSTOMS PROCEDURES FOR THE SUPERVISION OF INTERNATIONAL CIVIL AIRCRAFT

(Revised, promulgated and put into into effect by the Ministry of Foreign Trade on October 1, 1974)

I General Rules

Article 1 These Procedures are formulated for the purpose of ensuring the effective implementation of the state policies and customs decrees in the control of foreign trade and to facilitate international civil air transportation.

Article 2 The international civil aircraft referred to in these Procedures are all civil aircraft entering and leaving our country, excluding the special planes taken by the heads of states and governments.

Article 3 Except those specially permitted, international civil aircraft shall be permitted to land or take off only at the international airports provided with Customs houses.

International airports shall notify the Customs two hours before the landing or taking off of civil aircraft.

Article 4 If an international civil aircraft is to handle passengers, goods, postal items, luggage and other articles, it shall have to be authorised by Customs and do the work under the Customs' supervision.

II The Declaration, Examination and Clearance of Aircraft

Article 5 After the landing of an international civil aircraft, the commander or his agent shall submit the following documents to the Customs immediately:

(1) A manifest of entering and transit passengers and luggage;

(2) A manifest of import and transit goods, postal items and other articles and a copy of the airway bill relating to the goods;

(3) A list of the aircrew and their personal effects which include currencies, gold and silver.

Article 6 Before an international civil aircraft takes off, the commander or his agent shall submit the following documents to the Customs:

(1) A manifest of outgoing passengers and luggage;

(2) A manifest of export goods, postal items and other articles and a copy of the airway bill relating to the goods;

(3) A list of the aircrew and their personal effects which include currencies, gold and silver (which is exempt from submission if there is no change in the aircrew after entering the airport).

Article 7 When an international civil aircraft lands and takes off at the second and third international airports in our territory in the same flight, the commander or his agent shall submit the declaration documents to the Customs as stipulated in Article 5 and Article 6 of these Procedures.

The commander or the person assigned by him shall be responsible for carrying the customs envelope given him by the Customs intact to the Customs house at the next airport.

Article 8 If an international civil aircraft incidentally lands at a designated unscheduled airport with the consent of the civil aviation administration department because of the climate and other objective reasons, it shall be exempt from submission of declaration documents if it does not handle passengers and goods. However, the commander shall take necessary measures to keep all the goods and luggage on board intact.

Article 9 An international civil aircraft shall be examined by the Customs after landing or before taking off.

When the Customs examines the aircraft, the commander or the person assigned by him shall be present. When the Customs considers it necessary to open up the relevant parts of the plane and look into the flight log and other documents, the commander or the person assigned by him shall act upon the request and submit the same for examination.

Upon completion of the Customs' examination of the aircraft, the commander shall sign the examination record compiled by the Customs.

Article 10 An international civil aircraft shall only be permitted to take off after the Customs has finished examination, and signs and seals the export manifest for clearance.

III The Supervision of Passengers, Goods, Postal Items and Luggage

Article 11 Incoming or outgoing passengers and their luggage and articles shall go through customs formalities before going out of the airport or boarding the aircraft.

Article 12 Import or export goods, postal items, luggage and other articles shall go through customs formalities and the Customs shall sign and seal the airway bill or other relevant documents for clearance before the airport delivers or receives them for shipment.

Article 13 The passengers, goods, postal items, luggage and other articles in transit in the original aircraft shall be examined if the Customs considers it necessary to do so.

Article 14 The passengers in transit who have to change aircraft shall go through transit formalities in accordance with the relevant provisions of the Customs.

Article 15 The goods, postal items, luggage and other articles in transit by changing aircraft shall be landed and stored in the storage places approved by the Customs, put under the supervision of the Customs and go through transit formalities in accordance with the relevant provisions of the Customs.

Article 16 If a military aircraft or a special plane carrying the head of a state or a government entering or leaving our country also carries general goods and/or passengers, the department concerned shall give a notice to the Customs and the Customs shall supervise them in accordance with these Procedures and other relevant provisions.

IV The Supervision of Articles Carried by the Aircrew

Article 17 The articles, currencies, gold and silver carried by the aircrew for their own use shall be examined and cleared by the Customs when they enter or leave our country.

Article 18 The articles carried by the aircrew for import or export shall be restricted to the necessary or odd articles for their own use in the flight. The imported articles shall be prohibited from sale or transfer.

When the aircrew of a foreign civil aircraft buy reasonable quantities of articles for their own use and carry them abroad, the aircrew shall submit the foreign currency exchange memos and the sales memos of the stores which sold them to Customs for examination.

Article 19 The aircrew shall be prohibited from carrying articles into or out of our country on behalf of other persons.

V The Supervision of Aircraft's Fuel, Oil, Parts, and Supplies as well as Gold, Silver and Currencies

Article 20 The fuel, oil, parts, spares, normal equipment, and supplies as well as gold, silver and currencies shall be examined or sealed if the Customs thinks it necesssary to do so. The commander shall keep the Customs sealing marks intact.

The above articles shall be prohibited from sale or transfer for other purposes during the aircraft's stay at the airport.

Article 21 The fuel, oil, parts, spares, normal equipment, supplies, etc. obtained from an aircraft for use by the other aircraft belonging to the same civil aviation enterprise shall be listed in a separate certficate for clearance without a licence, signed by the commander, submitted to the Customs for examination and the articles should be stored in the storage places approved by the Customs under the supervision of the Customs. When they are to be used or transported out, a certificate for clearance without a licence shall be made, signed and submitted to the Customs for verification and cancellation.

The above articles are exempt from customs duties, but they shall be prohibited from sale or transfer for other purposes.

Article 22 An application shall be made to the Customs for supervision when an international civil aircraft is to replenish fuel, oil, parts, spares, normal equipment and supplies.

VI The Supervision of Import and Export Articles of International Civil Aviation Enterprises

Article 23 An international civil aviation enterprise shall make a list of the common articles transported in for its own use and such business materials as publicity materials, souvenirs, documents, forms, tickets, etc. and declare them at the Customs. After approval, the Customs shall tax and clear the public articles and such other articles as publicity materials without taxation, but prohibit them from sale.

Article 24 "Public postal items" received and sent by international civil aviation enterprises are confined to the letters between civil aviation listed in the manifest for the Customs examination and clearance when they are imported or exported.

VII Supplementary Provisions

Article 25 The captain or his agent or the civil aircraft is to replenish fuel, oil, parts, spares, a prompt notice to the Customs if an international civil aircraft is forced to drop passengers with parachutes and discard goods within our territory because of engine troubles or other reasons or if the airplane crashes in our country due to accidents.

Article 26 Those acts in violation of the relevant provisions of these Procedures shall be dealt with by the Customs in accordance with related decrees.

NOTICE OF THE MINISTRY OF PUBLIC SECURITY OF THE PEOPLE'S REPUBLIC OF CHINA

(March 15, 1981)

To ensure transportation safety in international civil aviation service, it has been decided that starting from April 1, 1981, technical security checks will be conducted on all Chinese and foreign passengers and luggage boarding international flights at all civil airports in the People's Republic of China.

1. Weapons, tools for criminal purposes, ammunition, explosives, combustibles, extremely poisonous or radioactive materials and other dangerous items hazardous to safety of the flight are strictly prohibited on board.

2. Except for those who have obtained special permission, all the passengers must pass through an inspection gate or detector check. Passengers' hand-carried items must pass the inspection of detectors. When necessary, bodily searches and open-luggage checks must be made. Passengers who refuse to go through inspection procedures are not allowed to board the plane and will be responsible for their own losses.

3. The above-mentioned dangerous items discovered in the course of the inspection must be handled by the airport security inspection department. Suspects of hijacking and other acts endangering safety of the flight must be turned over to the local public security organs.

The notice is hereby announced.

NOTICE OF THE MINISTRY OF PUBLIC SECURITY OF THE PEOPLE'S REPUBLIC OF CHINA

(October 15, 1981)

To ensure the safety of domestic civil flights, it has been decided to enforce a technical security inspection at all civil aviation airports in China of Chinese and foreign passengers on all regular domestic civil flights and their luggage and other belongings beginning from November 1, 1981.

1. It is strictly forbidden for anyone to carry aboard or put inside unaccompanied luggage or pieces of cargo any weapon, tool used for criminal purposes, ammunition, any explosive, inflammable, lethally poisonous or radioactive article, or any other dangerous item threatening flight safety.

2. Except where special exemption is granted, all passengers and their luggage and other belongings will be subjected to security inspection. When necessary, a body search may be conducted. Anyone who refuses the inspection will not be permitted to board the plane and will be solely responsible for any personal loss arising therefrom.

3. Cases of passengers found to be carrying any one of the above-mentioned dangerous items will be handled by the airport security inspection department concerned. Anyone suspected of hijacking a plane or committing any other act endangering flight safety will be handed over for investigation to a public security organ.

The notice is hereby announced.

THE PROCEDURES OF THE CUSTOMS FOR THE SUPERVISION OF INTERNATIONAL SAILING VESSELS AND THE GOODS ON BOARD

(Promulgated as Notice No. JHD-Sun-393(58) of the Ministry of Communications and No. GH-Lin-1159(58) of the Ministry of Foreign Trade on December 31, 1958)

Chapter I General Rules

Article 1 These Procedures are formulated for the purpose of ensuring the effective implementation of the foreign trade control system and facilitating the transportation of international sailing vessels (hereinafter simply referred to as "ship(s)").

Article 2 With the exception of those specially permitted by the Ministry of Communications jointly with the Ministry of Foreign Trade, ships shall only be permitted to berth and carry goods and passengers in the ports provided with Customs houses.

Article 3 The port authorities shall notify the Customs in advance of the time of arrival and departure of ships.

Article 4 The port authorities shall designate jointly with the Customs the places for ships to berth and carry goods and passengers in the ports. The port authorities shall obtain the Customs' consent of ships' changes of berths in the ports.

Article 5 Ships shall be put under the supervision of the Customs from their arrival in the ports till their departure from the ports. The Customs shall be entitled to examine them if it deems necessary to do so.

During the stay of a ship in a port, the ship shall be allowed to leave the port first if it is required by force majeure to do so temporarily and it is not possible to obtain the approval of the Customs; however, the captain shall report the cause and situation of the departure from the port upon returning to the port.

Article 6 If a ship is to carry goods, travellers' luggage, international mailbags and other articles, these jobs shall have the prior approval of the Customs and shall be done under the supervision of the Customs.

Chapter II The Customs Declaration, Examination and Clearance of Ships

Article 7 When a ship enters a port, the captain shall submit to the Customs a ship's import manifest (the form omitted) and the following documents:

(1) An import loading list;

(2) An incoming passenger list (including through transport travellers, but no submission is required if there are no passengers);

(3) A list (the form omitted) of the articles, currencies, gold and silver for the crew's personal use and as the ship's spares;

(4) A crew list;

(5) Other documents and papers required by the Customs.

If a ship calls at two or more ports of our country in succession on the same voyage, with the exception of its arrival at the first port, it shall be exempted from submitting the ship's import manifest and the document listed in the above item (3) when it arrives at the other ports. (Note: This article has been amended in accordance with Notice No. GH-Hu-73(59) of the Ministry of Foreign Trade.)

Article 8 When a ship applies for export or sails to other ports of our country, the captain shall submit the following documents to the Customs:

(1) An export loading list;

(2) An outgoing passenger list (no submission is required if there are no outgoing passengers);

(3) A crew list (exempt from submission if there are no changes);

(4) A list of Renminbi balance after use (see Article 18 of these Procedures);

(5) Other documents and papers required by the Customs.

Article 9 When a ship calls at two or more ports of our country in succession on the same voyage, the captain shall be responsible for carrying the Customs envelope given to him by the first Customs house intact to the Customs house in the next port. A ship shall not be allowed to sail to any foreign country on its voyage between the ports of our country.

Article 10 The crew shall not be allowed to leave the ship without the permit of the Customs between its arrival in the port and the completion of the Customs' examination of the ship and the crew's luggage and articles.

When a seaman carries his personal articles, currencies, gold and silver aboard the ship or on shore, he shall declare them at the Customs house and the Customs shall examine and clear them.

Article 11 When the Customs examines a ship, the captain shall dispatch personnel to be present and open the rooms, cabins and storage places on board as required by the Customs. The captain shall act upon the request as soon as the Customs thinks it necessary to open up the parts of the ship, which may be used to conceal smuggled goods.

When the Customs examines the crew's luggage and articles, the seamen concerned shall be present at the time as required by the Customs and open the luggage, packages and storage places.

When the Customs finishes examining the ship, the captain shall sign on the examination record prepared by the Customs.

Article 12 With the exception of the personnel engaged in examination and piloting, others shall not be allowed to go on board ships without the permit of the Customs before the completion of the Customs' examination of arriving ships and after the completion of the Customs' examination of leaving ships.

Article 13 The port authorities shall only permit a leaving ship or go out of the port after it has been cleared by the Customs.

Chapter III The Supervision of Ship's Fuel, Materials, Currencies, Gold and Silver

Article 14 During a ship's stay in a port, the ship's materials and the currencies, gold and silver in the possession of the ship and its crew shall be sealed if the Customs thinks it necessary to do so; the captain shall be responsible for keeping the Customs sealing marks intact.

Article 15 If a ship is to replenish fuel or materials, the captain or his agent shall prepare and submit a list to the Customs (an oral declaration shall be made for the replenishment of catering materials) for the Customs' verification and clearance.

Article 16 If an application is made for the mutual allotment and transfer of ship's fuel or materials between foreign ships or between the international sailing ships of Chinese registry, the captains or their agents shall prepare a list, submit it to the Customs for approval and carry out the allotment and transfer under the supervision of the Customs.

(Note: This article has been amended in accordance with Notice No. GH-Lin-463(63) of the Ministry of Foreign Trade.)

Article 17 The captain or his agent shall submit a "list of borrowed Renminbi" to the Customs for any Renminbi borrowed by the ship when he carries the Renminbi aboard the ship.

If the ship or its crew exchange foreign currencies or gold or silver for Renminbi, a clear declaration shall be made at the Customs and the exchange memos from the bank shall be submitted for examination.

Article 18 Before a ship sails out of port or to another port of our country, the captain shall prepare a "list of the Renminbi balance after use" and submit it to the Customs for verification (exempt from submission if there is no Renminbi borrowed or exchanged for).

If the ship sails directly to a port of a foreign country, the surplus Renminbi shall be handed over by the ship to its agent under the supervision of the Customs and he is prohibited from taking it abroad; if the ship sails to another port of our country, the surplus Renminbi shall be kept in the custody of the captain himself or the seamen themselves.

Article 19 [*Omitted*]

If a ship replenishes fuel or materials in our country, the Customs house at the place of exit shall make an examination according to the ship's record if necessary.

If an outgoing ship has to carry Renminbi, and intends to use the same in the ports along the coasts of our country, it shall declare it at the Customs, while the Customs house shall seal the Renminbi and give it to the captain who shall be responsible for having the custody of the money. At the next time of import, the money shall be declared at the Customs house in the place of entry for verification.

The provisions in Articles 14, 15, 16, 17 and 18 of these Procedures shall not apply to the ships of Chinese registry.

Chapter IV The Customs Declaration, Examination and Clearance of Goods

Article 20 The owner of import goods or his agents shall submit the import licence together with the bill of lading and invoice(s) to the Customs when or before they arrive in the port.

The owner or agents of export goods shall submit the export licence together with the shipping order to the Customs before the exports are loaded on board a ship.

For the import or export goods to undergo commodity inspection as stipulated by the law, the papers shall be submitted for examination in accordance with the relevant provisions of the commodity inspection authorities.

If there is a discrepancy with respect to exports, the shipper or his agent shall make a report to the Customs within the time fixed by the Customs.

Article 21 Import and export goods shall be examined by the Customs. When the Customs examines the goods, their owner or his agent shall be present at the time fixed by the Customs and handle such jobs as moving, measuring, opening and repacking as required by the Customs.

Article 22 When a ship handles goods, each lot of them shall be clearly differentiated in accordance with the shipping order or the bill of lading and the number of packages shall be correctly counted.

The Customs shall be entitled to verify the tally records of the ship and the port authorities at any time. If confusion of goods is found or the number of goods is not correct, the ship and the port authorities shall promptly check and correct the records as required by the Customs.

Article 23 Upon completion of a ship's handling of goods, the port authorities shall submit to the Customs a copy of the goods hand-over and take-over certificate prepared by them and the ship; if there is surplus, shortage or damage of the goods, a copy of relevant record prepared shall be submitted to the Customs.

Article 24 The import or export goods under the supervision of the Customs shall be stored in the storage places agreed to by the Customs.

Article 25 The port authorities, goods owner (or his agent) and ship shall only deliver, take delivery of or ship the export or import goods after they are cleared by the Customs and a seal is impressed on the bill of lading or the shipping order.

Chapter V The Supervision of Ship's Padding and Ballast

Article 26 If a ship is to unload padding and ballast (excluding those included in the import loading list), the captain or his agent shall make a list and submit it to the Customs for approval. The padding and ballast declared to be re-exported later shall be transported abroad within six months of the date of unloading and the Customs shall check and clear them on the basis of the list declared at the time of import; with regard to the padding and ballast not to be re-exported, the consignee shall go through import formalities within two months of the date of unloading. Those which are not re-exported or which go through import formalities after the time limit is exceeded shall be sold by the Customs and all the proceeds shall be paid into the state treasury after the deduction of transport, custody and other expenses.

In respect of the padding, ballast and footing declared by the captain for disposal, the captain or his agent or the take-over unit shall make an oral declaration at the Customs and the take-over unit shall dispose of them with the consent of the Customs.

Article 27 If a ship is to replenish padding and ballast, the captain or his agent shall make a list and submit it to the Customs for approval. Another list shall be prepared for the padding and ballast required to be re-imported and returned by the Customs after signing and certification.

The above padding and ballast to be re-imported shall be re-transported in within one year of the date of the Customs' signing and certification and the Customs house in the place of entry shall examine and clear them on the basis of the list signed and certified by the Customs.

Chapter VI Supplementary Provisions

Article 28 If a ship fails to reach a port with a Customs house but has to berth at another place in distress or due to other cases of force majeure, it shall report to the local port authorities or people's committee so that they can supervise it on behalf of the Customs and notify the nearest Customs house. If necessary, the Customs house shall dispatch an officer to exercise supervision.

Article 29 The power-driven ships with the register tonnage more than 300 tons coming from or sailing to Hong Kong and Macao shall be handled in accordance with these Procedures.

Article 30 These Procedures shall be put into effect as of March 1, 1959.

PROCEDURES OF THE CUSTOMS SERVICE FOR THE SUPERVISION OF IMPORT EXHIBITS

Promulgated and put into effect by the Ministry of Foreign Trade (November 3, 1975)

I. General Provisions

Article 1 These Procedures are to ensure the effective implementation of state policies in the control of foreign trade and to facilitate foreign countries, exhibitions of China.

Article 2 The import exhibits referred to in these Procedures include those transported into our country by foreign countries for the purpose of holding economic, cultural, scientific, technical and other exhibitions in China as well as publicity materials, decoration materials, service materials, small articles for sale and all other articles relating to the exhibitions.

Article 3 The unit which accommodates a foreign country in its holding of an exhibition in China shall send a duplicate of the relevant instrument of approval in advance to the Customs house at the place of exhibition.

Article 4 Import exhibits shall be put under the supervision of the Customs Service and go through the Customs formalities as stipulated in these Procedures.

Article 5 When the Customs dispatches officers to the place of exhibition to carry out the supervision duties, the exhibition or host organization shall provide them with offices and necessary office equipment.

II. The Declaration and Examination of Exhibits

Article 6 Before the import of the exhibits, the exhibition organization or its agent shall translate the exhibit list in duplicate into Chinese which should include such contents as marks, numbers, number of packages, weight, names, specifications, quantities, prices, etc., and declare them at the Customs house.

Article 7 When the exhibits are imported, the exhibition organization or its agent shall submit a foreign goods transfer permit, a bill of lading (or a waybill) and a loading list for further conveyance to the Customs house at the place of entry and after they are examined by the Customs, transfer them to the place of exhibition as "the goods under the supervision of the Customs."

Approval from the Customs is needed when the exhibits are required for some reason to be moved out of the place of exhibition.

Article 8 The exhibition organization shall notify the Customs before opening the cases of the exhibits so that the Customs officers can be present for examination.

When the Customs officers examine the exhibits, the exhibition organization or its agent shall be present.

Article 9 The exhibition organization shall submit in advance to the Customs house at the place of exhibition for examination and approval the publicity materials and technical data for exhibition or use, including movies, slides, sound recording tapes, video recording tapes, discs, photos, maps, manuals, advertisements, etc. and only after approval shall they be allowed to be exhibited or used.

The publicity materials and technical data which degenerate the politics, economy, culture, morality, etc. of the People's Republic of China shall not be exhibited or used and shall be confiscated, returned abroad or the exhibition organization shall be ordered to amend them before use as the case may be.

Article 10 If there are some articles in the exhibits which shall be controlled as stipulated by other decrees of the People's Republic of China, the exhibition organization or its agent shall go through examination or approval formalities in accordance with the provisions of those decrees concerned.

III. The Use, Presentation, Sale and Disposal of Exhibits

Article 11 The cigarettes, wine and food transported in by the exhibition organization used for serving in the exhibition shall be used duty-free after verification and approval by the

Customs, but shall not be transferred, sold or used for other purposes.

Article 12 The odd souvenirs or demonstration articles presented by the exhibition organization to the spectators and working personnel shall be examined and approved by the Customs before presentation.

Article 13 If any exhibits are to be presented as gifts or samples, the exhibition organization shall report the objects of presentation to the Customs and go through exemption or taxation formalities in accordance with the Customs' provisions for the administration of import gifts. (Note: The provisions for the administration of imported gifts have become invalid .)

Article 14 For all small articles for sale in the exhibition, the exhibition organization shall submit the permit signed and issued by the administration authorities of foreign trade of the People's Republic of China to the Customs for examination and pay the Customs duties and industrial and commercial consolidated tax.

Article 15 The following principles shall be applied to the exhibits to be sold by the exhibition organization:

(1) If the exhibits are to be sold to foreign trade import and export corporations of our country, the corporations concerned shall conduct the import formalities at the Customs.

(2) If the exhibits are to be sold (or presented) to the embassy or consulate of other countries in China or their diplomats, the embassy or consulate or diplomats concerned shall conduct the import formalities at the Customs.

(3) If they are to be sold to other Chinese or foreign organizations or individuals, the exhibition organization shall apply to the administration authorities of foreign trade of the People's Republic of China for permits and they shall be examined, taxed and cleared by the Customs in accordance with the permits.

Article 16 For the exhibits to be waived, the exhibition organization shall report their categories, quantities and values to the Customs. If there is any take-over unit, the takeover unit shall go through Customs formalities; if there is no take-over unit, they shall be disposed of by the Customs according to directions.

Article 17 After the exhibition has closed, the exhibition organization shall submit a disposition list of exhibits in time to the Customs house at the place of exhibition, which should separately list the details of consumption, presentation, sale, disposal, re-export, etc.

IV. The Transfer and Re-export of Exhibits

Article 18 If the exhibition organization is to transfer the exhibits to another part of our country for another exhibition, it shall go through transfer formalities at the Customs as provided in Article 20 of these Procedures.

Article 19 The exhibits to be re-exported shall be completed within 3 months from the date of the closing of the exhibition. If the exhibition organisation fails to carry out the re-export as scheduled, it shall apply to the Customs for extension of time. Those exhibits which are not re-exported abroad within the said time limit shall be disposed of by the Customs in accordance with the regulations.

The exhibits re-exported as scheduled shall be exempted from Customs duties.

Article 20 When the exhibits are transferred or re-exported, the exhibition organization or its agent shall submit to the Customs a foreign goods transfer permit and a loading list in duplicate and go through transfer formalities as "the goods under the supervision of the Customs."

INTERIM CUSTOMS PROCEDURES FOR THE SUPERVISION OF IMPORT AND EXPORT CONTAINERS AND THE GOODS CONTAINED THEREIN

(August 1, 1981)

Article 1 These Procedures are formulated for the purpose of strengthening the supervision of containers and the goods contained therein (hereinafter simply referred to as "container goods") entering and leaving our country.

Article 2 The containers used to ship import and export goods shall be examined by the Customs and comply with the requirements of the Customs for their supervision.

Article 3 If an incoming or outgoing means of transport carries import or export container goods, the person in charge of the means of transport shall make a declaration to the Customs with an import or export waybill (a manifest) or a loading list, indicating such contents as the number of containers carried, container numbers, measurement(s), descriptions of the import or export goods, quantities (weight), shipper, consignee, number of the bill of lading or the shipping order, etc. and attach the loading list of each container to such a document in submission.

Article 4 Import or export container goods shall be stored in the bonded warehouses authorized by the Customs. The units assigned by the Customs for the custody of the containers shall be responsible for keeping the sealing marks on the container intact and shall not break the said sealing marks or load or unload the containers without authorization and consent of the Customs. When the Customs examines container goods and supervises the loading and unloading of goods, the owner of the goods, the manager of the containers or their agent (hereinafter simply referred to as shipment declarer) shall be present and handle them as required by the Customs. Import and export container goods shall be cleared by the Customs before delivery or shipment.

Article 5 With regard to the import or export container goods going through supervision and clearance formalities on the spot at the port of entry or exit, the shipment declarer shall go through declaration formalities at least 24 hours before opening import containers or loading export containers and submit an import or export goods declaration in duplicate and other related documents.

Article 6 With regard to the import container goods to be directly transported from the Customs house at the place of entry to an inland Customs house for supervision and clearance, or the export container goods to be supervised by an inland Customs house until their clearance by the Customs house at the port of the place of exit, these goods shall go through the formalities as "goods under the supervision of the Customs," the shipment declarer shall submit an import or export goods declaration in triplicate and other related documents and the carrier shall be responsible for carrying the customs envelope (which shall contain the declaration in duplicate) to the Customs house at the destination so as to have the goods examined and cleared according to the declaration.

Article 7 With regard to the import or export of container goods which required supervision and clearance beyond the areas under the control of the Customs (including the container goods transported door to door), the shipment declarer or the unit concerned shall make a prior written application to the Customs, in order that Customs officers may carry out the supervision after approval and collect fees. The applicant unit concerned shall supply the means of transport and bear the travelling expenses thereon.

Article 8 All the container goods under the supervision of the Customs shall have customs sealing marks affixed at the Customs house and the declarer or the tallying department shall affix commercial transport sealing marks at the same time.

Article 9 All purchased containers duly approved and imported shall proceed to the Customs house for declaration and customs duties formalities.

Article 10 All temporary imported containers shall be declared at the Customs by the container management unit by filing declaration forms and the said unit shall submit a written guarantee for their re-transport out of our country within 3 months. This time limit can be extended for a further 3 months with the prior approval of the Customs on grounds of special circumstances. If the containers cannot be re-transported abroad within the time limit, they shall make a fresh application for import duty formalities at the Customs.

Article 11 With regard to the non-commercial goods or articles shipped in containers, the declaring unit shall go through declaration formalities in accordance with these Procedures and other relevant provisions.

Article 12 The Customs shall establish its setups at or dispatch its officers to be stationed at special container wharves, warehouses, or designated places for loading and unloading containers as the case may be and the units concerned shall provide them with working facilities and supply necessary offices gratis.

Article 13 No one is allowed to use container cargo transportation for smuggling and other illegal activities.

Article 14 The violations against the provisions in these Procedures shall be dealt within accordance with the related clauses of the Interim Law of the People's Republic of China on Customs.

Article 15 These Procedures shall be promulgated and put into effect from August 1, 1981.

INTERIM CUSTOMS PROCEDURES FOR THE SUPERVISION OF IMPORT AND EXPORT GOODS AND OTHER MATERIALS NEEDED IN THE COOPERATIVE EXPLORATION AND EXPLOITATION OF SEA OIL AND ENGINEERS' AND TECHNICIANS' LUGGAGE AND ARTICLES

(October 1, 1981)

Article 1 These Procedures are formulated in accordance with the relevant provisions of the "Interim Law of the People's Republic of China on Customs" and according to the spirit of Document No. GF-211(1980) of the State Council in order to facilitate the import and export of goods and materials needed in the cooperative exploration and exploitation of the sea oil of our country.

Article 2 The Customs shall exercise supervision over all kinds of goods and materials imported and exported by oil companies for the purpose of exploring and exploiting the sea oil of our country in accordance with the documents and contracts (including subcontracts – the same hereinafter) approved by the State Council or the authorities authorized by the Council.

After the determination of a certain project, the oil company concerned shall submit a list of approved planned import goods, equipment and materials (including supplementary lists) to the Customs house at the location of the project as well as at the port of entry and exit for examination before import in addition to the submission of the aforesaid approved documents and contracts. The production goods and materials which are examined and proved to be within the range of the project shall be imported by means of the above approved list without another application for licence(s) (but prior applications shall be made to the correct examination and approval authorities for approval with regard to the machinery and equipment to be imported). The import licence signed and issued by the administration authorities of foreign trade shall be submitted for examination in respect of goods and materials beyond the range of the project, those incidentally imported by the oil company concerned and not for direct use in production, and those which shall require an application for the import licence.

Article 3 When goods and materials are imported or exported, the oil company or its agent shall file an import or export goods declaration in duplicate and go through import or export formalities by submitting it together with such relevant documents as invoice, packing list, etc.

If the goods and materials are imported and exported via different places, the shipment declarer shall file an import or export goods declaration in triplicate and go through the transfer formalities at the Customs house in the place of entry or, if they are exported at the Customs-house, in its location. The shipment declarer shall be responsible for asking the carrier to carry the Customs envelope with the goods to the Customs house at the destination or at the place of exit as the case may be, and the carrier shall ensure the Customs sealing marks are intact on the goods or on the means of transport.

Article 4 When the Customs examines import or export goods or materials, the owner or his agent shall be present and responsible for opening their packages. If examination is required in a place outside the areas under the supervision of the Customs, a prior application shall be made to the Customs for approval and fees shall be paid as stipulated by the Customs.

Article 5 To import (including the imports on lease) goods and materials within the duty-free range approved by the state, the Customs shall clear the articles duty-free; with regard to the goods and materials beyond the above duty-free range, the Customs shall clear them after collecting Customs duties and industrial and commercial (consolidated) taxes in accordance with the regulations.

For goods and materials temporarily imported, the oil company concerned shall go through declaration formalities at the Customs house in its location and guarantee to re-export them within six months; the articles shall be exempted from Customs duties, but a deposit equivalent to the payable duties shall be paid and a guarantee shall be given for the re-export of them within the fixed period. The deposit shall be refunded when the goods and materials are re-transported abroad. If the time limit for re-exporting the above goods and materials temporarily imported shall be extended due to particular reasons, an application shall be made to the Customs for approval for proper extension of the time limit. If they are not re-transported abroad within the said time, the import formalities shall be supplemented as stipulated by these Procedures and Customs duties and industrial and commercial (consolidated) taxes collected accordingly.

Article 6 Import goods and materials shall go through Customs formalities or be specially permitted by the Customs for clearance before delivery and forwarding; export goods and materials shall go through Customs formalities and be shipped abroad under the supervision of the Customs.

Article 7 The consignment warehouses established by foreign firms in oil bases shall be handled by the Customs in accordance with the "Interim Procedures for the Supervision of Bonded Goods and Bonded Warehouses." But if goods and materials consigned and maintenance parts and components are turned for import, the taxation or tax exemption shall be conducted as stipulated in Article 5 of these Interim Procedures.

Article 8 Import goods and materials shall be dealt with by the Customs as stipulated if they are not declared at the Customs or their taxes are not paid at the expiration of three months from the date of the declaration for import by the means of transport.

Article 9 With regard to the foreign engineers and technicians who come to China to carry out the exploration and exploitation duties, the authorities concerned shall supply the Customs a list in quadruplicate, sending the copies separately to the Customs houses at the place of entry, their location, Guangzhou Customs house and Jiulong Customs house. The Customs shall handle their luggage and articles on the basis of the list and in accordance with the provisions for the administration of the import and export of luggage and articles and the incoming and outgoing mailed articles of the foreign engineers and technicians who are invited to work in China.

The luggage and articles carried by the engineers and technicians of our country who cross the borders as required by their work shall be handled in accordance with the "Provisions on the Luggage and Articles of Our Exit Working Personnel Crossing the Borders" and the provisions in the document of Supplementary Notice No. MGH 517 (79) of the four Ministries of Foreign Trade, Foreign Affairs, Foreign Economic Relations and Finance.

Article 10 Any of the following shall be dealt with by the Customs according to different conditions in accordance with the relevant clauses of the "Interim Law of the People's Republic of China on Customs:"

(1) False declarations;

(2) The delivery or shipment of the import or export goods and materials which have not been cleared by the Customs by a unit concerned without authorization;

(3) Smuggling by making use of the import or export goods and materials;

(4) Selling the goods which are cleared duty-free by the Customs without authorization;

(5) The goods which are permitted by the Customs to import temporarily are not re-exported as scheduled and their Customs formalities are not supplemented as stipulated;

(6) Opening Customs envelopes and sealing marks without authorization or losing the Customs envelopes;

(7) Other violations against the provisions of the Customs.

Article 11 According to the requirements of the work, the Customs shall establish offices or station officers in the cooperative exploration and exploitation bases of sea oil. Oil companies and their branches shall supply free working rooms and living facilities.

Article 12 These Procedures shall be put into effect as of October 1, 1981.

15 ACCOUNTANCY

TRIAL REGULATIONS ON THE POWERS OF ACCOUNTING PERSONNEL

(Adopted by the 122nd Meeting of the Plenary Sessions of the State Council on November 24, 1962)

I General Rules

1 These Regulations are formulated for the purpose of explicitly stipulating the duties and powers of accounting personnel as so to enable accounting personnel to do their best at accounting work and take full cognizance of the positive role of accounting in the socialist construction.

2 All state enterprises, institutions, organizations, bodies, banks, troops and schools shall, as required by their work, be provided with financial accounting setups or full-time accounting personnel to carry out their accounting work.

Accounting personnel includes accountants, bookkeepers, cashiers, accounting clerks, auditors and the personnel in charge of accounting, who take charge of accounting, and those who receive and pay money.

3 The duties of accounting personnel are to implement accounting regulations strictly, ensure the truthfulness and reliability of figures, report the situation of economic activities accurately, strengthen economic accounting through this work, protect state property, abide rigorously by state plans, execute state regulations, maintain state financial and credit discipline and strike at all illegal and discipline-violating activities.

4 The state vests accounting personnel with necessary authority so as to facilitate them to do their duties. Anyone shall not in any way obstruct them in exercising their authority as stipulated by the state.

5 The leaders of each department or each unit shall strengthen their leadership over accounting so as to ensure that accounting personnel shall do their duties, accurately exercise the authority granted by the state and do their best at accounting work. Accounting personnel shall also report in time to the leaders on the situation of their work and regularly interpret to them the rules and regulations relating to accounting. Accounting personnel shall be responsible if they do not report to the leadership when any of the leaders violates the provisions of accounting regulations; however, the leader shall be responsible if he has not taken any measures to rectify the situation although an accounting clerk has reported to him the irregularity in time.

6 The financial accounting department at each level shall assume the responsibility to direct the accounting work in its subordinate units. The financial accounting department at each level shall regularly direct its subordinate units in their accounting affairs and help them to solve the problems in their work.

II Accounting Personnel's Duties

7 Accounting personnel shall practically do well the jobs such as bookkeeping, ledger balancing, accounts checking and reporting in accordance with the following provisions:

(1) To establish and perfect the systems of original records and original vouchers relating to accounting business so as to ensure the completeness, accuracy and reliability of accounting data.

(2) To conscientiously examine and verify all accounting vouchers to check whether their contents are both rational and legal and to prevent them from confusion or incompleteness.

(3) To provide for accounting ledgers and use unified account headings as prescribed by the state and not use documents or forms instead of ledgers.

(4) Keep accounts on the basis of accounting vouchers and balance daily accounts that very day so as to ensure the accounts tally with the vouchers and prevent the ledgers from errors or omissions.

(5) Clear accounts on schedule and accurately calculate revenues, expenditures, costs, expenses and financial results.

(6) Regularly check accounts and verify credits and debts so as to ensure the accounts tally with each other.

(7) Settle accounts by the month, by the quarter and by the year and prepare accounting report forms to ensure that the accounts tally with the report forms, the figures are true, the contents are complete and the report and submission of them are duly made.

8 Accounting personnel shall strictly carry out the plans and budgets approved by the state:

(1) All the revenues which shall be paid into Treasury shall be duly and fully paid in accordance with the regulations on payment as stipulated by the state, and shall not delay in paying it or pay less. They shall be strictly prohibited from keeping any sum back for expenditure or from diverting any sum to any other purpose. The funds which shall be allocated to lower units shall be duly examined, approved and allocated to the subordinate units and they shall not be detained or diverted to other purposes.

(2) Pay all funds and supervise the use of funds so as to minimize expenditure on the basis of approved plans and budgets and in accordance with the limits and standards of expenditures as stipulated.

(3) Abide by the percentage-deducting regulations for such special-purpose funds as overhaul funds, enterprise rewarding funds, supplementary wages, etc. They shall be prohibited from raising the percentages deducted without authorization; special-purpose funds shall be used for special purposes only.

9 Accounting personnel shall carry out various regulations on credit, account settlements, cash administration, etc., as stipulated by the state:

(1) Put bank loans to proper use in accordance with the provisions in bank credit regulations; they shall duly repay the loans which have become due and shall not let the loans be in arrears.

(2) Handle bank account settlements and cash receipts and payments in accordance with the provisions in bank account settlement regulations and cash administration regulations. The receipts and payments which shall be transferred through banks shall be settled through banks. The cash in hand which exceeds the limit shall be duly deposited in banks. They shall put bank checks under strict control and shall not sign or issue blank checks or dud checks.

(3) Strictly execute account settlement discipline and duly clear up credits and debts. Receivable sums shall be duly pressed for payment; payable sums shall be duly paid off. They shall supervise and urge the departments or personnel concerned to duly reimburse or clear up the provisionally received or paid sums. They shall duly claim money compensations which shall be made by other units.

10 Accounting personnel shall protect state property through accounting work:

(1) Supervise the personnel concerned in the proper execution of such work on all property and materials as measurement, examination, receipt, dispatch, obtaining, return, allocation, transfer and rejection so as to ensure protection of state property from losses.

(2) Participate in regular checks of property and materials and the regular verification of the stock so as to ensure the accounts tally with actual stock.

11 Accounting personnel shall duly examine and analyse the economic activities and revenue and expenditure of their own unit on the basis of the accounting records, accounting report forms and other relevant data and report the following situations and problems to the leaders of their own unit, the higher financial or acccounting department and the finance and bank department:

(1) The situations of the execution of plans, budgets and various quotas and the causes of fulfillment or the failure to fulfil them;

(2) The situations and causes of surplus or deficient stock, stock lying idle or overstocking, damage or loss and mildewing or rotting or deterioration of property, commodities and materials;

(3) Whether the use of funds is rational, whether there are phenomena of arbitrary deviations to other purposes or abuses and the situations and causes of the saving on and waste of funds;

(4) Whether the costs of production and circulation of commodities are economical, whether there is overspending and the situations and causes of savings or overspending;

(5) Whether the plans for profits have been fulfilled and the situations and causes of profits or losses;

(6) Whether the authorized size of the staff and the wage funds have exceeded the norms fixed by the state and the situations and causes of the excess or deficiency of the fixed norms;

(7) The specific cases in which the financial regulations and financial discipline are upheld or violated.

12 Accounting personnel shall be responsible for supplying various accounting data to the leaders of their own unit or the account-checking personnel dispatched by higher authorities or financial, bank, tax or other department, answer questions according to the facts, not refuse to answer lawful questions nor give any false information.

13 Accounting personnel shall, jointly with the department(s) concerned, organize mass economic accounting, establish and perfect the economic activity analytical system at each level and promote the measures to increase production and practise economy.

14 When an accountant is transferred to another post or leaves his or her office for a long time for some reason, he or she shall work out a detailed list for transfer and, on handing his job over, explain clearly to his or her successor the vouchers, accounts, sums, accounting files and unfinished affairs of which he or she has been in charge. He or she shall not leave the post before the settlement of the handing-over procedure. When an accountant leaves the post for a short time for some reason, he or she shall apply to the leaders of his or her own unit for the assignment of a person to act specially for him or her and explain his or her job clearly to the agent on handing it over.

In the case of a unit which is determined by the state to wind up or merge with other units, the pesonnel in charge of accounting and the accounting personnel concerned shall be responsible for handling accounting work during the clearing period. All property, materials, credits, debts and the matters to be turned over to the higher authorities or allocated to lower units shall be cleared and all accounts shall be clearly explained to the take-over unit on handing them over before the personnel in charge of accounting and the accounting personnel concerned leave.

III. Accounting Personnel's Authority

15 Accounting personnel shall be entitled to request the departments and personnel concerned of their own unit to correctly carry out the plans, budgets and various financial or accounting regulations approved by the state and act according to accounting formalities and the departments and personnel concerned shall not refuse their request without reasonable grounds.

16 The personnel in charge of accounting and the accounting personnel concerned shall be entitled to participate in the formulation of all relevant plans, budgets and quotas of their own unit. The accounting report forms to be forwarded to other departments by each unit shall not become effective until they are signed by the leader and the person in charge of accounting of the unit.

17 Accounting personnel shall be entitled to supervise the transfer and allocation of property and materials. Various property and materials shall not be transported out of the unit until the transport is signed and testified by the officer in charge of accounting or by the accounting clerk assigned by the officer in charge of accounting. When an officer in charge of property and materials is transferred to another post and the handing-over procedure is conducted, the officer in charge of accounting or the accounting clerk assigned by him or her shall participate in the supervision of the procedure.

18 Accounting personnel shall be entitled to require the departments or personnel concerned of their own unit to supply the following situations and data:

(1) The situations and data of the execution of various relevant plans, budgets and quotas;

(2) The situations and data of the changes of property and materials;

(3) The situations and data of the use of various funds;

(4) The situations and data of various costs and expenses;

(5) The situations and data of the execution of various economic contracts;

(6) Other data relating to finance or accounting.

19 The officer in charge of accounting or the accounting clerk assigned by him or her shall be entitled to check the vouchers and accounts of each department concerned of the unit and each department and the personnel concerned shall not without reasonable grounds refuse to supply the information. If any irregularity is found in checking, the accountant shall find out the cause and duly report it to the leadership of the unit or higher authorities to deal with it.

20 Accounting personnel shall be entitled to refuse to pay for or reimburse or to carry out the following matters:

(1) The purchase of commodities, materials or goods beyond the provisions of plans or budgets or those which are inconsistent in quality, category or specifications or which are insufficient in quantity;

(2) The illegal sale of commodities, materials or goods or the illegal sale of commodities on credit or the illegal barter or the sale of commodities by raising or lowering prices without authorization;

(3) The arbitrary lending, selling-off, rejection or disposal of property or materials beyond the provisions of the state or the arbitrary reimbursement for the damages or losses of property or materials without approval;

(4) The use of circulating funds for capital construction, "four kinds of expenses," welfare, or other violations against the principle of earmarking special funds for specified purposes only;

(5) The arbitrary squeezing of the costs of production or that of circulating expenses of commodities beyond the state provisions for the

limits of costs, expenditures and the division of expenses;

(6) The arbitrary prepayment, advancement or payment in expectation of being repaid of any sum of money in violation of regulations;

(7) To pay in excess of the wage fund plan or arbitrarily raise wage grades, wage standards or the standards of enterprise rewarding funds and supplementary wages;

(8) To proceed with any capital construction outside plan;

(9) Various expenditures or expenses in excess of plans or budgets or in excess of the prescribed standards;

(10) Extravagance and waste or entertainment and presentation;

(11) The absence of approval, incomplete formalities, untrue vouchers and other matters not in accordance with regulations.

21 An accountant shall duly report to the leaders of his or her own unit the matters which he or she refuses to pay, to reimburse or to execute. If the leaders are of different opinion, the accountant shall report them to higher authorities and financial departments while acting in accordance with the decision of the leaders of his or her own unit. Accounting personnel shall resolutely refuse to do any illegal or discipline-violating acts, frauds and trickery, graft, deceiving superiors, etc. and shall report them to higher authorities.

An accountant shall bear joint liability with the illegal personnel if he does not refuse to pay, to reimburse or to execute the matters in violation of the provisions in decrees and regulations nor report them to the leaders and higher authorities and financial departments.

22 Higher authorities and financial department shall conscientiously and duly investigate and handle the report made by the accountant in relation to the violations against state provisions or illegal and discipline-violating acts and notify the accountant and personnel concerned of the results of investigation. Anyone shall not make things difficult for, stand in the way of or retaliate upon the accounting personnel who report the situations to their superiors or departments concerned.

IV. The Appointment, Dismissal and Rewards or Punishments of Accounting Personnel

23 Accounting personnel shall stay in one position as far as possible and shall not be transferred at will. With regard to the appointment or dismissal of general accounting personnel, consent shall be obtained from higher authorities and financial or accounting departments. The person in charge of accounting in each unit shall be directly appointed or dismissed by higher authorities.

Technical titles and grades of accounting personnel shall be fixed according to their working ability. The technical titles and grades of accounting personnel shall be fixed accordingly.

24 Accounting personnel shall strengthen their political viewpoint, production viewpoint and mass viewpoint, make every effort to study state policies, decrees and regulations, endeavour to gain professional proficiency and constantly improve the levels of their political thought and professional skills.

25 Accounting personnel shall conscientiously abide by the state security regulations, take good care of accounting files and shall not lose or damage them.

26 Necessary systems of rewards and punishments shall be established for accounting personnel's jobs. Praise or rewards shall be granted to those who work hard and conscientiously abide by the law, practise strict economy, protect state property, report situations as things really are and make remarkable achievements in the fulfillment of tasks. Criticisms or punishments shall be imposed on those who are not conscientious at work, do not exert themselves to execute regulations, or those who abuse their authority which results in the loss of work. Administrative disciplinary punishments or punishments according to the law shall be imposed in the light of different conditions on the accounting personnel who withhold the truth, resort to deception make false reports of figures, falsify accounts, disperse funds, practise graft and embezzlement or engage in malpractice for personal gains. Those who cases are serious, resulting in the great loss of state property, shall be severely punished.

V Supplementary Provisions

27 Joint state-private enterprises, handicraft cooperatives and supply and marketing cooperatives shall also execute various provisions in these Regulations.

28 The financial personnel concerned shall also execute the duties and powers of accounting personnel as stipulated.

29 Each department under the State

Council, the people's committee of each province, autonomous region or municipality directly under the Central Government shall formulate detailed rules for the implementation of these Regulations and submit them to the Ministry of Finance for filing accordingly.

INTERIM PROVISIONS FOR TECHNICAL TITLES OF ACCOUNTING CADRES

Annotated and Passed On by the State Council
(March 2, 1981)

These Provisions are formulated for the purpose of the better training and rational employment of accounting cadres and of the accomplishment of their examination and promotion so as to bring their initiative into full play, encourage them to endeavour to obtain professional proficiency and improve the professional and scientific levels of accounting to serve the socialist construction better.

Article 1 The technical titles of accounting cadres shall be defined as: Senior Accountants, Accountants, Assistant Accountants and Accounting Clerks.

Article 2 An accounting cadre who is going to have or be promoted to a technical title shall support the leadership of the Communist Party of China, be devoted to the socialist motherland, make great efforts to study Marxism, Leninism and Mao Zedong Thought. He or she shall carry out the Party's lines, guiding principles and policies conscientiously, maintain the financial and economic discipline, endeavour to obtain professional proficiency and work hard to serve the socialist cause.

Article 3 The determination or promotion of the technical titles of accounting cadres shall mainly be based on the degrees of their learning, their professional ability and merits. Consideration shall also be given to their records of education and their qualifications at financial or accounting posts.

Article 4 A graduate from the financial and economic faculty of a polytechnic school, who has undergone one year's probation at a financial or accounting post, or a person who has the same educational level shall be defined as an accounting clerk if he or she has the following qualifications:

(1) That he or she shall have the basic knowledge of accounting and finance and have a good command of general calculating techniques;

(2) That he or she shall be familiar with relevant financial or accounting regulations and able to execute them accordingly;

(3) That he or she shall be able to hold a general financial or accounting post and accomplish his or her own job.

Article 5 A graduate from the financial and economic department of an institution of higher learning, who has undergone one year's probation, or a person who has the same educational level or an accounting clerk shall be defined as or promoted to an assistant accountant if he or she has the following qualifications:

(1) That he or she shall have the basic theory and professional knowledge of the financial and accounting profession;

(2) That he or she shall be familiar with related guiding principles, policies, decrees and financial and accounting regulations and able to execute them;

(3) That he or she shall be familiar with the relevant production management and administration, able to hold a major financial or accounting post and accomplish tasks better;

(4) That he or she shall have a basic command of a foreign language.

Article 6 An assistant accountant or a person who has the same vocational training shall be defined as or promoted to an accountant if he or she has the following qualifications:

(1) That he or she has a relatively systematic command of the basic theory and professional knowledge of the financial and accounting profession;

(2) That he or she shall have a certain understanding of policy and be able to carry out relevant guiding principles, policies, decrees and financial and accounting regulations properly;

(3) That he or she shall have relatively rich experience in financial and accounting jobs and knowledge of production management and administration, be able to independently organize and direct the financial and accounting work of a general enterprise or unit or the financial and accounting work of a department, be able to handle relatively complicated problems in the job properly and have certain achievements in the work;

(4) That he or she shall have a good command of a foreign language.

Article 7 An accountant or a person who has the same vocational training shall be defined as or promoted to a senior accountant if he or she has the following qualifications:

(1) That he or she shall have a systematic

command of the theoretical knowledge of economy, finance and accounting, have made a more profound study of, or have greater attainments or achievements in the financial and accounting profession of a certain field and have written research papers, academic writings or work reports on a higher level;

(2) That he or she shall have a higher understanding of policy, be able to make an overall analysis of the economic activities of his or her own department or unit and make valuable suggestions of improvement in policy;

(3) That he or she shall have rich experience in financial and accounting jobs, be able to organize and direct the economic accounting and financial accounting of a department or a large economic unit, be able to solve major issues relating to the profession and have made remarkable achievements in strengthening economic accounting, improving economic effects and fostering qualified personnel;

(4) That he or she shall have a very good command of a foreign language.

Article 8 The determination or promotion of the technical title of an accounting cadre shall be made through examinations. An examination shall be arranged every one to three years on the basis of the usual achievements. Examinations shall be arranged at any time for those who have made outstanding achievements in order to promote them ahead of them. Those of them who have the same educational levels shall be tested in the basic theory, professional knowledge and level of a foreign language required by the financial and accounting profession in addition to the appraisal of their vocational achievements.

Article 9 The determination or promotion of the technical title of an accounting cadre shall be evaluated by a corresponding appraising and examining organization in accordance with the limits of authority in the administration of cadres. The composition of an appraising and examining organization at each level shall be approved by the authorities at the same level.

Article 10 To be defined as or promoted to a technical title of an accounting cadre, the person concerned shall make an application or be recommended by the organization. He shall file a professional resume and submit work reports or research papers or academic writings and the technical title shall be conferred by the authorities after the appraisal of the correponding appraising and examining organization.

A senior accountant shall be conferred by each department of the State Council or the people's government of each province, autonomous region or municipality directly under the Central Government; an accountant shall be conferred by the authorities at the same level of an administrative office; an assistant accountant or an accounting clerk shall be conferred by the authorities at a county level. The cadres who are conferred the technical titles above accountants shall be granted certificates.

Article 11 The determination or promotion of the technical titles of accounting cadres shall be practical and realistic as well as serious and conscientious. Those who practice graft or suppress accounting cadres shall be dealt with severely according to the degrees of seriousness. Those who forge the records of education or qualifications, make false reports of achievements or get technical titles by fraud shall have their technical titles withdrawn and be severely dealt with according to the degrees of seriousness.

Article 12 The technical titles of accounting cadres conferred before the promulgation of these Provisions shall be reviewed in accordance with these Provisions.

Article 13 These Provisions are applicable to the full-time cadres who are now engaged in finance or accounting.

Article 14 Each department of the State Council or the people's government of each province, autonomous region or municipality directly under the Central Government shall prescribe the detailed rules for the implementation of these Provisions in light of the actual conditions.

Article 15 These Provisions shall be put into effect from the date of promulgation.

16

LAWYER AND LEGAL ARBITRATION

Arbitration/ Lawyer

PROVISIONAL RULES OF PROCEDURE OF THE FOREIGN TRADE ARBITRATION COMMISSION OF THE CHINA COUNCIL FOR THE PROMOTION OF INTERNATIONAL TRADE

(Adopted on March 31, 1956 at the 4th Committee Meeting of the China Council for the Promotion of International Trade)

Article 1 The present Rules are made in accordance with Article 12 of the decision of the Government Administration Council of the Central People's Government adopted at its 215th Session on May 6, 1954 concerning the establishment of a Foreign Trade Arbitration Commission within the China Council for the Promotion of International Trade.

Article 2 The Foreign Trade Arbitration Commission (hereinafter referred to as the Arbitration Commission) exercises jurisdiction for the arbitration of disputes arising from contracts and transactions in foreign trade, particularly disputes between foreign firms, companies or other economic organizations on the one hand and Chinese firms, companies or other economic organizations on the other. It may also exercise jurisdiction for the arbitration of similar cases arising between foreign firms, companies or economic organizations as well as between Chinese firms, companies or other economic organizations.

Such disputes include all disputes arising from contracts for purchase or sale of merchandise in foreign countries or contracts for commissioning an agency to purchase or sell merchandise in foreign countries, disputes arising from transportation, insurance, safe-keeping or delivery of the merchandise in question and disputes arising from other matters of business in foreign trade.*

Article 3 The Arbitration Commission exercises jurisdiction for the arbitration of a dispute referred to in the preceding article upon the written application of one of the disputing parties and in accordance with the written agreement between the parties which stipulates the submission of the dispute to the Arbitration Commission for settlement.

The agreement referred to above means the arbitration clause stipulated in the original trade contract or trade agreement, or any other form of agreement to submit to arbitration (such as special agreement, exchange of correspondence or any specific stipulation contained in other relevant documents).

Article 4 The following items must be specified in the application for arbitration:

a. The name and address of the applicant and those of the respondent;

b. The claim of the applicant and the facts and evidence upon which the claim is based;

c. The name of an arbitrator chosen by the applicant from among the members of the Arbitration Commission or a statement authorizing the chairman of the Arbitration Commission to appoint the arbitrator on behalf of the applicant.

Article 5 Original documents (contracts, arbitration agreements, correspondence between the parties, etc.) relevant to the application, or certified duplicates or copies thereof, must accompany the application for arbitration.

Article 6 When submitting an application for arbitration, the applicant shall pay a sum equivalent to 0.5% of the amount of the claim as a deposit for the fee required to cover the costs of arbitration.

Such deposits shall be paid to the Arbitration Commission.

Article 7 The application for arbitration and its appended documents submitted to the Arbitration Commission shall be accompanied by as many duplicates as the number of respondents.

Article 8 Upon receipt of the application, the Arbitration Commission shall notify the defendant to that effect without delay and forward to him a duplicate of the application and all the appended documents.

Article 9 Within fifteen days from the date of receipt of the notice the respondent shall either choose an arbitrator from among the members of the Arbitration Commission and notify the Arbitration Commission of his choice or authorize the chairman of the Arbitration Commission to appoint the arbitrator on his behalf.

In case a different period of time is agreed upon between the parties, such agreement shall prevail.

The Arbitration Commission may also, upon

the request of the respondent, alter the period of fifteen days.

Article 10 Should the respondent fail to choose an arbitrator within the time specified in the preceding article, the chairman of the Arbitration Commission shall, upon the request of the applicant, appoint the arbitrator for the respondent.

Article 11 The Arbitration Commission shall notify the arbitrators, whether chosen by the parties or appointed by the chairman, to select an umpire from among the members of the Arbitration Commission within fifteen days from the date of receipt of the notice.

In case no agreement is reached between the chosen or appointed arbitrators regarding the selection of the umpire within the time limit stated in the preceding paragraph, the chairman of the Arbitration Commission shall select the umpire on their behalf.

Article 12 The disputing parties may jointly choose or authorize the chairman of the Arbitration Commission to appoint for them a sole arbitrator from among the members of the Arbitration Commission to arbitrate the case singly.

In case the parties separately delegate the choice of arbitrators to the chairman of the Arbitration Commission, the chairman may, after obtaining the consent of the parties, appoint a sole arbitrator from among the members of the Arbitration Commission to arbitrate the case singly.

Article 13 If an arbitrator is unable to perform his duties, the Arbitration Commission shall notify the party concerned to that effect and request him to choose a new arbitrator from among the members of the Arbitration Commission within fifteen days from the date of receipt of the notice.

Should the said party fail to choose a new arbitrator within that time, the chairman of the Arbitration Commission shall then appoint a new arbitrator on his behalf.

Article 14 If an umpire is unable to perform his duties, the Arbitration Commission shall notify the arbitrators for the parties to that effect and request them to select a new umpire from among the members of the Arbitration Commission within fifteen days from the date of receipt of the notice.

Should the arbitrators fail to agree on the selection of the new umpire within that time, the Chairman of the Arbitration Commission shall then select a new umpire on their behalf.

Article 15 Upon the request of one of the parties, the chairman of the Arbitration Commission may, for the purpose of safeguarding the interests of the disputing parties, prescribe provisional measures concerning the materials, property rights and/or other matters appertaining to the parties.

Article 16 The date for the hearing of the case shall be set by the chairman of the Arbitration Commission in consultation with the umpire or the sole arbitrator as the case may be.

Article 17 The Arbitration Commission may require the parties to give their explanations in writing before the date of hearing.

Article 18 A disputing party may confer with the Arbitration Commission on matters relating to the proceedings either in person or by attorney.

Such attorneys may be citizens of the People's Republic of China or foreign citizens.

Article 19 Hearings shall be held at the seat of the Arbitration Commission. When necessary, hearings may, upon the approval of the chairman of the Arbitration Commission, be held at other places within the Chinese territory.

Article 20 Proceedings for the arbitration of a case are conducted by an Arbitration Tribunal formed by one umpire and two arbitrators.

A sole arbitrator forms a Tribunal by himself and conducts the proceedings singly.

Article 21 The Arbitration Tribunal shall hear cases in open sessions, but it may, upon the request of both or either of the parties, decide to hold the hearings in closed sessions.

Article 22 At every session of the Arbitration Tribunal, records shall be taken, and these records shall be signed by the umpire or the sole arbitrator as the case may be.

The Arbitrator Tribunal may require the parties or their attorneys, witnesses or other persons to sign their names on the records for purpose of evidence.

Article 23 The Arbitration Commission shall notify the parties of the date of hearing to be held by the Arbitration Tribunal.

Article 24 The defendant may file a counter-claim against a claim over which the Arbitration Commission has assumed jurisdiction.

The provisions in Articles 2-7 of the present Rules apply likewise to counter-claims.

Article 25 The parties shall produce evidence in support of the facts upon which their claims or pleadings are based.

Article 26 The examination and appraisal of evidence shall be performed by the Arbitration Tribunal at its discretion.

An Arbitration Tribunal may decide to entrust one of its members with the work of the examination of evidence.

Article 27 The Arbitration Tribunal may consult experts for the clarification of any questions concerning technical or special matters or business practices.

Such experts may be designated from among citizens of the People's Republic of China or foreign citizens.

Article 28 Should one of the disputing parties or his attorney fail to appear at the hearing held by the Arbitration Tribunal, the Tribunal may, upon the request of the party present, proceed with the hearing or render the award.

Article 29 The award of an Arbitration Tribunal is decided by majority vote and the minority opinion may be made in writing and docketed into the file.

Article 30 The principal part of the award shall be read to the parties at the closing session of the hearings.

The full award together with the reasons for the decision shall be made in writing within fifteen days from the date of the reading of the principal part. It shall be signed by the umpire and the arbitrators or by the sole arbitrator as the case may be.

Article 31 The award given by the Arbitration Commission is final and neither party shall request revision before a court of law or any other organization.

Article 32 The award of the Arbitration Commission shall be executed by the parties themselves within the time fixed by the award. In case an award is not executed after the expiration of the fixed time, one of the parties may request the People's Court of the People's Republic of China to enforce it in accordance with law.

Article 33 To compensate for the costs of arbitration, the Arbitration Commission may collect from the parties a fee, the amount of which shall be determined by the Arbitration Tribunal in the award but shall not in any case exceed 1% of the amount of the claim.

The Arbitration Tribunal may, having regard to the circumstances of the case, determine in the award whether such a fee should be borne entirely by the losing party or proportionally by both parties.

Article 34 The Arbitration Tribunal may determine in the award the amount to be paid by the losing party to the winning party in compensation for the costs incurred in the action, which amount shall not in any case exceed 5% of the sum awarded to the winning party.

Article 35 In the event that a case over which the Arbitration Tribunal has already assumed jurisdiction is settled by conciliation between the parties, it shall be dismissed without delay. Prior to the forming of the Arbitration Tribunal the decision for dismissal shall be made by the chairman of the Arbitration Commission and after the forming of the Arbitration Tribunal by the Arbitration Tribunal itself.

Article 36 The Chinese language is the official language of the Arbitration Commission.

If, at the hearing, any one of the parties, their attorneys or witnesses, or any other person is unfamiliar with the Chinese language, the Arbitration Tribunal may designate an interpreter for him or direct the party concerned to furnish one himself.

Article 37 All notices of the Arbitration Commission to the parties shall be delivered by special messengers, registered mail or telegraph.

Article 38 The present Rules shall come into force from the date of adoption by the China Council for the Promotion of International Trade.

---

*According to the decision of the State Council on February 26, 1980, the Foreign Trade Arbitration Commission was renamed Arbitration Commission for External Economics and Foreign Trade.

PROVISIONAL PROCEDURAL RULES OF THE MARITIME ARBITRATION COMMISSION OF THE CHINA COUNCIL FOR THE PROMOTION OF INTERNATIONAL TRADE

(Adopted on January 8, 1959, at the 7th Committee Meeting of the China Council for the Promotion of International Trade)

Article 1 The present Rules are made in accordance with Article 12 of the decision of the State Council of the People's Republic of China adopted on November 21, 1958, concerning the establishment of a Maritime Arbitration Commission within the China Council for the Promotion of International Trade.

Article 2 The Maritime Arbitration Commission takes cognizance of:

a. Disputes regarding remuneration for salvage services rendered by sea-going vessels to each other or by a sea-going vessel to a river craft and vice versa;

b. Disputes arising from collisions between sea-going vessels or between sea-going vessels and river craft or from damages caused by sea-going vessels to harbour structures or installations;

c. Disputes arising from chartering sea-going vessels, agency services rendered to sea-going vessels, carriage by sea in virtue of contracts of affreightment, bills of lading or other shipping documents, as well as disputes arising from marine insurance.

Article 3 The Maritime Arbitration Commission takes cognizance of a dispute referred to in the preceding Article upon the written application of one of the disputing parties and in accordance with such written agreement as concluded between the parties either prior or subsequent to the arising of the dispute, which stipulates for the submission of the dispute to the Maritime Arbitration Commission for settlement.

The agreement referred to in the preceding paragraph means the arbitration clause stipulated in the original contract from which the dispute has arisen, or any other form of agreement in respect of submission to arbitration (such as special agreement, correspondence exchanged or any specific stipulation contained in other relevant documents).

Article 4 The following items must be specified in the application for arbitration:

a. The name and address of the applicant and those of the respondent,

b. The claim of the applicant and the facts and evidence upon which the claim is based;

c. The name of an arbitrator chosen by the applicant from among the members of the Maritime Arbitration Commission or a statement authorizing the chairman of the Maritime Arbitration Commission to appoint the arbitrator for the applicant.

Article 5 Original relevant documents (contracts, arbitration agreements, correspondence between the parties, etc.), or certified duplicates or copies thereof, must accompany the application for arbitration.

Article 6 When submitting an application for arbitration, the plaintiff shall pay a sum equivalent to 1% of the amount of the claim as a deposit for the arbitration fee.

Article 7 The application for arbitration and its appended documents shall be accompanied by as many duplicates as the number of respondents, all to be submitted to the Maritime Arbitration Commission.

Article 8 Upon receipt of the application, the Maritime Arbitration Commission shall notify the respondent to that effect without delay and forward to him a duplicate of the application and of all the appended documents.

Article 9 Within fifteen days from the date of receipt of the notice the respondent shall either choose an arbitrator from among the members of the Maritime Arbitration Commission and notify the Maritime Arbitration Commission of his choice or authorize the chairman of the Maritime Arbitration Commission to appoint the arbitrator for him.

In case a different period of time is agreed upon between the parties, such period of time shall prevail.

The Maritime Arbitration Commission may also, upon the request of the respondent, alter the period of fifteen days.

Article 10 Should the respondent fail to choose an arbitrator within the time specified in the preceding Article, the chairman of the Maritime Arbitration Commission shall, upon the request of the applicant, appoint the arbitrator for the respondent.

Article 11 The Maritime Arbitration Commission shall notify the arbitrators, whether chosen by the parties or appointed by the chairman, to select an umpire from among the members of the Maritime Arbitration Commission within fifteen days from the date of receipt of the notice.

In case no agreement is reached between the chosen or appointed arbitrators regarding the selection of the umpire within the time limit stated in the preceding paragraph the chairman of the Maritime Arbitration Commission shall then select an umpire for them.

Article 12 The disputing parties may either jointly choose or authorize the chairman of the Maritime Arbitration Commission to appoint for them a sole arbitrator from among the members of the Maritime Arbitration Commission.

In case the parties separately delegate the choice of arbitrators to the chairman of the Commission, the chairman may, after obtaining the consent of the parties, appoint a sole arbitrator from among the members of the Maritime Arbitration Commission.

Article 13 If an arbitrator is unable to perform his duties, the Maritime Arbitration Commission shall notify the party concerned to that effect without delay and request him to choose a new arbitrator from among the members of the Maritime Arbitration Commission within fifteen days from the date of receipt of the notice.

Should the said party fail to choose a new arbitrator within that time, the chairman of the Maritime Arbitration Commission shall then appoint a new arbitrator for him.

Article 14 If an umpire is unable to perform his duties, the Maritime Arbitration Commission shall notify the arbitrators for the parties to that effect without delay and request them to select a new umpire from among the members of the Maritime Arbitration Commission within fifteen days from the date of receipt of the notice.

Should the arbitrators fail to agree on the selection of the new umpire within that time, the chairman of the Maritime Arbitration Commission shall then select a new umpire for them.

Article 15 In cases within the cognizance of the Maritime Arbitration Commission, the chairman of the Maritime Arbitration Commission may, upon the request of one of the parties, make decisions in respect of measures of security and determine the amount and form of the security for the claim. If the amount and form of the required security have already been agreed upon between the parties, such amount and form shall prevail.

Article 16 Upon the request of one of the parties, the people's courts of the People's Republic of China shall enforce the decision of the chairman of the Maritime Arbitration Commission in respect to measures of security in accordance with law.

Article 17 The date for the hearing of the case shall be set by the chairman of the Maritime Arbitration Commission in consultation with the umpire or the sole arbitrator as the case may be.

Article 18 The Maritime Arbitration Commission may require the parties to give their explanations in writing before the date of hearing.

Article 19 The Maritime Arbitration Commission may endeavour to settle by conciliation any dispute of which it has taken cognizance.

Article 20 The disputing parties may appoint attorneys to protect their interests and to confer with the Maritime Arbitration Commission on matters relating to the proceedings of arbitration.

Such attorneys may be citizens of the People's Republic of China or foreign citizens.

Article 21 Hearings shall be held at the seat of the Maritime Arbitration Commission. When necessary, hearings may, upon the approval of the chairman of the Maritime Arbitration Commission, be held at other places within the Chinese territory.

Article 22 Proceedings for the arbitration of a case are conducted by an Arbitration Tribunal formed by one umpire and two arbitrators.

A sole arbitrator forms a Tribunal by himself and conducts the proceedings singly.

Article 23 The Maritime Arbitration Commission shall hear cases in open sessions, but it may, upon the request of both or either of the parties, hold the hearings in closed sessions.

Article 24 At every session of the Arbitration Tribunal, records shall be taken, and these records shall be signed by the umpire or the sole arbitrator as the case may be.

The Arbitration Tribunal may require the parties or their attorneys, witnesses or other persons to sign the records.

Article 25 The Maritime Arbitration Commission shall notify the parties in advance of the date of hearing to be held by the Arbitration Tribunal.

Article 26 The respondent may file a counterclaim against the applicant in cases of which the Maritime Arbitration Commission has taken cognizance.

The provisions in Article 2-7 of the present Rules apply likewise to counter-claims.

Article 27 The disputing parties shall produce evidence in support of the facts upon which their claims or pleadings are based. When necessary, the Arbitration Tribunal itself may make investigations or collect evidence.

Article 28 The examination and appraisal of evidence shall be performed by the Arbitration Tribunal at its discretion.

An Arbitration Tribunal may entrust one of its members with the work of the examination of evidence.

Article 29 The Arbitration Tribunal may consult experts for the clarification of any questions concerning technical or special matters or business practices.

Such experts may be designated from among citizens of the People's Republic of China or foreign citizens.

Article 30 Should one of the disputing parties or his attorney fail to appear at the hearing held by the Arbitration Tribunal, the Tribunal may, upon the request of the party present, proceed with the hearing or give summary verdict.

Article 31 The award of an Arbitration Tribunal is decided by majority vote and the minority opinion may be recorded in the file.

Article 32 The conclusion of the award shall be read to the parties at the end of the hearings.

The award shall be made in writing within fifteen days from the date of the reading of the conclusion. It shall include the reasons for the decision and shall be signed by the umpire and the arbitrators or by the sole arbitrator as the case may be.

Article 33 The award given by the Maritime Arbitration Commission is final and neither party shall request revision before a court of law or any other organization.

Article 34 The award of the Maritime Arbitration Commission shall be executed by the parties themselves automatically within the time fixed by the award. In case an award is not executed after the expiration of the fixed time, one of the parties may present petition to the People's Court of the People's Republic of China to enforce it in accordance with law.

Article 35 The Maritime Arbitration Commission may collect an arbitration fee the amount of which shall be determined by the Arbitration Tribunal in the award but shall in no case exceed 2% of the amount of the claim.

The Arbitration Tribunal may, with regard to the circumstances of the case, determine whether such a fee should be borne entirely by the unsuccessful party or proportionally by both parties.

For cases having been dismissed in accordance with Article 37, the Maritime Arbitration Commission may also collect a fee at its discretion.

Article 36 The Arbitration Tribunal may determine in the award the amount to be paid by the unsuccessful party to the successful party in compensation for the cost incurred in the action which amount shall in no case exceed 5% of the sum awarded to the successful party.

Article 37 If a case already taken cognizance of by the Maritime Arbitration Commission is settled by conciliation between the parties, it shall be dismissed without delay. Prior to the forming of the Arbitration Tribunal the decision for dismissal shall be made by the chairman of the Maritime Arbitration Commission and after the forming of the Arbitration Tribunal by the Arbitration Tribunal itself.

Article 38 The Chinese language is the official language of the Maritime Arbitration Commission.

If, at the hearing, any one of the parties, their attorneys or witnesses, or any other person is unfamiliar with the Chinese language, the Arbitration Tribunal may designate an interpreter for him or direct the party concerned to furnish one himself.

Article 39 All notices of the Maritime Arbitration Commission to the parties shall be delivered by special messengers, registered mail or telegraph.

Article 40 The present Rules shall come into force from the date of its adoption by the China Council for the Promotion of International Trade.

PROVISIONAL RULES FOR GENERAL AVERAGE ADJUSTMENT OF THE CHINA COUNCIL FOR THE PROMOTION OF INTERNATIONAL TRADE

(In short, "Beijing Adjustment Rules")

(January 1, 1975)

With a view to dealing properly with general average adjustment on the basis of equality and mutual benefit so as to enhance friendly relations among peoples of different countries and promote the development of international trade and marine transport, the China Council for the Promotion of International Trade has adopted the present Provisional Rules and set up the Department for Average Adjustment.

Article 1 Scope of general average

The following extraordinary loss or damage and reasonable extra expenses arising from measures properly taken for relieving a ship, cargo, etc. from common danger caused by natural calamities, accidents and/or other extraordinary circumstances in marine transport shall fall within the scope of general average:

a. Loss or damage reasonably caused to the ship, cargo, etc. for rescuing the same from danger;

b. Extra expenses incurred by the ship for entering a port of refuge, port charges incurred during the extra period of the ship's staying in a port of refuge and extra expenses for the ship's leaving the port of refuge subsequently with her original cargo or a part thereof;

c. Crew's wages and maintenance incurred as well as fuel and stores consumed during the prolongation of the voyage occasioned by the ship proceeding to a port of refuge and during the extra period of the ship's stay in a port of refuge;

d. Salvage expenses, expenses for forced discharge and reloading of the cargo, etc. and other extra expenses.

Where the ship needs repairs for the safe completion of the voyage in consequence of damage caused by an accident during the voyage, the port charges, crew's wages and maintenance and fuel and stores necessarily incurred or consumed during the reasonable period of detention of the ship in the port of repair, as well as the expenses and loss or damage arising from such discharging, reloading and handling on board of the cargo, etc. as are required for the repairs, may under the present circumstances be admitted as general average.

Where any expense is incurred to save another expense which would have been admissible in general average, such expense may be allowed in general average as a substituted expense. Unless otherwise agreed upon by and between the ship and cargo interests, the amount so allowable shall not exceed the amount of the expense saved.

With the exception of loss or damage and expenses referred to in the above three paragraphs, any other indirect loss, including loss or damage and expenses through delay, shall not fall within the scope of general average.

Article 2 Principle of adjusting general average

The principle of general average adjustment is the ascertainment of liability on the basis of investigation and study and dealing with the compensation for and contribution to various losses and expenses fairly, reasonably and in a truth-seeking way.

The onus of proof shall be upon the party applying for general average adjustment as well as other parties concerned to show that their respective loss or damage and expenses claimed for are allowable as general average according to the provisions of the Rules.

If the event giving rise to a claim submitted for adjustment as general average is due to a fault of one of the parties to the contract of affreightment, for which he is not entitled to exemption from liability, no general average adjustment shall be proceeded with, but the case may be otherwise appropriately dealt with through consultation according to the circumstances involved.

Article 3 Computation of amount of general average loss or damage

The amount to be admitted as general average for loss or damage to the ship, cargo and freight shall be computed on the following basis:

a. The amount allowable for loss or damage to the ship shall be computed in accordance with the actual reasonable cost of repairing such damage, including cost of temporary repairs and of replacements subject to reasonable deductions in respect of "wear and tear". Where no repairs have been effected, computation shall be made in accordance with the reasonably estimated cost of necessary repairs. The amount allowable for loss of or damage to fuel and stores, etc. shall be computed on the basis of their actual values.

b. The amount allowable for loss or damage to the cargo shall be computed on the basis of the CIF value, less the freight which would have been incurred but for such loss or damage. Where the cargo so damaged is sold and it is impossible to ascertain the extent of the damage, the amount shall be computed on the basis of the difference between the CIF value and the net proceeds of sale.

c. The amount allowable for loss of freight shall be computed on the basis of the freight lost owing to the loss of or damage to the cargo, less the operating costs of the ship, which would have been incurred but for such loss or damage.

Article 4 Contribution to general average

General average loss or damage and expenses shall be contributed to by the benefited interests in proportion to their respective contributory values.

The contributory value shall be computed on the following basis:

a. The contributory value of the ship shall be computed either in accordance with the value of the ship in sound condition at the time and place of the termination of the voyage, less the amount of loss or damage not allowable in general average, or in accordance with the actual net value of the ship at the time and place of the termination of the voyage, plus the amount allowable in general average.

b. The contributory value of the cargo shall be computed on the basis of the CIF value, less the amount of loss or damage not allowable in general average and the freight at the risk of the carrier. Undeclared or falsely declared cargo shall contribute on the actual value, but loss of or damage to such cargo, if any, shall not be admitted as general average.

Passengers' luggage and personal effects shall not contribute to general average except under extraordinary circumstances.

c. The contributory value of the freight shall be computed on the basis of the freight at the risk of the carrier and subsequently earned, subject to a deduction corresponding to the extent of the voyage still uncompleted at the time of the event giving rise to general average, plus the amount of loss of freight allowable in general average.

Article 5 Interest and commission

Interest shall be allowed on general average loss or damage and expenses at the rate of 7% per annum until the date of the completion of the general average adjustment.

A commission of 2% shall be allowed on general average expenses other than crew's wages and maintenance and fuel and stores.

Article 6 General average security

The contributing parties shall, at the request of the parties concerned, provide a security to ensure the contribution to general average. Such security may be in the form of a reliable letter of guarantee or a cash deposit. Where a cash deposit is provided, same shall be paid into an account in a bank in the name of the Department for Average Adjustment unless otherwise agreed upon by and between the parties concerned. Any use of the cash deposit shall be decided by the Department for Average Adjustment. The provision, use and refund of the cash deposit shall be without prejudice to the ultimate liability of the contributing parties.

Article 7 Time limit of general average

For the purpose of safeguarding the interests of all parties concerned and completing the adjustment of general average as promptly as possible, all parties shall, upon the occurrence of the event giving rise to general average, do everything necessary in time and declare general average and provide the Department for Average Adjustment with relevant materials within the following time limits:

a. *Declaration of General Average*

Within forty-eight hours upon the ship's arrival in the first port after the event, if it has occurred at sea, or within forty-eight hours after the event, if it has occured in a port;

b. *Provision of relevant materials*

For documentary evidence pertaining to the occurrence of general average and general average loss or damage, within one month after receipt thereof by the claiming party, but all materials shall in any case be provided within one year of the completion of the voyage.

In case of extraordinary circumstances the above time limits may be appropriately extended, provided reason for extension has been given within the respective time limits to the Department for Average Adjustment and its approval obtained.

In case of failure to observe the above stipulations on the part of any of the parties concerned, the Department for Average Adjustment may either decline to proceed with adjustment or adjust the case on the basis of the materials in its possession.

Article 8 Simplification of adjustment of general average

With a view to lightening the burden of all parties concerned and improving working efficiency, the adjustment of general average shall be made as simple as possible; unduly complicated procedures and calculations shall be avoided; adjustment shall be made as clear and concise as possible and easy to execute.

Summary adjustment may be applied in simple cases.

For cases in which the amount involved is small, adjustment may be dispensed with if consent has been obtained from the principal parties concerned.

PROVISIONAL REGULATIONS ON LAWYERS OF THE PEOPLE'S REPUBLIC OF CHINA

(Adopted by the 15th Session of the Standing Committee of the 5th National People's Congress on August 26, 1980)

I. The Functions and Rights of Lawyers

Article 1 Lawyers are the state's legal workers and function to give legal assistance to the state organs, enterprises, establishments, mass organizations, the people's communes and the citizens in order to ensure the correct implementation of law and protect the interests of the state and the collectives as well as the legitimate rights and interests of the citizens.

Article 2 The major services of the lawyers are:

a. To accept the instructions of the state organs, enterprises, establishments, mass organizations and the people's communes to act as their legal advisers;

b. To accept a litigant's instructions to act as a representative in a civil case;

c. To accept a defendant's instructions or the assignment of a people's court to act as an advocate in a criminal case; accept the instructions of a party who initiates a private prosecution and the instructions of a victim of a public prosecution or their close relatives to act as a representative in a lawsuit;

d. To accept instructions to act in noncontentious matters and to render legal assistance or to act as a representative in mediation and arbitration;

e. Explain questions on law and draft documents in a lawsuit and other related legal matters.

Lawyers must propagate the socialist legal system in all their work.

Article 3 In performing their services, lawyers must serve the cause of socialism and the interests of the people, act on the basis of facts and take the law as their criterion.

Lawyers must carry out their work according to the law and are protected by the law. No organization or person is permitted to interfere with lawyers' work.

Article 4 When acting as legal advisers, lawyers are responsible for giving advice, drafting and examining legal documents on legal questions that occur in the course of business of an organization that instructed them and act as representatives in law suits, mediation and arbitration in order to safeguard the legitimate rights and interests of the organization.

Article 5 Acting as representatives in litigation and nonlitigation matters, lawyers are responsible for safeguarding the legitimate rights and interests of the client within the authority of the entrustment.

The litigant acts and legal acts of the lawyer have the same legal effect as that of the client within his authority as a representative.

Article 6 Acting as advocates in a criminal case, lawyers are responsible for safeguarding the legitimate rights and interests of the accused on the basis of facts and the law.

In case of untruthful representation by the accused in a case, a lawyer can refuse to act as his advocate.

Article 7 In performing their work in lawsuits, lawyers are entitled to obtain research materials relevant to the case according to regulations and to make inquiries about related organizations and persons. In acting as advocates in criminal cases, lawyers have the right to meet and correspond with the accused in custody.

Organizations and persons concerned must assist lawyers on the above.

Lawyers have the responsibility to maintain secrecy when they come into contact with state secrets and personal secrets in their work.

II. The Qualifications of Lawyers

Article 8 Those citizens who cherish the PRC, support the socialist system and have the right to vote and stand for election are eligible to be lawyers after an examination and if they have the following qualifications:

a. Those who graduated from university or college law departments and have engaged for 2 or more years in judicial work, teaching or research or law;

b. Those who have professional legal training or worked as judges or procurators in the people's courts and the people's procuratorates;

c. Those who have received higher education, have done 3 or more years of economic, scientific and technological work, are well versed in their profession and in relevant laws and decrees related to the profession, have gone through professional legal training and are suitable for the position of a lawyers;

d. Those who have attained the same law level as listed in a and b possess the cultural level of higher schools and can perform the functions of a lawyer.

Article 9 After obtaining the necessary qualifications for lawyers, approval and a certificate must be obtained from the judicial departments (bureaus) of provinces, autonomous regions or municipalities directly under the central government; such certification must also be entered in the record of the PRC Ministry of Justice. Upon discovery of improper examination or approval, the ministry of Justice must instruct the judicial departments (bureau) to conduct an inquiry into the matter therewith.

Article 10 Those who have acquired the qualifications of a lawyer but are unable to leave their job can act as part-time lawyers. Organizations concerned must support such part-time lawyers.

Personnel who are in active service in the people's courts, the people's procuratorates and the people's public security organs cannot be part-time lawyers.

Article 11 Those who have graduated from university or college law departments or have gone through professional legal training can act as trainee-lawyers after obtaining approval from the judicial departments (bureaus) of provinces, autonomous regions or municipalities directly under the central government by passing an examination.

The training period for trainee-lawyers is 2 years. Upon completion of the training period, trainee-lawyers are qualified as lawyers in accordance with the procedure stipulated in Article 9 of the provisional regulations; the training period can be extended if the trainee-lawyers fail to pass the examination.

Article 12 Lawyers who are highly incompetent may be deprived of their qualifications by decision of the judicial departments (bureaus) of provinces, autonomous regions and municipalities directly under the central government and with the approval of the Ministry of Justice.

III Work Organs for Lawyers

Article 13 Legal advisory offices are work organs for lawyers to perform their duties.

Legal advisory offices are public institutions under the organizational leadership and professional supervision of state judicial administrative organs.

Article 14 Legal advisory offices are established at the country, city and municipal district levels. When necessary, specialized legal advisory offices can be established with the approval of the Ministry of Justice.

Legal advisory offices are not subordinate to each other.

Article 15 The principal functions of a legal advisory office are to help lawyers to carry out their professional work and to organize lawyers to study politics and acquire professional knowledge in fields of law as well as to sum up and exchange work experience.

Article 16 A legal advisory office shall have one director and may have deputy directors if necessary. The director and deputy directors are to be elected by the lawyers in that office and approved by the judicial departments (bureaus) of provinces, autonomous regions and municipalities directly under the central government. They are elected for a term of 3 years and are eligible for re-election.

The director and deputy directors of a legal advisory office shall lead the work of the legal advisory office and they must also perform legal work.

Article 17 When lawyers are requested to handle cases, instructions shall be accepted and service fees shall be collected by the legal advisory office on a unified basis.

In assigning cases to lawyers, the legal advisory office shall assign lawyers named by clients as far as possible to meet their requests and according to actual conditions.

Article 18 A legal advisory office may appoint lawyers to carry out professional activities in other localities and the local legal advisory office shall provide them with assistance.

Article 19 A lawyers' association shall be established to protect the legitimate rights and interests of lawyers, to exchange work experience, to promote lawyers' work and to promote contacts between legal workers both at home and abroad.

The lawyers' association is a social organization and its organizational statute shall be worked out by the lawyers association.

IV Supplementary Articles

Article 20 The standards for the title of a lawyer, the regulations on rewards and penalties for lawyers and the measures on their service fees will be separately worked out by the Ministry of Justice.

Article 21 These regulations shall go into force on January 1, 1982.

INTERIM REGULATIONS OF THE PEOPLE'S REPUBLIC OF CHINA ON NOTARIZATION

Promulgated by the State Council
(April 13, 1982)

I General Rules

Article 1 These Regulations are formulated in order to perfect our state notarization system, protect the socialist legal system, prevent disputes and reduce lawsuits.

Article 2 Notarization means that the state notarial organization, upon the application of a party concerned, certifies according to law the authenticity and legality of a legal act, a document or a fact of legal significance so as to protect public property and a citizen's rights and legitimate interests in status and property.

Article 3 A notary's office is a state notarial organization. A notary's office shall teach citizens to abide by the law and protect the socialist legal system through the notarization activities.

II The Business of a Notary's Office

Article 4 The business of a notary's office is as follows:

(1) To certify contracts (or agreements), commissions and testaments;

(2) To certify rights of inheritance;

(3) To certify the presentation or separation of property;

(4) To certify adoptive relations;

(5) To certify family relations;

(6) To certify status, record of formal learning or career;

(7) To certify birth, marriage, existence or death;

(8) To prove the signatures and/or seals on documents to be true;

(9) To prove the copies, abbreviated versions, translations or photostat copies of documents to tally with the originals;

(10) To certify the effect of enforcement on the documents used for demanding payment of debts or for claiming compensations if they are considered to be beyond doubt;

(11) To preserve evidence;

(12) To take custody of testaments or other documents;

(13) To draw up the applications for notarization for the parties concerned;

(14) To handle other notarial affairs upon the applications of the parties concerned in accordance with international practice.

III The Organization and Leadership of a Notary's Office

Article 5 A notary's office shall be set up in a municipality directly under the Central Government, a county (or an autonomous county, the same hereinafter) or a city. A notary's office shall also be set up in a district under the jurisdiction of a city with the approval of the judicial administration authorities of the province, autonomous region or municipality directly under the Central Government.

Article 6 A notary's office shall be under the control of the judicial administration authorities.

There are no subordinate relations between notaries' offices.

Article 7 A notary's office shall be provided with notaries and assistant notaries. It shall be provided with a director or vice-director(s) as required.

The posts of the director or vice-director(s) shall be held by notaries. The director and/or vice-director(s) shall exercise control over the business of a notary's office and carry out the duties of notaries.

The director, vice-director(s), notaries and assistant notaries shall be appointed or dismissed respectively in accordance with the provisions for the administration of cadres by the people's government of a municipality directly under the Central Government, a county or a city.

Article 8 A citizen who has the right to vote and to stand for election shall be appointed notary if he or she possesses any of the following qualifications:

(1) Graduation from the law speciality of an institution of higher learning, having passed probation and been engaged in a judicial job or in law teaching or law studies for more than one year;

(2) Service as a judge or a procurator in a people's court or in a people's procuratorate;

(3) Judicial vocational work in judicial administration authorities for more than two years, or work in another state organization, body, enterprise or institution for more than five years, and a knowledge of law equal to that of a graduate from a secondary law school;

(4) The title of assistant notary for more than two years.

Article 9 A graduate from a higher law instiution or a secondary law school who has passed probation, or a state worker who has the same educational qualification shall be appointed assistant notary.

IV. Jurisdiction

Article 10 Notarial affairs shall be under the jurisdiction of the notary's office at the location of the applicant's household register or at the place of occurrence of the legal act or fact.

Article 11 The notarial affairs relating to the transfer of property shall be under the jurisdiction of the notary's office at the location of the applicant's household register or at the location of the principal property.

Article 12 If the household registers of a number of applicants for the handling of the same notarial affair are not located within the area under the jurisdiction of a notary's office, or if the property is scattered in a number of areas under the jurisdiction of several notaries' offices, the parties concerned shall consult with each other and make the application to any of the notaries' offices. If the parties concerned fail to reach any agreement, the case shall be put under the jurisdiction of the notaries' offices concerned by means of consultation for the convenience of the people.

Article 13 If jurisdiction disputes occur between the notaries'offices, their common higher judicial administration authorities shall specify the jurisdiction.

Article 14 The Ministry of Justice and the judicial administration authorities of each province, autonomous region and municipality directly under the Central Government shall be entitled to assign a certain notarial affair to a certain notary's office.

Article 15 Our embassies and consulates accredited abroad shall handle notarial affairs at the request of our citizens in the countries where they are accredited.

V. The Procedure of Notarization

Article 16 In the application for notarization, the party concerned shall personally go to the notary's office and make a written or verbal application. If someone else is entrusted to do so, he shall present a power of attorney. However, an applicant for the certification by a notary of a commission, statement, adoption of child, testament or signature and seal shall not entrust someone else to act on his behalf; if the party has any real difficulty, the notary shall handle notarization at the party's location.

The state organizations, bodies, enterprises and institutions shall dispatch their representatives to the notaries' offices in making applications for notarization. The representatives shall present powers of attorney.

Article 17 A notary shall be prohibited from handling the notarial affairs applied for by himself or herself or his or her spouse or his or her own or spouse's close relatives, and also be prohibited from handling the notarial affairs in which he himself or she herself or his or her spouse has interests.

A party concerned shall be entitled to apply for the sidestepping of notaries.

Articles 18 A notary shall examine the status of a party concerned and his or her capacities in the exercise of rights and the fulfilment of obligations; examine whether the facts, documents and related papers of which the party concerned applies for the notarization are true and legal.

Article 19 When a notary's office considers the evidence supplied by the party concerned to be incomplete or doubtful, it shall be entitled to notify the party to make necessary supplements or make inquiries of the units or individuals concerned and ask for related papers and materials. The units or individuals concerned shall be obliged to give assistance.

Article 20 A notary shall make notarial deeds in the forms as stipulated or approved by the Ministry of Justice.

Article 21 A copy of a notarial deed shall be kept on file after its completion. A number of copies shall be made and issued to the party concerned together with the original in accordance with the needs of the party.

Article 22 A notary's office shall collect fees for handling notarial affairs. The procedures for the collection of notarial fees shall be separately formulated by the Ministry of Justice.

Article 23 All the notarial affairs handled by the notary's office shall be kept confidential.

Article 24 Either party concerned shall be entitled to apply to the people's court which has jurisdiction for the enforcement of the credit document which has been notarized by a notary's office to effect enforcement according to Clause (10) of Article 4 when the other party is in breach of the provisions in the said document.

Article 25 A notary's office shall refuse to notarize untrue and illegal facts and documents. When the notary's office refuses the party's application for notarization, it shall give the party the reasons for the refusal orally or in writing and explain the appeals procedure if he or she disagrees with the reasons of the refusal.

If a party concerned disagrees with the reason of the refusal of a notary's office or considers a notary to have handled his or her application improperly, he or she shall make an appeal to the city or county judicial administration authorities at the location of the office or to higher judicial administration authorities and the authorities concerned shall make a decision.

Article 26 A notarial deed issued shall be cancelled if it is found to be improper or wrong by the notary's office or the judicial administration authorities at its same level or higher judicial administration authorities.

Article 27 If a notarial deed applied for by a party concerned is intended to be used abroad, it shall also be submitted to the Ministry of Foreign Affairs or the foreign affairs office of the province, autonomous region or municipality directly under the Central Government and the embassy or consulate of the country concerned in China for attestation, in addition to being handled in the procedure as stipulated in these Regulations. However, these procedures do not apply to those which are otherwise stipulated by the country where the deed(s) is(are) to be sent and used or which are agreed by both parties to be exempt from consular attestations.

VI Supplementary Provisions

Article 28 These Regulations shall be applicable to the foreign citizens who live in China.

Article 29 The Ministry of Justice shall be responsible for the interpretation of these Regulations.

Article 30 These Regulations shall be put into effect from the date of promulgation.

17 MEASUREMENTS

PROVISIONAL REGULATIONS ON MEASUREMENTS OF THE PEOPLE'S REPUBLIC OF CHINA

Issued by the State Council
(May 27, 1977)

Chapter I General Principles

Article 1 These regulations are formulated in order to further unify China's system of measurements and improve the nationwide metrological setup, so that metrological work may meet the growing needs of socialist revolution and socialist construction.

Article 2 Metrological work must abide by Chairman Mao's proletarian revolutionary line. Under the centralized leadership of the Chinese Communist Party and with class struggle as the key link, metrological work must be made to serve the three great revolutionary movements of class struggle, the struggle for production and scientific experiment through better regulation, unifying measurement values, combining the efforts of professional personnel with mass campaigns, conducting measurements in conjunction with production and construction tasks and integrating calibration with repairs.

Chapter II System of Measurements

Article 3 China's system of measurements is in the main the metric system, with the International System of Units (SI) being adopted step by step.

The domestic system now still in use will be phased out gradually.

The British system may not be used except in special cases approved by metrological departments at the provincial, municipal, autonomous regional or higher level.

Article 4 The Chinese terms, symbols and usage of measurement units will be published separately.

Chapter III Establishment of Standards of Measurements and Transmission of Their Values

Article 5 The national standards of measurements are the foundation for achieving nationwide unification of measurement values. The National Bureau of Standards and Metrology of the People's Republic of China (NBSM) will organize research in metrology and establish these standards in the light of the needs of production and construction. These standards shall be put into service after certification by the state.

Standards at all other levels shall be established by the various localities under unified and overall state planning to ensure rational geographical distribution and on the principle of joint leadership by the central and local authorities with emphasis on the latter. The establishment by a lower metrological department of its most authoritative standards is subject to examination and approval by the next higher metrological department.

Article 6 The values of the national standards shall be transmitted to other standards maintained by the various localities and then onto the measuring instruments used in economic construction, defense building and scientific research so as to ensure nationwide uniformity of the values of standards. Arrangements for such transmission shall be made according to the principle of proximity.

Chapter IV Control on Measuring Instruments

Article 7 Enterprises engaged in the manufacture and repair of measuring instruments may apply for business registration with the local bureau of industry and commerce only after clearance by the local metrological department.

Such enterprises must put proletarian politics in command and strictly observe rules concerning verification in order to ensure the quality of their products. All new or repaired measuring instruments must be certified by the state. Such certification shall be carried out by the metrological departments or by enterprises approved by them. Substandard products may not be delivered.

The metrological departments shall exercise tighter control over the manufacture or repair of measuring instruments and supervise and inspect the quality of products.

The NBSM has the unified control of the allocation of standard measuring instruments. The specific scope and method of control shall be worked out by the NBSM in collaboration with other departments concerned.

Article 8 New types of measuring instruments may be put into serial production only after they have been proved satisfactory through technical evaluations. The specific procedures shall be laid down by the NBSM in collaboration with other departments concerned.

Article 9 Imported measuring instruments may be sold or used only after they have been calibrated or tested by the metrological departments and found to be up to standard. When compensation is to be demanded for substandard imported instruments, the papers of attestation shall be provided by metrological departments at the provincial, municipal, autonomous regional or higher level.

Plans for importing measuring instruments shall be examined and approved by the departments concerned in collaboration with the metrological departments. It is strictly forbidden to import measuring instruments which are not in conformity with China's system of measurements or which fail to meet the usage requirements.

Article 10 It is forbidden to purchase or market measuring instruments whose use is prohibited by the state or which is without qualification stamps or certificates.

Article 11 User units of measuring instruments should draw up and perfect a set of rules on metrological control, choose measuring instruments in the light of actual needs, and calibrate them at regular intervals so as to maintain their accuracy. Measuring instruments that have undergone repairs may be put into use only after being approved through technical evaluation.

The metrological departments exercise supervision, carry out inspection and provide technical guidance in regard to the use of measuring instruments by various units.

Article 12 Measuring instruments shall be calibrated in accordance with calibration specification. Those found up to standards will be issued certificates or will be duly stamped. Calibration specification shall be formulated and the certificates and stamps shall be stipulated and issued by the NBSM.

Article 13 The setting and collection of fees for the testing of measuring instruments shall be laid down by the NBSM in consultation with other departments concerned.

Article 14 These regulations shall be observed by all units and individuals who manufacture, import, market, use or repair measuring instruments. Those found guilty of violating state metrological regulations or who use measuring instruments in illicit activities detrimental to the socialist economy and public interests shall be dealt with by metrological departments in collaboration with other departments concerned. Cases of serious offence shall be referred to judicial departments.

Chapter V Metrological Departments and Their Functions

Article 15 The metrological departments are special organs charged with implementing state metrological regulations, exercising metrological supervision and control, establishing the standards of measurements, organizing the transmission of their values and measurement work so as to ensure nationwide unification of the system of measurements and the uniformity, accuracy and correct use of measuring instruments. They should be set up and improved on the principle of "streamlined organization and simpler administration."

Article 16 The NBSM is the functional department under the State Council in charge of standardization and metrological work for the country as a whole. It is responsible for formulating the guiding principles for standardization and metrological work, drawing up working programmes and administering standardization and metrological work throughout the country.

The provincial, municipal and autonomous regional departments of standards and metrology and the prefectural, city and county metrological offices are functional bodies of the revolutionary committees of the corresponding levels and are responsible for administering metrological work in the locality.

Institutions engaged in research, verification, repair and measurement as well as experimental workshops run by the metrological departments are public undertakings.

Article 17 A metrological office or a full-time or part-time metrologist shall be established or appointed by all ministries concerned under the State Council, all appropriate departments of the People's Liberation Army, all provincial, municipal and autonomous regional departments concerned, as well as all enterprises, institutions and army units in accordance with national or regional plans and requirements and, upon approval by higher authorities, shall take charge of the metrological work of the ministry, department, enterprise, institution or unit concerned.

Chapter VI Supplementary Provisions

Article 18 The provincial, municipal and autonomous regional revolutionary committees, the ministries concerned under the State Council and the appropriate departments of the People's Liberation Army may work out their own measures of implementation on the basis of these regulations.

Article 19 Interpretation of these regulations is the responsibility of the NBSM.

Article 20 These regulations shall be put into effect from the date of their issuance.

18

STANDARDIZATION AND QUALITY CONTROLS

Quality Control/ Standardization

PROVISIONAL REGULATIONS FOR TOTAL QUALITY CONTROL IN INDUSTRIAL ENTERPRISES

(Promulgated by the State Economic Commission on March 18, 1980)

Chapter I General Principles

Article 1 The present regulations are formulated for the purposes of popularizing total quality control in industrial enterprises, carrying out the policy of putting "quality in first place" and improving the quality of products steadily so as to meet the needs of the programme of Four Modernizations and the continuous rise in the people's living standards.

Article 2 Total quality control is a central link in enterprise management as well as a scientific method of quality control in modern industry. It means control of the quality of products in the entire process from designing, trial-production, and manufacture through post-sale service. All the workers and staff of an enterprise and all the departments therein should learn and take part in quality control.

Article 3 The tasks for those involved in total quality control are: keep abreast of the needs of national reconstruction and the people's livelihood and investigate the developments of similar products in China and other countries and their market conditions; educate the workers and staff to foster the concept of putting "quality in first place" and correctly carry out advanced and rational technical standards; adopt scientific methods (including mathematical statistics) and, through specialized technical research, control various factors affecting product quality; undertake technical-economic analysis of the quality of products; offer technical services to users; constantly improve quality in line with the requirements in their use and strive to turn out products that are good in quality, low in price, suited to buyer's requirements, satisfactory to users and competitive on both the domestic and overseas markets.

Chapter II Planning for Product Quality

Article 4 Planning for product quality is a constant and effective means of organizing total quality control. Such planning calls for a programme of action involving departments engaged in quality control. All industrial enterprises need to map out comprehensive plans for improving product quality, as well as specific plans for different items, periods and departments in line with the principle of achieving greater, faster, better and more economical results.

Article 5 Planning for product quality consists of:

1. Planning for catching up with or surpassing advanced levels in product quality. This means drafting plans for catching up with or surpassing advanced levels in trial-producing and manufacturing new products and improving existing products in line with users' requirements and the orientation of technological development. This requires the defining of concrete targets for catching up with or surpassing advanced levels in China and abroad and the setting of a time limit and rate of progress for fulfilling the targets.

2. Planning for quality targets. The comprehensive economic plan of an enterprise should embody the policy of putting "quality in first place." A separate plan defining the rates of first-grade and fine quality products should be drafted and examined in the light of specific circumstances.

3. Planning for measures to improve quality. This kind of plan defines the measures for quality improvement to be taken during the year and in each quarter and the departments to take the main responsibilities. The annual outlay for technical measures should, first of all, be spent on improvement of product quality and development of new products.

Article 6 Stress should be laid on the implementation of plans. Various plans for the quality of products should be carried out by all departments, brigades and individual workers, and their implementation should be linked up with examination, emulation, assessment, rewards and punishments.

Chapter III Quality Control at Design and Trial-Production Stage

Article 7 The stage of designing and trial-production means the whole process of technical preparations prior to the stage of regular production of a product. It covers investigation and research, programme drafting, product designing, technical designing, trial-production, testing and appraisal.

1. Investigation, research and drafting of programme. This means investigating users' requirements with respect to product quality, collecting relevant technical data in China and other countries, and studying ways of solving key technological problems. The work also includes the drafting of targets for quality and technical requirements that are suitable and reliable, satisfactory to customers, economical and rational.

2. Organization of users, sales, research, manufacturing, and quality control departments and a "three-in-one" combination of leading officials, technicians and workers for the examination of designs. Efforts should be made through such examination to meet the requirements of users, solve problems that may arise in the course of production, and select suitable design.

3. Work must be done well in the trial-production, testing and assessment of new products. After the completion of the trial-production of new products (including major improvements in existing products), the enterprise concerned should organize relevant personnel to make strict tests and appraisals. With regard to important products, the department in charge should organize user and other relevant units for appraisal and all-round technical and economic assessment.

4. Work must be done well in the examination of standardization. It is essential to ensure that product designs are up to or even above the various technical standards stipulated by the state and to raise the level of standardization, serialization and interchangeability of products.

Article 8 The following requirements must be met before a new product can go into serial production:

1. The technical standards of the product have been drawn up and have gone through the formalities of report and approval;

2. The technical papers must be complete, accurate and clear;

3. A certificate of quality must be obtained from the authorities for supervising and inspecting the product, and a product ready to go into the market must have its trademark registered;

4. There must be complete sets of equipment and devices for examining and testing product quality;

5. It must be in conformity with the requirements for environmental protection, security and sanitation.

Article 9 It is essential to adopt a scientific approach to the process of designing and trial-production and to act strictly according to the stipulated procedures; it is forbidden to proceed with designing, experimenting and manufacturing simultaneously.

Chapter IV Quality Control in Course of Production

Article 10 The tasks for those involved in quality control in the course of production are: establish a production system capable of constantly turning out qualified and top quality products, and do a good job of quality control at each link of the chain of production; strictly follow the technical standards, make sure that the quality of products reaches or surpasses all these standards, strive to turn out top quality products, and try to cut down rejects as far as possible.

Article 11 Close attention should be given to the following points if success is to be achieved in quality control in the course of production:

1. Establish or improve the system of responsibility for each and every workpost, map out or revise rules for various operations in good time, implement them strictly, and get everyone to observe technical dicipline.

2. Do a really good job of working in a scientific way and, in particular, maintaining good order in production, rationally equip the work places with tools and make sure that the passageways for production are free from obstacles and that the work sites are tidy and clean. Trees should be planted in the surroundings and pollution and dust prevented.

3. Make good preparations before production starts and arrange production plans rationally; improve production management, strengthen weak links in time, and take steps to achieve a harmonious flow in production.

4. Make full use and flexible employment of mathematical statistics and other methods of quality control to maintain the quality of products in the course of production and prevent rejects.

5. Map out or revise technical standards for existing products. Enterprises which do not have such standards should institute their standards and those whose standards are backward should revise them; all enterprises should strictly implement their standards after they are submitted to and approved by the appropriate authorities.

6. Strengthen metrological work. To ensure the quality of products, all enterprises should institute special metrological organizations or personnel to be responsible for unified control of metrological work in measurement, temperature, mechanics, electricity, chemistry, etc., to implement metrological laws and decrees and the system of metrological control, and to be responsible for the examination and maintenance of metrological instruments and the work of testing. It is essential to equip the enterprises with all necessary metrological devices and testing instruments and equipment and keep them constantly in good repair.

7. Establish or improve various systems for quality control centered round the system of responsibility for each workpost. Unqualified raw and other materials must not be used in production, unqualified semi-finished products must not be used, unqualified products must not be allowed to leave the factory as qualified products, nor must they be included in calculating the value and volume of production. Workpieces from one working procedure which are not up to standard must not be allowed to move to the next procedure; workers on the next shift have the right to refuse to take over if they find the equipment, the job being worked on and the environmental sanitation are not up to the standards for quality control. The principle of combining inspection by the workers themselves and by full-time personnel should be adopted in the inspection of product quality. Self-inspection and mutual inspection among the workers should be the main practice in the course of production whereas semi-finished and finished products should mainly be inspected by professional personnel. Records on quality should be established or improved and a good job should be done in keeping primary records about product quality and in making statistics and analysis.

8. Do a good job of quality control in the supply of materials. Examination and acceptance of materials going into storage should be done strictly according to rule. Materials that are not up to standard or not in conformity with the provisions of contracts may be returned or rejected. The caretakers of materials should take effective steps to avoid damage and deterioration. The quality of service should be raised so as to ensure timely supply of materials. Departments in charge of materials supply should assume total responsibility for the quality of those products whose purchase and marketing are monopolized by these departments.

9. Strengthen maintenance service so as to keep all equipment in good technical condition. Repaired equipment should be up to the specified requirements for quality. Tools and equipment should be kept well to ensure the required precision of tools, fixtures, measuring instruments and cutting tools.

10. Improve the quality of packing. Standards for packing should be instituted in line with the characteristics of products, packing and examination should be done in strict accordance with the standards, and packing of products that is not up to standard must be done over again. Packing and decoration of products should be improved continuously to make them attractive.

11. Delivery of products should be handled in line with the specific contracts signed with the customers. It is impermissible to compel the customers to accept them on the pretext that they are up to certain general norms or to accept a mixture of quality and inferior products.

Chapter V Quality in the Course of Use

Article 12 The assessement of product quality depends mainly on the users' evaluation. Quality control in the course of use is an extension of the work of an enterprise in quality control. The enterprise should constantly study and seek to improve product quality through visits to users and technical service for them.

Article 13 Active steps should be taken to develop technical service:

1. Compile manuals explaining the use of products. The contents of such manuals should generally include the characteristics, structure, installation, use and maintenance of the products, points for attention, the period of guarantee and conditions under which they are to be kept and transported, etc. Manuals for export products should be translated into foreign languages.

2. Impart techniques about the installation, use and maintenance of products and help train technicians in a variety of ways, and undertake to resolve knotty technical problems in the use of products.

3. Provide blueprints for the manufacture of parts that are easily worn out and supply users according to their needs with the spare parts and accessories for maintenance purposes (assembly plants responsible for supplying users; factories making elements and components and factories rendering assistance responsible for supplying assembly plants).

4. Set up a network of repair shops or retail shops and in certain cases take service to users' doorsteps.

5. Manufacturers should help users with the installation and trial run of certain complex products or provide technical guidance.

Article 14 Introduce and maintain such practices as visiting users, manning sales counters or holding users' discussions regularly. Links between industry and commerce, and between production and marketing, should be strengthened. Every enterprise should try through all possible channels to investigate the effects and requirements of its products in use, find out their flaws and problems, and feed these back in good time while comparing its own products with those of other enterprises and countries, so as to improve designs and raise product quality.

Article 15 All users (including units in the following working procedures) should, in the spirit of responsibility to the country and people and mutual assistance between enterprises, keep the manufacturing and supplying units informed of the quality of raw and other materials, parts and whole products. Assembly plants should keep abreast of the work of the quality control systems of supplying units and suggest improvements with respect to existing problems and take the initiative to solve the problems. All units involved should be organized in a coordinated effort to guarantee the quality of the end products. Manufacturing units should handle conscientiously problems concerning the quality of its ex-factory products. They should give prompt answers to criticisms and demands raised by users. They should enthusiastically help users acquire the techniques of using the products where problems have arisen because of inappropriate handling. In case of problems due to faulty manufacturing, the assembly plants should be responsible for repairing or substituting the parts concerned or for refunding, no matter whether the parts in question were made by themselves or bought from other factories. Damages should be paid in case of accidents occurring during the period of guarantee because of inferior product quality. Economic contracts should be concluded between assembly plants and factories supplying raw and other materials and accessories. The supplying units should deliver their consignments according to the quality, quantity and date of delivery specified in the contracts; those which fail to honour contracts should be held responsible for the economic losses thus incurred.

Chapter VI System of Quality Control

Article 16 All enterprises should conscientiously implement the principles, policies, rules and regulations for quality control laid down by the party and state. It is essential to give full play to the enthusiasm and initiative of the technical personnel and the workers in quality control and define explicitly the tasks that must be fulfilled by each department, unit and individual worker, the responsibilities they are charged with and the limits of their authority. All departments and units should draft their own standards for high quality work so as to use the high quality of work done to ensure the quality of products. A complete system for total quality control should be established, under which there should be people responsible for each product, each working procedure and each relevant piece of work.

Article 17 All enterprises should put total quality control as an important item on the agenda, and the managers or factory directors should bear full responsibility for the quality of products manufactured by their own enterprises. The chief engineers should, under the leadership of the factory directors, be responsible for the development and manufacture of new products, the drafting of plans for catching up with or surpassing advanced levels in product quality, and the solving of major technical problems concerning product quality.

Article 18 Establish comprehensive quality control organizations or full-time personnel whose major functions are: under the leadership of the managers or factory directors, assist the leadership in comprehensive, day-to-day work of quality control; be responsible for the tabulation of comprehensive statistics and examination of the implementation of the plans for quality control; study and popularize advanced methods of quality control; coordinate the work of quality control in related departments; organize investigations of the effects and requirements of use of products; take part in the assessment of new products; carry out publicity and education with regard to quality control; and organize mass participation in quality control.

All enterprises should establish or improve quality inspection organizations which are responsible for supervising the implementation of the standards for product quality. Their main tasks are: make strict inspection of product quality in accordance with the technical standards and orders for goods; undertake the inspection of the quality of raw and other materials, purchased parts, semi-finished products, finished products, and the principal working procedures; make comments on whether a new product can be put into regular production; sign certificates of inspection for products leaving the factory; and report to the managers or factory directors and the higher authorities on the actual quality of products manufactured by their own enterprises and parts supplied by support factories. The appointment and removal of chiefs of quality inspection divisions or sections should be done with the approval of the next higher authorities.

Article 19 Departments of distribution, materials supply and transportation should set up a system of responsibility for guaranteeing the quality of products during transportation and for improving the work of factories, workshops, warehouses and storage and transport facilities in this regard.

Chapter VII Mass Participation in Quality Control

Article 20 All enterprises should, in the light of their own characteristics, mobilize the masses extensively and carry out various forms of activity for quality control. Quality control groups in different forms should be set up on a voluntary basis and with reference to the actual conditions, and they should carry out constant activities concerning quality control and tackle major problems in order to improve quality. Records should be kept on the establishment of quality control groups and their activities.

Article 21 The workers should be organized to take an active part in the "quality month" drive, emulation campaigns should be launched to turn out high quality products, pace-setters in improving quality elected, and all kinds of meetings on the work of quality control held to exchange experience, commend advanced workers and promote the steady improvement of products.

Chapter VIII Education and Training

Article 22 Education in total quality control should be carried out in all enterprises, and leading cadres at various levels should take the lead in study and application. First of all, it is necessary to train a number of people as the backbone force in quality control.

Article 23 All workers should be given constant, repeated education in quality control. The contents and time of study should be stipulated according to the workers' different trades and needs. Education inside and outside of the factory should be integrated so that all concerned will be able to acquire the basic knowledge and methods of total quality control and apply them in a flexible way in the light of their own jobs.

Article 24 Effective steps should be taken ro run technical schools and various types of technical training courses. A variety of methods such as on-site training, technical demonstrations, competitions of skills and election of skilled hands should be adopted in conjunction with everyday production activities to encourage the workers to study techniques and raise their technical standards.

Article 25 New workers should be given basic technical training and education in total quality control following their recruitment. They must first pass the examination and acquire a certificate of qualification for operation before they are allowed to take over workposts and operate.

Article 26 All workers are subjected to technical and professional examinations on the improving of product quality according to rule. The results are to be entered in their records as an important basis for their promotion or upgrading.

Chapter IX Rewards and Punishments

Article 27 The principle to be followed is: high price for high quality, low price for low quality, and priority for advanced units in the supply of raw materials, fuel and power.

Article 28 The system of rewards in all enterprises should embody the policy of "putting quality in first place." Contributions to quality should be regarded as the foremost condition for winning overall rewards.

Separate terms should be drafted for rewarding full-time inspectors in enterprises. Examination of inspectors' records should be concentrated on the quality and amount of inspection they have done.

Article 29 Improvement of product quality should be integrated with the interests of the enterprises and the workers themselves. Outstanding groups and individuals who have made signal contributions to quality control and improvement of product quality should be given honorary diplomas and annual material rewards. Quality products up to the required standards may apply for regional, departmental or national rewards for quality.

Article 30 Those enterprises whose products are of inferior quality for long periods of time due to chaotic business management and therefore incur strong criticisms from users, must be ordered to make improvements within a set time. They should be ordered to stop production and straighten things out where necessary, and the wages of their leading cadres may be reduced appropriately and the bonuses for the workers suspended in the light of the circumstances, until the quality of their products attains the standard.

Article 31 Where accidents pertaining to product quality have occurred, the enterprises concerned should find out the causes, handle them seriously, and report to the departments in charge promptly in accordance with relevant stipulations. In case of major accidents pertaining to quality, the leadership should be held responsible and those who are directly responsible should be criticized or punished according to the seriousness of their cases and their own attitudes. Those whose cases are serious and whose attitudes are bad should be dealt with according to law. Anyone who practises fraud on product quality, trumps up data, palms off inferior products as qualified ones, cheats customers, or retaliates upon inspectors and others who expose his fraudulence, will be held responsible and dealt with severely.

Chapter X Supplementary Articles

Article 32 The present regulations shall go into force from the day of their promulgation. Various regions and departments concerned may formulate their own by-laws for application according to their specific circumstances.

Article 33 The right of explanation of these regulations rests with the State Economic Commission.

REGULATIONS ON STANDARDIZATION CONTROL OF THE PEOPLE'S REPUBLIC OF CHINA

Promulgated by the State Council
(July 31, 1979)

Chapter I General Principles

Article 1 Standardization is an important means of organizing modern production and an essential part of scientific management. Promoting standardization in the course of socialist construction is a major technical-economic policy of the state. Without standardization, there will be neither specialization, nor high quality, nor high-speed growth. These Regulations are formulated to strengthen standardization control, raise the level of standardization and bring its role into full play in the modernization of agriculture, industry, national defence, and science and technology.

Article 2 Technical standards (hereinafter, standards for short) provide a common technical basis for production, construction and the circulation of commodities. Standards must be worked out and implemented for all industrial goods in regular production, major farm products, engineering projects, and for environmental protection, safety, sanitation and other matters where the technical requirements should be unified.

Chapter II Formulation and Revision of Standards

Article 3 In formulating or revising standards, full consideration should be given to the needs of the users, to natural conditions and to the rational utilization of the country's resources, so that the standards shall be technically advanced, economically sound, and reliable for safe operation.

Article 4 The formulation or revision of standards must be based on a selection, proper classification and serialization of the varieties and specifications of the products of the same category; the scope of application should be enlarged as far as possible for widely used spare parts, components, elements, apparatus, structural parts and fittings so as to improve their interchangeability. Different types of standards should be well-coordinated and be complementary to one another; attention should be paid to their applicability for both military and civilian purposes.

Article 5 With regard to the quality indices for industrial and agricultural products, proper grading rules may be included in the relevant standards as required.

Article 6 Packaging standards should be worked out simultaneously with product standards and they must meet the quality and safety requirements, taking into consideration the conditions of loading, unloading, transportation and storage and paying attention to the economical use of materials.

Article 7 Internationally accepted standards and advanced foreign standards should be studied conscientiously and adopted as far as possible.

Article 8 With regard to products for export and the engineering projects China undertakes to build in foreign countries, standards geared to the needs of foreign trade markets should be worked out, if necessary, by the authorities in charge of production and construction, in cooperation with the departments in charge of foreign trade and foreign economic relations.

Article 9 Standards should be revised in time to keep pace with technical and economic development. They should be reviewed once every three to five years to see whether they should be reaffirmed, revised or abrogated.

Article 10 Standardization promoting programmes and plans shall be included in the national economic programmes and plans at all levels. The experimental and research projects necessary for the formulation of standards shall be included in the relevant scientific research plans of various levels.

Chapter III Classification, Endorsement and Promulgation of Standards

Article 11 Standards are divided into three

classes: state standards, ministry standards (specialized standards) and enterprise standards. Ministry standards should be replaced by specialized standards step by step. Neither ministry standards (specialized standards) nor enterprise standards should contravene state standards; and no enterprise standards should contravene ministry standards (specialized standards).

Article 12 State standards refer to those which are of cardinal importance to China's economic and technical development and which must be uniform throughout the country. They include mainly: standards for basic raw materials and semi-processed materials; standards for major industrial and agricultural products which are vital to the people's livelihood, used extensively and in large quantities and produced inter-departmentally; safety and sanitation standards for the protection of the public and the environment; basic standards for interchangeability and common technical terminology; standards for general-purpose spare parts, components, elements, apparatus, structural parts, fittings, tools and measuring instruments; standards for commonly adopted experimental and testing methods; and international standards adopted in China.

Article 13 State standards shall be drafted by the departments in charge under the State Council (or the technical committees in charge of specialized standardization) and, depending on the scope of application of the standards, reported to the following departments for examination, endorsement and promulgation:

–The State Administration of Standards (for standards relating to industrial and agricultural products and products for both military and civilian uses);
–The State Capital Construction Commission (for standards relating to engineering projects and environmental protection);
–The Ministry of Public Health (for standards relating to pharmaceuticals, public health and disease prevention); and
–The defence industry departments (for standards relating to defence industries).

Important standards shall be reported to the State Council for examination and approval.

Article 14 Ministry standards (specialized standards) refer mainly to those which are unified for a specialized trade throughout the country. They shall be drafted under the auspices of, and endorsed and promulgated by, the competent authorities and reported to the State Administration of Standards to be put on record.

Article 15 Enterprise standards should be worked out for all products that are not covered by state standards or ministry standards (specialized standards). To ensure constant improvement of their products, enterprises may draw up higher quality standards than those laid down in state and ministry standards (specialized standards). Measures governing enterprise standards shall be formulated separately by the State Administration of Standards.

Article 16 All organizations and individuals may propose draft standards. Proposals for state and ministry standards (specialized standards) shall be considered by the national organizations in charge of technical matters relating to specialized standardization; proposals for enterprise standards shall be considered by the higher authorities of the enterprises concerned.

Article 17 The revision or abrogation of standards shall be endorsed and announced by the departments which approved the standards in question. These departments or the organizations they appoint are responsible for the interpretation of the said standards.

Chapter IV Implementation of Standards

Article 18 As soon as standards are endorsed and promulgated, they become technical decrees, which must be strictly observed by all departments in charge of production, construction, scientific research and design and by all enterprises and undertakings; no organizations are allowed to alter or lower standards without authorization. Anyone who acts in violation of standards and thus causes ill consequences or even grave accidents shall be criticized, disciplined, given economic sanctions or brought to court, depending on the merits of each case.

Where there are real difficulties in implementing standards, the reasons must be explained and a report made on the time allowance requested and the measures to be adopted to apply the standards. After examination and endorsement by the higher authorities, the report shall be submitted to the standard-promulgating departments for approval.

Article 19 The material and technical conditions necessary for the implementation of standards should be guaranteed by the higher authorities; the major items should be included as part of the technical measures that are planned at various levels.

Article 20 All production enterprises must adhere to standards when checking raw materials, semi-processed materials and parts made by other enterprises, examining semi-finished products and inspecting finished products. Up-to-standard products shall be certified as such by the inspection departments; substandard products shall all be excluded from the statistics showing the fulfilment of plans and from output values, and are not allowed to be checked out.

Article 21 All engineering projects must be designed and built in accordance with standards. No project should start on substandard designs and no substandard project should be accepted as passed in final inspection.

Article 22 Full consideration should be given to the requirements of standardization in designing new products and projects, and the letters of designing assignments as well as the design papers must undergo standardization checks; the standardization control departments must be represented in such checks when a design is being examined and finalized.

No new product is allowed to go into serial production unless the standards for that product have been worked out.

Article 23 Full attention should be paid to standardization in reorganizing and improving old products, and the standardization control departments must be represented in the standardization checks.

Article 24 Full consideration must be given to the requirements of domestic standardization when importing equipment and techniques from abroad. There must be prior standardization checks by the departments concerned under the State Council, by the provincial, municipal or autonomous regional standardization control organizations or, if the imported items greatly affect domestic standardization, by the departments concerned under the auspices of the State Administration of Standards.

Chapter V Quality Supervision and Inspection

Article 25 The State Administration of Standards and the provincial, municipal and autonomous regional bureaus of standards are in charge of the work of supervising and inspecting the quality of products, and they shall coordinate and guide the specialized inspection organizations concerned in carrying out the task. Specific measures shall be drawn up separately by the State Administration of Standards in cooperation with the other departments concerned.

The provinces, municipalities and autonomous regions should establish and improve the organizations charged with quality supervision and inspection in those cities where industries are concentrated. These organizations shall work under the leadership of the standardization control departments of the same level.

Article 26 The tasks of the organizations charged with quality supervision and inspection are: supervising and inspecting the quality of products against the standards; acting as arbiter-inspector when there are disputes over the quality of products between the producer and the seller; keeping the higher authorities informed of the situation and problems in implementing standards, and proposing improvements in the quality of products; giving guidance and help to enterprises in checking up on the quality of products.

Article 27 The departments in charge of quality supervision and inspection have the power to conduct regular and irregular check-ups on the quality of products, either directly or by proxy. They have the power to stop the issuance of quality certificates by those enterprises which do not produce according to standards and the products of which are of low quality; for especially serious cases, they have the power to propose to the competent authorities the application of economic sanctions on the enterprises and the personnel concerned, or to order the enterprises to suspend operation, pending improvement.

Article 28 A new product must be certified up-to-standard by the organizations in charge of quality supervision and inspection before an application for the registration of its trademark is made.

Article 29 With regard to fine-quality products, a quality-indicating system, an award system and a policy of higher price for better quality are adopted. Symbols for good-quality products shall be issued if the products have been certified as such by the organizations in charge of quality supervision and inspection, recognized by the departments concerned and approved by the higher authorities in charge. Specific measures for this shall be formulated separately by the State Administration of Standards together with the other departments concerned.

Chapter VI Standardization Control Organizations and Personnel

Article 30 The main tasks of the standardization control departments are: enforcing the relevant principles and policies of the state; organizing the formulation and revision of standards; supervising and speeding up the implementation of standards; supervising and inspecting the quality of products and engineering projects; supervising and checking up on the work of standardization relating to the design of new products; the reorganization of old products and the importation of equipment and techniques.

Article 31 The State Administration of Standards is the functional department under the State Council in charge of all standardization work in the country. Its responsibility is to put forward principles and policies for standardization, organize the formulation and implementation of national standardization programmes and plans, and take charge of all standardization work and quality supervision and inspection in the country.

Article 32 The bureaus of standards of the provinces, municipalities, autonomous regions and industrial cities and the standardization control organizations of autonomous prefectures and counties are the functional departments under the revolutionary committees of the same level and are responsible for standardization control and quality supervision and inspection in their localities.

Article 33 The standardization control organizations of the departments concerned under the State Council and in the People's Liberation Army are responsible for standardization control within their respective departments.

Article 34 The standardization control organizations or standardization control personnel in the specialized bureaus, companies, enterprises and undertakings of the departments concerned under the direct leadership of the officials in municipalities and autonomous regions are under the direct leadership of the officials in charge of technical work (or the chief engineers) and are responsible for standardization work in their own units or as assigned by the higher authorities.

Article 35 The State Administration of Standards and the departments concerned under the State Council should set up and strengthen standardization research institutes and standardization information and data-processing centres. The provincial, municipal and autonomous regional bureaus of standards should set up and strengthen standardization information and data-processing centres.

Article 36 The national technical committees in charge of specialized standardization, the standardization research institutes of the departments concerned under the State Council and other organizations in charge of technical matters relating to specialized standardization shall conduct relevant scientific research, organize and undertake the formulation and revision of state standards and ministry standards (specialized standards), and participate in relevant international activities.

Article 37 Standardization and quality inspection are productive technical work. The scientists and technicians engaged in this work are part of the scientific and technical contingent, and they should enjoy the same political and economic treatment as the scientists and technicians of other departments. Those who have made outstanding achievements or important contributions should be awarded.

Chapter VII Appendices

Article 38 Measures for the implementation of these regulations shall be worked out by the revolutionary committees of the provinces, municipalities and autonomous regions, the departments concerned under the State Council, and the departments concerned of the People's Liberation Army.

Article 39 The State Administration of Standards is responsible for the interpretation of these regulations.

Article 40 These regulations shall come into force from the day they are promulgated, and the former "Measures Governing Technical Standards for Industrial and Agricultural Products and Engineering Projects" shall cease to be effective.

PROCEDURES FOR THE EXAMINATION AND ADMINISTRATION OF STANDARDIZATION OF NEW MECHANICAL AND ELECTRICAL PRODUCTS

(Promulgated jointly by the State Commission of Machine Building Industry, the State Economic Commission and the State Bureau of Standardization on March 14, 1981)

I General Rules

Article 1 These Procedures are formulated in accordance with the provision in the "Regulations of the People's Republic of China on the Administration of Standardization" that new products shall go through standardization examinations in order to strengthen the administration of the standardization of new mechanical and electrical products, carry out various technical standards, heighten the levels of standardization, develop categories of products rationally, contribute to the specialized cooperative production, simplify design and technology, shorten the cycles of design and trial production, ensure and improve the quality of products and speed up the socialist modernization construction.

Article 2 For the new mechanical and electrical substitute products to go through standardization examinations means to substitute for or make remarkable improvements in old products in such aspects as performance, structure, technical targets, etc. The articles required for examination include the machinery, instruments and meters and electrical, electronic, telecommunications, radio and other mechanical and electrical products which are listed in the plans of new products by all departments or all trades.

Article 3 The requirements for standardization shall be taken into full account throughout each stage as from the preparation of the specifications of a new product to its design, trial production, appraisal, etc. Each management of production, construction, scientific research or design or each enterprise or institution shall conscientiously carry out standardization examinations as stipulated in these Procedures.

II The Standardization Examinations of the Design of New Products

Article 4 The design of new products shall embody relevant state, technical and economic policies and various technical standards and be conscientiously implemented. For a product designed for the first time, the development trend of the product shall be considered and the serial standards for the development of new products shall be prescribed in time.

Article 5 The design and technological personnel of new products shall be familiar with relevant state standards, ministerial (specialized) and enterprise standards, adopt standard parts and components as far as possible under the prerequisites of ensuring the major technical performance of the new products and take the inheritance of parts, components and elements into full account. The standardized level of a new product is an important index for the examination of the design and technological quality. The standardization professional personnel shall participate in the discussion of the design plans of new products.

Article 6 Explicit requirements shall be made for standardization in the preparation of the specifications of a new product. The standardization professional personnel at the same level shall participate in the examination of the specifications. Before the design of a product, the person in charge of the design shall propose "Comprehensive Requirements for the Standardization of the New Product" jointly with the standardization professional personnel.

Article 7 The "Comprehensive Requirements for the Standardization of the New Product" are the basic ground for the preparation of the "Examination Report of the Standardization of the New Product." Its contents mainly include:

1. Conforming to the requirements of the serial standards of products and other current technical standards;

2. The standardization coefficient estimated to be attained by the new product;

3. The requirements for the standardization of materials and elements;

4. Contrasting the standardized levels of the same product both at home and abroad and put-

ting forward the requirements for the standardization of the new product.

5. Expected economic effects of the standardization.

Article 8 On the basis of the "Comprehensive Requirements for the Standardization of the New Product" and in the light of the task at each stage of the design of the new product, the product designing personnel shall work out the specific contents of standardization at each stage of the design jointly with the standardization professional personnel.

Article 9 The main contents of the standardization examination of the drawings and technical papers of a new product are as follows:

1. The accuracy of the drawings and technical papers in the implementation and employment of various standards;

2. The integrity and unity of the drawings and technical papers;

3. The standardized degrees of parts, components, elements and large modules;

4. The implementation of the material standards.

III The Standardization Examination for the Appraisal of New Products

Article 10 Before the appraisal of a new product, the "Examination Report of the Standardization of the New Product" shall be put forward. It is the summary of the implementation of the "Comprehensive Requirements for the Standardization of the New Product" and the standardization at each stage of design in the course of the design of the new product, the technical ground for evaluating whether the new product is qualified for formal production in respect of standardization and a technical paper which shall be provided for in the appraisal of the product.

Article 11 The main contents of the examination report for the appraisal of the standardization of the prototype new product are as follows:

1. The category, main applications and production batch number of the new product;

2. The quality level of the drawings and technical papers of the new product;

3. The standardization coefficient of the new product;

4. The estimated economic effects of the standardization of the new product;

5. The draft standards of the new product;

6. The implementation of various standards and the reasons of the failure to implement some standards;

7. The comprehensive appraisal of the standardization of the new product;

8. The conclusion from the standardization examination.

Article 12 The main contents of the examination report for the appraisal of the standardization of the trial of a new product produced in a small batch are as follows:

1. The standardization of the technology and equipment and their inheritance;

2. The execution of the suggestions as to the standardization proposed in the appraisal of the prototype;

3. The accuracy, integrity and unity of the technological papers;

4. The contents of the main literature cited;

5. The standardization coefficient of the equipment and the analysis of economic effects;

6. The existing problems and the measures to solve them;

7. The conclusion from the standardization examination.

Article 13 Some of the new products which have been put into formal production shall still have to go through the appraisal of their small-batch trial production and the standardization examination after they have been proved up to standard through the appraisal of the prototypes. Some shall only go through one appraisal. In the case of a product to be appraised once, the appraised items shall go through the standardization examination in accordance with the contents stipulated in Article 11 and Article 12. The standards for the new product shall be prescribed before it is put into production and the certificate of inspection for the new product shall be obtained, otherwise the production management shall not produce the same in large batches and the administration for industry and commerce shall not handle the registration of the trademark.

IV Forms and Duties of Examinations

Article 14 The standardization examination of new products shall generally be divided into four forms in accordance with the plan of the new products, i.e., state examination, departmental examination, local examination and grass-roots examination.

1. The State Bureau of Standardization and Metrology or the unit concerned entrusted it shall

participate in the standardization by examination of the items of the new products to be examined by the state.

2. The standardization management organization of a ministry, a commission or a state bureau concerned of the State Council or the subordinate unit concerned entrusted by it shall participate in the standardization examination of the items of the new products to be examined by the ministry, commission or state bureau.

3. A local bureau of standardization shall participate in or organize the standardization examination or entrust a department or a bureau (corporation) with the participation in or the organization of the standardization examination of the item of the new products to be examined by the locality.

4. The standardization professional personnel in an enterprise or an institution shall participate in the standardization examination of the items of the new products to be examined by the grass-roots unit. But the appraisal and production of the new products shall be reported to the authorities concerned for examination and approval jointly with the standardization management organization at the same level.

Article 15 The items in the standardization examination of new products at each level shall be arranged in particular on the work plans of the unit at each level which organizes the examination of the new products so as to ensure that the examination shall be carried on in a led, planned and organized way. In the examination of a new product, the unit which organizes the examination shall notify the standardization organization at the same level to participate.

Article 16 In the standardization examination of a new product, the standardization personnel shall be entitled to refuse to sign the technical papers or drawings which do not conform to the requirements for standardization. The technical papers or drawings without the signatures of the standardization personnel shall not become effective.

Article 17 Standardization professional personnel, product designing personnel and technological personnel shall coordinate of their own accord and cooperate closely with each other, conscientiously carry out the standardization policies and principles, duly solve the standardization problems in the design and technology and jointly make a good job of the standardization of new products.

Article 18 To make a good job of the standardization of new products is an important technical and economic policy of the state. The comprehensive standardization requirements and the standardization examination reports proposed for new products shall conscientiously be implemented by enterprises and institutions. If serious accidents or economic losses result from the unconscientious implementation of them, the standardization personnel shall propose the departments in charge of production to respectively impose criticisms, punishments, economic sanctions or even affix liability on the personnel concerned according to the degrees of seriousness.

V Supplementary Provisions

Article 19 The State Bureau of Standardization shall be responsible for the interpretation of these Procedures.

Article 20 These Proceduces shall be put into effect as from the date of promulgation.

A NUMBER OF PROVISIONS OF THE STATE COMMISSION OF MACHINE BUILDING INDUSTRY FOR THE STRENGTHENING OF STANDARDIZATION

(June 30, 1981)

Standardization is an important means for the organization of the modernized production and construction and for the achievement of scientific management. Standardization is also an important technical basic job for regulating the structure of production, increasing economic benefit and improving the levels of business management. It is mainly aimed at obtaining overall optimum economic effects and promoting the development of the national economy. Standardization will play an increasingly important part in the economic regulation of our country.

The machine building industry has made a lot of achievements in standardization for the last two years. However, there still exist a large number of problems and the achievements are still far from suiting the needs of the regulation and development of the machine building industry.

Each department concerned of the machine building industry does not have a sufficient understanding of and does not pay enough attention to the importance of standardization. The standardization management or research organizations are not perfect. There are no normal channels for the supply of standardization funds. Qualified standardization scientific and technical personnel are wanting. The progress is slow in the prescription or revision of standards. As the responsibilty is not clearly assigned, the standards are not vigorously implemented nor put under strict supervision. There are only a few specialized standards which are not unified as well. All these problems have seriously affected the specialized production and the economic and technical effects of the machine building industry.

Seeing that standardization is a very important economic and technical policy and technical basic job in the machine building industry, the following provisions are made for the purpose of strengthening the standardization in real earnest in the course of the economic regulation:

1. Each department concerned shall strengthen the leadership over the technical standardization and list it in important agendas. The deputy minister or deputy-director in charge of scientific and technical work in each department concerned shall be determined to make a real start of the technical standardization. He or she shall execute in real earnest the "Regulations of the People's Republic of China on the Administration of Standardization," make an overall deployment every half of the year for the examination of the technical standardization in the light of the concrete conditions in his or her own unit under the direction of the State Bureau of Standardization, and make a brief written report to the State Commission of Machine Building Industry on the situations of the prescription and implementation of standards.

2. The technical policies of standardization shall be executed in an all-round way and the standardization shall be brought into the regulation plans of the machine building industry. The regulation planning coordination group of each trade under the leadership of the State Commission of Machine Building Industry shall take charge of the technical standardization as a matter of great importance and prescribe the technical standards for various trades jointly with the State Bureau of Standardization and by relying on each national standardization technical committee concerned and each appropriate standardization unit (appropriate organization). In future, each department concerned shall lay stress on the prescription of state standards and specialized technical standards and gradually revise the existing technical standards of the department into specialized standards. In the case of a product without a state standard or a specialized standard (ministerial standard), the enterprise shall prescribe an enterprise standard on the basis of its own technical level and in the light of the current international standard. Each enterprise shall obey and execute an appropriate state standard or specialized standard as soon as it is prescribed and promulgated.

3. Each department concerned shall work out a feasible plan for the prescription of technical standards within this year and organize all research units and enterprises concerned to strive for the completion of the prescription of major technical standards within a period of about five years. Before drawing up the plan, a list of standardization systems shall be made first with the unified coordination of the State Bureau of Standardization so as to use it as the basis for drawing up the plan. At present, comprehensive and elementary technical standards shall first be prescribed and the technical standards (state and ministerial standards) which have been prescribed shall also be analysed and sorted out. Those which are still

applicable or which are applicable after amendments or which shall be abolished shall be promulgated and confirmed again before the end of August of 1982 after sorting them out separately. The standards prescribed in future shall make clear the date of execution for each. The standards shall be rechecked once every three to five years and respectively confirmed, revised or annulled. The fulfilment of the tasks to prescribe and revise standards shall be regarded as one of the examination targets for enterprises and research institutes in their fulfilment of plans.

Each department concerned shall make a good job of the prescription of state standards jointly with the State Bureau of Standardization and prescribe the standards for military industry jointly with the National Defence Industry Office.

4. Each department concerned shall perfect the standardization administration organization(or office or bureau) and research organization (in general, a ministry shall set up a standardization research institute and a state bureau shall set up a standardization research office). Leading cadres with professional knowledge and devotion to the cause shall be provided, the professional technical personnel with certain practical experience (those who have been transferred to the posts other than their professional ones shall be returned as far as possible) shall be fully manned and the staff shall be kept stable as far as possible.The standardization technical personnel shall make up one to three per cent of the total of the technical personnel of each unit (factory or institute) and this proportion shall be increased in a unit which undertakes the appropriate standardization tasks. The working conditions in a standardization research organization shall vigorously be improved. In order to speed up the prescription or revision of standards, each department concerned shall organize the existing technical personnel of the units under it to participate in the prescription of technical standards. The personnel, organization and duties shall be ensured. The standardization technical personnel are a component part of the scientific and technical contingents and shall enjoy the same remuneration and conditions.

5. Each department concerned shall select some key institutes or enterprises, make the best possible use of the existing equipment and forces in each appropriate specialized unit of the standardization systems, equip them with necessary measuring and testing equipment and instruments and enable them to become the appraising, examining, measuring, testing and verifying centres for the standards of products in each trade. Each enterprise shall also be provided with proper measuring and testing equipment so as to strictly examine and measure its own products in accordance with technical standards. The expenses required shall be paid from those of technical measures.

6. In the prescription of technical standards, international standards and foreign advanced standards shall vigorously be adopted; meanwhile consideration shall also be given to our country's conditions of resources and energy and current level of industrial technology so that they shall be advanced in technology, rational in economy and reliable in safety.

Each department shall dispatch the comrades who are really engaged in standardization to participate in various professional meetings of the International Standard Organization. It shall vigorously make a good job of the introduction, translation, publication, testing and verification of international standards, conscientiously consider and vigorously adopt international standards and foreign current technical standards.

7. The research and prescription of technical standards shall be included in the five-year scientific and technical development plan and the annual scientific and technical plan of each department concerned and transmitted to lower levels by stages. The expenses for the research and verification of important standards shall be included in the expenditure of scientific research outlays. The State Bureau of Standardization and each department concerned shall be requested to properly increase the subsidies for the prescription and revision of standards. The technical standards approved shall be part of scientific research achievements and shall be rewarded in accordance with relevant provisions.

8. The standardization in the introduction of technology shall be strengthened. Technical standards (which usually contain the achievements of advanced technology) are an important component part of the introduction of foreign advanced technology. Standardization shall be carried out in the introduction of technology in investigations, negotiations, translations, and in all applications up to production. Each department in charge shall in a unified way organize the collection, translation and analysis of the state standards of the countries from which they are to be introduced and relevant enterprise standards. With the prerequisite to ensure against the reduction of the level of the technology introduced or the quality of products, our state standards and specialized standards (ministerial standards) shall vigorously be adopted and improve the sub-

stitution or trial production of the materials made in our country. Otherwise, the introduced standards (the state standards of foreign countries or relevant enterprise standards) and international standards shall be adopted.

The introduced advanced technology and standards shall be absorbed with great efforts and constantly perfected so as to upgrade the standards of our country. Each department in charge of introduction shall be responsible for organizing the coordination and supply of standard interchangeable parts, components and fittings in the introduction of technology.

9. The technical standards of the mechanical and electrical products which conform to the export requirements shall be revised or prescribed and be strictly executed.

Our current standards for the mechanical and electrical products which have gone or are ready to go on the international market shall be revised in accordance with international standards or the current advanced technical standards abroad so that the products shall not be lower than the same kinds of foreign products in performance and quality index and shall be interchangeable so as to meet the demands of the international market and improve the competitive capacity of products. If it is not suitable or temporarily impossible to adopt a unified standard for the same products both for export and for domestic sale, each department shall as soon as possible work out interim specialized standards for the export products jointly with the trades and organizations concerned and report them to the State Commission of Machine Building Industry and the State Bureau of Standardization and Metrology for record. In the production of export mechanical and electrical products, each enterprise shall strictly implement the technical standards for export products so as to ensure the quality of export mechanical and electrical products.

10. The production sections of each department concerned shall conscientiously implement various technical standards in the arrangement for production. The technical standards which have been promulgated and executed are provided with legal effect and the products which do not correspond with the standards shall be unqualified products. The products made without the earnest implementation of various technical standards shall not be appraised to be those of high quality nor be qualified for obtaining various honours of quality or material rewards. All new mechanical and electrical products shall implement the "Procedures for the Examination and Administration of the Standardization of New Mechanical and Electrical Products."

The production permit regulations which are to be prescribed soon shall stipulate that the production of the products which do not implement state standards and specialized standards (ministerial standards) shall be stopped and rectified and no production permits shall be issued. The functionary organization which supervises technical standards is the quality control section of each department concerned. Each department concerned shall also assign a number of appraising and testing centres to conduct standardization examinations of related products and make public the results in the newspapers or magazines concerned.

These Provisions shall be put into effect from the date of promulgation.

PROCEDURES FOR THE ADMINISTRATION OF STANDARDIZATION OF INDUSTRIAL ENTERPRISES (FOR PROVISIONAL IMPLEMENTATION)

(Promulgated by the State Bureau of Standardization and Metrology on November 16, 1981)

Chapter I General Rules

Article 1 The standardization of industrial enterprises (including corporations, head offices of factories, factories, etc., hereinafter mentioned) is a component of business management and the base for the enterprises to achieve scientific management. Making a good job of enterprise standardization plays an important role in the stabilization and improvement of the quality of products, in the rational development of categories and specifications, in the improvement of management and in the increase of economic benefit. These Procedures are formulated in the spirit of the "Regulations of the People's Republic of China on the Administration of Standardization" for the purpose of strengthening the standardization of industrial enterprises.

Article 2 The tasks in the standardization of industrial enterprises are to work out and carry out standards in combination with the overall quality control and the overall economic accounting so as to rationalize the production and technical activities of enterprises and to attain the aims of high quality, high efficiency and low cost.

Article 3 Standardization runs through all aspects of the production and management of enterprises and is related to all departments. Therefore, all the departments and the whole staff of an enterprise shall cooperate closely and jointly make a good job of the standardization of the enterprise.

Chapter II The Objects of Enterprise Standards and Their Prescription, Revision, Examination, Approval and Issuance

Article 4 Technical standards are the backbones of enterprise standards. They are the provisions made for the objects, conditions and methods of production as well as for packing, storage and transportation. The technical standards include those of various products, raw materials and semi-finished products, spare parts and components, technology and equipment, safety measures, sanitation and environmental protection, etc.

To ensure the quality of products and increase economic benefit, appropriate standards of management shall be prescribed by means of the principle of standardization for relevant production and technical management, including the consumption quotas of raw materials and energy, the rules for the maintenance, use and service of equipment, the system for the examination and administration of technical documentation, operating regulations and the provisions for civilized production.

Article 5 The standards of an enterprise shall, in principle, be prescribed and revised by the enterprise with its own organization and approved and issued by the person(s) in charge of the enterprise. In the case of local enterprises, the standards of products used as the terms for the delivery of commodities or the standards used beyond the limits of an enterprise shall be examined, approved and issued by higher authorities of the enterprise or by the bureau of standardization as stipulated by the government of the province, municipality or autonomous region as the case may be; in the case of the enterprises directly under the Central Government (including those under dual leadership), they shall be examined, approved and issued by a specialized bureau or corporation under the department of the State Council in charge or by a unit entrusted therewith and the copies shall be delivered to the bureau of standardization of the province, municipality or autonomous region where the enterprise concerned is located for filing.

Article 6 Enterprise standards shall be prescribed for all products in mass production if there are no national standards or ministerial standards (specialized standards) available. In order to catch up with and surpass the advanced technical levels and satisfy the needs of better use, the quality standards of products shall be prescribed higher than the natural standards and ministerial standards (specialized standards) already established for certain products, and the prescription of the internal controlled standards or special-purpose standards of enterprises is strongly encouraged. Enterprise standards shall not be in conflict with national and ministerial standards (specialized standards).

Article 7 In order to satisfy the requirements of export, an enterprise may directly adopt international standards or foreign advanced standards and it may sign supply contracts or technical agreements as required by the customer.

Article 8 The standards approved by an enterprise shall be duly amended according to the requirements for use and to the development of production technology. The enterprise standards approved by the higher authorities shall generally be reexamined once every two to three years and respectively confirmed, revised or annulled.

Article 9 The contents to be written and the forms of expression of enterprise technical standards shall be handled in the light of the provisions in State Standard No. GB1.1-81.

Chapter III. The Implementation of Standards

Article 10 Enterprises shall conscientiously implement various standards upon their approval and issuing. The technical and material conditions required for the implementation of standards shall be brought into the related plans of the enterprises.

Article 11 All the products regularly made shall be manufactured and examined strictly according to the standards so that the raw materials which are not up to standard shall not be put into production, the semi-finished products which are not up to standard shall not be passed on to the next process and parts or components which are not up to standard shall not be assembled so as to ensure the stable production of the products up to standard and those of the best quality. Certificates of quality shall be signed and issued by the quality examination department of an enterprise as stipulated for the products in keeping with the standards; the products which are not in keeping with the standards shall not be delivered out of the factory. The products which are not up to standard and endanger personal safety or health shall strictly be prohibited from delivery out of the factory.

Article 12 Consideration shall be given to the domestic requirements for standardization when an enterprise introduces technology or equipment from abroad and the introduction shall go through the standardization examination by higher authorities jointly with the standardization administration department.

Article 13 An enterprise shall regularly keep abreast of the developments of the implementation of standards, duly report the problems arising in relation to prescribed standards to the departments concerned, make suggestions as to amendments and continue to implement the original standards until official approval of the amendments is obtained.

Article 14 If an enterprise really has difficulty in the implementation of the standards of higher authorities or the enterprise standards approved by the higher authorities, it shall give reasons in detail and make a report to postpone the time limit and measures for the implementation and shall only postpone the implementation after the examination and approval of the standard approving department.

Chapter IV Rewards and Punishments

Article 15 As technical standards are part of scientific and technical achievements, an enterprise or higher authorities shall give praise or rewards for those with good technical and economic effects and to the units and personnel that have made remarkable achievements in the standardization of the enterprise.

Article 16 Those who do not exert themselves to implement standards and cause adverse results shall be criticized; necessary punishments shall be imposed on those who violate the provisions of standards and cause serious accidents; economic responsibility shall be investigated and affixed on those who wilfully reduce the standards, deceive customers and cause economic losses and the cases shall even be dealt with according to law.

Chapter V Enterprise Standardization Working Organization, Personnel and Powers

Article 17 The enterprise standardization shall be under the direct leadership of the person in charge of production technical work of an enterprise (or the chief engineer) and an appropriate standardization working organization and full-time (or part-time) personnel shall be provided for in accordance with the scale of production and the demand of management. A large or medium enterprise shall set up a standardization office or a quality management and standardization office and shall set up a standardization group or provide full-time or part-time personnel in a technical office concerned or in a workshop according to the demand forming a standardization working system of the whole enterprise; a small enterprise shall be provided with standardization full-time and part-time personnel.

Article 18 Enterprise standardization technical personnel shall have a certain understanding of policy matters and organizing ability, possess full professional technical knowledge and be familiar with the management or production. In general, standardization technical personnel shall make up one to three per cent of the total number of technical personnel in an enterprise and this proportion shall correspondingly be increased in an enterprise with greater working volume of standardization. The number of standardization technical personnel shall be kept relatively stable.

Article 19 The tasks of an enterprise standardization organization (full-time personnel) are:

1. To carry out the standardization guiding principles and policies of higher authorities and work out the standardization plans of the enterprise;
2. To organize the prescription and revision of enterprise standards;
3. To organize the implementation of national standards, ministerial standards (specialized standards) and enterprise standards, participate in the supervision of the quality of products and deal with the problems in the implementation of standards;
4. To participate in the design of new products, put forward the requirement for standardization and conduct the standardization examination of technical documentation properly;
5. To unify, classify and manage various standards, set up a filing system and gather both domestic and overseas standardization information and data;
6. To make a good job of the statistics and analysis of results of standardization and sum up experience;
7. To assume the standardization tasks it is entrusted with by higher authorities.

Article 20 An enterprise standardization working organization (full-time personnel) is empowered to check an act of violation of the provisions of standards, make suggestions as to its disposition and report it to the person(s) in charge of the enterprise or directly to the higher department by bypassing the immediate leadership; it (they) shall be entitled to refuse to endorse a technical paper which is not up to standard.

Chapter VI Supplementary Provisions

Article 21 The basic principles of these Procedures shall also be applicable to enterprises of communications and transportation as well as construction projects.

Article 22 Each enterprise shall formulate the detailed rules for the implementation on the basis of these Procedures.

Article 23 These Procedures shall be put into provisional implementation as from the date of promulgation. "Several Provisions for Strengthening the Administration of the Enterprise Standards of Industrial and Agricultural Products" promulgated by the State Bureau of Standardization on February 16, 1979 shall be annulled at the same time.

Article 24 The State Bureau of Standardization and Metrology shall be responsible for the Interpretation of these Procedures.

(PROVISIONAL) PROCEDURES FOR THE ADMINISTRATION OF THE ADOPTION OF INTERNATIONAL STANDARDS:

(March 17, 1982)

I General Rules

Article 1 The adoption of international standards is a tendency developing in all countries in the world. These Procedures are formulated in accordance with the "Regulations of the People's Republic of China on the Administration of Standardization" and the relevant provisions of the state standardization organization in order to promote technical interchange, improve the quality of products, expand foreign trade, suit the domestic needs, increase the prescribing and revising speeds of standards and heighten the levels of standards.

Article 2 The vigorous adoption of international standards or foreign advanced standards is an important technical and economic policy of our country today. The adoption shall closely be combined with the national conditions of our country and in conformity to the relevant laws, regulations and policies of our country so that the standards adopted can be advanced in technology, economical and rational, safe and reliable as well as realistic and practical.

Article 3 International standards generally mean those prescribed by the International Standard Organization (ISO) and the International Electrotechnical Commission (IEC). The standards of other authoritative international organizations and those stipulated in relevant international pacts or conventions are also part of the ranges to be adopted.

Foreign advanced standards mean the foreign regional standards internationally recognized to be authoritative, the state standards of industrial advanced countries and the organization standards internationally in force. Each department shall choose and adopt the best after conscientious consideration in the light of the needs of its own profession and the international tendencies developed.

II The Principles of the Adoption of International Standards and Foreign Advanced Standards

Article 4 The guiding principles of conscientious consideration, vigorous adoption and dealing with different things in different ways shall be taken in the adoption of international standards and foreign advanced standards.

International standards are adopted into our state standards in two ways: one is equivalent adoption and the other is referential adoption.

The meanings of the equivalent adoption include the following:

(1) To be fully equivalent to international standards without any editorial amendments or with a few amendments;

(2) To be equivalent to international standards with few technical differences.

Referential adoption means that some changes shall be made in accordance with the natural resources and economic conditions of our country and the traditional features of our products, but the performance of products and the targets of their quality shall be equivalent to international standards and our standards shall be coordinated with international standards in such aspects as interchangeability, safety, public health and so on.

Article 5 In general, the current basic ones in international standards, such as technical terms, symbols, tolerance and fitness, mechanical drawings, international system of units, etc., shall equivalently be adopted.

Article 6 In general, the current methodological ones in international standards, such as sampling methods, testing methods, measuring methods, counting methods, etc., shall equivalently be adopted.

Article 7 Measures shall be taken to adopt equivalently as far as possible those relating to personal safety, public health, environmental protection, etc. in international standards.

Article 8 Those products in international standards which are advanced in technology and economic and rational shall conscientiously be considered and vigorously be adopted in the light of the actual conditions of the specialized trade itself:

(1) Technical specifications, quality indices, installation and connection dimensions and requirements for interchangeability and the

standards which are advantageous to the upgrading and generation renewal of domestic products and to the export of foreign trade shall equivalently be adopted. If necessary, the relevant provisions which are not included in international standards shall be supplemented.

(2) Those with some changes required in accordance with different conditions in our country shall referentially be adopted. The referential adoption shall accord with the provisions in Article 4.

(3) Except for those which are really irrational, a small number of quality indices and requirements in the current standards of our country which are higher than the international ones shall, in general, not be lowered.

Article 9 There is often the recommendation of several schemes or the mere reference to the main functions of products in international standards and in order to prevent the disorder of categories and specifications, the international current standards for a certain product shall, in principle, be selected in the adoption of such international standards and necessary provisions shall be supplemented for the basic parameters, standard series, design specifications, raw materials, etc. of the product.

Article 10 The international standards in the developing technical fields such as laser, optical-fiber communication, electronic computers, etc. shall generally be equivalently adopted.

Article 11 The adoption of foreign advanced standards into the state standards is also divided into two kinds as stipulated in Article 4, i.e., the equivalent (fully equivalent or equivalent) adoption and the referential adoption which are analogous to those in the adoption of international standards. Their meanings are also identical.

III The Ways to Adopt International Standards and Foreign Advanced Standards

Article 12 When an international standard or a foreign advanced standard is to be adopted, investigations or necessary tests and verifications shall be carried out according to different conditions in respect of technical terms, symbols, testing methods, specifications, etc.. The other relevant international standards cited in the international standards shall also vigorously be adopted as our state standards and if necessary, tests and verifications shall be carried out so as to make them feasible.

Article 13 An international standard shall be adopted in conformity to the provisions in ISO/IEC "Guiding Rule 3" and "Guiding Rule 21" (1981 edition). In the introduction, there shall be the same title, number and publishing year as in the international standards and the following shall be indicated:

(1) The equivalent degree between the state standard and the international standard;

(2) What editorial amendments have been made to the international standard;

(3) What technical differences there are from the international standard.

Article 14 In the equivalent adoption of an international standard, dual numbers shall be used on the cover and the first page.

A state standard which is fully equivalent to an international standard shall be numbered as follows:

GB x x x x − x x = ISO x x x x − x x

A state standard which is equivalent to an international standard shall be numbered as follows:

GB x x x x − x x ≈ IEC x x x x − x x

If the product performance, quality index and other aspects of a state standard in which an international standard is referentially adopted are analogous to those of the international standard, this shall be clearly indicated in the notes attached to the state standard. For example:

GB x x x x − x x ~ ISO x x x x − x x

Article 15 In addition to the brief explanations in the introduction, the explanatory notes, editorial amendments or technical differences made in the equivalent adoption shall be annotated at the bottom of the page where a related clause is located so as to indicate its difference from the international standard by adding any one of the following headings:

(1) If the contents are only confined to editorial amendments, the heading shall be "The Notes in Adoption;"

(2) If the contents are not confined to editorial amendments, the heading shall be "The Differences in Adoption."

In the case of a state standard into which an international standard is equivalently adopted, each department in charge shall strictly examine, proofread and ratify the technical contents and editorial aspects of the translation in conformity to the requirements in ISO/IEC "Guiding Rule 3" and "Guiding Rule 21" (1981 edition).

Article 16 If a foreign advanced standard is used in a state standard, the same title, number and publishing year shall be clearly marked in the introduction as in the foreign advanced standard adopted. And in the notes attached to the state standard, the adoption degree (i.e., fully equivalent, equivalent or referential), editorial amendments or technical differences shall be indicated in brief.

IV The Working Procedure for the Adoption of International Standards and Foreign Advanced Standards

Article 17 Each department in charge (or the standardization specialized technical committee) shall list the international standards and foreign advanced standards to be adopted as state standards in the standardization long-term and annual plans of the department after conscientious consideration on the basis of working out the list of standard systems. They shall also be submitted to the State Bureau of Standardization and Metrology for gathering, synthesizing and balancing and the bureau shall bring them into the national standardization long-term and annual plans.

Article 18 In accordance with the plan of the items to adopt international standards, the department in charge shall assign the undertaking unit to take the international standard for the draft state standard, print it and distribute it among the member units of the drafting group to invite comments and, if necessary, enlarge the distribution to major production, use and scientific research units and to institutions of higher education for examination; the time limit should be generally not less than two months and not more than three months. Those which do not return their comments when the time limit is exceeded shall be considered as having agreed to the draft.

Tests and verifications shall be arranged for those to be tested and verified.

The undertaking unit shall gather the comments from different quarters, the situations of their disposition and relevant data and submit them to the department in charge within two months.

Article 19 On the basis of the comments from the undertaking unit and from different quarters and relevant data, the department in charge shall conclude through synthesis and analysis whether it shall be adopted. If the requirements of an international standard can be attained within two to three years, it shall be adopted as a state standard and meanwhile the enterprise shall be provided with a definite time limit for the preparation for production.

Article 20 With regard to the state standard by means of the equivalent adoption or the referential adoption, the department in charge shall write an examination report and submit it together with the explanations of the preparation, the draft standard, the original of the international standard, the summary and disposition list of the comments from various departments and necessary verification reports to the State Bureau of Standardization for examination and approval. The number of copies to be submitted shall be handled in accordance with the relevant provisions for the prescription of state standards.

The department in charge shall simplify the formalities of examination and verification and shorten the time for them, which generally shall not exceed two months; the time for the State Bureau of Standardization to examine and approve of a standard shall not exceed one month.

Article 21 The similarly equivalent adoption or the referential adoption of a foreign advanced standard as a state standard shall be handled in accordance with this working procedure.

V The Division of Labour in and the Material Conditions for the Adoption of International Standards and Foreign Advanced Standards

Article 22 The Standard Library under the State Bureau of Standardization and Metrology shall be responsible for establishing contact for and supplying international standards, foreign advanced standards and related documents and data.

The Technical Standards Publishing House shall be responsible for the publication or printing of the translations of international standards and foreign advanced standards.

Article 23 The appropriate standardization unit shall notify the department concerned of the data of international or foreign standards obtained by various departments through professional channels. One photocopy of the original and three copies of the translation published for each standard shall be submitted to the Standard Library and the library shall circulate a notice of it in the "Reports on the Data of Foreign Standards."

The standardization research organization of each department shall be responsible for organizing the translation, examination, proofreading and ratification of international standards and foreign advanced standards and regularly circulate notices of translation and publication to the State Bureau of Standardization, each department concerned and the standardization organization of each province, municipality or autonomous region.

Article 24 The standardization research organization and the appropriate specialized unit of each department shall regularly keep abreast of the developments of the prescription or revision of international standards and urge the units concerned to duly consider the draft international standards and relevant documents and put forward the comments on their positions.

Each department shall vigorously recommend the advanced standards of our country to the International Standard Organization so as to have them brought into international standards.

Article 25 The expenses of data, verifications, conferences and official business required for the adoption of international standards and foreign advanced standards shall be handled in the light of the relevant provisions for outlays and expenditures jointly printed and distributed by the Ministry of Finance and the State Bureau of Standardization according to the grades of the standards.

Article 26 The studies and verifications of important standards shall be brought into scientific research plans.

The measuring or testing equipment, test benches, etc. which shall be purchased for verifications shall be brought into the plans of the department in charge for the construction of measuring and testing bases.

The department in charge shall guarantee the material and technical conditions such as the additional equipment and measuring or testing instruments required for the implementation of standards in production and bring them into the plans of renewal, transformation and technical organizational measures.

Article 27 The adoption of international standards or foreign advanced standards to our state standards shall be treated equally to the prescription or revision of state standards and rewards shall be given to the excellent ones.

VI Supplementary Provisions

Article 28 The adoption of international standards or foreign advanced standards into professional or enterprise standards shall be carried out in the light of the provisions in these Procedures.

These Procedures shall also be applicable to construction and other departments.

Each department or each province, municipality or autonomous region shall separately formulate the specific rules for the implementation on the basis of these Procedures.

Article 29 These Procedures shall be put into effect as from the date of promulgation. The "Interim Provisions for the Procedures for the Direct Adoption of International Standards as Our State Standards" promulgated by the State Bureau of Standardization and Metrology as Document No. Guo-Biao-Fa 081(1979) shall be annulled at the same time.

Article 30 The State Bureau of Standardization shall be responsible for the interpretation of these Procedures.

THE ANNOTATIONS OF (PROVISIONAL) PROCEDURES FOR THE ADMINISTRATION OF THE ADOPTION OF INTERNATIONAL STANDARDS AND FOREIGN ADVANCED STANDARDS

I The Range of International Standards

(1) They generally mean the standards prescribed by the International Standard Organization (ISO) and the International Electrotechnical Commission (IEC).

(2) Various organizations of the United Nations, such as the International Telecommunication Union (ITU), the Consultative Committee of International Telegraph and Telephone (CCITT), Comité Consultatif Internationale des Radiocommunication (CCIR), Union Internationale des Chemines de Fer (UIC), Union Postale Universelle (UPU), the United Nations Food and Agriculture Organization (UNFAO), the World Health Organization (WHO), the Intergovernmental Maritime

Consultative Organization (IMCO), etc, also have their own standards or proposals and there are also standards and proposals in international conventions. Although these organizations are not specialized standardization organizations, the standards prescribed by them carry certain authority and are internationally recognized.

II The Range of Foreign Advanced Standards

(1) Influential regional standards, such as the standards prescribed by Comité Européen de Normalisation (CEN), Comité Européen de Normalisation Electrotechnique (CENELEC), etc.;

(2) The state standards of industrial advanced countries, such as the American National Standards Institute (ANSI), Deutsche Institute fur Normen (DIN), the British Standards (BS), the Japanese Industrial Standards (JIS), Norm Francaise (NF), the state standards of the Soviet Union (IOCT), etc.

(3) The organization standards internationally recognized to be authoritative, such as those of the American Society of Testing Material (ASTM), those of the American Petroleum Institution (API), those the Electronic Industry Association (EIA) of the U.S.A., the military (MIL) standards of the U.S.A., the American Underwriters' Laboratory Safety Standards (UL), "Ship Classification Specifications and Regulations" of the Lloyd's Register of Shipping of the United Kingdom, etc.

19

AWARDS AND PROTECTION OF INVENTION

Awards/ Patents

REGULATIONS OF THE PEOPLE'S REPUBLIC OF CHINA ON AWARDS FOR INVENTIONS

(Promulgated by the State Council on December 18, 1978)

Article 1 These Regulations are formulated for the purpose of encouraging inventions by granting awards, promoting the modernization of science and technology and speeding up the socialist construction.

Article 2 An invention referred to in these Regulations is a significant new scientific and technical achievement and it must be accompanied with the following three conditions before becoming qualified:

(1) Being original;

(2) Being advanced;

(3) Proved applicable through actual use.

Article 3 The State Scientific and Technological Commission of the People's Republic of China (hereinafter simply referred to as the SSTC) exercises the unified leadership of the awards for inventions countrywide. Each department of the State Council and the scientific and technological commission of each province, municipality or autonomous region (hereinafter simply referred to as the STC of the province, municipality or autonomous region) shall be responsible for the leadership of the report and examination of the inventions in the department and the area.

Article 4 The report of an invention by (collective or individual) inventor(s) shall include the following contents:-

(1) Name of the invention;

(2) Detailed contents of the invention;

(3) Identity of the inventor (s);

(4) Reasons for the invention;

(5) Time of completion of the invention;

(6) Date of report;

(7) Opinions of examination of the reporting unit.

Article 5 The procedure for the report and approval of an invention is as follows:

(1) The report of an invention by inventor(s) shall be submitted level by level in accordance with the related establishments. Meanwhile, its copies shall be submitted to the STC of the province, municipality or autonomous region and the department of the State Council in charge.

(2) The department or bureau of each province, municipality or autonomous region shall duly examine the reported inventions upon receipt and report those which conform to the provisions in Article 2 of these Regulations to the STC of the province, municipality or autonomous region and the department of the State Council in charge.

(3) The scientific and technological association at each level below the province, municipality or autonomous region and each society shall recommend the inventions to the department or bureau concerned of the province, municipality or autonomous region; the Scientific and Technological Association of China and each society shall recommend inventions to each relevant department of the State Council in charge.

(4) The STC of each province, municipality or autonomous region and each department of the State Council in charge shall duly examine the reported inventions upon receipt, appraise and determine the grades of the awards for those which conform to the provisions in Article 2 of these Regulations and report them to the State Scientific and Technological Commission.

(5) The State Scientific and Technological Commission (SSTC) sets up an inventions appraisal and selection committee which shall take charge of the appraisal and selection of inventions, the evaluation of the grades of awards and the report of the approved ones to the SSTC for examination, approval and granting of award.

(6) The procedure for the report, examination and approval of the inventions for the special use of national defence shall be otherwise stipulated by the Science and Technology Commission for National Defence and the Office in Charge of National Defence Industry (hereinafter simply referred to the STCND and the OCNDI); the STCND and the OCNDI shall examine the inventions for the special use of national defence, evaluate the grades of awards and report the approved one to the State Scientific and Technological Commission for examination, approval and granting of award.

Metrology or the unit concerned entrusted it shall

Article 6 On granting awards for inventions, the parties concerned shall insist on putting the proletarian politics in command and implement the principle of combining moral encouragement and material reward with the stress on the former.

The awards for inventions shall be divded into four grades according to the degrees of their effect and significance as follows:

Grade of Award	Award of Honour	Money Reward
1st	Invention Certificate & Medal	10,000 yuan
2nd	Invention Certificate & Medal	5,000 yuan
3rd	Invention Certificate & Medal	2,000 yuan
4th	Invention Certificate & Medal	1,000 yuan

Article 7 An especially significant invention shall be classified as special-grade and granted a special-grade award. The report for such shall be made by the SSTC to the State Council for approval and a separate award will be granted accordingly.

Article 8 The monetary reward obtained for a collective invention (including one from a cooperative unit) shall be reasonably distributed according to the degrees of the contributions from the inventors. The monetary reward for an individual's invention shall be given to the individual.

Article 9 All inventions belong to the state. Every unit in the whole country (including those of collective ownership) can make use of the invention(s) when it needs to.

Article 10 With regard to the announcement of the contents of an invention and the classifications of its secrecy, the department of the State Council in charge shall put forward the suggestions to the SSTC for approval; the announcement of the contents of an invention for the special use of national defence and the classifications of its secrecy shall be approved by the STCND or the OCNDI.

Article 11 The supply of the classified contents of an invention to foreign trade or other causes must be approved by the SSTC.

Article 12 The overseas Chinese residing abroad and foreigners may report their inventions to the SSTC for awards as stipulated in these Regulations after examination and approval.

Article 13 If there is any dispute on an invention, it shall be reported to higher authorities which shall conscientiously investigate and handle the matter.

Article 14 With regard to the inventions of the masses, every department or unit shall give encouragement to them and take serious and earnest as well as realistic and practical attitudes towards them. In the implementation of the rewarding system, every department or unit shall strengthen the ideological and political work, advocate the spirit of the socialist extensive cooperation and oppose such unhealthy tendencies as selfish departmentalism, individualism, mutual resistance against cooperation, etc. It shall criticize and check such acts as stifling inventions, playing trickery in inventions or plagiarizing the fruits of others' hard work and impose punishments on those whose cases are vile or even have them punished according to law.

Article 15 These Regulations shall be put into effect from the date of the promulgation of the State Council.

REGULATIONS ON AWARDS FOR QUALITY PRODUCTS OF THE PEOPLE'S REPUBLIC OF CHINA

(Approved by the State Council and Promulgated by the State Economic Commission on June 30, 1979)

Chapter I General Principles

Article 1 In order to encourage industrial enterprises to keep improving the quality of their products and strive to make more high-quality goods as required by China's socialist modernization programme and the need to steadily raise the people's living standards and increase exports, the state has decided to confer State Quality Awards on fine-quality industrial products.

Article 2 State Quality Awards are issued annually after evaluation, selection, consideration and approval of the eligible products. The awards are divided into two classes: Class A — gold medals; and Class B — silver medals.

Chapter II Qualifications

Article 3 All products to be granted State Quality Awards must conform to the following qualifications:

1. They are suited to the needs of, are reliable and satisfactory to the users, and are sought for and appreciated in domestic and world markets;
2. Their quality indices are higher than those laid down in all existing technical standards, on a par with or close to the advanced international standards for the same category or products, or the products are unique and original in design and possess fine traditional qualities;
3. The products are placed first in quality contests among Chinese products of the same kind; and
4. Their designs have been finalized and approved for serial production, and the quality of the products improves steadily.

Chapter III Selection and Approval

Article 4 Applications for State Quality Awards shall be submitted by the producers of high-quality products and studied by the organizations concerned under the auspices of the revolutionary committees of the provinces, municipalities and autonomous regions. If the applications are accepted, the products shall be tested, evaluated and selected nationally by the departments in charge under the State Council. The results shall be re-examined by the State Administration of Standards and the General Administration for Industry and Commerce and reported to the State Quality Award Board for consideration and approval.

Article 5 The selection and approval of products for State Quality Awards must follow the principal of "high standards and strict demands." Resort to deceit or deception is strictly forbidden and offenders shall be dealt with seriously on the merits of each case.

Chapter IV Awards

Article 6 All State Quality Awards shall be issued by the State Economic Commission, generally during the annual "Quality Promotion Month."

Article 7 The issuing of State Quality Awards represents a major policy to encourage the development of fine-quality products and must be regarded seriously. The localities, departments and units shall no longer issue medals, badges or cups as prizes for any industrial products.

Chapter V Symbols of Honour

Article 8 Symbols of honour indicative of medal-winning high-quality products may be affixed to the products which have won State Quality Awards and to their directions and trademarks.

Article 9 The quality of all award-winning products may only be improved and not lowered. No unqualified products are allowed to use the symbols for State Quality Awards.

Article 10 If the quality of any award-winning products should deteriorate, the producer should immediately stop using the symbols for State Quality Awards and promptly report this to the relevant authorities. When the original quality is restored through improvement, the producer may apply to the departments concerned for using these symbols again.

Chapter VI Appendices

Article 11 The policy toward quality products is to give them higher prices and priority in the supply of raw and semi-processed materials, fuel and electricity.

Article 12 The expenses involved in the issuance of State Quality Awards shall be defrayed by special allocations from the state treasury.

Article 13 The right of interpretation of these Regulations is vested in the State Economic Commission.

Article 14 These Regulations shall be put into effect from the day they are promulgated.

REGULATIONS REGARDING THE NATURAL SCIENCE AWARDS OF THE PEOPLE'S REPUBLIC OF CHINA

Promulgated by the State Council
(December 21, 1979)

Article 1 In order to encourage and bring into full play the initiative and creativeness of scientific workers, speed up the development of China's sciences and promote socialist modernization, the present regulations are hereby formulated.

Article 2 Awards for natural sciences shall be conferred on those collectives or individuals whose research into the phenomena, characteristics or laws of nature have produced results with great significance for scientific and technological development.

Article 3 Awards for natural sciences are divided into four grades:

First-class awards include a certificate of honour, a first-class medal and a monetary award of 10,000 yuan.

Second-class awards include a certificate of honour, a second-class medal and a monetary award of 5,000 yuan.

Third-class awards include a certificate of honour, a third-class medal and a monetary award of 2,000 yuan.

Fourth-class awards include a certificate of honour, a fourth-class medal and a monetary award of 1,000 yuan.

Article 4 A special award shall be given to those whose scientific research results, as provided in Article 2, are of especially great significance. Separate awards for such cases shall be reported by the Scientific and Technological Commission of China to the State Council for approval.

Article 5 Recommendations for awards can be made by research institutes, institutions of higher learning, national academic societies or by a group of over ten scientific workers at or above the level of associate research fellows.

Article 6 Preliminary examination of the items recommended for award shall be organized, in accordance with their special fields, by the Chinese Academy of Sciences, the Ministry of Education, the Scientific and Technological Association of China, the State Agriculture Commission, the Ministry of Public Health, the State Economic Commission, the Science and Technology Commissions for National Defence and the Office in Charge of National Defence Industry of the State Council. In the preliminary examination, the related units should hold meetings, with the participation of those in the same trade or occupation, to choose items for award through public evaluation and make suggestions on the grade of the award.

Article 7 The issuance of awards is under the unified leadership of the Scientific and Technological Commission.

The Natural Science Awards Committee under the Commission is in charge of evaluating items and grades for awards. Its recommendations will be examined and approved by the Commission which will confer the awards.

Article 8 When the natural science award belongs to an individual, the certificate of honour, medal and monetary award will be conferred on the individual; when the award belongs to a collective, the certificate of honour will go to the collective, the medal will go to the collective and the personnel who made the biggest contributions in the scientific research, and the monetary award will be distributed among the participants in the research effort in proportion to their contributions.

Article 9 The natural science awards may be conferred, in accordance with the regulations, upon those Chinese nationals residing in foreign countries and foreigners who are engaged in natural science research and whose outstanding achievements have contributed enormously to the development of science and technology in the People's Republic of China.

Article 10 Recommendation and assessment of items for awards should be practical, realistic and serious. Cases of malpractice for selfish ends and deception will be dealt with sternly according to the seriousness of each case.

Article 11 The regulations will be put into effect on the date of promulgation. In cases of contravention with previous regulations regarding the natural science awards, the present regulations will hold.

SUPPLEMENTARY PROVISIONS FOR IMPLEMENTATION OF THE "REGULATIONS ON AWARDS FOR QUALITY PRODUCTS OF THE PEOPLE'S REPUBLIC OF CHINA"

(Printed and issued by the State Economic Commission on February 28,1981)

Since the implementation in 1979, the "Regulations on Awards for Quality Products of the People's Republic of China" have played a good driving role in mobilizing the broad masses of workers and staff members on the industrial and communications fronts to launch quality emulation, carry out overall quality management, endeavour to improve the quality of products and meet the demands of users. In order to implement these Regulations better and further improve the selection of quality products through public appraisal, the following supplementary provisions are made on the basis of the summary of practical experience.

I Qualifications for Awards

1. The products with applications for State Quality Awards shall be provided with the following in overall conformity to the four qualifications for awards stipulated in the "Regulations on Awards for Quality Products of the People's Republic of China:"

(1) The quality products named by the departments of the State Council in charge and by provinces, municipalities and autonomous regions.

(2) The enterprises have carried out overall quality management and are therefore provided with the necessary conditions for ensuring the production of quality products.

(3) The enterprises have prescribed and implemented the internally-controlled standards or norms which are better than the current technical standards; the products with trademarks customarily used shall be provided with the trademarks approved by the General Administration for Industry and Commerce for registration; provided with the product quality examination records of the last two years; provided with the inspection data and conclusive certificates of the inspection organizations designated by the departments concerned of the State Council or the economic commissions (or departments of standardization) of provinces, municipalities and autonomous regions; with the appraisals of major users; with the data of quality contrast with the advanced levels of the products of the same kinds at home and abroad.

2. The following products shall be selected through public appraisal in priority under the conditions of the overall conformity to the four qualifications for awards stipulated in the "Regulations on Awards for Quality Products of the People's Republic of China:"

(1) The products which have greater influences on the national economy and the people's livelihood;

(2) Good and cheap products which are popular with the broad masses of the people;

(3) Those which enjoy good reputation and have strong competitive capacity and which can be exported in exchange for more foreign currencies;

(4) Those in large batches, at low cost and with less material consumption in production.

3. The following products shall not be appraised for State Quality Awards:

(1) Agricultural and sideline products;

(2) The industrial products which do not go through production processing (e.g., raw coal, ores, crude oil, natural gas, logs, etc.) and electricity.

(3) The industrial products which fall into disuse;

(4) Those which are assembled with the parts and components supplied from abroad, Hong Kong and Macao.

II Methods of Appraisal and Examination

The following amendments and supplements shall be made to the ways of appraisal and examination:

(1) The methods of appraisal by stages and in groups shall be adopted for State Quality Awards, namely, some products shall be appraised each year and each category of products shall, in principal, be appraised once every three to five years.

(2) The department in charge of products shall formulate the plan for the appraisal of the

products for State Quality Awards by stages and in groups according to the characteristics of the trade and notify each province, municipality or autonomous region and the departments concerned of the plan.

(3) The producing enterprises shall apply for State Quality Awards in stipulated forms in accordance with the qualifications for awards and the above plan for the appraisal. The enterprises directly under each department of the State Council shall directly apply to the department in charge; the applications from local enterprises shall be submitted to the departments in charge by means of the appropriate channels of products after the examination and consent of the economic commission of the province, municipality or autonomous region jointly with the department of standardization and the administration for industry and commerce.

(4) Each department of the State Council in charge of products shall make a strict examination and a scientific appraisal of the products for which the provinces, municipalities and autonomous regions or the enterprises directly under it apply for State Quality Awards and put forward a list of the appraisal in advance of the State Quality Awards before July 15 each year. The list shall be published by the Office of the State Quality Award Board in a unified way so as to solicit opinions from the general public, and the Office shall examine and report the opinions to the State Quality Award Board for examination and determination after each department in charge gathers and considers them. The Board shall grant gold medals or silver medals in the "Quality Promotion Month."

(5) A product which has won a State Quality Award shall participate again in the next selection through public appraisal and shall win an additional award if it is selected again.

(6) A quality product which has won a State Quality Award shall be regularly or irregularly rechecked during the appraisal and competition period. The products of the enterprises directly under each department and those under the dual leadership of the central and local authorities shall be rechecked by the department in charge; the products of local enterprises shall be rechecked by the economic commission of each province, municipality or autonomous region jointly with the bureau of standardization, the administration for industry and commerce and the specialized department (or bureau). The results of the rechecking shall be submitted to each ministry in charge and the State Bureau of Standardization. If the reduction of the quality of a product is found, it shall be improved within a definite time or an application shall be made to the State Quality Award Board for the cancellation of the title of "State Quality Product."

(7) A quality inspection and evaluation unit shall take charge of the scientific selective examination and evaluation of the quality of products and furnish the data. An enterprise which sends products for examination and evaluation shall pay it certain examination and evaluation charges as stipulated.

III Guideline Provisions for the Selection of Products under an Appropriate Department in Charge

1. The products for civil use and those for the common use of the military and the people but mainly for civil use which are produced by military industries shall be selected by means of the appropriate channels of civil products.

2. The products produced by civil enterprises for military use shall be selected by means of the appropriate channels of military industrial products, of which the raw materials and accessory equipment to form complete sets of military industrial products shall be selected by the departments in charge of the enterprises.

3. The products for military use shall be selected by the departments of the State Council in charge and each province, municipality or autonomous region shall no longer select or name local military industrial quality products.

4. The products produced by several departments shall be appraised and selected by the ministry in specific charge of them; or appraised and selected through the consultation between each department concerned with the ministry in charge for determination or by the joint appraisal and examination team organized.

When a ministry in specific charge of the products organizes the appraisal and competition of products, it shall pay attention to the invitation of the enterprises under other departments which produce the products of the same kinds to participate in the appraisal and competition.

5. Each prefecture, city or county under the province, municipality or autonomous region or each specialized department (bureau) of the province, municipality or autonomous region shall organize the appraisal and competition of the quality of products according to specific conditions , but shall not name any quality products.

REGULATIONS ON REWARDS FOR RATIONALIZATION PROPOSALS AND TECHNOLOGICAL IMPROVEMENTS

(Promulgated by the State Council on March 16, 1982)

Chapter I General Rules

Article 1 These Regulations are formulated for the purpose of encouraging workers and staff members to put forward rationalization proposals energetically, endeavour to carry out technological innovations, promote the development of the national economy and speed up the socialist modernization construction.

Article 2 Rewards shall be given in accordance with these Regulations for the rationalization proposals of improving production or the technological improvements put forward by workers and staff members (collectively or individually) which enable the production or work of a certain unit to make remarkable benefit through experiments, research and practical application.

Article 3 Rationalization proposals and technological improvements include the following contents:

(1) The improvement or the improvement of the quality of industrial products or building structures, the improvement or development of the varieties or breeds of biologic species and the development of new products.

(2) The improvement of technological methods, testing or examining methods, cultivation techniques, plant protection techniques, breeding techniques, safety techniques, medical or hygienic or labour safety techniques and the storage, maintenance and transport techniques of materials and so on.

(3) The improvement of tools, equipment, instruments or devices.

(4) The technical measures to make more effective use of raw materials, other materials, fuel, power, equipment and natural conditions.

(5) The improvement of designs, statistics, calculation and other techniques.

Article 4 These Regulations shall be applicable to the enterprises and institutions of the people's ownership. The units not under the people's ownership shall execute these Regulations accordingly.

Chapter II Rewards

Article 5 To give rewards for rationalization proposals and technological improvemnts, the principle of combining moral encouragement and material reward with the emphasis on the former shall be put into implementation. Commendation, certificates of merit and monetary rewards shall be given to those who contribute to rationalization proposals or technological improvements.

Article 6 The rewards for the rationalization proposals or technological improvements adopted shall be divided into four grades according to the degrees of their annual economic benefit:

Grade of Reward	Annual Economic Benefit	Money Reward	Reward of Honour
1st	more than 1,000,000 yuan	1,000 to 2,000 yuan	Certificate of Merit
2nd	more than 100,000 yuan	500 to 1,000 yuan	Certificate of Merit
3rd	more than 10,000 yuan	200 to 500 yuan	Certificate of Merit
4th	less than 10,000 yuan	less than 200 yuan	Commendation

The annual economic benefit of a rationalization proposal or a technological improvement shall be calculated as that of the year from the time of adoption.

Article 7 The rewards shall be graded according to the degree of effect and significance of a rationalization proposal or a technological improvement which improves labour conditions, ensures safe production or eliminates environmental pollution, the economic benefit of which cannot be directly calculated.

Article 8 The monetary reward for a project collectively completed shall be rationally distributed according to the degrees of contributions.

Article 9 The limits of authority for the examination and approval of rewards: The rewards for rationalization proposals and technological improvements shall be examined and approved by the adopting units and reported to higher authorities in charge for filing.

Article 10 Rewards shall be paid by the adopting units. The rewards paid by producing units shall be included in the costs of production and those paid by non-productive units shall be reimbursed from the operating expenses.

Chapter III Examination and Handling

Article 11 An enterprise or an institution shall be provided with an appropriate organization or personnel to take charge of the examination, implementation and rewarding of rationalization proposals and technological improvements. When any dispute arises between a proposer and an examination unit, it shall be submitted to a higher department in charge for handling.

Article 12 Significant rationalization proposals or technological improvements or those which cannot be handled by a unit itself shall be submitted to the higher department in charge for handling. Rewards shall be given by the adopting units after adoption.

Article 13 A rationalization proposal or a technological improvement shall be proved successful through tests or appraisal before adoption.

Article 14 Those who seek honour through fraud and deception shall be criticized, the rewards given shall be recovered by deducting them from their income or deposits and disciplinary punishments shall be imposed on those whose cases are serious.

Chapter IV Supplementary Provisions

Article 15 The State Economic Commission shall be responsible for the interpretation of these Regulations.

Article 16 The people's government of each province, municipality or autonomous region and each department of the State Council shall formulate the rules for the implementation of these Regulations in the light of specific conditions.

Article 17 These Regulations shall be put into effect from the date of promulgation. The "Regulations on the Rewards for Technological Improvements" promulgated in 1963 shall be annulled at the same time.

PROVISIONAL REGULATIONS ON THE GUARANTEE OF INVENTION RIGHTS AND PATENT RIGHTS

(Approved by the 45th Government Administrative Meeting of the Government Administration Council on August 11, 1950)

Article 1 These Regulations are formulated for the purpose of encouraging citizens' research of the science of production and promoting the development of the national economic construction.

Article 2 All the inventions of the citizens of the People's Republic of China, whether collective or individual, in production shall be reported to the central authorities in charge for examination and verification and the inventors shall be entitled to apply for invention rights or patent rights on their own free will.

Article 3 The inventions referred to in these Regulations mean the new methods of production created in production which can actually raise the efficacy of production or the new products manufactured which can actually increase their value of use.

The above inventions shall also be restricted to those which can directly be manifested in industrial manufacture or agricultural production.

The procedures for the guarantee of the invention of medical methods and of the academic inventions which are not directly related to production shall be otherwise formulated.

Article 4 If the inventors apply for invention rights or patent rights, the central authorities in charge shall issue invention certificates or patent certificates to protect them after they have examined and determined them to be qualified.

The central authorities in charge referred to above are the Central Administration for Technology of the Financial and Economic Commission of the Government Administration Council.

Article 5 No invention certificates or patent certificates shall be issued as stipulated in Article 3 of these Regulations for all the substances which are obtained through chemical process, but they shall be issued for the new methods of their manufacture.

Article 6 The owner of an invention right shall enjoy the following rights except for the rights to use and disposal of his or her invention which belongs to the state:

(1) To accept monetary rewards, medals, certificates of merit, medals of merit or honorary degrees in accordance with the procedures for rewards stipulated by the state; the procedures shall be otherwise formulated;

(2) To use a prize-winning invention as a legacy and the person who inherits the legacy shall be entitled to accept the monetary reward;

(3) To name the invention after his or her own name or other special name with the approval of the central authorities as required by the inventor.

Article 7 The owner of a patent right shall enjoy the following rights:

(1) To be entitled to run an enterprise with his or her own capital or by raising capital with shares so as to be engaged in production with his or her invention;

(2) To transfer the patent right to another person or give licence to any organization or individual to use his or her invention for remuneration and the terms and conditions shall be prescribed by the owner of the patent right and the user in a contract;

(3) No person shall be entitled to use his or her invention without the licence of the owner of the patent right; those who violate this provision shall indemnify the owner of the patent right for losses according to law;

(4) The person who inherits the legacy of a patent right shall have the same rights as the original patent right owner;

(5) To be entitled to apply to the central authorities for the examination and approval of changing the patent right into an invention right within the patent period if the owner of the patent right (including his or her inheritor, the same hereinafter mentioned) has not transferred his or her rights or granted any licence to use his or her invention.

Article 8 Only an invention certificate shall be issued for any of the following inventions and no patent certificate shall be issued:

(1) The inventions relating to national defence secrets, military techniques or armament manufacturing industries;

(2) Those which have a bearing on the welfare of the majority of the people and are required for rapid popularization, such as those of medicines and varieties or breeds in agriculture or animal husbandry;

(3) Those which are completed by inventors within the scope of their employment in state factories, mines, scientific research institutes, administrations for technology, laboratories or other research organizations;

(4) Those which are completed by inventors on trust of state organizations, enterprises or social bodies by receiving remuneration.

Article 9 The invention right or a patent right shall be valid for three to 15 years, which shall be determined by the central authorities when the certificate is issued.

Article 10 The owner of a patent right shall abide by the following provisions:

(1) He or she shall not solely exercise the patent right without the consent of each common owner if the right is in common ownership;

(2) The transfer of a patent right and the issue of a licence to use an invention shall be approved by the central authorities in charge.

Article 11 The owner of a patent right shall have his or her rights taken and his or her patent certificate returned in any of the following cases:

(1) Selling his or her patent right illicitly abroad without examination or approval within the patent period;

(2) Having not applied for the approval of extension for two years after receiving the patent certificate and having not exercised his or her patent right in the practice of manufacture;

(3) Having stopped manufacture without cause or reason for two years within the patent period and having not applied for examination or approval.

Article 12 The person who is in any of the following cases shall assume the responsibility to compensate and criminal responsibility:

(1) Being in the case in Clause (1) of Article 11 of these Regulations;

(2) Publishing an invention abroad without the examination and approval of the central authorities;

(3) The inventor or another person has disclosed the secret of the invention which has been classified by the central authorities in charge as not for publication;

(4) Plagiarizing the invention of another person or divulging another person's secret before the invention is published.

(5) Using without authorization the invention rights which are to be used and disposed of by the state only.

Article 13 Those who have adopted an invention or who have made all necessary preparations for the adoption before the inventor makes an application shall be entitled to continue to adopt it or to adopt with priority.

Article 14 The central authorities in charge shall be entitled to consult with the owner of a patent right about an invention with a patent certificate issued if they think it necessary to have the invention used and disposed of by the state and ask him or her to transfer the patent right to the state. If no agreement can be reached in the consultation, the Government Administration Council shall be entitled to make the final decision, grant the owner of the patent right an invention right instead and fix the amount of the reward given.

Article 15 An inventor shall give positive assistance to the implementation of his or her invention and to its further improvement.

Article 16 The inventor who applies for an invention right shall be entitled to apply again for a patent right if the invention is not adopted by the government or shall directly be given the patent right by the central authorities in charge. If the government need not adopt an invention when an invention certificate is issued, the central authorities in charge shall give the inventor a patent certificate instead.

Article 17 If a citizen of the People's Republic of China has specific plans and drawings in the research of science and technology which is considered by the central authorities in charge through examination to be of real value and promise success, an enterprise or a research or experiment organization concerned shall be designated to provide him or her with the facilities for research or experiments and give him or her material subsidies as it thinks fit.

Article 18 The foreigners residing in China shall apply for invention rights or patent rights in accordance with these Regulations.

Article 19 The procedure for the application for an invention right or a patent right and the handling of it is as follows:

(1) The inventor fills in an application form, signs it, attaches to it detailed plans, drawings, specifications and other data enough to give full proof of the effects of the invention and makes the application to the central authorities. The authorities shall give a notice of acceptance of the application within 10 days upon its receipt except for the special inventions which shall undergo long-term consideration and examination, but the examination of which shall be completed within three months so as to let the applicants know the results of the examinations.

(2) The central authorities in charge shall be entitled to ask the inventor to complement his or her data if they think them to be inadequate and shall keep all the examined data confidential.

(3) The central authorities in charge shall make an annoucement after the application is examined and proved up to standard and the examination shall be taken as confirmed if no one has an objection within three months of the date of announcement. However, the inventions concerning military secrets shall not be announced.

(4) After the examination is confirmed, an invention certificate or a patent certificate shall be issued; the validity of the invention right or patent right shall be calculated from the date of the issue of the certificate.

(5) If it is examined and proved not up to standard, the central authorities in charge shall give the applicant a letter of examination, giving the reasons in detail; the applicant shall be entitled to ask for the knowledge of all data from which the conclusion of the examination is drawn.

(6) The applicant shall apply for re-examination by giving reasons in detail within 45 days of the arrival of the letter of examination if the previous application is examined and proved not up to standard; if he or she still refuses to accept the decision of the re-examination as final, he or she shall take proceedings according to law within 90 days.

Article 20 The central authorities in charge shall announce the loss of effectiveness of an invention certificate or a patent certificate at its expiration or the cancellation of it for other reasons.

Article 21 The invention or patent right of an invention jointly compoleted by more than two persons is their common ownership; the proportions of the distribution of the common right shall be determined by the common owners through an agreement. If they cannot reach an agreement, the data contributed by each to the invention shall be supplied and submitted to the central authorities in charge for ruling.

Article 22 These Regulations shall be promulgated and put into effect by the Financial and Economic Commission of the Government Administration Council with the approval of the Government Administration Council of the Central People's Government. The rules for the implementation shall be otherwise formulated by the Commission.

20

LABOUR WELFARE AND ORGANIZATION

Unions/ Welfare

THE TRADE UNION LAW OF THE PEOPLE'S REPUBLIC OF CHINA

(June 29, 1950)

The trade union law is promulgated as follows in order to clearly stipulate the legal status and duties of a trade union under the new-democratic regime, enable the working class of the whole country to organize themselves better and give play to their proper role in the new-democratic construction:

Chapter I General Rules

Article 1 Trade unions are the mass organizations of the voluntary unity of the working class. All physical and mental paid labourers in all enterprises, Party and government organizations and schools within the boundaries of China whose income of wages is the whole or major source of their means of livelihood and paid labourers without permanent employers shall have the right to organize trade unions.

Article 2 In accordance with the provisions in the constitution of the All-China Federation of Trade Unions adopted by the National Labour Congress, the organizational principle of trade unions shall be democratic centralism (i.e., centralism on the basis of democracy and democracy under centralized guidance). The trade union committee at each level shall come into being through the election of a general member meeting or a congress. Union members have the right to dismiss or replace the representatives or committee members elected by them at any time in accordance with the provisions in the union constitution. The trade union committee at each level shall be accountable to the masses of members it represents or their congress and obey the resolutions or instructions of higher trade union organizations.

Article 3 Trade unions are mass organizations made up on the basis of the constitutions and resolutions adopted by the National Labour Congress and the congresses of various industrial trade unions (including cultural and educational workers' trade unions, government functionaries' trade unions, etc.), and they have a national independent and unified organizational system with the All-China Federation of Trade Unions as their supreme leading body. When a trade union is to be formed, a report shall be made to the All-China Federation of Trade Unions or an industrial trade union or a local trade union under it which shall examine and approve of its formation and then pass it on to the local people's government for registration and filing.

Article 4 Any other bodies that are not organized in accordance with the provisions in Article 3 of this Law shall not be named trade unions nor enjoy the rights provided for by this Law.

Chapter II The Rights and Duties of Trade Unions

Article 5 In state-operated and cooperative enterprises, the trade unions have the right to participate in production management and sign collective contracts with the administrations on behalf of the masses of employed workers and staff.

Article 6 In private enterprises, the trade unions have the right to make representations to or hold negotiations with the owners or attend labour and capital consultative meetings or sign collective contracts with the owners on behalf of the masses of employed workers and staff.

Article 7 Trade unions have the responsibility to protect the interests of the masses of workers and staff, supervise the conscientious execution by the administrations or the owners of the labour protection, labour insurance, standards of wage payments, factory hygiene and technical safety rules stipulated in government decrees and other relevant regulations, orders, etc., and improve various material and cultural living facilities of the masses of workers and staff.

Article 8 In a state-operated or cooperative enterprise, the trade union organization at each level has the right to ask the administrative authority of the enterprise at the same level to report its work at a general members' meeting or a congress of the trade union committee and has the right to participate in the management committee or administrative meetings of the enterprise on behalf of the masses of employed workers and staff.

Article 9 For the purpose of protecting

the essential interests of the working class, trade unions provide the following services in accordance with their constitutions and resolutions:

1. Educate and organize the masses of workers and staff to safeguard the decrees of the people's government and to implement the policies of the people's government so as to consolidate the people's regime under the leadership of the working class;

2. Educate and organize the masses of workers and staff to cultivate a new attitude towards labour and observe labour discipline and organize production emulation drives and other production campaigns so as to ensure the fulfillment of production plans;

3. Protect public property, oppose corruption, waste and bureaucracy and struggle against saboteurs in state-operated and cooperative enterprises and in Party and government organizations and schools.

4. Carry out the policies of developing production to benefit both labour and capital and oppose all acts in violation of government decrees and impairing production in private enterprises.

Article 10 The government at each level shall allocate necessary houses and equipment to the All-China Federation of Trade Unions, industrial trade unions and local ones for use to conduct their official business, meetings, education, recreation and set up collective welfare facilities; the government shall also give them the same treatment as enjoyed by the government organizations at the same levels in the use of postal, telegraphic, telephone, railway, highway, shipping and other services.

Article 11 If the administration or the owner is going to transfer a member of the trade union committee elected by the masses to another post or discharge him, prior consent shall be obtained from the trade union committee which shall pass it on to the higher trade union committee for approval before it is put into effect.

Article 12 The committee members of the trade union organization at each level or the representatives dispatched by it who hold the credentials of the organization shall be entitled to inspect the working places, dormitories and so on of the enterprises, Party and government organizations and schools within the limits under the trade union organization and the administration or the owner shall not refuse. However, those with special stipulations shall be excepted.

Chapter III Grass-roots Trade Union Organizations

Article 13 A grass-roots trade union committee shall be set up in such a producing or administrative unit as a factory, a mine, a store, a farm, a Party or government organization, a school, etc., with more than 25 workers and a staff (such as a factory committee, a mine committee, a Party or government organization committee, etc.); in the case of a unit with fewer than 25 workers and staff, an organizer shall be elected and enjoy the same rights as a grass-roots trade union committee. The procedures for the organization of a grass-roots trade union committee shall be formulated by the All-China Federation of Trade Unions or the national committee of each industrial trade union.

Article 14 In such producing or administrative units as factories, mines, stores, farms, Party and government organizations, schools, etc., no other organizations shall enjoy the rights which are enjoyed only by grass-roots trade union organizations except the grass-roots trade union organizations approved by industrial or local trade unions as stipulated by Article 3 and Article 13 of this Law.

Article 15 The number of committee members of a grass-roots trade union organization who are released from production or original work to concentrate on the work of the trade union shall be determined according to the number of workers and staff employed by such a producing or administrative unit as the factory, mine, store, farm, Party or government oragnization, school, etc. The standards are as follows:

1 committee member for 200 to 500 workers and staff;

2 committee members for 501 to 1000 workers and staff;

3 committee members for 1001 to 1500 workers and staff;

4 committee members for 1501 to 2500 workers and staff;

5 committee members for 2501 to 4000 workers and staff.

An additional committee member shall be released from production or original work for every 2000 workers and staff more than 4000. If the grass-roots trade union committee in a unit with fewer than 200 workers and staff requires any of its members to be released from production or original work, it shall be approved by the higher trade union committee.

Article 16 After a grass-roots trade union committee is elected, it shall notify the administration or the owner of the list of its members. The administration or the owner shall relieve the committee members who are required to be released from production or original work from their posts in accordance with the resolution of the grass-roots trade union committee.

Article 17 The wages of the committee members who are released from production or original work shall be paid by the trade union and the sums shall not be less than their original wages. They shall continue to enjoy the labour insurance and other welfare treatments paid by the administration or the owner. After their terms of office are expired, the administration or the owner shall ensure the resumption of their posts or the assignment of them to positions with equivalent wages as their original posts.

Article 18 The administration or the owner of such a producing or administrative unit as a factory, a mine, a store, a farm, a Party or government organization, a school, etc. shall not interfere in the activities of the grass-roots trade union committee and the general members' meetings or congresses convened by it. However, various meetings convened by the trade union organization shall be held outside production or office hours. If any meeting shall be held within production or office hours due to special conditions, the consent of the administration or the owner shall be obtained. If the members of the grass-roots trade union committee who are not released from production or original work have to take up production or office hours for the activities of the trade union, the union shall notify the administration or the owner of this; however, no individual person shall take up production or office hours for more than two working days per month and the wages for these two days so taken up shall still be paid by the administration or the owner.

Article 19 If necessary, the elections shall be held within production or office hours when a trade union elects the representatives for a people's representative assembly or a people's congress in accordance with the instruction of the people's government above the city (or county) level or when it elects the representatives for a trade union congress in accordance with the instruction of the trade union committee above the provincial or city level. The representatives of the workers and staff in private enterprises to attend the above meetings or other meetings shall have their wages during the meetings paid by the Party or government organizations that convene the meetings.

Article 20 The administration or the owner of such a producing or administrative unit as a factory, a mine, a store, a farm, a Party or government organization, a school, etc. which employs more than 100 persons shall provide the grass-roots trade union committee with free necessary buildings and facilities (such as water, electricity, furniture, etc.) so as to be used as the offices of the committee and provide it with or temporarily lend to it a proper place for the purpose of holding general members' meetings or representative assemblies. If a unit which employs fewer than 100 persons cannot provide the trade union with an office, the trade union organization shall be entitled to set up desks in a public building and hold various meetings there.

Article 21 The administration or the owner of such a producing or administrative unit as a factory, a mine, a store, a farm, a Party or government organization, a school, etc. shall notify the grass-roots trade union committee of the employment of a worker or a staff member and the grass-roots trade union committee shall be entitled to lodge a protest within three days if it finds the employment in violation of the decrees of the people's government or the collective contracts. If a dispute emerges because the administration or the owner does not agree to the protest of the grass-roots trade union committee, it shall be handled in accordance with the settlement of labour disputes.

Article 22 When any workers or staff members are to be discharged, the administration or the owner of such a producing or administrative unit as a factory, a mine, a store, a farm, a Party or government organization, a school, etc. shall notify the grass-roots trade union committee 10 days before of the list of the personnel to be discharged and the reasons therefor. The grass-roots trade union committee shall be entitled to lodge a protest within seven days if it finds the discharge in violation of the decrees of the people's government or the collective contracts. If a dispute emerges because the administration or the owner does not agree to the protest of the grass-roots trade union committee, it shall be handled in accordance with the procedure for the settlement of labour disputes.

The provisions in the previous article and this one are not applicable to personnel appointed by the people's government at each level.

Chapter IV Outlays of Trade Unions

Article 23 Trade unions shall set up their own systems of budgets, final accounts, accounting, examination, etc. on the principle of the independence in outlays.

Article 24 The sources of the outlays of trade unions are as follows:

1. The membership dues paid by the members of trade unions as stipulated in the Constitution of the All-China Federation of Trade Unions;

2. The administration or the owner of such a producing or administrative unit as a factory, a mine, a store, a farm, a Party or government organization, a school, etc. shall allocate by the month two percent of the total of the actual wages (including the part in cash, that in kind and food) of all the staff and workers employed (excluding the owner's agent(s) in a private enterprise) to the trade union organization as the outlays of the trade union (among which the 1.5 per cent of the total of the actual wages is used as the cultural and educational expenses of the staff and workers);

3. The income from the cultural, sport or other undertakings run by trade unions;

4. The subsidies from the people's government at each level.

Article 25 The procedures for the expenditure of the outlays of the trade union committee at each level shall be formulated by the All-China Federation of Trade Unions.

Chapter V Supplementary Provisions

Article 26 This Law shall be promulgated and put into effect after adoption by the Committee of the Central People's Government.

ORGANIC RULES FOR WOMEN WORKERS' COMMITTEES

Issued by the All-China Federation of Trade Unions
(September 19, 1951)

I The tasks of a women workers' committee are to inspect and supervise each committee of the trade union under the leadership of the grass-roots trade union committee to see if it pays attention to women workers and their special interests; meanwhile, to mobilize and teach women workers to take an active part in productive emulation drives and in cultural and technical studies; to study and overcome difficulties of immediate concern to women workers; to encourage and urge women workers to play a positive role in all the activities of the trade union.

II A women workers' committee shall be set up under the grass-roots trade union committee with more than 50 women members; women workers' committee members shall be provided for that with fewer than 50 women workers.

A women workers' committee shall be composed of three to 15 members chosen by the grass-roots trade union committee from the women staff members and workers' congress or from the women staff members and workers' representative assembly. The post of the director of the women workers' committee shall be concurrently held by a member of the grass-roots trade union committee, and one to two deputy-directors shall be provided if necessary.

III The specific jobs of a women workers' committee are:

1. To mobilize and organize women workers to take part in productive emulation drives, immerse itself among the masses of women workers to find out, study and care for their specific misgivings and difficulties in production and livelihood and duly report them to and impel the quarters concerned to settle them properly so as to ensure the fulfillment of production plans.

2. To supervise the administration or the owner in the implementation of the provisions for the treatment of women workers in the regulations on labour protection and labour insurance and in labour legislation and make specific suggestions as to the protection of the special interests of women workers.

3. To help the administration or the owner to run a nursery and direct and supervise its work regularly. To help and teach the child-care workers to convene mothers' meetings to heed the opinions and suggestions as to the nursery so as to duly improve their work.

4. To frequently organize doctors and medical personnel in explaining the elementary knowledge of maternity and child hygiene to women staff members and workers.

5. To explain the decrees and policies concerning women in the light of the current specific problems occurring among the masses of women staff members and workers.

6. To publicize among and mobilize women staff members and workers to participate in various literacy classes, training classes, sparetime schools and studies of production technology and in various cultural and art groups organized by the workers' club. To help the cultural and educational committee to find out and dispel the misgivings and difficulties of the women staff members and workers in the studies.

7. To care for and discover the activists among women workers and help the grass-roots trade union committee to train and promote woman worker cadres in a planned way.

8. In a factory with more women workers, the meeting of the workshop women workers' committee members shall be regularly called under the leadership of the women workers' committee and women workers' representative assemblies and various relevant special meetings shall also be called if necessary.

IV

1. The women workers' committee shall work out a working plan every month and put it into effect with the approval of the grass-roots trade union committee.

2. The session of the women workers' committee shall be called once a month and reports shall be made on its work to the grass-roots trade union committee and the women workers' representative assembly so as to sum up experience.

WORKING REGULATIONS ON THE LABOUR PROTECTION WORKING COMMITTEES OF GRASS-ROOTS AND WORKSHOP TRADE UNIONS

(Draft for Provisional Implementation, February, 1963)

The Regulations are formulated in order to mobilize and organize the masses of staff and workers to implement the Party's and the state's guiding principles of safe production and various labour protection policies and decrees, make good jobs of labour protection, improve labour conditions, guarantee the safety and health of staff and workers, increase labour productivity and fulfill and overfulfill state plans.

I Organization

1. A grass-roots or workshop trade union shall set up a labour protection working committee or labour protection committee according to the needs of production and work.

2. The members of a grass-roots or workshop labour protection working committee shall come forward in a democratic way and those on the committee shall be old workers, advanced workers, administrative personnel concerned and other activists who are enthusiastic in promoting labour protection. Their terms of office are the same as those of the grass-roots or workshop trade union committee and the vacancies for committee members shall be duly filled.

3. A labour protection working committee shall be provided with a director and with a number of deputy-directors if necessary. The post of the director shall be held by a member of the grass-roots or workshop trade union committee. The division of labour of a labour protection working committee shall be carried out according to the specialty of each member or on the principle of convenience for work.

II Duties

4. To publicize among the masses of staff and workers the Party's and the state's guiding principles of safe production and various labour protection policies and decrees; to help the administration to educate the staff and workers in thinking about safe production, safety technical knowledge, rules and regulations and labour discipline.

5. To urge and help the administration of the enterprise to improve various kinds of safety equipment, inspect if the tools, machines and the safety devices of various kinds of equipment are in good condition and teach the staff and workers to make proper use and take good care of various kinds of equipment and safety devices.

6. To help the administration of the enterprise to work out the plans for safety technical measures and regularly examine their implementation. To supervise the administration in the rational use of the labour protection expenses.

7. To urge and help the administration of the enterprise to take various effective measures to bring the density of dust, the contents of poisonous gases, temperature, humidity, lighting, etc. up to the state standards, make good jobs of industrial hygiene and prevent the occurrence of occupational diseases. To supervise and urge the administration of the enterprise to have health checks on the staff and workers as stipulated and give positive treatment to the patients of occupational diseases.

8. To supervise and urge the administration of the enterprise to duly supply cleaning water, drinking water, cold drinks and healthy food as stipulated. To supervise and urge the administration to set up necessary lounges, locker rooms, bathrooms, women workers' clinics and other facilities according to the specific conditions of the enterprise and regularly make inspections; to teach the staff and workers to take good care of public equipment and maintain sanitation and hygiene.

9. To supervise and urge the administration of the enterprise to supply labour protection necessities as stipulated and educate the staff and workers in the good care of various labour protection necessities and in the best possible economy on their use.

10. To help the administration to conscientiously implement the Party's policy of striking a proper balance between work and rest, teach the staff and workers to make full use of the working hours, supervise the administration not to

put in extra hours wantonly and ensure the eight hours' sleep of the staff and workers so as to practically strike a proper balance between work and rest.

11. Jointly with the women workers' working committee, to help the administration of the enterprise to assign to the women workers the jobs they can do according to the physiological features of the female and make good jobs conscientiously of the special protection of women staff members and workers in their menstrual, gestation, parturient and breast-feeding periods.

12. To energetically participate in the investigation and disposition of injuries and deaths, conscientiously analyse causes, draw lessons, take measures and prevent the occurrence of injuries and deaths.

III Methods of Work

13. The labour protection working committee shall direct the work of group labour protection inspectors. It shall support their reasonable suggestions, strengthen the ideological education and professional training of them, exchange their experience in work and constantly enhance their understanding of policies and their vocational skills.

14. The labour protection working committee shall arrange its working plans around the Party's central tasks in the light of the key matters in the protection of each period, establish the system of meeting reports and regularly report its work to the grass-roots or workshop trade union committee.

15. The labour protection working committee shall do its work by relying upon the activists and the broad masses. It shall make in-depth investigations and strengthen its links and close cooperation with the departments concerned on its own initiative.

16. It shall conscientiously study the Party's and the state's policies and decrees. Proceeding from actual conditions, it shall adhere to principle and struggle against all thoughts and acts in violation of the guiding principles of safe production, labour protection policies and decrees and those of operations against rules and regulations.

WORKING REGULATIONS ON LABOUR PROTECTION INSPECTORS OF TRADE UNION GROUPS

(Draft for Provisional Implementation, February, 1963)

I. These Regulations are formulated in order to mobilize the masses to implement the Party's and the state's guiding principles of safe production and various labour protection policies and decrees as well as the safety rules and regulations of enterprises, prevent injuries and deaths and occupational diseases, ensure the health of staff members and workers, improve labour productivity and accomplish safe production.

II. A trade union group shall be provided with one to three labour protection inspectors according to the demands of production, who shall come forward from the group in a democratic way. The posts of labour protection inspectors shall be held by those who have rather high technical levels and knowledge of safe production, are enthusiastic in promoting the protection, have good links with the masses and are brave in upholding principles. Their terms of office are the same as those of the head of the trade union group.

III. Labour protection inspectors shall do their work under the leadership of the head of the trade union group and under the direction of the workshop labour protection working committee.

IV. The duties of labour protection inspectors are:

(1) To organize the staff members and workers in the group to study the state labour protection policies and decrees, the enterprise's safety rules and regulations and safety technical knowledge, exchange experience in safe operations and enhance the understanding of policies and the levels of safety techniques.

(2) To help the head of the group or the team leader to regularly educate new workers and the workers who have their types of work changed in safety and examine the results of the education.

(3) To regularly examine various machines, tools, safety devices and ventilation, heating, lighting and other equipment. They shall duly supervise and urge the departments concerned to handle the problems if found.

(4) To help the head of the group, team leader and departments concerned to check the transportation, storage and use of such dangerous goods as poisonous goods, combustibles, explosives, etc. and teach the staff members and workers to strictly implement the rules of production and storage.

(5) To help the head of the group and team leader to regularly check if the density of dust, the contents of poisonous gases, temperature, humidity, lighting, etc. conform to the state standards, regularly check the state of sanitation and hygiene of the working sites and organize the staff members and workers to duly remove waste and rearrange the finished and semi-finished products so as to maintain unimpeded passage.

(6) To supervise and urge the head of the group or team leader to duly obtain labour protection necessities as stipulated and teach the staff members and workers to use them properly and pay attention to their saving.

(7) To regularly examine the supply of healthy food, cold drinks, drinking water and cleaning water and duly report the problems to the quarters concerned if found.

(8) To teach the workers of the group to observe labour discipline, make full use of working hours and pay attention to the proper balance between work and rest.

(9) In a group with women staff members and workers, to care for their safety and health and supervise and urge the administration to conscientiously solve the problems of the special protection of them in their menstrual, gestation, parturient and breast-feeding periods.

(10) When an injury or a death occurs, to make a prompt report to the head of the trade union group or the workshop labour protection working committee and help the head of the group or the team leader to organize the workers of the group or team to analyse the causes of the accident, draw experience and lessons, take effective measures and prevent the occurrence of accidents.

V. They shall conscientiously study the Party's and the state's labour protection policies and decrees and the provisions of the enterprises for labour protection and constantly heighten their ideological and vocational levels. They shall implement various rules and regulations in an exemplary way, proceed from the production, uphold principles and struggle against various ideas and acts in violation of the state policies, decrees, rules and regulations.

VI. They shall do their work by relying upon the activists in the same group, show warm solicitude for the safety and health of the workers in the same group, heed the opinions and requirements of the masses with an open mind and regularly report to the head of the trade union group, the workshop trade union labour protection working committee and the administration safety technical department on the conditions of labour protection.

NOTICE OF THE ALL-CHINA FEDERATION OF TRADE UNIONS, THE PEOPLE'S BANK OF CHINA AND THE MINISTRY OF FINANCE CONCERNING THE ALLOTMENT OF TRADE UNION OUTLAYS IN STRICT ACCORDANCE WITH THE PROVISIONS OF THE "LAW ON TRADE UNIONS"

(December 31, 1980)

In order to ensure the smooth progress of the trade union work and the cultural, educational and sports activities of the masses of staff and workers, the state stipulated in the "Law on Trade Unions" promulgated in June of 1950 that the administration of every enterprise, institution or Party or government organ where a trade union organization is established should allot trade union outlays to the trade union organization by the month. During the Ten-year Catastrophe, trade union organizations were destroyed and the provision for the allotment of trade union outlays was suspended. After the Ninth National Trade Union Congress, the Ministry of Finance and the All-China Federation of Trade Unions gave a joint notice on December 22, 1978 to resume the implementation of the provision for the allotment of trade union outlays. According to the reports from various places, since the resumption of the allotment of trade union outlays, the majority of units have allotted them as stipulated, but there are still a small number of units that have not done so as stipulated even though they have been urged many times to do so. A very few departments in charge of enterprises and institutions have not supervised and urged the units under them to allot trade union outlays but have even gone so far as to stand in the way of the allotment. As the outlays of trade union organizations are not well collected in many places, the resumption and development of the normal activities of the masses of staff and workers and the trade union work have been affected.

In order to ensure the conscientious implementation of the state provision and the allotment of trade union outlays on schedule and in full, the following suggestions and procedures have been put forward and approved by the State Council and you are requested to implement them accordingly.

(1) All the units with trade union organizations set up shall allot trade union outlays to the trade unions in strict accordance with the provision in the "Law on Trade Unions" and that in the joint notice of the Ministry of Finance and the All-China Federation of Trade Unions of December 22, 1978. The higher departments in charge shall be responsible for the supervision and inspection of the allotment of trade union outlays by the units under them.

(2) If any unit does not allot any trade union outlays when the time limit is exceeded, the trade union organization shall explain to it the significance of the allotment of trade union outlays and the provisions for it and duly urge it to do so or demand its payment. If many demands are in vain, the district trade union of a county or a city (the trade union immediately higher than a grass-roots one in case the outlays are managed by an industrial trade union) shall give an official written notice to the bank with which the paying unit has opened an account so that the bank shall deduct them from the deposit of the unit for payment and make the daily deduction of 0.5 per cent of the amount in arrears for the payment of the fine for late payment.

(3) As for the enterprises which the state has officially resolved to close during the regulation of the national economy and have stopped production, they shall be exempted from the allotment of trade union outlays except for bearing the necessary expenses of the grass-roots trade unions; if an enterprise which has been determined by the state to stop production really has actual difficulty and fails to allot the outlays for the time being, it shall give reasons to the higher trade union and shall suspend the payment of trade union outlays within a definite time with the consent of the trade union. The necessary expenses of the grass-roots trade union during the suspension of payment shall be settled by the administration of the enterprise.

INTERIM REGULATIONS ON STAFF AND WORKERS' CONGRESSES OF STATE INDUSTRIAL ENTERPRISES

(June 15, 1981)

Chapter I General Rules

Article 1 According to the provision in Article 17 of the Constitution of the People's Republic of China that "the state upholds the principle of socialist democracy and ensures the participation of the people in the administration of the state, in the administration of various economic and cultural undertakings and in the supervision of state organs and state personnel," all enterprises shall establish and perfect the system of the staff and workers' congresses under the leadership of Party committees while practising the system of factory directors' responsibility under the leadership of Party committees, so as to give play to the staff and workers' sense of responsibility as masters and ensure the democratic rights of the masses of staff and workers to be the masters in the administration of enterprises.

Article 2 A staff and workers' congress (or a staff and workers' general meeting) is a basic form for an enterprise to practise democratic management and a setup of power for the masses of staff and workers to participate in policy-making and management and supervision of cadres.

Article 3 A staff and workers' congress shall act in accordance with the Party's guiding principles and policies and the state's laws and orders, exercise its functions and powers under the leadership of the Party committee, maintain a proper balance in the relationship between the state, the enterprise and the staff and workers themselves, compromise the internal contradictions in the enterprise, ensure the fulfillment of state plans and various tasks and run a socialist enterprise well.

Article 4 The organizational principle of a staff and worker's congress is democratic centralism (centralism on the basis of democracy and democracy under centralized guidance).

Chapter II Functions and Powers

Article 5 The staff and workers' congress of an enterprise shall exercise the following functions and powers in accordance with the state policies, decrees and planned requirements:

(1) Discussing and considering the factory director's work reports, production and construction plans or financial budgets and final accounts and significant plans of potentialities-tapping, innovation or transformation or major issues in business management and then making relevant resolutions.

(2) Discussing and deciding on the use of enterprise labour protection measure funds, staff and workers' welfare funds or rewarding funds and the matters in the aspects of immediate concern to the staff and workers such as the procedures for the rewards and punishments of the staff and workers, the plans for the allotment of dwelling houses to the staff and workers, etc.

(3) Discussing and adopting the matters of the reform of the enterprise's system, the schemes for the readjustment of wages, the plans for training the staff and workers and the important rules and regulations relating to the whole factory.

(4) Supervising the leading cadres and working personnel at each level of the enterprise; recommending to the higher authorities to praise or reward the cadres who always work hard and have made outstanding achievements; recommending to the higher authorities to promote the cadres who have made special contributions; suggesting that the higher authorities should criticize, punish or dismiss the cadres who are not conscientious or cause losses; suggesting that the Party's discipline inspecting organs or the state political and legal authorities should deal severely with the cadres who seriously neglect their duties and violate laws and discipline.

(5) Electing the administrative leading personnel of the enterprise in accordance with the deployment of the organ in charge of the enterprise. The cadres elected through democratic election shall be reported to the organ in charge within the limits of the administration of cadres for examination, approval and appointment.

Article 6 The factory director shall regularly report his work to the staff and workers' congress, be responsible for executing and handling the resolutions and motions of the staff and workers' congress relating to the production or administration of the enterprise and subject himself to the examination and supervision of the staff and workers' congress. The staff and workers' congress shall support the factory director to exercise his functions and powers, safeguard the high degree of authority of the production command system and teach the staff and workers to constantly enhance their sense of responsibility as the masters, conscientiously observe labour discipline and strictly execute various systems of productive or technical responsibility.

Article 7 The staff and workers' congress shall make suggestions if it has any objection to a decision or an instruction of the organ in charge of the enterprise. If the organ in charge maintains the original decision or instruction after consideration, the staff and workers' congress shall implement it.

Chapter III Staff and Workers' Deputies

Article 8 The deputies to the staff and workers' congress shall come forward through the direct election of the staff and workers by the team or group, by the section or by the workshop (or department or office). The official staff members and workers who enjoy civil rights in the unit shall be eligible for election as deputies.

The permanent system shall be practised with regard to the staff and workers' deputies who shall be re-elected every two years and who shall renew the term of office if they are re-elected. The staff and workers' deputies shall subject themselves to the supervision of the staff and workers of the electing unit and the original electing unit shall be entitled to dismiss and replace the deputies of its own unit according to the stipulated procedure.

Among the deputies, there shall be workers, scientific and technical personnel, management personnel, leading cadres and other working personnel, of which, in general, the workers' deputies shall not be fewer than 60 percent of the total of the staff and workers' deputies. The deputies of scientific and technical personnel, management personnel, young and women staff members and workers shall respectively take up certain proportions.

The staff and workers' deputies shall form deputations (or deputies' groups) by the workshop or by the department or office (or by a number of sections or offices) and elect a head and a number of assistant heads.

Article 9 The rights of the staff and workers' deputies:

(1) To have the rights to elect, to stand for election and to vote at the staff and workers' congress.

(2) To be entitled to participate in inspecting the implementation of the resolutions and motions of the staff and workers' congress by the units concerned in the enterprise and to be entitled to participate in addressing inquiries to the leading personnel of the enterprise.

(3) To be entitled to enjoy the deserved treatments as on normal duty even though they have to take up the production or working hours for participation in the activities of the staff and workers' congress.

(4) To be entitled to appeal to or lodge complaints with the departments concerned if they suffer retaliation due to the exercise of their just democratic rights.

Article 10 The duties of the staff and workers' deputies:

(1) To observe the Party's guiding principles and policies and the state's laws and orders in an exemplary way, abide conscientiously by labour discipline, rules and regulations and do their own jobs well.

(2) To energetically publicize and take the lead in executing the resolutions of the staff and workers' congress and make good jobs of various tasks assigned by the congress.

(3) To represent the interests of the masses properly, maintain close links with the masses and report the masses' opinions as things really are.

(4) To study hard so as to constantly heighten their political consciousness, their vocational or technical competence and their management capacity.

(5) To observe social morality in an exemplary way and guide the masses in the cultivation of new socialist habits.

(6) To help, teach and urge the staff members and workers who do not observe the rules and regulations of the factory or who violate labour discipline to correct their shortcomings or mistakes conscientiously.

Chapter IV Organizational System

Article 11 In the convention of the staff and workers' congress, the congress presidium shall be elected to preside over the congress. The members of the presidium shall include workers, scientific and technical personnel, management personnel and the chief leading cadres of the Party, administration, trade union and Youth League organizations of the enterprise. In general, workers shall constitute the majority. No standing body shall be established for the staff and workers' congress and the permanent system shall be practised in respect of the congress presidium.

Article 12 The staff and workers' congress shall be convened every half year at least. There shall be more than two thirds of the deputies attending each meeting. A provisional meeting shall be convened on the motion of one third of the deputies when any major issue arises. An election or a resolution of the staff and workers' congress shall be passed by the majority of all the deputies before it becomes effective.

Article 13 The opinions of the masses shall be extensively heeded in regard to the topics for discussion at the staff and workers' congress, which shall be submitted to the congress for adoption after the examination and approval of the congress presidium.

Article 14 The staff and workers' congress shall organize a number of special working committees or groups (without being released from production or original work) as required. Their main tasks are: to make investigations into and suggestions as to the major issues to be discussed at the staff and workers' congress; to gather and verify relevant motions; to examine and urge the departments concerned to execute the resolutions of the congress.

Article 15 If any important matter is to be solved immediately when the staff and workers' congress is not in session, the permanent presidium shall call a meeting attended by the heads of the staff and workers' deputations (or deputies' groups) and the staff and workers' representatives concerned to handle it.

Chapter V Working Organization

Article 16 The grass-roots trade union committee shall assume the tasks of the working organization of the staff and workers' congress and jointly with the departments concerned, make the preparations for its session, conduct the congress business and routine organizational work when the congress is not in session and handle the matters assigned by the staff and workers' congress or the presidium.

Chapter VI Supplementary Provisions

Article 17 Each enterprise shall formulate the detailed rules for the implementation of these Regulations for the staff and workers' congress (or the staff and workers' general meeting) of its own unit,in the light of actual conditions.

Article 18 In principle, these Regulations shall also be applicable to communications and transportation, capital construction, state farms and forestry centres, water conservancy facilities, commercial, foreign trade and other enterprises or units. Scientific research, educational, cultural and other institutions or units shall also practise democratic administration by relying on the masses and shall formulate the interim regulations of their own staff and workers' congresses in the light of their own actual conditions in the spirit of these Regulations.

INTERIM PROVISIONS FOR THE LIVING HARDSHIP SUBSIDIES TO SURVIVING FAMILY MEMBERS OF DECEASED WORKING PERSONNEL OF STATE ORGANS AND INSTITUTIONS

(February 13, 1980)

As regards the living hardship of the surviving family members of the deceased working personnel of state organs and institutions, the Ministry of Internal Affairs, the Ministry of Finance and the Bureau of Personnel of the State Council stipulated in principle in their joint notices in 1957 and 1964 that provisional or regular subsidies could be given. However, each area and each department have been inconsistent in the implementation for many years, affecting each other. For this reason, the following interim provisions are made according to present conditions and the requirements of each area in order to overcome the living difficulties of the surviving family members properly, contribute to stability and unity, relieve the broad masses of working personnel of the fear of disturbance in the rear and give full play to their enthusiasm so as to make more contributions to the accomplishment of the socialist four modernizations.

I If the surviving family members of a functionary of a state organ or institution have difficulty in their livelihood after his or her death, the unit where the deceased was located before his or her death shall give them regular or provisional subsidies on the principles of "more subsidies for greater hardship, less subsidies for small hardship and no subsidies for no hardship."

II In general, the standards of the living hardship subsidies to the surviving family members shall be based on the principle of keeping their livelihood at the living standards of the local masses and the specific standards shall be prescribed by each province, municipality or autonomous region (the central and state organs and institutions shall implement the standards of the areas where they are located). With regard to the personnel who sacrifice their lives to protect or save state assets or in the struggle against the enemy, the standards of the living hardship subsidies to their surviving family members shall be properly raised a little higher.

The subsidies to the surviving family members shall be calculated in accordance with the number of persons who enjoy the surviving family member subsidies and with the standards and the total shall not exceed the wages of the deceased before his or her death.

III The subsidized targets refer to the following directly related family members and other family members who are supported by the deceased before his or her death:

1. The deceased's father (including the person who brings the deceased up) or husband who has reached the age of 60 or who has basically lost his ability to work;
2. The deceased's mother (including the person who brings the deceased up) or wife who has reached the age of 50 or who has basically lost her ability to work;
3. Children (including posthumous children, adopted children, the children left by the former wife or the former husband) who are under the age of 16, or who are still studying at middle school even though they have reached the age of 16 or who have basically lost their ability to work;
4. Younger brother or sister (including the younger brother or sister with the same father but different mother or with the same mother but different father) who is under the age of 16, or who is still studying at middle school even though he or she has reached the age of 16 or who has basically lost his or her ability to work.

IV The remuneration obtained by the above subsidized targets by participating in the work or agricultural production shall be used as their own living expenses and these revenues shall be taken into account in the calculation of the standards of living hardship subsidies.

V If the deceased's spouse has fixed income, the balance of the income after the deduction of his or her own necessary living expenses shall be used as the living expenses of the other surviving family members and subsidies shall be given if it still falls short. The standards of deduction shall be determined by each area according to the living standards of general working personnel in the area.

VI After the surviving family members enjoy regular subsidies, the unit where the deceased was located before his or her death shall give provisional subsidies as it thinks fit when they have other special difficulties.

VII If the surviving family members enjoying subsidies have their economic income increased, obtain employment or have their number decreased, their living hardship subsidies shall be reduced or stopped according to new conditions.

VIII The living hardship subsidies to the surviving family members shall be paid from the funds of the unit where the deceased was located before his or her death.

NOTICE OF THE STATE BUREAU OF LABOUR AND THE MINISTRY OF FINANCE CONCERNING THE REQUEST OF STAFF MEMBERS AND WORKERS OF STATE ENTERPRISES FOR MARITAL, FUNERAL OR JOURNEY LEAVE

(February 20, 1980)

Notice No. Zhong-Lao-Xin 67 (59) promulgated by the original Ministry of Labour on June 1, 1959 stipulated that the wages should still be paid out to the staff members and workers of enterprises who had less than three days' marital or funeral leave. Since this procedure was put into trial implementation, a number of units, staff members and workers have let us know that some staff members and workers have run up against some actual difficulties because they have no journey leave if any of them is going to marry a person who is working in another place or if any of them has to go personally to a place other than his or hers for the purpose of making arrangements for a funeral when a directly-related family member of his or hers dies. After consideration, the following notice is given with regard to the request of staff members and workers for marital or funeral leave or journey leave.

1. When a staff member or a worker is going to marry or when a directly-related family member (father, mother, spouse, son or daughter) of his or hers dies, he or she shall have one to three days' marital or funeral leave with the approval of the administrative leadership of his or her unit as it thinks fit according to specific conditions.

2. A staff member or a worker shall additionally have journey leave according to the length of the journey when he or she is going to marry another person who is working in another place or when he or she has to go personally to a place other than his or hers for the purpose of making arrangements for a funeral when a directly-related family member of his or hers dies there.

3. The wages of the staff members and workers shall still be paid during their marital or funeral leave and journey leave approved and the vehicle or vessel fares, etc. on their journeys shall all be provided by themselves.

4. The above provisions shall be put into effect as from the month of the transmission of this Notice to lower levels.

PROVISIONS ON LIVING ALLOWANCE FOR FUNCTIONARIES OF STATE ORGANS DURING SICK LEAVE
(Promulgated by the State Council on April 6, 1981)

In order to properly overcome the living difficulties of the functionaries of state organs on sick leave and to help sick and recuperating personnel to get well as soon as possible, the following Provisions are made in respect of the living allowance to the functionaries of state organs on sick leave in accordance with the principle of distribution according to work:

1. Original pay shall be given to a functionary who has been on sick leave for less than two months.

2. If a functionary has been on sick leave for more than two months, his or her pay during sick leave shall be given according to the following standards as from the third month:

(1) 90 per cent of his or her pay shall be given if he or she has worked for less than 10 years;

(2) 100 per cent of his or her original pay shall be given if her or she has worked for more than 10 years.

3. If a functionary has been on sick leave for more than six months, his or her pay during sick leave shall be given according to the following standards as from the seventh month:

(1) 70 per cent of his or her pay shall be given if he or she has worked for less than 10 years;

(2) 80 per cent of his or her pay shall be given if he or she has worked for 10 years or for more than 10 years;

(3) 90 per cent of his or her pay shall be given if he or she took part in revolutionary work before September 2, 1945.

If the functionaries stated in the above Items (1), (2) and (3) have obtained the titles of labour heroes or model workers conferred by the people's government of each province, municipality or autonomous region or each department of the State Council and still retain the honour for the time being, their pay during sick leave shall be appropriately increased with the approval of the people's government of the province, municipality or autonomous region or each department of the State Council.

4. The pay during sick leave shall be paid out as usual to a deputy commissioner of a prefectural administrative office or a person holding the post of equal rank or a cadre above the fourteenth administrative grade who took part in revolutionary work before the end of September of 1949 or to a county magistrate or a deputy county magistrate of a county people's government or a person holding a post of equal rank, or a cadre above the eighteenth administrative grade who took part in revolutionary work before September 2, 1945 or to a functionary who took part in revolutionary work before July 6, 1937.

5. The pay below 30 yuan when on sick leave shall be paid at 30 yuan and the original pay below 30 yuan shall be paid at the original amount.

6. A functionary shall, on sick leave, continue to enjoy the welfare treatment of the unit where he or she is stationed.

7. If a functionary is to enjoy the living allowance in these Provisions during sick leave, he or she shall have the certificate of a medical institution and meet with the approval of the leading body in charge.

8. The calculation of the working hours of a functionary shall be handled in accordance with the current relevant provisions of the State Council.

9. The institutions under state organs shall implement these Provisions accordingly.

10. The State Bureau of Personnel shall be responsible for the interpretation of these Provisions.

11. These Provisions shall be put into effect from the date of promulgation. The "Provisional Procedures for the Living Allowance to the Functionaries of State Organs on Sick Leave" promulgated by the State Council on December 29, 1955 shall be annulled at the same time.

THE PROVISIONS OF THE MINISTRY OF FINANCE FOR TRAVELLING EXPENSES FOR HOME VISITS OF STAFF MEMBERS AND WORKERS

(April 8, 1981)

Article 1 These Provisions are made on the basis of the "Provisions of the State Council for the Living Allowance to Staff Members and Workers during Home Visits".

Article 2 The vehicle and vessel fares on the journey to and fro for a staff member or a worker to go home to visit his or her family or relatives shall be reimbursed in accordance with the following standards:

1. If he or she travels by train (including through express or special express), he or she shall be reimbursed for the hard seat fares no matter what official rank he or she holds. Anyone who is over the age of 50 and travels by train in succession for more than 48 hours shall be reimbursed for hard sleeper charges.
2. Anyone who travels by ship shall be reimbursed for Class 4 cabin (the cabin one class higher than the steerage) seat fares.
3. Anyone who travels by long-distance bus or by other means of civil communications shall be reimbursed for the actual expenses of the tickets. The limits of the other means of civil communications and the requirements for taking them shall be prescribed by each province or municipality directly under the Central Government for itself.
4. The urban traffic expenses on the journey of a home visit shall be reimbursed by the tickets of through-route trams, buses and ferries showing the starting points and termini. But the expenses for taking urban taxis shall be provided by the staff member or worker for himself or herself and shall not be reimbursed.
5. Airline tickets shall not be reimbursed for a home visit of a staff member or a worker. If he or she has to travel by plane for some reason, he or she shall be reimbursed in accordance with the through-route vehicle and/or vessel fares and provide the excess parts for himself or herslef.

Article 3 If a staff member or a worker has to change vehicles or vessels halfway and has to put up at the transfer place(s) on the journey to and fro of a home visit due to limited conditions of communications, he or she shall have the accommodation expenses reimbursed for an ordinary room bed one day per transfer by the receipt. If the days for transfer accommodation expenses are more than those stipulated, the excessive expenses shall be provided by the staff member or worker for himself or herself.

If a staff member or a worker travels by long-distance bus or other means of civil communications in succession on the journey of a home visit and has to put up due to the stopping of the vehicle, the accommodation expenses shall be reimbursed on the receipts of the hotel or inn.

If an unexpected traffic accident (such as a collapse obstructing the road, a flood destroying the bridge) causes the suspension of traffic on the journey of a home visit of a staff member or a worker, the accommodation expenses during the waiting for the resumption of traffic shall be reimbursed on the certificate of the local communications authorities and on the receipt(s) of the accommodation expenses.

Article 4 If the travelling expenses (including vehicle and vessel fares, urban traffic expenses, accommodation charges) to and fro for a married staff member or worker to visit his or her parents are less than 30 per cent of his or her own standard wages, they shall be provided by the staff member or worker for himself or herself and those in excess of this percentage shall be borne by the unit where he or she is stationed.

Article 5 Such expenses of a staff member or a worker during a home visit as board expenses, checkroom charges, consignment charges and those for him or her to look round or go on sightseeing at his or her convenience shall be provided by him or her for himself and herself and shall not be reimbursed.

Article 6 Each province or municipality directly under the Central Government shall formulate the specific procedures for the implementation of these Provisions, put them into effect in a unified way within the province or municipality and submit them to the Ministry of Finance for record. The provisions of an autonomous region for the travelling expenses for the home visits of staff members and workers shall be formulated by the region in the spirit of these Provisions and submitted to the Ministry of Finance for record.

Article 7 These Provisions shall be put into effect as from the date of the promulgation of the

"Provisions of the State Council for the Remuneration to Staff Members and Workers during Home Visits". The past provisions for the travelling expenses for the home visits of staff members and workers shall be annulled at the same time.

INTERIM PROVISIONS FOR THE ADMINISTRATION OF STAFF AND WORKERS' EDUCATIONAL FUNDS AND THEIR EXPENDITURE LIMITS

(Promulgated by the Ministry of Finance on May 8, 1981)

According to the "Decision on the Strengthening of the Education of Staff and Workers" of the Central Committee of the Communist Party of China and the State Council, the following interim provisions are now made for the administration of staff and workers' educational funds and their expenditure limits:

I Each area, department, enterprise, institution or administrative unit shall energetically run well various types of the education of the cadres, staff members and workers at their posts as required in the "Decision" in the spirit of striving arduously and practising thrift and hard work. Short-term training classes can be run and various types of staff and workers' education can also be set up, such as staff and workers' schools, broadcast and television universities (middle schools), correspondence universities (middle schools), night universities, etc. Sparetime education can be run and released-from-work or semi-released-from-work studies can also be organized. Each of them shall be run solely by a unit or jointly by several units or staff members and workers shall be selected and recommended for training to various types of schools run by educational departments, higher departments in charge or other brotherly units.

II The funds required for the above-mentioned types of staff and workers' education shall be expanded from the staff and workers' educational funds in accordance with expenditure limits and the sources of funds stipulated. The funds for the joint running of a school shall be rationally shared by the running units.

III The Sources of Funds:

1. Staff and workers' educational funds of an enterprise: According to the current developments of staff and workers' education and the possibility of state financial resources, an enterprise or a corporation with unified accounting (including construction enterprises) shall control their expenditure in this respect within the limits of one percent of the total wages and directly include it in the cost of production (circulation cost). Some of these funds shall also be drawn from the enterprise funds, profit reserves, undertaking surplus or profits reserved after tax payment for the purpose of staff and workers' education.

The expenditure of the trade union outlays for the purpose of staff and workers' sparetime education shall still be controlled for use in the range of 25 to 37.5 percent of the trade union outlays allotted by the administration of the enterprise.

The funds concerning staff and workers' education which were originally stipulated to be expended from the cost of the enterprise or its extra-business expenditure shall be expended within the limits of one percent of the total wages instead and no longer included in the extra-business expenditure.

The funds for capital construction units to run staff and workers' education shall be expended from the capital construction investments.

The funds for closed or stopped enterprises or the units with capital construction stopped or delayed to run staff and workers' education shall be expended from the clearing and maintenance expenses of the closed or stopped enterprises or from the maintenance expenses of the units with construction stopped or postponed.

2. Staff and workers' educational funds of an administrative unit or an institution: The units without trade union organizations shall settle the expenditure by redistributing the funds themselves. If a small number of grass-roots units really have difficulty, the revenue office at each level shall consider and settle it.

3. The funds for educational departments to run staff and workers' education: All the expenditure shall be made within the items of funds in the educational operating expenses allotted by the state for the funds of the staff and workers' education run by the educational department at each level, such as broadcast and television universities, correspondence or night universities and those attached to various common institutions of higher learning, sparetime literacy schools, primary or secondary broadcast and television education, correspondence education and literacy education, schools (institutions) for teachers' vocational studies, teacher training classes and their subordinate correspondence education and those run in a centralized way during vacations, etc.

IV The Limits of the Expenditure of Funds:

The enterprises, capital construction units, administrative organs and institutions which run staff and workers' education shall make the expenditure of staff and workers' educational funds within the following limits:

1. Official business expenses: including teaching and administrative staff and workers' administrative expenses, miscellaneous and travelling expenses and the maintenance costs of teaching appliances.

2. Vocational expenses: including teachers' teaching experiment expenses and those for the purchase of teaching materials, data, etc.

3. Additional teaching remuneration: meaning that for inviting part-time teachers. The standards of remuneration shall be implemented in accordance with the provisions of the Ministry of Education, the Ministry of Finance and the State Bureau of Labour in 1978 respectively numbered Jiao-Ji 987 (78), Cai-Shi 241 (78) and Lao-Xin 54 (78).

4. Practice and research expenses: the expenses incurred for students to do production practice in their own units or do practice and research in other units with approval and those incurred for graduation designs. If any proceeds come from the products of the production practice, they shall be used to set off the expenditure.

5. Equipment purchase costs: mainly meaning the costs for the purchase of general appliances, instruments, books, etc.

6. The funds for entrusting other units with training: referring to the vocational study and training expenses which shall be paid in accordance with the state provisions for selecting and recommending the staff members and workers of their units for training to institutions of higher learning, polytechnic schools, higher departments in charge or brotherly units, etc.

7. The expenditure of other funds: meaning miscellaneous odd expenses.

The following items which are not included in staff and workers' educational funds shall be expended in accordance with relevant provisions:

1. The wages of the full-time teaching and administrative staff members and workers, various labour protection funds, welfare funds, rewards, etc. and the wages given the students who are released from work for study as stipulated shall not be included in the staff and workers' educational funds and shall be paid as stipulated by the units where the individuals are located.

2. The textbooks, reference materials, slide rules (calculators), small drawing instruments (such as protractors, set squares, compasses, etc.) and so on used by students in study and other studying stationery such as pens, pencils, ink, paper, etc. shall be provided by the students for themselves and shall not be paid for out of the staff and workers' educational funds.

3. If the equipment required to be purchased for running staff and workers' education conforms to the standards of fixed assets it shall be paid for as stipulated separately out of capital construction investments, enterprise renewal and transformation funds, administrative or operating expenses and shall not be included in the staff and workers' educational funds.

4. The classrooms, school buildings or educational bases needed for running staff and workers' education shall be settled as far as possible by redistributing the existing buildings on the principle of doing things simply and thriftily. If they are to be newly built, old enterprises shall settle them by making arrangements in the enterprise renewal and transformation funds; administrative units and institutions shall pay for them out of the capital construction investments; newly-built units shall take the necessary facilities for staff and workers' education into account in designing and settle the funds required within the general investments of the newly-built projects.

V The administration of staff and workers' educational funds shall be strengthened.

1. The staff and workers' educational funds shall strictly be expended according to the limits stipulated and the amounts controlled. The revenue and financial departments at each level shall strengthen their supervision over the administration and use of staff and workers' educational funds so as to ensure the implementation of these Provisions.

2. Grass-roots enterprises, administrative units and institutions shall strengthen the administration of staff and workers' educational funds under the unified leadership of the Party committees, sum up the experience in the administration and improve the levels of the administration.

VI These Provisions are applicable to state enterprises, administrative units and institutions. The units of collective ownership shall implement them accordingly.

VII Each province, municipality or autonomous region or each department of the central authorities in charge shall make specific supplementary provisions in the light of the concrete conditions of its area or department on the principles of these Provisions with the prerequisites not to extend the limits of expenditure, not to raise the standards of expenditure and not to break through the general controlled amounts and submit them to the Ministry of Finance for record.

VIII These Provisions shall be put into trial implementation as of January 1, 1981. If any previous procedures go against these Provisions, these Provisions shall be taken as standard.

21

WAGES

Bonus/ Over-Time Allowance/ Piece Rate

PROVISIONS OF THE STATE COUNCIL FOR PROPERLY IMPLEMENTING THE REWARDS SYSTEM AND RESOLUTELY CHECKING THE RECKLESS GRANTING OF REWARDS

(January 16, 1981)

Since its resumption in 1978, the rewards system has been playing a positive role in mobilizing the enthusiasm of the broad masses of staff and workers and impelling enterprises to improve business management, enforce the increase of production and strict economy, improve the quality of products and reduce the costs of production, and its achievements are positive. However, owing to inconsistencies in the understanding of this system, the ideological and political work of staff and workers has slackered; serious equalitarianism exists in the course of providing rewards and some enterprises are even acting as if they are vying with each other for the excessive or reckless granting of rewards because of an imperfect rewards system and procedures for the drawing of reward funds and unstrengthened management systems of enterprises, and moreover because some leading cadres have taken the granting of rewards as an exclusive means to increase the income of staff and workers, all of which have caused the granting of rewards to get out of control. Some enterprises have even gone so far as to violate law and discipline by raising the prices of commodities wilfully at the expense of the state and consumers' interests so as to seek illicit profits and give more rewards by means of this. If an end is not put to such a state of affairs, it will not only cause the rewards system to go against the principle of distribution according to work, lose its effect of encouraging the advanced, corrupt the ideology of staff and workers and affect their unity, but also waste state funds and add difficulty to the regulation of the national economy. Therefore, the proper implementation of the rewards system and the resolute checking of the reckless granting of rewards have become an urgent task at present to make a good job of regulation and stabilizing the economy. We hope the government and the departments in charge of enterprises at each level shall regard this task as a major issue and conscientiously and earnestly pay close attention to and make a good job of it while relaying and implementing the spirit of the Central Working Conference of December of 1980. The following provisions are now made for rewards during the regulation of the national economy:

1 In the implementation of the rewards system, an enterprise shall strengthen the ideological and political work of the staff and workers so as to enable it to contribute to the regulation of the national economy and to promote the development of the enterprise's production.

It shall teach the broad masses of cadres, staff members and workers to cultivate the communist attitude towards labour, give full play to their own intelligence and wisdom and make more contributions to the accomplishment of the four modernizations by doing their work according to their ability. Everyone shall display his revolutionary spirit in being selfless, putting others before himself, building the country through thrift and hard work and striving arduously and criticize and oppose the bourgeois decadent ideas of benefiting oneself at the expense of others, being bent solely to profit or "turning all towards money."

At present, it is the issue concerning all and where the essential interests of the whole nation lie to make good jobs of the regulation of the national economy, stabilize the economy and maintain the livelihood of the people. The implementation of the rewards system and the granting of rewards shall be subordinated to this issue with consideration given to the interests of the state, the enterprise and the individual. It shall not be allowed to give consideration merely to those of one party. In particular, they shall be subordinated to the state interests and advantageous to the accomplishment of the regulation of the national economy.

The implementation of the rewards system by an enterprise is aimed at mobilizing the enthusiasm of the masses better, impelling the enterprise to improve its business management and encouraging its staff and workers to raise their technical or professional standards, heighten their labour productivity, develop production, increase social wealth, make more profits and increase the income of the staff and workers on the basis of the increase of production and income and the guarantee of the most income for the state. Rewards are an encouragement for overfulfilled labour. Therefore, in the implementation of the rewards system, the enterprise shall conscientiously implement the principle of distribution according to work, oppose equalitarianism and closely combine the sums of the rewards for the staff and workers with the enterprise's production or operation achievements and the staff and workers' labour contributions. The rate of the increase of enterprise rewards shall be lower than that of its production and profits.

Honorary and material rewards shall be combined with equal emphasis laid on both and without the overemphasis on either of them at the expense of the other. Necessary honorary rewards shall be given to the collectives and individuals who have made outstanding contributions to the state so as to further kindle their enthusiasm for socialism.

2 The equalitarianism in the rewards system between enterprises shall be overcome and the grant of rewards shall be strictly controlled.

All enterprises shall only draw and give rewards under the conditions of fulfilling or overfulfilling such major economic and technical targets as yields, qualities, profits, supply contracts, etc., as stipulated in state plans.

The granting of rewards shall be controlled in accordance with the following procedures:

The annual total of rewards given by a bureau (or a corporation analogous to a bureau) in charge as the calculating unit of the enterprises under each province, municipality or autonomous region or under each department of the State Council shall be controlled within the total of one to two months' standard wages of the staff members and workers in the subordinate enterprises, who implement the rewards system. The annual total of rewards given by each bureau or each corporation shall be examined and determined by the people's government of each province, municipality or autonomous region or by each department of the State Council in charge respectively according to the situations of production and profits of each subordinate bureau or corporation. In some bureaux or corporations, it shall be equal to the total of one month's standard wages; in others, it shall be equal to that of more than one month's wages; in those with good production and more profits, it shall amount to that of two months' wages; however, it shall not be allowed that every bureau or corporation gives rewards equal to the total of two months' standard wages.

Specific provisions shall be made by each bureau in charge of enterprises or each corporation for the annual total of rewards given by each enterprise within the limits of the annual total of rewards which shall be given by the bureau or corporation with the examination and determination of the people's government of the province, municipality or autonomous region or the department of the State Council in charge according to different situations of enterprises in the fulfillment or overfulfillment of various major economic or technical targets and different conditions of enterprises for the degrees of increase of profits and those of difficulty in obtaining profits; different enterprises shall be dealt with in different ways, advanced enterprises to be given more, and less advanced ones to be given less, and no equal grants shall be allowed. The maximum limit of various rewards (excluding the invention, technical improvement or rationalization proposal rewards stipulated by the state and specific fuel or raw material economy rewards) annually given by an enterprise shall, in general, not exceed the total of the two months' standard wages of its staff and workers; a very few enterprises with the outstanding fulfillment of various economic or technical targets or with especially great contributions shall give some more rewards with the approval of the economic commission, labour and financial departments of the province, municipality or autonomous region or the department of the State Council in charge, but they shall not be more than the total of three months' standard wages in each enterprise.

If an enterprise with losses due to policies reduces the amount of losses checked and ratified, such a reduction shall be regarded to be the same with the increase of profits and proper rewards shall be given.

In the case of closed or discontinued enterprises, no rewards shall be given. With regard to the enterprises with seriously insufficient production tasks within plans and without any profits, no rewards shall be given as well. However, in order to encourage these enterprises to undertake production tasks by themselves according to the needs of the market, proper rewards shall be given with the approval of the bureau in charge of the enterprises as it thinks fit, according to the quantities of the undertaken production tasks and the degrees of the economic effect obtained.

The total of rewards given by a subordinate enterprise at the prefectural or county level shall be prescribed by the people's government of the province, municipality or autonomous region itself in the light of specific conditions on the above principles.

The surplus of the reward funds drawn by an enterprise after the granting of rewards shall be used to build the dwelling houses of its staff members and workers and run other collective welfare facilities or shall be carried forward for use in the next year.

3 In the granting of rewards, an enterprise

shall pay practical attention to their economic effect, combine them with the production and with the labour emulation and shall not distribute the rewards equally between workshops, offices, staff members or workers.

Each enterprise shall be entitled to work out its own procedures for production rewards by itself within the limits of the total of rewards which shall be given by it according to the needs of production and the features of work.

An enterprise shall clearly stipulate the various rewarded economic and technical targets and the procedures for appraisal and calculation of rewards for each workshop or each office. Each workshop or each office shall stipulate the granting of the individual rewards to the staff members and workers according to their specific production or working conditions. In the case of the production workers for whom labour quotas shall be prescribed and other production targets shall be appraised, the rewards shall be calculated and given according to the degrees of their fulfillment or overfulfillment of the labour quotas or other production targets. Rewards shall be given to the personnel for whom labour quotas shall not be prescribed and other production targets shall not be appraised as well according to their fulfillment of their personal responsibility and their own work.

The rewards given to advanced collectives and advanced individuals in labour emulation shall be drawn from the enterprise rewarding funds or enterprise funds and shall not be more than one per cent of the total of the standard wages of the staff members and workers.

4 Each enterprise shall give full play to the role of the staff and workers' congress or the staff and workers' general meeting. The procedures for the use of enterprise rewarding funds and for the rewarding shall be discussed and passed by the staff and workers' congress or the staff and workers' general meeting.

5 The reckless granting of rewards, allowances, subsidies or material objects shall be resolutely checked.

The following fall under the reckless granting of rewards, allowances, subsidies or material objects in violation of state provisions:

(1) An enterprise has given rewards even though it suffers losses in its business or even though it has not fulfilled the state plans for major economic or technical targets.

(2) The total of rewards given is in excess of these Provisions and the specific provisions of the people's government of the province, municipality or autonomous region or of each department of the State Council in charge.

(3) Prices are raised or covertly raised without authorization in violation of state policies of prices so as to seek illicit profits and give rewards by means of this.

(4) Various pretexts are concocted to give rewards by such illegal means as taking a share of sales money, forcibly taking up part of the cost, cashing fraudulently, etc.

(5) Rewards are given on the excuse of promoting the sale of idle commodities or purchasing short goods and materials.

(6) "Rewards" are presented between enterprises or units for the purpose of trying to establish a relationship with each other, or the higher department in charge asks the enterprises under it for "rewards."

(7) Various rewards in kind (for example, desk lamps, electric fans, furniture, etc. are sold to the staff members and workers at low prices) are covertly given.

(8) Allowances or subsidies are recklessly given in violation of state provisions or the scopes of giving allowances or subsidies or the standards of allowances or subsidies are wilfully extended or raised.

If a violation of the provisions as aforesaid occurs in a bureau in charge of enterprises, a corporation or an enterprise, its immediate higher department in charge shall duly handle it and resolutely put it right. Some shall have the granting of their rewards stopped and some others shall have their rewards, allowances or subsidies deducted for reimbursement. With regard to the rewards in kind covertly given, compensations shall be paid at rational prices and the excessively given ones shall be recovered. The leading personnel concerned shall be criticized and necessary punishments shall be imposed on those whose cases are serious.

In general, the rewards, allowances, subsidies or material objects which had been excessively given before the transmission of these Provisions shall no longer be dealt with again. However, the responsibility shall be investigated and affixed on the leading personnel concerned in respect of the violations of law and discipline, the deliberate violations of state provisions or vile cases and they shall be severely dealt with.

6 The enterprises which are qualified for the implementation of the piece rate wage system shall implement this wage system in accordance with the provisions in the "(Draft) Interim Procedures for Piece Rate Wages in State Enterprises" promulgated by the State Planning Commission, the State Economic Commission and the State Bureau of Labour in April of 1980. No regular

production rewards shall be implemented any longer for the staff members and workers who practise the piece rate wage system (including the share-drawing or profit sharing wage system) with the exception of the practice of the specific fuel or raw material economy rewards. In the enterprises which practise profit reserves, the excessive parts of piece rate wages shall be paid from their profit reserves.

7 The administration and supervision of rewards shall be strengthened.

In the enterprises which implement profit reserves and which assume sole responsibility for their own profits or losses, the production rewards given out of the rewarding funds shall be drawn from the "Special-Purpose Fund Accounts" opened by them with banks.

With regard to the production rewards given by the enterprises which have not implemented profit reserves or the economy rewards given by the enterprises which implement specific fuel or raw material economy prices, the enterprises shall take the certificates of the totals of rewards approved by the department in charge of them to the banks with which their accounts are opened and the banks shall pay the money by the certificates.

If the above provisions are violated, each bank shall be entitled to refuse to pay the rewards.

The department in charge of enterprises shall strengthen the supervision and inspection of the drawing and granting of rewards by the enterprises under it and shall not neglect its duty. The economic commission, financial and trade office, labour department, financial department and people's bank at each level shall also assume the responsibility of supervision and inspection. If a problem which is difficult to handle occurs, a report shall be submitted to the people's government of the province, municipality or autonomous region or even to the State Council.

8 The people's government of each province, municipality or autonomous region or each department concerned of the State Council shall formulate specific stipulations on the basis of these provisions in the light of the actual conditions of the area or the department, transmit them to lower levels and put them into effect. In the formulation of the specific stipulations, the opinions of the trade union at the same level shall be solicited. The copies of the specific stipulations shall be submitted to the State Bureau of Labour, the State Economic Commission, the Ministry of Finance, the head office of the People's Bank of China and at the same time to the All-China Federation of Trade Unions.

The provisons for the rewards system of the enterprises of collective ownership (including the enterprises jointly run by the units of the whole people's ownership and those of collective ownership) shall be made by the people's government of each province, municipality or autonomous region itself in the spirit of these Provisions, transmitted to lower levels and put into effect, and their copies shall be submitted to the State Bureau of Labour, the State Economic Commission, the Ministry of Finance, the head office of the People's Bank of China and the All-China Federation of Trade Unions.

9 These Provisions shall be applicable to industrial, communications, capital construction, financial and trade, agricultural and forestry and other enterprises and put into effect as of January of 1981. If the relevant provisions in the past go against these Provisions, these Provisions shall be implemented instead.

In the implementation of these Provisions, each area, department or enterprise shall be sure to sum up their experiences conscientiously, make good jobs of thoroughgoing and painstaking ideological and political work and handle the current existing problems carefully and skillfully so as to really accomplish the proper implementation of the rewards system, promote the development of production and maintain stability and unity.

SUPPLEMENTARY PROVISIONS OF THE STATE COUNCIL ON PROBLEMS IN IMPLEMENTATION OF THE NO.10 DOCUMENT OF THE STATE COUNCIL

(May 31, 1981)

Since the resumption and implementation of the rewarding system of enterprises in 1978, it has played a positive role in mobilizing the enthusiasm of the broad masses of workers and staff members, impelling the development of production and promoting stability and unity, so the main trend is good. However, the problem of the abusive grant of rewards and the tendency towards equalitarianism actually exist and shall be conscientiously put right.

In January this year, the State Council issued "Several Provisions for Properly Implementing the Rewarding System and Resolutely Checking the Abusive Grant of Rewards" (i.e., the No. 10 (1981) Document of the State Council). Each area or each department is implementing the document. In order to implement the No. 10 Document of the State Council, the following supplementary provisions are made:

1 In the implementation of the No. 10 Document of the State Council, each area, department or unit shall make good jobs of the following links:

First, strengthen the political and ideological work on the workers and staff members, quicky made the No. 10 Document of the State Council and these Supplementary Provisions directly known by the masses of workers and staff members, make clear the current economic situation and tasks, state explicitly that there is still rather great difficulty in the current state finance and explain the relations between the increase of production, that of profits and that of rewards in the light of the actual conditions of the area, department or unit itself. Educate the broad masses of workers and staff members to proceed from the situation as a whole and adopt a correct attitude towards the interests of the state, the collective and the individuals. Meanwhile, by relying upon the broad masses of workers, technical personnel and management cadres, make great efforts to improve the business management of enterprises, rigorously increase production and practise strict economy, put the production on a regular basis and accomplish the increase of production and revenue.

Secondly, both the people's and collective units shall conscientiously implement the principle of distribution according to work and resolutely overcome equalitarianism. In the current granting of rewards by enterprises, some enterprises do not conscientiously implement the principle of distribution according to work and the equalitarianism in them is serious, which is disadvantageous to the mobilization of the enthusiasm of the enterprises and workers and staff members. In future, the granting of rewards shall be closely combined with the overall economic results of an enterprise and with the degrees of the labour contributions of workers and staff members. More rewards shall be given for an enterprise with full productive tasks, satisfactory fulfillments of various economic and technical targets and high levels of profits; less rewards shall be given for an enterprise with insufficient productive tasks, common fulfillments of various economic and technical targets and reduction of profits which is not caused by objective causes; the granting of rewards shall be resolutely stopped for a closed or dissolved enterprise or an enterprise which suffers operational losses or which has not fulfilled the state plans of major economic and technical targets.

Thirdly, all enterprises shall make a conscientious final account and reorganize the granting of rewards. They shall continue to persist in the practice which is rational and advantageous to the mobilization of the enthusiasm of workers and staff members and the promotion of production. They shall resolutely correct and check the eight cases of the abusive granting of rewards in violation of the state provisions as pointed out in the No. 10 Document of the State Council and the misuse and wrongful application of capital to issue "subsidies" and those in kind. They shall rationally organize production and strictly control overtime work.

Fourthly, they shall combine the proper implementation of the rewarding system with the consolidation of enterprise management, establish and perfect a set standard of personal administration and the system of personal responsibility and strengthen the economic accounting of the enterprise at each level.

2 The Control of the Levels of Rewards:

In principle, the procedures for the control of the levels of rewards shall still be executed as stipulated in the No. 10 Document of the State Council, namely, the rewards shall be controlled within the total of one to two months' standard wages with the bureau in charge or the corporation at the same level of the bureau as the calculating unit. If some areas have difficulty in the execution of the above-mentioned procedures, they shall be controlled by the "trade organizational system" (such as the industrial and communications trade organizational system, the capital construction trade organizational system, the finanical and trade organizational system) with the approval of the people's government of the province, municipality or autonomous region or controlled by the prefecture or city in the province by the "trade organizational system" so as to facilitate the regulation between trades.

The total of the rewards actually given this year shall be remarkably reduced as compared with that of last year. This can be accomplished so long as an enterprise or a bureau makes a conscientious consolidation of the granting of rewards, resolutely corrects and checks such phenomena as giving rewards abusively, giving "subsidies" or those in kind by extruding the cost wantonly, etc., and overcomes equalitarianism. In the case of an area or a department with the total of the rewards actually given last year within one and a half months' standard wages, the total of rewards this year shall, in principle, not exceed that of last year. But the total shall be properly increased with the approval of the people's government of the province, municipality or autonomous region in the case of an enterprise with better fulfillments of various economic and technical targets and higher levels of profits than last year and with outstanding achievement.

3 According to the provisions in the No. 10 Document of the State Council, the total of rewards given the whole year shall be a little more with the approval of the department concerned in the case of a very few enterprises which have fulfilled various economic and technical targets in an outstanding way and have made especially great contributions, but it shall not be more than the total of three months' standard wages. The parts of the rewards of such enterprises in excess of the totals of two months' standard wages shall also be included in the controlled limits of rewards of the bureau in charge (or corporation) or of the "trade organizational system."

4 In order to raise labour efficiency and contribute to the strengthening of the contingent of workers and staff members, an enterprise shall make a good job of the fixing of norms and persons and organize production in strict accordance with the fixed norms and fixed persons. An enterprise shall train all its workers and staff members in rotation by stages and in groups and the number of persons to be trained each stage shall be determined according to the surplus persons after the fixing. In order to encourage the trained workers and staff members to endeavour to acquire literacy and learn techniques and raise the level of production technology, proper scholarships shall be given to the workers and staff members who get excellent results in their studies during the training. The scholarships for the trained workers and staff members shall be included in the limits of rewards of the enterprise.

5 The drawing proportions of rewarding funds and their sources for each unit shall still be implemented in accordance with the provisions of the State Council and the departments concerned of the State Council. The surplus of the rewarding funds drawn after the granting of rewards shall be used for collective welfare facilities or carried forward for use in the next year.

6 An enterprise with full productive tasks shall implement the piece rate wage system for the workers who are suitable for such implementation on the basis of establishing the system of responsibility and the system of appraisal and perfecting the fixed-norm administration by making the levels of the fixed norms advanced and rational. The piece rate shall be reckoned by the collective or by the individual. The workers who practise the piece rate wage system shall no longer obtain regular production rewards. Those who cannot practise the piece rate wage system shall have their rewards calculated by recording their workpoints.

The implementation of the piece rate wage system shall be linked up with the economic results of the enterprise so as to ensure the quality, reduce labour cost and achieve a greater increase of production and revenue. With this prerequisite, an enterprise which practises profit reserves shall pay the piece rate wages out of its cost and check and reduce the proportion of the enterprise's profit reserves accordingly. The rewarding funds drawn by the enterprise out of the profit reserves shall not include the wages of the workers who practise the piece rate system so as to avoid double expenditure which may cause waste.

7 An enterprise shall launch socialist labour emulation drives and implement the principle of combining moral encouragement and material reward with the stress laid on the former. The labour emulation rewards which make up one per cent of the total of standard wages shall be well used, paid by the grass-roots unit out of the enterprise rewarding funds or enterprise funds and not included in the limits of rewards given by the

enterprise. The rewards of the model workers conferred by each level above the grass-roots shall be given by the grass-roots unit and no rewards shall be doubly given by the organization at each level above the grass-roots, which shall mainly give them honorable rewards.

8 While grasping production, the economic commission at each level shall handle the rewarding work well. The department of labour at each level shall cooperate closely with the economic commission and other departments concerned and conscientiously and responsibly do the overall administration work of rewarding well.

The rewarding and piece rate reckoning work of the units directly under the central authorities shall be arranged for by the central departments in charge; the rewarding and piece rate reckoning work of the units under local authorities or those under dual leadership with the local leadership as the major one shall be arranged for by the people's government of the province, municipality or autonomous region.

The people's government of each province, municipality or autonomous region or each central department concerned shall make specific provisions for the implementation of the No. 10 Document of the State Council and its supplementary provisions in the light of actual conditions.

9 Having drawn the lesson in the preceding period that the reckless or excessive granting of rewards increased the difficulty in the state revenue, the leading cadres at each level shall proceed from the situation as a whole, rigorously enforce financial and economic discipline, struggle resolutely against the unhealthy tendencies of dishonest practices, combine the consolidation of rewards with that of the enterprise and pay close attention to and make a good job of these consolidations so as to enable our economic work to make a new advance.

The people's government of each province, municipality or autonomous region or each central department concerned shall duly report to the State Council on the implementation of the No. 10 Document of the State Council and these Supplementary Provisions.

NOTICE OF THE MINISTRY OF COMMERCE CONCERNING THE TRANSMISSION TO LOWER LEVELS OF "PROVISIONAL PROCEDURES FOR THE IMPLEMENTATION OF THE SYSTEM OF FIXED WAGES PLUS DIVIDEND WAGES IN STATE CATERING AND SERVICE ENTERPRISES"

(July 27, 1981)

In order to implement the principle of work according to ability and distribution according to work and mobilize the labour enthusiasm of workers and staff members, we are now issuing to you the "Provisional Procedures for the Implementation of the System of Fixed Wages plus Dividend Wages in State Catering and Service Enterprises" with the consent of the State Bureau of Labour and the Ministry of Finance in the spirit of the No. (81) 10 Document of the State Council, namely, "Several Provisions for Properly Implementing the Rewarding System and Resolutely Checking the Abusive Grant of Rewards" and the supplementary provisions of the State Council for the implementation of the No. 10 Document, and you are requested to put them into trial implementation step by step in a planned way under the leadership of the people's government of the province, municipality or autonomous region and pay attention to handling the following problems well in your work:

1 You shall conscientiously estimate and calculate well so as to enable the dividend rates to properly embody and consider the interests of the state, the enterprise and the workers and staff members. You shall ensure the increase of the state accumulation and that of the enterprise's income and cause the income of workers and staff members to be on the increase, preventing the tendency or giving one-sided consideration.

2 You shall conscientiously consolidate grass-roots enterprises, make great efforts to improve business management and accomplish the increase of revenue and the economy on expenditure in accordance with the requirements of the "Regulations on the Administration of State Catering and Service Enterprises," but it shall never be allowed to seek profits and expend dividend wages by means of such wrong practices as violating policies, raising prices, driving up prices covertly and deteriorating service quality.

3 The commercial and service administrations at each level shall strengthen leadership, do ideological and political work well and educate the broad masses of cadres and workers and staff members to proceed from the overall situation of carrying out the further economic regulation and achieving further political stability, struggle arduously and work hard. They shall go down to the grass-roots units, duly study and settle the new situations and problems emerging in the course of the implementation, sum up experience and perfect the implementation so as to push this work healthily forward.

PROVISIONAL PROCEDURES FOR THE IMPLEMENTATION OF THE SYSTEM OF FIXED WAGES PLUS DIVIDEND WAGES IN STATE CATERING AND SERVICE ENTERPRISES

(September 7, 1981)

Chapter I General Rules

Article 1 These Procedures are formulated for the purpose of fully mobilizing the labour enthusiasm of workers and staff members, improving the business management of enterprises and enhancing working efficiency and service quality so as to serve production and the people's livelihood better.

Article 2 The system of fixed wages plus dividend wages is a better form of wages to suit the features of the productive labour and management of the catering trade and other service trades and embody the principle of distribution according to work, i.e., more pay for more work, less pay for less work and equal pay for equal work. In the implementation of this system of wages, consideration shall be given to the interests of the four parties, i.e., the state, the collective of the enterprise, the individual workers and staff members and the consumers, and the income of workers and staff members shall be increased on the basis of the increase of production and revenue and the guarantee of more gains for the state and for the enterprise.

Article 3 An enterprise shall be provided with certain favourable conditions for the implementation of the system of fixed wages plus dividend wages, such as rather stable operations, rather rational labour organizations, rather sound systems of management (such as the records of work volumes, the examination system of service quality, etc.), independent financial accounting and strict calculation of economic results.

Chapter II The Concrete Forms of Dividend Wages

Article 4 An enterprise which practises the system of fixed wages plus dividend wages shall share the dividend wages separately by the group or by the enterprise. The share-out by the group shall be practised if turnovers or the sums of profits can be calculated and examined independently by the group, while the share-out by the enterprise shall be practised if they can only be calculated and examined by the enterprise.

Article 5 In order to ensure the relative stability of the livelihood of workers and staff members and avoid a too great disparity between the income of workers and staff members in the off seasons and that in the peak periods, the current standard wages with a certain discount (for example, 20% less) shall be taken as the parts of the fixed wages and the shares according to the sums of profits or to the turnovers shall be taken as the parts of the dividend wages. But each area shall properly expand or reduce the proportions of the parts of fixed wages according to local conditions.

Article 6 With regard to the parts of dividend wages, it is, in general, better to practise the share out of the full profits. An enterprise practising profit share out shall take appropriate measures to ensure the quality of products and services so as to protect the interests of consumers and guarantee proper expenditure of expenses and state accumulation. An enterprise which practises the share-out according to the turnovers shall prescribe rational norms of raw material consumption, expenses and labour so as to prevent the pure pursuit of high turnovers regardless of costs or the interests of the state and the enterprise.

Article 7 An enterprise which implements the system of fixed wages plus dividend wages shall strictly execute state policies and decrees. If the enterprise suffers loss, only the parts of the fixed wages shall be paid. The part of the income obtained in violation of policies or at the expense of the interests of the state or of consumers shall be deducted from the profits to be shared out. For example, the income of the catering trade in excess of the scope of gross profits stipulated by the higher authorities or the irrational reductions of other service trades of the consumption of materials or articles or of the expenditure which is determined to ensure service quality shall not be included in the share-out of the dividend wages of workers and staff members. In addition, their causes shall be discovered and they shall be put right.

Chapter III The Determination and Revision of Dividend Rates

Article 8 The determination of dividend rates shall be rational. So-called rational standards mean that the actual income of individual workers and staff members is properly increased while the workers and staff members endeavour to improve their service and fulfill various economic targets under the circumstances of rather rational labour organizations and rather normal operating conditions and it is ensured that the state and the enterprise obtain more of the increased profits. The concrete proportions of dividend wages shall be controlled according to areas and trades and checked and ratified by the commercial and service department or bureaux of each province, municipality or autonomous region jointly with the labour and financial departments according to different trades and on the basis of local conditions. Equalitarianism shall not be settled in one attempt and it shall be prevented to show a tendency towards higher standards with the reluctance to reduce them according to actual conditions and toward the pursuit of dividend wages in high proportions.

Article 9 The dividend rates of each enterprise shall be determined by the departments of each area in charge of catering and service trades according to different trades and different types, grades, sections, and business conditions of enterprises and submitted to the local administrations for commercial and service trades for approval before implementation.

In order to increase the gains of workers and staff members properly on the basis of ensuring more gains for the state, the progressive decrease of dividend rates by stages shall generally be adopted at present without the provision for the maximum limits of individual dividend wages.

Article 10 Dividend rates shall be kept stable under normal conditions and, in general, examined and revised once a year (a period of trial implementation shall be set for the dividend rates prescribed for the first time, for example, three to six months' trial implementation), but they shall be duly revised if there is a major change in the scale, grade, business scope, operating conditions or labour organizations of the enterprise.

Article 11 In general, the dividend rates in the off seasons and in the peak periods shall be identical and it shall not be allowed to raise the dividend rates in the off seasons for the purpose of ensuring the income of workers and staff members. The correct practice shall be adjusting the labour organizations rationally according to different business conditions in the off seasons and the peak periods so as to expand the business and increase profits, or storing up in the peak periods to make up for the off seasons, namely, transferring the surplus after the distribution of dividend wages in the peak periods to be used in the off seasons.

Chapter IV The Distribution of Dividend Wages

Article 12 The dividend wages obtained by a group or an enterprise shall be rationally distributed according to the degrees of the working achievements or the labour results of each member on the principle of "distribution according to work and more pay for more work." In general, the leading and management personnel who are released from production or original work in an enterprise shall participate in the distribution of dividend wages in the light of the fulfillment of their tasks at their posts.

Article 13 With regard to the specific procedures for the distribution of dividend wages, the method of "changeable value for fixed share" or "changeable value for changeable share" shall be adopted or the way of combining "fixed share and changeable share" but calculating the pay in "changeable value" shall be used. The assessment of "fixed share" shall mainly be based on such actual conditions as each worker's or each staff member's technical level, responsibility, labour intensity, labour conditions and the amount of his or her original wages and it shall be rationally determined through democratic appraisal. "Fixed shares" shall be assessed once a quarter, a half year or a year, during which the "fixed shares" shall be kept fixed and unchanged. In the determination of "changeable shares," the method of "recording workpoints" shall be adopted as far as possible, namely, the points of the "changeable share" of each worker or staff member shall be recorded and calculated according to his or her actual labour results and the requirements for the reward or forfeiture of workpoints.

Article 14 Dividend wages shall be paid out of the item of wages. The surplus of the amount of dividend wages after the rational distribution of them among workers and staff members shall be carried forward for use in the next year.

Chapter V The Administration of Dividend Wages

Article 15 The commercial and service departments or bureaux of each province, municipality or autonomous region shall formulate the specific procedures which are suited to the area in the spirit of these Procedures and obtain the consent of the provincial bureau of labour and department (bureau) of finance before implementation.

Article 16 A grass-roots enterprise shall submit the specific procedures and rules for the implementation of dividend wages to the higher unit in charge for approval.

Article 17 An enterprise shall implement the same system of wages for the workers or staff members who do the same work in the same period and it shall not be allowed to implement the system of fixed wages plus dividend wages for some persons, while practising the time wage system for the others.

Article 18 The department in charge of enterprises or an enterprise shall strengthen the administration of wages, put someone in charge of it, pay regular attention to the analysis and examination of the operation of the enterprise, the workers' and staff members' income of wages and the wage relations between the workers and staff members inside the enterprise and those outside it and between new workers and staff members and old ones, duly sum up and improve the wage work and strictly implement the wage policies and decrees stipulated by the state.

Article 19 An enterprise which implements the system of fixed wages plus dividend wages shall no longer grant regular production or service rewards or overall rewards except for the invention, technological improvement and fuel saving rewards stipulated by the state. No overtime wages shall be paid as well except for statutory festivals and holidays. If a worker or a staff member is transferred out of the enterprise, his or her standard wages shall be taken as the criterion. Long-term sick leave, resignations or retirements shall be handled in accordance with the provisions in the labour protection regulations.

Article 20 An enterprise which implements the system of fixed wages plus dividend wages shall not only oppose equalitarianism in the distribution, but also prevent such unhealthy tendencies as the mere pursuit of quantity to the neglect of quality and at the expense of equipment or appliances, putting in excessive extra hours which affects the health of workers and staff members, etc., for the purpose of obtaining more dividend wages.

Article 21 An enterprise which implements the system of fixed wages plus dividend wages shall strengthen political and ideological work and educate the broad masses of workers and staff members to cultivate the communist attitide towards labour, serve the people wholeheartedly and develop the revolutionary spirit of being selfless, putting others before oneself, building up the country through thrift and hard work and struggling arduously so as to make more contributions to the socialist modernization construction. Material reward shall be well combined with moral encouragement and necessary honorable rewards shall be given to the collectives and individuals who have made contributions to the state so as to further arouse the socialist enthusiasm of workers and staff members.

Article 22 These Procedures shall only be applicable to independent accounting grass-roots enterprises. The business management units at each level shall implement the procedures for reward like commercial business management units.

REGULATIONS ON REWARDS AND PUNISHMENTS FOR ENTERPRISE WORKERS AND STAFF MEMBERS

(Adopted by the Ordinary Meeting of the State Council on March 12, 1982 and promulgated and put into effect on April 10)

Chapter I General Rules

Article 1 These Regulations are formulated in accordance with the relevant provisions in the Constitution of the People's Republic of China in order to enhance the sense of responsibility of enterprise workers and staff members as the masters of the state, encourage their initiative and creativity, maintain normal productive and working order, improve labour productivity and working efficiency and promote the socialist modernization construction.

Article 2 Enterprise workers and staff members shall abide by state policies, laws and decrees, observe labour discipline, comply with various rules and regulations of each individual enterprise, take good care of public property, learn and master cultural, technical and professional knowledge and skills required for their own jobs, unite and cooperate with each other and fulfil production and working tasks.

Article 3 In the implementation of the regulations on rewards and punishments, an enterprise shall combine ideological and political work with economic means. The principles of the combination of moral encouragement and material reward with emphasis on the former shall be upheld in the rewards; the principles of emphasizing ideological education with the punishments as the supplementary means shall be maintained with regard to the workers and staff members who violate discipline.

Article 4 These Regulations shall be applicable to all the workers and staff members of enterprises of the people's ownership and those of collective ownership in cities and towns. With regard to the rewards or punishments given to the working personnel in the enterprises who are appointed by state administrative authorities, the limits of authority of approval and the procedures of examination and approval shall be handled in accordance with the "Interim Provisions of the State Council for the Rewards and Punishments of the Working Personnel of State Administrative Authorities."

Chapter II Rewards

Article 5 Rewards shall be given to a worker or a staff member who has any of the following manifestations:

(1) Having made remarkable achievements in such aspects as fulfilling productive tasks or working tasks, improving product quality or service quality, saving on state assets and energy, etc.;

(2) Having made inventions, technical improvements or rationalization proposals or having yielded significant results or made remarkable achievements in such aspects as production, scientific research, technological design, product design, improving labour conditions, etc.;

(3) Having made remarkable achievements and relatively great contributions to the state in the improvement of the business management of the enterprise and the increase of the economic benefit;

(4) Having made contributions to the protection of public property or the prevention or remedy of accidents so as to protect the interests of the state and the people from great losses;

(5) Having made outstanding merits in the struggle against evildoers and evil deeds and in the maintenance of normal productive order or working order and social public order;

(6) Having performed outstanding deeds in safeguarding financial and economic discipline and resisting unhealthy trends and evil practices;

(7) Being always devoted to his or her duty, energetic and responsible, honest in performing his or her official duties, having sacrificed his or her own interests for the sake of others and having performed outstanding deeds;

(8) Others deserving rewards.

Article 6 The rewards for workers and staff members are divided into: citations for merit, citations for great merit, promotions, orders of commendation and conferring of honorable titles such as advanced producer (worker), model worker, etc. When the above rewards are given, money rewards shall also be given at the same time.

Article 7 With regard to the citation for merit, the citation for great merit, the grant of money rewards or the conferring of honorable title of advanced producer (worker), a proposal shall be made by the trade union and a decision shall be made by the enterprise or the higher department in charge of the enterprise. In general, money rewards shall be given once a year and paid out of the total of the labour emulation rewards of the enterprise.

The orders of commendation shall be determined by the people's government at each level or by the higher department in charge of the enterprise.

The procedures for conferring the honorable title of model worker shall be otherwise formulated.

Article 8 In giving rewards to workers and staff members, the masses in the unit where they are located shall have discussions or choices through public appraisal, which shall be handled within the limits of authority stipulated in Article 7. If a worker or a staff member obtains a reward, the enterprise shall enter it into his or her personal file.

Article 9 Rewards shall be given to a worker or a staff member who has made an invention, a technical improvement or a rationalization proposal in conformity with the provision in Item (2) of Article 5 in accordance with the "Regulations on the Rewards for Inventions" and the "Regulations on the Rewards for Rationalization Proposals and Technical Improvements" and no further money rewards shall be given.

Article 10 The granting principles, sources of money rewards and procedures for proposing rewards of regular production rewards and saving rewards shall be handled in accordance with the relevant provisions of the state.

Chapter III Punishments

Article 11 Disciplinary punishments or economic sanctions shall be imposed according to different conditions on a worker or a staff member who has committed any of the following deeds and refuses to mend his or her ways despite criticism and admonition:

(1) Violating labour discipline, frequently being late for work and leaving the post early and staying away from work without leave, being slack in work and failing to fulfill productive tasks or working tasks;

(2) Refusing to obey the assignment, transfer or direction of jobs without proper reasons or making troubles wilfully, ganging up to create disturbances or coming to blows so as to affect productive, working and social public order;

(3) Neglecting duty, violating technical operating rules and safety rules or giving orders against regulations so as to cause accidents and result in losses to the life and property of the people;

(4) Being irresponsible at work, frequently producing waste products, damaging equipment and tools and wasting raw materials and energy, resulting in economic losses;

(5) Abusing his or her powers, violating policies and decrees, contravening financial and economic discipline, evading taxes, intercepting and retaining profits to be turned over, giving money rewards recklessly, squandering and wasting state assets and benefiting himself or herself at the expense of the public so as to cause economic losses to the state and to the enterprise;

(6) Practising graft and embezzlement, speculation and profiteering, smuggling and selling smuggled goods, offering and accepting bribes, extortion and blackmail or other unlawful or discipline-violating activities;

(7) Committing other serious mistakes. If a worker or a staff member who has committed any of the above deeds has such a serious case as to violate the criminal law, he or she shall be punished by the judicial authorities according to law.

Article 12 The disciplinary punishments of workers and staff members are divided into: warnings, records of demerits, records of serious offences, demotions, dismissals from posts, placing on probation within the enterprise and discharges. While the above disciplinary punishments are affixed, fines shall also be imposed at the same time.

Article 13 The discharge of a worker or a staff member shall be proposed by the factory director (manager) and discussed and resolved by the staff and workers' congress or by the staff and workers' general meeting and then reported to the department in charge of the enterprise and the department of labour or personnel at the location of the enterprise for filing.

Article 14 If a worker or a staff member is placed on probation within the enterprise, the period of probation shall be one to two years. During the period of probation, the issue of his or her wages shall be stopped and living expenses shall be given. The standards of the living expenses shall be lower than those of his or her original wages, which shall be determined by the enterprise according to conditions. After the expiration of his or her probation, he or she shall be reinstated as an official worker or staff member and his or her wages shall be reassessed if he or she has done well on probation; he or she shall be discharged if he or she acts badly.

Article 15 If a worker or a staff member is dismissed from his or her post, the grade of his or her wages shall be reduced at the same time if necessary.

In general, the scope of the demotion punishment of a worker or a staff member shall be one grade and not more than two grades.

Article 16 The sums of the fines on workers and staff members shall be decided upon by the enterprise and, in general, shall not be more than 20 per cent of their monthly standard wages.

Article 17 The workers and staff members who have performed the deeds in Items (3) and (4) of Article 11 shall be ordered to compensate for the economic losses. The sums of the compensations for economic losses shall be determined by the enterprise according to specific conditions and deducted from the wages of the workers amd staff members, but the monthly deducted sums shall not be more than 20 per cent of their monthly standard wages. If they can promptly correct their mistakes and have done very well, the sums of compensations shall be reduced as the enterprise thinks fit.

Article 18 The enterprise shall be entitled to remove from the rolls the name of a worker or a staff member who frequently stays away from work without leave and proper reasons and refuses to mend his or her own ways despite criticism and admonition if he or she stays away from work without leave in succession for more than 15 days or for more than 30 days by the cumulative total within a year.

Article 19 To impose disciplinary punishments and economic sanctions on a worker or a staff member, the facts shall be straightforward and the evidence shall be obtained, certain meetings shall be held to discuss them, the opinions of the trade union shall be solicited, the punished shall be permitted to argue his or her own case and the decision shall be prudently made.

Article 20 With regard to the time for the examination and approval of a punishment of discharge on a worker or a staff member, it shall not be more than five months from the date of the worker's or the staff member's commitment of the mistake and shall not be more than three months for another punishment.

The enterprise shall notify the worker or staff member in writing of the disciplinary punishment, economic sanction or removal of title imposed on him or her and enter it in his or her personal file.

Article 21 After the approval of the punishment of a worker or a staff member, the punished may make a written appeal to the higher leading authorities within 10 days of the announcement of the punishment if he or she refuses to accept it as final. But the original punishment decision shall still be executed before the higher leading authorities make any decision to alter the original punishment.

Article 22 In general, a worker or a staff member shall settle in the place where the enterprise is located after he or she is discharged or after his or her name is removed from the rolls.

If he or she asks to return to his or her native place, his or her request shall be handled on the principles of removing from a large city to a medium or small one, from a coastal area to an inland or border one or from a city or town to the countryside.

If he or she conforms to the provisions in this Article, the department in charge of the enterprise shall get in prior touch with the public security department at the destination of his or her move. The public security department at the destination shall handle the settlement formalities by the certificate of the department in charge of the enterprise. A production team shall allow the one who returns to the countryside to settle there.

Article 23 The punished workers and staff members shall be treated in the same way as other workers and members according to the stipulated qualifications in respect of the assessment of rewards, promotion, etc., if they have been punished by means of warnings, records of demerits or records of serious mistakes for more than half a year or if they have been dismissed from their posts for more than one year or if they have been approved to be reinstated as official workers and staff members after being placed on probation within the enterprise.

Article 24 Necessary punishments shall be imposed on the workers and staff members who seek rewards through fraud and deception according to the degrees of seriousness.

Article 25 Severe punishments shall be imposed on or even criminal responsibility shall be investigated and affixed on the personnel who abuse their powers to make use of punishments to retaliate upon workers and staff members or who harbour the workers and staff members who shall be punished.

Chapter IV Supplementary Provisions

Article 26 The people's government of each province, municipality or autonomous region and each department of the State Council shall formulate the procedures for the implementation of the provisions in these Regulations.

Article 27 The department of labour at each level shall be entitled to exercise supervision and examination over the execution of these Regulations.

Article 28 These Regulations shall be put into effect from the date of promulgation.

NOTICE OF THE STATE COUNCIL TO RIGOROUSLY CURTAIL ABUSIVE PAYMENTS OF OVERTIME WAGES BY ENTERPRISES

(April 8, 1982)

In recent years, enterprises have organized workers and staff members to work too many extra hours and paid very large sums of overtime wages, some of which are required for the production (work) but a large part of which are not necessary. An important cause of working too many extra hours is that some enterprises regard it as the means to increase the income of workers and staff members and some others have even gone so far as to violate financial and economic discipline, concoct various pretexts and employ trickery so as to make fraudulent applications for claims of overtime wages. This practice of organizing workers and staff members wilfully to work extra hours and paying overtime wages abusively has not only decreased the state revenue, reduced the economic benefit of enterprises and been disadvantageous to the regulation of the national economy, but also affected the health of workers and staff members and corroded their ideology. In order to effectively control the overtime work of enterprises and curtail the reckless payment of overtime wages, this Notice is given as follows:

1. Each enterprise or each department in charge of enterprises shall strengthen ideological and political work and teach workers and staff members to enhance the sense of responsibility as masters, make full attendance, work full hours, raise the utilization rates of working hours, increase working efficiency and labour productivity and endeavour to fulfill or overfulfill productive (working) tasks within normal working hours. Meanwhile, it shall strengthen enterprise management, organize balanced production well, pay attention to the proper balance between the work and rest of workers and staff members and protect their health. It shall correct such wrong practices as relying upon working extra hours to fulfill productive tasks, paying overtime wages as a means to increase the income of workers and staff members covertly, etc.

2. No enterprise shall work extra hours under normal circumstances and shall organize its workers and staff members to work overtime only under the following conditions:

(1) The work cannot be interrupted and the production, transportation or business must be continued on statutory festivals or public holidays.

(2) It is required to make use of the suspension of production during statutory festivals or public holidays to overhaul or maintain and install equipment.

(3) Rush repairs must be done because of the temporary troubles of production equipment, communications and transportation lines, public facilities, etc.

(4) Rescues shall be carried out because the people's safety or health or state assets are being seriously endangered by a serious natural disaster or other calamity.

(5) Overtime work is required for the purpose of fulfilling urgent productive tasks for national defence or fulfilling other urgent productive tasks arranged by higher authorities outside state plans, or commercial and supply and marketing enterprises have to fulfill the urgent tasks of purchasing, transporting or processing agricultural and sideline products in peak seasons.

3. To organize workers and staff members to work overtime under any of the above circumstances, an enterprise shall, in advance, put forward its reasons, estimate the volume of work and the number of workers and staff members who will work overtime, obtain the consent of the trade union organization at the same level and then go through the formalities of examination and approval; if it is really difficult to estimate the volume of work and the number of workers and staff members required in advance in a few special cases, the enterprise shall go through the formalities of examination and approval afterwards. The limits of authority to examine and approve the overtime work shall be considered and determined by the people's government of each province, municipality or autonomous region and each department of the State Council.

4. If an enterprise worker is granted substitute leave after working extra hours on a statutory festival, he or she shall be given the same number of hours as substitute leave and no overtime wages shall be paid; overtime wages can only be given when arrangement for substitute leave is impossible. In principle, no overtime wages shall be paid and only the same number of hours shall be given for substitute leave after working extra hours on a public holiday; overtime wages shall only be given to a small number of persons who really cannot have substitute leave due to the

demand of production (work). If the extra hours are added to the normal working hours, only the same hours shall be given for substitute leave and no overtime wages shall be given and accumulation of extra working hours is not allowed.

With regard to the payment of overtime wages for working on a statutory festival day, a worker or a staff member who practises the time wage system shall be paid at 200 percent of his or her daily standard wages; a worker or a staff member who practises the piece rate wage system shall be paid overtime wages at 100 percent of his or her daily standard wages in addition to the deserved piece rate wages paid according to the norm fulfilled that day and the unit piece rate fixed. With regard to the payment of overtime wages for a public holiday, a worker or a staff member who practises the time wage system shall be paid at 100 percent of his or her daily standard wages; a worker or a staff member who practises the piece rate wage system shall be paid the deserved piece rate wages and no overtime wages shall be paid. The people's government of each province, municipality or autonomous region or each department of the State Council shall consider and determine the ways.

5. No overtime pay shall be given after working extra hours to a leading cadre of an enterprise above the rank of section head or deputy or a cadre or a worker who is under the system where he or she will be paid the usual wages even though he or she is enjoying casual leave within a fixed number of days. Overtime pay shall be given to a workshop head or a deputy, a general cadre or worker who must work extra hours together with productive workers and who does not practise the system of getting paid the wages as usual even if he or she has casual leave within a fixed number of days. The overtime pay given to the cadres of the coal mine enterprises under the unified distribution shall still be implemented as stipulated in Document No. Jing-Ran 36 (1979) of the State Economic Commission.

The workers and staff members who have drawn overtime wages shall not enjoy night meal allowances simultaneously. Night meal allowances shall be given in accordance with current provisions to those who work extra hours later than 11 o'clock at night without overtime pay. The giving of night meal allowances shall also be strictly controlled and they shall not be given wantonly at will.

6. The time for a make-up rest after a worker or a staff member works extra hours shall be duly arranged by the enterprise under the conditions of ensuring the normal progress of production (work) and it shall not be delayed too long. It shall not be replaced by overtime wages at will and the worker or staff member shall be taught to observe and implement it.

7. Overtime wages shall not be paid by an enterprise which has insufficient productive tasks or which has not fulfilled the productive tasks as planned if it puts in extra hours for the purpose of doing a rush job of fulfilling the tasks or doing a rush job of fulfilling the productive tasks provisionally undertaken.

8. The total of overtime wages paid shall strictly be controlled. The department in charge of enterprises shall check and ratify the annual total of overtime wages to be paid by each enterprise separately according to the different situation of production of each enterprise in the spirit of this Notice and submit it to the local department of labour for examination and approval. The part of the total of overtime wages annually paid by an enterprise in excess of the checked and ratified limit shall be deducted from the total of rewards which has been checked and ratified and can be used for the grant that year.

9. The administration and supervision of the payment of overtime wages shall be strengthened. The department in charge of enterprises and the department of labour at each level shall conscientiously check, ratify, examine and approve of the overtime plans and the total of overtime wages which are put forward by an enterprise. In checking and ratifying an enterprise's annual total of overtime wages, the copy of the total shall be sent to a local bank so that it can supervise its implementation. If the limit of overtime wages has not been checked and ratified, the bank shall not pay the overtime wages. The department in charge of enterprises and the department of labour at each level shall strengthen the supervision and examination of the payment of overtime wages, deal seriously with the units which pay overtime wages abusively by illegitimate means and the departments which approve wantonly overtime wages in violation of current provisions and financial and economic discipline, put them right resolutely and impose disciplinary punishments on the leading personnel concerned who violate law and discipline seriously.

PROVISIONAL REGULATIONS CONCERNING PIECE-RATE WAGES IN STATE-OWNED ENTERPRISES (DRAFT)

Issued by the State Planning Commission, the State Economic Commission and the State Bureau of Labour

(April 1, 1980)

With a view to better carrying out the principle of "from each according to his ability, to each according to his work," to arousing the labour enthusiasm of the workers and staff members, to enhancing labour productivity and impelling the enterprises to improve their management so as to speed up the development of socialist production and construction, the present regulations have been worked out:

1 Those enterprises which carry out the piece-rate wage system must possess the following conditions:

a) They should have adequate production tasks and a normal supply of raw and processed materials, fuels and power and a stable market for their products;

b) They should have advanced, rational production quotas and strict standards for measuring the quantity of products and for checking on their quality;

c) They should have a fairly sound management system (with original records of production, statistical data, check-up and acceptance of products and economic accounting).

2 The enterprises which possess the necessary conditions for the implementation of the piece-rate wage system may apply it to all workers for whom the system is suitable.

3 In the course of carrying out the piece-rate wage system, the enterprises must guarantee that their products are up to the fixed standards, and that the quota for material consumption is not exceeded, and they must bring about a clear-cut reduction in the costs of per-unit products and wages. If, after an enterprise has adopted the piece-rate wage system, the quality of its products is lowered, its consumption of materials exceeds the fixed quota, or the costs of per-unit products and wages are increased, it should immediately stop practising the system. Meanwhile, the leadership of the enterprise must to a certain degree be held responsible for resultant economic losses and must recover that portion of wages that should not have been paid to the workers.

4 In practising the piece-rate wage system, an enterprise must strengthen the management of production quotas. Wherever there are unified production quotas set by the department in charge, the enterprise should adopt these quotas for its workers. Where there are no unified quotas, the enterprise may set its own quotas, but it must report them for approval to the higher authorities in charge before adopting these production quotas.

The production quotas of an enterprise, be they stipulated by the department in charge or set by the enterprise itself, must always be advanced, rational quotas. As a rule, they should be reexamined and revised every six months or each year. A timely revision must be made if any of the following cases arises:

a) Major changes made in the specifications of products or raw materials;

b) Major changes made in production equipment, instruments and in the technological process;

c) The worksite or geological conditions have changed obviously;

d) The level of some quotas has been set too low or too high;

e) The level of quotas is seriously affected by the adoption of inventions, technical innovations or rationalization proposals (the collective or individuals who have made the inventions, innovations or rationalization proposals may be allowed to keep the original level of quotas unchanged for half a year, in addition to receiving the bonuses due to them).

When production quotas are introduced by an enterprise, they first should be tried out for a certain period, but generally for not more than three months.

5 In practising the piece-rate wage system, an enterprise should fix reasonable piece prices per unit. The unit piece price of a product will be fixed on the basis of production quotas to be fulfilled by workers within a prescribed time, the standard-time wages corresponding to the equivalent grade of the object of work and the current level of workers' wages. The grade of the object of work is determined by the technical complexity, the strenuousness of the work, the weight of responsibility and the condition of the production equipment involved.

When a production quota has been revised, the unit piece price must be changed accordingly.

6 To encourage workers to raise the quality of products, the piece prices of all products that are classified according to quality should be fixed according to the principle of "higher price for better quality." The piece prices of high-quality products shall be set a little higher than that of average up-to-standard products.

To facilitate the upgrading and renewal of products, the piece price of a new variety of product may also be set higher when it is trial-produced.

7 An enterprise may apply the piece-rate wage system to the collective or to the individual according to the characteristics of its production. But among the workers of the same group or team, it shall not apply the collective piece-rate wage system to some and a time wage system to others.

8 Whether the piece-rate wage system is applied to a collective or to individual workers, an enterprise should pay the wages on the basis of piece price according to how well the collective or the workers fulfill their production quotas.

Provided that production quotas are advanced and rational, no limit should be imposed on extra wages earned by workers who overfulfill their quotas.

9 In groups or teams to which the collective piece-rate wage system is applied, the piece-rate wage received should be distributed according to the respective contributions of their members in production. It should not be distributed on a basis of equal portions.

10 The workers to whom the piece-rate wage system is applied may be given economy bonuses in accordance with the Tentative Regulations (Draft) on Bonuses for Saving Specially Designated Fuels and Raw Materials in State-Owned Industrial and Transport Enterprises as jointly promulgated on December 10, 1979 by the Ministry of Finance, the State Bureau of Labour and the State Administration of Supplies. But they shall no longer receive regular production bonuses.

11 When a worker who is paid according to the piece-rate wage system produces items that are rejected due to his own fault, the enterprise concerned shall not pay wages for the rejects but shall ask him to compensate for a part or the whole of the loss according to the seriousness of the loss he has caused. While a basic living standard is guaranteed to the worker, the maximum amount of the compensation he pays per month should not exceed 25% of his standard monthly wage and generally the compensation should be paid off within a period not exceeding six months.

12 Before an enterprise introduces the piece-rate wage system, it must make a plan and send it to the department in charge for approval and then report the system to the local labour management department for the record.

13 An enterprise practising the piece-rate wage system should at three-month intervals inform the bank with whom it has opened an account how the system is being carried out so that the bank may supervise its execution. If the bank discovers that the unit costs of a product and wages have increased after the enterprise introduced the piece-rate wage system, it has the right to examine the financial affairs of the enterprise and refuse to pay the piece wages.

14 While practising the piece-rate wage system, the enterprises should strengthen political ideological work among the workers and staff members, educating them to adopt a communist attitude towards labour, to cooperate well with each other in production, and to strictly observe labour discipline and the operating rules. Those who practise fraud, who damage equipment and tools and who waste too much raw material should be given disciplinary sanctions in accordance with the relevant regulations. The portion of wages received through fraud should be ascertained and all of it returned.

15 The provinces, municipalities and autonomous regions as well as the various departments of the State Council may, in light of their specific conditions, work out concrete rules according to the provisions of these regulations to be transmitted to their subordinate units and, at the same time, send copies of these rules to the State Planning Commission, the State Economic Commission and the State Bureau of Labour for the record.

22 INDIVIDUAL AND COLLECTIVE ENTERPRISES

Collective Enterprise/ Individual Enterprises

REGULATIONS ON QUESTIONS CONCERNING THE DEVELOPMENT OF ENTERPRISES RUN BY RURAL PEOPLE'S COMMUNES AND PRODUCTION BRIGADES

Promulgated by the State Council (Draft for Trial Use)
(July 3, 1979)

I The Significance of Developing Commune- and Brigade-Run Enterprises

In accordance with the Decision on Questions Concerning the Acceleration of Agricultural Development (Draft) adopted at the Third Plenary Session of the Eleventh Central Committee of the Communist Party of China, there should be a big expansion of enterprises run by rural people's communes and production brigades. The expansion of such enterprises can, above all, better serve the development of agricultural production, strengthen the collective economy at the commune and brigade levels and provide the funds required for mechanization. At the same time, it will open up new avenues of employment in production for the labour power which will be released by mechanization, make fuller use of local resources, aid the development of a diversified rural economy, increase collective income and raise the living standards of commune members. It will also gradually create the conditions for the people's communes to undergo the transition from the system of small-scale collective ownership to that of large-scale collective ownership and then to the system of ownership by the whole people. A big expansion of industries run by rural people's communes can provide society in general with large amounts of raw and semi-finished materials and industrial products, thus accelerating the development of China's industry as a whole; it can also avoid the disadvantage of over-concentration of industry in large and medium-sized cities. It is an important way gradually to narrow the differences between town and country, worker and peasant, and manual and mental labour.

II Guiding Principles for Development

Commune- and brigade-run enterprises must persist in the socialist orientation and strive to produce what is needed by society, serving mainly agricultural production and the people's livelihood and also the needs of large-scale industry and exports.

These enterprises must develop in line with local conditions and in accordance with local resources and social needs, and they must grow from small to big and from a lower to a higher stage. They must not be initiated if their machines cannot be "fed," nor, in the case of processing industries, should they be built with excessive production capacity. They must not compete with large-scale, advanced industries for raw materials and energy, and they must not cause damage to the natural resources of the country.

They must persist in self-reliance and hard struggle, democratic management and thrift, and must practice strict economic accounting.

Active attempts must be made to run enterprises which combine agricultural, industrial and commercial functions.

III Business Scope

Crop cultivation, animal husbandry and fish-breeding must be expanded energetically. Where local conditions are favourable, forestry centres, orchards, tea plantations, silkworm farms, medicinal herb plantations, seed-production centres, edible-mushroom farms, livestock and poultry farms, and fish hatcheries must be set up. All these can provide the basis for developing processing industries for farm and side-line products. Farms can be set up where there is virgin territory.

Efforts must be made to develop processing industries for farm and side-line products. In accordance with the principle of economic rationality, all farm, forestry, animal husbandry and fishery products and special local products which are suitable for processing by communes and brigades can be processed by them. As to those products already being processed by factories set up by the state, whether they should be handed over to commune and brigade-run enterprises is to be decided by the revolutionary committees of provinces or autonomous regions in consultation with the departments concerned and after weighing both advantages and disadvantages.

Efforts must be made to run agriculture-related industries well. Small and medium-sized farm tool manufacturing and repair shops must be set up to process spare parts under the unified plans for local farm machinery undertakings. Where the necessary conditions exist, enterprises can be set up to produce humic acid fertilizer, bacterial fertilizer, insecticides and herbicides, and veterinary medicines, and to process fodder.

In line with local conditions, more fuel and raw materials extraction industries such as bio-gas stations, small coal fields, small iron, non-ferrous metal and other mines must be initiated, and small works for producing building materials – brick yards, lime kilns, quarries and cement plants – set up. Saltworks and saline chemical works can be set up where there are abundant resources of bittern.

A major effort must be made to develop the power industry. In the light of concrete conditions, hydro- and thermal-power stations with generating capacities of 12,000 kilowatts and less can be set up.

Localities with the necessary conditions can undertake the production of spare parts or certain products subcontracted to them by large-scale industries. In accordance with the demands of the market and with the availability of energy, small chemical works, hardware factories, smelters, and workshops turning out daily necessities must be set up to make use of leftover bits and pieces of industrial material, urban and rural wastes and old materials, as well as waste residue, waste water and waste gas.

Where it is necessary and feasible, building squads and transport teams can be organized to undertake certain tasks in urban and rural capital construction, transport and loading.

Efforts must be made to produce traditional handicrafts and goods for export where there are local resources or favourable technical conditions. Production bases for export commodities must be built up step by step, based on the requirements of foreign trade. When conditions permit, compensatory trade should be promoted.

Service trades such as sewing and repair, hotel and restaurant operation, should be initiated where they are needed.

IV Plans for the Readjustment and Development of Enterprises

In the light of the spirit of the Third Plenary Session of the Eleventh Central Committee of the Communist Party, the percentage of income from nationwide commune- and brigade-run enterprises in the total income of rural people's communes at three levels should increase from 29.7 percent in 1978 to around 50 percent in 1985. The various provinces, municipalities, autonomous regions and counties must work out long-term plans for the development of commune- and brigade-run enterprises, plans which are tied closely to local plans for production in farming, forestry, animal husbandry and fisheries, industrial and transportation undertakings and for urban and rural construction, and they must see to it that these plans are implemented at the commune level. In mapping out such plans, they must seek truth from facts, take the overall situation into account, and aim at rational distribution.

The first thing in working out development plans is to adhere to the general policy for readjusting the national economy, pursuing both progress and consolidation in the course of readjustment, and accomplishing the readjustment of commune- and brigade-run enterprises as soon as possible. Efforts must be made to increase the production of raw and semi-finished materials, fuels and power, and of all badly needed commodities for the home market and for export. Enterprises with excessive capacity for spare-part production and those where the technology is not up to standard or where the problem of supplies and marketing cannot be solved must readjust the orientation of their production, merge or close down according to the unified arrangement of the county revolutionary committees.

New enterprises must not be initiated blindly, but must be set up in a planned way with the approval of the departments in charge of commune- and brigade-run enterprises, and they must be rationally distributed. Industrial and commercial enterprises must be approved and licensed by the departments in charge of industry and commerce.

V Sources of Funds

1. Capital must be accumulated mainly by the enterprises themselves through their own efforts. When an enterprise is first started, or where the necessary conditions prevail, appropriate sums can be drawn from the public reserve funds of production brigades or teams and treated as shares with the approval of the congresses of commune or brigade members.

2. Local revolutionary committees at the various levels must do their best to support commune- and brigade-run enterprises by allocating part of their reserve funds to the departments in charge of such enterprises for this purpose.

3. Normally, not less than half of the investment made by the state to support rural people's communes must be allocated to the departments in charge of commune-and brigade-run enterprises to support the poorer brigades in their effort to set

up enterprises. The departments in charge may entrust these investment funds and those provided by local financial departments to the banks for disbursement and retrieval for continued use.

4. The Agricultural Bank must assign a certain proportion of annual agricultural loans as low-interest loans to support commune-and brigade-run enterprises. Those loans which are spent on buying equipment are normally to be repaid over a period of three to five years.

VI Ownership

Commune- and brigade-run enterprises are collectively owned socialist enterprises. Those run by communes are owned by those communes, and those run by brigades are owned by the brigades. Economic exchanges between state enterprises and those run by communes and brigades, or between commune- and brigade-run enterprises and other collective economic units, should be exchanges of equal value. No organization or individual may obtain funds, products, equipment, or raw or semi-finished materials from commune- and brigade-run enterprises without compensation, or borrow money from them. The power of these enterprises to make their own decisions must be respected.

Nationalization of commune- and brigade-run enterprises is forbidden. Those enterprises taken over by the state after the First National Conference on Learning from Dazhai in Agriculture must be returned to their original owners; the pay and working conditions of workers and staff need not be affected.

In order to improve rational distribution, strengthen coordination, raise quality and reduce costs, it is necessary to encourage joint enterprises. These can be run by several communes or brigades, or by communes and brigades together. Hereafter, industrial enterprises should be run mainly by communes or by several communes jointly under the auspices of county authorities with cadres appointed by the county authorities and economic activities carried on in the capacity of county-run factories.

Joint enterprises can also be set up on a trial basis between communes and counties, the profits made to be shared between the two sides according to an agreed ratio. It is forbidden to nationalize joint enterprises, either those involving several communes which resemble county-owned factories in form or those run by counties and communes.

The revolutionary committees of various provinces, municipalities and autonomous regions should readjust unreasonable management fees and administrative charges levied against commune- and brigade-run enterprises by the departments concerned.

VII The Farming Out of Production by Urban Industries

According to the needs of expanding production and the capacity of communes and brigades, urban industries can divert the production of some products or spare parts to rural communes.

When organizing the farming out of certain products from urban industries, it is necessary to give good technical guidance and in some cases to transfer special equipment and tools at fixed prices. For cooperation between urban industries and rural people's communes and brigades to be maintained, supplies of raw and semi-finished materials and marketing channels must not be interrupted. Commune- and brigade-run enterprises must guarantee the quality of products and fulfill their assumed tasks on time. Contracts must be signed and strictly observed by both parties. An overall solution to the problem of duplicated taxation must be worked out by the Ministry of Finance with respect to products turned out through such cooperative efforts.

Only after effective measures have been taken to prevent or deal with the discharge of poisonous substances in the production process can commune- and brigade-run enterprises be assigned the tasks of such production. Those goods that are unsalable and those that are already obsolete must not be assigned to commune- and brigade-run enterprises for production.

Urban industrial equipment lying idle or discarded in the course of retooling but suitable for use in commune- and brigade-run enterprises should be transferred to such enterprises at reasonable prices and may be paid for in a single or in several installments.

VIII Improved Planning in Production, Supply and Marketing

Commune- and brigade-run enterprises are becoming an increasingly important component of the national economy. The planning commissions at all levels and all departments concerned, especially the industrial departments, must take charge of state and commune- and brigade-run enterprises. Every possible means must be employed to improve planning as related to the production, supply and marketing of commune- and brigade-run enterprises so that their plans dovetail with state economic plans at the various levels.

1. The departments in charge of commune- and brigade-run enterprises and the other departments concerned should give guidance to the people's communes when plans are being worked out for the production of such enterprises. For some products, the production plans proposed by the departments concerned are to be brought into overall balance by the State Planning Commission and directly incorporated into the state economic plans at the various levels. The production plans for other products can be indirectly incorporated into the state economic plans at the various levels through contracts signed with the clients. As for those products which are not included in one or another level of the state economic plans but which are needed by society and are assured of raw and semi-finished materials and power supply, production plans can be worked out by the people's communes themselves.

Medium-sized and small farm tools, building materials and processed farm and side-line products turned out by commune- and brigade-run enterprises should be managed by the departments in charge of such enterprises. State and local funds and materials used for this purpose should also be managed and distributed by them. As to which other products can also be managed by the local departments in charge of commune-and brigade-run enterprises, this is a question to be decided by the revolutionary committees of the same level according to the terms of their jurisdiction.

Planning commissions at the various levels should pool the output value and revenue figures of commune- and brigade-run enterprises as well as the investment indices for agricultural production and capital construction and incorporate them into their respective comprehensive plans.

2. Materials required for the production of products directly included in the plans of various levels should be allocated according to plan by the planning commissions and departments responsible for arranging production. Special-use equipment should be provided by the departments in charge of the product category concerned. Materials required for the production of products which are only indirectly included in the plans should be provided by those ordering the products according to the terms of their contracts.

Local planning commissions at the various levels are to list the materials required by commune- and brigade-run enterprises for capital construction, the maintenance of equipment and technical improvement which are to be allotted by the state, and the means of transportation to be acquired by the enterprises themselves, and to work out overall arrangements; the State Planning Commission is to give them the necessary allotments. A certain amount of substandard steel and other waste materials recovered by the localities is to be allotted by the local planning commissions to commune- and brigade-run enterprises.

The departments in charge of commune- and brigade-run enterprises are to apply to the departments concerned (in accordance with the supplies system provisions) for the second and third-category materials and for labour protection articles required by the enterprises in order to fulfill production plans. Such materials can also be acquired through exchanges organized by offices of the same level in charge of coordination of materials, or can be purchased directly by commune- and brigade-run enterprises and the departments in charge of such enterprises.

3. Products which are directly included in the plans at various levels are to be purchased by the departments concerned and contracts are to be signed between the concerned parties on production and marketing. Products which are indirectly involved in the plans at various levels are to be purchased by those ordering the products according to contract. Products which are produced according to the plans of commune- and brigade-run enterprises themselves and surplus products which are produced according to the plans of various levels or according to contract and which are not to be allocated by the state are to be sold by the departments in charge of commune- and brigade-run enterprises or by the enterprises themselves. If such products are not purchased within the localities concerned, no restrictions should be placed on their sale outside.

With the approval of the state, a certain proportion of the products to be allotted by the state can be kept by the commune- and brigade-run enterprises themselves provided there is a genuine need for such products within the production process.

4. Applications by commune- and brigade-run enterprises for the transportation of the required raw and semi-finished materials, fuels, equipment and of finished products should be arranged by railway, transport and shipping authorities and such transportation should be included in their plans.

Departments in charge of commune- and brigade-run enterprises can sign contracts for production, supply, marketing and transportation with the departments or units concerned on behalf of such enterprises.

IX All Trades and Lines of Work Must Actively Support Commune- and Brigade-Run Enterprises

All trades and lines of work must treat support for the development of commune- and brigade-run enterprises as an important task. They must work out plans, adopt measures and do their part in greatly expanding commune- and brigade-run enterprises.

Planning departments must take all factors into consideration and make overall arrangements to see that commune- and brigade-run enterprises mesh with state enterprises, each displaying its own strong points and developing in close coordination with the other.

The various industrial departments must have regard for those commune- and brigade-run industrial enterprises which turn out the same line of products as themselves or which cooperate to produce spare parts as their competent assistants; they must guide these enterprises in developing in a planned way, help them to raise their technical levels, and provide them with special equipment and the necessary materials. The state should not set up new factories to produce products which can be produced by commune- and brigade-run industries.

Departments engaged in capital construction must guide and assist the communes and production brigades in their efforts to run construction enterprises, and must make overall arrangements for construction tasks, train construction teams for them and gradually mechanize these teams.

The railway, transport and shipping departments must guide and assist communes and brigades in their efforts to run transport and loading enterprises and must help commune- and brigade-run enterprises to solve effectively the problems of materials transportation.

Departments of commerce, supply and marketing, and foreign trade must guide commune- and brigade-run enterprises in their efforts to determine the needs of the market, to improve the quality of their products and to increase their variety, and must support them in the supply of materials and in product marketing. Commune- and brigade-run enterprises must be given their shares of the profits made from the sale of export commodities in foreign currency, in accordance with the unified regulations of the state.

Financial departments, banks and credit cooperatives must support commune- and brigade-run enterprises with funds while strengthening their guidance and supervision over the use of such funds. The banks should assist the departments in charge of such enterprises to do a good job of coaching in accounting so as to help the commune- and brigade-run enterprises institute business accounting; and the banks should make it convenient for them to open or close accounts.

Departments in charge of farming, forestry and aquatic products must help communes and brigades to expand planting and breeding activities, to develop the processing and comprehensive use of forest and aquatic products. Commune- and brigade-run enterprises must be encouraged to produce the agriculture-related industrial products which fall within the jurisdiction of farming and forestry departments.

Scientific and technological departments and educational institutions must help communes and brigade-run enterprises train management and technical personnel, conduct scientific research, and exchange scientific and technological information.

Labour and public health departments must actively aid commune- and brigade-run enterprises in improving dust and poison prevention work so as to guarantee safety in production and protection of the environment.

Geological departments must help the people's communes solve problems arising in mineral prospecting so as to promote the expansion of mining by communes and brigades.

Administrative departments in charge of industry and commerce must actively help coordinate production, supply and marketing relationships and ensure the conduct of business in accordance with law through the registration of enterprises and the management of contracts.

X Pricing Policy and Subsidies to Encourage Sales

Commune- and brigade-run enterprises must follow state pricing policies. In principle, products to be purchased by the state must be priced the same as those of similar quality turned out by state enterprises. The prices of products to be sold by the enterprises themselves are to be fixed through discussion between the buying and selling parties within the price limits set by the pricing departments.

Materials allotted by the state to commune- and brigade-run enterprises according to plan must be paid for at the state-determined prices for allotted or supplied materials; large batches of raw materials supplied by the market may be paid for at wholesale prices.

Awards, subsidies and advance purchases of certain products of commune- and brigade-run enterprises by the state and departments concerned must be continued and honoured. Materials awarded to encourage the sale of certain products and subsidies or compensatory materials which should be turned over to the production units must not be intercepted by the departments handling them or, indeed, by any other department.

XI Tax Policy

The state applies reduced-tax or tax-exemption policies to the commune-and brigade-run enterprises. They, in turn, are duty-bound to pay state taxes according to the regulations and not to default or evade.

According to the concrete conditions prevailing in the localities, and with the approval of the revolutionary committees of the various provinces, municipalities or autonomous regions, those commune- and brigade-run enterprises directly serving agricultural production and the livelihood of the commune members may register specific products and services for exemption from industrial, commercial and income taxes.

In accordance with the stipulations set forth in Document Cai Shui Zi No. 21 issued by the Ministry of Finance in 1978, small iron mines, coal fields, power stations, and cement works are to be exempt from industrial, commercial and income taxes for a period of three years commencing in 1978. New enterprises of this kind are to be exempt from taxes for a period of three years from the time they are established. Other new enterprises which have difficulty in paying taxes in the initial stage may be exempted from industrial, commercial and income taxes for a period of two to three years with the approval of the revolutionary committees of the provinces, municipalities or autonomous regions.

In order to accelerate the growth of the rural economy in border areas and in areas inhabited by the minority nationalities, commune- and brigade-run enterprises in counties, autonomous counties or banners in such areas are to be exempt from income tax for a period of five years as from 1979. The revolutionary committees of the various provinces, municipalities and autonomous regions should also make up lists of those old revolutionary base areas which still suffer from difficult economic conditions and which should therefore be similarly exempted from taxes; these lists should be submitted to the State Council for approval.

Self-help undertakings run by communes and brigades in areas struck by natural disasters may be exempt from some or all industrial, commercial and income taxes for a set period of time, with the approval of the revolutionary committees of the provinces, municipalities or autonomous regions.

Commune- and brigade-run enterprises are to be taxed at the present tax rate of 20 percent. This rate will also apply to the income tax to be paid by the supply and marketing organs of the departments in charge of commune- and brigade-run enterprises or of specialized corporations.

XII The Labour System, Labour Remuneration and Labour Protection

The labour system of the commune- and brigade-run enterprises involves both industrial and agricultural aspects. The labour force required by the enterprises is to be provided by communes or brigades in accordance with the principle of overall consideration and arrangement and through the transfer of personnel in consultation with the basic accounting units, on the precondition that a sufficient labour force remains in agricultural production. This labour force will gradually grow as the mechanization of agriculture goes forward. Enterprises should not recruit workers on their own or hand out jobs to friends or relatives.

Payment for labour in commune- and brigade-run enterprises must follow the principle of "to each according to his work." The common practice is "to have workers' grades determined by the factories, their work-points calculated by their production teams, their remuneration worked out by the factories and teams together, and their earnings distributed to them by their teams." Other systems can also be implemented. Where conditions are ripe, a wage system can be implemented. In the case of personnel whose registered permanent residence is in an urban area and who live on commodity grain, the wage system should apply. Technical subsidies should be granted by the enterprises to those personnel who are highly skilled and who contribute the most to the enterprises. The system of fixed production quotas should be implemented and material incentives given as appropriate to those groups or individuals who overfulfill their quotas and who guarantee the quality of the products. Men and women should enjoy equal pay for equal work.

An extra allowance for living expenses should be given to personnel who engage in high-temperature operations; work in mines or high above the ground; work at jobs detrimental to health or in particularly heavy labour; and to those who cannot take meals at home. The extra grain ration for these jobs is to be drawn from the extra grain put aside by the collectives for extra-grain subsidies.

Payment by the enterprises to the production teams for labour should in general be higher than the distribution levels in the teams and, as far as possible, rich teams must not be left at a disadvantage. Accounts must be settled on time and obligations must be honoured. In the case of enterprises which are temporarily without income and, therefore, have difficulty in honouring payrolls, the communes or brigades can use the profits handed in by other enterprises, or can keep clear accounts and wait for such time as these enterprises begin to acquire an income.

Commune- and brigade-run enterprises should attach importance to production safety and strengthen education in this respect. Continued efforts must be made in improving working conditions, labour protection must be handled well, care must be given to the health of personnel, and attention paid to the special needs of women workers. Accidents resulting in injury or death in the course of duty must be reported and investigated promptly and dealt with seriously. Medical treatment should be provided to those injured while on duty and to those contracting occupational diseases; extra living allowances should be given to those who are disabled and pensions given to the families of any deceased.

The environment must be well protected. New enterprises must not pollute the environment, and existing ones should make an effort to eliminate pollution. Those that cause serious pollution must be required to provide remedies within fixed time limits.

In those rural handicraft enterprises that have been transferred to commune management in accordance with Document No. 66 issued by the State Council in 1977, the wages of workers and staff, their grain rations, and the regulations concerning withdrawal or retirement, labour protection and other welfare conditions remain the same as before the transfer.

XIII The Use of Profits

The use of the profits of the commune- and brigade-run enterprises is to be decided by the conferences of the representatives of members of the brigades and communes, and then approved by the communes or counties respectively. Leaders are strictly forbidden to give arbitrary personal instructions on the use of profits. Apart from expanded reproduction and the setting up of new enterprises, profits must be expended mainly on farm capital construction, the mechanization of agriculture and in giving support to the poor teams. A certain proportion may also be distributed among the commune members or spent on commune or brigade welfare undertakings. Waste and extravagance are prohibited and it is forbidden to spend profits on entertainment or gifts.

A certain proportion of the profits made can be left as enterprise funds in the hands of those enterprises which have fulfilled or overfulfilled their production plans.

XIV The Establishment and Perfection of a System of Management Rules and Regulations

Commune- and brigade-run enterprises must persist in the principles of democratic management and thrift, give full play to the initiative of their personnel, and establish and perfect rules and regulations of business management.

Planning must be strengthened. Plans must be made by relying on the masses and regular checks must be conducted to guarantee their fulfillment. As production expands and management skills improve, the eight economic and technical indices – output, variety, quality, consumption, labour productivity, costs, profits, fixed assets and circulating funds – should be worked out and assessment procedures initiated.

Labour management must be strengthened. The labour force must be organized rationally and a system of fixed production quotas implemented. A system in which specialized groups or individuals take responsibility for each section of a production line must be established. Discipline must be strict, and awards and punishments fair.

Technical management must be improved. A system of personal responsibility for technical matters must be set up. Operational regulations must be worked out in accord with the special characteristics of the enterprises. Enterprise personnel should be graded according to technical proficiency as determined through regular assessments and they should be granted the titles appropriate for technical personnel.

Product quality control must be strengthened and the principle of "quality first" adhered to. Production must be organized according to the demands of variety, specification and quality. Strict product inspection rules must be formulated so that quality can catch up with or surpass advanced levels for the various product lines. Substandard products must not be allowed to leave the factories and must not be included in total output values.

Materials management must be strengthened. There must be fixed quotas for the consumption of raw and semi-finished materials and other goods and there must be detailed rules governing the stocking or removal of materials from storehouses. Fixed assets such as machinery, equipment and means of transportation must be maintained by people especially assigned for the job and must be overhauled regularly. As regards abnormal losses, it is necessary to find out where the responsibility lies and to deal with such cases seriously.

Financial management must be strengthened. State regulations governing financial matters and the management of cash must be strictly implemented. The magnitude of circulating funds must be fixed and the depreciation funds for fixed assets set aside; mining operations must also set aside funds for technical transformation. Accounting must be improved and efforts must be made to practise strict economy while increasing production so as to reduce costs and boost profits. Commune- and brigade-run enterprises must make public their income and expenditures regularly and must report to the congresses or conferences of the representatives of commune members, accepting the supervision of the masses.

XV Technical Innovation and Transformation

Commune- and brigade-run enterprises must actively engage in technical innovation and technical transformation, make an effort to tap production potentials and constantly raise production levels. Small groups or individuals that make contributions to technical innovation and technical transformation must be commended and awarded.

Depreciation funds generally and the technical transformation funds for mines must be expended on the renewal of equipment and on technical transformation; the surplus must be deposited in banks and must not be used otherwise. Departments in charge of commune- and brigade-run enterprises and other departments concerned must give active support to such enterprises in the renewal of equipment involved in their technical transformation so as to help change their production step by step. Those enterprises which have the necessary conditions can make use of their shares of foreign-currency profits to import advanced technology and equipment from abroad.

The study of science and training in technology must be strengthened, with commune- and brigade-run enterprises becoming schools for helping raise the scientific and cultural level of the rural population.

XVI Consolidation of Enterprises

It is necessary to make a real effort to consolidate commune- and brigade-run enterprises this year and next. Consolidation must be centered on production and mainly on the improvement of management and the establishment of a national production order so as to lay the foundation for large-scale development.

It is necessary to teach cadres to work in close cooperation with technical personnel and all other personnel in the enterprises, to encourage rationalization proposals, to set up a proper production order, and to establish and perfect business management, especially the system of fixed responsibility for each section of the production line and the system of democratic management of financial matters. It is imperative that all waste and extravagance, graft and embezzlement, speculation and profiteering be combatted.

It is necessary to help the cadres to learn production skills and business management, to persist in ideological work, to take the lead in observing rules and regulations and discipline, and to accept the supervision of the masses.

It is necessary to establish the system of electing the leading cadres of the enterprises democratically and to form good leading groups through consolidation. The leading cadres of an enterprise are to be elected by the personnel of that enterprise and approved by the leading organ at the higher level. Government functionaries who are assigned work in factories jointly run by several communes continue to enjoy remuneration and other conditions as state functionaries and, just as everybody else, they can assume leading posts only when elected to them and when their election is approved by leading organs of a higher level.

From now on, we must check the work of the enterprises regularly, sum up experiences and solve problems as they arise so as to enable commune- and brigade-run enterprises to develop in a healthy manner.

XVII The Establishment of Efficient Administrative Organs

Commune- and brigade-run enterprises have broad prospects for development involving many sectors of the economy, and it is therefore necessary to set up powerful and efficient organs to take charge.

A General Administration for Commune- and Brigade-Run Enterprises is being established under the Ministry of Agriculture to take direct charge of the investments, materials and equipment allotted to such enterprises by the State Planning Commission and the State General Administration for Materials. Administrative bureaus for these enterprises are to be set up at the provincial and county levels, with corresponding organs at the prefectural level. The people's communes must assign persons to take special charge of commune- and brigade-run enterprises. Planning commissions at the various levels and the other departments concerned should also set up functional organs or assign persons to take special charge.

Departments in charge of commune- and brigade-run enterprises at various levels must implement the line, policies and principles formulated by the party and state for the development of these enterprises, work out and fulfill annual and long-term plans, do a good job of managing the products entrusted to them and of the materials and funds allotted to the enterprises. They must coordinate their relations with the other departments concerned, mediate between producers, suppliers and sellers, and help the enterprises to improve management, popularize new techniques and sum up and exchange experiences.

The staff of the departments in charge of commune- and brigade-run enterprises at the various levels must be kept as small as possible (their actual size to be decided by the revolutionary committees of the various provinces, municipalities and autonomous regions) and must be drawn from existing staff. Expenses are to be included in the general financial expenditures at the various levels.

Departments in charge of commune- and brigade-run enterprises at the various levels must set up supply and marketing agencies and specialized corporations, which are themselves in the nature of enterprises. The tasks of such agencies and corporations are to organize production, exchange economic information, mediate between producers, suppliers and sellers, organize cooperative ventures, and do a good job of procuring materials and selling products. The expenses of their staffs must be paid out of commissions collected. The circulating funds required are to be provided through allocations by financial departments or through bank loans.

XVIIJ The Strengthening of Leadership

Commune- and brigade-run enterprises are forging ahead and changing day by day. New circumstances, problems and experiences will inevitably keep presenting themselves. The leading organs at all levels must make unified plans and strengthen their leadership; they must listen to reports regularly, study and solve major problems, and sum up and popularize advanced experience.

It is necessary, under the leadership of the party committees of the various levels, to strengthen the political work in commune- and brigade-run enterprises and to arouse the masses in unfolding socialist labour emulation drives and campaigns to increase production and practice economy, and in exerting themselves to turn their enterprises into advanced operations and become model workers themselves. It is important to build up party and youth league organizations and give full play to the role of the party organizations as fighting bastions and the role of the youth league as the party's aide.

In accordance with the instructions of the Party Central Committee and Comrade Hua Guofeng, the leadership at all levels must display the spirit of the foolish old man who removed the mountains and make persistent and redoubled efforts to turn all bright hopes into reality as soon as possible.

The revolutionary committees of the various provinces, municipalities and autonomous regions should work out concrete plans for the implementation of the above regulations.

PROVISIONS OF THE STATE COUNCIL FOR COMMUNE AND BRIGADE ENTERPRISES' IMPLEMENTATION OF THE GUIDING PRINCIPLES FOR THE REGULATION OF THE NATIONAL ECONOMY

(May 4, 1981)

Commune and brigade enterprises have a remarkable effect on utilizing and developing local resources, arranging rural surplus labour force, consolidating and strengthening collective economy and increasing the income of commune members; they have also played a positive role in the gradual change of rural and agricultural economic structure, the support of agricultural development and the promotion of the construction of small towns; they have also made contributions to developing the production of commodities, stimulating the market, expanding export and increasing state revenue. Commune and brigade enterprises have become important component parts of the rural economy and conform to the direction of the overall development of the rural economy.

At present, the main problems existing in commune and brigade enterprises include: the blindness existing in their development and the inadequate attention to making the most economic benefit and turning resources to full exploitation; the rather few economic interests directly obtained by production teams and commune members in the use of the profits; the confused financial administration in a lot of enterprises and the fairly serious unhealthy tendencies.

Commune and brigade enterprises shall implement the guiding principles of the central authorities concerning the further regulation of the national economy and carry out conscientious regulation and consolidation in accordance with the features of commune and brigade enterprises and the existing problems by proceeding from the requirements of the macroscopic economy.

1. Commune and brigade enterprises have a bearing on farmers' economic interests, on the employment of nearly thirty million persons and on the supply of some indispensable market commodities. While they shall carry out regulation by submitting resolutely to the situation as a whole, the powers of communes and brigades to act on their own shall be esteemed. Prudent steps shall be taken to make good jobs of fact-finding and distinguish between conditions so as to give play to their positive roles while restricting their negative factors and develop the production of products in short supply while reducing that of excessive ones for the purpose of enabling the enterprises to develop healthily. In the regulation, the supervising and regulating functions of finance, credit, taxes and prices shall be brought into play. The enterprises which do not vie with big factories for raw materials, whose products find markets or which make profits in their business shall not be forcibly closed or stopped.

In the regulation and consolidation, preferential treatment and support shall be particularly given to the commune and brigade enterprises in minority nationality regions, mountain areas, outlying districts and impoverished areas.

2. They shall be planned in a unified way and deployed rationally in combination with state enterprises and big collective ones by the county. They shall also join national or local trade organizations and subject themselves to the plans of supply, production and marketing jointly formulated.

Commune and brigade enterprises shall energetically exploit and fully utilize resources to develop the production of consumer goods with great efforts in line with local conditions. They shall start with planting, raising and aquaculture as the basis and develop the productive trades and living service facilities to serve agricultural production, the people's livelihood, the construction of small towns, big industries and foreign trade export, especially emphasizing the development of traditional labour concentrated trades, energy industry, raw material industry and building material industry. In minority nationality regions, commune and brigade enterprises shall pay attention to developing the production of the products specially needed in the localities.

Commune and brigade enterprises shall promote and bring along the development of the household sideline and handicraft production of commune members and the industrial and sideline production undertakings run by commune members in partnership.

3. With regard to the agricultural and sideline products to be purchased with state monopoly or assignment, the state shall prescribe the bases of allocation and transfer for each province, municipality or autonomous region and pursue the system of purchase contracts step by step for communes and brigades. Communes and brigades shall

ensure the fulfillment of the tasks stipulated in contracts or bases. In the case of the surplus products after the fulfillment of the tasks, some shall still be sold to the state in accordance with the relevant provisions of the State Council; some others shall also be used for the economic combination with state enterprises or be processed by the state enterprises for the return of profits or products; still others shall be processed and sold by themselves. In future if state enterprises have surplus processing capacity, communes and brigades shall no longer set up the enterprises of the same kinds or expand their own processing capacity; as regards the products which are made of or from agricultural and sideline products as raw materials and which are suitable for rural processing, the state shall, in general, no longer set up new factories in cities or expand the processing capacity there, and shall emphasize supporting the development of the processing industries of collective ownership on the principles of economy and rationality.

4. The development of commune and brigade cotton mills, cigarette factories and small saltworks shall be stopped. The cigarette factories which have been built shall have their production stopped or transferred to that of another product. The cotton mills shall also be organized to transfer their production except for those which have been brought into the state plans of supply, production and marketing, which process the supplied materials or which make use of cotton waste. The small saltworks which have been built shall be consolidated and upgraded and the production of unrefined salt shall be stopped. The medicines produced by small pharmaceutical factories shall be appraised by the departments concerned and the production of those which are not up to standard shall resolutely be stopped. Fur tanneries shall make full use of social waste and old resources and make a good job of processing with the supplied materials, or run the factories jointly with bigger tanneries with the reserved materials so as to execute the procedures for the centralized treatment of raw materials and the decentralized processing of finished products. Small distilleries shall be regulated and the use of forage grain to make wine shall be controlled, which shall not exceed 20 per cent of the forage calculated by the county.

5. The machining factories of commune and brigade enterprises shall centre on making good jobs of the production of medium and small farm tools and the servicing of farm machines and tools so as to ensure the needs of agricultural production; or be engaged in the cooperation with big industries for the production of complete sets so as to produce parts and components for them. They shall also serve scientific research units by trial producing new products. Those which find no market shall have their production transferred in a planned way.

6. Commune and brigade mining industry shall be consolidated. The mining points shall be rationally arranged and mining shall be carried out in a planned way. It shall strictly be forbidden to dig wantonly or mine recklessly and the destruction of resources shall be prohibited. Technological transformation shall be carried out for the mines which are not qualified for production and the production of those which cannot be transformed for the time being shall resolutely be stopped. The technological transformation expenses shall be drawn as stipulated. Those to be used for the technological transformation of commune and brigade mines shall not be diverted to any other purpose and the materials allotted by the state shall not be partially embezzled. If there are any disputes on mineral resources, overall consideration shall be given and rational arrangement shall be made.

7. Commune and brigade enterprises shall organize and participate in many types of combination in line with local conditions in accordance with the "Interim Provisions for the Promotion of Economic Combination" so as to suit the objective needs of the economic development. The combination of the same trades between counties and communes and brigades shall be developed so as to arrange supply, production and marketing in a unified way. Good jobs shall be made of the combination between areas so as to give play to the respective superiority of each area and achieve common development. In various types of economic combination, each party shall maintain its own ownership and independent accounting unchanged.

At present, commune and brigade enterprises shall pay particular attention to the combination with production teams to enable commune members to share economic results so as to strengthen the mass foundation of commune and brigade enterprises.

With regard to commune members' household handicraft, planting, raising and aquaculture and the industrial and sideline production run by commune members in partnership, combination shall be practised in the supply of improved varieties and fine breeds, in technical directions and in supply and marketing and they shall be fostered.

In the places where favourable conditions exist, agricultural-industrial-commercial (or animal husbandry-industrial-commercial or forestry-industrial-commercial or fishery-industrial-commercial) combined enterprises shall be energetically run as experiments. The distribution of enterprises shall be rationally regulated through combination.

8. The supervisory role of the administrations for industry and commerce shall be brought into play. The enterprises run by communes and brigades shall be examined and approved by the departments in charge of commune and brigade enterprises above the county level within the limits of authority in their administration; industrial and commercial enterprises shall make applications to the administrations for industry and commerce as stipulated for examination and issue of business licences, otherwise they shall not be allowed to commence business.

9. The administration of the capital construction of commune and brigade enterprises shall be strengthened. The present stress of work shall be laid on giving full play to the potentialities of the existing enterprises and on making good jobs of tapping potentialities, innovating equipment and technology and reforming the system. The newly-built projects shall be built according to capabilities, strictly controlled and administered by levels according to different trades of different scales, the specific procedures for which shall be formulated by each province, municipality or autonomous region. The existing capital construction projects shall be sorted out and those which have no favourable factors for capital construction or which seriously pollute the environment shall be stopped or rebuilt. Those which are up to standard shall be resubmitted for approval. The projects to be newly built in future shall strictly follow the procedure for capital construction so as to give play to the supervisory roles of finance and credit.

10. The development of commune and brigade enterprises shall be combined with the construction of small towns, planned in a unified way, arranged rationally and concentrated properly. While developing industrial production, various cultural welfare facilities and living service trades shall be developed so as to make the small towns prosper step by step.

In the construction of new enterprises, the idle land of towns shall be turned into full use and cultivated or good land shall not be occupied as far as possible. The land for capital construction shall strictly be controlled and the bureau of commune and brigade enterprises of each province, municipality or autonomous region shall prescribe the limits of land occupied for capital construction according to different trades and scales of production, submit them for approval in accordance with the limits of authority in examination and approval and pay land compensations. The land excessively taken up or taken up but unused shall be returned to production teams.

11. Commune and brigade enterprises shall conscientiously implement the Notice of the State Council of the Strict Control of Prices and the Consolidation of Negotiated Prices and the relevant provisions of each province, municipality or autonomous region. The future changes of the selling prices of commodities shall be approved within the limits of authority in the administration of prices. It shall strictly be forbidden to practise speculation and profiteering, drive up prices, manufacture in a rough and slipshod way, pass off the inferior as the good or seek exorbitant profits.

12. Commune and brigade enterprises shall pay taxes according to regulations in accordance with "A Number of Provisions for the Regulation of Industrial and Commercial Tax Burdens of Rural Commune and Brigade Enterprises" and it shall be forbidden to concoct various pretexts or employ trickery to evade taxes.

13. Each province, municipality or autonomous region shall select a number of factories (or farms) to conduct the experiments of reforming the system of commune and brigade enterprises so as to change the collective enterprises both run and owned by communes or by brigades into those jointly run by production teams. The present stress shall be laid on regulating the relations between communes or brigades and production teams or commune members so as to increase the material benefit of commune members; on regulating the relations between communes or brigades and enterprises so as to expand the powers of the enterprises to act on their own.

14. The business management of commune and brigade enterprises shall be seriously and generally consolidated. Such major matters as the directions of commune and brigade enterprises' production, the new construction or the expansion of enterprises, the distribution and use of profits, etc. shall be discussed and determined by the commune members' representative assemblies or by the shareholders' meetings. The democratic management of enterprises shall be strengthened so as to give play to the supervisory roles of the staff and workers.

The system of being both workers and peasants shall be upheld in respect of the personnel system and labour administration of enterprises. The prospective employees shall go through examinations so that the best of them shall be employed and it shall be forbidden to put personal kin or friends in the vacant positions; the employees in rather highly technical trades shall be kept stable so as to contribute to the improvement of management and technical levels; a strict system of productive responsibility shall be pursued and the policy of distribution according to work shall be implemented so as to combine the operation results of enterprises with the material interests of staff and workers.

Commune and brigade enterprises shall practise economic accounting, tap their potentialities, reduce their costs and consumption, increase production, improve product quality and strengthen the competitive capacity.

They shall consolidate financial administration, strengthen accounting work, train financial and accounting personnel, set up strict financial and accounting regulations and give play to the functionary roles of the financial and accounting personnel; they shall check up on assets and funds, clear up credits and debts, set up the perfect administrative system of funds and materials, oppose the wanton diversion or use of funds, oppose corruption, waste, entertainment, giving gifts or bribery; oppose the reckless issue of rewards and check all unhealthy tendencies.

15. Commune and brigade enterprises shall strengthen labour protection and make good jobs of safe production. They shall energetically control pollution and beautify the environment. The enterprises which seriously damage resources, pollute the environment or do not possess the factors for safe production shall be improved within a definite time and if these problems cannot be solved, the enterprises shall be closed, stopped, merged or transferred.

The food industry shall strictly implement the food hygienic standards promulgated by the state and the food which is not up to standard shall not be sold.

16. The people's government at each level shall further strengthen its leadership over commune and brigade enterprises and perfect the management organizations of commune and brigade enterprises to strengthen them in accordance with the relevant provisions in Document No. 170 (1979) of the State Council. It shall carry out the investigation of resources and formulate the plans of regulation and development. Good jobs shall be made of the legislation of commune and brigade enterprises. The economic and technical services of commune and brigade enterprises shall be unfolded step by step. The government shall strengthen the supply and marketing of commune and brigade enterprises, forecast the market situation well and develop combined purchase or sale or commission purchase or sale so as to clear the channels of supply and marketing. It shall strengthen economic and technical information, technical training and technical services.

NOTICE OF THE STATE BUREAU OF LABOUR, THE GENERAL ADMINISTRATION OF MUNICIPAL CONSTRUCTION, THE MINISTRY OF PUBLIC SECURITY AND THE GENERAL ADMINISTRATION FOR INDUSTRY AND COMMERCE TO SOLVE THE PROBLEMS OF SITES REQUIRED FOR THE DEVELOPMENT OF COLLECTIVE AND INDIVIDUAL ECONOMIES IN CITIES AND TOWNS

(May 6, 1981)

In order to continue to implement the guiding principle of employment put forward in Document No.64 (1980) of the central authorities, promote the healthy development of collective and individual economies in cities and towns and improve labour employment work, a positive attitude shall be adopted and an overall plan shall be made to rationally solve the problems of sites required by the collective producing and service network points run by local people, the small collective ones run by neighbouring committees and those run by labour services and required by individual industrial and commercial firms. For this reason, the following Notice is given:

1. With regard to the new network points and factory buildings required to be increased for the development of various types of collective and individual economies in cities and towns, the departments of local labour, house property management, city planning, public security, administration for industry and commerce and other departments concerned shall make joint considerations and overall plans. The sites required shall be arranged by the city planning and management departments by consulting with departments concerned in the cities and towns where the sites are located. The departments concerned shall give energetic support, afford facilities and pay close attention to the solution of the problems. A good job shall be made of the rational layout of sites so as to prevent blind development.

2. In order to invigorate the market and make things convenient for the masses, proceeding from the local actual conditions, it shall be allowed to delimit a certain section of a city after the examination and determination of the city planning department and the administration for industry and commerce and with the consent of the local public security bureau to resume the traditional stall market (morning or evening market) and small commodity market and permit collectives and individuals to set up stalls and salespoints there to provide commercial services.

3. If civil defence works in urban areas are suitable for being transformed into business premises, they shall be rented to collective units or individual industrial and commercial firms for use under the unified arrangement of the civil defence and the house property management departments.

4. The ground floor of a newly-built dormitory building on the streetside of a city or a town, which is assigned for commercial purpose, shall be rented by the house property management department to collective enterprises or individual firms for use as the business shop front. (The rents shall be calculated on the basis of such five factors as maintenance costs, management fees, depreciation rates, taxes and interest.)

5. If any room of an original business shop front alongside a street has been transformed into a storeroom or dormitory or for other purposes, it shall be vacated as far as possible and rented to collective enterprises or individual firms for business use. With regard to the streetside residences or public houses in the downtown districts, the house property management departments shall assist in exchanging residences and transform them into business shops.

6. In the case of a section within the "red lines" of a city plan, in which no construction can be carried out within a short period, the local labour service shall enter into a temporary renting agreement with the city planning department and on the approval of the department, build temporary sheds there, but the sheds shall conform to the requirements of fire prevention and guarantee their removal at the appointed time. They shall not affect the construction.

You are requested to consider and put forward specific procedures jointly in the light of the actual conditions in each place and in accordance with the above requirements, submit them to local people's governments for examination and determination and organize and supervise their implementation.

JOINT NOTICE OF THE GENERAL ADMINISTRATION FOR INDUSTRY AND COMMERCE, THE MINISTRY OF COMMERCE, THE MINISTRY OF FOOD, THE NATIONAL FEDERATION OF SUPPLY AND MARKETING COOPERATIVES, THE STATE BUREAU OF SUPPLIES AND THE STATE BUREAU OF LABOUR CONCERNING PROBLEMS SUCH AS THE SUPPLY OF SOURCES OF GOODS TO INDIVIDUAL INDUSTRIAL AND COMMERCIAL FIRMS IN CITIES AND TOWNS

(June 22, 1981)

Since the Third Plenary Session of the Party's 11th Central Committee, individual industrial and commercial firms in cities and towns have made certain developments and played a positive role in promoting stability and unity, invigorating the economy and expanding employment. However, owing to the insufficient understanding of the objective inevitability of the development of the individual economy in cities and towns and because a series of policies have not been well implemented, such problems as the sources of products, taxation, recklessness in collecting charges, etc., have not been solved so that the development of individual industrial and commercial firms is considerably affected and falls far short of the demands of the people's livelihood and labour employment. In the spirit of the recent written instructions of Comrade Hu Yaobang concerning the development of individual industrial and commercial firms, the following notice is now given regarding the questions concerned:

1. Individual industrialists and businessmen are independent labourers who support themselves by their own labour. Individual industrial and commercial firms shall be treated without discrimination in politics and economy equally to the units of the whole-people's ownership and of collective ownership and shall be energetically supported by each department in the aspects of funds, raw materials, taxes, etc. At present, the discrimination against individual industrial and commercial firms existing in some places shall be altered. We hope that each area shall make a conscientious examination of the problems existing in the implementation of the policy to develop individual industry and commerce and report to us on the results of the examination.

2. With regard to the raw materials and the sources of goods needed by the individual industrialists and businessmen with official residency in cities or towns and who have obtained "business licences," the local state commercial, food, supply and marketing, material and other departments shall energetically supply them within the dealing ranges of commodities approved and the individual firms shall enjoy wholesale prices in the same way as state and collective units. In accordance with the limits of distribution of labour in the trade, the state commercial, supply and marketing, material and other departments shall properly set up more wholesale network points and properly reduce the starting points for wholesale so as to facilitate the individual firms to replenish their stock. In the case of the limited materials required for repairing services, the needs of the individual industrial and commercial firms shall also be taken into account and the material department shall pay attention to arrangements for them in the distribution of supplies. In the supply of food and oils, the food department shall supply raw grains by grain coupons in the planned amounts of supply and shall ration food oils in proportion to the individual catering traders who hold the official residency in towns with municipal organizational systems, and in cities and towns above county seats without municipal organizational systems, and who have obtained 'business licences" according to the demands of the market, treating them in the same way as the whole-people's and collective catering units. With regard to the foods and oils beyond the plans, they shall be supplied at negotiated prices according to the conditions of the local sources of foods and oils.

As regards the raw materials and the sources of goods which the state does not supply or which are in short supply, the individual industrial and commercial firms shall purchase them by themselves in the specified markets with the approval of the departments concerned.

3. A small amount of transaction service charges shall only be collected by the stall from the individual industrial and commercial firms that set up stalls in country fairs. No department shall collect any charges without authorization and approval of the people's government of the province, municipality or autonomous

region to increase the burdens of the individual firms.

4. The administrations for industry and commerce, commercial departments, food departments, supply and marketing departments, material and labour departments at each level shall cooperate closely with each other, strengthen the direction and administration of individual industrial and commercial firms, protect their legal operations and prohibit illegal activities. The individual industrial and commercial firms that enjoy the treatment of state wholesale prices shall strictly implement the retail prices stipulated by the state in a unified way and pay taxes in accordance with the unified provisions of the state and they shall be prohibited from reselling for profits, driving up prices or evading taxes.

POLICIES ON THE NON-AGRICULTURAL INDIVIDUAL ECONOMY IN URBAN AREAS ISSUED BY THE STATE COUNCIL

(July 7, 1981)

Under socialism in China, the individual economy which abides by the policies and laws of the state, serves the cause of socialist construction and does not exploit others, is a complementary part of the state and collective economies. Citizens engaged in individual business are independent labourers earning their own living. Because the level of development of the productive forces in our country are low and commodity economy is not well developed, it is ienvitable to let the diversified economic composition and varied forms of management exist side by side for quite a long historical period. Practice has shown, provided the state and collective economies hold a dominant position, the resumption and development of non-agricultural individual economy in the urban areas is of great significance to increasing production, stimulating the market, meeting the needs of the people and giving more opportunities for employment. All local governments, and departments concerned with finance, commerce, light industries, comm dities, banking, industrial and commercial bureaux must give practical support to the development of non-agricultural individual economy in urban areas. In the matter of funds, supply of commodities, provision of business space, taxation, and marketing, all the necessary assistance and facilities should be extended to them. Any discrimination, interference, or passive attitude toward individual economy will run counter to the development of socialist economy and are therefore fallacious. With a view to promoting the sound development of non-agricultural individual economy in the urban areas, the following policies are laid down for observance:

1. Urban non-agricultural individual economy refers to all kinds of handicrafts, retail sales, restaurants, service trades, repair work, transport by non-motor vehicles and house-repairing, run on a small scale by non-agricultural individuals in urban areas.

2. The state encourages and supports job-waiting youths to engage in those trades which are needed by the masses and left open by the state and collective economy, so as to play a complementary role.

3. In accordance with the needs and possibilities, the state-owned and collective-owned enterprises may rent or assign a part of handicraft, repair work, service trades and network of shops suitable for decentralized management to the individual economic workers.

4. All unemployed urban youths and middle aged people with formal residence registration may apply for individual work. Retired workers who have special skills or managerial experience in urgent need for the society and who will teach and pass on their skills to the apprentices may also apply for such work.

Individual workers are to run their business only after their applications have been commented on by the neighbourhood committees and approved by the industrial and commercial administrative bureaux, who will issue the necessary business license. They should go through the formalities according to the regulations of the industrial and commercial administrative bureaux before they are allowed to close, transfer, combine with other units, or turn over their business to others.

5. The individual workers generally do their business all by themselves or with their families. If necessary and when approved by the industrial and commercial administrative bureaux, an individual worker may employ one or two helpers. If the work needs higher techniques or special skills, two, three or at most no more than five apprentices may be employed. In employing helpers and apprentices, a contract should be signed by both parties setting forth the rights, duties, time limit and remuneration, and approved by the local administrative bureaux of industry and commerce.

6. All local governments and departments concerned should actively arrange through overall planning the business sites, shops, stalls and spaces necessary for the development of the individual economy. The latter may also arrange with the parties concerned to loan, rent, or buy the houses, instruments and equipment needed.

7. For bringing into full play the characteristic of their flexible management to suit the convenience of the people, they are allowed to do their business in a number of ways. They may

process materials supplied by customers, make and sell their own products, retail commodities for the state, and set stalls or send out street peddlers to sell sundries at the doors of the customers. They are also allowed within certain limits to convey and sell certain fresh and live commodities, whose free purchase and sale are permitted by the state. They are, however, forbidden to deal wholesale.

8. Raw materials and commodities required by the individual workers, the supply of which falls into the state plan, should be included in an overall plan by the local commercial and commodity departments concerned without discrimination and reasonably distributed according to a positive arrangement.

9. Commodities supplied to individual workers by the state-owned industry and commerce or by collective-owned enterprises at wholesale prices should sell according to retail prices stipulated by the state. Prices of products made from raw materials provided by commodity departments, should be fixed according to their quality and in line with prices of same products made by the state-owned enterprises. Commodities purchased by themselves at negotiated prices, may sell according to the market price. Remuneration of service trades, repair work and transport by non-motor vehicles may be fixed by the society of individual workers or agreed to by both parties concerned.

10. When funds raised by the individual workers themselves are found not sufficient, the local governments and departments concerned should find ways to help. If they meet with difficulties in finance, they may apply for a bank loan.

11. In order to encourage individual workers to engage in repairing, processing, eating business and service trades which fall short of the needs of the society, exemption or reduction of taxes may be considered on their merits. When some of the trades needed by the masses are really in difficulties or running at too small a profit, they may apply for an exemption of taxes.

12. The state protects legitimate business activities, profits and capital of individual workers. No department or unit may interfere in their business activities which are permitted by the state policy and law. No unit may occupy shops and places approved by the department concerned. The supply of material already included in the plan of the local department concerned should not be discontinued at will. Exept for the taxes and fees they pay according to the state rules and regulations, no department or unit may collect fees under any pretext whatsoever.

13. Individual workers enjoy the same political rights and social status as the workers in state-owned and collective-owned units. Departments and units concerned should treat the individual working youths equally without discrimination for joining the army, or entering a higher school. Individual workers may pay social insurance premiums to the insurance companies and establish labour security, welfare and retirement system step by step. Concrete measures will be stipulated later. Individual workers are to count their period of service according to practical length of work starting from the day of approval to run their business.

14. Individual workers may at their own will set up a society or federation of individual workers according to trades. Their tasks are: provide service to the members, exchange experiences, transfer techniques, transmit the policies of the state and the government and organize their study, inspect and supervise the members to observe conscientiously the policies and laws of the state and reflect their opinions and requirements to the departments concerned.

The society or federation of individual workers is placed under the leadership of the industrial and commercial bureau or of another department appointed by the local government.

15. Individual workers should abide by the policies and laws of the state, engage in regular business, and accept supervision of the masses. They are forbidden to engage in speculation and profiteering, evading taxes, adulteration, and driving up prices. Those who violate the provisions should be given warnings or an economic penalty or be liable to the withdrawal of their business licenses or legal actions according to the seriousness of their cases.

Those who have committed serious offences against the law for engaging in speculation and profiteering or other illegal activities are not allowed to do business independently.

16. The above regulations are in principle also applicable to the non-agricultural individual workers in the rural areas.

Policies and rules of individuals engaged in

cultural, educational, medical, and hygienic work will be stipulated separately.

17. In carrying out the above policies to develop non-agricultural individual economy in urban areas, the people's governments in all provinces, municipalities and autonomous regions should conduct investigations, train cadres and make out a general plan before putting them into practise step by step, and not rush headlong into mass action without effective leadership.

18. The people's governments in all provinces, municipalities and autonomous regions may make detailed and supplementary rules on the basis of the above regulations and practical conditions of local areas.

DECISION ON OPENING UP MORE AVENUES AND STIMULATING ECONOMIC DEVELOPMENT FOR SOLVING THE URBAN EMPLOYMENT PROBLEM

Issued by the Central Committee of The Chinese Communist Party and The State Council (Excerpts) (October 17, 1981)

1. Arranging jobs for the young people in urban areas has an important bearing on the national economy.

The question is also of great importance to the interest of the people and to the stability and unity of the country in realizing its aim of four modernizations. Therefore, proceeding from the needs of economic readjustment and development, we must solve the problem step by step in a planned way. We must make continuous investigations and sum up experiences in order to gradually formulate a whole set of employment systems favourable to the development of national economy and to the improvement of the living standard of the people within a short period of time.

After the Third Plenary Session of the 11th Party Central Committee, the central authorities decided to open up more avenues for developing the collectively owned economy so as to solve the employment problem in cities and towns. In 1980, a national working conference on labour and employment set forth further the following principle: "Under the state's overall planning and guidance, while the labour departments continue to provide employment opportunities, those waiting for jobs may organize collective enterprises on a voluntary basis or they may individually create jobs." Practice has shown that this principle is correct. In the last three years, great achievements have been made in employment, jobs having been provided for more than 20 million people in the urban areas. Nonetheless, a number of problems remain unsolved. This refers mainly to the fact that to the neglect of opening up more avenues, some places have put undue emphasis on arranging jobs in already overstaffed state-owned enterprises and undertakings with the result that the overstaffed situation has been made more serious to the detriment of the improvement of management. Experiences must be summed up conscientiously, in order to draw a lesson and improve this work actively.

Employment in the urban areas is a long-term and arduous task. But it should be realized that with the correction of "leftist" errors after the Third Plenary Session, the whole situation is getting better, and that conditions for solving the employment problem are improving day after day. While facing up to all kinds of difficulties, we must not lose sight of beneficial conditions so that we should persist in solving the problem according to the principle set forth by the central authorities and in coordination with our efforts to readjust the national economy.

2. Efforts to open up more avenues for employment should be dovetailed with efforts to readjust the structure of industry and ownership and should proceed on the basis of developing the economy and various construction projects.

Historical experiences, present requirements and future trends have told us that based on local conditions, the development of commerce, service trades and consumer goods industry, all of which are closely related to the livelihood of the people, has broad prospects, and there exists, therefore, a great potential for solving the problem of urban employment. We must make great efforts in studying and trying to solve this important question of developing these trades.

In the future, while readjusting the structure of industry, emphasis should be placed on creating jobs in the collective and individual sectors of the economy. In China, state-owned and collective-owned enterprises are the basic forms of the socialist economy, with individual economy of the working people within certain areas as their necessary complement. With the state-owned economy as the leading role in the various forms of economy, we must, in the meantime, give play to the active role of collective and individual forms of economy, in order to suit the development of the productive forces and to meet the manifold needs of the people. Given the predominance of the socialist public economy, the various forms of economy and management will coexist for a long time; this is a strategic decision of our Party, rather than an expediency. The central authorities call on all members of the Party, with leaders of all walks of life in the first place, to achieve a clarified and unanimous guiding ideology and make concerted efforts to reach the goal.

3. Strive to operate the urban collective economy efficiently, encourage and direct the job-waiting young people to organize and work in collective enterprises.

According to the experience gained in certain districts, under the state's overall planning, guidance and support, the collective economy in urban areas should follow the principles of organizing on a voluntary basis, bearing the responsibility for gains and losses on its own, giving remuneration on the basis of work done and carrying out democratic management. Observing these principles, the party committees and governments at all levels should within a few years strive to realize a marked development of the various forms of collective economy.

Generally speaking, the various existing forms of collective economy have played an active role in developing economy, offering facilities to the life of the people and enlarging opportunities for employment. This should be fully confirmed. But due to the long-standing "leftist" influence, not a few of the enterprises have more or less the defects of "eating from the same pot" and "iron rice bowl"* or have the inclination to follow suit. These problems have existed for a long time in such collective enterprises and should be readjusted and reformed through active and reliable steps in the course of continuous development in accordance with the formulated principles, so that the collective enterprise could give full play to its original strong points and active role. While adopting economic policies and methods, we should always bear in mind to create favourable conditions for future reforms, and be careful not to put up new obstacles.

4. According to the needs of national economy, appropriately develop the individual economy of working people in the urban areas and open up more avenues for people to create their own jobs.

At present, the individual economy of working people in the urban areas has been restored and made some progress, but it still falls short of the needs of the national economic development. In order to relieve misgivings of cadres, the masses and the job-waiting youths, and to assure sound development of the individual economy of working people in the urban areas, it is necessary to further readjust policies, give more publicity to Party principles and explain the important role of this economic sector in developing production, stimulating economy, meeting people's needs and creating job opportunities.

Individual workers are socialist workers in China. They should be treated on the same footing as workers in state-owned and collective-owned enterprises with regard to their social and political status. Among them, advanced personnel who are in accord with the demands of a Party member or a Youth League member, should be admitted into the Party or Youth League according to their respective rules and regulations.

5. The departments concerned under the Central Committee of the Party and the State Council should actively formulate speedy and resolute measures to guide, encourage, promote and support collective and individual economies, instead of discrimination, restriction, attacking and annexing against collective and individual economy.

The relevant regulations made in the past should be seriously checked up and concrete measures of reform put forward within a certain time limit. Party committees and governments at all levels should call upon the State Planning Commission, National Economic Commission, State Capital Construction Commission and the various departments dealing with finance, commerce, supply and marketing, commodities, food, prices, banking, taxes, industrial and commercial bureaus, foreign trade, city construction, public safety, overseas Chinese, education, health, labour, educated youth and all production units, as well as such organizations as trade unions, Communist Youth Leagues, Women's Leagues, Overseas Chinese Leagues, the Democratic Party of National Construction and the Associations of Industry and Commerce — all to coordinate their efforts under overall planning and take up their respective duties to develop the urban collective and individual economy.

The ownership of property, regular business activities and revenues of the collective and individual enterprises should be protected by the law and no department or unit is allowed, without authorization, to interfere in their affairs, transfer their property and resources or swallow them up. They are required to pay taxes and other fees according to state laws and the rules and regulations of the various provinces, municipalities and autonomous regions, and no department or unit is allowed to change them under any pretext. It is necessary to educate those engaged in collective or individual enterprises to abide by the laws and policies of the state, accept the supervision and control of the departments concerned and not to engage in any such illegal activities as smuggling, speculating, driving up prices, tax evasion and offering or accepting bribes. Those violating the law will be dealt with on their merits.

6. Restructure the economic and labour systems in state-owned enterprises step by step and improve the management and administration effectively and achieve better economic results.

At present, one of the drawbacks of state-owned enterprises is the practice of "eating from the same pot." Another drawback is the "iron rice bowl" practice. State-owned enterprises should be restructed so as to eliminate the existing shortcomings.

Every prospective worker should be fully examined and priority given to the best qualified. A multiform employment system should be instituted: some work according to contracts, some on a temporary basis and others on a regular basis, and the requirement should be carried out step by step that workers are made subject to movement according to the need of the enterprises. Labour discipline should be enforced. As to those workers and staff members who violate the law, breach discipline and refuse to mend their ways after repeated education, they should be disciplined or dismissed. Any decision to dismiss a worker or staff member should be examined and discussed by the congress of workers and staff members and approved by the trade union organization at the same level.

7. Establish, improve and expand labour service companies, provide adequate staff workers and give free rein to their functions.

The various labour service companies are now doing the work to organize social labour force, carry out economic activities and perform part of the administrative functions for the government labour departments. They should be gradually developed into a multipurpose body capable of organizing economic undertakings, arranging jobs according to overall planning, supplying and administering a labour force to meet the temporary needs of various enterprises and providing job training. The necessary preparatory work should be done for the establishment of the China General Labour Service Company in order to strengthen the work along these lines.

For the labour service companies and the collective units organized by all walks of life mainly for the purpose of enlarging employment, the departments concerned should give the necessary support and assistance by way of supply, production, marketing, bank loans, business spaces, taxes and funds needed for their establishment. Where appropriate, factories, mines, enterprises, government and public organizations may give guidance to and provide work for the job-waiting children of the workers and staff members by setting up labour service companies and developing collective and individual economic units which practise independent accounting and bear their own responsibility for gains and losses.

8. Step up vocational and technical training and raise political consciousness and technical level of the workers and staff members step by step.

Job training should be provided gradually for every urban job-waiting youth before he or she is assigned work. Let everyone who needs to be trained get such opportunities before being employed. The training should cover both skills and political and ideological understanding and take various forms to meet the needs of economic development and social life. The period of training may be long or short and the classes big or small. Work-study programmes should be encouraged, and vocational schools and training classes should play an active role in training competent personnel for the collective and individual economy. After having finished their training and passed the necessary examination, the trainees will receive a diploma, but not necessarily a job, which they should seek at the open recruiting examination held by the various units who will choose those with the best performance on the examination for employment. Assistance may also be given for them to organize themselves to work collectively or to find jobs individually.

9. Strictly control the flow of rural workers into cities and towns.

Surplus labour forces in the countryside should be used locally to develop a diversified economy, including commune- or brigade-run enterprises, instead of being allowed to flow into cities and towns. Under the present economic condition of China, the flow of rural population and labour forces to the cities and towns should be strictly controlled according to government policies.

Active measures should be taken to improve the management of the various farms and sideline occupation centres in suburban, afforestation, and industrial and mining areas, which are specially run for educated youths. Political mobilization should be combined with material incentives to encourage job-waiting youths in urban areas to join them and participate in farming, stock-raising, fish-breeding and developing a diversified economy. Where possible, some enterprises should be developed and transformed into combines, which intergrate farming, industry and commerce, and thus they can accommodate more job-waiting urban youths. Those educated youths who have settled down in the countryside and got married to the peasants should be employed near or right at the place where they live. For those job- waiting youths who though living in the countryside do not belong to the agricultural population, more avenues of employment should be provided locally, and commune- or brigade-run enterprises in the countryside should welcome them and give them employment there.

10. Strengthen leadership over employment work in the urban areas.

The work of employment cannot be undertaken successfully by the labour departments alone; the party committees and governments at all levels must give strong leadership and provide efficient working personnel. The chief leading cadre should tackle the problem himself, overcome all kinds of obstacles with persistence, and arrive at a practical solution of it.

For solving the labour employment problem we depended in the past on the recruitment programmes of state-owned enterprises; now we have opened up new avenues through state-owned, collectively owned and individual enterprises. This tremendous change has already evoked all sorts of response among the cadres and the masses. Therefore, party committees at all levels, political organs, propaganda, educational, cultural, news and publishing, and theoretical departments and various people's organizations should strengthen their ideological and educational work to the cadres, the masses and job-waiting youths to continue to eliminate the leftist influences and rectify those old concepts of looking down upon the collective and individual units, or despising consumer, commercial and service trades. The broad masses of cadres, especially leading cadres, should take the lead in implementing the decisions made by the Party Central Committee and the State Council and encourage their job-waiting children and relatives to work in collective and individual economic units and service trades.

* The expressions "eating from the same pot" and "iron rice bowl" refer to the fact that everyone gets his or her remuneration regardless of the amount and quality of work done, and once a worker or staff member gets on an enterprise's payroll, his or her job is permanently secured, no matter how he or she works.

23

STATISTIC

INTERIM PROVISIONS FOR THE TECHNICAL TITLES OF STATISTICAL CADRES

(Approved and Promulgated by the State Council on May 16, 1980)

Article 1 These Provisions are formulated for the purpose of bringing the enthusiasm of the masses of statistical cadres into full play and encouraging statistical cadres to love their own work, endeavour to gain professional proficiency and heighten the scientific levels of their statistical work so as to suit statistics better to the needs of the socialist modernization construction.

Article 2 The technical titles of statistical cadres shall be defined as: Senior Statisticians, Statisticians, Assistant Statisticians and Statistical Clerks.

Article 3 A statistical cadre who is given a technical title or promoted to such a degree shall support the leadership of the Communist Party of China, have deep love for the socialist motherland, study Marxism, Leninism and Mao Zedong Thought conscientiously, probe energetically into statistical science and technology and endeavour to serve the socialist modernization construction.

Article 4 The determination and promotion of the technical titles of statistical cadres shall mainly be based on their working ability, professional skills and working contributions with proper consideration of their records of education and qualifications.

Article 5 A graduate from a polytechnic school or a statistical cadre who has the same educational level shall be defined as a statistical clerk at the expiration of one year's probation if he or she possesses the following qualifications:

1. Having a good command of general statistical professional knowledge and calculating skills;
2. Being able to fill in report forms accurately as stipulated in the statistical system and statistical method;
3. Being able to process and sort out statistical data and make a preliminary analysis and study of them.

Article 6 A graduate from a regular course in an institution of higher learning who has undergone one year's probation, or a statistical cadre who has the same educational level or a statistical clerk who has been engaged in statistical work for more than three years shall be defined as or promoted to an assistant statistician if he or she possesses the following qualifications:

1. Having a good command of the basic knowledge of statistical theory and relevant professional knowledge;
2. Being familiar with relevant statistical systems and statistical methods and being able to make simpler statistical investigation plans;
3. Being able to make more systematic processing, sorting, analysis and study of statistical data, having the ability to carry out investigations and studies independently and being able to write out general statistical investigation reports.

Article 7 An assistant statistician shall be promoted to a statistician if he or she possesses the following qualifications:

1. Having a good command of high systematic statistical theoretical knowledge and more relevant professional knowledge;
2. Having richer experience in statistical work, being able to make related statistical investigation plans, being capable of directing the statistical work of a unit or a specialized trade and having made good achievements;
3. Being able to make investigation and comprehensive analyses of social and economic problems and write out statistical investigation reports in appropriate standards.

Article 8 A statistician shall be promoted to a senior statistician if he or she has the following qualifications:

1. Having a good command of systematic statistical theoretical knowledge and richer relevant professional knowledge;
2. Having rich experience in statistical work and the ability to solve major technical problems in statistical work, being able to direct the statistical work of an area, a department, a specialized trade or a large enterprise, and having made remarkable achievements;
3. Being able to make scientific research of statistical theory, statistical systems and statistical methods and put forward scientific writings up to a higher standard, or being able to make systematic investigations into social and economic problems, write out statistical investigation reports up to a higher standard and make suggestions of important value;
4. Having a good command of a foreign language.

Article 9 The determination and promotion of the technical titles of statistical cadres shall go through examinations. An examination shall take place every two to three years on the basis of the routine testing of achievements. Those who have made outstanding achievements shall be examined at any time and promoted out of turn.

Article 10 The examination of the statistical cadres at every level shall be the appraisal based mainly on their achievements in work, working reports or statistical academic writings. Those of them who have the same educational levels shall be put to the tests of statistical theoretical knowledge and relevant professional knowledge. Those who are to be promoted to senior statisticians shall be put to the tests of their levels of foreign languages.

Article 11 The determination and promotion of the technical titles of statistical cadres shall be appraised and determined by the corresponding organizations in charge of the appraisal and examination of the technical titles of statistical cadres in accordance with the limits of the authority of administration of cadres. The composition of the appraisal and examination organization at each level shall be approved by the authorities at each level.

Article 12 To have a technical title of the statistical cadre defined or promoted, the person himself or herself shall apply or be recommended by the organization and put forward working reports or academic writings and the authorities shall confer on him or her the technical title after the appraisal and examination of the appraisal and examination organization and record it on the files of personnel and business achievement examinations.

Article 13 The determination and promotion of the technical titles of statistical cadres shall be practical and realistic as well as serious and conscientious. Those who practise graft and strike and suppression on statistical cadres shall be seriously dealt with according to the degrees of seriousness.

Article 14 A statistical cadre whose technical title is changed to engineering or technical cadre shall no longer have the technical title of a statistical cadre appraised and determined.

Article 15 The detailed rules for the implementation of these Provisions shall be formulated by the State Bureau of Statistics.

Article 16 These Provisions shall prevail when they come into conflict with the past provisions for technical titles.

INTERIM PROVISIONS OF THE STATE BUREAU OF STATISTICS FOR THE ADMINISTRATION OF STATISTICAL REPORT FORMS

(November 17, 1980)

1 These Interim Provisions are formulated in accordance with the instruction of the State Council that statistical report forms shall be under the unified administration of the statistical department at each level for the purpose of suiting the system of statistical report forms to the needs of the socialist modernization construction without adding too much burden to grass-roots units and for the purpose of preventing the reckless issues of statistical report forms.

2 Both periodical (including the statistics of progress) and single (including brief outline of investigation similar to statistical report) report forms shall be under the unified administration of the statistical department at each level, in charge by levels and under strict control.

3 Both demand and possibility shall be taken into consideration in making and issuing statistical report forms. In the selection of investigation plans, attention shall be paid to the use of the least possible manpower, material resources and financial resources to get the best possible investigation results. Only those which are indispensable to the socialist modernization construction and can really be executed by grass-roots units and statistical departments shall be made and issued. The report forms made and issued shall be:

(1) Brief and to the point without trivial details, repetitions or contradictions.

(2) A variety of investigating ways shall be adopted to reveal the situations. If a single investigation can solve the problem, no periodical report forms shall be made; if a sampling investigation or a key or a typical one can solve the problem, no overall statistical report forms shall be made.

(3) The frequency of reports shall be reduced. If a monthly report can satisfy the needs, no ten-day or daily report shall be made; if an annual report can satisfy the needs, no monthly or quarterly report shall be made; if the statistics can be made once every once every three to five years, no annual report shall be made.

(4) The existing statistical data shall be brought into full play. If the data can be collected from the departments concerned or if the existing statistical data can be processed or sorted out, no statistical report forms shall be made and issued to the grass-roots units.

(5) There shall be detailed investigation plans which clearly stipulate the purposes of investigation, the ways to investigate, the scope of statistics, the contents of classification, the interpretation of targets, the method of counting, the units to make and report, the time limit for completion, the authorities to receive the forms, etc. so as to help fill them in for report.

(6) Investigations and necessary experiments shall be undergone in advance so as to prevent the separation from reality and improve them continuously in practice.

4 The limits of authority to make and issue statistical report forms and the procedure of examination and approval:

(1) The basic statistical report forms of nationwide social and economic situations (including grass-roots forms and comprehensive forms) shall be worked out by the State Bureau of Statistics and transmitted in a unified way to lower levels or jointly worked out and transmitted down by the State Bureau of Statistics and the business departments concerned. Important statistical report forms shall be submitted to the State Council for approval before being transmitted to lower levels. The report forms issued to rural people's communes, production brigades and production teams shall strictly be controlled. Any report forms or targets which have been transmitted to lower levels by the State Bureau of Statistics in a unified way or jointly with the business departments concerned shall not be made and issued by the business departments at any level repeatedly; if it is required by special needs to supplement some report forms or targets, applications shall be made to the government statistical department at the same level for examination and approval.

(2) The specialized statistical report forms worked out by each business department of the State Council are necessary supplements to the basic statistical report forms of social and economic situations made by the State Bureau of Statistics and shall be organized, examined and managed in a unified way by the synthesizing and statistical organ of the department itself. It shall resolutely be changed that each functionary organ within a department makes and issues statistical report forms by itself. The statistical report forms to be issued to the enterprises and institutions directly under the same department or under the jurisdiction of the same system shall be approved to be transmitted down by the person in charge

of the department and submitted to the State Bureau of Statistics for filing; the statistical report forms to be issued to the enterprises and institutions which are not under the jurisdiction of the same system shall be signed by the person in charge of the department which makes the investigations and submitted to the State Bureau of Statistics for examination and approval.

(3) The regional statistical report forms worked out by the bureaus of statistics of provinces, municipalities and autonomous regions shall be reported to the State Bureau of Statistics for filing. Applications shall be made to the people's government of a province, a municipality or an autonomous region for approval of the transmission of important statistical report forms.

(4) The specialized statistical report forms made by each business department of a province, a municipality or an autonomous region shall be organized, examined and managed in a unified way by the synthesizing and statistical organ of the department itself. The statistical report forms to be issued to the enterprises and institutions directly under the same department or under the jurisdiction of the same system shall be approved to be transmitted down by the person in charge of the department and submitted to the bureau of statistics of the province, municipality or autonomous region for filing; the statistical report forms to be issued to the enterprises and institutions which are not under the jurisdiction of the same system shall be signed by the person in charge of the department which conducts the investigations and submitted to the bureau of statistics of the province, municipality or autonomous region for examination and approval.

(5) The procedure for the statistical department and the business department of a prefecture, a city or a county to work out, examine and approve of statistical report forms shall be formulated by the bureau of statistics of the province, municipality or autonomous region in accordance with the specific conditions of each area, submitted to the people's government of the province, municipality or autonomous region for approval of the transmission to lower levels and submitted to the State Bureau of Statistics for filing.

(6) In general, the central task offices or various provisional offices set up by each department of the State Council and the leading bodies of provinces, municipalities and autonomous regions shall not directly issue statistical report forms; and statistical data required by their work shall be gathered from the departments concerned for sorting out. If it is really necessary to make and issue a small number of statistical report forms, applications shall be made to the government statistical department at the same level for examination and approval in accordance with the above provisions.

(7) The procedure for examination and approval in the making and issuing of statistical report forms by people's bodies or scientific research organizations shall be handled in accordance with the above provisions.

5 The contents of the report forms, the interpretation of targets, the method of counting, the time limit for completion, etc. in the specialized statistical report forms made and issued by the business department at each level shall not contradict the relevant statistical report forms made and issued by the government statistical department at the same level and repetitions should be avoided.

The statistical concepts, scopes, methods, classifications, forms, numbers, etc. prescribed in the basic statistical report forms of nation wide social and economic situations worked out by the State Bureau of Statistics or jointly with the business departments concerned shall not be amended or changed by the government statistical department in each area or by each business department without authorization so as to facilitate the nationwide unified implementation. If it is really necessary to make some supplements, deletions or alterations, they shall be examined and approved by the State Bureau of Statistics.

6 In the case of the statistical report forms which have been approved or kept on file, the form-making organization, approving organization or filing organization and the number of the paper of approval shall be clearly marked on the right upper corner of each form for the convenience of administration and supervision.

7 The government statistical department at each level shall be serious and responsible in exercising strict control over the examination and approval of report forms. If the statistical report forms submitted for approval or for filing do not conform to Articles 3 through 6 of these Provisions, the government statistical department at each level shall be entitled to notify the form-making organization(s) to amend or annul them.

8 The statistical report forms which have been approved for transmittal to lower levels shall be filled in and submitted by the units concerned conscientiously in accordance with various provisions. If they have any objections, they shall make them known by the form-making organizations but shall execute them in accordance

with the original provisions before adding any amendments or alterations.

If a statistical report form is not examined and approved or kept on file or if no form-making organization, approving organization or filing organization is indicated on the form and the number of the paper of approval is not clearly marked on its right upper corner, the filling-in and submitting unit shall refuse to fill it in and submit it and shall expose and denounce such form.

department at each level shall make a serious inspection of the unit which recklessly issues report forms in violation of these Provisions, deal sternly with it and check the further execution of the report forms without approval.

If the reckless issuing of report forms has resulted in losses to the grass-roots units, the government statistical department at each level shall circulate a notice of criticism and investigate and affix the responsibility according to the degrees of seriousness.

9 The government statistical department and the business department at each level shall regularly examine and sort out statistical report forms and the statistical report forms or targets which have been out of date or no longer applicable shall be duly annulled or revised. Upon completion of an annual examination and sorting, the results of the sorting shall be reported to the government statistical department at the higher level and to the people's government at the same level.

10 Each business department of the State Council and the bureau of statistics of each province, municipality or autonomous region shall formulate the detailed rules for the implementation on the principles of these Provisions and submit them to the State Bureau of Statistics for filing.

INTERIM PROVISIONS FOR THE QUARTERLY PROMULGATION OF THE DEPARTMENTAL TARGETS OF MAJOR ECONOMIC EFFECTS AND THE INSTITUTION OF THE ANALYTICAL SYSTEM OF ECONOMIC ACTIVITIES

(July 1982)

In order to promote the activities of emulating, learning from, catching up with, helping and in turn surpassing each other among all departments, all trades and all enterprises with the improvement of economic benefit as the key purpose and strengthen the analyses of economic activities so as to duly take effective measures, it is now determined to, from the first half of this year, submit monthly (temporarily quarterly this year) and promulgate quarterly the fulfilment of the targets of the major economic effects of each industrial or communications department of the State Council in addition to continuing to promulgate quarterly the fulfilment of the targets of the major economic effects in industry of each province, municipality or autonomous region. Each economic responsible department of the State Council shall quarterly submit the circulation of the targets of the major economic effects of its subordinate trades and key enterprises. Each economic responsible department of the State Council shall institute the quarterly analytical system of economic activities. Now the relevant matters are provided for as follows:

I The 14 Targets of Major Economic Effects to Be Submitted Monthly (Temporarily Quarterly This Year) and Promulgated Quarterly by the Industrial and Communications Departments of the State Council:

1. Gross industrial output value and rate of increase (converted turnover for communications departments and gross business volume and rate of increase for the Ministry of Posts and Telecommunications);

2. The fulfilment of the plans of the output of major industrial products. (the fulfilment of the plans of the volume of major materials traffic for communications departments);

3. Stable improvement rate of the quality of major industrial products (rate of starting and running punctually passenger trains and cargo trains for the Ministry of Railway; rate of goods damage and rate of goods shortage of the water transport and port enterprises for the Ministry of Communications);

4. Rate of reduction of major raw materials and fuel power consumption (rate of reduction of coal, oil and power consumption converted into that of standard coal for transport departments);

5. Sales (business) income and rate of increase of industrial and communications enterprises;

6. Profits achievement and rate of increase of industrial and communications enterprises (balance of business revenue and expenditure and rate of increase for the Ministry of Posts and Telecommunications);

7. Turned-over profits and rate of increase of industrial and communications enterprises;

8. Rate of profits and taxes in output value and rate of increase;

9. Rate of profits in sales (business) income and rate of increase of industrial and communications enterprises;

10. Days of turnover of rated circulating funds and rate of acceleration of industrial and communications enterprises;

11. Percentage of production capital and rate of reduction thereof;

12. Amount of reduction of comparable product cost and rate of reduction of industrial and communications enterprises (converted ton-kilometre cost and rate of reduction for communications departments; the expenditure per 100 yuan income and rate of reduction for the Ministry of Posts and Telecommunications);

13. Full staff labour productivity and rate of increase thereof;

14. Death rate at work per 1,000 workers and rate of reduction thereof.

You are requested to list the totals of the enterprises directly under the above 14 targets under the departmental totals. Those with the marks "▲" are the targets for counting the comprehensive indices of economic developments. The counting ranges, counting methods and those for counting the comprehensive indices of economic developments shall be implemented in the light of relevant provisions in the "Detailed Rules for the Implementation of the Periodical Promulgation of the Targets of Major Economic Effects" as Document No. Jing-Zong 140(1982).

If the number of product quality and consumption targets determined to be examined by each department is more than 10, the provisions in the above "Detailed Rules for the Implementation" shall be executed; if it is less than 10, they shall be counted and recorded according to the degree of importance of every target. After the targets and recording standards are decided upon, they shall be submitted to the State Economic Commission and the State Bureau of Statistics for future reference and shall not be altered within the year.

II Each economic responsible department of the State Council is requested, from the first half of this year, to make a periodical internal circulation of the fulfilment of the targets of major economic effects by the trades and key enterprises under it. The ranges include:

Industry: Industries under the administration in the system of each responsible department and only the enterprises directly under are listed;

Communications: Railway, communications, post and telecommunications, civil aviation enterprises;

Commerce: Commercial and food units, supply and marketing cooperatives;

Foreign Trade: Branches of each province, municipality or autonomous region under the administration in the system of the Ministry of Foreign Economic Relations and Trade;

Capital Construction: Building and installing enterprises and independent accounting processing enterprises (the industrial and communications departments shall periodically promulgate the targets of major economic effects such as improvement of quality, reduction of building costs, shortening of building time, etc. for the capital construction units and building and installing enterprises directly under them);

Agriculture: State farms, forestry centres, fishing and processing enterprises;

Geology: Geological prospecting enterprises and processing enterprises.

Each economic responsible department of the State Council is requested to formulate specific procedures on the basis of its own features for the promulgated targets, the concrete division of trades, the list of key enterprises (construction units) and specific procedures for the implementation.

III The Institution of the Regular Analytical System of Economic Activities

Each economic department of the State Council is requested to regularly organize the functional subdepartments and bureaux concerned to make the analyses of economic activities for all trades directly under it and is requested to assign the persons in charge. Stress shall be laid on the analysis of the subjective and objective causes of the good or poor fulfilment of the targets of major economic effects and the disparities between trades and between key enterprises in order to duly popularize the advanced experience in the improvement of economic benefit and take specific measures in a countering manner, examining and supervising the implementation. Each province, municipality or autonomous region shall handle them in the light of the aforesaid.

IV The Time for Submission

Each industrial or communications department of the State Council shall assign a synthesizing section to take charge of gathering and sorting. The 14 targets of major economic effects quarterly submitted shall be submitted 25 days before the end of each quarter and the targets of major economic effects promulgated by the industrial, communications, financial and commercial departments for the trades and key enterprises under them and the situations of their circulation shall be submitted 35 days before the end of each quarter to the State Economic Commission, the State Planning Commission, the State Bureau of Statistics and the Ministry of Finance. The regular analytical reports of economic activities of each department shall be submitted 40 days before the end of each quarter to the State Economic Commission, the State Planning Commission, the State Bureau of Statistics, the Ministry of Finance, the Ministry of Labour and Personnel and the People's Bank of China.

The time for state agricultural enterprises, aquatic catching or breeding enterprises and geological prospecting enterprises to promulgate the targets of major economic effects and the time for the departments concerned to submit to us the situations of their circulation and the analytical reports of economic activities shall be determined by the authorities concerned.

V The units which make clear achievements in the overall improvement of economic benefit shall, at the end of a year, be recommended and submitted by each department or each area to the State Economic Commission for gathering and balancing and promulgated after the approval of the State Council (specific procedures shall separately be formulated).

Each department or each area shall be praised as a group or by units with better and improved economic benefit in addition to those promulgated and praised by the state.

VI It is a new task and one of important significance to promulgate the departmental targets of major economic effects and institute the regular analytical system of economic activities.

In order to start this new task as soon as possible, the authorities at each level shall be required to make concerted efforts, act in close cooperation, do it well and conscientiously and ensure timely submissions. As we are short of practical experience, some provisions are still imperfect and shall be gradually improved in the course of execution.

24 ENVIRONMENTAL PROTECTION

THE ENVIRONMENTAL PROTECTION LAW OF THE PEOPLE'S REPUBLIC OF CHINA

(Provisional)

(Adopted in Principle at the 11th Meeting of the Standing Committee of the Fifth National People's Congress on September 13, 1979)

Chapter I General Provisions

Article 1 This law is established in accordance with Article 11 of the Constitution of the People's Republic of China which provides that "the State protects the environment and natural resources and prevents and eliminates pollution and other hazards to the public."

Article 2 The function of the Environmental Protection Law of the People's Republic of China is to ensure, during the construction of a modernized socialist state, rational use of the natural environment, prevention and elimination of environmental pollution and damage to ecosystems, in order to create a clean and favourable living and working environment, protect the health of the people and promote economic development.

Article 3 For the purposes of this law, "environment" means: the atmosphere, water, land, mineral resources, forests, grassland, wildlife, wild plants, aquatic plants and animals, famous spots and historic sites, scenic spots for sightseeing, hot springs, health resorts, nature conservation areas, residential districts, etc.

Article 4 The guidelines governing environmental protection work are: overall planning, rational layout, comprehensive utilization, conversion of harm into good, reliance upon the masses with everybody taking part in the protection of the environment for the benefit of the people.

Article 5 The State Council and its subordinate bodies, and the local people's governments at all levels shall endeavour to carry out environmental protection work in earnest and do a good job of it. They shall make overall plans for the protection and improvement of the environment in planning for national economic development and take practical measures for its implementation. Where pollution of the environment and other hazards to the public have already been caused, plans should be worked out to eliminate such in a systematic and orderly manner.

Article 6 All enterprises and institutes shall pay adequate attention to the prevention of pollution and damage to the environment when selecting their sites, designing, constructing and planning production. In planning new construction, reconstruction and extension projects, a report on the potential environmental effects shall be submitted to the environmental protection department and other relevant departments for examination and approval before designing can be started. The installations for the prevention of pollution and other hazards to the public should be designed, built and put into operation at the same time as the main project. Discharge of all kinds of harmful substances shall be in compliance with the criteria set down by the State.

The units which have caused pollution and other hazards to the environment shall, according to the principle of "whoever causes pollution shall be responsible for its elimination," make plans to actively eliminate such, or alternatively submit an application to the competent authorities for approval to transfer the property or move to some other place.

Article 7 In rebuilding old cities or building new ones, assessments shall be made of the potential environmental effects in industrial and residential areas, public utility facilities, and green belts by reference to the meteorological, geographical, hydrological and ecological conditions; and overall planning and rational layout shall be made to prevent pollution and other hazards to the public so as to build a clean modern city in a planned way.

Article 8 The citizen has the right to supervise, accuse and bring a complaint before the court against the unit or the individual who has caused pollution and damage to the environment. The unit or the individual thus accused and charged shall not take any retaliatory action.

Article 9 Foreigners or foreign aircraft, ships, vehicles, goods, plants and animals, etc. entering or passing through Chinese territory, territorial waters, or airspace shall be subject to the present law and other regulations and rules relating to the protection of the environment.

Chapter II Protection of the Natural Environment

Article 10 Use the land rationally according to local conditions, improve the soil and increase the vegetation to prevent soil erosion, hardening, alkalinization, desertification, and water losses.

Comprehensive scientific surveys shall be carried out before going ahead with plans to reclaim wasteland, put up dykes along the seacoast or lakes, and construct new large- or medium-sized water conservancy facilities. Practical measures for protection and improvement of the environment shall be taken to prevent damage to the eco-systems.

Article 11 Keep bodies of water such as rivers, lakes, seas, reservoirs, etc., from being polluted so as to preserve the quality of water in a good state.

Protect, develop and utilize aquatic flora and fauna in a rational way. Fishing to the extent of threatening extinction of, and damage to, living resources is prohibited.

Exercise tight control over, and economize, use of water in industry, agriculture, and in daily life. Exploit rationally the subsoil waters to prevent exhaustion of water resources and surface subsidence.

Article 12 In exploiting mineral resources, comprehensive surveying, evaluation and utilization should be carried out. Excavating and mining at random is strictly forbidden, and tailings and slags should be appropriately disposed of, to prevent damage to resources and pollution of the natural environment.

Article 13 Strictly adhere to the National Forestry Law; protect and develop forest resources; fell trees in a rational way; tend trees and reforest at the appropriate time. Destroying forest to reclaim land and arbitrary cutting and felling are strictly forbidden. Preventive measures should be taken against forest fires.

Efforts should be made to plant trees everywhere and make barren hills, wasteland, desert areas and semi-desert areas green; tree planting should be vigorously carried out in villages, towns, and industrial and mining districts. Make good use of all available scattered open spaces inside and outside factory compounds, mining districts, school campuses, office compounds, along roadsides, river banks, and around villages and houses by planting trees and grass so as to turn the whole country into a big park.

Article 14 Protect and develop forage resources. Actively.plan and carry out the grassland development programme; herd sheep and cattle rationally; maintain and improve the regenerating capacity of the grasslands, and prevent the grasslands from deteriorating. Abusive exploitation of grassland is strictly forbidden. Efforts should be made to prevent grassland fires.

Article 15 Protect, develop, and utilize rationally wildlife and wild plant resources. National regulations forbid hunting of rare animals and felling of precious trees.

Chapter III Prevention and Elimination of Pollution and Other Hazards to the Public

Article 16 Actively prevent and control noxious substances from factories, mines, enterprises and urban life, such as waste gas, waste water, waste residues, dust, garbage, radioactive material, etc., as well as noise, vibration, and bad odours from polluting and damaging the environment.

Article 17 Enterprises or institutions that will cause pollution of the environment shall not be set up in the residential areas of the cities and towns, water resource protection zones, places of historic interest and scenic beauty, scenic spots for sightseeing, hot springs, health resorts and nature conservation areas. Where such units have been established, a target date shall be set for elimination and control of the pollution, or making necessary adjustments, or removal.

Article 18 Actively conduct experiments and adopt new technology, techniques and devices which are pollution-free or will reduce pollution.

Strengthen business management and carry out civilized production; make comprehensive use of such environment-polluting substances as waste gas, waste water and waste residues, and transform them into useful things. Discharge of such substances where necessary shall be in compliance with the criteria laid down by the State. Where such national criteria cannot be met for the time being, a later date will be set for compliance; if national standards still cannot be met by the deadline, a limit shall be set to production.

In cases where release of pollutants goes beyond the limits of the specified national standards, a fee shall be charged towards dealing with the release of such pollutants according to the quantities and concentrations of the pollutants released as specified in the relevant regulations.

Article 19 All smoke-discharging devices, industrial furnaces, motor vehicles, ships, etc. shall take effective measures to eliminate smoke and dust, and discharge of noxious gas shall be in compliance with the standards laid down by the State.

Develop and use on a large scale coal gas, liquefied petroleum gas (LPG), natural gas, marsh gas, solar energy, terrestrial heat and other non-polluting or less polluting energy sources. In the cities, district central heating should be promoted.

Article 20 Dumping garbage and waste residues into the waters is prohibited. Discharge of sewage shall be in compliance with the standards set down by the State.

Ships are prohibited from discharging substances containing oil, poison, and other harmful wastes into the waters protected by the law of this country.

It is strictly prohibited to discharge poisonous and harmful waste water by way of seepage pits, crevices, lava holes, or dilution methods. Prevent seepage of water containing industrial filth to ensure that subsoil water is not contaminated.

Take strong measures to protect sources of drinking water from contamination and gradually perfect the sewage discharge piping system and sewage purification facilities.

Article 21 Actively develop effective, low-toxin and low-residue agricultural pesticides. Promote comprehensive and biological methods of prevention and control; use rationally sewage for irrigation so as to prevent pollution of the soil and crops.

Article 22 Step up control of noise and vibration in urban and industrial districts. All kinds of noisy machines, motor vehicles, aircraft, etc. with heavy vibrations are required to install noise suppressors and antivibration devices.

Article 23 The units which emit harmful gases or dust should actively adopt sealed production equipment and technology, and install ventilating, dust collecting and purifying, and recovery facilities. The amount of harmful gases and dust in the working environment must conform with the standards for industrial hygiene specified by the law of this country.

Article 24 Registration and control of toxic chemicals must be strictly carried out. Highly toxic substances should be tightly sealed to prevent leakage during storage and tranportation.

Radioactive materials, electro-magnetic radiation, etc. should be strictly monitored and controlled according to the applicable law of this country.

Article 25 Strict precautions shall be taken to prevent pollution of food in the course of production, processing, packing, transportation, storage, and marketing. Food inspection shall be strengthened, and the sale, export and import of foods not meeting the requirements of national hygienic standards shall be prohibited.

Chapter IV Environmental Protection Office and its Functions

Article 26 The State Council has established an Environmental Protection Office whose main functions are:

a) To implement and supervise the carrying out of national guidelines, policies, laws and acts relating to environmental protection;

b) To draft regulations, rules, standards, economic and technical policies relating to environmental protection in conjunction with relevant departments;

c) To develop long-term programmes and annual plans for protection of the environment in conjunction with relevant departments and to encourage and supervise their implementation;

d) To make unified plans for organizing the monitoring of the environment; carry out investigations and keep under review the environmental situation and development trends of the whole country, and recommend improvement measures;

e) To organize and coordinate, in conjunction with relevant departments, research and educational programmes in environmental science, actively promote foreign as well as domestic advanced experiences and techniques in the field of environmental protection;

f) To direct the environmental protection work of all the departments under the State Council, and of the provinces, autonomous regions, and municipalities directly under the central government;

g) To organize and coordinate international cooperation and communication in the field of environmental protection.

Article 27 The people's government of the provinces, autonomous regions, and municipalities directly under the central government shall establish environmental protection bureaus in their respective areas. The people's governments of the municipalities, autonomous prefectures, counties, and autonomous counties may establish environmental protection organizations as required.

The main functions of the local environmental protection organizations at every level are: To supervise and urge the implementation of the national guidelines, policies, laws and acts relating to the protection of environment in the various departments and units within their jurisdictions; to draft applicable local standards and specifications concerning environmental protection; to organize monitoring of the environment and keep under review the local environmental situation and development trends; to develop long-term programmes and annual plans applicable locally for the protection of the environment in conjunction with the relevant departments, and supervise their implementation; to organize local research and educational programmes in environmental science in conjunction with relevant departments; to actively promote foreign as well as domestic advanced experiences and techniques in the field of environmental protection.

Article 28 The relevant departments under the State Council, the local people's governments at all levels, large- and medium-size enterprises, and relevant institutions shall establish, as required, environmental protection offices separately responsible for the protection of the environment within their own system of affiliated organizations, departments, and units.

Chapter V Scientific Research, Propaganda and Education

Article 29 China Environmental Science Research Institute, relevant scientific institutes, universities and colleges should devote major efforts to research in the following areas: fundamental principles of environmental science, environmental management, environmental economics, comprehensive control techniques, environmental quality evaluation, environmental pollution and human health, rational use and protection of the natural environment, etc.

Article 30 Cultural and publicity departments should actively carry out publicity and educational programmes to disseminate the knowledge of environmental science so as to enhance the understanding of the general public about the significance of environmental protection work and to raise the scientific and technical standards in the environmental field.

Environmental protection specialists should be trained in a planned way. The educational departments should establish a required course or speciality in environmental protection in the relevant departments of the universities and colleges. Middle and primary school textbooks should include appropriate texts relating to environmental protection.

Chapter VI Rewards and Punishments

Article 31 The State will give commendations and rewards to units and individuals who have made outstanding achievements and contributions to the work of environmental protection.

The State will grant tax reductions or exemptions on, and apply a preferential pricing policy to, products manufactured by utilizing waste gas, waste water, and waste residues as main material, and the profits originating therefrom need not be turned over to the higher authorities but will be used by the manufacturers concerned to control pollution and improve the environment.

Article 32 Units which have violated this law and other environmental protection regulations and rules by polluting and damaging the environment and causing hazards to the people's health shall, according to the merit of each case, be criticized, warned, fined, or ordered to pay damages and stop production and control and eliminate such pollution, by the environmental protection organizations at various levels subject to the approval of the people's government of the corresponding level.

Unit leaders, persons directly responsible or other citizens who have caused serious pollution and damage to the environment resulting in casualties or substantial damage to farming forestry, animal husbandry, side-line production and fishery shall be held responsible administratively, economically, and even criminally, as the case may be, according to law.

Chapter VII Supplementary Articles

Article 33 The State Council may establish regulations and rules relating to environmental protection according to the present law.

NOTICE OF THE STATE COUNCIL RELATING TO THE PROMULGATION OF THE "INTERIM PROCEDURES FOR THE COLLECTION OF POLLUTANT DISCHARGE PENALTIES"

(February 5, 1982)

We are now delivering to you the "Interim Procedures for the Collection of Pollutant Discharge Penalties" and you are requested to implement them in light of the actual conditions of each area.

The collection of pollutant discharge penalties is a better way to strengthen environmental protection by economic means for the purpose of urging enterprises and institutions to give more effective management and administration, save and put resources to comprehensive use, bring pollution under control and improve the environment. As the collection of pollutant discharge penalties covers a wide range and bears much on policies, we hope the people's governments at every level will strengthen your leadership and popularize and implement them step by step in a planned and focused way. If each area or department has any suggestions as to the implementation of these Procedures, please make them known in time by the office of the Environmental Protection Leading Group of the State Council.

Interim Procedures for The Collection of Pollutant Discharge Penalties

Article 1 These Procedures are formulated on the basis of the provisions in Article 18 of the "The Environmental Protection Law of The People's Republic of China (Provisional)" that pollutant discharge penalties shall be collected as stipulated on the pollutants discharged in excess of the standards stipulated by the state in accordance with the numbers or quantities and concentrations or densities of the discharged pollutants.

Article 2 The collection of pollutant discharge penalties is aimed at urging enterprises and institutions to give more effective management and administration, save and put resources to comprehensive use, bring pollution under control and improve the environment.

Article 3 All enterprises and institutions shall observe such relevant standards as the "Provisional Standards of the Discharge of the Three Industrial Wastes (i.e., waste water, waste gas and industrial residue)" promulgated by the state. If the people's government of a province, an autonomous region or a municipality directly under the Central Government has approved and promulgated regional standards of discharge, the enterprises and institutions in the locality shall observe the regional standards of discharge.

Pollutant discharge penalties shall be collected from the enterprises and institutions which discharge pollutants in excess of the above standards; heating boiler smoke and dust discharge penalties shall be collected from other pollutant discharge units.

Although a pollutant discharge unit pays pollutant discharge penalties, it shall not be exempted from the responsibilities of bringing pollution under control and compensating for damages which shall be borne by it and from other responsibilities stipulated by the law.

Article 4 A pollutant discharge unit shall report the kinds, numbers or amounts and concentrations or densities of the pollutants discharged as circumstances are to the local environmental protection department and register them with it, which shall serve as the grounds for the collection of pollutant discharge penalties after being examined and ratified by the environmental protection department or the monitoring unit assigned by it.

Article 5 The standards for the collection of pollutant discharge penalties shall be implemented as stipulated in the attached lists of these Procedures. A very few large or medium cities which have concentrated industries and are particularly seriously polluted shall properly readjust the standards of the charges with the approval of the Environmental Protection Leading Group of the State Council.

The penalties shall be calculated in accordance with the highest rate if the waste water or waste gas or industrial residue discharged by a pollutant discharge unit contains more than two harmful substances in the same discharge outlet.

The standards of the collection for the additional items to regional standards of discharge shall be prescribed by the people's government of a province, an autonomous region or a municipality directly under the Central Government in light of the attacted lists of these Procedures.

Article 6 If a pollutant discharge unit is below the standards of discharge after payment of pollutant discharge penalties, the standards of collection shall be increased by 5% every year from the third year of the beginning of collection. If the pollutant discharge unit has observed the standards of discharge or has remarkably reduced the numbers or quantities and concentrations or densities of pollutants discharged through control and strengthened administration, it shall make an application to the local environmental protection department and the collection shall be stopped or the penalties shall be reduced after it is proved to be true through monitoring.

The penalties shall be doubled if the pollutants discharged by newly-built, extended, rebuilt, productivity-enhanced, improved or transformed projects exceed the standards after the promulgation of the The Environmental Protection Law of the People's Republic of China (Provisional) or if they have pollutant treatment facilities but fail to put them into operation or if the pollutants discharged exceed the standards again after the removal of the treatment facilities without authorization.

Each province, autonomous region or municipality directly under the Central Government shall make other provisions for the increase or reduction of penalties according to actual conditions.

Article 7 Pollutant discharge penalties shall be paid monthly or quarterly. Regardless of its relations of jurisdiction and ownership, any pollutant discharge unit shall pay the pollutant discharge penalties to the specified bank within 20 days in accordance with the notice of payment from the local environmental protection department. If the payment is not made within the time limit, a fine for one thousandth of the amount in default shall be additionally collected every day.

The pollutant discharge penalties paid by the pollutant discharge units under the jurisdiction of the ministries of the Central Government and of provinces (autonomous regions and municipalities directly under the Central Government) shall be turned over to the provincial revenue and those paid by other pollutant discharge units shall be turned over to local revenue. In the cities where the enterprises under the jurisdiction of the central ministries and provinces are concentrated, the pollutant discharge penalties shall be turned over to the local revenue with the approval of the provincial people's governments.

Article 8 The pollutant discharge penalties paid by an enterprise shall be included in the cost of production. Those above the standards of collection shall be paid from the profit reserves or business funds of an enterprise of the whole people's ownership; they shall be paid from the profits after the payment of the income tax in the case of an enterprise of the whole people's ownership or of collective ownership which practises "paying taxes instead of turning over profits, independent accounting and assuming sole responsibility for its profits or losses." The pollutant discharge penalties paid by an institution shall be paid from the balance after completion of unit payments and extra-budgetary funds, and if they are still insufficient, the penalties shall be paid from the unit operating expenses.

Article 9 The pollutant discharge penalties collected shall be brought into the budget as environmental protection subsidies which shall be administered as special funds and shall not take part in the system division of net gains.

The environmental protection subsidies shall be planned and arranged for use in a unified way by the environmental protection departments jointly with the financial departments. The departments shall adhere to earmarking funds for their specified purposes only, collecting first and using later, keeping expenditures within the limits of income and guarding against overspending or diversion. Any surplus shall be carried forward for use in the next year.

Article 10 Environmental protection subsidies shall be mainly used to subsidize key pollutant discharge units for the control of the sources of pollution and for the comprehensive control measures of environmental pollution.

When a pollutant discharge unit takes measures to bring pollution under control, it shall first make use of its own financial resources and if they are really insufficient, it shall report the case to the authorities in charge. The authorities shall examine it, gather the same cases from the units concerned under their jurisdiction and then make an application to the environmental protection department and the financial department for the granting of a certain amount of subsidies out of the environmental production subsidies. In general, these subsidies shall not be more than 80 percent of the pollutant discharge penalties paid. It shall also be allowed to grant 80 percent of the environmental protection subsidies to every bureau in charge to arrange for use to subsidize enterprises and institutions to bring pollution under control under the supervision of the environmental protection department and the financial department. The units in the case as stated in Clause 2 of Article 6 shall not be subsidized.

Environmental protection subsidies shall be appropriately used to subsidize an environmental protection department for the purchase of the monitoring instruments and equipment, but shall not be used for administrative outlays and such non-business expenses as building offices, dormitories, etc.

Article 11 Environmental protection subsidies shall be allocated under the supervision of the Construction Bank.

Article 12 The people's government of each province, autonomous region and municipality directly under the Central Government shall formulate specific procedures for implementation on the basis of these Procedures.

Article 13 These Procedures shall be put into effect as of July 1, 1982.

Attached Lists:

Standards of Collection of Pollutant Discharge Penalties

I. Waste Gas

Unit: Yuan

<table>
<tr><th colspan="2">Names of Harmful Substances</th><th>Discharge Amount above Standard (per kg.)</th><th colspan="3">Concentration above Standard (per 10 cu.m.)</th></tr>
<tr><td colspan="2">sulfur dioxide, carbon disulfide, hydrogen sulfide, fluorides, nitrogen oxides, chlorine, hydrogen chloride, carbon oxide.</td><td>0.04</td><td colspan="3"></td></tr>
<tr><td colspan="2">sulfuric acid (mist), lead, mercury, beryllides</td><td></td><td colspan="3">0.03 – 0.10</td></tr>
<tr><td rowspan="3">production dust</td><td>glass wool, slag wool, rock wool, aluminides</td><td>0.10</td><td colspan="3"></td></tr>
<tr><td>power station coal dust, cement dust</td><td>0.02</td><td colspan="3"></td></tr>
<tr><td>steel-making furnace dust, other dust</td><td>0.04</td><td colspan="3"></td></tr>
<tr><td rowspan="3">industrial & heating boiler smoke & dust</td><td>multiple more than standard</td><td>less than 4</td><td>4.1 – 6</td><td>6.1 – 9</td><td>over 9</td></tr>
<tr><td>Ringelman density</td><td>Scale 2</td><td>Scale 3</td><td>Scale 4</td><td>Scale 5</td></tr>
<tr><td>charge per ton fuel</td><td>3.00</td><td>4.00</td><td>5.00</td><td>6.00</td></tr>
</table>

Notes: (1) No penalties shall be charged for the time being for the smoke discharged from steam locomotives and other mobile sources of pollution.

(2) Pollutant discharge penalties for the waste gas from thermal power stations, industrial and heating boilers shall now temporarily be charged as smoke and dust. No penalties shall be charged for other harmful substances for the time being.

II. Waste Water

Unit: Yuan/Ton Water

Names of Harmful Substances or Items	Multiple of Concentration More than Standard				
	below 5	5 – 10	10 – 20	20 – 50	over 50
mercury, cadmium, arsenic, lead and their inorganic compounds, 6-valence chromium compounds	0.15 – 0.20	0.20 – 0.30	0.30 – 0.45	0.45 – 0.90	0.90 – 2.00
sulfides, petroleum and the like, volatile phenol, cyanides, organic phosphorus, copper, zinc, fluorine and their compounds, nitrobenzene, phenyl amines	0.10 – 0.15	0.15 – 0.20	0.20 – 0.35	0.35— 0.60	0.60 – 1.00
suspended substances, COD, BOD, PH value	0.04 – 0.06	0.06 – 0.10	0.10 – 0.15	0.15 – 0.20	0.20 – 0.30
pathogens			0.08		

Notes: If the PH values are beyond 6 – 9, one value above or below those values shall be calculated as one-fold of the base (0.04 – 0.06 yuan) for the multiple below 5 exceeding standard.

III. Residue

Unit: Yuan

Names of Harmful Substances	Dumped or Discharged into Water Bodies (per ton)	Piled without Precautions against Water or Seepage (per ton/ month)	Piled without Specially provided Piling Places (per ton/ month)
residues containing mercury, cadmium, arsenic, 6-valence chromium, lead, cyanides, yellow phosphorus and other soluble deadly poisons	36.00	2.00	
power plant powdered coal ash	1.20		0.10
other industrial residues	5.00		0.30

Notes: (1) Such acts as discharging, dumping or piling deadly poisonous residues without any precautions against water or seepage shall be promptly checked and the offenders shall be ordered to remove them in addition to the penalties.

(2) The item of "power plant powdered coal ash" is only applicable to the coal-burning power plants which have been completed and put into production before the promulgation of the "The Environmental Protection Law (Provisional)" and are not provided with ash yards with the ash discharged into water bodies. The standard for "other industrial residues" is applicable to the powdered coal ash discharged by other power plants (including the above ones which have been extended).

(3) No penalties shall be charged for the time being for the residues piled in such facilities as tailing dams, ash yards , residues (including gangue), special-purpose piling yards, etc.

經 濟 管 理
"ECONOMIC MANAGEMENT" MONTHLY

歡 迎 訂 閱

※ 內 容 簡 介 ※

《經濟管理》月刊以基層經濟單位領導與管理幹部爲對象，主要內容是：宣傳黨和國家的方針政策，探討有關管理的理論與實踐問題，介紹國內外先進管理經驗，普及有關管理的基本知識。

編輯者：《經濟管理》編輯委員會
出版者：經濟管理雜誌社
社　址：北京埠外月壇北小街２號（郵政編號100037）電　話：89-1013
Address: No. 2 Yuetan Beixiaojie, Beijing · Tel: 89-1013

國外總發行：**中國國際書店**（北京399信箱）
Oversea Distributor:
GUOJI SHUDIAN (CHINA PUBLICATIONS CENTRE)
P.O. Box 399, Beijing, China.

國內期刊代號：2-839
國外期刊代號：M107
國 內 定 價：0.30元

白葡萄酒

制釘機 Nail-making Machine

吊滑輪 Pulleys

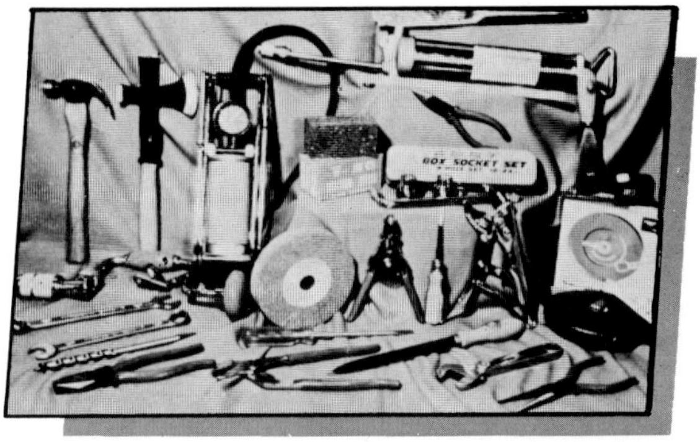

工具 Tools

石墨電極 Graphite Electrodes

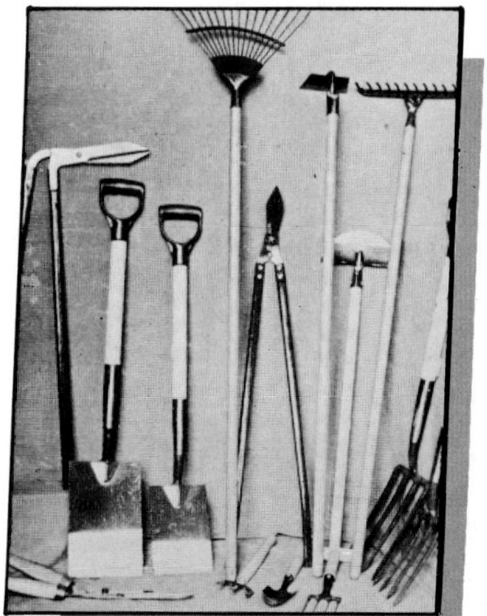

農具 Agricultural Implements

河南抽紗

河南抽紗是中國著名的工藝品之一，歷史悠久，暢銷世界。產品包括衣料、枱布、床褥、被套、枕袋、盤墊、圍布、手絹等。每類產品均品質優良，花式新款，美觀而實用。

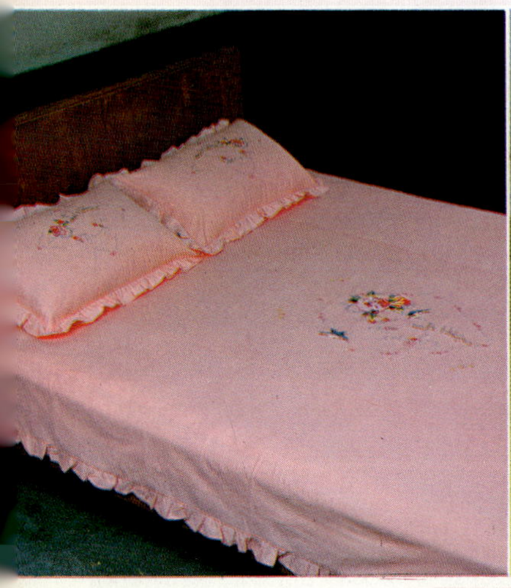

中國工藝品進出口公司河南省分公司・地址：河南鄭州文化路六十九號

China National Arts & Crafts Imp. & Exp. Corp. Henan Branch • Address: 69, Wenhua Road, Zhengzhou,China

GUANGDONG CHEMICALS

廣東化工原料

ETHYL ALCOHOL 酒精

HIGH ABRASION FURNACE BLACK (H. A. F. BLACK) 高耐磨炭黑

LITHOPONE 立德粉

MANGANESE SULPHATE 硫酸錳

中國化工進出口總公司廣東省分公司經營

經營範圍：化工原料、醫藥原料、藥品、醫療器械、石油及副產品、橡膠製品、塑料。

承辦：進口和出口業務，來料加工，來件裝配，補償貿易，委托代理，合資經營，合作生產。

CHINA NATIONAL CHEMICALS IMPORT & EXPORT CORPORATION
GUANGDONG BRANCH

61, Yan Jiang Road (West), Guangzhou, China.
Cable Address: "SINOCHEMIC" Guangzhou Telex: 44076 HAGON CN

中國化工進出口公司廣東省分公司

中國廣州市沿江西路61號　電報掛號：廣州"SINOCHEMIC"　電傳掛號：44076 HAGON CN

向陽牌人參蜂王漿

RENSHENFENGWANGJIANG

向陽牌
HSIANG YANG BRAND

常服人參蜂王漿　身强體健精神爽

Regular administrations will strengthen your body and maintain vitality!

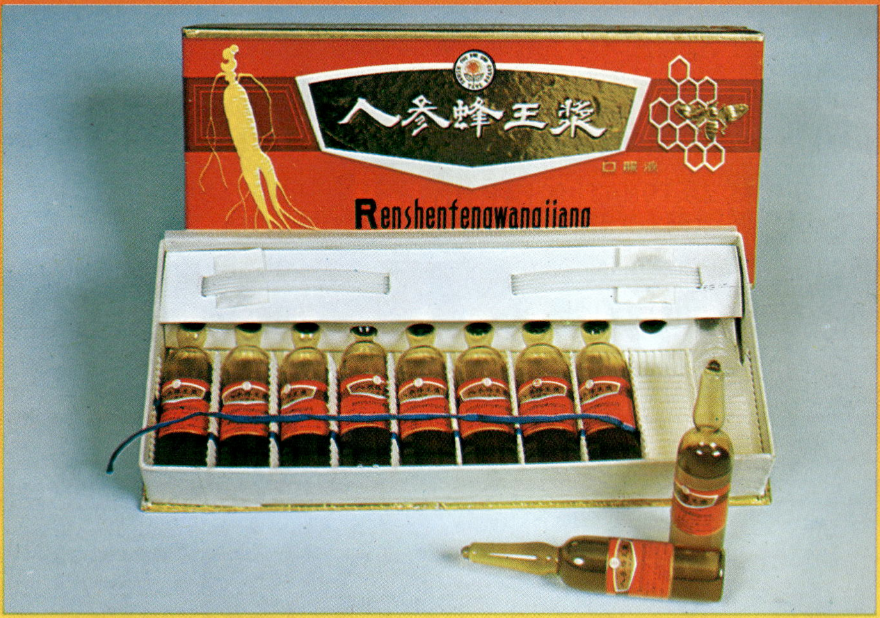

人參蜂王漿系採用東北珍貴特產人參和蜂王漿爲原料精製而成，營養豐富、服用方便，對勞倦厭食、神經衰弱、營養不良、貧血消瘦、毛髮脫落及關節炎、胃潰瘍及老年疾病等症功效極佳，確爲當代理想的滋補强壯佳品。

Ginseng-Royal Jelley is prepared with ginseng, a treasure products of North China, and Royal Jelley, and is nourishing and convenient to take. It is especially efficacious for cases of mental and physical tiredness, poor appetite, neurasthenia, malnutrition, over-fatigue, falling of hair, arthritis, gastric ulcer and sensile degeneration. It is indeed an ideal supertonic for all ages.

中國土產畜產進出口總公司黑龍江省分公司經營
地址：哈爾濱市和平路55號
電報掛號：“HNAIEC” HARBIN

CHINA NATIONAL NATIVE PRODUCE & ANIMAL BY-PRODUCTS IMPORTS & EXPORT CORPORATION, HEILONGJIANG BRANCH
Address: 55 Heping Road, Harbin, China
Cable: “HNAIEC” HARBIN

TMT
CEILING FAN
TMT牌吊扇
中國輕工業品進出口公司廣東省分公司
CHINA NATIONAL LIGHT INDUSTRIAL
PRODUCTS IMP. & EXP. CORP.
GUANGDONG BRANCH
中國廣州市僑光路2號
電報掛號：0675廣州
電傳：44147 KLIPC CN
, QIAO GUANG ROAD, GUANGZHOU, CHINA
CABLE: "INDUKT" GUANGZHOU
TELEX: 44147 KLIPC CN
TMT Trading Co. Ltd.
12/F., Block B,
11-13 Hong Kong Industrial Centre,
489-491 Castle Peak Road, Kowloon,
Hong Kong. G.P.O. Box 10381 H.K.
Telex: 42524 TMTCO HX Cable: TMTFAN
Tel: 3-7455225 (5 lines).

河北抽紗

河北省是中國抽紗主要產地之一，歷史悠久、暢銷世界。主要制品分手綉、機綉、手編、印花、提花等五類。產品包括枱布、被單套、童單套、中西式枕袋、盤墊、圍裙、披肩、午餐套、揩手巾等各種實用品。
“河北抽紗”品質優良、花色新穎、素雅大方，經久耐用。歡迎洽購。

中國工藝品進出口公司河北省分公司

地址：中國石家庄市機場路八號
電報掛號：6877
電傳：22547
電話：1638

CHINA NATIONAL ARTS & CRAFTS IMPORT & EXPORT CORPORATION HEBEI BRANCH

ADD: 8, AIRPORT ROAD SHIJIAZHUANG, CHINA.
CABLE: CRAFTS
TELEX: 22547 WHBFC CN
TELEPHONES: 3300/416

旅行衣箱

A.B.S. Suitcases

長城牌A.B.S.旅行衣箱，選用高級A.B.S.
，精工製作而成，配有雙筋合金鋁口及橫
鎖，美觀耐用。衣箱內全舖上華麗綢裏，
有活動隔檔，高貴大方。衣箱特配有尼龍
，方便携帶。誠旅行者必備的恩物。

貨號：P732　尺碼：25″×28″×31″

顏色：紅、棕、灰、綠　四色。

"Great Wall" brand A.B.S. suitcases from Beijin
practical, compact, lightweight and come in all
and colours like red, brown, grey, and light gr
Artical No. P732 Size: 25" x 28" x 31"

中國輕工業品進出口公司北京市分公司

China National Light Industrial Products
Imp. & Exp. Corp. Beijing Branch

北京市西長安街76號

Address: 76 Changan Street, West, Beijing, China.
Cable: INDUSPK BEIJING Telex: 22142 LITPK CN

Lucky Star

浙江棉針織品

本公司經營出口各種文化衫、男女童毛巾衫、翻領
、男女睡衣、睡袍、綉花衣（機綉、手綉）、多種枱
，產品具有色澤鮮艷、做工精細、透氣性强、易洗易
靜特點。歡迎客戶蒞臨洽購，或來函來電，我們將給
你滿意的答覆。

you are looking for quaility sleeping
its/gowns, children sweaters, with scall-
ed collar, embroider garments, under-
ars and table-cloths, please contact us!

中國紡織品進出口公司浙江省分公司
China National Textiles
Imp. & Exp. Corp. Zhejiang Branch
190, Baochu Road, Hangzhou, China.
Cable: TEXTILES HANG ZHOU
Telex: 35026 TEX CM
Telephone: 25396

田七 TIENCHI (NOTO-GINSENG)
A special product of Yunnan, China

Tienchi (Noto-ginseng), also known as San-chi, is a famous tonic drug indigenous to Yunnan and the best variety of the genus Panax Linn. Tienchi is remarkably effective for nourishing and strengthening the function of the heart, promoting the circulation of blood, lowering the level of cholesterol in the blood vessels, etc. It is an ideal natural health-preserving tonic which help prevent and cure cardiovascular diseases.

TIENCHI POWDER
A Natural Health Preserving Tonic Drug for Increasing Vitality and Energy

茶花牌
CAMELLIA BRAND

Tienchi powder is prepared from high quality Tienchi
It nourishes and vitalizes the human body
It strengthens the functioning of the heart and helps prevent cardiovascular diseases
It promotes the growth of child and is good for all ages

Orders and business enquiries are welcome

China National Native Produce & Animal By-products Import & Export Corporation

Yunnan Native Produce Branch

Address: 113 Hua Shan Road (South), Kunming   Cable Address: PROEXCORP KUNMING

鎮痛膏

玉泉牌鎮痛膏由麝香草腦、冬綠油等藥物製成。藥物能滲入皮下組織，刺激神經，擴張血管，促進血液循環，起消炎鎮痛作用。對神經痛、關節痛等特別有效。輕輕一貼，藥力可持久十二小時以上，誠運動者及家居保健的必備良藥。

經營出口：
中國化工進出口公司北京市分公司
北京朝陽門內大街一九〇號
電報掛號：SINOCHEMIP 北京
電傳：22470 BFTCC-A CN

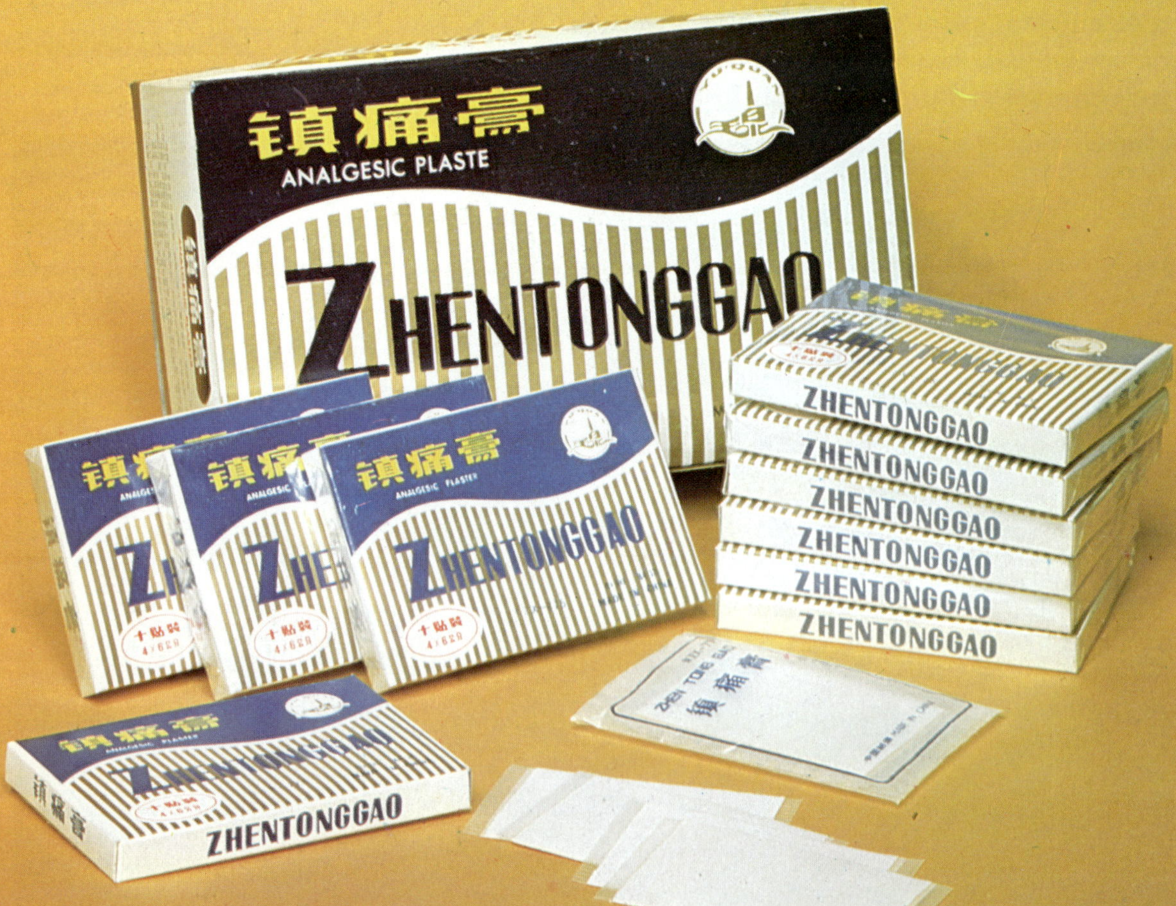